Readings in
Managerial
Psychology

Edited by
Harold J.
Leavitt,
Louis R.
Pondy,
and
David M.
Boje

Readings in Managerial Psychology

Fourth Edition

The University of Chicago Press
Chicago and London

The University of Chicago Press, Chicago 60637
The University of Chicago Press, Ltd., London
© 1964, 1973, 1980, 1989 by The University of Chicago
All rights reserved. First edition 1964
Second edition 1973. Third edition 1980
Fourth edition 1989
Printed in the United States of America

98 97   5 4

Library of Congress Cataloging in Publication Data

Readings in managerial psychology.

  Includes bibliographies.
    1. Psychology, Industrial.   2. Industrial management.
I. Leavitt, Harold J.   II. Pondy, Louis R.   III. Boje,
David M.
HF5548.8.R375   1989   658   88-1159
ISBN 0-226-46991-3
ISBN 0-226-46992-1 (pbk.)

This book is
dedicated
to the memory of our
friend and colleague
Louis R. Pondy
1938–1987

Contents

Preface   ix

1 Motivation: The Driving Force

Introduction   1

Motivation: A Diagnostic Approach   3
David A. Nadler and Edward E. Lawler III

A Theory of Human Motivation   20
A. H. Maslow

Intrinsic and Extrinsic Motivation   36
Barry M. Staw

On the Folly of Rewarding A, while Hoping for B   72
Steven Kerr

2 Mind: Thinking, Creating, Analyzing

Introduction   88

Cognitive Processes in Creative Acts   90
John R. Hayes

Emotional Blocks   107
James L. Adams

The Science of "Muddling Through"   117
Charles E. Lindblom

3 Opinions, Beliefs, and Attitudes: The Balancing Act

Introduction   132

The Rationalizing Animal   134
Elliot Aronson

Commitment and Consistency:
Hobgoblins of the Mind   145
Robert B. Cialdini

Training the Woman to Know Her Place:
The Power of a Nonconscious
Ideology   183
Sandra L. Bem and Daryl J. Bem

Self-fulfilling Stereotypes   195
Mark Snyder

4 Communicating in Organizations: Talk, Talk, Talk

Introduction   202

Language and Organization   204
Richard L. Daft and John C. Wiginton

Leadership Is a Language Game   224
Louis R. Pondy

On the Dynamics of the Helping
Relationship   234
David A. Kolb and Richard E. Boyatzis

The Art of Saying No: Linking Power to
Culture   253
Dafna M. Izraeli and Todd D. Jick

5 Leading: Inspiration and Direction

Introduction   276

The Role of the Founder in Creating
an Organizational Culture   278
Edgar H. Schein

Managers and Leaders: Are They
Different?   297
Abraham Zaleznik

The Human Side of Enterprise 314
Douglas M. McGregor

Female Leadership in Formal Organizations: Must the Female Leader Go
Formal? 325
Jean Lipman-Blumen

**6 Power: Over and
Under the Table**

Introduction 345

Who Gets Power—and How They Hold
on to It: A Strategic-contingency Model
of Power 346
Gerald R. Salancik and Jeffrey Pfeffer

Power Enactment through Language
and Ritual 367
Michael Moch and Anne S. Huff

Power Tactics 389
Norman H. Martin and John Howard
Sims

Why the Powerless Do Not Revolt 397
Jean Lipman-Blumen

**7 Groups: Group
Pressures, Group
Decisions, Group
Conflicts**

Introduction 408

Suppose We Took Groups
Seriously 410
Harold J. Leavitt

Management Development as a Process of Influence 421
Edgar H. Schein

Groupthink 439
Irving L. Janis

An Intergroup Perspective on Individual
Behavior 451
Kenwyn K. Smith

8 Managing Conflict: Making Friends and Making Enemies

Introduction   469

The Absorption of Protest   471
Ruth Leeds Love

Organizational Culture and Counter-culture: An Uneasy Symbiosis   498
Joanne Martin and Caren Siehl

Organizational Conflict: Concepts and Models   513
Louis R. Pondy

9 The Manager's Job

Introduction   532

What Effective General Managers Really Do   534
John P. Kotter

Trade Routes: The Manager's Network of Relationships   554
Robert E. Kaplan

Managerial Work: Analysis from Observation   573
Henry Mintzberg

Pathfinding, Problem Solving, and Implementing: The Management Mix   591
Harold J. Leavitt

10 Designing Organizational Cultures: Myth, Ritual, and Symbol

Introduction   606

Myth Making: A Qualitative Step in OD Interventions   608
David M. Boje, Donald B. Fedor, and Kendrith M. Rowland

The Role of Ceremonials in Organizational Behavior   622
Harrison M. Trice, James Belasco, and Joseph A. Alutto

Symbols, Patterns, and Settings: An Optimistic Case for Getting Things Done   636
Thomas J. Peters

Fitting New Employees into the Company Culture   655
Richard Pascale

11 Strategy, Structure, and Adaptation

Introduction   664

Choosing Strategies for Change   665
John P. Kotter and Leonard A. Schlesinger

Managing Strategies Incrementally   679
James Brian Quinn

Managing the Stages of Organizational Growth   705
Eric G. Flamholtz

12 Organizations and Their Environments

Introduction   720

Strategies for Survival: How Organizations Cope with Their Worlds   722
Harold J. Leavitt, William R. Dill, and Henry B. Eyring

Transorganizational Development: Contributions to Theory and Practice   733
David M. Boje and Terance J. Wolfe

Beyond Management and Worker: The Institutional Function of Management   755
Jeffrey Pfeffer

Preface

This fourth edition of *Readings in Managerial Psychology* is both different from and similar to its predecessors. A little more than half of the papers are new—new, that is, to this edition. Once again some of the "new" ones are not newly written, but newly relevant, as we rediscover the value of works that had not yet reached their time. We have also tried very hard to seek out those pieces that meet the twin criteria of high quality and high readability. As both students and teachers know, not very many papers pass through both of those filters.

The overall structure of this edition is the same as in the past. The book moves from the smaller to the larger. We start with the individual as the focal unit, move to two-person relationships, and onward to issues of leadership, power, small groups, and whole organizations.

This edition focuses more than ever on the managing process—on whole organizations and on managing relationships with other organizations. To underline that emphasis, we have included a new section called "The Manager's Job." That section deals with what managers do, how they do it, why they do it, and how they should do it.

"Soft" issues also play an even bigger part in this edition—issues such as managing creativity and imagination, issues of the manager's values and beliefs, and issues of organization culture.

While this book is intended to stand alone, readers familiar with the new fifth edition of *Managerial Psychology* (Leavitt and Bahrami) will note that the two are designed in parallel, so that they can be used together.

We are grateful to many people for help in putting together this edition of *Readings in Managerial Psychology,* to students, executives, and faculty colleagues, and especially to Mrs. Arleen Danielson.

H. J. L., D. M. B., and L. R. P.

1

Motivation:
The Driving Force

We are driven. We are motivated. People are creatures who search, explore, and inquire. They don't spend much of their time just sitting on their duffs. They undertake and implement an astonishing variety of tasks and projects. Everywhere in the world, and since it all began, human beings have been movers and shakers, driven sometimes by hunger, thirst, greed, and lust, and sometimes by love and affection.

Perhaps the most frequent questions managers ask of psychologists and other behavioral types are motivational questions: "How do I motivate my people?" "What does one do with someone who's lost motivation?" "How does one motivate older managers these days?"

Interestingly, the whole concept of motivation hasn't been around very long. Managers fifty years ago apparently didn't think much about what motivates people. They thought much more in terms of work specifications and specialization.

So the notion that is now taken for granted that people strive and work in response to some kinds of internal "wants" or "drives" is a *relatively* new notion.

Motivation is also a very "soft" notion, still subject to great controversy within the discipline of psychology. But controversial or not, it is important for the manager to try to understand the concept of human motivation. The more fully we understand what drives the human being, the more effectively can we design organizations in which human beings can live and work productively.

The four papers in this first section try to give the manager and prospective manager a useful perspective on human motivation. We do not try to cover the field, but rather to hit some major and particularly useful points.

The first paper, by David Nadler and Edward Lawler, outlines a way of looking at motivation known as "expectancy theory." It is a straightforward approach treating both internal and situational forces acting on the person, and treating the person as a cognitively competent creature who can make sensible decisions. The paper then goes on to relate that theory to managerial practice, like the design of reward systems and jobs.

1

The second paper is a classic by Abraham Maslow. His name, more than that of any other American psychologist, is associated with the concept of motivation. Maslow was a clinician who observed individuals over extended periods and with great care and sensitivity. He evolved the idea of a *hierarchy of needs,* the notion that people tend to move from one level of motivation onward and upward to higher levels as each lower level reaches some degree of satisfaction. Thus the satisfaction of an existing set of needs becomes not the end but the beginning, the opening up of a new level of motives. Maslow sees humans as "growth" oriented, with old achievements forever triggering new interests. The validity of Maslow's theory is still debated, but its utility to the manager as a tool for thinking seems beyond question.

The third paper, by Barry Staw, is a more contemporary piece, dealing with a motivational problem that has important implications for the managing process. The issue is intrinsic versus extrinsic motivation. Some behavioral people like to say (with good reason) that one should not ask the question "How do I motivate people?" They argue that we cannot motivate anyone else; only God can. The more proper question would be something like, "What are the conditions under which people's intrinsic, built-in motivation can be nurtured to grow and bloom?" By that view, motivation is an *intrinsic* phenomenon, bubbling up out of the human soul. Yet we all know that, to some degree at least, we *can* get more work out of people, by paying them more or by offering them other *extrinsic* incentives. Staw reviews what is known about those two interacting, and not always harmonious, aspects of motivation. Sometimes, for example, when we add extrinsic motivation to intrinsic, we don't enhance intrinsic motivation; we kill it. If I began paying you to do something you now do for fun, would the extrinsic and intrinsic motivating forces simply sum? Or would they conflict?

The last paper, Steven Kerr's, goes after some practical issues of the use and misuse of financial rewards and other incentives to motivate people in organizations. He reviews cases of two companies, along with many other examples, to emphasize that managers must make sure that their reward systems do indeed reward the behavior they want, instead of its opposite.

So the papers in this section move from theory to practice, a pattern we will follow in several later sections. We have not, of course, either covered all major theories of motivation or all major practices that have been extrapolated from them. But these four papers are relevant and, we believe, useful for the manager and the student of management.

Motivation: A Diagnostic Approach
David A. Nadler
Edward E. Lawler III

What makes some people work hard while others do as little as possible?

How can I, as a manager, influence the performance of people who work for me?

Why do people turn over, show up late to work, and miss work entirely?

These important questions about employees' behavior can only be answered by managers who have a grasp of what motivates people. Specifically, a good understanding of motivation can serve as a valuable tool for *understanding* the causes of behavior in organizations, for *predicting* the effects of any managerial action, and for *directing* behavior so that organizational and individual goals can be achieved.

Existing approaches

During the past twenty years, managers have been bombarded with a number of different approaches to motivation. The terms associated with these approaches are well known—"human relations," "scientific management," "job enrichment," "need hierarchy," "self-actualization," etc. Each of these approaches has something to offer. On the other hand, each of these different approaches also has its problems in both theory and practice. Running through almost all of the approaches with which managers are familiar are a series of implicit but clearly erroneous assumptions.

Assumption 1: All Employees Are Alike. Different theories present different ways of looking at people, but each of them assumes that all employees are basically similar in their makeup: Employees all want economic gains, or all want a pleasant climate, or all aspire to be self-actualizing, etc.

Assumption 2: All Situations Are Alike. Most theories assume that all

Reprinted with permission of the authors from *Perspectives on Behavior in Organizations,* Second Edition, edited by J. Richard Hackman, Edward E. Lawler, and Lyman W. Porter (New York: McGraw-Hill). © 1977 by David A. Nadler and Edward E. Lawler III.

managerial situations are alike, and that the managerial course of action for motivation (for example, participation, job enlargement, etc.) is applicable in all situations.

Assumption 3: One Best Way. Out of the other two assumptions there emerges a basic principle that there is "one best way" to motivate employees.

When these "one best way" approaches are tried in the "correct" situation they will work. However, all of them are bound to fail in some situations. They are therefore not adequate managerial tools.

A new approach

During the past ten years, a great deal of research has been done on a new approach to looking at motivation. This approach, frequently called "expectancy theory," still needs further testing, refining, and extending. However, enough is known that many behavioral scientists have concluded that it represents the most comprehensive, valid, and useful approach to understanding motivation. Further, it is apparent that it is a very useful tool for understanding motivation in organizations.

The theory is based on a number of specific assumptions about the causes of behavior in organizations.

Assumption 1: Behavior Is Determined by a Combination of Forces in the Individual and Forces in the Environment. Neither the individual nor the environment alone determines behavior. Individuals come into organizations with certain "psychological baggage." They have past experiences and a developmental history which has given them unique sets of needs, ways of looking at the world, and expectations about how organizations will treat them. These all influence how individuals respond to their work environment. The work environment provides structures (such as a pay system or a supervisor) which influence the behavior of people. Different environments tend to produce different behavior in similar people just as dissimilar people tend to behave differently in similar environments.

Assumption 2: People Make Decisions about Their Own Behavior in Organizations. While there are many constraints on the behavior of individuals in organizations, most of the behavior that is observed is the result of individuals' conscious decisions. These decisions usually fall into two categories. First, individuals make decisions about *membership behavior*—coming to work, staying at work, and in other ways being a member of the organization. Second, individuals make decisions about the amount of *effort* they will direct *towards performing their jobs*. This includes decisions about how hard to work, how much to produce, at what quality, etc.

Assumption 3: Different People Have Different Types of Needs, Desires and Goals. Individuals differ on what kinds of outcomes (or rewards) they desire. These differences are not random; they can be examined systematically by an understanding of the differences in the strength of individuals' needs.

Assumption 4: People Make Decisions among Alternative Plans of Behavior Based on Their Perceptions (Expectancies) of the Degree to Which a Given Behavior will Lead to Desired Outcomes. In simple terms, people tend to do those things which they see as leading to outcomes (which can also be called "rewards") they desire and avoid doing those things they see as leading to outcomes that are not desired.

In general, the approach used here views people as having their own needs and mental maps of what the world is like. They use these maps to make decisions about how they will behave, behaving in those ways which their mental maps indicate will lead to outcomes that will satisfy their needs. Therefore, they are inherently neither motivated nor unmotivated; motivation depends on the situation they are in, and how it fits their needs.

The theory

Based on these general assumptions, expectancy theory states a number of propositions about the process by which people make decisions about their own behavior in organizational settings. While the theory is complex at first view, it is in fact made of a series of fairly straightforward observations about behavior. (The theory is presented in more technical terms in Appendix A.) Three concepts serve as the key building blocks of the theory:

Performance-Outcome Expectancy. Every behavior has associated with it, in an individual's mind, certain outcomes (rewards or punishments). In other words, the individual believes or expects that if he or she behaves in a certain way, he or she will get certain things.

Examples of expectancies can easily be described. An individual may have an expectancy that if he produces ten units he will receive his normal hourly rate while if he produces fifteen units he will receive his hourly pay rate plus a bonus. Similarly an individual may believe that certain levels of performance will lead to approval or disapproval from members of her work group or from her supervisor. Each performance can be seen as leading to a number of different kinds of outcomes and outcomes can differ in their types.

Valence. Each outcome has a "valence" (value, worth, attractiveness) to a specific individual. Outcomes have different valences for different individuals. This comes about because valences result from individual needs and perceptions, which differ because they in turn reflect other factors in the individual's life.

For example, some individuals may value an opportunity for promotion or advancement because of their needs for achievement or power, while others may not want to be promoted and leave their current work group because of needs for affiliation with others. Similarly, a fringe benefit such as a pension plan may have great valence for an older worker but little valence for a young employee on his first job.

Effort-Performance Expectancy. Each behavior also has associated with it in the individual's mind a certain expectancy or probability of success. This expectancy represents the individual's perception of how hard it will be to achieve such behavior and the probability of his or her successful achievement of that behavior.

For example, you may have a strong expectancy that if you put forth the effort, you can produce ten units an hour, but that you have only a fifty-fifty chance of producing fifteen units an hour if you try.

Putting these concepts together, it is possible to make a basic statement about motivation. In general, the motivation to attempt to behave in a certain way is greatest when:

a. The individual believes that the behavior will lead to outcomes (performance-outcome expectancy)

b. The individual believes that these outcomes have positive value for him or her (valence)

c. The individual believes that he or she is able to perform at the desired level (effort-performance expectancy)

Given a number of alternative levels of behavior (ten, fifteen, and twenty units of production per hour, for example) the individual will choose that level of performance which has the greatest motivational force associated with it, as indicated by the expectancies, outcomes, and valences.

In other words, when faced with choices about behavior, the individual goes through a process of considering questions such as, "Can I perform at that level if I try?" "If I perform at that level, what will happen?" "How do I feel about those things that will happen?" The individual then decides to behave in that way which seems to have the best chance of producing positive, desired outcomes.

A general model

On the basis of these concepts, it is possible to construct a general model of behavior in organizational settings (see Figure 1). Working from left to right in the model, motivation is seen as the force on the individual to expend effort. Motivation leads to an observed level of effort by the individual. Effort alone, however, is not enough. Performance results from a combination of the effort that an individual puts forth *and* the level of ability which he or she has (reflecting skills, training, information, etc.) Effort thus combines with ability to produce a given level of performance. As a result of performance, the individual attains certain outcomes. The model indicates this relationship in a dotted line, reflecting the fact that sometimes people perform but do not get desired outcomes. As this process of performance-reward occurs, time after time, the actual events provide in-

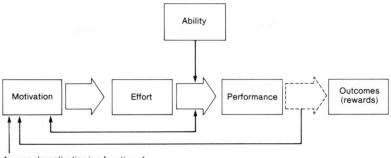

A person's motivation is a function of:

   a. Effort-to-performance expectancies
   b. Performance-to-outcome expectancies
   c. Perceived valence of outcomes

Figure 1. The basic motivation-behavior sequence

formation which influences the individual's perceptions (particularly expectancies) and thus influences motivation in the future.

Outcomes, or rewards, fall into two major categories. First, the individual obtains outcomes from the environment. When an individual performs at a given level he or she can receive positive or negative outcomes from supervisors, co-workers, the organization's reward systems, or other sources. These environmental rewards are thus one source of outcomes for the individual. A second source of outcomes is the individual. These include outcomes which occur purely from the performance of the task itself (feelings of accomplishment, personal worth, achievement, etc.). In a sense, the individual gives these rewards to himself or herself. The environment cannot give them or take them away directly; it can only make them possible.

Supporting evidence

Over fifty studies have been done to test the validity of the expectancy-theory approach to predicting employee behavior.[1] Almost without exception, the studies have confirmed the predictions of the theory. As the theory predicts, the best performers in organizations tend to see a strong relationship between performing their jobs well and receiving rewards they value. In addition they have clear performance goals and feel they can perform well. Similarly, studies using the expectancy theory to predict how people

1. For reviews of the expectancy-theory research, see T. R. Mitchell, "Expectancy models of job satisfaction, occupational preference and effort: A theoretical, methodological and empirical appraisal," *Psychological Bulletin* 81 (1974): 1053–77. For a more general discussion of expectancy theory and other approaches to motivation, see E. E. Lawler, *Motivation in work organizations* (Belmont, Calif.: Brooks/Cole, 1973).

choose jobs also show that individuals tend to interview for and actually take those jobs which they feel will provide the rewards they value. One study, for example, was able to correctly predict for 80 percent of the people studied which of several jobs they would take.[2] Finally, the theory correctly predicts that beliefs about the outcomes associated with performance (expectancies) will be better predictors of performance than will feelings of job satisfaction since expectancies are the critical causes of performance and satisfaction is not.

Questions about the model

Although the results so far have been encouraging, they also indicate some problems with the model. These problems do not critically affect the managerial implications of the model, but they should be noted. The model is based on the assumption that individuals make very rational decisions after a thorough exploration of all the available alternatives and on weighing the possible outcomes of all these alternatives. When we talk or observe individuals, however, we find that their decision processes are frequently less thorough. People often stop considering alternative behavior plans when they find one that is at least moderately satisfying, even though more rewarding plans remain to be examined.

People are also limited in the amount of information they can handle at one time, and therefore the model can indicate a process that is much more complex than the one that actually takes place. On the other hand, the model does provide enough information and is consistent enough with reality to present some clear implications for managers who are concerned with the question of how to motivate the people who work for them.

Implications for managers

The first set of implications is directed towards the individual manager who has a group of people working for him or her and is concerned with how to motivate good performance. Since behavior is a result of forces both in the person and in the environment, you as manager need to look at and diagnose both the person and the environment. Specifically, you need to do the following:

Figure Out What Outcomes Each Employee Values. As a first step, it is important to determine what kinds of outcomes or rewards have valence for your employees. For each employee you need to determine "what turns him or her on." There are various ways of finding this out, including (a) finding out employees' desires through some structured method of data collection, such as a questionnaire, (b) observing the employees' reactions

2. E. E. Lawler, W. J. Kuleck, J. G. Rhode, and J. E. Sorenson, "Job choice and post–decision dissonance," *Organizational Behavior and Human Performance* 13 (1975): 133–45.

to different situations or rewards, or (c) the fairly simple act of asking them what kinds of rewards they want, what kind of career goals they have, or "what's in it for them." It is important to stress here that it is very difficult to change what people want, but fairly easy to find out what they want. Thus, the skillful manager emphasizes diagnosis of needs, not changing the individuals themselves.

Determine What Kinds of Behavior You Desire. Managers frequently talk about "good performance" without really defining what good performance is. An important step in motivating is for you yourself to figure out what kinds of performances are required and what are adequate measures or indicators of performance (quantity, quality, etc.). There is also a need to be able to define those performances in fairly specific terms so that observable and measurable behavior can be defined and subordinates can understand what is desired of them (e.g., produce ten products of a certain quality standard—rather than only produce at a high rate).

Make Sure Desired Levels of Performance are Reachable. The model states that motivation is determined not only by the performance-to-outcome expectancy, but also by the effort-to-performance expectancy. The implication of this is that the levels of performance which are set as the points at which individuals receive desired outcomes must be reachable or attainable by these individuals. If the employees feel that the level of performance required to get a reward is higher than they can reasonably achieve, then their motivation to perform well will be relatively low.

Link Desired Outcomes to Desired Performances. The next step is to directly, clearly, and explicitly link those outcomes desired by employees to the specific performances desired by you. If your employee values external rewards, then the emphasis should be on the rewards systems concerned with promotion, pay, and approval. While the linking of these rewards can be initiated through your making statements to your employees, it is extremely important that employees see a clear example of the reward process working in a fairly short period of time if the motivating "expectancies" are to be created in the employees' minds. The linking must be done by some concrete public acts, in addition to statements of intent.

If your employee values internal rewards (e.g., achievement), then you should concentrate on changing the nature of the person's job, for he or she is likely to respond well to such things as increased autonomy, feedback, and challenge, because these things will lead to a situation where good job performance is inherently rewarding. The best way to check on the adequacy of the internal and external reward system is to ask people what their perceptions of the situation are. Remember it is the perceptions of people that determine their motivation, not reality. It doesn't matter for example whether you feel a subordinate's pay is related to his or her performance. Motivation will be present only if the subordinate sees the relationship.

Many managers are misled about the behavior of their subordinates because they rely on their own perceptions of the situation and forget to find
out what their subordinates feel. There is only one way to do this: ask.
Questionnaires can be used here, as can personal interviews. (See Appendix B for a short version of a motivation questionnaire.)

Analyze the Total Situation for Conflicting Expectancies. Having set up
positive expectancies for employees, you then need to look at the entire
situation to see if other factors (informal work groups, other managers, the
organization's reward systems) have set up conflicting expectancies in the
minds of the employees. Motivation will only be high when people see a
number of rewards associated with good performance and few negative
outcomes. Again, you can often gather this kind of information by asking
your subordinates. If there are major conflicts, you need to make adjustments, either in your own performance and reward structure, or in the other
sources of rewards or punishments in the environment.

Make Sure Changes in Outcomes Are Large Enough. In examining the
motivational system, it is important to make sure that changes in outcomes
or rewards are large enough to motivate significant behavior. Trivial rewards
will result in trivial amounts of effort and thus trivial improvement in performance. Rewards must be large enough to motivate individuals to put forth
the effort required to bring about significant changes in performance.

Check the System for Its Equity. The model is based on the idea that
individuals are different and therefore different rewards will need to be
used to motivate different individuals. On the other hand, for a motivational system to work it must be a fair one—one that has equity (not equality). Good performers should see that they get more desired rewards than
do poor performers, and others in the system should see that also. Equity
should not be confused with a system of equality where all are rewarded
equally, with no regard to their performance. A system of equality is guaranteed to produce low motivation.

Implications for organizations

Expectancy theory has some clear messages for those who run large organizations. It suggests how organizational structures can be designed so that
they increase rather than decrease levels of motivation of organization
members. While there are many different implications, a few of the major
ones are as follows:

Implication 1: The Design of Pay and Reward Systems. Organizations
usually get what they reward, not what they want. This can be seen in many
situations, and pay systems are a good example.[3] Frequently, organizations

---

3. For a detailed discussion of the implications of expectancy theory for pay and reward
systems, see E. E. Lawler, *Pay and organizational effectiveness: A psychological view* (New
York: McGraw-Hill, 1971).

reward people for membership (through pay tied to seniority, for example) rather than for performance. Little wonder that what the organization gets is behavior oriented towards "safe," secure employment rather than effort directed at performing well. In addition, even where organizations do pay for performance as a motivational device, they frequently negate the motivational value of the system by keeping pay secret, therefore preventing people from observing the pay-to-performance relationship that would serve to create positive, clear, and strong performance-to-reward expectancies. The implication is that organizations should put more effort into rewarding people (through pay, promotion, better job opportunities, etc.) for the performances which are desired, and that to keep these rewards secret is clearly self-defeating. In addition, it underscores the importance of the frequently ignored performance evaluation or appraisal process and the need to evaluate people based on how they perform clearly defined specific behaviors, rather than on how they score on ratings of general traits such as "honesty," "cleanliness," and other, similar terms which frequently appear as part of the performance appraisal form.

Implication 2: The Design of Tasks, Jobs, and Roles. One source of desired outcomes is the work itself. The expectancy-theory model supports much of the job enrichment literature, in saying that by designing jobs which enable people to get their needs fulfilled, organizations can bring about higher levels of motivation.[4] The major difference between the traditional approaches to job enlargement or enrichment and the expectancy-theory approach is the recognition by the expectancy theory that different people have different needs and, therefore, some people may not want enlarged or enriched jobs. Thus, while the design of tasks that have more autonomy, variety, feedback, meaningfulness, etc., will lead to higher motivation in some, the organization needs to build in the opportunity for individuals to make choices about the kind of work they will do so that not everyone is forced to experience job enrichment.

Implication 3: The Importance of Group Structures. Groups, both formal and informal, are powerful and potent sources of desired outcomes for individuals. Groups can provide or withhold acceptance, approval, affection, skill training, needed information, assistance, etc. They are a powerful force in the total motivational environment of individuals. Several implications emerge from the importance of groups. First, organizations should consider the structuring of at least a portion of rewards around group performance rather than individual performance. This is particularly important where group members have to cooperate with each other to produce a group product or service, and where the individual's contribu-

---

4. A good discussion of job design with an expectancy theory perspective is in J. R. Hackman, G. R. Oldham, R. Janson, and K. Purdy, "A new strategy for job enrichment," *California Management Review* (Summer 1975): 57.

tion is often hard to determine. Second, the organization needs to train managers to be aware of how groups can influence individual behavior and to be sensitive to the kinds of expectancies which informal groups set up and their conflict or consistency with the expectancies that the organization attempts to create.

Implication 4: The Supervisor's Role. The immediate supervisor has an important role in creating, monitoring, and maintaining the expectancies and reward structures which will lead to good performance. The supervisor's role in the motivation process becomes one of defining clear goals, setting clear reward expectancies, and providing the right rewards for different people (which could include both organizational rewards and personal rewards such as recognition, approval, or support from the supervisor). Thus, organizations need to provide supervisors with an awareness of the nature of motivation as well as the tools (control over organizational rewards, skill in administering those rewards) to create positive motivation.

Implication 5: Measuring Motivation. If things like expectancies, the nature of the job, supervisor-controlled outcomes, satisfaction, etc., are important in understanding how well people are being motivated, then organizations need to monitor employee perceptions along these lines. One relatively cheap and reliable method of doing this is through standardized employee questionnaires. A number of organizations already use such techniques, surveying employees' perceptions and attitudes at regular intervals (ranging from once a month to once every year-and-a-half) using either standardized surveys or surveys developed specifically for the organization. Such information is useful both to the individual manager and to top management in assessing the state of human resources and the effectiveness of the organization's motivational systems.[5] (Again, see Appendix B for excerpts from a standardized survey.)

Implication 6: Individualizing Organizations. Expectancy theory leads to a final general implication about a possible future direction for the design of organizations. Because different people have different needs and therefore have different valences, effective motivation must come through the recognition that not all employees are alike and that organizations need to be flexible in order to accommodate individual differences. This implies the "building in" of choice for employees in many areas, such as reward systems, fringe benefits, job assignments, etc., where employees previously have had little say. A successful example of the building in of such choice can be seen in the experiments of TRW and the Educational Testing Service with "cafeteria fringe-benefits plans" which allow employees to choose the fringe benefits they want, rather than taking the expensive

---

5. The use of questionnaires for understanding and changing organizational behavior is discussed in D. A. Nadler, *Feedback and organizational development: Using data-based methods* (Reading, Mass.: Addison-Wesley, 1977).

and often unwanted benefits which the company frequently provides to everyone.[6]

Summary

Expectancy theory provides a more complex model of man for managers to work with. At the same time, it is a model which holds promise for the more effective motivation of individuals and the more effective design of organizational systems. It implies, however, the need for more exacting and thorough diagnosis by the manager to determine (a) the relevant forces in the individual, and (b) the relevant forces in the environment, both of which combine to motivate different kinds of behavior. Following diagnosis, the model implies a need to act—to develop a system of pay, promotion, job assignments, group structures, supervision, etc.—to bring about effective motivation by providing different outcomes for different individuals.

Performance of individuals is a critical issue in making organizations work effectively. If a manager is to influence work behavior and performance, he or she must have an understanding of motivation and the factors which influence an individual's motivation to come to work, to work hard, and to work well. While simple models offer easy answers, it is the more complex models which seem to offer more promise. Managers can use models (like expectancy theory) to understand the nature of behavior and build more effective organizations.

APPENDIX A: The expectancy theory model in more technical terms

A person's motivation to exert effort towards a specific level of performance is based on his or her perceptions of associations between actions and outcomes. The critical perceptions which contribute to motivation are graphically presented in Figure 2. These perceptions can be defined as follows:

a. The effort-to-performance expectancy ($E{\rightarrow}P$): This refers to the person's subjective probability about the likelihood that he or she can perform at a given level, or that effort on his or her part will lead to successful performance. This term can be thought of as varying from 0 to 1. In general, the less likely a person feels that he or she can perform at a given level, the less likely he or she will be to try to perform at that level. A person's $E{\rightarrow}P$ probabilities are also strongly influenced by each situation and by previous experience in that and similar situations.

b. The performance-to-outcomes expectancy ($P{\rightarrow}O$) and valence (V): This refers to a combination of a number of beliefs about what the out-

---

6. The whole issue of individualizing organizations is examined in E. E. Lawler, "The individualized organization: Problems and promise," *California Management Review* 17, no. 2 (1974): 31–39.

comes of successful performance will be and the value or attractiveness of these outcomes to the individual. Valence is considered to vary from +1 (very desirable) to −1 (very undesirable) and the performance-to-outcomes probabilities vary from +1 (performance sure to lead to outcome) to 0 (performance not related to outcome). In general, the more likely a person feels that performance will lead to valent outcomes, the more likely he or she will be to try to perform at the required level.

c. Instrumentality: As Figure 2 indicates, a single level of performance can be associated with a number of different outcomes, each having a certain degree of valence. Some outcomes are valent because they have direct value or attractiveness. Some outcomes, however, have valence because they are seen as leading to (or being "instrumental" for) the attainment of other "second level" outcomes which have direct value or attractiveness.

d. Intrinsic and extrinsic outcomes: Some outcomes are seen as occurring directly as a result of performing the task itself and are outcomes which the individual thus gives to himself (i.e., feelings of accomplishment, creativity, etc.). These are called "intrinsic" outcomes. Other outcomes that are associated with performance are provided or mediated by external factors (the organization, the supervisor, the work group, etc.). These outcomes are called "extrinsic" outcomes.

Along with the graphic representation of these terms presented in Figure 2, there is a simplified formula for combining these perceptions to arrive at a term expressing the relative level of motivation to exert effort towards performance at a given level. The formula expresses these relationships:

a. The person's motivation to perform is determined by the $P{\rightarrow}O$ ex-

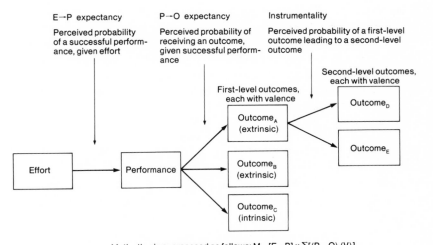

Motivation is expresssed as follows: $M = [E{\rightarrow}P] \times \sum[(P{\rightarrow}O)(V)]$

Figure 2. Major terms in expectancy theory

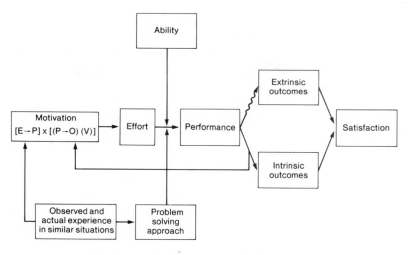

Figure 3. Simplified expectancy-theory model of behavior

pectancy multiplied by the valence (*V*) of the outcome. The valence of the first order outcome subsumes the instrumentalities and valences of second order outcomes. The relationship is multiplicative since there is no motivation to perform if either of the terms is zero.

b. Since a level of performance has multiple outcomes associated with it, the products of all probability-times-valence combinations are added together for all the outcomes that are seen as related to the specific performance.

c. This term (the summed *P→O* expectancies times valences) is then multiplied by the *E→P* expectancy. Again the multiplicative relationship indicates that if either term is zero, motivation is zero.

d. In summary, the strength of a person's motivation to perform effectively is influenced by (1) the person's belief that effort can be converted into performance, and (2) the net attractiveness of the events that are perceived to stem from good performance.

So far, all the terms have referred to the individual's perceptions which result in motivation and thus an intention to behave in a certain way. Figure 3 is a simplified representation of the total model, showing how these intentions get translated into actual behavior.[7] The model envisions the following sequence of events:

a. First, the strength of a person's motivation to perform correctly is most directly reflected in his or her effort—how hard he or she works. This

---

7. For a more detailed statement of the model, see E. E. Lawler, "Job attitudes and employee motivation: Theory, research and practice," *Personnel Psychology* 23 (1970): 223–37.

effort expenditure may or may not result in good performance, since at least two factors must be right if effort is to be converted into performance. First, the person must possess the necessary abilities in order to perform the job well. Unless both ability and effort are high, there cannot be good performance. A second factor is the person's perception of how his or her effort can best be converted into performance. It is assumed that this perception is learned by the individual on the basis of previous experience in similar situations. This "how to do it" perception can obviously vary widely in accuracy, and—where erroneous perceptions exist—performance is low even though effort or motivation may be high.

b. Second, when performance occurs, certain amounts of outcomes are obtained by the individual. Intrinsic outcomes, not being mediated by outside forces, tend to occur regularly as a result of performance, while extrinsic outcomes may or may not accrue to the individual (indicated by the wavy line in the model).

c. Third, as a result of the obtaining of outcomes and the perceptions of the relative value of the outcomes obtained, the individual has a positive or negative affective response (a level of satisfaction or dissatisfaction).

d. Fourth, the model indicates that events which occur influence future behavior by altering the $E{\rightarrow}P$, $P{\rightarrow}O$, and V perceptions. This process is represented by the feedback loops running from actual behavior back to motivation.

APPENDIX B: Measuring motivation using expectancy theory

Expectancy theory suggests that it is useful to measure the attitudes individuals have in order to diagnose motivational problems. Such measurement helps the manager to understand why employees are motivated or not, what the strength of motivation is in different parts of the organization, and how effective different rewards are for motivating performance. A short version of a questionnaire used to measure motivation in organizations is included here.[8] Basically, three different questions need to be asked (see Tables 1, 2, and 3).

Using the questionnaire results

The results from this questionnaire can be used to calculate a *work-motivation score*. A score can be calculated for each individual and scores can be combined for groups of individuals. The procedure for obtaining a work-motivation score is as follows:

a. For each of the possible positive outcomes listed in questions 1 and 2, multiply the score for the outcome on question 1 ($P{\rightarrow}O$ expectancies)

---

8. For a complete version of the questionnaire and supporting documentation, see D. A. Nadler, C. Cammann, G. D. Jenkins, and E. E. Lawler, eds., *The Michigan organizational assessment package* (Progress Report II) (Ann Arbor: Survey Research Center, 1975).

Table 1. Question 1: Here are some things that could happen to people if they do their jobs *especially well*. How likely is it that each of these things would happen if you performed your job *especially well?*

a	You will get a bonus or pay increase	(1)	(2)	(3)	(4)	(5)	(6)	(7)
b	You will feel better about yourself as a person	(1)	(2)	(3)	(4)	(5)	(6)	(7)
c	You will have an opportunity to develop your skills and abilities	(1)	(2)	(3)	(4)	(5)	(6)	(7)
d	You will have better job security	(1)	(2)	(3)	(4)	(5)	(6)	(7)
e	You will be given chances to learn new things	(1)	(2)	(3)	(4)	(5)	(6)	(7)
f	You will be promoted or get a better job	(1)	(2)	(3)	(4)	(5)	(6)	(7)
g	You will get a feeling that you've accomplished something worthwhile	(1)	(2)	(3)	(4)	(5)	(6)	(7)
h	You will have more freedom on your job	(1)	(2)	(3)	(4)	(5)	(6)	(7)
i	You will be respected by the people you work with	(1)	(2)	(3)	(4)	(5)	(6)	(7)
j	Your supervisor will praise you	(1)	(2)	(3)	(4)	(5)	(6)	(7)
k	The people you work with will be friendly with you	(1)	(2)	(3)	(4)	(5)	(6)	(7)

Note: Numbers indicate a range of likelihood: (1), not at all likely; (3), somewhat likely; (5), quite likely; (7) extremely likely.

Table 2. Question 2: Different people want different things from their work. Here is a list of things a person could have on his or her job. How *important* is each of the following to you?

How Important Is . . . ?

a	The amount of pay you get	(1)	(2)	(3)	(4)	(5)	(6)	(7)
b	The chances you have to do something that makes you feel good about yourself as a person	(1)	(2)	(3)	(4)	(5)	(6)	(7)
c	The opportunity to develop your skills and abilities	(1)	(2)	(3)	(4)	(5)	(6)	(7)
d	The amount of job security you have	(1)	(2)	(3)	(4)	(5)	(6)	(7)

How Important Is . . . ?

e	The chances you have to learn new things	(1)	(2)	(3)	(4)	(5)	(6)	(7)
f	Your chances for getting a promotion or getting a better job	(1)	(2)	(3)	(4)	(5)	(6)	(7)
g	The chances you have to accomplish something worthwhile	(1)	(2)	(3)	(4)	(5)	(6)	(7)
h	The amount of freedom you have on your job	(1)	(2)	(3)	(4)	(5)	(6)	(7)

How Important Is . . . ?

i	The respect you receive from the people you work with	(1)	(2)	(3)	(4)	(5)	(6)	(7)
j	The praise you get from your supervisor	(1)	(2)	(3)	(4)	(5)	(6)	(7)
k	The friendliness of the people you work with	(1)	(2)	(3)	(4)	(5)	(6)	(7)

Note: Numbers indicate range of importance: (1), moderately important or less; (4), quite important; (7) extremely important.

Table 3. Question 3: Below you will see a number of pairs of factors that look like this:

Warm weather → sweating   (1) (2) (3) (4) (5) (6) (7)

You are to indicate by checking the appropriate number to the right of each pair how often it is true for *you* personally that the first factor leads to the second on *your job*. Remember, for each pair, indicate how often it is true by checking the box under the response which seems most accurate.

a Working hard → high productivity	(1)	(2)	(3)	(4)	(5)	(6)	(7)
b Working hard → doing my job well	(1)	(2)	(3)	(4)	(5)	(6)	(7)
c Working hard → good job performance	(1)	(2)	(3)	(4)	(5)	(6)	(7)

Note: Numbers indicate frequency range: (1), Never; (3), sometimes; (5), often; (7), almost always.

by the corresponding score on question 2 (valences of outcomes). Thus, score 1a would be multiplied by score 2a, score 1b by score 2b, etc.

   b. All of the 1 times 2 products should be added together to get a total of all expectancies times valences ———.

   c. The total should be divided by the number of pairs (in this case, eleven) to get an average expectancy-times-valence score ———.

   d. The scores from question 3 (*E→P* expectancies) should be added together and then divided by three to get an average effort-to-performance expectancy score ———.

   e. Multiply the score obtained in step c (the average expectancy times valence) by the score obtained in step d (the average E→P expectancy score) to obtain a total work-motivation score ———.

Additional comments on the work-motivation score

A number of important points should be kept in mind when using the questionnaire to get a work-motivation score. First, the questions presented here are just a short version of a larger and more comprehensive questionnaire. For more detail, the articles and publications referred to here and in the text should be consulted. Second, this is a general questionnaire. Since it is hard to anticipate in a general questionnaire what may be valent outcomes in each situation, the individual manager may want to add additional outcomes to questions 1 and 2. Third, it is important to remember that questionnaire results can be influenced by the feelings people have when they fill out the questionnaire. The use of the questionnaire as outlined above assumes a certain level of trust between manager and subordinates. People filling out questionnaires need to know what is going to be done with their answers and usually need to be assured of the confidentiality of their responses. Finally, the research indicates that, in many cases, the score obtained by simply averaging all the responses to question 1 (the P→O expectancies) will be as useful as the fully calculated work-motivation score. In each situation, the manager should experiment and find out whether the additional information in questions 2 and 3 aid in motivational diagnosis.

A Theory of Human Motivation
A. H. Maslow

Dynamics of the basic needs

The "physiological" needs

The needs that are usually taken as the starting point for motivation theory are the so-called physiological drives. Two recent lines of research make it necessary to revise our customary notions about these needs: first, the development of the concept of homeostasis, and second, the finding that appetites (preferential choices among foods) are a fairly efficient indication of actual needs or lacks in the body.

Homeostasis refers to the body's automatic efforts to maintain a constant, normal state of the blood stream. Cannon[1] has described this process for (1) the water content of the blood, (2) salt content, (3) sugar content, (4) protein content, (5) fat content, (6) calcium content, (7) oxygen content, (8) constant hydrogen-ion level (acid-base balance), and (9) constant temperature of the blood. Obviously this list can be extended to include other minerals, the hormones, vitamins, and so on.

Young in a recent article[2] has summarized the work on appetite in its relation to body needs. If the body lacks some chemical, the individual will tend to develop a specific appetite or partial hunger for that food element.

Thus it seems impossible as well as useless to make any list of fundamental physiological needs for they can come to almost any number one might wish, depending on the degree of specificity of description. We cannot identify all physiological needs as homeostatic. That sexual desire, sleepiness, sheer activity, and maternal behavior in animals are homeostatic has not yet been demonstrated. Furthermore, this list would not in-

Abridged from A. H. Maslow, "A Theory of Human Motivation," *Psychological Review* 50 (1943): 370–96. Copyright 1943 by the American Psychological Association, and reproduced by permission.
1. W. B. Cannon, *Wisdom of the Body* (New York: Norton, 1932).
2. P. T. Young, "The Experimental Analysis of Appetite," *Psychological Bulletin* 38 (1941): 129–64.

clude the various sensory pleasures (tastes, smells, tickling, stroking) which are probably physiological and which may become the goals of motivated behavior.

In a previous paper[3] it has been pointed out that these physiological drives or needs are to be considered unusual rather than typical because they are isolable and because they are localized somatically. That is to say, they are relatively independent of each other, of other motivations, and of the organism as a whole, and, in many cases, it is possible to demonstrate a localized, underlying somatic base for the drive. This is true less generally than has been thought (exceptions are fatigue, sleepiness, maternal responses), but it is still true in the classic instances of hunger, sex, and thirst.

It should be pointed out again that any of the physiological needs and the consummatory behavior involved with them serve as channels for all sorts of other needs as well. The person who thinks he is hungry may actually be seeking more for comfort or dependence than for vitamins or proteins. Conversely, it is possible to satisfy the hunger need in part by other activities such as drinking water or smoking cigarettes. In other words, these physiological needs are only relatively isolable.

Undoubtedly these physiological needs are the most prepotent of all needs. What this means specifically is that, in the human being who is missing everything in life in an extreme fashion, it is most likely that the major motivation would be the physiological needs rather than any others. A person who is lacking food, safety, love, and esteem would most probably hunger for food more strongly than for anything else.

If all the needs are unsatisfied, and the organism is then dominated by the physiological needs, all other needs may become simply nonexistent or be pushed into the background. It is then fair to characterize the whole organism by saying that it is hungry, for consciousness is almost completely preempted by hunger. All capacities are put into the service of hunger-satisfaction, and the organization of these capacities is almost entirely determined by the one purpose of satisfying hunger. The receptors and effectors, the intelligence, memory, habits, all may now be defined simply as hunger-gratifying tools. Capacities that are not useful for this purpose lie dormant or are pushed into the background. The urge to write poetry, the desire to acquire an automobile, the interest in American history, the desire for a new pair of shoes are, in the extreme case, forgotten or become of secondary importance. For the man who is extremely and dangerously hungry, no other interests exist but food. He dreams food, he remembers food, he thinks about food, he emotes only about food, he perceives only food, and he wants only food. The more subtle determinants

3. A. H. Maslow, "A Preface of Motivation Theory," *Psychosomatic Medicine* 5 (1943): 85–92.

that ordinarily fuse with the physiological drives in organizing even feeding, drinking, or sexual behavior, may now be so completely overwhelmed as to allow us to speak at this time (but *only* at this time) of pure hunger drive and behavior, with the one unqualified aim of relief.

Another peculiar characteristic of the human organism when it is dominated by a certain need is that the whole philosophy of the future tends also to change. For our chronically and extremely hungry man, utopia can be defined very simply as a place where there is plenty of food. He tends to think that, if only he is guaranteed food for the rest of his life, he will be perfectly happy and will never want anything more. Life itself tends to be defined in terms of eating. Anything else will be defined as unimportant. Freedom, love, community feeling, respect, philosophy may all be waved aside as fripperies which are useless, since they fail to fill the stomach. Such a man may fairly be said to live by bread alone.

It cannot possibly be denied that such things are true, but their *generality* can be denied. Emergency conditions are, almost by definition, rare in the normally functioning peaceful society. That this truism can be forgotten is due mainly to two reasons. First, rats have few motivations other than physiological ones, and since so much of the research on motivation has been made with these animals, it is easy to carry the rat-picture over to the human being. Second, it is too often not realized that culture itself is an adaptive tool, one of whose main functions is to make the physiological emergencies come less and less often. In most of the known societies, chronic extreme hunger of the emergency type is rare rather than common. In any case, this is still true in the United States. The average American citizen is experiencing appetite rather than hunger when he says, "I am hungry." He is apt to experience sheer life-and-death hunger only by accident and then only a few times through his entire life.

Obviously a good way to obscure the "higher" motivations, and to get a lopsided view of human capacities and human nature, is to make the organism extremely and chronically hungry or thirsty. Anyone who attempts to make an emergency picture into a typical one and who will measure all of man's goals and desires by his behavior during extreme physiological deprivation is certainly being blind to many things. It is quite true that man lives by bread alone—when there is no bread. But what happens to man's desires when there *is* plenty of bread and when his belly is chronically filled?

At once other (and "higher") needs emerge and these, rather than physiological hungers, dominate the organism. And when these in turn are satisfied, again new (and still "higher") needs emerge, and so on. This is what we mean by saying that the basic human needs are organized into a hierarchy of relative prepotency.

One main implication of this phrasing is that gratification becomes as important a concept as deprivation in motivation theory, for it releases the organism from the domination of a relatively more physiological need, permitting thereby the emergence of other more social goals. The physiological needs, along with their partial goals, when chronically gratified cease to exist as active determinants or organizers of behavior. They now exist only in a potential fashion in the sense that they may emerge again to dominate the organism if they are thwarted. But a want that is satisfied is no longer a want. The organism is dominated and its behavior organized only by unsatisfied needs. If hunger is satisfied, it becomes unimportant in the current dynamics of the individual.

This statement is somewhat qualified by a hypothesis to be discussed more fully later, namely, that it is precisely those individuals in whom a certain need has always been satisfied who are best equipped to tolerate deprivation of that need in the future; furthermore, those who have been deprived in the past will react to current satisfactions differently from the one who has never been deprived.

The safety needs

If the physiological needs are relatively well gratified, there then emerges a new set of needs, which we may categorize roughly as the safety needs. All that has been said of the physiological needs is equally true, although in lesser degree, of these desires. The organism may equally well be wholly dominated by them. They may serve as the almost exclusive organizers of behavior, recruiting all the capacities of the organism in their service, and we may then fairly describe the whole organism as a safety-seeking mechanism. Again we may say of the receptors, the effectors, of the intellect and the other capacities that they are primarily safety-seeking tools. Again, as in the hungry man, we find that the dominating goal is a strong determinant not only of his current world-outlook and philosophy but also of his philosophy of the future. Practically everything looks less important than safety (even sometimes the physiological needs which, being satisfied, are now underestimated). A man, in this state, if it is extreme enough and chronic enough, may be characterized as living almost for safety alone.

Although in this paper we are interested primarily in the needs of the adult, we can approach an understanding of his safety needs perhaps more efficiently by observation of infants and children, in whom these needs are much more simple and obvious. One reason for the clearer appearance of the threat or danger reaction in infants is that they do not inhibit this reaction at all, whereas adults in our society have been taught to inhibit it at all costs. Thus even when adults do feel their safety to be threatened, we may not be able to see this on the surface. Infants will react in a total fashion and as if they were endangered, if they are disturbed or dropped suddenly, startled by loud noises, flashing light, or other unusual sensory stimulation, by rough handling, by general loss of support in the mother's arms, or by inadequate support.[4]

In infants we can also see a much more direct reaction to bodily illnesses of various kinds. Sometimes these illnesses seem to be immediately and per se threatening and seem to make the child feel unsafe. For instance, vomiting, colic, or other sharp pains seem to make the child look at the whole world in a different way. At such a moment of pain, it may be postulated that, for the child, the appearance of the whole world suddenly changes from sunniness to darkness, so to speak, and becomes a place in which anything at all might happen, in which previously stable things have suddenly become unstable. Thus a child who because of some bad food is taken ill may, for a day or two, develop fear, nightmares, and a need for protection and reassurance never seen in him before his illness.

Another indication of the child's need for safety is his preference for some kind of undisrupted routine or rhythm. He seems to want a predictable, orderly world. For instance, injustice, unfairness, or inconsistency in the parents seems to make a child feel anxious and unsafe. This attitude may not be so much because of the injustice per se or any particular pains involved, but rather because this treatment threatens to make the world look unreliable or unsafe or unpredictable. Young children seem to thrive better under a system which has at least a skeletal outline of rigidity, in which there is a schedule of a kind, some sort of routine, something that can be counted upon, not only for the present, but also far into the future. Perhaps one could express this more accurately by saying that the child needs an organized world rather than an unorganized or unstructured one.

The central role of the parents and the normal family setup are indisputable. Quarreling, physical assault, separation, divorce, or death within the family may be particularly terrifying. Also parental outbursts of rage or threats of punishment directed to the child, calling him names, speaking to him harshly, shaking him, handling him roughly, or actual physical punishment sometimes elicit such total panic and terror in the child that we must assume more is involved than the physical pain alone. While it is true that in some children this terror may represent also a fear of loss of parental love, it can also occur in completely rejected children, who seem to cling to the hating parents more for sheer safety and protection than because of hope of love.

Confronting the average child with new, unfamiliar, strange, unmanageable stimuli or situations will too frequently elicit the danger or terror reaction, as, for example, getting lost or even being separated from the parents

---

4. As the child grows up, sheer knowledge and familiarity as well as better motor development make these "dangers" less and less dangerous and more and more manageable. Throughout life it may be said that one of the main conative functions of education is this neutralizing of apparent dangers through knowledge, e.g., I am not afraid of thunder because I know something about it.

for a short time, being confronted with new faces, new situations, or new tasks, the sight of strange, unfamiliar, or uncontrollable objects, illness, or death. Particularly at such times, the child's frantic clinging to his parents is eloquent testimony to their role as protectors (quite apart from their roles as food-givers and love-givers).

From these and similar observations, we may generalize and say that the average child in our society usually prefers a safe, orderly, predictable, organized world which he can count on and in which unexpected, unmanageable, or other dangerous things do not happen and in which, in any case, he has all-powerful parents who protect and shield him from harm.

That these reactions may so easily be observed in children is in a way a proof of the fact that children in our society feel too unsafe (or, in a word, are badly brought up). Children who are reared in an unthreatening, loving family do *not* ordinarily react as we have described above.[5] In such children the danger reactions are apt to come mostly to objects or situations that adults too would consider dangerous.[6]

The healthy, normal, fortunate adult in our culture is largely satisfied in his safety needs. The peaceful, smoothly running, "good" society ordinarily makes its members feel safe enough from wild animals, extremes of temperature, criminals, assault and murder, tyranny, and so on. Therefore, in a very real sense, they no longer have any safety needs as active motivators. Just as a sated man no longer feels hungry, a safe man no longer feels endangered. If we wish to see these needs directly and clearly we must turn to neurotic or near-neurotic individuals, and to the economic and social underdogs. In between these extremes, we can perceive the expressions of safety needs only in such phenomena as, for instance, the common preference for a job with tenure and protection, the desire for a savings account, and for insurance of various kinds (medical, dental, unemployment disability, old age).

Other broader aspects of the attempt to seek safety and stability in the world are seen in the very common preference for familiar rather than unfamiliar things, or for the known rather than the unknown. The tendency to have some religion or world-philosophy that organizes the universe and the men in it into some sort of satisfactorily coherent, meaningful whole is also in part motivated by safety-seeking. Here too we may list science and philosophy in general as partially motivated by the safety needs (we shall see

5. M. Shirley, "Children's Adjustments to a Strange Situation," *Journal of Abnormal and Social Psychology* 37 (1942): 201–17.

6. A "test battery" for safety might be confronting the child with a small exploding firecracker or with a bewhiskered face, having the mother leave the room, putting him upon a high ladder, giving him a hypodermic injection, having a mouse crawl up to him, and so on. Of course I cannot seriously recommend the deliberate use of such "tests," for they might very well harm the child being tested. But these and similar situations come up by the score in the child's ordinary day-to-day living and may be observed. There is no reason why these stimuli should not be used with, for example, young chimpanzees.

later that there are also other motivations to scientific, philosophical, or religious endeavor).

Otherwise the need for safety is seen as an active and dominant mobilizer of the organism's resources only in emergencies, e.g., war, disease, natural catastrophes, crime waves, societal disorganization, neurosis, brain injury, chronically bad situations.

Some neurotic adults in our society are, in many ways, like the unsafe child in their desire for safety, although in the former it takes on a somewhat special appearance. Their reaction is often to unknown, psychological dangers in a world that is perceived to be hostile, overwhelming, and threatening. Such a person behaves as if a great catastrophe were almost always impending, i.e., he is usually responding as if to an emergency. His safety needs often find specific expression in a search for a protector, or a stronger person on whom he may depend, or perhaps a *Führer*.

The neurotic individual may be described in a slightly different way with some usefulness as a grown-up person who retains his childish attitudes toward the world. That is to say, a neurotic adult may be said to behave "as if" he were actually afraid of a spanking or of his mother's disapproval or of being abandoned by his parents or of having his food taken away from him. It is as if his childish attitudes of fear and threat reaction to a dangerous world had gone underground and, untouched by the growing up and learning processes, were now ready to be called out by any stimulus that would make a child feel endangered and threatened.[7]

The neurosis in which the search for safety takes its clearest form is in the compulsive-obsessive neurosis. Compulsive-obsessives try frantically to order and stabilize the world so that no unmanageable, unexpected, or unfamiliar dangers will ever appear.[8] They hedge themselves about with all sorts of ceremonials, rules, and formulas so that every possible contingency may be provided for and so that no new contingencies may appear. They are much like the brain-injured cases, described by Goldstein,[9] who manage to maintain their equilibrium by avoiding everything unfamiliar and strange and by ordering their restricted world in such a neat, disciplined, orderly fashion that everything in the world can be counted upon. They try to arrange the world so that anything unexpected (dangers) cannot possibly occur. If, through no fault of their own, something unexpected does occur, they go into a panic reaction as if this unexpected occurrence constituted a grave danger. What we can see only as a none-too-strong preference in the healthy person, e.g., preference for the familiar, becomes a life-and-death necessity in abnormal cases.

---

7. Not all neurotic individuals feel unsafe. Neurosis may have at its core a thwarting of the affection and esteem needs in a person who is generally safe.

8. A. H. Maslow and B. Mittelmann, *Principles of Abnormal Psychology* (New York: Harper & Bros., 1941).

9. K. Goldstein, *The Organism* (New York: American Book Co., 1939).

The love needs

If both the physiological and the safety needs are fairly well gratified, then there will emerge the love and affection and belongingness needs, and the whole cycle already described will repeat itself with this new center. Now the person will feel keenly, as never before, the absence of friends or a sweetheart or a wife or children. He will hunger for affectionate relations with people in general, namely, for a place in his group, and he will strive with great intensity to achieve this goal. He will want to attain such a place more than anything else in the world and may even forget that once, when he was hungry, he sneered at love.

In our society the thwarting of these needs is the most commonly found core in cases of maladjustment and more severe psychopathology. Love and affection, as well as their possible expression in sexuality, are generally looked upon with ambivalence and are customarily hedged about with many restrictions and inhibitions. Practically all theorists of psychopathology have stressed thwarting of the love needs as basic in the picture of maladjustment. Many clinical studies have therefore been made of this need and we know more about it perhaps than any of the other needs except the physiological ones.[10]

One thing that must be stressed at this point is that love is not synonymous with sex. Sex may be studied as a purely physiological need. Ordinarily sexual behavior is multidetermined, that is to say, determined not only by sexual but also by other needs, chief among which are the love and affection needs. Also not to be overlooked is the fact that the love needs involve both giving *and* receiving love.[11]

The esteem needs

All people in our society (with a few pathological exceptions) have a need or desire for a stable, firmly based, (usually) high evaluation of themselves, for self-respect, or self-esteem, and for the esteem of others. By firmly based self-esteem, we mean that which is soundly based on real capacity, achievement, and respect from others. These needs may be classified into two subsidiary sets. These are, first, the desire for strength, for achievement, for adequacy, for confidence in the face of the world, and for independence and freedom.[12] Second, we have what we may call the desire

10. Maslow and Mittelmann, *Principles of Abnormal Psychology.*

11. For further details see A. H. Maslow, "The Dynamics of Psychological Security-Insecurity," *Character and Personality* 10 (1942): 331–44, and J. Plant, *Personality and the Cultural Pattern* (New York: Commonwealth Fund, 1937), chap. 5.

12. Whether or not this particular desire is universal we do not know. The crucial question, especially important today, is, "Will men who are enslaved and dominated inevitably feel dissatisfied and rebellious?" We may assume on the basis of commonly known clinical data that a man who has known true freedom (not paid for by giving up safety and security but rather built on the basis of adequate safety and security) will not willingly or easily allow his

for reputation or prestige (defining it as respect or esteem from other people), recognition, attention, importance, or appreciation.[13] These needs have been relatively stressed by Alfred Adler and his followers, and have been relatively neglected by Freud and the psychoanalysts. More and more today, however, there is appearing widespread appreciation of their central importance.

Satisfaction of the self-esteem need leads to feelings of self-confidence, worth, strength, capability, and adequacy, of being useful and necessary in the world. But thwarting of these needs produces feelings of inferiority, of weakness, and of helplessness. These feelings in turn give rise to either basic discouragement or else compensatory or neurotic trends. An appreciation of the necessity of basic self-confidence and an understanding of how helpless people are without it can be easily gained from a study of severe traumatic neurosis.[14]

The need for self-actualization

Even if all these needs are satisfied, we may still often (if not always) expect that a new discontent and restlessness will soon develop, unless the individual is doing what he is fitted for. A musician must make music, an artist must paint, a poet must write, if he is to be ultimately happy. What a man *can* be, he *must* be. This need we may call self-actualization.

This term, first coined by Kurt Goldstein, is being used in this paper in a much more specific and limited fashion. It refers to the desire for self-fulfillment, namely, to the tendency for one to become actualized in what one is potentially. This tendency might be phrased as the desire to become more and more what one is, to become everything that one is capable of becoming.

The specific form that these needs take will of course vary greatly from person to person. In one individual it may be expressed maternally, as the desire to be an ideal mother, in another athletically, in still another aesthetically, in the painting of pictures, and in another inventively, in the creation of new contrivances. It is not necessarily a creative urge, although in people who have any capabilities for creation it will take this form.

The clear emergence of these needs rests upon prior satisfaction of the physiological, safety, love, and esteem needs. We shall call people who are

---

freedom to be taken away from him. But we do not know that this is true for the person born into slavery. The events of the next decade should give us our answer. See discussion of this problem in E. Fromm, *Escape from Freedom* (New York: Farrar & Rinehart, 1941), chap. 5.

13. Perhaps the desire for prestige and respect from others is subsidiary to the desire for self-esteem or confidence in one's self. Observation of children seems to indicate that this is so, but clinical data give no clear support of such a conclusion.

14. A. Kardiner, *The Traumatic Neuroses of War* (New York: Hoeber, 1941). For more extensive discussion of normal self-esteem, as well as for reports of various researches, see A. H. Maslow, "Dominance, Personality, and Social Behavior in Women," *Journal of Social Psychology* 10 (1939): 3–39.

satisfied in these needs, basically satisfied people, and it is from these that we may expect the fullest (and healthiest) creativeness.[15] Since, in our society, basically satisfied people are the exception, we do not know much about self-actualization, either experimentally or clinically. It remains a challenging problem for research.

The preconditions for the basic need satisfactions

There are certain conditions which are immediate prerequisites for the basic need satisfactions. Danger to these is reacted to almost as if it were a direct danger to the basic needs themselves. Such conditions as freedom to speak, freedom to do what one wishes so long as no harm is done to others, freedom to express one's self, freedom to investigate and seek for information, freedom to defend one's self, justice, fairness, honesty, orderliness in the group are examples of such preconditions for basic need satisfactions. Thwarting in these freedoms will be reacted to with a threat or emergency response. These conditions are not ends in themselves but they are *almost* so, since they are so closely related to the basic needs, which are apparently the only ends in themselves. These conditions are defended because without them the basic satisfactions are quite impossible, or, at least, very severely endangered.

If we remember that the cognitive capacities (perceptual, intellectual, learning) are a set of adjustive tools, which have, among other functions, that of satisfaction of our basic needs, then it is clear that any danger to them, any deprivation or blocking of their free use, must also be indirectly threatening to the basic needs themselves. Such a statement is a partial solution of the general problems of curiosity, the search for knowledge, truth, and wisdom, and the ever-persistent urge to solve the cosmic mysteries.

We must therefore introduce another hypothesis and speak of degrees of closeness to the basic needs, for we have already pointed out that *any* conscious desires (partial goals) are more or less important as they are more or less close to the basic needs. The same statement may be made for various behavior acts. An act is psychologically important if it contributes directly to satisfaction of basic needs. The less directly it contributes, or the weaker this contribution is, the less important this act must be conceived to be from the point of view of dynamic psychology. A similar statement may be made for the various defense or coping mechanisms. Some are very directly related to the protection or attainment of the basic needs, others are

15. Clearly creative behavior, like painting, is like any other behavior in having multiple determinants. It may be seen in "innately creative" people whether they are satisfied or not, happy or unhappy, hungry or sated. Also, it is clear that creative activity may be compensatory, ameliorative, or purely economic. It is my impression (as yet unconfirmed) that it is possible to distinguish the artistic and intellectual products of basically satisfied people from those of basically unsatisfied people by inspection alone. In any case, here too we must distinguish, in a dynamic fashion, the overt behavior itself from its various motivations or purposes.

only weakly and distantly related. Indeed, if we wished, we could speak of more basic and less basic defense mechanisms and then affirm that danger to the more basic defenses is more threatening than danger to less basic defenses (always remembering that this is so only because of their relationship to the basic needs).

The desires to know and to understand

So far, we have mentioned the cognitive needs only in passing. Acquiring knowledge and systematizing the universe have been considered as, in part, techniques for the achievement of basic safety in the world, or, for the intelligent man, expressions of self-actualization. Also freedom of inquiry and expression have been discussed as preconditions of satisfactions of the basic needs. True though these formulations may be, they do not constitute definitive answers to the question as to the motivation role of curiosity, learning, philosophizing, experimenting, and so on. They are, at best, no more than partial answers.

This question is especially difficult because we know so little about the facts. Curiosity, exploration, desire for the facts, desire to know may certainly be observed easily enough. The fact that they often are pursued even at great cost to the individual's safety is an earnest of the partial character of our previous discussion. In addition, the writer must admit that, though he has sufficient clinical evidence to postulate the desire to know as a very strong drive in intelligent people, no data are available for unintelligent people. It may then be largely a function of relatively high intelligence. Rather tentatively, then, and largely in the hope of stimulating discussion and research, we shall postulate a basic desire to know, to be aware of reality, to get the facts, to satisfy curiosity, or as Wertheimer phrases it, to see rather than to be blind.

This postulation, however, is not enough. Even after we know, we are impelled to know more and more minutely and microscopically, on the one hand, and, on the other, more and more extensively in the direction of a world philosophy, religion, and so on. The facts that we acquire, if they are isolated or atomistic, inevitably get theorized about, and either analyzed or organized or both. This process has been phrased by some as the search for "meaning." We shall then postulate a desire to understand, to systematize, to organize, to analyze, to look for relations and meanings.

Once these desires are accepted for discussion, we see that they too form themselves into a small hierarchy in which the desire to know is prepotent over the desire to understand. All the characteristics of a hierarchy of prepotency that we have described above seem to hold for this one as well.

We must guard ourselves against the too-easy tendency to separate these desires from the basic needs we have discussed above, i.e., to make a sharp dichotomy between "cognitive" and "conative" needs. The desire to know and to understand are themselves conative, i.e., have a striving character, and are as much personality needs as the "basic needs" we have already discussed.[16]

Further characteristics of the basic needs

The degree of fixity of the hierarchy of basic needs

We have spoken so far as if this hierarchy were a fixed order but actually it is not nearly as rigid as we may have implied. It is true that most of the people with whom we have worked have seemed to have these basic needs in about the order that has been indicated. However, there have been a number of exceptions.

1. There are some people in whom, for instance, self-esteem seems to be more important than love. This most common reversal in the hierarchy is usually due to the development of the notion that the person who is most likely to be loved is a strong or powerful person, one who inspires respect or fear and who is self-confident or aggressive. Therefore, such people who lack love and seek it, may try hard to put on a front of aggressive, confident behavior. But essentially they seek high self-esteem and its behavior expressions more as a means-to-an-end than for its own sake; they seek self-assertion for the sake of love rather than for self-esteem itself.

2. There are other, apparently innately creative people in whom the drive to creativeness seems to be more important than any other counter-determinant. Their creativeness might appear as self-actualization released not by basic satisfaction but in spite of lack of basic satisfaction.

3. In certain people the level of aspiration may be permanently deadened or lowered. That is to say, the less prepotent goals may simply be lost and may disappear forever, so that the person who has experienced life at a very low level, i.e., chronic unemployment, may continue to be satisfied for the rest of his life if only he can get enough food.

4. The so-called psychopathic personality is another example of permanent loss of the love needs. There are people who, according to the best data available,[17] have been starved for love in the earliest months of their lives and have simply lost forever the desire and the ability to give and to receive affection (as animals lose sucking or pecking reflexes that are not exercised soon enough after birth).

5. Another cause of reversal of the hierarchy is that when a need has been satisfied for a long time, this need may be underevaluated. People who have never experienced chronic hunger are apt to underestimate its effects and to look upon food as a rather unimportant thing. If they are

16. M. Wertheimer, unpublished lectures at the New School for Social Research.
17. D. M. Levy, "Primary Affect Hunger," *American Journal of Psychiatry* 94 (1937): 643–52.

dominated by a higher need, this higher need will seem to be the most important of all. It then becomes possible, and indeed does actually happen, that they may, for the sake of this higher need, put themselves into the position of being deprived in a more basic need. We may expect that after a long-time deprivation of the more basic need there will be a tendency to reevaluate both needs so that the more prepotent need will actually become consciously prepotent for the individual who may have given it up very lightly. Thus, a man who has given up his job rather than lose his self-respect, and who then starves for six months or so, may be willing to take his job back even at the price of losing his self-respect.

6. Another partial explanation of *apparent* reversals is seen in the fact that we have been talking about the hierarchy of prepotency in terms of consciously felt wants or desires rather than of behavior. Looking at behavior itself may give us the wrong impression. What we have claimed is that the person will *want* the more basic of two needs when deprived in both. There is no necessary implication here that he will act upon his desires. Let us say again that there are many determinants of behavior other than needs and desires.

7. Perhaps more important than all these exceptions are the ones that involve ideals, high social standards, high values, and the like. With such values people become martyrs; they will give up everything for the sake of a particular ideal or value. These people may be understood, at least in part, by reference to one basic concept (or hypothesis) which may be called "increased frustration-tolerance through early gratification." People who have been satisfied in their basic needs throughout their lives, particularly in their earlier years, seem to develop exceptional power to withstand present or future thwarting of these needs simply because they have strong, healthy character structure as a result of basic satisfaction. They are the "strong" people who can easily weather disagreement or opposition, who can swim against the stream of public opinion, and who can stand up for the truth at great personal cost. It is just the ones who have loved and been well loved and who have had many deep friendships who can hold out against hatred, rejection, or persecution.

I say all this in spite of the fact that there is a certain amount of sheer habituation which is also involved in any full discussion of frustration tolerance. For instance, it is likely that those persons who have been accustomed to relative starvation for a long time are partially enabled thereby to withstand food deprivation. What sort of balance must be made between these two tendencies, of habituation on the one hand, and of past satisfaction breeding present frustration tolerance on the other hand, remains to be worked out by further research. Meanwhile we may assume that they are both operative, side by side, since they do not contradict each other. In respect to this phenomenon of increased frustration tolerance, it seems probable that the most important gratifications come in the first two years of life. That is to say, people who have been made secure and strong in the earliest years tend to remain secure and strong thereafter in the face of whatever threatens.

Degrees of relative satisfaction

So far, our theoretical discussion may have given the impression that these five sets of needs are somehow in a stepwise, all-or-none relationship to one another. We have spoken in such terms as the following: "If one need is satisfied, then another emerges." This statement might give the false impression that a need must be satisfied 100 percent before the next need emerges. In actual fact, most members of our society who are normal are partially satisfied in all their basic needs at the same time. A more realistic description of the hierarchy would be in terms of decreasing percentages of satisfaction as we go up the hierarchy of prepotency. For instance, if I may assign arbitrary figures for the sake of illustration, it is as if the average citizen is satisfied perhaps 85 percent in his physiological needs, 70 percent in his safety needs, 50 percent in his love needs, 40 percent in his self-esteem needs, and 10 percent in his self-actualization needs.

As for the concept of emergence of a new need after satisfaction of the prepotent need, this emergence is not a sudden, saltatory phenomenon but rather a gradual emergence by slow degrees from nothingness. For instance, if prepotent need A is satisfied only 10 percent then need B may not be visible at all. However, as this need A becomes satisfied 25 percent, need B may emerge 5 percent; as need A becomes satisfied 75 percent, need B may emerge 90 percent; and so on.

Unconscious character of needs

These needs are neither necessarily conscious nor unconscious. On the whole, however, in the average person, they are more often unconscious. It is not necessary at this point to overhaul the tremendous mass of evidence which indicates the crucial importance of unconscious motivation. It would by now be expected, on a priori grounds alone, that unconscious motivations would on the whole be rather more important than the conscious motivations. What we have called the basic needs are very often largely unconscious although they may, with suitable techniques and with sophisticated people, become conscious.

The role of gratified needs

It has been pointed out above several times that our higher needs usually emerge only when more prepotent needs have been gratified. Thus gratification has an important role in motivation theory. Apart from this, however, needs cease to play an active determining or organizing role as soon as they are gratified.

What this means, for example, is that a basically satisfied person no longer has the needs for esteem, love, safety, and so on. The only sense in which he might be said to have them is in the almost metaphysical sense that a sated man has hunger or a filled bottle has emptiness. If we are interested in what *actually* motivates us and not in what has, will, or might motivate us, then a satisfied need is not a motivator. It must be considered for all practical purposes simply not to exist, to have disappeared. This point should be emphasized because it has been either overlooked or contradicted in every theory of motivation I know.[18] The perfectly healthy, normal, fortunate man has no sex needs or hunger needs, or needs for safety or for love or for prestige or for self-esteem, except in stray moments of quickly passing threat. If we were to say otherwise, we should also have to aver that every man had all the pathological reflexes, e.g., Babinski, etc., because if his nervous system were damaged, these would appear.

It is such considerations as these that suggest the bold postulation that a man who is thwarted in any of his basic needs may fairly be envisaged simply as a sick man. This is a fair parallel to our designation as "sick" of the man who lacks vitamins or minerals. Who is to say that a lack of love is less important than a lack of vitamins? Since we know the pathogenic effects of love starvation, who is to say that we are invoking value-questions in an unscientific or illegitimate way, any more than the physician does who diagnoses and treats pellagra or scurvy? If I were permitted this usage, I should then say simply that a healthy man is primarily motivated by his needs to develop and actualize his fullest potentialities and capacities. If a man has any other basic needs in any active, chronic sense, then he is simply an unhealthy man. He is as surely sick as if he had suddenly developed a strong salt-hunger or calcium hunger.[19]

If this statement seems unusual or paradoxical, the reader may be assured that this is only one among many such paradoxes that will appear as we revise our ways of looking at man's deeper motivations. When we ask what man wants of life, we deal with his very essence.

Summary

1. There are at least five sets of goals which we may call basic needs. These are briefly physiological, safety, love, esteem, and self-actualization. In addition, we are motivated by the desire to achieve or maintain the various conditions upon which these basic satisfactions rest and by certain more intellectual desires.

18. Note that acceptance of this theory necessitates basic revision of the Freudian theory.

19. If we were to use the "sick" in this way, we should then also have to face squarely the relations of man to his society. One clear implication of our definition would be that (1) since a man is to be called sick who is basically thwarted, and (2) since such basic thwarting is made possible ultimately only by forces outside the individual, the (3) sickness in the individual must come ultimately from a sickness in the society. The "good" or healthy society would then be defined as one that permitted man's highest purposes to emerge by satisfying all his prepotent basic needs.

2. These basic goals are related to one another, being arranged in a hierarchy of prepotency. This means that the most prepotent goal will monopolize consciousness and will tend of itself to organize the recruitment of the various capacities of the organism. The less prepotent needs are minimized, even forgotten or denied. But when a need is fairly well satisfied, the next prepotent ("higher") need emerges, in turn to dominate the conscious life and to serve as the center of organization of behavior, since gratified needs are not active motivators.

Thus man is a perpetually wanting animal. Ordinarily the satisfaction of these wants is not altogether mutually exclusive but only tends to be. The average member of our society is most often partially satisfied and partially unsatisfied in all of his wants. The hierarchy principle is usually empirically observed in terms of increasing percentages of nonsatisfaction as we go up the hierarchy. Reversals of the average order of the hierarchy are sometimes observed. Also it has been observed that an individual may permanently lose the higher wants in the hierarchy under special conditions. There are not only ordinarily multiple motivations for usual behavior but, in addition, many determinants other than motives.

3. Any thwarting or possibility of thwarting of these basic human goals, or danger to the defenses which protect them or to the conditions upon which they rest, is considered to be a psychological threat. With a few exceptions, all psychopathology may be partially traced to such threats. A basically thwarted man may actually be defined as a "sick" man.

4. It is such basic threats which bring about the general emergency reactions.

5. Certain other basic problems have not been dealt with because of limitations of space. Among these are (a) the problem of values in any definitive motivation theory, (b) the relation between appetites, desires, needs, and what is "good" for the organism, (c) the etiology of the basic needs and their possible derivation in early childhood, (d) redefinition of motivational concepts, i.e., drive, desire, wish, need, goal, (e) implication of our theory for hedonistic theory, (f) the nature of the uncompleted act, of success and failure, and of aspiration-level, (g) the role of association, habit, and conditioning, (h) relation to the theory of interpersonal relations, (i) implications for psychotherapy, (j) implication for theory of society, (k) the theory of selfishness, (l) the relation between needs and cultural patterns, (m) the relation between this theory and Allport's theory of functional autonomy. These as well as certain other less important questions must be considered as motivation theory attempts to become definitive.

Intrinsic and Extrinsic Motivation

Barry M. Staw

The study of motivation is not only a specialized research area within the field of psychology, but also an important pursuit for nearly everyone. People engage widely in the art of untangling the causes of human behavior and stand ready to predict the future actions of others. The scientific study of motivation is an organized effort to go beyond these native skills or common sense in explaining, predicting, and possibly controlling, individual behavior.

Typically, explanations of motivational phenomena attempt to answer such questions as, "Why does this worker spend so much time at his job?" or "Why did that student write a fifty-page term paper when everyone else stopped at ten?" To the layman these questions are often answered, or the behavior is "explained," by verbally linking a given action with a recognized goal or desirable outcome (Koch 1956; Lawler 1973). For example, if Person X performs a given act y, his behavior can be made intelligible to the lay person by completing the sentence, "X did y in order to . . ." Thus, acceptable commonsense explanations of a worker's behavior would include such reasons as "in order to increase his salary" or "to be promoted to a better job," while a student's high level of performance could be explained by such goals as "to receive the highest grade" or "to please others."

Commonsense theorizing, however, rarely constitutes a scientific explanation of behavior. It does not specify why a particular goal or end state was valued by an individual or why particular behaviors were chosen to reach the goal. As noted by Vroom (1964), the study of motivation by psychologists has been in large part directed toward filling in this missing empirical content of commonsense reasoning. The scientific effort basically has been one of specifying which objects or outcomes have value to the individual (e.g., those which reduce primary, biologically based drives or accomplish ends ultimately related to these basic needs), how attraction

Reprinted by permission from Barry M. Staw, *Intrinsic and Extrinsic Motivation*, © 1976 by Silver Burdett Company (Morristown, N.J.: General Learning Press).

to various end states undergoes change (e.g., via deprivation, satiation, stimulus generalization), and how behavior directed toward particular outcomes is acquired, refined, and persists over time.

In this module we would like to emphasize, as Koch (1956) has done earlier, that there is an important similarity between commonsense reasoning and scientific theories of motivation. Both are based on an assumption of instrumentalism such that individuals are considered to be doing things for specifiable ends. For example, two of the most dominant approaches to the study of motivation—drive theory (Hull 1943; Spence 1956) and expectancy × value theory (Lewin 1938; Tolman 1932)—include the notion of a reward or desired outcome and posit a learned connection within the organism. For drive theory this learned connection is an S-R habit strength; for expectancy × value theory it is a behavior-outcome expectancy which is perceived by the individual (Campbell et al. 1970). In sum, the instrumentalism present in scientific theories of motivation is not far removed from the layman's "in order to . . ." explanation.

The instrumental view of human behavior is most readily apparent in several formulations of the expectancy × value theory of motivation. As shown in table 1, the formal statements of expectancy × value theory specify that motivation is a product of the utility or valence of a particular goal and the probability of achieving the desired outcome. For each theoretical formulation, the individual is assumed to take the shortest or most direct path toward a valued goal. However, it is important to recognize that in each case the valued goal is also considered to be *external* to the process of "doing." That is, in analyzing behavior, an individual will probably be considered to be performing an act for some goal independent of the activity itself (e.g., higher pay, promotion to a better job). Unfortunately, these expectancy × value formulations (like many others in motivational psychology) do not easily allow for the fact that a worker may be highly productive simply because he enjoys working hard or is satisfied by good work. Likewise, the theories do not readily lead one to an explanation that a student's work is due to a sheer love of writing or a desire to get something fully explained regardless of the grade or praise to be received from others.

Viewed as a whole, the expectancy × value theories outlined in table 1 can be classified as theories of extrinsic motivation, since each assumes a specific goal that provides satisfaction independent of the activity itself.[1] But, actions may sometimes be valued for their own sake, and they may be self-sustained without any external inducement. In these situations, behavior can be said to be intrinsically motivated. Thus whereas extrinsic moti-

---

1. Although Lewin's construct of "resultant force" emphasized the goal-directed nature of motivation, its formulation did actually include the intrinsic valence associated with a behavioral path as well as the extrinsic ends of an action.

Table 1. Summary of expectancy × value theories

Theorist	Major Motivational Constructs			Resultant
Lewin et al. (1944)	Subjective probability of achieving desired outcome	× (Valence) value of desired outcome		→ Force
Tolman (1955)	Expectation of achieving desired outcome	× Demand level for given outcome	× Level of given outcome	→ Performance vector
Edwards (1955)	Subjective probability of achieving desired outcome	× Utility of desired outcome		→ Behavior choice
Rotter (1954)	Expectancy of achieving desired reinforcement	× Value of reinforcement		→ Behavior potential
Atkinson (1966)	Probability of achieving desired outcome	× Motive level for achieving desired outcome	× Incentive level of desired outcome	→ Resultant motivation
Vroom (1964)	Expectancy of achieving desired outcome	× (Valence) value of desired outcome		→ Force

Source: Abraham K. Korman, *The Psychology of Motivation.* © 1974. Reprinted by permission of Prentice-Hall, Inc., Englewood Cliffs, N.J.

vation emphasizes the value an individual places on the ends of an action and the probability of reaching these ends, intrinsic motivation refers to the pleasure or value associated with the activity itself. Let us examine more closely the theoretical and empirical basis of intrinsic motivation so that we may explicitly build this factor into a revised theory of motivation that takes both factors into account.

The basis of intrinsic motivation

Value inherent in behavior

There is strong evidence that many activities such as manipulation, exploration, and information processing provide satisfaction in and of themselves. For example, in some early studies on animal behavior, Harlow and his associates (Harlow et al. 1950; Harlow and McClearn 1954) demonstrated that monkeys will learn to disassemble puzzles for no reward other than the opportunity to manipulate things. Similarly, Montgomery (1954) showed that rats will systematically select the path in a maze which leads to an opportunity to explore additional mazes. Also, in studies using human subjects it has been shown that the absence of stimulation and environmental change can lead to extreme discomfort. In one of the most vivid demonstrations of the need for stimulation, Bexton et al. (1954) employed college students to lie on a cot for 24 hours a day in a sound-deadened room (with time out for meals and toilet needs). In this study visual and tactile stimulation was also minimized since subjects were required to wear translucent goggles and special gloves. Although the participants were paid extremely well for their time ($20 in 1954 currency), few could tolerate the experiment for as long as two or three days.

In general, research has shown that in the absence of either external pleasureful-painful stimulation or basic homeostatic needs, an individual is not quiescent. In fact, there is some evidence that it is precisely when external pressures (e.g., hunger, thirst, sex) are minimized that play, exploration, manipulation, and curiosity behaviors are most likely to be manifested (Hunt 1965). As a result of these findings, several psychologists have gone so far as to posit new human needs for manipulation (Harlow and McClearn 1954), exploration (Montgomery 1954), and curiosity (Berlyne 1960). Tasks engaging these needs can be considered intrinsically motivating, since the activity provides value to the individual independent of any external sources of satisfaction.

Value inherent in accomplishment

In addition to the value an individual may derive from the physical or mental activities involved in a task, he may also gain satisfaction from knowing that his efforts have led to a completed product or accomplishment. McClelland (1951, 1961) has conceptualized this source of satisfaction as the fulfillment of a need for achievement. Using a projective test (the TAT) to assess the strength of achievement motivation, it has been shown that situations involving competition or the testing of individual abilities produce the greatest motive arousal (McClelland 1971). A learned drive to achieve is thought to be activated when performance can be readily evaluated as a success or failure, and the affect potentially associated with a task (the incentive value of success) is hypothesized to be a function of both the strength of this achievement need and the probability of success. The greatest satisfaction or pride in accomplishment would therefore be derived by persons with high need for achievement who are successful in performing a difficult task (see Litwin [1966] and Cook [1970] for empirical tests of this hypothesis).

Also consistent with the notion that many people seek out or value accomplishment are the theoretical statements of White (1959) and Maslow (1954, 1970). White posits that individuals are motivated toward competence or mastery over their environments—that they not only manipulate and explore their surroundings but strive to master them through higher levels of motor and mental coordination. In a similar vein, Maslow states that many individuals possess active higher-order needs for esteem and self-actualization. Esteem needs include a need for personal feelings of achievement or success, while a self-actualization need is considered to be a striving for personal growth and development through one's *own* actions. Thus like McClelland's formulation of achievement motivation, both White's and Maslow's theoretical statements suggest that individuals may be motivated to perform certain tasks without an apparent need for external reward. If a task involves the opportunity for one to use new skills or is challenging to one's ability, it may therefore provide satisfaction in and of itself.

A revised expectancy × value theory

Although expectancy × value theories were originally conceived as models of extrinsic motivation, they can be amended to include intrinsic factors. As we have seen, it is important to recognize two sources of individual satisfaction that are not generally included in an expectancy × value model. First, a person may work on a task merely for the activity and stimulation involved regardless of whether his actions lead to a specific accomplishment or tangible rewards provided by others. Second, individual accomplishments may provide satisfaction regardless of whether they lead to external rewards such as money, praise, or increased status. We may thus think of task performance as involving three distinct sources of value to an individual: (1) value associated with a behavior itself, (2) value associated with accomplishment, and (3) value associated with rewards presented by others. The first two sources of value are mediated by the individual and can be considered intrinsic to his performance, while the third comprises an extrinsic source of satisfaction.

Several recent formulations of task motivation within organizational settings have incorporated intrinsic as well as extrinsic factors into the expectancy $\times$ value framework. Galbraith and Cummings (1967), Porter and Lawler (1967), and Lawler (1971, 1973) have each noted that task accomplishment can be rewarding to an individual independent of any externally mediated rewards. However, their models of motivation have each defined intrinsic rewards as those derived only from achievement, and they have not specifically considered the intrinsic rewards associated with behavior irrespective of task accomplishment. A recent expectancy model put forth by House and his associates (House 1971; House et al., 1974) is most inclusive in that it specifies both these potential sources of intrinsic motivation. A slightly amended version of the model is presented below.

$$M = IV_a + (P_1)(IV_b) + [\sum_{i=1}^{n} (P_{2i})(EV_i)]$$

where

    M = task motivation
    IV_a = intrinsic valence associated with task behavior
    IV_b = intrinsic valence associated with task accomplishment
    EV_i = extrinsic valences associated with task accomplishment
    P_1 = perceived probability that one's behavior will lead to accomplishment of the task
    P_{2i} = perceived probabilities that one's task accomplishment will lead to extrinsic valences

House's theory of task motivation posits that the individual estimates the instrumentality of his behavior, P_1, for accomplishing a task goal and also the likelihood, P_2, that a task accomplishment will lead to valued extrinsic rewards. In assessing P_1 the individual may take into consideration such factors as the level of his abilities relevant to the task, barriers to work goal accomplishment in the environment (e.g., not getting sufficient materials to finish a job correctly), and the help or support he will receive from others in the work setting. In assessing P_2 the individual may consider the likelihood that his supervisor will recognize good performance through praise, favoritism, a salary raise, or promotion to a better job. In addition, the individual is assumed to place some subjective value upon the behaviors involved in task performance, task accomplishment, and the extrinsic rewards potentially available through work performance. Thus a worker who is bored at home may possess a high IV_a, a worker who has a high need for achievement will be high on IV_b, while the person in dire need of a bigger paycheck should have a high EV_i. We will make use of this revised version of expectancy $\times$ value theory in predicting individual task motivation and formulating specific strategies for changing motivation.[2]

Methods of increasing task motivation

Extrinsic factors

Probably the most common action individuals take to change another's task behavior is to alter extrinsic motivation. From the expectancy $\times$ value model presented above, we can see that extrinsic motivation can be increased by changing either the extrinsic valences associated with task accomplishment (EV_i) or the perceived probabilities linking accomplishment to rewards (P_{2i}).

One procedure by which the valence of extrinsic rewards can be altered is through deprivation. Numerous laboratory studies have shown that by depriving a subject of a valued commodity (e.g., food, water, sex), motivation can be increased for any task which leads to its attainment. The same principle no doubt holds in everyday life, but the use of deprivation to motivate someone to perform a task is considered an ethically undesirable way to change behavior. Fortunately, few allocators of rewards have the amount of control over the lives of others necessary to use it successfully. At present, for example, if an industrial firm chose to restrict workers' pay, it would, in addition to increasing the perceived value of money, cause workers to transfer quickly to another job. Only when the workers' options are extremely limited (e.g., during periods of high unemployment or a government-controlled labor market) would deprivation be an effective motivational tool.

A preferable way to increase extrinsic motivation is to assess the desires or needs of the individuals performing a task and to make available those extrinsic rewards with the greatest utility. For instance, one purpose of periodic meetings between supervisors and subordinates within small task groups and attitude surveys within large organizations could be to assess regularly the changing needs of employees. Ideally, extrinsic rewards could be tailored to groups of individuals with similar needs (e.g., for security, money, verbal praise) or provided on an individual basis. By simply

2. Clearly, any effort to change the motivation or behavior of another individual implies certain ethical considerations. For example, as a change agent, one must assess the likely consequences of a change intervention; the results of not intervening; and the rights, both legal and ethical, of the "target" individual. In the sections that follow, several motivational strategies are described in terms of increasing another person's intrinsic and/or extrinsic motivation to perform a task. The examples that illustrate these strategies consider the change agent to be someone in control of resources or other sources of social power, such as a task supervisor, educational instructor, or group leader. Obviously, there may be alternative initiators of change interventions (workers, students, outside consultants), and some of the strategies illustrated here may be (justifiably) rejected by a change agent on the basis of local values and social norms.

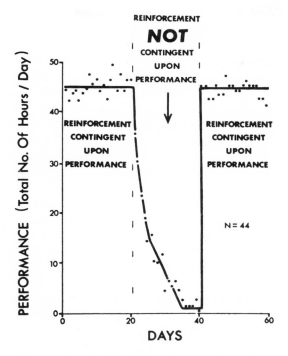

Figure 1. Total number of hours of onward performance by a group of 44 patients under contingent and noncontingent reinforcement schemes

SOURCE: T. Allyon and N. H. Azrin, "The Measurement and Reinforcement of Behavior of Psychotics," *Journal of the Experimental Analysis of Behavior* 8 (1965): 357–383. Copyright 1965 by the Society for the Experimental Analysis of Behavior, Inc. (Additional information and related research can be found in *The Token Economy: A Motivational System for Therapy and Rehabilitation* by T. Allyon and N. Azrin, published by Appleton-Century-Crofts, 1968.)

restructuring the mix of rewards to achieve the greatest extrinsic valences, motivation to perform a task could thus be increased (see Lawler [1971] for a discussion of "cafeteria-style" pay schemes as applied to industry).

In addition to the valences associated with extrinsic rewards, considerable attention should also be given to the perceived probability that task accomplishment will lead to rewards. The most effective procedure in terms of increasing motivation is to make rewards contingent upon performance. As shown in figure 1, dramatic changes in behavior can result from tying extrinsic rewards to behavior. Depicted in the figure is the level of desired behavior emitted by patients of a mental hospital when rewards are both contingent and noncontingent on behavior. The extrinsic rewards used in the study were tokens which could be exchanged for food, cigarettes, or other valued commodities.

In practice, there are many ways of designing a contingent reward system. When task accomplishments are easily defined and measurable, it is often feasible to institute some sort of piece-rate incentive system. In these cases, the level of extrinsic rewards is based upon the quantity and/or quality of performance. Often, however, task accomplishments are neither clearly defined nor easily measured. In these cases, a judgment of the individual's performance is required by a supervisor or allocator of rewards. Obviously, any error in evaluation or sudden change in the criteria of performance will sharply reduce the individual's perception that task accomplishment leads to rewards. As a consequence, the perceived objectivity or fairness of the appraisal system can be as important a determinant of the individual's task motivation as the actual contingency between rewards and performance.

Making valued extrinsic rewards contingent upon performance is generally an effective motivational strategy. However, it is not without some problems. First, it requires that a supervisor possess a sufficient quantity of extrinsic rewards to motivate workers to complete a task. Although most formal organizations (e.g., industry, government) can afford literally to purchase a worker's services, a lack of valued extrinsic rewards can present a motivational problem in many informal work settings (e.g., social clubs, volunteer organizations, home environment). Also, as discussed, an effective strategy of extrinsic motivation requires that performance be accurately assessed by supervisors so that rewards can be dispensed on a contingent basis. Although this is no problem on a routine task for which the supervisor can clearly set the criteria of performance and measure it, frequently (on tasks involving a great deal of skill and creativity) the supervisor may actually know less about the job than the worker and be in a very poor position to evaluate his performance.

Intrinsic factors

From the revised expectancy $\times$ value model we can see that intrinsic motivation results from the perception of rewards inherent in either task behavior (IV_a) or accomplishment (IV_b). Several factors can be expected to account for the intrinsic valences associated with both behavior and accomplishment, but not all of them are easily alterable. For example, it would be most difficult to change individual needs for activity, manipulation, or exploration, except on a temporary basis. McClelland and his associates have had some success in increasing an individual's achievement needs and motivating entrepreneurial behavior through intensive training sessions (McClelland and Winter 1969). However, it is doubtful that achievement motivation can, by itself, affect the performance of persons on routine organizational tasks or other activities which are not highly achievement oriented (McClelland 1973a, 1973b).

Perhaps the most practical method of increasing a person's intrinsic motivation to perform a task is to purposely alter the characteristics of his work activities. Assuming that individuals possess at least a moderate need for activity and achievement, many tasks can be changed so that individuals derive greater satisfaction from either task behavior or accomplishment. Many industrial firms have, in effect, followed these principles in programs of job enlargement and job enrichment. For example, the intrinsic rewards associated with task behavior are often improved by increasing the variety of skills necessary to perform a task or by rotating workers among several different tasks. Similarly, the intrinsic rewards associated with task accomplishment can be improved by increasing the responsibility of workers or the importance of the tasks they perform.

Increasing intrinsic motivation has several advantages as a motivational strategy. When individuals can derive satisfaction from task behaviors or accomplishment, there may, for example, be a reduced need for extrinsic rewards to motivate behavior. This may be especially important in cases where supervisors have a limited supply of extrinsic inducements or where individuals do not value those that are readily available. A second advantage of intrinsic motivation is that the need to monitor another's task behavior is reduced. With intrinsic motivation, it may not be necessary to rely totally upon piece-rate incentive systems or periodic performance appraisals to induce a high level of task performance. Instead, a task can be designed so that the quantity and/or quality of performance fulfills the individual's needs for achievement. When this is done, the worker who values achievement can monitor his own task accomplishment and reward himself on a completely contingent basis.

There are a number of ways a task can be changed to increase intrinsic motivation and some of the most important ones are listed in figure 2. The job characteristics shown in the figure are based heavily upon the recent research and theory of Hackman and Oldham (1975, in press), but are framed within the expectancy $\times$ value model of motivation discussed earlier. It should be noted that the research underlying the model presented

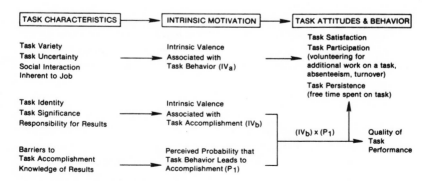

Figure 2. Task determinants of intrinsic motivation

here has been conducted largely within industrial organizations. However, the characteristics of tasks are stated in rather general terms and may be applicable to many other settings (e.g., educational organizations). A brief consideration of each of these task characteristics and how they might be altered follows.

Task variety

In order to increase the intrinsic valence associated with task behavior (IV_3), greater variety can often be introduced into a job. A greater assortment of tasks can be performed by the individual on a single job or, if this is impossible, he can be rotated periodically from job to job. Many industrial firms have followed this procedure to reduce boredom, and increases in task satisfaction commonly result from such changes. Within educational organizations, a similar increase in the variety of learning tasks can often be used to maintain student interest.

Task uncertainty

Very mechanistic tasks, even if they comprise a varied set of activities, may not be totally satisfying to most individuals. Because of our needs for exploration and cognitive stimulation, a task that involves information processing and/or the resolution of uncertainty may be of greater intrinsic interest (e.g., Hune 1971, Lanzetta 1971). Obviously, there may be some upper limit to the degree of uncertainty satisfying to an individual. Both the individual's level of task-relevant skills needed to resolve uncertainty and his personal tolerance for ambiguity may therefore determine the optimal task design.

Social interaction inherent to the job

The fact that individuals generally derive satisfaction from interacting with others can be an important inducement for working. For most persons, the intrinsic valence associated with task behavior is greater when social interaction is an integral part of the job. The formation of task groups and exchange of information are techniques used by schools for increasing the intrinsic interest of students. Also, within industry, there are now experiments in which previously isolated workers can increase their contact with the ultimate users of their services as well as with their co-workers (Hackman et al. 1975).

Task identity

Another way to improve the intrinsic valence associated with task accomplishment might be to increase the "wholeness" or identity of a person's work output. At present, within industry, many jobs are so specialized that the worker cannot see the relationship between his small task and the final finished product. In order to increase task identity, jobs can often be redesigned. The individual can be allowed to produce a larger module of work, or a small team of workers can be formed to complete an entire assembly process.

Task significance

The intrinsic valence associated with task accomplishment (IV_b) can often be improved by increasing the perceived significance of a person's work output. This can be done either by changing the individual to a more important job or by increasing the salience of his present work output. An example of the latter course of action would be to emphasize the usefulness of the person's work or to place the person in direct contact with the ultimate users of his product. Within the educational setting, an increase of task significance may translate itself into a stress for "relevance" in learning activities.

Responsibility for results

If an individual does not feel responsible for his work output, it is doubtful that he will place a high value on task accomplishment. Only when the person can experience success or failure on a task is he likely to value the intrinsic rewards associated with accomplishment. Therefore, to increase intrinsic motivation, the person might be given a larger amount of discretion over his task activities and held more accountable for his results. In industry, the autonomy of workers is often increased by allowing them to schedule their own work activities, decide on work methods, and check the quantity of their own output. Quite similar procedures could be devised within a school environment in order to increase the felt responsibility of students for their own learning.

Barriers to task accomplishment

Within any task setting (e.g., industrial, educational, etc.) the perceived probability that behavior leads to accomplishment (P_2) may depend on the extent to which there are barriers to task accomplishment. Some of these barriers may be internal to the individual such as his ability or training to perform a task; others may be related to his immediate task environment (e.g., not getting the necessary material or social support to complete the job). Restructuring a job (or educational task) to remove external barriers to accomplishment and providing requisite training and supervision may thus serve to increase an individual's intrinsic motivation.

Knowledge of results

Knowledge of results can also be expected to affect a person's intrinsic motivation to perform a task. Clearly, if the individual receives no feedback on the quality of his performance, it will be difficult for him to derive satisfaction from accomplishment. Thus it is important for supervisors to relate to workers exactly how they are doing. This feedback should be on a continuous basis so that the individual can quickly change his behavior, and not merely on a periodic review basis. Ideally, a feedback system should be built into the work itself. At present many industrial tasks do contain their own quality checks which can be performed by the worker, and within the educational context, computerized instruction provides a good example of learning tasks in which immediate feedback is provided so that changes in behavior can be effected by the individual.

Effects of intrinsic motivation

Figure 2 shows that intrinsic motivation can influence both an individual's task attitudes and his behavior. If the individual values the behaviors associated with a task actively (IV_a), he can be expected to participate in the task, be satisfied with it, and perhaps even to volunteer for additional tasks of a similar nature. If the individual values task accomplishment and perceives a strong link between his behavior and accomplishment $[(IV_b) (P_1)]$, he can also be expected to produce high-quality work. Empirical support for these hypotheses is derived from research on both task design and work effectiveness within organizational settings (see Hackman and Lawler 1971; Hackman and Oldham 1975, 1976; House 1971; Oldham 1974).

Combining intrinsic and extrinsic motivation

It is apparent from our discussion that both intrinsic and extrinsic motivation can be effective methods of energizing behavior. Either of these motivational strategies can be used to get an individual to perform a task, and both intrinsic and extrinsic rewards can bring satisfaction to the individual. The question remains, however, whether these two sources of motivation can be combined effectively to yield overall positive effects on the individual's task attitudes and behavior.

In the expectancy $\times$ value model presented above, intrinsic and extrinsic factors are added to form an overall measure of motivation. This model, like those of Galbraith and Cummings (1967), Porter and Lawler (1967), and Lawler (1971, 1973), *assumes* that the perception of intrinsic rewards and the perception of extrinsic rewards are additive in their effect on anticipated work satisfaction. It assumes that intrinsic motivation $[(IV_a) + (P_1) (IV_b)]$ and extrinsic motivation

$$[\sum_{i=1}^{n} (P_{2i}) (EV_i)]$$

summate to produce overall motivation and that intrinsic and extrinsic motivation are separate, independent factors.

Whether or not intrinsic and extrinsic sources of motivation are independent or do in fact have an effect upon each other is a question of considerable practical as well as theoretical significance. For example, if they are positively interrelated, we might expect extrinsic rewards to increase a person's intrinsic interest in a task, whereas if they are negatively interrelated, the administration of an extrinsic reward could drive out intrinsic motivation. This issue is of importance to any setting (e.g., industrial organizations, schools, or voluntary work situations) in which extrinsic rewards are administered and the allocator of the rewards is interested in the individual's resultant task attitudes and behavior.

The interrelationship of intrinsic and extrinsic motivation

Historically, the interrelationship of intrinsic and extrinsic motivation has been the subject of considerable controversy. In fact, it can be said that there exist psychological theories which will predict either a positive relationship between intrinsic and extrinsic motivation, a negative relationship, or no relationship at all. As a consequence, we will examine each of these theoretical positions in some detail and, in the light of recent empirical research, attempt to formulate a unified view of the interrelationship between intrinsic and extrinsic factors.

Long ago, Woodworth (1918) suggested that in the process of acquiring a set of skills toward some end, the skills themselves could develop their own motivating force that might endure even after the end is no longer sought. He made the point in the following context:

> . . . while a man may enter a certain line of business from a purely external economic motive, he develops an interest in the business for its own sake . . . and the motive force that drives him in the daily task, provided of course this does not degenerate into mere automatic routine, is precisely an interest in the problems confronting him and in the processes by which he is able to deal with those problems. The end furnishes the motive force for the search for means but once the means are found, they are apt to become interesting on their own account. [P. 104]

Allport (1937) has argued in a similar vein that certain behaviors develop their own motive power or "functional autonomy." He noted that while many activities, such as making money and solving problems, originally may have served some other motive, their persistence in the absence of external force necessitates their having developed a value on their own.

The notion that an activity or task behavior can become valued by an individual through its continued association with an external reward can be explained by the process of *secondary reinforcement*. Secondary reinforcement refers to a process by which an originally neutral stimulus acquires reinforcing properties through its pairing with a primary reinforcer (Ferster and Skinner 1957; Uhl and Young 1967). Thus in these terms it is possible to assert that an intrinsically motivating activity is simply one in which the reinforcement value of an extrinsic goal has associatively rubbed off on the behavior. Irrespective of temporal considerations (i.e., how long it might take for an activity to acquire reinforcing properties on its own), we can therefore predict, through secondary reinforcement, that there will be a positive relationship between intrinsic and extrinsic motivation. In short, no matter what a person's original reaction to a task, secondary reinforcement predicts that it may improve over time if it leads to valued extrinsic rewards.

Other psychologists, as we have seen, might disagree with the notion that all activities currently valued by individuals are merely those which have previously led to positive external outcomes. As noted by Harlow (1950), Montgomery (1954), and Berlyne (1960), an intrinsically motivated activity may stem from an innate human need for stimulation, information, or knowledge and is not necessarily dependent upon external reinforcement. Since certain activities may be valued independently of homeostatic needs or acquired drives based upon them, we might therefore posit that there is no clear relationship between intrinsic and extrinsic motivation.

A new approach to the problem

Recently, investigations have been undertaken into the relationship between intrinsic and extrinsic motivation from an entirely different perspective. Instead of asking how intrinsic motivation might be derived from extrinsic reward contingencies or independent human motives, several researchers have concluded that both intrinsic and extrinsic motivation may be more usefully studied as perceptions on the part of individuals. From a perceptual approach it is not necessary to know how specific behaviors originally acquired reinforcing properties, but only that an individual at a given point in time may perceive a task to be rewarding in and of itself. That is, if individuals *think* they are intrinsically motivated, this self-perception alone may be enough to influence future behavior and attitudes. This new approach is consistent with our expectancy $\times$ value formulation of motivation, since in that model individuals are assumed to hold perceptions of rewards to be derived from their actions, and behavior is assumed to be based on the direction and magnitude of these perceptual states.

Within the area of interpersonal perception, it has been noted (Heider 1958) that an individual may infer the causes of another's actions to be a function of personal and environmental force:

$$\text{Action} = f(\text{personal force} + \text{environmental force})$$

This is quite close to saying that individuals attempt to determine whether another person is intrinsically motivated to perform an activity (action due to personal force), or extrinsically motivated (action due to environmental force), or both. The extent to which an individual will infer intrinsic motivation on the part of another is predicted to be affected by the clarity and strength of external forces within the situation (Kelley 1967; Jones and Davis 1965; Jones and Nisbett 1971). When there are strong forces bearing on the individual to perform an activity, there is little reason to assume that a behavior is self-determined, whereas a high level of intrinsic motivation might be inferred if environmental force is minimal. Several studies dealing with interpersonal perception have supported this general conclusion (Jones et al. 1961; Thibaut and Riecken 1955; Jones and Harris 1967; Strickland 1958).

Bem (1967a, 1967b) extrapolated this interpersonal theory of causal attribution to the study of self-perception or how one views his *own* behavior within a social context. Bem hypothesized that the extent to which external pressures are sufficiently strong to account for one's behavior will determine the likelihood that a person will attribute his own actions to internal causes. Thus if a person acts under strong external rewards or punishments, he is likely to assume that his behavior is under external control. However, if extrinsic contingencies are not strong or salient, the individual is likely to assume that his behavior is due to his own interest in the activity or that his behavior is intrinsically motivated. De Charms has made a similar point in his discussion of individuals' perceptions of personal causation (1968, p. 328):

> As a first approximation, we propose that whenever a person experiences himself to be the locus of causality for his own behavior (to be an Origin), he will consider himself to be intrinsically motivated. Conversely, when a person perceives the locus of causality for his behavior to be external to himself (that he is a Pawn), he will consider himself to be extrinsically motivated.

De Charms emphasized that the individual may attempt psychologically to label his actions on the basis of whether or not he has been instrumental in affecting his own behavior; that is, whether his behavior has been intrinsically or extrinsically motivated.

The case for a negative relationship between intrinsic and extrinsic motivation

The self-perception approach to intrinsic and extrinsic motivation leads to the conclusion that there may be a negative interrelationship between these two motivational factors. The basis for this prediction stems from the assumption that individuals may work backward from their own actions in inferring sources of causation (Bem 1967a, 1967b, 1972). For example, if external pressures on an individual are so high that they would ordinarily cause him to perform a given task regardless of the internal characteristics of the activity, then the individual might logically infer that he is extrinsically motivated. In contrast, if external reward contingencies are extremely low or nonsalient, the individual might then infer that his behavior is intrinsically motivated. What is important is the fact that a person, in performing an activity, may *seek out* the probable cause of his own actions.

Since behavior has no doubt been caused by something, it makes pragmatic, if not scientific, sense for the person to conclude that the cause is personal (intrinsic) rather than extrinsic if he can find no external reasons for his actions.

Two particular situations provide robust tests of the self-perception prediction. One is a situation in which there is insufficient justification for a person's actions, a situation in which the intrinsic rewards for an activity are very low (e.g., a dull task) and there are no compensating extrinsic rewards (e.g., monetary payment, verbal praise). Although rationally, one ordinarily tries to avoid these situations, there are occasions when one is faced with the difficult question of "why did I do that?" The self-perception theory predicts that in situations of insufficient justification, the individual may cognitively reevaluate the intrinsic characteristics of an activity in order to justify or explain his own behavior. For example, if the individual performed a dull task for no external reward, he may "explain" his behavior by thinking that the task was not really so bad after all.

Sometimes a person may also be fortunate enough to be in a situation in which his behavior is oversufficiently justified. For example, a person may be asked to perform an interesting task and at the same time be lavishly paid for his efforts. In such situations, the self-perception theory predicts that the individual may actually reevaluate the activity in a downward direction. Since the external reward would be sufficient to motivate behavior by itself, the individual may mistakenly infer that he was extrinsically motivated to perform the activity. He may conclude that since he was forced to perform the task by an external reward, the task probably was not terribly satisfying in and of itself.

Figure 3 graphically depicts the situations of insufficient and overly sufficient justification. From the figure, we can see that the conceptual framework supporting self-perception theory raises several interesting issues. First, it appears from this analysis that there are only two fully stable attributions of behavior: (1) the perception of extrinsically motivated behavior in which the internal rewards associated with performing an activity are low while external rewards are high, and (2) the perception of intrinsically motivated behavior in which the task is inherently rewarding but external rewards are low. Furthermore, it appears that situations of insufficient justification (where intrinsic and extrinsic rewards are both low) and oversufficient justification (where intrinsic and extrinsic rewards are both high) involve unstable attribution states. As shown in figure 4, individuals apparently resolve this attributional instability by altering their perceptions of intrinsic rewards associated with the task.

An interesting question posed by the self-perception analysis is why individuals are predicted to resolve an unstable attribution state by cognitively reevaluating a task in terms of its intrinsic rewards rather than changing their perceptions of extrinsic factors. The answer to this question

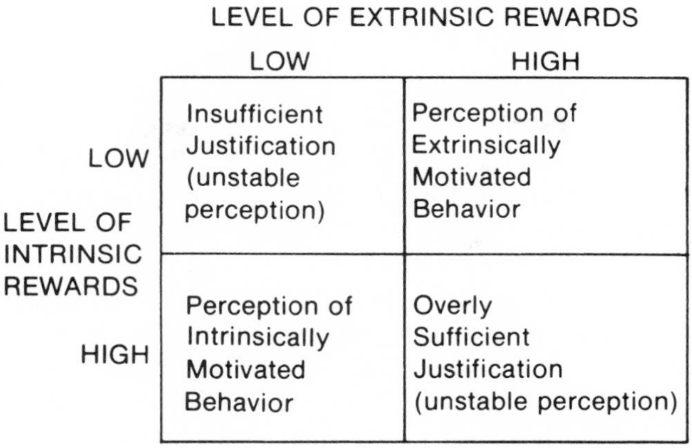
LEVEL OF EXTRINSIC REWARDS
LOW
HIGH
LEVEL OF INTRINSIC REWARDS
LOW
HIGH
Insufficient Justification (unstable perception)
Perception of Extrinsically Motivated Behavior
Perception of Intrinsically Motivated Behavior
Overly Sufficient Justification (unstable perception)

Figure 3. A conceptual framework of self-perception theory

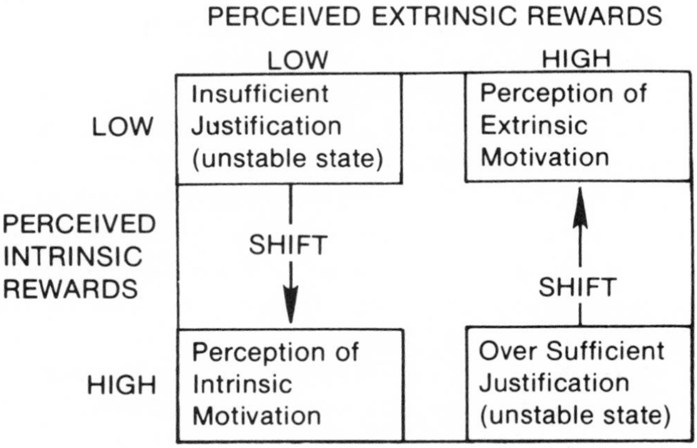
PERCEIVED EXTRINSIC REWARDS
LOW
HIGH
PERCEIVED INTRINSIC REWARDS
LOW
HIGH
Insufficient Justification (unstable state)
Perception of Extrinsic Motivation
SHIFT
SHIFT
Perception of Intrinsic Motivation
Over Sufficient Justification (unstable state)

Figure 4. A schematic analysis of the self-perception of intrinsic and extrinsic motivation

may lie in the relative clarity of extrinsic as compared with intrinsic rewards, and the individual's relative ability to distort the two aspects of the situation. Within many settings (and especially within laboratory experiments) extrinsic rewards are generally quite salient and specific, whereas an individual must judge the intrinsic nature of a task for himself. Any shifts in the perception of intrinsic and extrinsic rewards may therefore be more likely to occur in the intrinsic factor. As shown in figure 4, it is these predicted shifts in perceived intrinsic rewards that may theoretically underlie a negative relationship between intrinsic and extrinsic motivation.

Empirical evidence

Insufficient justification

Several studies have shown that when an individual is induced to commit an unpleasant act for little or no external justification, he may subsequently conclude that the act was not so unpleasant after all. Actually, the first scientific attempt to account for this phenomenon was the theory of cognitive dissonance (Festinger 1957). It was predicted by dissonance theorists (Festinger 1957; Aronson 1966) that, since performing an unpleasant act for little or no reward would be an inconsistent (and seemingly irrational) thing to do, an individual might subsequently change his attitude toward the act in order to reduce the inconsistency or to appear rational. Bem's self-perception theory yields the same predictions but does not require one to posit that there is a motivating state such as dissonance reduction or self-rationalization. To Bem, since the individual examines his own behavior in light of the forces around him, he is simply more likely to come to the conclusion that his actions were intrinsically satisfying if they were performed under minimal external force.

In general, two types of experiments have been designed to assess the consequences of insufficient justification. One type of design has involved the performance of a dull task with varied levels of reward (Brehm and Cohen 1962; Weick 1964; Freedman 1963; Weick and Penner 1965). A second and more popular design has involved some form of counterattitudinal advocacy, either in terms of lying to a fellow subject about the nature of an experiment or writing an essay against one's position on an important issue (Festinger and Carlsmith 1959; Carlsmith et al. 1966; Linder et al. 1967). Fundamentally, the two types of designs are not vastly different. Both require subjects to perform an intrinsically dissatisfying act under varied levels of external inducement, and both predict that, in the low payment condition, the subject will change his attitude toward the activity (i.e., think more favorably of the task or begin to believe the position advocated).

The most well-known experiment designed to test the insufficient justification paradigm was conducted by Festinger and Carlsmith (1959). Subjects participated in a repetitive and dull task (putting spools on trays and turning pegs) and were asked to tell other waiting subjects that the experiment was enjoyable, interesting, and exciting. Half the experimental subjects were paid $1 and half were paid $20 for the counterattitudinal advocacy (and to be "on call" in the future), while control subjects were not paid and did not perform the counterattitudinal act. As predicted, the smaller the reward used to induce subjects to perform the counterattitudinal act, the greater the positive change in their attitudes toward the task. Al-

though the interpretation of the results of this study have been actively debated (e.g., between dissonance and self-perception theorists) the basic
findings have been replicated by a number of different researchers. It
should be noted, however, that several mediating variables have also been
isolated as being necessary for the attainment of this dissonance or self-
perception effect: free choice (Linder et al. 1967), commitment or irrevo-
cability of behavior (Brehm and Cohen 1962), and substantial adverse
consequences (Calder et al. 1973; Collins and Hoyt 1972).

Recently, a strong test of the insufficient justification paradigm was also
conducted outside the laboratory (Staw 1974a). A natural field experiment
was made possible by the fact that many young men had joined an organization (Army ROTC) in order to avoid being drafted, and these same
young men subsequently received information (a draft lottery number) that
changed the value of this organizational reward. Of particular relevance
was the fact that those who joined ROTC did so not because of their intrinsic interest in the activities involved (drills, classes, and summer camp),
but because they anticipated a substantial extrinsic reward (draft avoidance). As a result, those who received draft numbers that exempted them
from military service subsequently faced a situation of low extrinsic as
well as intrinsic rewards, a situation of insufficient justification. In contrast, persons who received draft numbers that made them vulnerable to
military call-up found their participation in ROTC perfectly justified—they
were still successfully avoiding the draft by remaining in the organization.
To test the insufficient justification effect, both the attitudes and the performance of ROTC cadets were analyzed by draft number before and after the
national draft lottery. The results showed that those in the insufficient justification situation enhanced their perception of ROTC and even performed
somewhat better in ROTC courses after the lottery. It should be recognized, however, that this task enhancement occurred only under circumstances very similar to those previously found necessary for the dissonance
or self-perception effect (i.e., high commitment, free choice, and adverse
consequences).

Overly sufficient justification

There have been several empirical studies designed to test the self-perception
prediction within the context of overly sufficient justification. Generally, a
situation in which an extrinsic reward is added to an intrinsically rewarding
task has been experimentally contrived for this purpose. Following self-
perception theory, it is predicted that an increase in external justification
will cause individuals to lose confidence in their intrinsic interest in the
experimental task. Since dissonance theory cannot make this prediction (it
is neither irrational nor inconsistent to perform an activity for too many
rewards), the literature on overly sufficient justification provides the most

important data on the self-perception prediction. For this reason, we will examine the experimental evidence in some detail.

In an experiment specifically designed to test the effect of overly sufficient justification on intrinsic motivation, Deci (1971) enlisted a number of college students to participate in a problem-solving study. All the students were asked to work on a series of intrinsically interesting puzzles for three experimental sessions. After the first session, however, half of the students (the experimental group) were told that they would also be given an extrinsic reward (money) for correctly solving the second set of puzzles, while the other students (the control group) were not told anything about the reward. In the third session, neither the experimental nor the control subjects were rewarded. This design is schematically outlined below:

	Time 1	TIme 2	Time 3
Experimental group	No payment	Payment	No payment
Control group	No payment	No payment	No payment

Deci had hypothesized that the payment of money in the second experimental session might decrease subjects' intrinsic motivation to perform the task. That is, the introduction of an external force (money) might cause participants to alter their self-perception about why they were working on the puzzles. Instead of being intrinsically motivated to solve the interesting puzzles, they might find themselves working primarily to get the money provided by the experimenter. Thus Deci's goal in conducting the study was to compare the changes in subjects' intrinsic motivation from the first to third sessions for both the experimental and control groups. If the self-perception hypothesis was correct, the intrinsic motivation of the previously paid experimental subjects would decrease in the third session, whereas the intrinsic motivation of the unpaid controls should remain unchanged.

As a measure of intrinsic motivation, Deci used the amount of free time participants spent on the puzzle task. To obtain this measure, the experimenter left the room during each session, supposedly to feed some data into the computer. As the experimenter left the room, he told the subjects they could do anything they wanted with their free time. In addition to the puzzles, current issues of *Time, The New Yorker,* and *Playboy* were placed near the subjects. However, while the first experimenter was out of the laboratory, a second experimenter, unknown to the subjects, observed their behavior through a one-way mirror. It was reasoned that if the subject worked on the puzzles during this free time period, he must be intrinsically motivated to perform the task. As shown in table 2, the amount of free time spent on the task decreased for those who were previously paid to perform the activity, while there was a slight increase for the unpaid controls. Although the difference between the experimental and control groups was only marginally significant, the results are suggestive of the fact that an

Table 2. Mean number of seconds spent working on the puzzles during the free time periods

Group	Time 1	Time 2	Time 3	Time 3– Time 1
Experimental (n = 12)	248.2	313.9	198.5	−49.7
Control (n = 12)	213.9	202.7	241.8	27.9

Source: E. L. Deci, "The effects of externally mediated rewards on intrinsic motivation," *Journal of Personality and Social Psychology* 18 (1971): 105–15. Copyright 1971 by the American Psychological Association. Reprinted by permission.

overly sufficient extrinsic reward may decrease one's intrinsic motivation to perform a task.

Lepper et al. (1973) also conducted a study that tested the self-perception prediction in a situation of overly sufficient justification. Their study involved having nursery school children perform an interesting activity (playing with Magic Markers) with and without the expectation of an additional extrinsic reward. Some children were induced to draw pictures with the markers by promising them a Good Player Award consisting of a big gold star, a bright red ribbon, and a place to print their name. Other children either performed the activity without any reward or were told about the reward only after completing the activity. Children who participated in these three experimental conditions (expected reward, no reward, unexpected reward) were then covertly observed during the following week in a free-play period. As in the Deci (1971) study, the amount of time children spent on the activity when they could do other interesting things (i.e., playing with other toys) was taken to be an indicator of intrinsic motivation.

The findings of the Lepper et al. study showed that the introduction of an extrinsic reward for performing an already interesting activity caused a significant decrease in intrinsic motivation. Children who played with Magic Markers with the expectation of receiving the external reward did not spend as much subsequent free time on the activity as did children who were not given a reward or those who were unexpectedly offered the reward. Moreover, the rated quality of drawings made by children with the markers was significantly poorer in the expected reward group than either the no-reward or unexpected reward groups.

The results of the Lepper et al. study help to increase our confidence in the findings of the earlier Deci experiment. Not only are the earlier findings replicated with a different task and subject population, but an important methodological problem is minimized. By reexamining table 2, we can see that the second time period in the Deci experiment was the period in which payment was expected by subjects for solving the puzzles. However, we can also see that in time 2 there was a whopping increase in the free time subjects spent on the puzzles. Deci explained this increase as an attempt by subjects to practice puzzle solving to increase their chances of earning money. However, what Deci did not discuss is the possibility that the subsequent decrease in time 3 was due not to the prior administration of rewards but to the effect of satiation or fatigue. One contribution of the Lepper et al. study is that its results are not easily explained by this alternative. In the Lepper et al. experiment, there was over one week's time between the session in which an extrinsic reward was administered and the final observation period.

Although both the Deci and Lepper et al. studies support the notion that the expectation of an extrinsic reward may decrease intrinsic interest in an activity, there is still one important source of ambiguity in both these studies. You may have noticed that the decrease in intrinsic motivation follows not only the prior administration of an extrinsic reward, but also the withdrawal of this reward. For example, in the Deci study, subjects were not paid in the third experimental session in which the decrease in intrinsic motivation was reported. Likewise, subjects were not rewarded when the final observation of intrinsic motivation was taken by Lepper et al. It is therefore difficult to determine whether the decrease in intrinsic interest is due to a change in the self-perception of motivation following the application of an extrinsic reward or merely to frustration following the removal of the reward. An experiment by Kruglanski et al. (1971) helps to resolve this ambiguity.

Kruglanski et al. induced a number of teenagers to volunteer for some creativity and memory tasks. To manipulate extrinsic rewards, the experimenters told half the participants that because they had volunteered for the study, they would be taken on an interesting tour of the psychology laboratory; the other participants were not offered this extrinsic reward. The results showed that teenagers offered the reward were less satisfied with the experimental tasks and were less likely to volunteer for future experiments of a similar nature than were teenagers who were not offered the extrinsic reward. In addition, the extrinsically rewarded group did not perform as well on the experimental task (in terms of recall, creativity, and the Zeigarnik effect) as the nonrewarded group. These findings are similar to those of Deci (1971) and Lepper et al. (1973), but they cannot be as easily explained by a frustration effect. Since in the Kruglanski et al. study the reward was never withdrawn for the experimental group, the differences between the experimental (reward) and control (no reward) conditions are better explained by a change in self-perception than by a frustration effect.

The designs of the three overly sufficient justification studies described above have varying strengths and weaknesses (Calder and Staw 1975a), but taken together, their results can be interpreted as supporting the notion that extrinsic rewards added to an already interesting task can decrease intrinsic motivation. This effect, if true, has important ramifications for educational, industrial, and other work settings. There are many situations in which people are offered extrinsic rewards (grades, money, special privileges) for accomplishing a task which may already be intrinsically interesting. The self-perception effect means that, by offering external rewards, we may sometimes be sacrificing an important source of task motivation and not necessarily increasing either the satisfaction or the performance of the participant. Obviously, because the practical implications of the self-perception effect are large, we should proceed with caution. Thus, in addition to scrutinizing the validity of the findings themselves (as we have done above), we should also attempt to determine the exact conditions under which they might be expected to hold.

Earlier, Deci (1971, 1972) had hypothesized that only rewards contingent on a high level of task performance are likely to have an adverse effect on intrinsic motivation. He had reasoned that a reward contingent upon specific behavioral demands is most likely to cause an individual to infer that his behavior is extrinsically rather than intrinsically motivated and that a decrease in intrinsic motivation may result from this change in self-perception. Although this assumption seems reasonable, there is not a great deal of empirical support for it. Certainly in the Kruglanski et al. and Lepper et al. studies all that was necessary to cause a decrease in intrinsic motivation was for rewards to be contingent upon the completion of an activity. In each of these studies what seemed to be important was the cognition that one was performing an activity *in order to get an extrinsic reward* rather than a prescribed goal for a particular level of output. Thus as long as it is salient, a reward contingency based upon the completion of an activity may decrease intrinsic motivation just like a reward contingency based on the quality or quantity of performance.

Ross (1975) recently conducted two experiments that dealt specifically with the effect of the salience of rewards on changes in intrinsic motivation. In one study, children were asked to play a musical instrument (drums) for either no reward, a nonsalient reward, or a salient reward. The results showed that intrinsic motivation, as measured by the amount of time spent on the drums versus other activities in a free play situation, was lowest for the salient reward condition. Similar results were found in a second study in which some children were asked to think either of the reward (marshmallows) while playing a musical instrument, think of an extraneous object (snow), or not think of anything in particular. The data for this second study showed that intrinsic motivation was lowest when children consciously thought about the reward while performing the task.

In addition to the salience of an external reward, there has been empirical research on one other factor mediating the self-perception effect, the existing norms of the task situation. In examining the prior research using situations of overly sufficient justification, Staw et al. (1975) reasoned that there is one common element which stands out. Always, the extrinsic reward appears to be administered in a situation in which persons are not normally paid or otherwise reimbursed for their actions. For example, students are not normally paid for laboratory participation, but the Deci (1971) and Kruglanski et al. (1971) subjects were. Likewise, nursery school children are not normally enticed by special recognition or rewards to play with an interesting new toy, but both the Lepper et al. (1973) and Ross (1975) subjects were. Thus Staw et al. (1975) manipulated norms for payment as well as the actual payment of money for performing an interesting task. They found an interaction of norms and payment such that the introduction of an extrinsic reward decreased intrinsic interest in a task only when there existed a situational norm for no payment. From these data and the findings of the Ross study, it thus appears that an extrinsic reward must be both salient and situationally inappropriate for there to be a reduction in intrinsic interest.

Reassessing the self-perception effect

At present there is growing empirical support for the notion that intrinsic and extrinsic motivation *can* be negatively interrelated. The effect of extrinsic rewards on intrinsic motivation has been replicated by several researchers using different classes of subjects (males, females, children, college students) and different activities (puzzles, toys), and the basic results appear to be internally valid. As we have seen, however, the effect of extrinsic rewards is predicated on certain necessary conditions (e.g., situational norms and reward salience), as is often the case with psychological findings subjected to close examination.

To date, the primary data supporting the self-perception prediction have come from situations of insufficient and overly sufficient justification. Empirical findings have shown that individuals may cognitively reevaluate intrinsic rewards in an upward direction when their behavior is insufficiently justified and in a downward direction when there is overly sufficient justification. In general, it can be said that the data of these two situations are consistent with the self-perception hypothesis. Still, theoretically, it is not immediately clear why previous research has been restricted to these two particular contexts. No doubt it is easier to show an increase in intrinsic motivation when intrinsic interest is initially low (as under insufficient justification) or a decrease when intrinsic interest is initially high (as under overly sufficient justification). Nevertheless, the theory should support a negative interrelationship of intrinsic and extrinsic factors at *all levels,* since it makes the rather general prediction that the greater the extrinsic rewards, the less likely is the individual to infer that he is intrinsically motivated.

One recent empirical study has tested the self-perception hypothesis by manipulating *both* intrinsic and extrinsic motivation. Calder and Staw (1975*b*) experimentally manipulated both the intrinsic characteristics of a task as well as extrinsic rewards in an attempt to examine the interrelationship of these two factors at more than one level. In the study male college students were asked to solve one of two sets of puzzles identical in all respects except the potential for intrinsic interest. One set of puzzles contained an assortment of pictures highly rated by students (chiefly from *Life* magazine but including several *Playboy* centerfolds); another set of puzzles was blank and rated more neutrally. To manipulate extrinsic rewards, half the subjects were promised $1 for their 20 minutes of labor (and the dollar was placed prominently in view), while for half of the subjects, money was neither mentioned nor displayed. After completing the task, subjects were asked to fill out a questionnaire on their reactions to the puzzle-solving activity. The two primary dependent variables included in the questionnaire were a measure of task satisfaction and a measure of subjects' willingness to volunteer for additional puzzle-solving exercises. The latter consisted of a sign-up sheet on which subjects could indicate the amount of time they would be willing to spend (without pay or additional course credit) in future experiments of a similar nature.

The results of the Calder and Staw experiment showed a significant interaction between task and payment on subjects' satisfaction with the activity and a marginally significant interaction on subjects' willingness to volunteer for additional work without extrinsic reward. These data provided empirical support for the self-perception effect in a situation of overly sufficient justification, but not under other conditions. Specifically, when the task was initially interesting (i.e., using the picture puzzle activity), the introduction of money caused a reduction of task satisfaction and volunteering. However, when the task was initially more neutral (i.e., using the blank puzzle activity), the introduction of money increased satisfaction and subjects' intentions to volunteer for additional work. Thus if we consider Calder and Staw's dependent measures as indicators of intrinsic interest, the first finding is in accord with the self-perception hypothesis, while the latter result is similar to what one might predict from a reinforcement theory. The implications of these data, together with previous findings, are graphically depicted in figure 5.

As shown in the figure, self-perception effects have been found *only* at the extremes of insufficient and overly sufficient justification. Thus it may be prudent to withhold judgment on the general hypothesis that there is a uniformly negative relationship between intrinsic and extrinsic motivation. Perhaps we should no longer broadly posit that the greater external rewards and pressures, the weaker the perception of intrinsic interest in an activity; and the lower external pressures, the stronger intrinsic interest. Certainly, under conditions other than insufficient and overly sufficient justification,

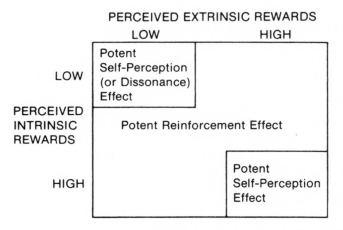

Figure 5. The relative potency of self-perception and reinforcement mechanisms

reinforcement effects of extrinsic rewards on intrinsic task satisfaction have readily been found (Cherrington et al. 1971; Cherrington 1973; Greene 1974).

At present it appears that only in situations of insufficient or overly sufficient reward will there be attributional instability of such magnitude that shifts will occur in the perception of intrinsic rewards. We might therefore speculate that either no attributional instability is evoked in other situations or it is just not strong enough to overcome a countervailing force. I would place my confidence in the latter theoretical position. It seems likely that both self-perception *and* reinforcement mechanisms hold true, but that their relative influence over an individual's task attitudes and behavior varies according to the situational context. For example, only in situations with insufficient or overly sufficient justification will the need to resolve attributional instability probably be strong enough for external rewards to produce a decrease in intrinsic motivation. In other situations we might reasonably expect a more positive relationship between intrinsic and extrinsic factors, as predicted by reinforcement theory.

Although this new view of the interrelationship between intrinsic and extrinsic motivation remains speculative, it does seem reasonable in light of recent theoretical and empirical work. Figure 6 graphically elaborates this model and shows how the level of intrinsic and extrinsic motivation may depend on the characteristics of the situation. In the figure, secondary reinforcement is depicted to be a general force for producing a positive relationship between intrinsic and extrinsic motivation. However, under situations of insufficient and oversufficient justification, self-perception (and dissonance) effects are shown to provide a second but still potentially effective determinant of a negative interrelationship between intrinsic and

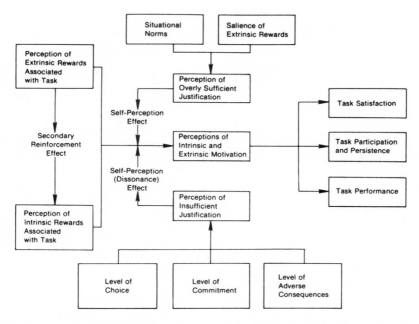

Figure 6. The interrelationship of intrinsic and extrinsic motivation as a function of situational characteristics

extrinsic motivation. Figure 6 shows the joint operation of these two theoretical mechanisms and illustrates their ultimate effect on individuals' satisfaction, persistence, and performance on a task.

Implications of intrinsic and extrinsic motivation

In this discussion we have noted that the administration of both intrinsic and extrinsic rewards can have important effects on a person's task attitudes and behavior. Individually, extrinsic rewards may direct and control a person's activity on a task and provide an important source of satisfaction. By themselves, intrinsic rewards can also motivate task-related behavior and bring gratification to the individual. As we have seen, however, the joint effect of intrinsic and extrinsic rewards may be quite complex. Not only may intrinsic and extrinsic factors not be additive in their overall effect on motivation and satisfaction, but the interaction of intrinsic and extrinsic factors may under some conditions be positive and under other conditions negative. As illustrated in figures 5 and 6, a potent reinforcement effect will often cause intrinsic and extrinsic motivation to be positively interrelated, although on occasion a self-perception mechanism may be so powerful as to create a negative relationship between these two factors.

The reinforcement predictions of figures 5 and 6 are consistent with our common sense. In practice, extrinsic rewards are relied upon heavily to induce desired behaviors, and most allocators of rewards (administrators, teachers, parents) operate on the theory that extrinsic rewards will positively affect an individual's intrinsic interest in a task. We should therefore concentrate on those situations in which our common sense may be in error—those situations in which there may in fact be a negative relationship between intrinsic and extrinsic motivation.

Motivation in educational organizations

One of the situations in which intrinsic and extrinsic motivation may be negatively interrelated is our schools. As Lepper and Greene (1975) have noted, many educational tasks are inherently interesting to students and would probably be performed without any external force. However, when grades and other extrinsic inducements are added to the activity, we may, via overly sufficient justification, be converting an interesting activity into work. That is, by inducing students to perform educational tasks with strong extrinsic rewards or by applying external force, we may be converting learning activities into behaviors that will not be performed in the future without some additional outside pressure or extrinsic force.

Within the educational context, a negative relationship between intrinsic and extrinsic motivation poses a serious dilemma for teachers who allocate external rewards. For example, there is no doubt that grades, gold stars, and other such incentives can alter the direction and vigor of specific "in school" behaviors (e.g., getting students to complete assigned exercises by a particular date). But because of their effect on intrinsic motivation, extrinsic rewards may also weaken a student's general interest in learning tasks and decrease voluntary learning behavior that extends beyond the school setting. In essence, then, the extrinsic forces that work so well at motivating and controlling specific task behaviors may actually cause the extinction of these same behaviors within situations devoid of external reinforcers. This is an important consideration for educational organizations, since most of an individual's learning activity will no doubt occur outside the highly regulated and reinforced setting of the classroom.[3]

In order to maintain students' intrinsic motivation in learning activities it is recommended that the use of extrinsic rewards be carefully controlled. As a practical measure, it is recommended that when a learning task is inherently interesting (and would probably be performed without any external force) all external pressures on the individual be minimized. Only when a task is so uninteresting that individuals would not ordinarily perform it should extrinsic rewards be applied. In addition, it is suggested that

---

3. It is interesting to note that Kazdin and Bootzin (1972) have made a quite similar point in their recent review of research on token economies. They noted that while operant conditioning procedures have been quite effective in altering focal behaviors within a controlled setting, seldom have changes been found to generalize to natural, nonreinforcing environments.

the student role be both enlarged and enriched to increase rather directly the level of intrinsic motivation. The significance of learning tasks, responsibility for results, feedback, and variety in student activities are all areas of possible improvement.

Motivation in work organizations

Voluntary work organizations are very much like educational organizations; their members are often intrinsically motivated to perform certain tasks and extrinsic rewards are generally not necessary to induce the performance of many desired behaviors. Moreover, if for some reason extrinsic rewards were to be offered to voluntary workers for performing their services, we would expect to find, as in the educational setting, a decrease in intrinsic motivation. As in the educational context, we would expect an external reward to decrease self-motivated (or voluntary) behavior in settings free from external reinforcement, although the specific behaviors which are reinforced might be increased. As a concrete example, let us imagine a political candidate who decides to "motivate" his volunteer campaign workers by paying them for distributing fliers to prospective voters. In this situation, we might expect that the administration of an extrinsic reward will increase the number of fliers distributed. However, the political workers' subsequent interest in performing other campaign activities *without pay* may subsequently be diminished. Similarly, the volunteer hospital worker who becomes salaried may no longer have the same intrinsic interest in his work. Although the newly professionalized worker may exert a good deal of effort on the job and be relatively satisfied with it, his satisfaction may stem from extrinsic rather than intrinsic sources of reward.

Let us now turn to the implications of intrinsic and extrinsic motivation for nonvoluntary work organizations. Deci (1972), in reviewing his research on intrinsic motivation, cautioned strongly against the use of contingent monetary rewards within industrial organizations. He maintained that paying people contingently upon the performance of specific tasks may reduce intrinsic motivation for these activities, and he recommended noncontingent reinforcers in their stead. As we have seen, however, a decrease in intrinsic motivation does not always occur following the administration of extrinsic rewards; certain necessary conditions must be present before there is a negative relationship between intrinsic and extrinsic motivation. Generally, industrial work settings do not meet these necessary conditions.

First, within industrial organizations, a large number of jobs are not inherently interesting enough to foster high intrinsic motivation. Persons would not ordinarily perform many of the tasks of the industrial world (e.g., assembly-line work) without extrinsic inducements, and this initial lack of intrinsic interest will probably preclude the effect of overly sufficient justification. Second, even when an industrial job is inherently interesting, there exists a powerful norm for extrinsic payment. Not only do workers specifically join and contribute their labor in exchange for particular inducements, but the instrumental relationship between task behavior and extrinsic rewards is supported by both social and legal standards. Thus the industrial work situation is quite unlike that of either a voluntary organization or an educational system. In the former cases, participants may be initially interested in performing certain tasks without external force, and the addition of overly sufficient rewards may convey information that the task is not intrinsically interesting. Within industrial organizations, on the other hand, extrinsic reinforcement *is* the norm, and tasks may often be perceived to be even more interesting when they lead to greater extrinsic rewards.

The very basic distinction between nonvoluntary work situations and other task settings (e.g., schools and voluntary organizations) is that, without extrinsic rewards, nonvoluntary organizations would be largely without participants. The important question for industrial work settings is therefore not one of payment versus nonpayment, but of the recommended degree of contingency between reward and performance. On the basis of current evidence, it would seem prudent to suggest that, within industrial organizations, rewards continue to be made contingent upon behavior. This could be accomplished through performance evaluation, profit sharing, or piece-rate incentive schemes. In addition, intrinsic motivation should be increased directly via the planned alteration of specific job characteristics (e.g., by increasing task variety, complexity, social interaction, task identity, significance, responsibility for results, and knowledge of results).

A final comment

Although the study of the interaction of intrinsic and extrinsic motivation is a relatively young area within psychology, it has been the intent of this paper to outline a theoretical model and provide some practical suggestions based upon the research evidence available to date. As we have seen, the effects of intrinsic and extrinsic motivation are not always simple, and several mediating variables must often be taken into account before specific predictions can be made. Thus in addition to providing "answers" to theoretical and practical problems, this paper may illustrate the complexities involved in drawing conclusions from a limited body of research data. The main caution for the reader is to regard these theoretical propositions and practical recommendations as working statements subject to the influence of future empirical evidence.

Bibliography

G. W. Allport, *Personality, A Psychological Interpretation.* Holt, 1937.
E. Aronson, "The Psychology of Insufficient Justification: An Analysis of Some Conflicting Data." In S. Feldman, ed., *Cognitive Consistency:*

Motivational Antecedents and Behavior Consequences. Academic Press, 1966.

J. W. Atkinson, *An Introduction to Motivation.* Van Nostrand, 1964.

T. Ayllon and N. H. Azrin, "The Measurement and Reinforcement of Behavior of Psychotics." *Journal of Experimental Analysis of Behavior,* 1965, 8 : 357 – 383.

D. J. Bem, "Self-perception: An Alternative Interpretation of Cognitive Dissonance Phenomena." *Psychological Review,* 1967*a,* 74 : 183 – 200.

———. "Self-perception: The Dependent Variable of Human Performance." *Organizational Behavior and Human Performance,* 1967*b,* 2 : 105 – 121.

———, "Self-perception Theory." In L. Berkowitz, ed., *Advances in Experimental Social Psychology,* Vol. 6, Academic Press, 1972.

D. E. Berlyne, *Conflicts, Arousal, and Curiosity.* McGraw-Hill, 1960.

W. H. Bexton, W. Heron, and T. H. Scott, "Effects of Decreased Variation in the Sensory Environment." *Canadian Journal of Psychology,* 1954, 8 : 70 – 76.

J. W. Brehm and A. R. Cohen, *Explorations in Cognitive Dissonance.* Wiley, 1962.

B. J. Calder, M. Ross, and C. A. Insko, "Attitude Change and Attitude Attribution: Effects of Incentive, Choice, and Consequences." *Journal of Personality and Social Psychology,* 1973, 25 : 84 – 100.

B. J. Calder and B. M. Staw, "The Interaction of Intrinsic and Extrinsic Motivation: Some Methodological Notes." *Journal of Personality and Social Psychology,* 1975*a,* 31 : 76 – 80.

———, "Self-perception of Intrinsic and Extrinsic Motivation." *Journal of Personality and Social Psychology,* 1975*b,* 31 : 599 – 605.

J. P. Campbell, M. D. Dunnette, E. E. Lawler, and K. E. Weick, *Managerial Behavior, Performance, and Effectiveness.* McGraw-Hill, 1970.

J. M. Carlsmith, B. E. Collins, and R. L. Helmreich, "Studies in Forced Compliance: The Effect of Pressure for Compliance on Attitude Change Produced by Face-to-Face Role Playing and Anonymous Essay Writing." *Journal of Personality and Social Psychology,* 1966, 4 : 1 – 13.

D. J. Cherrington, "The Effects of a Central Incentive—Motivational State on Measures of Job Satisfaction." *Organizational Behavior and Human Performance,* 1973, 10 : 271 – 289.

D. J. Cherrington, H. J. Reitz, and W. E. Scott, "Effects of Reward and Contingent Reinforcement on Satisfaction and Task Performance." *Journal of Applied Psychology,* 1971, 55 : 531 – 536.

B. E. Collins and M. F. Hoyt, "Personal Responsibility-for-Consequences: An Integration and Extension of the Forced Compliance Literature." *Journal of Experimental Social Psychology,* 1972, 8 : 558 – 594.

R. E. Cook, "Relation of Achievement Motivation and Attribution to Self-reinforcement," Ph.D. dissertation. University of California, 1970.

R. de Charms, *Personal Causation: The Internal Affective Determinants of Behavior.* Academic Press, 1968.

E. L. Deci, "The Effects of Externally Mediated Rewards on Intrinsic Motivation." *Journal of Personality and Social Psychology,* 1971, 18: 105–115.

——, "The Effects of Contingent and Noncontingent Rewards and Controls on Intrinsic Motivation." *Organizational Behavior and Human Performance,* 1972, 8:217–229.

W. Edwards, "The Prediction of Decision among Bets." *Journal of Experimental Psychology,* 1955, 50:201–214.

C. B. Ferster and B. F. Skinner, *Schedules of Reinforcement.* Appleton-Century-Crofts, 1957.

L. Festinger, *A Theory of Cognitive Dissonance,* Stanford University Press, 1957.

L. Festinger and J. M. Carlsmith, "Cognitive Consequences of Forced Compliance." *Journal of Abnormal and Social Psychology,* 1959, 58:203–210.

J. L. Freedman, "Attitudinal Effects of Inadequate Justification." *Journal of Personality,* 1963, 31:371–385.

J. Galbraith and L. L. Cummings, "An Emprical Investigation of the Motivational Determinants of Task Performance: Interactive Effects Between Instrumentality-Valence and Motivation-Ability." *Organizational Behavior and Human Performance,* 1967, 2:237–257.

C. N. Greene, "Causal Connections among Managers' Merit Pay, Job Satisfaction, and Performance." *Journal of Applied Psychology,* 1974, 58:95–100.

J. R. Hackman and E. E. Lawler, "Employee Reactions to Job Characteristics." *Journal of Applied Psychology,* 1971, 55:259–286.

J. R. Hackman and G. R. Oldham, "Development of the Job Diagnostic Survey." *Journal of Applied Psychology,* 1975, 60:159–170.

——, "Motivation through the Design of Work." *Organizational Behavior and Human Performance,* 1976, 16:250–279.

J. R. Hackman, G. R. Oldham, R. Janson, and K. Purdy, "A New Strategy for Job Enrichment." *California Management Review,* 1975.

H. F. Harlow, "Learning and Satiation of Response in Intrinsically Motivated Complex Puzzle Performance by Monkeys." *Journal of Comparative and Physiological Psychology,* 1950, 43:289–294.

H. F. Harlow, M. K. Harlow, and D. R. Meyer, "Learning Motivated by a Manipulation Drive." *Journal of Experimental Psychology,* 1950, 40: 228–234.

H. F. Harlow and G. E. McClearn, "Object Discrimination Learned by Monkeys on the Basis of Manipulation Motives." *Journal of Comparative and Physiological Psychology,* 1954, 47:73–76.

F. Heider, *The Psychology of Interpersonal Relations.* Wiley, 1958.

R. J. House, "A Path-Goal Theory of Leader Effectiveness." *Administrative Science Quarterly,* 1971, 16:321–338.

R. J. House, H. J. Shapiro, and M. A. Wahba, "Expectancy Theory as a Predictor of Work Behavior and Attitude: A Reevaluation of Empirical Evidence." *Decision Sciences,* 1974, 5:481–506.

C. L. Hull, *Principles of Behavior,* Appleton-Century-Crofts, 1943.

J. McV. Hunt, "Intrinsic Motivation and Its Role in Psychological Development." In D. Levine, ed., *Nebraska Symposium on Motivation.* University of Nebraska Press, 1965.

———, "Toward a History of Intrinsic Motivation." In H. I. Day, D. E. Berlyne, and D. E. Hunt, eds., *Intrinsic Motivation: A New Direction in Education.* Holt, Rinehart, and Winston of Canada, 1971.

E. E. Jones and K. E. Davis, "From Acts to Dispositions: The Attribution Process in Person Perception." In L. Berkowitz, ed., *Advances in Experimental Psychology,* Vol. 2, Academic Press, 1965.

E. E. Jones, K. E. Davis, and K. E. Gergen, "Role Playing Variations and Their Informational Value for Person Perception." *Journal of Abnormal and Social Psychology,* 1961, 63:302–310.

E. E. Jones and V. A. Harris, "The Attribution of Attitudes," *Journal of Experimental Social Psychology,* 1967, 3:1–24.

E. E. Jones and R. E. Nisbett, *The Actor and the Observer: Divergent Perceptions of the Causes of Behavior.* General Learning Press, 1971.

A. E. Kazdin and R. R. Bootzen, "The Token Economy: An Evaluative Review." *Journal of Applied Behavior Analysis,* 1972, 5:343–372.

F. S. Keller, *Learning: Reinforcement Theory,* 2d ed. Random House, 1969.

H. H. Kelley, "Attribution Theory in Social Psychology." In D. Levine, ed., *Nebraska Symposium on Motivation,* Vol. 15. University of Nebraska Press, 1967.

———, *Attribution in Social Interaction.* General Learning Press, 1971.

S. Koch, "Behavior as 'Intrinsically' Regulated: Work Notes towards a Pretheory of Phenomena Called Motivational." In M. R. Jones, ed., *Nebraska Symposium on Motivation.* University of Nebraska Press, 1956.

A. K. Korman, *The Psychology of Motivation.* Prentice-Hall, 1974.

A. W. Kruglanski, I. Freedman, and G. Zeevi, "The Effects of Extrinsic Incentives on Some Qualitative Aspects of Task Performance." *Journal of Personality,* 1971, 39:606–617.

J. T. Lanzetta, "The Motivational Properties of Uncertainty." In H. I. Day, D. E. Berlyne, and D. E. Hunt, eds., *Intrinsic Motivation: A New Direction in Education.* Holt, Rinehart, and Winston of Canada, 1971.

E. E. Lawler, *Pay and Organizational Effectiveness: A Psychological View.* McGraw-Hill, 1971.

———, *Motivation in Work Organizations.* Brooks/Cole, 1973.

M. R. Lepper and D. Greene, "Turning Play into Work: Effects of Adult

Surveillance and Extrinsic Rewards on Children's Intrinsic Motivation." *Journal of Personality and Social Psychology,* 1975, 31:479–486.

M. R. Lepper, D. Greene, and R. E. Nisbett, "Undermining Children's Intrinsic Interest with Extrinsic Rewards: A Test of the 'Overjustification' Hypothesis." *Journal of Personality and Social Psychology,* 1973, 28:129–137.

K. Lewin, *The Conceptual Representation and the Measurement of Psychological Forces,* Duke University Press, 1938.

K. Lewin, T. Dembo, L. Festinger, and P. W. Sears, "Level of Aspiration." In J. McV. Hunt, ed., *Personality and the Behavior Disorders,* Vol. 1, Ronald Press, 1944.

D. E. Linder, J. Cooper, and E. E. Jones, "Decision Freedom as a Determinant of the Role of Incentive Magnitude in Attitude Change." *Journal of Personality and Social Psychology,* 1967, 6:245–254.

G. H. Litwin, "Motives and Expectancies as Determinants of Preference for Degrees of Risk." In J. W. Atkinson and N. T. Feather, eds., *A Theory of Achievement Motivation,* Wiley, 1966.

A. H. Maslow, *Motivation and Personality.* Harper and Row, 1954.

————, *Motivation and Personality,* 2d ed. Harper and Row, 1970.

D. C. McClelland, "Measuring Motivation in Phantasy: The Achievement Motive." In H. Guetzkow, ed., *Groups, Leadership, and Man.* Carnegie Press, 1951.

————, *The Achieving Society.* Van Nostrand, 1961.

————, *Assessing Human Motivation.* General Learning Press, 1971.

————, "The Role of Educational Technology in Developing Achievement Motivation." In D. C. McClelland and R. W. Steele, eds., *Human Motivation: A Book of Readings.* General Learning Press, 1973*a*.

————, "What Is the Effect of Achievement Motivation Training in the Schools?" In D. C. McClelland and R. S. Steele, eds., *Human Motivation: A Book of Readings.* General Learning Press, 1973*b*.

D. C. McClelland and D. G. Winter, *Motivating Economic Achievement.* Free Press, 1969.

K. C. Montgomery, "The Role of the Exploratory Drive in Learning." *Journal of Comparative Physiological Psychology,* 1954, 47:60–64.

G. R. Oldham, "Intrinsic Motivation: Relationship to Job Characteristics and Performance." Paper presented at Eastern Psychological Association, 1974.

L. W. Porter and E. E. Lawler, *Managerial Attitudes and Performance.* Irwin Dorsey Press, 1967.

M. Ross, "Salience of Reward and Intrinsic Motivation." *Journal of Personality and Social Psychology,* 1975, 32:245–254.

J. B. Rotter, "Generalized Expectancies for Internal Versus External Control of Reinforcement." *Psychological Monographs,* 1966, 80: (1), 1–28.

K. W. Spence, *Behavior Theory and Conditioning,* Yale University Press, 1956.

B. M. Staw, "Attitudinal and Behavioral Consequences of Changing a Major Organizational Reward: A Natural Field Experiment." *Journal of Personality and Social Psychology,* 1974a, 6:742–751.

————, "Notes toward a Theory of Intrinsic and Extrinsic Motivation." Paper presented at Eastern Psychological Association. 1974b.

————, "Attribution of the 'Causes' of Performance: A New Alternative Interpretation of Cross-sectional Research on Organizations." *Organizational Behavior and Human Performance,* 1975, 13:414–432.

B. M. Staw, B. J. Calder, and R. Hess, "Intrinsic Motivation and Norms about Payment." Working paper, Northwestern University, 1975.

L. H. Strickland, "Surveillance and Trust." *Journal of Personality,* 1958, 26:200–215.

J. W. Thibaut and H. W. Riecken, "Some Determinants and Consequences of the Perception of Social Causality." *Journal of Personality,* 1955, 24:113–133.

E. C. Tolman, *Purposive Behavior in Animals and Men.* Appleton-Century-Crofts, 1932.

————, "Principles of Performance." *Psychological Review,* 1955, 62:315–326.

C. N. Uhl and A. G. Young, "Resistance to Extinction as a Function of Incentive, Percentage of Reinforcement, and Number of Non-reinforced Trials." *Journal of Experimental Psychology,* 1967, 73:556–564.

V. H. Vroom, *Work and Motivation.* Wiley, 1964.

K. E. Weick, "Reduction of Cognitive Dissonance through Task Enhancement and Effort Expenditure." *Journal of Abnormal and Social Psychology,* 1964, 68:533–539.

K. E. Weick and D. D. Penner, "Justification and Productivity." Unpublished manuscript, University of Minnesota, 1965.

R. W. White, "Motivation Reconsidered: The Concept of Competence." *Psychological Review,* 1959, 66:297–333.

R. S. Woodworth, *Dynamic Psychology.* Columbia University Press, 1918.

On the Folly of Rewarding A, While Hoping for B

Steven Kerr

Whether dealing with monkeys, rats, or human beings, it is hardly controversial to state that most organisms seek information concerning what activities are rewarded and then seek to do (or at least pretend to do) those things, often to the virtual exclusion of activities not rewarded. The extent to which this occurs of course will depend on the perceived attractiveness of the rewards offered, but neither operant nor expectancy theorists would quarrel with the essence of this notion.

Nevertheless, numerous examples exist of reward systems that are fouled up in that behaviors which are rewarded are those which the rewarder is trying to *discourage* while the behavior he desires is not being rewarded at all.

In an effort to understand and explain this phenomenon, this paper presents examples from society, from organizations in general, and from profit-making firms in particular. Data from a manufacturing company and information from an insurance firm are examined to demonstrate the consequences of such reward systems for the organizations involved, and possible reasons why such reward systems continue to exist are considered.

Societal examples

Politics

Official goals are "purposely vague and general and do not indicate . . . the host of decisions that must be made among alternative ways of achieving official goals and the priority of multiple goals . . ." (8, p. 66). They usually may be relied on to offend absolutely no one, and in this sense can be considered high acceptance, low quality goals. An example might be "build better schools." Operative goals are higher in quality but lower in acceptance, since they specify where the money will come from, what alternative goals will be ignored, etc.

Reprinted with permission from *Academy of Management Journal* 18, no. 4 (1975): 769–83.

The American citizenry supposedly wants its candidates for public office to set forth operative goals, making their proposed programs "perfectly clear," specifying sources and uses of funds, etc. However, since operative goals are lower in acceptance, and since aspirants to public office need acceptance (from at least 50.1 percent of the people), most politicians prefer to speak only of official goals, at least until after the election. They of course would agree to speak at the operative level if "punished" for not doing so. The electorate could do this by refusing to support candidates who do not speak at the operative level.

Instead, however, the American voter typically punishes (withholds support from) candidates who frankly discuss where the money will come from, rewards politicians who speak only of official goals, but hopes that candidates (despite the reward system) will discuss the issues operatively. It is academic whether it was moral for Nixon, for example, to refuse to discuss his 1968 "secret plan" to end the Vietnam war, his 1972 operative goals concerning the lifting of price controls, the reshuffling of his cabinet, etc. The point is that the reward system made such refusal rational.

It seems worth mentioning that no manuscript can adequately define what is "moral" and what is not. However, examination of costs and benefits, combined with knowledge of what motivates a particular individual, often will suffice to determine what for him is "rational."[1] If the reward system is so designed that it is irrational to be moral, this does not necessarily mean that immorality will result. But is this not asking for trouble?

War

If some oversimplification may be permitted, let it be assumed that the primary goal of the organization (Pentagon, Luftwaffe, or whatever) is to win. Let it be assumed further that the primary goal of most individuals on the front lines is to get home alive. Then there appears to be an important conflict in goals—personally rational behavior by those at the bottom will endanger goal attainment by those at the top.

But not necessarily! It depends on how the reward system is set up. The Vietnam war was indeed a study of disobedience and rebellion, with terms such as "fragging" (killing one's own commanding officer) and "search and evade" becoming part of the military vocabulary. The difference in subordinates' acceptance of authority between World War II and Vietnam is reported to be considerable, and veterans of the Second World War often have been quoted as being outraged at the mutinous actions of many American soldiers in Vietnam.

Consider, however, some critical differences in the reward system in use

---

1. In Simon's (10, pp. 76–77) terms, a decision is "subjectively rational" if it maximizes an individual's valued outcomes so far as his knowledge permits. A decision is "personally rational" if it is oriented toward the individual's goals.

during the two conflicts. What did the GI in World War II want? To go home. And when did he get to go home? When the war was won! If he disobeyed the orders to clean out the trenches and take the hills, the war would not be won and he would not go home. Furthermore, what were his chances of attaining his goal (getting home alive) if he obeyed the orders compared to his chances if he did not? What is being suggested is that the rational soldier in World War II, *whether patriotic or not,* probably found it expedient to obey.

Consider the reward system in use in Vietnam. What did the man at the bottom want? To go home. And when did he get to go home? When his tour of duty was over! This was the case *whether or not* the war was won. Furthermore, concerning the relative chance of getting home alive by obeying orders compared to the chance if they were disobeyed, it is worth noting that a mutineer in Vietnam was far more likely to be assigned rest and rehabilitation (on the assumption that fatigue was the cause) than he was to suffer any negative consequence.

In his description of the "zone of indifference," Barnard stated that "a person can and will accept a communication as authoritative only when . . . at the time of his decision, he believes it to be compatible with his personal interests as a whole" (1, p. 165). In light of the reward system used in Vietnam, would it not have been personally irrational for some orders to have been obeyed? Was not the military implementing a system which *rewarded* disobedience, while *hoping* that soldiers (despite the reward system) would obey orders?

Medicine

Theoretically, a physician can make either of two types of error, and intuitively one seems as bad as the other. A doctor can pronounce a patient sick when he is actually well, thus causing him needless anxiety and expense, curtailment of enjoyable foods and activities, and even physical danger by subjecting him to needless medication and surgery. Alternately, a doctor can label a sick person well and thus avoid treating what may be a serious, even fatal ailment. It might be natural to conclude that physicians seek to minimize both types of error.

Such a conclusion would be wrong.[2] It is estimated that numerous Americans are presently afflicted with iatrogenic (physician *caused*) illnesses (9). This occurs when the doctor is approached by someone complaining of a few stray symptoms. The doctor classifies and organizes these symptoms, gives them a name, and obligingly tells the patient what further symptoms may be expected. This information often acts as a self-fulfilling

---

2. In one study (4) of 14,867 films for signs of tuberculosis, 1,216 positive readings turned out to be clinically negative; only 24 negative readings proved clinically active, a ratio of 50 to 1.

prophecy, with the result that from that day on the patient for all practical purposes is sick.

Why does this happen? Why are physicians so reluctant to sustain a type 2 error (pronouncing a sick person well) that they will tolerate many type 1 errors? Again, a look at the reward system is needed. The punishments for a type 2 error are real: guilt, embarrassment, and the threat of lawsuit and scandal. On the other hand, a type 1 error (labeling a well person sick) "is sometimes seen as sound clinical practice, indicating a healthy conservative approach to medicine" (9, p. 69). Type 1 errors also are likely to generate increased income and a stream of steady customers who, being well in a limited physiological sense, will not embarrass the doctor by dying abruptly.

Fellow physicians and the general public therefore are really *rewarding* type 1 errors and at the same time *hoping* fervently that doctors will try not to make them.

General organizational examples

Rehabilitation centers and orphanages

In terms of the prime beneficiary classification (2, p. 42) organizations such as these are supposed to exist for the "public-in-contact," that is, clients. The orphanage therefore theoretically is interested in placing as many children as possible in good homes. However, often orphanages surround themselves with so many rules concerning adoption that it is nearly impossible to pry a child out of the place. Orphanages may deny adoption unless the applicants are a married couple, both of the same religion as the child, without history of emotional or vocational instability, with a specified minimum income and a private room for the child, etc.

If the primary goal is to place children in good homes, then the rules ought to constitute means toward that goal. Goal displacement results when these "means become ends-in-themselves that displace the original goals" (2, p. 229).

To some extent these rules are required by law. But the influence of the reward system on the orphanage's management should not be ignored. Consider, for example, that the:

1. Number of children enrolled often is the most important determinant of the size of the allocated budget.
2. Number of children under the director's care also will affect the size of his staff.
3. Total organizational size will determine largely the director's prestige at the annual conventions, in the community, etc.

Therefore, to the extent that staff size, total budget, and personal prestige are valued by the orphanage's executive personnel, it becomes rational for them to make it difficult for children to be adopted. After all, who wants to be the director of the smallest orphanage in the state?

If the reward system errs in the opposite direction, paying off only for placements, extensive goal displacement again is likely to result. A common example of vocational rehabilitation in many states, for example, consists of placing someone in a job for which he has little interest and few qualifications, for two months or so, and then "rehabilitating" him again in another position. Such behavior is quite consistent with the prevailing reward system, which pays off for the number of individuals placed in any position for 60 days or more. Rehabilitation counselors also confess to competing with one another to place relatively skilled clients, sometimes ignoring persons with few skills who would be harder to place. Extensively disabled clients find that counselors often prefer to work with those whose disabilities are less severe.[3]

Universities

Society *hopes* that teachers will not neglect their teaching responsibilities but *rewards* them almost entirely for research and publications. This is most true at the large and prestigious universities. Clichés such as "good research and good teaching go together" notwithstanding, professors often find that they must choose between teaching and research oriented activities when allocating their time. Rewards for good teaching usually are limited to outstanding teacher awards, which are given to only a small percentage of good teachers and which usually bestow little money and fleeting prestige. Punishments for poor teaching also are rare.

Rewards for research and publications, on the other hand, and punishments for failure to accomplish these, are commonly administered by universities at which teachers are employed. Furthermore, publication oriented resumés usually will be well received at other universities, whereas teaching credentials, harder to document and quantify, are much less transferable. Consequently, it is rational for university teachers to concentrate on research, even if to the detriment of teaching and at the expense of their students.

By the same token, it is rational for students to act based upon the goal displacement which has occurred within universities concerning what they are rewarded for. If it is assumed that a primary goal of a university is to transfer knowledge from teacher to student, then grades become identifiable as a means toward that goal, serving as motivational, control, and feedback devices to expedite the knowledge transfer. Instead, however, the grades themselves have become much more important for entrance to graduate school, successful employment, tuition refunds, parental respect, etc., than the knowledge or lack of knowledge they are supposed to signify.

3. Personal interviews conducted during 1972–1973.

It therefore should come as no surprise that information has surfaced in recent years concerning fraternity files for examinations, term paper writing services, organized cheating at the service academies, and the like. Such activities constitute a personally rational response to a reward system which pays off for grades rather than knowledge.

Business related examples

Ecology

Assume that the president of XYZ Corporation is confronted with the following alternatives:

1. Spend $11 million for antipollution equipment to keep from poisoning fish in the river adjacent to the plant; or
2. Do nothing, in violation of the law, and assume a one-in-ten chance of being caught, with a resultant $1 million fine plus the necessity of buying the equipment.

Under this not unrealistic set of choices it requires no linear program to determine that XYZ Corporation can maximize its probabilities by flouting the law. Add the fact that XYZ's president is probably being rewarded (by creditors, stockholders, and other salient parts of his task environment) according to criteria totally unrelated to the number of fish poisoned, and his probable course of action becomes clear.

Evaluation of training

It is axiomatic that those who care about a firm's well-being should insist that the organization get fair value for its expenditures. Yet it is commonly known that firms seldom bother to evaluate a new GRID, MBO, job enrichment program, or whatever, to see if the company is getting its money's worth. Why? Certainly it is not because people have not pointed out that this situation exists; numerous practitioner oriented articles are written each year to just this point.

The individuals (whether in personnel, manpower planning, or wherever) who normally would be responsible for conducting such evaluations are the same ones often charged with introducing the change effort in the first place. Having convinced top management to spend the money, they usually are quite animated afterwards in collecting arigorous vignettes and anecdotes about how successful the program was. The last thing many desire is a formal, systematic, and revealing evaluation. Although members of top management may actually *hope* for such systematic evaluation, their reward systems continue to *reward* ignorance in this area. And if the personnel department abdicates its responsibility, who is to step into the breach? The change agent himself? Hardly! He is likely to be too busy collecting anecdotal "evidence" of his own, for use with his next client.

Miscellaneous

Many additional examples could be cited of systems which in fact are rewarding behaviors other than those supposedly desired by the rewarder. A
few of these are described briefly below.

Most coaches disdain to discuss individual accomplishments, preferring
to speak of teamwork, proper attitude, and a one-for-all spirit. Usually,
however, rewards are distributed according to individual performance. The
college basketball player who feeds his teammates instead of shooting will
not compile impressive scoring statistics and is less likely to be drafted by
the pros. The ballplayer who hits to right field to advance the runners will
win neither the batting nor home run titles and will be offered smaller
raises. It therefore is rational for players to think of themselves first and the
team second.

In business organizations where rewards are dispensed for unit performance or for individual goals achieved without regard for overall effectiveness, similar attitudes often are observed. Under most Management by
Objectives (MBO) systems, goals in areas where quantification is difficult
often go unspecified. The organization therefore often is in a position
where it *hopes* for employee effort in the areas of team building, interpersonal relations, creativity, etc., but it formally *rewards* none of these. In
cases where promotions and raises are formally tied to MBO, the system
itself contains a paradox in that it "asks employees to set challenging, risky
goals, only to face smaller paychecks and possibly damaged careers if
these goals are not accomplished" (5, p. 40).

It is *hoped* that administrators will pay attention to long-run costs and
opportunities and will institute programs which will bear fruit later on.
However, many organizational reward systems pay off for short-run sales
and earnings only. Under such circumstances it is personally rational for
officials to sacrifice long-term growth and profit (by selling off equipment
and property, or by stifling research and development) for short-term advantages. This probably is most pertinent in the public sector, with the result that many public officials are unwilling to implement programs which
will not show benefits by election time.

As a final, clear-cut example of a fouled-up reward system, consider the
cost-plus contract or its next of kin, the allocation of next year's budget as a
direct function of this year's expenditures. It probably is conceivable that
those who award such budgets and contracts really hope for economy and
prudence in spending. It is obvious, however, that adopting the proverb "to
him who spends shall more be given," rewards not economy, but spending
itself.

Two companies' experiences

A manufacturing organization

A midwest manufacturer of industrial goods had been troubled for some time by aspects of its organizational climate it believed dysfunctional. For research purposes, interviews were conducted with many employees, and a questionnaire was administered on a companywide basis, including plants and offices in several American and Canadian locations. The company strongly encouraged employee participation in the survey and made available time and space during the workday for completion of the instrument. All employees in attendance during the day of the survey completed the questionnaire. All instruments were collected directly by the researcher, who personally administered each session. Since no one employed by the firm handled the questionnaires, and since respondent names were not asked for, it seems likely that the pledge of anonymity given was believed.

A modified version of the Expect Approval scale (7) was included as part of the questionnaire. The instrument asked respondents to indicate the degree of approval or disapproval they could expect if they performed each of the described actions. A seven point Likert scale was used, with one indicating that the action would probably bring strong disapproval and seven signifying likely strong approval.

Although normative data for this scale from studies of other organizations are unavailable, it is possible to examine fruitfully the data obtained from this survey in several ways. First, it may be worth noting that the questionnaire data corresponded closely to information gathered through interviews. Furthermore, as can be seen from the results summarized in Table 1, sizable differences between various work units, and between employees at different job levels within the same work unit, were obtained. This suggests that response bias effects (social desirability in particular loomed as a potential concern) are not likely to be severe.

Most importantly, comparisons between scores obtained on the Expect Approval scale and a statement of problems which were the reason for the survey revealed that the same behaviors which managers in each division thought dysfunctional were those which lower-level employees claimed were rewarded. As compared to job levels 1 to 8 in Division B (see Table 1), those in Division A claimed a much higher acceptance by management of "conforming" activities. Between 31 and 37 percent of Division A employees at levels 1–8 stated that going along with the majority, agreeing with the boss, and staying on everyone's good side brought approval; only once (level 5–8 responses to one of the three items) did a majority suggest that such actions would generate disapproval.

Furthermore, responses from Division A workers at levels 1–4 indicate that behaviors geared toward risk avoidance were as likely to be rewarded as

Table 1. Summary of two divisions' data relevant to conforming and risk-avoidance behaviors (extent to which subjects expect approval)

Dimension	Item	Division and sample	Total responses	percentage of workers responding		
				1, 2, or 3 disapproval	4	5, 6, or 7 approval
Risk avoidance	Making a risky decision based on the best information available at the time, but which turns out wrong	A, levels 1–4 (lowest)	127	61	25	14
		A, levels 5–8	172	46	31	23
		A, levels 9 and above	17	41	30	30
		B, levels 1–4 (lowest)	31	58	26	16
		B, levels 5–8	19	42	42	16
		B, levels 9 and above	10	50	20	30
	Setting extremely high and challenging standards and goals and then narrowly failing to make them	A, levels 1–4	122	47	28	25
		A, levels 5–8	168	33	26	41
		A, levels 9+	17	24	6	70
		B, levels 1–4	31	48	23	29
		B, levels 5–8	18	17	33	50
		B, levels 9+	10	30	0	70
	Setting goals which are extremely easy to make and then making them	A, levels 1–4	124	35	30	35
		A, levels 5–8	171	47	27	26
		A, levels 9+	17	70	24	6
		B, levels 1–4	31	58	26	16
		B, levels 5–8	19	63	16	21
		B, levels 9+	10	80	0	20

Conformity					
Being a "yes man" and always agreeing with the boss	A, levels 1–4	126	46	17	37
	A, levels 5–8	180	54	14	31
	A, levels 9+	17	88	12	0
	B, levels 1–4	32	53	28	19
	B, levels 5–8	19	68	21	11
	B, levels 9+	10	80	10	10
Always going along with the majority	A, levels 1–4	125	40	25	35
	A, levels 5–8	173	47	21	32
	A, levels 9+	17	70	12	18
	B, levels 1–4	31	61	23	16
	B, levels 5–8	19	68	11	21
	B, levels 9+	10	80	10	10
Being careful to stay on the good side of everyone, so that everyone agrees that you are a great guy	A, levels 1–4	124	45	18	37
	A, levels 5–8	173	45	22	33
	A, levels 9+	17	64	6	30
	B, levels 1–4	31	54	23	23
	B, levels 5–8	19	73	11	16
	B, levels 9+	10	80	10	10

to be punished. Only at job levels 9 and above was it apparent that the reward system was positively reinforcing behaviors desired by top management. Overall, the same "tendencies toward conservatism and apple-polishing at the lower levels" which divisional management had complained about during the interviews were those claimed by subordinates to be the most rational course of action in light of the existing reward system. Management apparently was not getting the behaviors it was *hoping* for, but it certainly was getting the behaviors it was perceived by subordinates to be *rewarding*.

An insurance firm

The Group Health Claims Division of a large eastern insurance company provides another rich illustration of a reward system which reinforces behaviors not desired by top management.

Attempting to measure and reward accuracy in paying surgical claims, the firm systematically keeps track of the number of returned checks and letters of complaint received from policyholders. However, underpayments are likely to provoke cries of outrage from the insured, while overpayments often are accepted in courteous silence. Since it often is impossible to tell from the physician's statement which of two surgical procedures, with different allowable benefits, was performed, and since writing for clarifications will interfere with other standards used by the firm concerning "percentage of claims paid within two days of receipt," the new hire in more than one claims section is soon acquainted with the informal norm: "When in doubt, pay it out!"

The situation would be even worse were it not for the fact that other features of the firm's reward system tend to neutralize those described. For example, annual "merit" increases are given to all employees, in one of the following three amounts:

1. If the worker is "outstanding" (a select category, into which no more than two employees per section may be placed): 5 percent.
2. If the worker is "above average" (normally all workers not "outstanding" are so rated): 4 percent.
3. If the worker commits gross acts of negligence and irresponsibility for which he might be discharged in many other companies: 3 percent.

Now, since (*a*) the difference between the 5 percent theoretically attainable through hard work and the 4 percent attainable merely by living until the review date is small and (*b*) since insurance firms seldom dispense much of a salary increase in cash (rather, the worker's insurance benefits increase, causing him to be further overinsured), many employees are rather indifferent to the possibility of obtaining the extra one percent reward and therefore tend to ignore the norm concerning indiscriminant payments.

However, most employees are not indifferent to the rule which states that, should absences or latenesses total three or more in any six-month period, the entire 4 or 5 percent due at the next "merit" review must be forfeited. In this sense the firm may be described as *hoping* for performance, while *rewarding* attendance. What it gets, of course, is attendance. (If the absence-lateness rule appears to the reader to be stringent, it really is not. The company counts "times" rather than "days" absent, and a ten-day absence therefore counts the same as one lasting two days. A worker in danger of accumulating a third absence within six months merely has to remain ill [away from work] during his second absence until his first absence is more than six months old. The limiting factor is that at some point his salary ceases, and his sickness benefits take over. This usually is sufficient to get the younger workers to return, but for those with 20 or more years' service, the company provides sickness benefits of 90 percent of normal salary, tax-free! Therefore . . .)

Causes

Extremely diverse instances of systems which reward behavior A although the rewarder apparently hopes for behavior B have been given. These are useful to illustrate the breadth and magnitude of the phenomenon, but the diversity increases the difficulty of determining commonalities and establishing causes. However, four general factors may be pertinent to an explanation of why fouled up reward systems seem to be so prevalent.

Fascination with an "objective" criterion

It has been mentioned elsewhere (6, p. 92) that:

> Most "objective" measures of productivity are objective only in that their subjective elements are (a) determined in advance, rather than coming into play at the time of the formal evaluation, and (b) well concealed on the rating instrument itself. Thus industrial firms seeking to devise objective rating systems first decide, in an arbitrary manner, what dimensions are to be rated, . . . usually including some items having little to do with organizational effectiveness while excluding others that do. Only then does Personnel Division churn out official-looking documents on which all dimensions chosen to be rated are assigned point values, categories, or whatever.

Nonetheless, many individuals seek to establish simple, quantifiable standards against which to measure and reward performance. Such efforts may be successful in highly predictable areas within an organization but are likely to cause goal displacement when applied anywhere else. Overconcern with attendance and lateness in the insurance firm and with the number of people placed in the vocational rehabilitation division may have been largely responsible for the problems described in those organizations.

Overemphasis on highly visible behaviors

Difficulties often stem from the fact that some parts of the task are highly visible while other parts are not. For example, publications are easier to demonstrate than teaching, and scoring baskets and hitting home runs are more readily observable than feeding teammates and advancing base runners. Similarly, the adverse consequences of pronouncing a sick person well are more visible than those sustained by labeling a well person sick. Team-building and creativity are other examples of behaviors which may not be rewarded simply because they are hard to observe.

Hypocrisy

In some of the instances described the rewarder may have been getting the desired behavior, notwithstanding claims that the behavior was not desired. This may be true, for example, of management's attitude toward apple-polishing in the manufacturing firm (a behavior which subordinates felt was rewarded, despite management's avowed dislike of the practice). This also may explain politicians' unwillingness to revise the penalties for disobedience of ecology laws, and the failure of top management to devise reward systems which would cause systematic evaluation of training and development programs.

Emphasis on morality or equity rather than efficiency

Sometimes consideration of other factors prevents the establishment of a system which rewards behaviors desired by the rewarder. The felt obligation of many Americans to vote for one candidate or another, for example, may impair their ability to withhold support from politicians who refuse to discuss the issues. Similarly, the concern for spreading the risks and costs of wartime military service may outweigh the advantage to be obtained by committing personnel to combat until the war is over.

It should be noted that only with respect to the first two causes are reward systems really paying off for other than desired behaviors. In the case of the third and fourth causes the system *is* rewarding behaviors desired by the rewarder, and the systems are fouled up only from the standpoints of those who believe the rewarder's public statements (cause 3), or those who seek to maximize efficiency rather than other outcomes (cause 4).

Conclusions

Modern organization theory requires a recognition that the members of organizations and society possess divergent goals and motives. It therefore is unlikely that managers and their subordinates will seek the same outcomes. Three possible remedies for this potential problem are suggested.

Selection

It is theoretically possible for organizations to employ only those individuals whose goals and motives are wholly consonant with those of management. In such cases the same behaviors judged by subordinates to be rational would be perceived by management as desirable. State-of-the-art reviews of selection techniques, however, provide scant grounds for hope that such an approach would be successful (for example, see 12).

Training

Another theoretical alternative is for the organization to admit those employees whose goals are not consonant with those of management and then, through training, socialization, or whatever, alter employee goals to make them consonant. However, research on the effectiveness of such training programs, though limited, provides further grounds for pessimism (for example, see 3).

Altering the reward system

What would have been the result if:

1. Nixon had been assured by his advisors that he could not win reelection except by discussing the issues in detail?
2. Physicians' conduct was subjected to regular examination by review boards for type 1 errors (calling healthy people ill) and to penalties (fines, censure, etc.) for errors of either type?
3. The President of XYZ Corporation had to choose between (a) spending $11 million dollars for antipollution equipment, and (b) incurring a 50–50 chance of going to jail for five years?

Managers who complain that their workers are not motivated might do well to consider the possibility that they have installed reward systems which are paying off for behaviors other than those they are seeking. This, in part, is what happened in Vietnam, and this is what regularly frustrates societal efforts to bring about honest politicians, civic-minded managers, etc. This certainly is what happened in both the manufacturing and the insurance companies.

A first step for such managers might be to find out what behaviors currently are being rewarded. Perhaps an instrument similar to that used in the manufacturing firm could be useful for this purpose. Chances are excellent that these managers will be surprised by what they find—that their firms are not rewarding what they assume they are. In fact, such undesirable behavior by organizational members as they have observed may be explained largely by the reward systems in use.

This is not to say that all organizational behavior is determined by formal rewards and punishments. Certainly it is true that in the absence of formal reinforcement some soldiers will be patriotic, some presidents will be ecology minded, and some orphanage directors will care about children. The point, however, is that in such cases the rewarder is not *causing* the behaviors desired but is only a fortunate bystander. For an organization to *act* upon its members, the formal reward system should positively reinforce desired behaviors, not constitute an obstacle to be overcome.

It might be wise to underscore the obvious fact that there is nothing really new in what has been said. In both theory and practice these matters have been mentioned before. Thus in many states Good Samaritan laws have been installed to protect doctors who stop to assist a stricken motorist. In states without such laws it is commonplace for doctors to refuse to stop, for fear of involvement in a subsequent lawsuit. In college basketball additional penalties have been instituted against players who foul their opponents deliberately. It has long been argued by Milton Friedman and others that penalties should be altered so as to make it irrational to disobey the ecology laws, and so on.

By altering the reward system the organization escapes the necessity of selecting only desirable people or of trying to alter undesirable ones. In Skinnerian terms (as described in 11, p. 704), "As for responsibility and goodness—as commonly defined—no one . . . would want or need them. They refer to a man's behaving well despite the absence of positive reinforcement that is obviously sufficient to explain it. Where such reinforcement exists, 'no one needs goodness.'"

Reference notes

1. Barnard, Chester I. *The functions of the executive.* Cambridge, Mass.: Harvard University Press, 1964.

2. Blau, Peter M., and Scott, W. Richard. *Formal organizations.* San Francisco: Chandler, 1962.

3. Fiedler, Fred E. Predicting the effects of leadership training and experience from the contingency model, *Journal of Applied Psychology,* 1972, 56:114–19.

4. Garland, L. H. Studies of the accuracy of diagnostic procedures, *American Journal Roentgenological, Radium Therapy Nuclear Medicine,* 1959, 82:25–38.

5. Kerr, Steven. Some modifications in MBO as an OD strategy, *Academy of Management Proceedings,* 1973, 39–42.

6. Kerr, Steven. What price objectivity? *American Sociologist,* 1973, 8:92–93.

7. Litwin, G. H., and Stringer, R. A., Jr. *Motivation and organizational climate.* Boston: Harvard University Press, 1968.

8. Perrow, Charles. The analysis of goals in complex organizations, in A. Etzioni (ed.), *Readings on modern organizations.* Englewood Cliffs, N.J.: Prentice-Hall, 1969.

9. Scheff, Thomas J. Decision rules, types of error, and their consequences in medical diagnosis, in F. Massarik and P. Ratoosh (eds.), *Mathematical explorations in behavioral science*. Homewood, Ill.: Richard D. Irwin, Inc., 1965.

10. Simon, Herbert A. *Administrative behavior*. New York: Free Press, 1957.

11. Swanson, G. E. Review symposium: Beyond freedom and dignity, *American Journal of Sociology*, 1972, 78:702–705.

12. Webster, E. *Decision making in the employment interview*. Montreal: Industrial Relations Center, McGill University, 1964.

2

Mind: Thinking, Creating, Analyzing

In section 1 we looked at people as emotionally motivated creatures, pushed by their inner wants and pulled by the carrots of incentives and rewards. But human beings are more than that. They also use their heads. They are thinking beings: reasoners, imaginers, analyzers.

The three papers in this section focus on the way human beings think, as well as create and solve problems. They seem especially relevant to the managing process, particularly relevant at this time in our history. How managers ought to be thinking, and about what, are the major questions that Western society is pressing its contemporary managers to reconsider.

John Hayes's piece, the first one, is about creativity. So is the second, by James Adams. Hayes, at Carnegie-Mellon University, draws from current cognitive theory about creativity, much of which has been developed at Carnegie-Mellon. But its focus is on how creativity happens and how we might make it happen.

Adams's paper is almost a how-to-do-it article about creative thinking. It is taken from his book, *Conceptual Blockbusting*. Adams is an engineer with interests in design and ways of finding original and unusual solutions to difficult and complex problems. He offers a set of rules of thumb, or heuristics, for escaping from traditionally constrained ways of thinking. He advocates looking at problems upside down, backward, with a microscope, and with a telescope to find new ways to break through old thought barriers.

The third article, a classic piece by Charles Lindblom, is quite different. It may be a little harder to follow than some of the other papers in this book, but it is very much worth reading. Lindblom, a senior political scientist, makes a strong and sensible challenge to the notion that the only "right" way to think is the logical, analytic, systematic way. He raises questions about alternative strategies that may be messier, more contingent, and more "muddling," but nevertheless more effective than purist advance planning. Indeed, Lindblom's article represents the start of a strong and growing literature that challenges the preeminence of analytic, logical, planful models of the managing process. This more "muddling" kind of orientation, this argument that managing requires flexibility, adjustment, and intuition as well as analytic skills will recur again and again later in this book.

So the focal issue of this section is how people use their heads, and how they might use them better.

Cognitive Processes in Creative Acts
John R. Hayes

In this chapter, we will define creativity and discuss four of the cognitive processes underlying creative acts: problem finding, idea generation, planning, and preparation. In addition, we will describe some procedures which can increase your problem finding and idea generation skills.

The main point that we want to make is that you can exercise some control over the cognitive processes and the social conditions which influence your creative abilities. To this extent, you can increase your chances of becoming a creative person.

What is a creative act?

Creative acts come in a great variety of forms. A creative act may be quite ordinary and inconsequential—for example, it might be something as simple as making up a bedtime story to tell our children—or it may be world shaking—as was Galileo's invention of the science of physics. A creative act may involve years of concentrated work—consider the decades Darwin devoted to developing the evidence for the theory of evolution—or it may be brief—condensed into a sudden flash of insight—the sort of insight that drove Archimedes naked from his bath shouting, "Eureka!"

What is there about these very different acts that leads us to call them all "creative"? Typically, we apply fairly stringent criteria in judging creativity. In most cases, we require an act to pass three tests before we call it creative. First, we must believe that the act is *original*. Second, we must believe that it is *valuable*. And third, it must suggest to us that the person who performed the act has special mental *abilities*. For example, when we see what the person has done, we ask ourselves, "How did she ever think of that?" or, "How did he have the patience to work all that out?"

Let's examine these conditions in order.

Reprinted, with some changes, from John R. Hayes, *The Complete Problem Solver* (Philadelphia: Franklin Institute Press, 1981).

Originality

We certainly wouldn't judge a painter creative who simply copied the pictures of other painters. To be judged creative, painters must use their own resources to shape the painting. They must paint their *own* pictures.

We don't mean though that everything in a creative work must be original. Painters, writers, and inventors routinely use ideas borrowed from others. However, the creative person combines or interprets these borrowed ideas in ways that are original. Renaissance artists very frequently painted the Madonna and Child, but each great artist presented the theme in an individual way.

Sometimes a person will do something original which is not new. For example, a scientist may make a discovery, quite independent of their people, only to find later that the discovery has been made several times before. In our society newness is important. We are very careful to give special credit to the person who is *first* to invent something. Still, we attribute creativity to the scientist above on the grounds of originality, even though the discovery is not new.

Value

Even if an act is original, we won't consider it creative unless we also judge it to be valuable. Suppose, for example, you were to turn all the furniture in your house upside down. That would be original, but it would hardly be valuable. Your friends would not ask admiringly, "How did you think of that?" Rather, they would ask, "Why did you think of that?" and worry a bit about your mental health.

Judging whether something is valuable or not is tricky. Perfectly reasonable people may disagree with each other about the value, say, of contemporary music. Further, opinions change over time. In the 1860s, both the critics and the public much preferred the painters of the French Academy to the Impressionists. Now both critical and popular judgment is reversed. Today the work of Impressionists such as Renoir, Degas, and Monet is much better known than that of French Academy painters such as Greuze or Gérôme.

If judgments of value can change with time, then judgments of creativity can change, too. An act which is judged creative by one generation may not seem so to the next.

Abilities

Our final condition for judging an act creative is that it must suggest that the person who performed the act has special mental abilities. Imagine the following scene: A housepainter is retouching the ceiling in a museum gallery. Just as he is about to finish, his foot slips. He knocks over the ladder, splattering paint everywhere, and does a double flip into a potted palm. He regains consciousness several hours later, just in time to hear members of the museum selection committee saying, "Brilliant!!" "A work of genius!" "What freedom of movement!" Peering through the palm fronds, he sees that they are referring to the aftermath of his accident on the wall.

Now, while the housepainter produced something original and valuable, we can't call his act creative. Falling off the ladder doesn't in any way cause us to admire the housepainter's mental abilities. It only suggests that he may have a tendency toward clumsiness.

You might be inclined to say that the housepainter's act wasn't creative because it was unintentional. You should notice, though, that some very creative acts are unintentional. For example, Becquerel's discovery of radioactivity was unintentional. He had no idea that uranium ore would fog a photographic film. We admire Becquerel for making the discovery because, while it was unintentional, he had the wit to recognize its significance.

Creativity and IQ

If creative acts require special mental abilities, we might expect that creative people have especially high IQ's. While creative people do have higher than average IQ's, the relation between creativity and IQ is complex. The simplest way to summarize it is to say that people with below average IQ's tend not to be creative. However, if we look just at people above a certain IQ level, such as 120, then there is very little relation between creativity and IQ. It is as if there is a certain minimum IQ required for creativity, after which IQ doesn't matter.

An alternative view (see Hayes, 1978) is that IQ has nothing to do with creative ability, and that the reason people with low IQ's are not creatively productive is that they aren't given the opportunity. IQ does predict how well a person will do in school. People who do poorly in school may have difficulty getting into good schools and getting good jobs in which there is a chance to be creative. Thus, our society may actually *prevent* people with low IQ's from being creative.

The important point about creativity and IQ that you should understand is this: You shouldn't give up on yourself as a creative person just because your IQ is not outstanding. For example, the IQ's of such famous people as Copernicus, Rembrandt, and Faraday have been estimated at 110 or less!

Creativity and ill-defined problems

In discussing the nature of a creative act, we will follow the lead of Newell, Shaw, and Simon (1964). These authors proposed that a creative act is a special kind of problem solving, that it is the act of solving an ill-defined problem.

In Chapter 1, we defined ill-defined problems as ones which require problem solvers to contribute to the definition of the problem from their *own* resources. To solve an ill-defined problem, you may be required either to make decisions based on your own knowledge and values (gap-filling decisions) or to discover new information through your own active exploration of the problem (jumping in), or both.

Your solutions to ill-defined problems are very much *your* solutions. They depend on your knowledge and your values. Other people would almost certainly have arrived at different solutions because their knowledge and values differ from yours. It is just because we put our own knowledge and values into the solution of ill-defined problems that it is possible to solve them creatively. It is by drawing on private resources—different in each person and largely hidden from the outside viewer—that we are able to produce solutions which dazzle and astound.

Cognitive processes underlying creative acts

Creative acts depend on a great many of our cognitive processes working together in harmony—processes of representation, search, memory, and decision making. We will focus on just four of these processes which are especially important for creativity: problem finding, idea generation, planning, and preparation.

Problem finding

Many problems come to us with neat labels which say in effect, "Solve me. I'm a problem!" Problems in exams, IQ tests, and puzzle books are like that. When we open an exam booklet, we are likely to find labels such as "Question #1" or "Problem 3." Whether we can solve the problems or not, we have no trouble finding them.

Some problems aren't as neatly labeled, though. There is a special class of ill-defined problems in which what we have to contribute to the definition of the problem is the discovery that there *is* a problem.

Here is an uncomplicated example in which I discovered a problem: Over the years, I have searched through the theater pages of the newspaper hundreds of times to find what was playing at my local theater. On the average, the search involved examining about half of the ads before finding the one I wanted. While this was a minor annoyance, until recently I hadn't seen it as a problem—that is, as a difficulty for which one could find a sensible solution. When I did see it as a problem—when I finally said to myself, "Something could be done about that"—it was easy enough to think of solutions, e.g., standardize the positions of the ads or alphabetize them. Finding this problem was a great deal more difficult than finding methods for its solution.

Problem finding and creativity

The process of problem finding plays a very important role both in artistic and in scientific creativity. For example, in the early 1900's, a group of American artists called the "ashcan school" discovered esthetic values in the everyday appearance of the city—people shopping or crossing at an intersection. They took it as their problem to capture these values in their paintings. No one told them to do this. In fact, a horrified artistic establishment told them not to. They had to discover their artistic problem for themselves.

Problem finding is important in scientific discovery as well. Einstein and Infeld (1938, p. 95) comment:

> Galileo formulated the problem of determining the velocity of light, but did not solve it. The formulation of a problem is often more essential than its solution, which may be merely a matter of mathematical or experimental skill. To raise new questions, new possibilities, to regard old problems from a new angle, requires creative imagination and marks real advance in science.

Here are three cases in point.

Case 1

In the heyday of the telegraph, hundreds of operators listened to the dots and dashes of the Morse ticker and transcribed them into words on paper. When the connection was bad, the messages were hard to hear. Most simply shrugged their shoulders and did the best they could in a difficult situation. Edison distinguished himself from the others by seeing the difficulty as a problem to be solved. He solved it by constructing a device which would record the dots and dashes as visible marks on a rotating disk. When the device was complete, however, others didn't necessarily see it as the solution to a problem. Edison's employers, for example, thought that reading from a disk rather than listening to the ticker was a complete waste of time.

The pattern of events that led to Edison's invention has been repeated in a number of scientific discoveries. What many had observed and dismissed as a trivial annoyance, one person recognized as an important problem to be solved.

Case 2

As many bacteriologists do, Alexander Fleming was growing colonies of bacteria on sterile agar plates. An accident, such as must have happened thousands of times in other laboratories, contaminated some of the plates with dust. The bacteria Fleming was trying to grow died in the neighborhood of the dust specks. Rather than throwing the plates out as "spoiled," Fleming saw that they posed an interesting problem—"Why did the bacteria die?" The answer was that the dust contained the mold which produces Penicillin—a substance whose existence was unknown at that time. Thus a major medical discovery depended on someone seeing a problem in some spoiled agar plates.

Case 3

As a part of a study of digestion, the physiologist, Ivan Pavlov, investigated the salivary reflex of dogs. Dogs salivate automatically when food is put into their mouths. The experiments went well at first, but then to Pavlov's surprise, the dogs began to salivate before they had any food in their mouths at all. He found that they would salivate at the sight or sound of the food dishes or to any other signal that had frequently been associated with feeding. These developments seriously complicated Pavlov's experiments. But, rather than seeing them simply as an annoyance, as most would have done, he saw that they revealed an important problem—"What was the nature of these anticipatory responses?" Pavlov received stern warning from his colleagues that he would be risking his very promising career in physiology if he pursued these "unscientific" psychological interests. Fortunately, Pavlov had the courage to ignore these warnings and to continue to work on the problem he had discovered. This work on conditioned reflexes earned him the Nobel prize.

Improving your problem-finding skills

The three procedures we are about to describe are not likely to earn you a Nobel prize, but they can help to make you a better problem finder. The first is intended as an aid to aspiring inventors. The second and third are *critical thinking* techniques, that is, techniques for finding flaws in arguments. Critical thinking skills are important for creativity because detecting a flaw in an accepted theory can be a very powerful source of inspiration for creating a new theory. Critical thinking skills are also very useful in such mundane activities as defending ourselves against politicians and encyclopedia salesmen.

Bug listing

Bug listing is a technique that Adams (1974) recommends to help inventors find promising problems to work on. The basic idea is that things which bother you, such as ice cream cones that drip or typewriters that won't spell, probably bother other people as well. An invention created to solve one of your bugs could have a wide market.

A bug list is simply a list of things that bother you. To make a bug list, you should carry a notebook with you so that you can record the bugs when you notice them. (Bugs are often so commonplace that they are hard to remember.) Here is a representative bug list:

1. remembering to mail letters
2. taking out the trash
3. fastening seatbelts
4. putting tops back on toothpaste, ketchup, etc.
5. changing the cat box

6. washing dishes
7. making my bed
8. keeping clean and dirty laundry separate
9. turning off lights
10. sliding doors that stick
11. cupboard doors that don't close
12. crumbs on the table, counter, and floor
13. cat fur
14. people with dirty ears
15. hanging up my coat
16. restaurants with dim lights that make your eyes go buggy
17. places that are crowded
18. stupid teachers
19. people in pants that are too tight
20. shorts that are too short
21. men who wear their shirts open to the navel
22. music in supermarkets
23. fight songs
24. stupid radio and television personalities
25. sour milk
26. sunburn
27. tangled hair
28. razor stubble
29. dirty glasses
30. dirt under contact lenses
31. food that drips on your clothes (like tacos)
32. getting teeth cleaned at the dentist
33. dark nail polish
34. dirty fingernails
35. registering for classes
36. drying my hair
37. humid days
38. crying babies
39. dripping faucets
40. passport photos

Each of these bugs can be viewed as a problem to be solved, and as the potential source of a useful invention.

Searching for counterexamples

The employment argument

This argument is not very popular today, but it was widely accepted in the '50's. "When a company is filling a job, it should hire men in preference to women, because men have to support families."

A common way for people to test an argument is to search for positive instances (Wason, 1968)—that is, to think of a case in which the argument seems right. For example, a person might say, "Well, if a man is supporting a wife and three kids, it *is* more important for him to have a job than for a single woman to have one." Having found a positive instance, many stop their search and accept the argument.

While searching for positive instances is a very common technique, it is, unfortunately, a very uncritical one. It ignores cases in which the argument is false. A much more critical approach to testing arguments is one widely used by philosophers and mathematicians—searching for counterexamples. A counterexample is a case in which the argument we are testing is false. A person searching for a counterexample to the employment argument might say, "Well, a woman who is supporting her crippled husband certainly deserves to have a job as much as a bachelor does." Clearly, we are much less likely to accept a faulty argument if we test it by searching for counterexamples. Here is another case.

The pre-cognition argument

Some claim that certain people can have accurate knowledge of events before they happen.

> Positive Instance: "Yeah! Last week my aunt dreamt that something good was going to happen to me and today I won the lottery!"
> Counterexample: "Sure, but two weeks ago, she dreamt that your turtle was going to have puppies."

Searching for counterexamples is only one of many techniques which philosophers have developed for detecting problems in arguments. An interesting and highly readable introduction to some of these techniques is provided by Thomas Schwartz in his book, *The Art of Logical Reasoning* (1980).

Searching for alternative interpretations

Our second technique for finding problems in arguments borrows from the critical spirit of scientific research. It is the technique of searching for alternative interpretations.

Case 1: Singing the baby to flab

Suppose that someone tried to convince us that singing to children makes them grow. They tell us that they have systematically observed 20 kindergarten children whose mothers sing to them every day, and that over a period of eight months, these children gained an average of four pounds.

Fortunately, the main problem in this argument is easy to find. We know that kindergarten children are growing rapidly, so we can readily formulate an alternate interpretation of the data. Those children might have gained four pounds even if they hadn't been sung to.

The problem with the argument is that the observations do not include *control* measurements, for example, weight gains of 20 kindergarten children whose mothers do *not* sing to them. We would be much more inclined to accept the argument if the children who were sung to gained *more* than the children who were not.

Case 2: Hypnotizing chickens

Once, in my wasted youth, I ran across an enterprising salesman who was selling a device for hypnotizing chickens. Indeed, the device was impressive. The salesman held a chicken down on a table and placed the device, which emitted a soft buzzing, next to the chicken's head. When he released the chicken, it just lay there and stared as if all active chicken thoughts had been chased from its head. It was completely gorked out. Then, after 30 seconds of complete immobility, it suddenly scrambled up and ran off.

One can easily understand that many people, perhaps even the salesman himself, would be convinced of the efficacy of the device—some to the extent of buying one.

I wasn't convinced, however, because I had an alternative interpretation of the demonstration. For no good reason, at that time, I was the local expert on "animal hypnosis." I knew that various animals—guinea pigs, snakes, alligators, and yes, chickens—could be "hypnotized" simply by putting them into certain postures. In particular, a chicken can be hypnotized by holding its head down on a table for a few seconds. My alternative interpretation was that what we were seeing was just another case of animal hypnosis and that a control observation in which the chicken's head was held on the table *without* the buzzer would have produced the same result, i.e., a gorked-out chicken.

Case I Revisited: Singing to children

Suppose that the person studying singing and weight gain had made the control observation we suggested above. Suppose that they had found that children of mothers who sing to them gain two pounds more on the average than children of mothers who do not. Would we then be forced to accept the argument that singing to children makes them grow? The answer is "No." The argument still has problems as we can see by considering some alternative interpretations. Perhaps there were other differences between the two groups of mothers. Perhaps if we interviewed the mothers, the non-singers would say, "Sing to my kid? Hell, I don't even feed 'm!", while the singers insist that a healthy child needs at least nine meals a day.

Clearly, searching for alternate interpretations can help us to find problems in persuasive arguments.

Summary

In some cases finding a problem is the most difficult part of solving it. Many discoveries depend on finding a problem that others have ignored. We frequently hear persuasive arguments that have problems hidden in them. If we fail to find the problems, we are likely to be persuaded of something that is false. By asking the following three questions, we can increase our chances of finding such problems:

1. Can I think of a counterexample?
2. Have appropriate control measurements been made?
3. Are there alternate interpretations of the result?

Exercises

1. Design a study of singing and weight gain that would avoid the problems we found above.
2. What problems can you find in the following arguments?
   a. Nine out of 10 doctors interviewed said that they prescribe our brand in preference to all others. Buy our brand.
   b. In clinical tests, eight out of 10 felt relief within 10 minutes after using our brand. Buy it.
   c. Four leading pain relievers contain 650 mg of aspirin per tablet, but our brand contains 800 mg. Buy our brand.

Generating ideas

Many of the difficulties in creative problem solving arise not in finding the problem but in generating ideas for a solution. When faced with a problem like The Loser (remember the man who always lost at gambling because the fortune teller cast a spell on him?), some people are terrific at thinking up ideas and some are terrible. This section is designed for people who have trouble generating ideas.

Many methods have been proposed to help make ideas flow. We will discuss just two: (1) brainstorming, and (2) finding analogies.

Brainstorming

Brainstorming is a technique developed by Alex Osborn, an executive of a major New York advertising firm, and first described in his book, *Your Creative Power* (1948). It is designed to increase the flow of ideas in small group meetings. The most important principle underlying brainstorming is that the process of generating ideas is completely separated from the process of evaluating them. Brainstorming sessions take place in two phases—an *idea generation* phase and an *idea evaluation* phase. During the idea generation phase, all judging and criticism of the produced ideas is eliminated—or rather deferred—until the evaluation phase.

In most conferences, such as town meetings and informal planning sessions, the standard format is debate, that is, proposal and criticism. This format is not notably successful in producing new ideas. Typically in such sessions, each new idea is met with a welter of criticism. Brainstorming is quite different from most meeting situations.

During the idea generation phase:

1. All criticism of ideas is withheld until the evaluation phase.
2. Wild or even silly ideas are welcomed.
3. Quantity of ideas is encouraged.
4. Participants are encouraged to combine or improve on ideas already suggested.
5. The group acts as a whole, not breaking up into several small groups.
6. One person acts as a secretary to record the list of ideas.

A brainstorming group needs a leader who will enforce the rules. The first and most important task of the leader is to be sure that criticism is withheld. There seems to be a strong tendency in many people to respond to an idea by saying, "Oh, that won't work because. . . ." An idea which is proposed as a joke may not be useful in itself as a solution of the problem, and yet it may aid the solution by suggesting a new dimension of the problem or by opening a new line of inquiry.

In a typical brainstorming session, the members of the group are allowed to propose ideas whenever they please. The possibility exists in this situation that one or a few of the group members will dominate the session, with the result that others may be prevented from contributing all that they could. To eliminate this possibility, Bouchard (1972) has modified the typical brainstorming procedure by adding a sequencing rule in which the members of the group take turns in offering ideas. He reported that groups using the sequencing rule produced more ideas than groups that did not use it.

If the group begins to run out of ideas during the idea-generating phase, it sometimes helps to review the list of ideas already suggested. When the group's ideas have been exhausted, it is time to move to the evaluation phase.

In the evaluation phase, each idea is reviewed critically to determine if it is in fact a practical solution. A list of the ideas that the group considers most practical is then submitted as the group's problem-solving recommendations.

Osborn feels that brainstorming is helpful in producing new ideas for two reasons. First, the reduction in criticism during the generation phase allows ideas to be born and developed that otherwise might never have been suggested, or might have been rejected before they had received sufficient positive consideration. Second, Osborn feels that brainstorming sessions promote a kind of social contagion in which one person's idea inspires a better idea in another—an idea that the second person wouldn't have thought of otherwise.

Studies reviewed by Stein (1975) indicate that groups using the brainstorming technique do produce more ideas than groups that generate and evaluate ideas simultaneously. Further, most of these studies also show that the brainstorming groups produce more high-quality ideas.

We should note that Osborn recommends brainstorming only for certain types of "simple and talkable" problems—problems like, "How can we prevent stealing from the library?" and, "How can we get more foreign visitors to come to the United States?" Indeed, research on group problem solving suggests that groups do better than individuals on some kinds of problems but not on others. Individuals are as good or better than groups in solving arithmetic problems (Hudgins, 1960), and in solving problems where each individual has all the necessary information. Groups are superior to individuals in tasks where the pooling of skills and information is important. For example, groups are superior to individuals for remembering a complex story (Perlmutter, 1953), and for solving prejudice-provoking syllogisms (Barnlund, 1959). Barnlund suggests that the group is more objective than the individual because prejudices are not completely shared among the members of the group.

Exercise

Form a group and conduct a brainstorming session. Suggested topics are: ways to save time; ways to keep the city clean; and, uses for discarded styrofoam cups.

Individual brainstorming

While the brainstorming technique was designed to be used with groups, it can also be used by a single person in private idea-generating sessions. The principles to be applied are the same. Separate idea generation from evaluation. Start with the idea generation phase, writing down ideas as they occur, without criticism. You should welcome wild or silly ideas, and you should try to combine or improve ideas that were generated earlier. The hard part in this phase is to control your internal editor—the internal voice of criticism which may lead you to ignore an idea that seems too dumb or trivial.

Just as with group brainstorming, when you begin to run out of ideas, you can review the list as a source to stimulate further production. When the ideas really have stopped coming, it is time to move on to the evaluation phase. Here you review each idea to select those that seem best for solving the problem.

Exercise

Conduct a brainstorming session by yourself. Suggested topics: how to increase your own efficiency; how to make your favorite annoyance less annoying; and, how to persuade someone to give you a job.

Individual brainstorming sessions can be very helpful when you are writing (see Flower, 1980). Suppose that you are planning a magazine article on architecture for a teenage audience. To brainstorm, first generate all of the ideas you can think of that a teenager might find interesting or important about architecture. As you do this, scratch down rapid notes in the form of scattered words and phrases that will remind you of the ideas. When idea generation is complete, evaluate the ideas—that is, decide which ideas you want to include in your article—and then organize them into an outline. At this point, you are well started in producing your article.

Discovering analogies

Analogies are an important source of ideas when we are searching for problem solutions. Several systems have been proposed for stimulating the formation of useful analogies. In essence, all of these systems employ some checklist of analogy types. The user of the system works through the checklist and tries to find analogies of each type.

In Gordon's synectics system (Gordon, 1961), the checklist consists of four analogy types: personal, direct, symbolic, and fantasy. Suppose that we were members of a synectics group looking for ideas to improve automobile brakes. First, we would try to form personal analogies in which we put ourselves directly into the problem situation. For example, we could imagine ourselves as the brakes of a car. Next, we would search for a direct analogy if the same function is accomplished in some other setting, such as a cat trying to stop on a slippery floor. Third, we would try to form symbolic analogies. I would tell you about this kind of analogy if I could, but unfortunately, I have been unable to find an intelligible description of it.

Finally, we think of fantasy analogies in which anything including magic and science fiction are allowed, for instance, claws reaching out of the road to grab our wheels.

In Koberg and Bagnall's (1974) attribute analogy system, the checklist is a list of attributes of an object—its name, form, function, color, and material. If we are trying to improve some object, say, a fireplace, we first list its attributes and then attach analogies to each one. Table 1 illustrates the process.

As yet there appears to be no solid experimental evidence that either synectics or attribute analogies actually work. However, the synectics system has received a good deal of favorable comment from users in industry (see Stein, 1975).

Table 1. The attribute analogy system

Assuming the problem is to improve a fireplace, its attributes are:
Name: Fireplace
Form: Geometric, angular, conical, etc.
Function: Heat room, psychologically soothing, etc.
Color: Black, brick red, etc.
Material: Steel, masonry, etc.

Analogy Chains (similarities)
Name: Combustion chamber, tea pot, auto engine, cigarette lighter, etc.
Form: Architectural constructions, crystals, prisms, etc.
Function: Cat on lap, robe, intimate friend, etc.

Ideas Produced (for improving fireplace)
Change name to energy transformer.
Try forms which are derived from crystal structures.
Use robe insulation principle to conserve radiant heat, etc.

Source: Koberg and Bagnall (1974).

Planning and creativity

A plan is a set of directions we use to guide us in solving a problem. The more effort we put into planning, the more likely we are to construct a good map which will guide us efficiently to the best solution. Since creative acts are problem-solving acts, it shouldn't surprise us that planning is also important for creativity. Flower and Hayes (1980) have shown that good expository writers plan much more effectively than do poor writers.

A path-breaking study by Getzels and Csikszentmihalyi (1976) indicates that planning is critically important in art. They showed that the amount of planning* that an art student did in preparing to draw a picture predicted not only the quality of the resulting picture, but also whether or not the student would become a productive artist years later.

The investigators tested 31 male second- and third-year students at a prestigious art school. Each student was brought into an experimental room supplied with drawing materials, an empty table, and a variety of objects. The students were asked to select any of the objects they wanted, arrange them on the table as they chose, and then to draw a picture. They were told, "The important thing is that the drawing should be pleasing to you."

The experimenter then noted three things about the students' behavior before they started drawing and three things about their behavior while they were drawing. These six behaviors (listed in table 2) were chosen to reflect

---

*These authors claim to measure problem finding rather than planning. However, as these terms are used in this text, and, I believe, in cognitive science generally, it is more appropriate to say that they have measured planning.

Table 2. Six behaviors used to measure planning

Before drawing:
  B1. How many objects were manipulated?
  B2. Were unusual objects chosen—that is, did a student choose objects which
       few other students chose?
  B3. How carefully did the student examine the objects?
While drawing:
  W1. How much time elapsed from the beginning of drawing to the time at
       which the final structure appeared? (judged later by looking at a sequence
       of timed photographs)
  W2. Did the subject start the drawing over or change the arrangement of the
       objects?
  W3. Was the drawing simply a copy of the arrangement of objects, or were the
       objects in the drawing modified in size, position, or number?

Table 3. Correlations among planning behaviors, the quality of the drawing, and
later success: Art critics' judgments

Planning behaviors	Originality	Crafts-manship	Overall worth	Success (7 years later)
B1—number of objects	.52[b]	.17	.48[b]	.45[b]
B2—unusualness of objects	.42[b]	.21	.35[a]	.21
B3—careful examination of objects	.58[c]	.34[a]	.44[b]	.43[b]
W1—delay in final structure	.08	−.18	.09	.48[b]
W2—restarts and changes in arrangement	.37[a]	.01	.22	.31[a]
W3—difference between drawing and arrangement	.61[c]	.37[a]	.44[b]	.20

[a] There is only one chance in 20 that a correlation this large would be obtained by chance.
[b] There is only one chance in 100 that a correlation this large would be obtained by chance.
[c] There is only one chance in 1,000 that a correlation this large would be obtained by chance.

the amount of planning the students did in executing the drawing. For example, students were scored high on planning if they examined many objects or if they made many drafts and took considerable time in arriving at
the final structure of their drawings.

The drawings that the students produced were then evaluated independently by five art critics for originality, craftsmanship, and overall value.
Table 3 shows the correlations between the average of the five critics' judgments and the planning behaviors. Five of the six planning behaviors show
strong correlations with the critics' judgments. (In this study, a correlation
of 0.3 or larger should be considered significant.) Planning, then, appears
to be very helpful in creating a good drawing.

In a follow-up study seven years later, Getzels and Csikszentmihalyi tried to determine how successful the 31 students were in pursuing artistic careers. By contacting art critics, directors of art galleries, and the students themselves, they found that about half of the students had dropped out of art completely. The rest were pursuing careers in the fine arts with varying degrees of success. Seven were using their skills in related professions, such as teaching art, but had not yet exhibited their work publicly. The remaining nine had all exhibited. Some were represented by major galleries and one had achieved a very notable degree of success. His work is hung in the best galleries, and articles about his work appear in the most respected art journals.

The last column of Table 1 shows the correlation between success as an artist and the planning behaviors measured seven years earlier. Four of the six behaviors show strong correlations with success. The simplest way to interpret this remarkable result is to assume that the successful artists habitually make planning part of their approach to artistic problems. Planning leads to high quality in all their artistic work just as it led to high quality in the experimental drawings.

Summary

A creative act is one which:

1. is original,
2. valuable, and,
3. suggests that the person performing the act has unusual mental abilities.

A creative act is a problem-solving act, and, in particular it is the solution of an ill-defined problem. Four cognitive processes especially important for creativity are: problem finding, idea generation, planning, and preparation.

Problem finding—the discovery of a new problem not suggested by anyone else—is important in initiating new directions in science and art. Three procedures that can help us to find problems are: bug listing, searching for counterexamples, and searching for alternative interpretations.

Sometimes, when we are trying to solve an ill-defined problem, we are blocked by difficulty in *generating ideas* for solution. Brainstorming and discovering analogies can help us out of this difficulty.

Planning is important in creative activities as it is in any form of problem solving. Good writing and good art depend on good planning.

Extensive *preparation* is essential for acts of outstanding creativity. Composers require about 10 years of preparation before they can produce works of outstanding quality.

References

Adams, J. L. *Conceptual Blockbusting*. San Francisco: W. H. Freeman & Co., 1974.

Barnlund, D. C. "A Comparative Study of Individual, Majority, and Group Judgment." *Journal of Abnormal and Social Psychology* 58 (1959):55–60.

Bouchard, T. J., Jr. "A Comparison of Two Group Brainstorming Procedures." *Journal of Applied Psychology* 56 (1972):418–21.

Einstein, A., and Infeld, L. *The Evolution of Physics.* New York: Simon and Schuster, Inc., 1938.

Flower, L. *Problem Solving Strategies for Writing.* New York: Harcourt, Brace, Jovanovich, Inc., 1980.

Flower, L., and Hayes, J. R. "The Cognition of Discovery: Defining a Rhetorical Problem." *College Composition and Communication* 2, no. 3 (1980):21–32.

Getzels, J. W., and Csikszentmihalyi, M. *The Creative Vision: A Longitudinal Study of Problem Finding in Art.* New York: John Wiley & Sons, Inc., 1976.

Gordon W. J. J. *Synectics.* New York: Collier, 1961.

Grove's Dictionary of Music and Musicians, Fifth Edition. New York: St. Martin's Press, Inc., 1955.

Hayes, J. R. *Cognitive Psychology: Thinking and Creating.* Homewood, IL: The Dorsey Press, 1978.

Hudgins, B. B. "Effects of Group Experience on Individual Problem Solving." *Journal of Educational Psychology* 51 (1960):37–42.

Koberg, D., and Bagnall, J. *The Universal Traveler,* Third Edition. Los Altos, CA: William Kaufmann, Inc., 1974.

Koechel ABC, Fifth Edition. Wiesbaden: Breitkopf and Hartel, 1965.

Newell, A., Shaw, J. C., and Simon, H. A. "The Processes of Creative Thinking." In *Contemporary Approaches to Creative Thinking,* Third Edition, edited by H. E. Gruber, G. Terrell, and M. Wertheimer. New York: Atherton Press, 1964.

Osborn, A. *Your Creative Power.* New York: Charles Scribner's Sons, 1948.

Perlmutter, H. V. "Group Memory of Meaningful Material." *Journal of Psychology* 35 (1953):361–370.

Schonberg, H. C. *The Lives of the Great Composers.* New York: W. W. Norton & Co., Inc., 1970.

Schwann-1 Record and Tape Guide. Boston: ABC Schwann, August, 1979.

Schwartz, T. *The Art of Logical Thinking.* New York: Random House, Inc., 1980.

Simon, H. A., and Chase, W. G. "Skill in Chess." *American Scientist* 61 (1973):394–403.

Stein, M. I. *Stimulating Creativity,* Volume 2. New York: Academic Press, Inc., 1975.

Wason, P. C. "Reasoning About a Rule." *Quarterly Journal of Experimental Psychology* 20 (1968): 273–281.

Emotional Blocks
James L. Adams

This chapter will begin with a game—a game which requires a group of people, the larger the better, so try it at a party. It was, I think, invented by Bob McKim and is called "Barnyard."

Exercise

Divide your group and assign them to be various animals as follows:

If their last names begin with:	they are:
A-E	sheep
F-K	pigs
L-R	cows
S-Z	turkeys

Now tell each person to find a partner (preferably someone he does not know too well) and to look this partner in the eye. You will then count to three, at which time everyone is to make the sound of his animal as loudly as he possibly can. See how loud a barnyard you can build.

The participants in this game will be able to experience a common emotional block to conceptualization—namely, that of feeling like an ass. If you did not play the game and want to experience the feeling, merely stand alone on any busy corner (or wherever you are right now) and loudly make the sound of one of the animals.

As mentioned in the previous chapter, conceptualization is risky and new ideas are hard to evaluate. The expression of a new idea, and especially the process of trying to convince someone else it has value, sometimes makes one feel like an ass, since you are doing something that possibly exposes your imperfections. In order to avoid this feeling, people will often avoid conceptualization, or at least avoid publicizing the output.

Before we discuss specific emotional blocks, let me make a few comments about psychological theory. Although, as I stated earlier, psychological theory does not offer a complete model for explaining the conceptual process, many theories exist and have commonalities which are pertinent to understanding emotional blocks. Of particular importance are the theories of Freud and his followers and of the contemporary humanistic psychologists (Rogers, Maslow et al.).

Freud

Much of Freudian theory is based upon conflicts between the *id* (the instinctive animal part of ourselves) and the *ego* (the socially aware and conscious aspect) and *superego* (the moralistic portion of ourselves that forbids and prohibits). The motive force in the Freudian model is the id, which resides in the unconscious and is concerned with satisfying our needs. According to Freud, ideas originating in the unconscious must be subjected to the scrutiny of the ego (which may reject them because we cannot realistically carry them out), and the superego (which may reject them because we should not have let ourselves have such ideas in the first place). If these ideas are rejected, they will either be completely repressed or they will contribute to neurotic behavior because of unresolved conflict. If they are accepted, they will be admitted to the conscious mind. (This acceptance may be accompanied by anxiety, since once the ego and superego identify with an idea one can be hurt by its rejection.) If the ego and superego are overly selective, relatively few creative ideas will reach the conscious mind. If they are not selective enough, a torrent of highly innovative but extremely impractical ideas will emerge.

Since the time of Freud, his theory has been elaborated upon by his followers. A good example of this can be seen in Lawrence S. Kubie's book *Neurotic Distortion of the Creative Process.* Kubie utilizes the Freudian concept of *preconscious* in his model of creative thinking. He relegates the subconscious portions of creative thought and problem-solving to this preconscious, reserving the unconscious for unsettled conflicts and repressed impulses. In this model, the preconscious mental processes are hindered both by the conscious and the unconscious processes. As Kubie states in *Neurotic Distortion:*

> Preconscious processes are assailed from both sides. From one side they are nagged and prodded into rigid and distorted symbols by unconscious drives which are oriented away from reality and which consist of rigid compromise formations, lacking in fluid inventiveness. From the other side they are driven by literal conscious purpose, checked and corrected by conscious retrospective critique.

Like Freud, Kubie has a model of the mind in which creative thinking is inhibited by the conscious ego and superego and in which creativity occurs at least partly below the conscious level. However, neuroses play a much more villainous role in Kubie's model than in Freud's.

The humanistic psychologists

Although humanistic psychologists agree that creativity is a response to basic inner needs in people, they have a somewhat broader hierarchy of needs than the Freudians. They maintain that people create in order to grow and to fulfill themselves, as well as to solve conflicts and to answer the cravings of the id. They are more concerned with reaching upward and outward. Carl Rogers, in an article entitled "Toward a Theory of Creativity" in *Creativity and its Cultivation* (edited by Harold Anderson) explains:

> The mainspring of creativity appears to be the same tendency which we discover so deeply as the curative force in psychotherapy—man's tendency to actualize himself, to become his potentialities. By this I mean the directional trend which is evident in all organic and human life—the urge to expand, extend, develop, mature—the tendency to express and activate all the capacities of the organism, to the extent that such activation enhances the organism or the self. This tendency may become deeply buried under layer after layer of encrusted psychological defenses; it may be hidden behind elaborate façades which deny its existence; it is my belief, however, based on my experience, that it exists in every individual and awaits only the proper conditions to be released and expressed.

The humanistic psychologists feel that the creative person is emotionally healthy and sensitive both to the needs and the capabilities of his unconscious to produce creative ideas. Like Freud's creative person, he possesses a strong ego and a realistic superego which allow him to be a prolific conceptualizer and relatively free of distracting neuroses.

We can now come to several interesting and believable conclusions, based upon our brief psychoanalytic discussion:

1. Man creates for reasons of inner drive, whether it be for purposes of conflict resolution, self-fulfillment, or both. He can, of course, also create for other reasons, such as money.
2. At least part of creativity occurs in a part of the mind which is below the conscious level.
3. Although creativity and neuroses may stem from the same source, creativity tends to flow best in the absence of neuroses.
4. The conscious mind, or ego, is a control valve on creativity.
5. Creativity can provoke anxieties.

Now I will continue with our discussion of emotional blocks.

Emotional blocks may interfere with the freedom with which we explore and manipulate ideas, with our ability to conceptualize fluently and flexibly—and prevent us from communicating ideas to others in a manner which will gain them acceptance. Let me list a few of them, which I will then discuss:

1. Fear to make a mistake, to fail, to risk
2. Inability to tolerate ambiguity; overriding desires for security, order; "no appetite for chaos"
3. Preference for judging ideas, rather than generating them
4. Inability to relax, incubate, and "sleep on it"
5. Lack of challenge; problem fails to engage interest
6. Excessive zeal; overmotivation to succeed quickly
7. Lack of access to areas of imagination
8. Lack of imaginative control
9. Inability to distinguish reality from fantasy

Fear of taking a risk

Fear to make a mistake, to fail, or to take a risk is perhaps the most general and common emotional block. Most of us have grown up rewarded when we produce the "right" answer and punished if we make a mistake. When we fail we are made to realize that we have let others down (usually someone we love). Similarly we are taught to live safely (a bird in the hand is worth two in the bush, a penny saved is a penny earned) and avoid risk whenever possible. Obviously, when one produces and tries to sell a creative idea he is taking a risk: of making a mistake, failing, making an ass of himself, losing money, hurting himself, or whatever.

This type of fear is to a certain extent realistic. Something new is usually a threat to the status quo, and is therefore resisted with appropriate pressure upon its creator. The risks involved with innovation often can result in real hardship. Far be it from me to suggest that people should not be realistic in assessing the costs of creativity. For instance, I spend a great amount of time attempting to explain to students that somehow the process of making money out of a commercially practical idea seems to require at least eight years, quite a bit of physical and emotional degradation, and often the sacrifice of such things as marriages and food. However, as I also try to explain to students, the fears which inhibit conceptualization are often *not* based upon a realistic assumption of the consequences. Certainly, a slightly "far-out" idea submitted as an answer to a class assignment is not going to cost the originator his life, his marriage, or even financial ruin. The only possible difficulty would arise if I, the teacher, were annoyed with his answer (and I happen to like such responses from students). The fear which is involved here is a more generalized fear of taking a chance.

One of the better ways of overcoming such a block is to realistically assess the possible negative consequences of an idea. As is sometimes asked, "What are your catastrophic expectations?" If one has an idea for a better bicycle lock and is considering quitting a job and founding a small business based upon the lock and a not-yet-conceived product line to go with it, the risks are considerable (unless the innovator happens to have large sums of money and important commercial contacts). If one invents a new method of flight (say, wings of feathers held together with wax) the risks may also be considerable in perfecting the product. However, if one thinks of a new way to schedule his day, paint his bathroom, or relate to others in his dormitory, the risks are considerably less.

In my experience, people do not often realistically assess the probable consequences of a creative act. Either they blithely ignore any consequences, or their general fear of failure causes them to attach excessive importance to any "mistake," no matter how minor it will appear in the eyes of future historians. Often the potential negative consequences of exposing a creative idea can be easily endured. If one has an idea which seems risky, it is well worth the time to do a brief study of the possible consequences. During the study, one should include "catastrophic expectations" (assume everything goes badly) and look at the result. By doing this, it will become apparent whether you want to take the risk or not.

Exercise

Next time you are having difficulty deciding whether to push a "creative" idea, write a short (two-page) "catastrophic expectations" report. In it detail as well as you can precisely what would happen to you *if everything went wrong*. By making such information explicit and facing it, you swap your analytical capability for your fear of failure—a good trade.

No appetite for chaos

The fear of making a mistake is, of course, rooted in insecurity, which most people suffer from to some extent. Such insecurities are also responsible for the next emotional block, the "inability to tolerate ambiguity; overriding desire for order; 'no appetite for chaos.'" Once again, some element of this block is rational. I am not suggesting that in order to be creative one should shun order and live in a totally chaotic situation. I am talking more of an excessive fondness for order in all things. The solution of a complex problem is a messy process. Rigorous and logical techniques are often necessary, but not sufficient. One must usually wallow in misleading and ill-fitting data, hazy and difficult-to-test concepts, opinions, values, and other such untidy quantities. In a sense, problem-solving is *bringing order to chaos*. A desire for order is therefore necessary. However, the ability to tolerate chaos is a must.

We all know compulsive people, those who must have everything always in its place and who become quite upset if the order of their physical lives is violated. If this trait carries over into a person's mental process, he is severely impaired in his ability to work with certain types of problems. One reason for extreme ordering of the physical environment is efficiency. Another may be the aesthetic satisfaction of precise physical relationships. However, another reason is insecurity. If one's underwear is precisely folded and "dressed right," one has precise control over one's underwear, and thus there is one less thing out of control to be threatening. I do not actually care how your underwear is stored. However, if your thoughts are precisely folded and dressed right you are probably a fairly limited problem-solver. The process of bringing widely disparate thoughts together cannot work too well because your mind is not going to allow widely disparate thoughts to coexist long enough to combine.

Judging rather than generating ideas

The next emotional block, the "preference for judging ideas, rather than generating them," is also the "safe" way to go. Judgment, criticism, tough-mindedness, and practicality are of course essential in problem-solving. However, if applied too early or too indiscriminately in the problem-solving process, they are extremely detrimental to conceptualization. In the Design Division, we often speak of analysis, judgment, and synthesis as three distinct types of thinking. In *analysis,* there is usually a right answer. I am an engineer: if you pay me to tell you how large a beam is needed to hold up a patio roof, you rightly expect *the* answer. Fortunately, I know how to analyze such things mathematically and can give it to you. *Judgment* is generally used in a problem where there are several answers and one must be chosen. A court case (the Angela Davis trial) is a good example. A situation such as Watergate is another. Judgments are made by sensible people as to guilt or innocence, and the situation is sufficiently complex that disagreements can occur. *Synthesis* is even more of a multianswer situation. A design problem (design a better way to serve ice cream) has an infinitude of answers, and there are few rigorous techniques to help in deciding between them.

If one analyzes or judges too early in the problem-solving process, he will reject many ideas. This is detrimental for two reasons. First of all, newly formed ideas are fragile and imperfect—they need time to mature and acquire the detail needed to make them believable. Secondly, as we will discuss later, ideas often lead to other ideas. Many techniques of conceptualization, such as brainstorming, depend for their effectiveness on maintaining "way-out" ideas long enough to let them mature and spawn other more realistic ideas. It is sometimes difficult to hold onto such ideas because people generally do not want to be suspected of harboring impractical thoughts. However, in conceptualization one should not judge too quickly.

The judgment of ideas, unfortunately, is an extremely popular and rewarded pastime. One finds more newspaper space devoted to judgment (critic columns, political analyses, editorials, etc.) than to the *creation* of ideas. In the university, much scholarship is devoted to judgment, rather than creativity. One finds that people who heap negative criticism upon all ideas they encounter are often heralded for their practical sense and sophistication. Bad-mouthing everyone else's concepts is in fact a cheap way to attempt to demonstrate your own mental superiority.

If you are a professional idea-haver, your criticism tends to be somewhat more friendly. Professional designers are often much more receptive to the ideas of our students than non-design-oriented faculty members. Professional problem-solvers have a working understanding of the difficulty in having ideas and a respect for ideas, even if they are flawed. If you are a compulsive idea-judger you should realize that this is a habit which may exclude ideas from your own mind before they have had time to bear fruit. You are taking little risk (unless you are excluding ideas that could benefit you) and are perhaps feeding your ego somewhat with the thrill of being able to judge the outputs of others, but you are sacrificing some of your own creative potential.

Inability to incubate

The "inability to relax, incubate, and 'sleep on it'" is also a somewhat common emotional block. There is general agreement that the unconscious plays an extremely important role in problem-solving. Everyone has had the experience of having the answer to a problem suddenly occur in his mind. One maddeningly familiar phenomenon to many people is a late answer to an important problem. One may work for days or weeks on a problem, complete it, and go on to other activities. Then, at some seemingly random point in time, a better answer "appears." Since the original problem was probably completed in order to reach a deadline, this "better" answer often only serves to annoy one that he did not think of it sooner. This better answer came straight from the unconscious as a result of the "incubation" process it was going through. I have found in my own case that this "incubation" process works and is reliable. I have the confidence to think hard about a problem (charging up my unconscious) and then forget about it for a period of time. When I begin work on it again, new answers are usually present.

Many "symptoms" of incubation are common. There is a widespread belief among students that they do their best work just before deadlines. If, in fact, they worked on the material when they received it long enough to store the data in their unconscious, then incubation can occur, and a better solution may emerge at a later time. Incubation does often seem to produce the right answer at the appropriate time. Students often claim to have come up with a winning idea the morning that it is due, after struggling futilely with the problem for days.

One must allow the unconscious to struggle with problems. Incubation is important in problem-solving. It is poor planning not to allow adequate time for incubation in the solution of an important problem. It is also important to be able to relax in the midst of problem-solving. One's overall compulsiveness is less fanatical when he is relaxed, and the mind is more likely to deal with seemingly "silly" combinations of thoughts. If one is never relaxed, his mind is usually on guard against nonserious activities, with resulting difficulties in the type of thinking necessary for fluent and flexible conceptualization.

Lack of challenge and excessive zeal

"Lack of challenge" and "excessive zeal" are opposite villains. One cannot do his best on a problem unless he is motivated. Professional problem-solvers learn to be motivated somewhat by money and future work which may come their way if they succeed. However, challenge must be present for at least some of the time, or the process ceases to be rewarding. On the other hand, an excessive motivation to succeed, especially to succeed quickly, can inhibit the creative process. The tortoise-and-the-hare phenomenon is often apparent in problem-solving. The person who thinks up the simple elegant solution, although he may take longer in doing so, often wins. As in the race, the tortoise depends upon an inconsistent performance from the rabbit. And if the rabbit spends so little time on conceptualization that he merely chooses the first answers that occur, such inconsistency is almost guaranteed.

Reality and fantasy

"Lack of access to areas of imagination," "lack of imaginative control," and "inability to distinguish reality from fantasy" will be discussed in more detail in chapter 7 [not reproduced here]. In brief, the imagination attempts to create objects and events. The creative person needs to be able to control his imagination and needs complete access to it. If all senses are not represented (not only sight, but also sound, smell, taste, and touch) his imagination cannot serve him as well as it otherwise could. All senses need representation not only because problems involving all senses can be attacked, but also because imagery is more powerful if they are all called upon. If one thinks purely verbally, for instance, there will be little imagery available for the solving of problems concerning shapes and forms. If visual imagery is also present, the imagination will be much more useful, but still not as potent as if the other senses are also present. One can usually imagine a ball park much more vividly if one is able to recall the smell of the grass, the taste of the peanuts and beer, the feel of the seats and the sunshine, and the sounds of the crowd.

The creative person must be able not only to vividly form complete images, but also to manipulate them. Creativity requires the *manipulation* and *recombination* of experience. An imagination which cannot manipulate experience is limiting to the conceptualizer. One should be able to imagine a volcano being born in his ball park, or an airplane landing in it, or the ball park shrinking as the grass simultaneously turns purple, if one is to make maximum use of his imagination. Chapter 7 will contain some exercises to allow you to gauge your ability to control your imagination as well as discussions on how to strengthen the "mental muscle" used in imagining.

"The inability to distinguish reality from fantasy" is a more unusual, but equally severe, block. The creative person needs the ability to fantasize freely and vividly. Yet, if his fantasies become too realistic, they may be less controllable. If you cannot go through the following exercise without a sense of acute physical discomfort, you may have difficulty distinguishing reality from fantasy. This exercise is taken from *Put Your Mother on the Ceiling* by Richard de Mille. Stay with each fantasy (marked off by slashes) until you have it fully formed in your imagination. This game is called *breathing*.

Let us imagine that we have a goldfish in front of us. Have the fish swim around. / Have the fish swim into your mouth. / Take a deep breath and have the fish go down into your lungs, into your chest. / Have the fish swim around in there. / Let out your breath and have the fish swim out into the room again. /

Now breathe in a lot of tiny goldfish. / Have them swim around in your chest. / Breathe them all out again. /

Let's see what kind of things you can breathe in and out of your chest. / Breathe in a lot of rose petals. / Breathe them out again. / Breathe in a lot of water. / Have it gurgling in your chest. / Breathe it out again. / Breathe in a lot of dry leaves. / Have them blowing around in your chest. / Breathe them out again. / Breathe in a lot of raindrops. / Have them pattering in your chest. / Breathe them out again. / Breathe in a lot of sand. / Have it blowing around in your chest. / Breathe it out again. / Breathe in a lot of little firecrackers. / Have them all popping in your chest. / Breathe out the smoke and bits of them that are left. / Breathe in a lot of little lions. / Have them all roaring in your chest. / Breathe them out again. /

Breathe in some fire. / Have it burning and crackling in your chest. / Breathe it out again. / Breathe in some logs of wood. / Set fire to them in your chest. / Have them roaring as they burn up. / Breathe out the smoke and ashes. /

Have a big tree in front of you. / Breathe fire on the tree and burn it all up. / Have an old castle in front of you. / Breathe fire on the castle and have it fall down. / Have an ocean in front of you. / Breathe fire on the ocean and dry it up. /

What would you like to breathe in now? / All right. / Now what? / All right. / What would you like to burn up by breathing fire on it? / All right. /

Be a fish. / Be in the ocean. / Breathe the water of the ocean, in and out. / How do you like that? / Be a bird. / Be high in the air. / Breathe the cold air, in and out. / How do you like that? / Be a camel. /

Be on the desert. / Breathe the hot wind of the desert, in and out. / How does that feel? / Be an old-fashioned steam locomotive. / Breathe out steam and smoke all over everything. / How is that? / Be a stone. / Don't breathe. / How do you like that? / Be a boy (girl). / Breathe the air of this room, in and out. How do you like that?

It would certainly be uncomfortable to inhale sand. Whether you can imagine the feeling of inhaling sand depends somewhat upon your ability to fantasize. No danger exists from imagining such an act, and any pain felt is imagined, not real. However, if one's fantasies are confused with reality, it can be very difficult to fantasize such things. The imagination is extremely powerful because it can go beyond reality. But in order to do this, the imagination must be set free of the constraints placed upon *real* acts and events.

The Science of
"Muddling Through"
Charles E. Lindblom

Suppose an administrator is given responsibility for formulating policy with respect to inflation. He might start by trying to list all related values in order of importance, e.g., full employment, reasonable business profit, protection of small savings, prevention of a stock market crash. Then all possible policy outcomes could be rated as more or less efficient in attaining a maximum of these values. This would of course require a prodigious inquiry into values held by members of society and an equally prodigious set of calculations on how much of each value is equal to how much of each other value. He could then proceed to outline all possible policy alternatives. In a third step, he would undertake systematic comparison of his multitude of alternatives to determine which attains the greatest amount of values.

In comparing policies, he would take advantage of any theory available that generalized about classes of policies. In considering inflation, for example, he would compare all policies in the light of the theory of prices. Since no alternatives are beyond his investigation, he would consider strict central control and the abolition of all prices and markets on the one hand and elimination of all public controls with reliance completely on the free market on the other, both in the light of whatever theoretical generalizations he could find on such hypothetical economies. Finally, he would try to make the choice that would in fact maximize his values.

An alternative line of attack would be to set as his principal objective, either explicitly or without conscious thought, the relatively simple goal of keeping prices level. This objective might be compromised or complicated by only a few other goals, such as full employment. He would in fact disregard most other social values as beyond his present interest, and he would for the moment not even attempt to rank the few values that he regarded as immediately relevant. Were he pressed, he would quickly admit

Reprinted from *Public Administration Review* 19, no. 2 (1952): 78–88, by permission of the author and the American Society for Public Administration.

117

that he was ignoring many related values and many possible important consequences of his policies.

As a second step, he would outline those relatively few policy alternatives that occurred to him. He would then compare them. In comparing his limited number of alternatives, most of them familiar from past controversies, he would not ordinarily find a body of theory precise enough to carry him through a comparison of their respective consequences. Instead he would rely heavily on the record of past experience with small policy steps to predict the consequences of similar steps extended into the future.

Moreover, he would find that the policy alternatives combined objectives or values in different ways. For example, one policy might offer price level stability at the cost of some risk of unemployment; another might offer less price stability but also less risk of unemployment. Hence, the next step in his approach—the final selection—would combine into one the choice among values and the choice among instruments for reaching values. It would not, as in the first method of policy making, approximate a more mechanical process of choosing the means that best satisfied goals that were previously clarified and ranked. Because practitioners of the second approach expect to achieve their goals only partially, they would expect to repeat endlessly the sequence just described, as conditions and aspirations changed and as accuracy of prediction improved.

By root or by branch

For complex problems, the first of these two approaches is of course impossible. Although such an approach can be described, it cannot be practiced except for relatively simple problems and even then only in a somewhat modified form. It assumes intellectual capacities and sources of information that men simply do not possess, and it is even more absurd as an approach to policy when the time and money that can be allocated to a policy problem are limited, as is always the case. Of particular importance to public administrators is the fact that public agencies are in effect usually instructed not to practice the first method. That is to say, their prescribed functions and constraints—the politically or legally possible—restrict their attention to relatively few values and relatively few alternative policies among the countless alternatives that might be imagined. It is the second method that is practiced.

Curiously, however, the literatures of decision making, policy formulation, planning, and public administration formalize the first approach rather than the second, leaving public administrators who handle complex decisions in the position of practicing what few preach. For emphasis I run some risk of overstatement. True enough, the literature is well aware of limits on man's capacities and of the inevitability that policies will be approached in some such style as the second. But attempts to formalize rational policy formulation—to lay out explicitly the necessary steps in the process—usually describe the first approach and not the second.[1]

The common tendency to describe policy formulation even for complex problems as though it followed the first approach has been strengthened by the attention given to, and successes enjoyed by, operations research, statistical decision theory, and systems analysis. The hallmarks of these procedures, typical of the first approach, are clarity of objective, explicitness of evaluation, a high degree of comprehensiveness of overview, and, wherever possible, quantification of values for mathematical analysis. But these advanced procedures remain largely the appropriate techniques of relatively small-scale problem solving where the total number of variables to be considered is small and value problems restricted. Charles Hitch, head of the Economics Division of RAND Corporation, one of the leading centers for application of these techniques, has written:

> I would make the empirical generalization from my experience at RAND and elsewhere that operations research is the art of suboptimizing, i.e., of solving some lower-level problems, and that difficulties increase and our special competence diminishes by an order of magnitude with every level of decision making we attempt to ascend. The sort of simple explicit model which operations researchers are so proficient in using can certainly reflect most of the significant factors influencing traffic control on the George Washington Bridge, but the proportion of the relevant reality which we can represent by any such model or models in studying, say, a major foreign-policy decision, appears to be almost trivial.[2]

Accordingly, I propose in this paper to clarify and formalize the second method, much neglected in the literature. This might be described as the method of _successive limited comparisons_. I will contrast it with the first approach, which might be called the rational-comprehensive method.[3] More impressionistically and briefly—and therefore generally used in this article—they could be characterized as the "branch method" and "root

---

1. James G. March and Herbert A. Simon similarly characterize the literature. They also take some important steps, as have Simon's other recent articles, to describe a less heroic model of policy making. See _Organizations_ (New York: John Wiley & Sons, 1958), p. 137.

2. "Operations Research and National Planning—A Dissent." _Operations Research_ 5 (October 1957): 718. Hitch's dissent is from particular points made in the article to which his paper is a reply; his claim that operations research is for low-level problems is widely accepted. For examples of the kind of problems to which operations research is applied see C. W. Churchman, R. L. Ackoff, and E. L. Arnoff, _Introduction to Operations Research_ (New York: John Wiley & Sons, 1957); and J. F. McCloskey and J. M. Coppinger, eds., _Operations Research for Management,_ vol. 2 (Baltimore: Johns Hopkins Press, 1956).

3. I am assuming that administrators often make policy and advise in the making of policy and am treating decision making and policy making as synonymous for purposes of this paper.

method," the former continually building out from the current situation, step-by-step and by small degrees; the latter starting from fundamentals anew each time, building on the past only as experience is embodied in a theory, and always prepared to start completely from the ground up.

Let us put the characteristics of the two methods side by side in simplest terms.

Rational-Comprehensive *(Root)*	*Successive Limited* *Comparisons (Branch)*
1*a*. Clarification of values or objectives distinct from and usually prerequisite to empirical analysis of alternative policies.	1*b*. Selection of value goals and empirical analysis of the needed action not distinct from one another but closely intertwined.
2*a*. Policy-formulation is therefore approached through means-end analysis: First the ends are isolated, then the means to achieve them are sought.	2*b*. Since means and ends are not distinct, means-end analysis is often inappropriate or limited.
3*a*. The test of a "good" policy is that it can be shown to be the most appropriate means to desired ends.	3*b*. The test of a "good" policy is typically that various analysts find themselves directly agreeing on a policy (without their agreeing that it is the most appropriate means to an agreed objective).
4*a*. Analysis is comprehensive; every important relevant factor is taken into account.	4*b*. Analysis is drastically limited: 　(i) Important possible outcomes are neglected. 　(ii) Important alternative potential policies are neglected. 　(iii) Important affected values are neglected.
5*a*. Theory is often heavily relied upon.	5*b*. A succession of comparisons greatly reduces or eliminates reliance on theory.

Assuming that the root method is familiar and understandable, we proceed directly to clarification of its alternative by contrast. In explaining the second, we shall be describing how most administrators do in fact approach complex questions, for the root method, the "best" way as a blueprint or model, is in fact not workable for complex policy questions, and administrators are forced to use the method of successive limited comparisons.

Intertwining evaluation and empirical analysis (1*b*)

The quickest way to understand how values are handled in the method of successive limited comparisons is to see how the root method often breaks down in *its* handling of values or objectives. The idea that values should be clarified, and in advance of the examination of alternative policies, is appealing. But what happens when we attempt it for complex social problems? The first difficulty is that on many critical values or objectives, citizens disagree, congressmen disagree, and public administrators disagree. Even where a fairly specific objective is prescribed for the administrator, there remains considerable room for disagreement on subobjectives. Consider, for example, the conflict with respect to locating public housing, described in Meyerson and Banfield's study of the Chicago Housing Authority[4]—disagreement which occurred despite the clear objective of providing a certain number of public housing units in the city. Similarly conflicting are objectives in highway location, traffic control, minimum wage administration, development of tourist facilities in national parks, or insect control.

Administrators cannot escape these conflicts by ascertaining the majority's preference, for preferences have not been registered on most issued; indeed, there often *are* no preferences in the absence of public discussion sufficient to bring an issue to the attention of the electorate. Furthermore, there is a question of whether intensity of feeling should be considered as well as the number of persons preferring each alternative. By the impossibility of doing otherwise, administrators often are reduced to deciding policy without clarifying objectives first.

Even when an administrator resolves to follow his own values as a criterion for decisions, he often will not know how to rank them when they conflict with one another, as they usually do. Suppose, for example, that an administrator must relocate tenants living in tenements scheduled for destruction. One objective is to empty the buildings fairly promptly, another is to find suitable accommodation for persons displaced, another is to avoid friction with residents in other areas in which a large influx would be unwelcome, another is to deal with all concerned through persuasion if possible, and so on.

How does one state even to himself the relative importance of these partially conflicting values? A simple ranking of them is not enough; one needs ideally to know how much of one value is worth sacrificing for some of another value. The answer is that typically the administrator chooses—and must choose—directly among policies in which these values are combined in different ways. He cannot first clarify his values and then choose among policies.

A more subtle third point underlies both the first two. Social objectives do not always have the same relative values. One objective may be highly prized in one circumstance, another in another circumstance. If, for example, an administrator values highly both the dispatch with which his agency can carry through its projects *and* good public relations, it matters little which of the two possibly conflicting values he favors in some ab-

---

4. Martin Meyerson and Edward C. Banfield, *Politics, Planning, and the Public Interest* (Glencoe, Ill.: Free Press, 1955).

stract or general sense. Policy questions arise in forms which put to administrators such a question as: Given the degree to which we are or are not
already achieving the values of dispatch and the values of good public relations, is it worth sacrificing a little speed for a happier clientele, or is it
better to risk offending the clientele so that we can get on with our work?
The answer to such a question varies with circumstances.

The value problem is, as the example shows, always a problem of adjustments at a margin. But there is no practicable way to state marginal
objectives or values except in terms of particular policies. That one value is
preferred to another in one decision situation does not mean that it will be
preferred in another decision situation in which it can be had only at great
sacrifice of another value. Attempts to rank or order values in general and
abstract terms so that they do not shift from decision to decision end up by
ignoring the relevant marginal preferences. The significance of this third
point thus goes very far. Even if all administrators had at hand an agreed
set of values, objectives, and constraints, and an agreed ranking of these
values, objectives, and constraints, their marginal values in actual choice
situations would be impossible to formulate.

Unable consequently to formulate the relevant values first and then
choose among policies to achieve them, administrators must choose directly among alternative policies that offer different marginal combinations
of values. Somewhat paradoxically, the only practicable way to disclose
one's relevant marginal values even to oneself is to describe the policy one
chooses to achieve them. Except roughly and vaguely, I know of no way to
describe—or even to understand—what my relative evaluations are for,
say, freedom and security, speed and accuracy in governmental decisions,
or low taxes and better schools than to describe my preferences among specific choices that might be made between the alternatives in each of the
pairs.

In summary, two aspects of the process by which values are actually
handled can be distinguished. The first is clear: evaluation and empirical
analysis are intertwined; that is, one chooses among values and among
policies at one and the same time. Put a little more elaborately, one simultaneously chooses a policy to attain certain objectives and chooses the objectives themselves. The second aspect is related but distinct: the
administrator focuses his attention on marginal or incremental values.
Whether he is aware of it or not, he does not find general formulations of
objectives very helpful and in fact makes specific marginal or incremental
comparisons. Two policies, X and Y, confront him. Both promise the same
degree of attainment of objectives $a, b, c, d,$ and e. But X promises him
somewhat more of f than does Y, while Y promises him somewhat more of
g than does X. In choosing between them, he is in fact offered the alternative of a marginal or incremental amount of f at the expense of a marginal or incremental amount of g. The only values that are relevant to his

choice are these increments by which the two policies differ; and, when he finally chooses between the two marginal values, he does so by making a choice between policies.[5]

As to whether the attempt to clarify objectives in advance of policy selection is more or less rational than the close intertwining of marginal evaluation and empirical analysis, the principal difference established is that for complex problems the first is impossible and irrelevant, and the second is both possible and relevant. The second is possible because the administrator need not try to analyze any values except the values by which alternative policies differ and need not be concerned with them except as they differ marginally. His need for information on values or objectives is drastically reduced as compared with the root method; and his capacity for grasping, comprehending, and relating values to one another is not strained beyond the breaking point.

Relations between means and ends (2*b*)

Decision making is ordinarily formalized as a means-ends relationship: means are conceived to be evaluated and chosen in the light of ends finally selected independently of and prior to the choice of means. This is the means-ends relationship of the root method. But it follows from all that has just been said that such a means-ends relationship is possible only to the extent that values are agreed upon, are reconcilable, and are stable at the margin. Typically, therefore, such a means-ends relationship is absent from the branch method, where means and ends are simultaneously chosen.

Yet any departure from the means-ends relationship of the root method will strike some readers as inconceivable. For it will appear to them that only in such a relationship is it possible to determine whether one policy choice is better or worse than another. How can an administrator know whether he has made a wise or foolish decision if he is without prior values or objectives by which to judge his decisions? The answer to this question calls up the third distinctive difference between root and branch methods: how to decide the best policy.

The test of "good" policy (3*b*)

In the root method, a decision is "correct," "good," or "rational" if it can be shown to attain some specified objective, where the objective can be specified without simply describing the decision itself. Where objectives are defined only through the marginal or incremental approach to values described above, it is still sometimes possible to test whether a policy does in fact attain the desired objectives; but a precise statement of the objec-

---

5. The line of argument is, of course, an extension of the theory of market choice, especially the theory of consumer choice, to public policy choices.

tives takes the form of a description of the policy chosen or some alternative to it. To show that a policy is mistaken one cannot offer an abstract argument that important objectives are not achieved; one must instead argue that another policy is more to be preferred.

So far, the departure from customary ways of looking at problem solving is not troublesome, for many administrators will be quick to agree that the most effective discussion of the correctness of policy does take the form of comparison with other policies that might have been chosen. But what of the situation in which administrators cannot agree on values or objectives, either abstractly or in marginal terms? What then is the test of "good" policy? For the root method, there is no test. Agreement on objectives failing, there is no standard of "correctness." For the method of successive limited comparisons, the test is agreement on policy itself, which remains possible even when agreement on values is not.

It has been suggested that continuing agreement in Congress on the desirability of extending old-age insurance stems from liberal desires to strengthen the welfare programs of the federal government and from conservative desires to reduce union demands for private pension plans. If so, this is an excellent demonstration of the ease with which individuals of different ideologies often can agree on concrete policy. Labor mediators report a similar phenomenon; the contestants cannot agree on criteria for settling their disputes but can agree on specific proposals. Similarly, when one administrator's objective turns out to be another's means, they often can agree on policy.

Agreement on policy thus becomes the only practicable test of the policy's correctness. And for one administrator to seek to win the other over to agreement on ends as well would accomplish nothing and create quite unnecessary controversy.

If agreement directly on policy as a test for "best" policy seems a poor substitute for testing the policy against its objectives, it ought to be remembered that objectives themselves have no ultimate validity other than that they are agreed upon. Hence agreement is the test of "best" policy in both methods. But where the root method requires agreement on what elements in the decision constitute objectives and on which of these objectives should be sought, the branch method falls back on agreement wherever it can be found.

In an important sense, therefore, it is not irrational for an administrator to defend a policy as good without being able to specify what it is good for.

Noncomprehensive analysis (4*b*)

Ideally, rational-comprehensive analysis leaves out nothing important. But it is impossible to take everything important into consideration unless "important" is so narrowly defined that analysis is in fact quite limited. Limits on human intellectual capacities and on available information set definite limits to man's capacity to be comprehensive. In actual fact, therefore, no one can practice the rational-comprehensive method for really complex problems, and every administrator faced with a sufficiently complex problem must find ways drastically to simplify.

An administrator assisting in the formulation of agricultural economic policy cannot in the first place be competent on all possible policies. He cannot even comprehend one policy entirely. In planning a soil bank program, he cannot successfully anticipate the impact of higher or lower farm income on, say, urbanization—the possible consequent loosening of family ties, the possible consequent need for revisions in social security and further implications for tax problems arising out of new federal responsibilities for social security and municipal responsibilities for urban services. Nor, to follow another line of repercussions, can he work through the soil bank program's effects on prices for agricultural products in foreign markets and consequent implications for foreign relations, including those arising out of economic rivalry between the United States and the USSR.

In the method of successive limited comparisons, simplification is systematically achieved in two principal ways. First, it is achieved through limitation of policy comparisons to those policies that differ in relatively small degree from policies presently in effect. Such a limitation immediately reduces the number of alternatives to be investigated and also drastically simplifies the character of the investigation of each. For it is not necessary to undertake fundamental inquiry into an alternative and its consequences; it is necessary only to study those respects in which the proposed alternative and its consequences differ from the status quo. The empirical comparison of marginal differences among alternative policies that differ only marginally is, of course, a counterpart to the incremental or marginal comparison of values discussed above.[6]

Relevance as well as realism

It is a matter of common observation that in Western democracies public administrators and policy analysts in general do largely limit their analyses to incremental or marginal differences in policies that are chosen to differ only incrementally. They do not do so, however, solely because they desperately need some way to simplify their problems; they also do so in order to be relevant. Democracies change their policies almost entirely through incremental adjustments. Policy does not move in leaps and bounds.

The incremental character of political change in the United States has often been remarked. The two major political parties agree on fundamentals; they offer alternative policies to the voters only on relatively small points of difference. Both parties favor full employment, but they define

6. A more precise definition of incremental policies and a discussion of whether a change that appears "small" to one observer might be seen differently by another is to be found in my "Policy Analysis," *American Economic Review* 48 (June 1958): 298.

it somewhat differently; both favor the development of water power resources, but in slightly different ways; and both favor unemployment compensation, but not the same level of benefits. Similarly, shifts of policy within a party take place largely through a series of relatively small changes, as can be seen in their only gradual acceptance of the idea of governmental responsibility for support of the unemployed, a change in party positions beginning in the early thirties and culminating in a sense in the Employment Act of 1946.

Party behavior is in turn rooted in public attitudes, and political theorists cannot conceive of democracy's surviving in the United States in the absence of fundamental agreement on potentially disruptive issues, with consequent limitation of policy debates to relatively small differences in policy.

Since the policies ignored by the administrator are politically impossible and so irrelevant, the simplification of analysis achieved by concentrating on policies that differ only incrementally is not a capricious kind of simplification. In addition, it can be argued that, given the limits on knowledge within which policy makers are confined, simplifying by limiting the focus to small variations from present policy makes the most of available knowledge. Because policies being considered are like present and past policies, the administrator can obtain information and claim some insight. Nonincremental policy proposals are therefore typically not only politically irrelevant but also unpredictable in their consequences.

The second method of simplification of analysis is the practice of ignoring important possible consequences of possible policies, as well as the values attached to the neglected consequences. If this appears to disclose a shocking shortcoming of successive limited comparisons, it can be replied that, even if the exclusions are random, policies may nevertheless be more intelligently formulated than through futile attempts to achieve a comprehensiveness beyond human capacity. Actually, however, the exclusions, seeming arbitrary or random from one point of view, need be neither.

Achieving a degree of comprehensiveness

Suppose that each value neglected by one policy-making agency were a major concern of at least one other agency. In that case, a helpful division of labor would be achieved, and no agency need find its task beyond its capacities. The shortcomings of such a system would be that one agency might destroy a value either before another agency could be activated to safeguard it or in spite of another agency's efforts. But the possibility that important values may be lost is present in any form of organization, even where agencies attempt to comprehend in planning more than is humanly possible.

The virtue of such a hypothetical division of labor is that every important interest or value has its watchdog. And these watchdogs can protect the interests in their jurisdiction in two quite different ways: first, by redressing damages done by other agencies; and, second, by anticipating and heading off injury before it occurs.

In a society like that of the United States in which individuals are free to combine to pursue almost any possible common interest they might have and in which government agencies are sensitive to the pressures of these groups, the system described is approximated. Almost every interest has its watchdog. Without claiming that every interest has a sufficiently powerful watchdog, it can be argued that our system often can assure a more comprehensive regard for the values of the whole society than any attempt at intellectual comprehensiveness.

In the United States, for example, no part of government attempts a comprehensive overview of policy on income distribution. A policy nevertheless evolves, and one responding to a wide variety of interests. A process of mutual adjustment among farm groups, labor unions, municipalities and school boards, tax authorities, and government agencies with responsibilities in the fields of housing, health, highways, national parks, fire, and police accomplishes a distribution of income in which particular income problems neglected at one point in the decision processes become central at another point.

Mutual adjustment is more pervasive than the explicit forms it takes in negotiations between groups; it persists through the mutual impacts of groups upon one another even where they are not in communication. For all the imperfections and latent dangers in this ubiquitous process of mutual adjustment, it will often accomplish an adaptation of policies to a wider range of interests than could be done by one group centrally.

Note, too, how the incremental pattern of policy making fits with the multiple pressure pattern. For when decisions are only incremental— closely related to known policies, it is easier for one group to anticipate the kind of moves another might make and easier too for it to make correction for injury already accomplished.[7]

Even partisanship and narrowness, to use pejorative terms, will sometimes be assets to rational decision making, for they can doubly insure that what one agency neglects, another will not; they specialize personnel to distinct points of view. The claim is valid that effective rational coordination of the federal administration, if possible to achieve at all, would require an agreed set of values[8]—if "rational" is defined as the practice of the root method of decision making. But a high degree of administrative coordination occurs as each agency adjusts its policies to the concerns of the other agencies in the process of fragmented decision making I have just described.

7. The link between the practice of the method of successive limited comparisons and mutual adjustment of interests in a highly fragmented decision-making process adds a new facet to pluralist theories of government and administration.

8. Herbert Simon, Donald W. Smithburg, and Victor A. Thompson, *Public Administration* (New York: Alfred A. Knopf, 1950), p. 434.

For all the apparent shortcomings of the incremental approach to policy alternatives with its arbitrary exclusion coupled with fragmentation, when compared to the root method, the branch method often looks far superior. In the root method, the inevitable exclusion of factors is accidental, un-systematic, and not defensible by any argument so far developed, while in the branch method the exclusions are deliberate, systematic, and defensible. Ideally, of course, the root method does not exclude; in practice it must.

Nor does the branch method necessarily neglect long-run considerations and objectives. It is clear that important values must be omitted in consid-ering policy, and sometimes the only way long-run objectives can be given adequate attention is through the neglect of short-run considerations. But the values omitted can be either long-run or short-run.

Succession of comparisons (5b)

The final distinctive element in the branch method is that the comparisons, together with the policy choice, proceed in a chronological series. Policy is not made once and for all; it is made and remade endlessly. Policy making is a process of successive approximation to some desired objectives in which what is desired itself continues to change under reconsideration.

Making policy is at best a very rough process. Neither social scientists nor politicians nor public administrators yet know enough about the social world to avoid repeated error in predicting the consequences of policy moves. A wise policy maker consequently expects that his policies will achieve only part of what he hopes and at the same time will produce un-anticipated consequences he would have preferred to avoid. If he proceeds through a *succession* of incremental changes, he avoids serious lasting mistakes in several ways.

In the first place, past sequences of policy steps have given him knowl-edge about the probable consequences of further similar steps. Second, he need not attempt big jumps toward his goals that would require predictions beyond his or anyone else's knowledge, because he never expects his pol-icy to be a final resolution of a problem. His decision is only one step, one that if successful can quickly be followed by another. Third, he is in effect able to test his previous predictions as he moves on to each further step. Lastly, he often can remedy a past error fairly quickly—more quickly than if policy proceeded through more distinct steps widely spaced in time.

Compare this comparative analysis of incremental changes with the as-piration to employ theory in the root method. Man cannot think without classifying, without subsuming one experience under a more general cate-gory of experiences. The attempt to push categorization as far as possible and to find general propositions which can be applied to specific situations is what I refer to with the word "theory." Where root analysis often leans heavily on theory in this sense, the branch method does not.

The assumption of root analysts is that theory is the most systematic and economical way to bring relevant knowledge to bear on a specific problem.

Granting the assumption, an unhappy fact is that we do not have adequate theory to apply to problems in any policy area, although theory is more adequate in some areas—monetary policy, for example—than in others. Comparative analysis, as in the branch method, is sometimes a systematic alternative to theory.

Suppose an administrator must choose among a small group of policies that differ only incrementally from each other and from present policy. He might aspire to "understand" each of the alternatives—for example, to know all the consequences of each aspect of each policy. If so, he would indeed require theory. In fact, however, he would usually decide that, *for policy-making purposes,* he need know, as explained above, only the consequences of each of those aspects of the policies in which they differed from one another. For this much more modest aspiration, he requires no theory (although it might be helpful, if available), for he can proceed to isolate probable differences by examining the differences in consequences associated with past differences in policies, a feasible program because he can take his observations from a long sequence of incremental changes.

For example, without a more comprehensive social theory about juvenile delinquency than scholars have yet produced, one cannot possibly understand the ways in which a variety of public policies—say on education, housing, recreation, employment, race relations, and policing—might encourage or discourage delinquency. And one needs such an understanding if he undertakes the comprehensive overview of the problem prescribed in the models of the root method. If, however, one merely wants to mobilize knowledge sufficient to assist in a choice among a small group of similar policies—alternative policies on juvenile court procedures, for example— he can do so by comparative analysis of the results of similar past policy moves.

Theorists and practitioners

This difference explains—in some cases at least—why the administrator often feels that the outside expert or academic problem solver is sometimes not helpful and why they in turn often urge more theory on him. And it explains why an administrator often feels more confident when "flying by the seat of his pants" than when following the advice of theorists. Theorists often ask the administrator to go the long way round to the solution of his problems, in effect ask him to follow the best canons of the scientific method, when the administrator knows that the best available theory will work less well than more modest incremental comparisons. Theorists do not realize that the administrator is often in fact practicing a systematic method. It would be foolish to push this explanation too far, for sometimes practical decision makers are pursuing neither a theoretical approach nor successive comparisons, nor any other systematic method.

It may be worth emphasizing that theory is sometimes of extremely limited helpfulness in policy making for at least two rather different reasons. It is greedy for facts; it can be constructed only through a great collection of observations. And it is typically insufficiently precise for application to a policy process that moves through small changes. In contrast, the comparative method both economizes on the need for facts and directs the analyst's attention to just those facts that are relevant to the fine choices faced by the decision maker.

With respect to precision of theory, economic theory serves as an example. It predicts that an economy without money or prices would in certain specified ways misallocate resources, but this finding pertains to an alternative far removed from the kind of policies on which administrators need help. Yet it is not precise enough to predict the consequences of policies restricting business mergers, and this is the kind of issue on which the administrators need help. Only in relatively restricted areas does economic theory achieve sufficient precision to go far in resolving policy questions; its helpfulness in policy making is always so limited that it requires supplementation through comparative analysis.

Successive comparison as a system

Successive limited comparisons is, then, indeed a method or system; it is not a failure of method for which administrators ought to apologize. Nonetheless, its imperfections, which have not been explored in this paper, are many. For example, the method is without a built-in safeguard for all relevant values, and it also may lead the decision maker to overlook excellent policies for no other reason than that they are not suggested by the chain of successive policy steps leading up to the present. Hence, it ought to be said that under this method, as well as under some of the most sophisticated variants of the root method—operations research, for example—policies will continue to be as foolish as they are wise.

Why then bother to describe the method in all the above detail? Because it is in fact a common method of policy formulation, and is, for complex problems, the principal reliance of administrators as well as of other policy analysts.[9] And because it will be superior to any other decision-making method available for complex problems in many circumstances, certainly superior to a futile attempt at superhuman comprehensiveness. The reac-

9. Elsewhere I have explored this same method of policy formation as practiced by academic analysis of policy ("Policy Analysis," *American Economic Review*, vol. 48). Although it has been here presented as a method for public administrators, it is no less necessary to analysts more removed from immediate policy questions, despite their tendencies to describe their own analytical efforts as though they were the rational-comprehensive method with an especially heavy use of theory. Similarly, this same method is inevitably resorted to in personal problem solving, where means and ends are sometimes impossible to separate, where aspirations or objectives undergo constant development, and where drastic simplification of the complexity of the real world is urgent if problems are to be solved in the time that can be given to them. To an economist accustomed to dealing with the marginal or incremental concept in market processes, the central idea in the method is that both evaluation and empirical analysis are incremental. Accordingly I have referred to the method elsewhere as "the incremental method."

tion of the public administrator to the exposition of method doubtless will be less a discovery of a new method than a better acquaintance with an old. But by becoming more conscious of their practice of this method, administrators might practice it with more skill and know when to extend or constrict its use. (That they sometimes practice it effectively and sometimes not may explain the extremes of opinion on "muddling through," which is both praised as a highly sophisticated form of problem solving and denounced as no method at all. For I suspect that insofar as there is a system in what is known as "muddling through," this method is it.)

One of the noteworthy incidental consequences of clarification of the method is the light it throws on the suspicion an administrator sometimes entertains that a consultant or adviser is not speaking relevantly and responsibly when in fact by all ordinary objective evidence he is. The trouble lies in the fact that most of us approach policy problems within a framework given by our view of a chain of successive policy choices made up to the present. One's thinking about appropriate policies with respect, say, to urban traffic control is greatly influenced by one's knowledge of the incremental steps taken up to the present. An administrator enjoys an intimate knowledge of his past sequences that "outsiders" do not share, and his thinking and that of the "outsider" will consequently be different in ways that may puzzle both. Both may appear to be talking intelligently, yet each may find the other unsatisfactory. The relevance of the policy chain of succession is even more clear when an American tries to discuss, say, antitrust policy with a Swiss, for the chains of policy in the two countries are strikingly different and the two individuals consequently have organized their knowledge in quite different ways.

If this phenomenon is a barrier to communication, an understanding of it promises an enrichment of intellectual interaction in policy formulation. Once the source of difference is understood, it will sometimes be stimulating for an administrator to seek out a policy analyst whose recent experience is with a policy chain different from his own.

This raises again a question only briefly discussed above on the merits of like-mindedness among government administrators. While much of organization theory argues the virtues of common values and agreed organizational objectives, for complex problems in which the root method is inapplicable, agencies will want among their own personnel two types of diversification: administrators whose thinking is organized by reference to policy chains other than those familiar to most members of the organization and, even more commonly, administrators whose professional or personal values or interests create diversity of view (perhaps coming from different specialties, social classes, geographical areas) so that, even within a single agency, decision making can be fragmented and parts of the agency can serve as watchdogs for other parts.

3

Opinions, Beliefs, and Attitudes: The Great Balancing Act

In the first section of this book we considered issues of drive and motivation. In the second, we looked at the thinking and reasoning side of human beings. In this one we try to bring the two together, to look at how people put the whole show together. We look into the world of attitudes, beliefs, and values.

Most readers are probably familiar with culture shock. In a few hours we can fly from a Western culture into an Eastern one and into a whole host of new sights, sounds, beliefs, and customs. The shock part of culture shock seems to result from our initial inability to straighten ourselves out in this new world, to simplify it and find perceptual order in this jungle of new stimulation. But we soon get past that.

We human beings are quite able to cope, after a bit, with massive quantities of discrete inputs from our environments. We do it by simplifying, filtering, stabilizing, and classifying information about the world. This section is about those simplifying, filtering, stabilizing, and classifying processes.

Consider the following statements. "A woman's place is in the home." "Smoking pot won't lead to using the hard stuff." "White folks don't have soul." "People should be objective in dealing with others on the job, and not let personal considerations enter into their decisions." "It's not right for public employees to strike." Each of those statements expresses an attitude, either about some factual matter or about rights and wrongs. Each of those attitudes, true or not, justified or not, helps its holder to simplify part of the world. The man who believes that a woman's place *is* in the home avoids having to deal with his spouse's career aspirations. He just denies them. The person who believes that pot won't lead to harder stuff will find it easier to decide whether or not to accept the offer of a joint. Attitudes (and stereotypes and values), by categorizing chunks of the world, enable us to deal more simply with it. But while simplifying, our attitudes also partially blind us; for some of the simplification results from filtering out some of what is really out there. And there is no guarantee that our filters will only filter out the irrelevant or unimportant.

132

This section is about attitudes and perceptions, about how attitudes are formed, how they influence our behavior, how we can change them, and how and why what we perceive may be different from what is really there. Like motives, attitudes are a state of mind. But whereas motives provide the driving force for behavior, attitudes provide the *premises* for behavior. They play a vital role both in influencing our perceptions and providing cues for behavior. Indeed, attitudes provide the meeting place of the emotional and reasoning sides of people.

The first paper in this section, by Elliot Aronson, is about the dynamics of just such processes—the processes by which we balance our feelings, cognitions, and perceptions to maintain some kind of total integrity as human beings. That paper pulls together a large amount of theorizing and researching on the dynamics of human attitude formation and decision making. It treats human beings as skillful rationalizing and self-balancing creatures, intolerant of inconsistent information—indeed, as organisms that *must* reduce, simplify, clarify, and rationalize in order to keep it together.

The second paper, from a recent book by Robert Cialdini, carries on from Aronson, but in a more applied way. Again, the model of man offered by Cialdini is self-balancing, rationalizing, and often self-deluding. How, given such characteristics, can one influence, change, or persuade such creatures? Cialdini shows how and why some techniques for influencing human behavior work and some don't.

The now classic article by Sandra Bem and Daryl Bem draws from the same basic model, showing how some of our most central attitudes and values are initiated during early childhood and infancy. Once formed, such attitudes and values become the screens through which we filter and access new information. The Bems show the extent to which the attitudes held by adult women in our culture, at least until recently, were inculcated early in life, and how our society managed to shape a huge range of rules and attitudes about what women were or were not supposed to do.

The last paper in this section, Mark Snyder's "Self-Fulfilling Stereotypes," carries the balancing/rationalizing model one step further, to the active side. Our need for internal consistency is not just a key to shaping our beliefs and attitudes. Once shaped, those attitudes shape much of our behavior and our perception. We tend to "enact" the world that fits our beliefs and attitudes.

Section 3 is an important section for the aspiring manager. It points at a core aspect of human behavior that many managers do not, at their peril, understand—the complex but quite comprehensible human balancing act, an act that blends faith with reason, emotion with cold logic, and prejudice with objectivity.

The Rationalizing Animal
Elliot Aronson

Man likes to think of himself as a rational animal. However, it is more true that man is a *rationalizing* animal, that he attempts to appear reasonable to himself and to others. Albert Camus even said that man is a creature who spends his entire life in an attempt to convince himself that he is not absurd.

Some years ago a woman reported that she was receiving messages from outer space. Word came to her from the planet Clarion that her city would be destroyed by a great flood on December 21. Soon a considerable number of believers shared her deep commitment to the prophecy. Some of them quit their jobs and spent their savings freely in anticipation of the end.

On the evening of December 20, the prophet and her followers met to prepare for the event. They believed that flying saucers would pick them up, thereby sparing them from disaster. Midnight arrived, but no flying saucers. December 21 dawned, but no flood.

What happens when prophecy fails? Social psychologists Leon Festinger, Henry Riecken, and Stanley Schachter infiltrated the little band of believers to see how they would react. They predicted that persons who had expected the disaster, but awaited it alone in their homes, would simply lose faith in the prophecy. But those who awaited the outcome in a group, who had thus admitted their belief publicly, would come to believe even more strongly in the prophecy and turn into active proselytizers.

This is exactly what happened. At first the faithful felt despair and shame because all their predictions had been for naught. Then, after waiting nearly five hours for the saucers, the prophet had a new vision. The city had been spared, she said, because of the trust and faith of her devoted group. This revelation was elegant in its simplicity, and the believers accepted it enthusiastically. They now sought the press that they had previously avoided. They turned from believers into zealots.

Living on the fault

In 1957 Leon Festinger proposed his theory of *cognitive dissonance,* which describes and predicts man's rationalizing behavior. Dissonance occurs whenever a person simultaneously holds two inconsistent cognitions (ideas, beliefs, opinions). For example, the belief that the world will end on a certain day is dissonant with the awareness, when the day breaks, that the world has not ended. Festinger maintained that this state of inconsistency is so uncomfortable that people strive to reduce the conflict in the easiest way possible. They will change one or both cognitions so that they will "fit together" better.

Consider what happens when a smoker is confronted with evidence that smoking causes cancer. He will become motivated to change either his attitudes about smoking or his behavior. And as anyone who has tried to quit knows, the former alternative is easier.

The smoker may decide that the studies are lousy. He may point to friends ("If Sam, Jack, and Harry smoke, cigarettes can't be all that dangerous"). He may conclude that filters trap all the cancer-producing materials. Or he may argue that he would rather live a short and happy life with cigarettes than a long and miserable life without them.

The more a person is committed to a course of action, the more resistant he will be to information that threatens that course. Psychologists have reported that the people who are least likely to believe the dangers of smoking are those who tried to quit—and failed. They have become more committed to smoking. Similarly, a person who builds a $100,000 house astride the San Andreas Fault will be less receptive to arguments about imminent earthquakes than would a person who is renting the house for a few months. The new homeowner is committed; he doesn't want to believe that he did an absurd thing.

When a person reduces his dissonance, he defends his ego, and keeps a positive self-image. But self-justification can reach startling extremes; people will ignore danger in order to avoid dissonance, even when that ignorance can cause their deaths. I mean that literally.

Suppose you are Jewish in a country occupied by Hitler's forces. What should you do? You could try to leave the country; you could try to pass as "Aryan"; you could do nothing and hope for the best. The first two choices are dangerous: if you are caught you will be executed. If you decide to sit tight, you will try to convince yourself that you made the best decision. You may reason that while Jews are indeed being treated unfairly, they are not being killed unless they break the law.

Now suppose that a respected man from your town announces that he has seen Jews being butchered mercilessly, including everyone who has recently been deported from your village. If you believe him, you might have a chance to escape. If you don't believe him, you and your family will be slaughtered.

Dissonance theory would predict that you will not listen to the witness, because to do so would be to admit that your judgment and decisions were wrong. You will dismiss his information as untrue, and decide that he was lying or hallucinating. Indeed, Elie Wiesel reported that this happened to the Jews in Sighet, a small town in Hungary, in 1944. Thus people are not passive receptacles for the deposit of information. The manner in which they view and distort the objective world in order to avoid and reduce dissonance is entirely predictable. But one cannot divide the world into rational people on one side and dissonance reducers on the other. While people vary in their ability to tolerate dissonance, we are all capable of rational or irrational behavior, depending on the circumstances—some of which follow.

Dissonance because of effort

Judson Mills and I found that if people go through a lot of trouble to gain admission to a group, and the group turns out to be dull and dreary, they will experience dissonance. It is a rare person who will accept this situation with an "Oh, pshaw. I worked hard for nothing. Too bad." One way to resolve the dissonance is to decide that the group is worth the effort it took to get admitted.

We told a number of college women that they would have to undergo an initiation to join a group that would discuss the psychology of sex. One third of them had severe initiation: they had to recite a list of obscene words and read some lurid sexual passages from novels in the presence of a male experimenter (in 1959, this really was a "severe" and embarrassing task). One third went through a mild initiation in which they read words that were sexual but not obscene (such as "virgin" and "petting"); and the last third had no initiation at all. Then all of the women listened to an extremely boring taped discussion of the group they had presumably joined. The women in the severe initiation group rated the discussion and its drab participants much more favorably than those in the other groups.

I am not asserting that people enjoy painful experiences, or that they enjoy things that are associated with painful experiences. If you got hit on the head by a brick on the way to a fraternity initiation, you would not like that group any better. But if you volunteered to get hit with a brick *in order to join* the fraternity, you definitely would like the group more than if you had been admitted without fuss.

After a decision—especially a difficult one that involves much time, money, or effort—people almost always experience dissonance. Awareness of defects in the preferred object is dissonant with having chosen it; awareness of positive aspects of the unchosen object is dissonant with having rejected it.

Accordingly, researchers have found that *before* making a decision, people seek as much information as possible about the alternatives. Afterward, however, they seek reassurance that they did the right thing, and do so by seeking information in support of their choice or by simply changing the information that is already in their heads. In one of the earliest experiments on dissonance theory, Jack Brehm gave a group of women their choice between two appliances, such as a toaster or a blender, that they had previously rated for desirability. When the subjects reevaluated the appliances after choosing one of them, they increased their liking for the one they had chosen and downgraded their evaluation of the rejected appliance. Similarly, Danuta Ehrlich and her associates found that a person about to buy a new car does so carefully, reading all ads and accepting facts openly on various makes and models. But after he buys his Volvo, for instance, he will read advertisements more selectively, and he will tend to avoid ads for Volkswagens, Chevrolets, and so on.

The decision to behave immorally

Your conscience, let us suppose, tells you that it is wrong to cheat, lie, steal, seduce your neighbor's husband or wife, or whatever. Let us suppose further that you are in a situation in which you are sorely tempted to ignore your conscience. If you give in to temptation, the cognition "I am a decent, moral person" will be dissonant with the cognition "I have committed an immoral act." If you resist, the cognition "I want to get a good grade (have that money, seduce that person)" is dissonant with the cognition "I could have acted so as to get that grade, but I chose not to."

The easiest way to reduce dissonance in either case is to minimize the negative aspects of the action one has chosen, and to change one's attitude about its immorality. If Mr. C. decides to cheat, he will probably decide that cheating isn't really so bad. It hurts no one; everyone does it; it's part of human nature. If Mr. D. decides not to cheat, he will no doubt come to believe that cheating is a sin, and deserves severe punishment.

The point here is that the initial attitude of these men is virtually the same. Moreover, their decisions could be a hairs breadth apart. But once the action is taken, their attitudes diverge sharply.

Judson Mills confirmed these speculations in an experiment with sixth-grade children. First he measured their attitudes toward cheating, and then put them in a competitive situation. He arranged the test so that it was impossible to win without cheating, and so it was easy for the children to cheat, thinking they would be unwatched. The next day, he asked the children again how they felt about cheating. Those who had cheated on the test had become more lenient in their attitudes; those who had resisted the temptation adopted harsher attitudes.

The data are provocative. They suggest that the most zealous crusaders are not those who are removed from the problem they oppose. I would hazard to say that the people who are most angry about "the sexual promiscuity of the young" are *not* those who have never dreamed of being promiscuous. On the contrary, they would be persons who had been seriously tempted by illicit sex, who came very close to giving in to their desires, but who finally resisted. People who almost live in glass houses are the ones who are most likely to throw stones.

Insufficient justification

If I offer George $20 to do a boring task, and offer Richard $1 to do the same thing, which one will decide that the assignment was mildly interesting? If I threaten one child with harsh punishment if he does something forbidden, and threaten another child with mild punishment, which one will transgress?

Dissonance theory predicts that when people find themselves doing something and they have neither been rewarded adequately for doing it nor threatened with dire consequences for not doing it, they will find *internal* reasons for their behavior.

Suppose you dislike Woodrow Wilson and I want you to make a speech in his favor. The most efficient thing I can do is to pay you a lot of money for making the speech, or threaten to kill you if you don't. In either case, you will probably comply with my wish, but you won't change your attitude toward Wilson. If that were my goal, I would have to give you a *minimal* reward or threat. Then, in order not to appear absurd, you would have to seek additional reasons for your speech—this could lead you to find good things about Wilson and hence, to conclude that you really do like Wilson after all. Lying produces great attitude change only when the liar is undercompensated.

Festinger and J. Merrill Carlsmith asked college students to work on boring and repetitive tasks. Then the experimenters persuaded the students to lie about the work, to tell a fellow student that the task would be interesting and enjoyable. They offered half of their subjects $20 for telling the lie, and they offered the others only $1. Later they asked all subjects how much they had really liked the tasks.

The students who earned $20 for their lies rated the work as deadly dull, which it was. They experienced no dissonance: they lied, but they were well paid for that behavior. By contrast, students who got $1 decided that the tasks were rather enjoyable. The dollar was apparently enough to get them to tell the lie, but not enough to keep them from feeling that lying for so paltry a sum was foolish. To reduce dissonance, they decided that they hadn't lied after all; the task was fun.

Similarly, Carlsmith and I found that mild threats are more effective than harsh threats in changing a child's attitude about a forbidden object, in this case a delightful toy. In the severe-threat condition, children refrained from playing with the toys and had a good reason for refraining—the very severity of the threat provided ample justification for not playing with the toy. In the mild-threat condition, however, the children refrained from playing with the toy but when they asked themselves, "How come I'm not playing with the toy?" they did not have a superabundant justification (because the threat was not terribly severe). Accordingly, they provided additional justification in the form of convincing themselves that the attractive toy was really not very attractive and that they didn't really want to play with it very much in the first place. Jonathan Freedman extended our findings, and showed that severe threats do not have a lasting effect on a child's behavior. Mild threats, by contrast, can change behavior for many months.

Perhaps the most extraordinary example of insufficient justification occurred in India, where Jamuna Prasad analyzed the rumors that were circulated after a terrible earthquake in 1950. Prasad found that people in towns that were *not* in immediate danger were spreading rumors of impending doom from floods, cyclones, or unforeseeable calamities. Certainly the rumors could not help people feel more secure; why then perpetrate them? I believe that dissonance helps explain this phenomenon. The people were terribly frightened—after all, the neighboring villages had been destroyed—but they did not have ample excuse for their fear, since the earthquake had missed them. So they invented their own excuse; if a cyclone is on the way, it is reasonable to be afraid. Later, Duriganand Sinha studied rumors in a town that had actually been destroyed. The people were scared, but they had good reason to be; they didn't need to seek additional justification for their terror. And their rumors showed no predictions of impending disaster and no serious exaggerations.

The decision to be cruel

The need for people to believe that they are kind and decent can lead them to say and do unkind and indecent things. After the National Guard killed four students at Kent State, several rumors quickly spread: the slain girls were pregnant, so their deaths spared their families from shame; the students were filthy and had lice on them. These rumors were totally untrue, but the townspeople were eager to believe them. Why? The local people were conservative, and infuriated at the radical behavior of some of the students. Many had hoped that the students would get their comeuppance. But death is an awfully severe penalty. The severity of this penalty outweighs and is dissonant with the "crimes" of the students. In these circumstances, any information that put the victims in a bad light reduces dissonance by implying, in effect, that it was good that the young people died. One high-school teacher even avowed that anyone with "long hair, dirty clothes, or [who goes] barefooted deserves to be shot."

Keith Davis and Edward Jones demonstrated the need to justify cruelty. They persuaded students to help them with an experiment, in the course of which the volunteers had to tell another student that he was a shallow, untrustworthy, and dull person. Volunteers managed to convince themselves that they didn't like the victim of their cruel analysis. They found him less attractive than they did before they had to criticize him.

Similarly, David Glass persuaded a group of subjects to deliver electric shocks to others. The subjects, again, decided that the victim must deserve the cruelty; they rated him as stupid, mean, etc. Then Glass went a step further. He found that a subject with high self-esteem was most likely to derogate the victim. This led Glass to conclude, ironically, that it is precisely because a person thinks he is nice that he decides that the person he has hurt is a rat. "Since nice guys like me don't go around hurting innocent people," Glass's subjects seemed to say, "you must have deserved it." But individuals who have *low* self-esteem do not feel the need to justify their behavior and derogate their victims; it is *consonant* for such persons to believe they have behaved badly. "Worthless people like me do unkind things."

Ellen Berscheid and her colleagues found another factor that limits the need to derogate one's victim: the victim's capacity to retaliate. If the person doing harm feels that the situation is balanced, that his victim will pay him back in coin, he has no need to justify his behavior. In Berscheid's experiment, which involved electric shocks, college students did not derogate or dislike the persons they shocked if they believed the victims could retaliate. Students who were led to believe that the victims would not be able to retaliate *did* derogate them. Her work suggests that soldiers may have a greater need to disparage civilian victims (because they can't retaliate) than military victims. Lt. William L. Calley, who considered the "gooks" at My Lai to be something less than human, would be a case in point.

Dissonance and the self-concept

On the basis of recent experiments, I have reformulated Festinger's original theory in terms of the self-concept. That is, dissonance is most powerful when self-esteem is threatened. Thus the important aspect of dissonance is not, "I said one thing and I believe another," but "I have misled people— and I am a truthful, nice person." Conversely, the cognitions, "I believe the task is dull," and "I told someone the task was interesting," are not dissonant for a psychopathic liar.

David Mettee and I predicted in a recent experiment that persons who had low opinions of themselves would be more likely to cheat than persons with high self-esteem. We assumed that if an average person gets a temporary blow to his self-esteem (by being jilted, say, or not getting a promotion), he will temporarily feel stupid and worthless, and hence do any number of stupid and worthless things—cheat at cards, bungle an assignment, break a valuable vase.

Mettee and I temporarily changed 45 female students' self-esteem. We gave one third of them positive feedback about a personality test they had taken (we said that they were interesting, mature, deep, etc.); we gave one third negative feedback (we said that they were relatively immature, shallow, etc.); and one third of the students got no information at all. Then all the students went on to participate in what they thought was an unrelated experiment, in which they gambled in a competitive game of cards. We arranged the situation so that the students could cheat and thereby win a considerable sum of money, or not cheat, in which case they were sure to lose.

The results showed that the students who had received blows to their self-esteem cheated far more than those who had gotten positive feedback about themselves. It may well be that low self-esteem is a critical antecedent of criminal or cruel behavior.

The theory of cognitive dissonance has proved useful in generating research; it has uncovered a wide range of data. In formal terms, however, it is a very sloppy theory. Its very simplicity provides both its greatest strength and its most serious weakness. That is, while the theory has generated a great deal of data, it has not been easy to define the limits of the theoretical statement, to determine the specific predictions that can be made. All too often researchers have had to resort to the very unscientific rule of thumb, "If you want to be sure, ask Leon."

Logic and psychologic

Part of the problem is that the theory does not deal with *logical* inconsistency, but *psychological* inconsistency. Festinger maintains that two cognitions are inconsistent if the opposite of one follows from the other. Strictly speaking, the information that smoking causes cancer does not make it illogical to smoke. But these cognitions produce dissonance because they do not make sense psychologically, assuming that the smoker does not want cancer.

One cannot always predict dissonance with accuracy. A man may admire Franklin Roosevelt enormously and discover that throughout his marriage FDR carried out a clandestine affair. If he places a high value on fidelity and he believes that great men are not exempt from this value, then he will experience dissonance. Then I can predict that he will either change his attitudes about Roosevelt or soften his attitudes about fidelity. But, he may believe that marital infidelity and political greatness are totally unrelated; if this were the case, he might simply shrug off these data without modifying his opinions either about Roosevelt or about fidelity.

Because of the sloppiness in the theory, several commentators have criticized a great many of the findings first uncovered by dissonance theory. These criticisms have served a useful purpose. Often, they have goaded us to perform more precise research, which in turn has led to a clarification of some of the findings which, ironically enough, has eliminated the alternative explanations proposed by the critics themselves.

For example, Alphonse and Natalia Chapanis argued that the "severe initiation" experiment could have completely different causes. It might be that the young women were not embarrassed at having to read sexual words, but rather were aroused, and their arousal in turn led them to rate the dull discussion group as interesting. Or, to the contrary, the women in the severe-initiation condition could have felt much sexual anxiety, followed by relief that the discussion was so banal. They associated relief with the group, and so rated it favorably.

So Harold Gerard and Grover Mathewson replicated our experiment, using electric shocks in the initiation procedure. Our original findings were supported—subjects who underwent severe shocks in order to join a discussion group rated that group more favorably than subjects who had undergone mild shocks. Moreover, Gerard and Mathewson went on to show that merely linking an electric shock with the group discussion (as in a simple conditioning experiment) did not produce greater liking for the group. The increase in liking for the group occurred only when subjects volunteered for the shock *in order* to gain membership in the group—just as dissonance theory would predict.

Routes to consonance

In the real world there is usually more than one way to squirm out of inconsistency. Laboratory experiments carefully control a person's alternatives, and the conclusions drawn may be misleading if applied to everyday situations. For example, suppose a prestigious university rejects a young Ph.D. for its one available teaching position. If she feels that she is a good scholar, she will experience dissonance. She can then decide that members of that department are narrow-minded and senile, sexist, and wouldn't recognize talent if it sat on their laps. Or she could decide that if they could reject someone as fine and intelligent as she, they must be extraordinarily brilliant. Both techniques will reduce dissonance, but note that they leave this woman with totally opposite opinions about professors at the university.

This is a serious conceptual problem. One solution is to specify the conditions under which a person will take one route to consonance over another. For example, if a person struggles to reach a goal and fails, he may decide that the goal wasn't worth it (as Aesop's fox did) or that the effort was justified anyway (the fox got a lot of exercise in jumping for the grapes). My own research suggests that a person will take the first means when he has expended relatively little effort. But when he has put in a great deal of effort, dissonance will take the form of justifying the energy.

This line of work is encouraging. I do not think that it is very fruitful to demand to know what *the* mode of dissonance reduction is; it is more instructive to isolate the various modes that occur, and determine the optimum conditions for each.

Ignorance of absurdity

No dissonance theorist takes issue with the fact that people frequently work to get rewards. In our experiments, however, small rewards tend to be associated with greater attraction and greater attitude change. Is the reverse ever true?

Jonathan Freedman told college students to work on a dull task after first telling them (*a*) their results would be of no use to him, since his experiment was basically over, or (*b*) their results would be of great value to him. Subjects in the first condition were in a state of dissonance, for they had unknowingly agreed to work on a boring chore that apparently had no purpose. They reduced their dissonance by deciding that the task was enjoyable.

Then Freedman ran the same experiment with one change. He waited until the subjects finished the task to tell them whether their work would be important. In this study he found incentive effects: students told that the task was valuable enjoyed it more than those who were told that their work was useless. In short, dissonance theory does not apply when an individual performs an action in good faith without having any way of knowing it was absurd. When we agree to participate in an experiment we naturally assume that it is for a purpose. If we are informed afterward that it *had* no purpose, how were we to have known? In this instance we like the task better if it had an important purpose. But if we agreed to perform it *knowing* that it had no purpose, we try to convince ourselves that it is an attractive task in order to avoid looking absurd.

Man cannot live by consonance alone

Dissonance reduction is only one of several motives, and other powerful drives can counteract it. If human beings had a pervasive, all-encompassing need to reduce all forms of dissonance, we would not grow, mature, or admit to our mistakes. We would sweep mistakes under the rug or, worse, turn the mistakes into virtues; in neither case would we profit from error.

But obviously people do learn from experience. They often do tolerate dissonance because the dissonant information has great utility. A person cannot ignore forever a leaky roof, even if that flaw is inconsistent with having spent a fortune on the house. As utility increases, individuals will come to prefer dissonance-arousing but useful information. But as dissonance increases, or when commitment is high, future utility and information tend to be ignored.

It is clear that people will go to extraordinary lengths to justify their actions. They will lie, cheat, live on the San Andreas Fault, accuse innocent bystanders of being vicious provocateurs, ignore information that might save their lives, and generally engage in all manner of absurd postures. Before we write off such behavior as bizarre, crazy, or evil, we would be wise to examine the situations that set up the need to reduce dissonance. Perhaps our awareness of the mechanism that makes us so often irrational will help turn Camus' observation on absurdity into a philosophic curiosity.

Commitment
and Consistency:
Hobgoblins of the Mind
Robert B. Cialdini

A study done by a pair of Canadian psychologists uncovered something fascinating about people at the racetrack: Just after placing a bet, they are much more confident of their horse's chances of winning than they are immediately before laying down that bet.[1] Of course, nothing about the horse's chances actually shifts; it's the same horse, on the same track, in the same field; but in the minds of those bettors, its prospects improve significantly once that ticket is purchased. Although a bit puzzling at first glance, the reason for the dramatic change has to do with a common weapon of social influence. Like the other weapons of influence, this one lies deep within us, directing our actions with quiet power. It is, quite simply, our nearly obsessive desire to be (and to appear) consistent with what we have already done. Once we have made a choice or taken a stand, we will encounter personal and interpersonal pressures to behave consistently with that commitment. Those pressures will cause us to respond in ways that justify our earlier decision.

Take the bettors in the racetrack experiment. Thirty seconds before putting down their money, they had been tentative and uncertain; thirty seconds after the deed, they were significantly more optimistic and self-assured. The act of making a final decision—in this case, of buying a ticket—had been the critical factor. Once a stand had been taken, the need for consistency pressured these people to bring what they felt and believed into line with what they had already done. They simply convinced themselves that they had made the right choice and, no doubt, felt better about it all.

Before we see such self-delusion as unique to racetrack habitués, we should examine the story of my neighbor Sara and her live-in boyfriend, Tim. They met at a hospital where he worked as an X-ray technician and she as a nutritionist. They dated for a while, even after Tim lost his job,

Reprinted with permission from *Influence: Science and Practice* by Robert B. Cialdini, © 1985 by Scott, Foresman and Company.
1. The racetrack study was done twice, with the same results, by Knox and Inkster (1968).

and eventually they moved in together. Things were never perfect for Sara: She wanted Tim to marry her and to stop his heavy drinking; Tim resisted both ideas. After an especially difficult period of conflict, Sara broke off the relationship and Tim moved out. At the same time, an old boyfriend of Sara's returned to town after years away and called her. They started seeing each other socially and quickly became serious enough to plan a wedding. They had gone so far as to set a date and issue invitations when Tim called. He had repented and wanted to move back in. When Sara told him her marriage plans, he begged her to change her mind; he wanted to be together with her as before. But Sara refused, saying she didn't want to live like that again. Tim even offered to marry her, but she still said she preferred the other boyfriend. Finally, Tim volunteered to quit drinking if she would only relent. Feeling that under those conditions Tim had the edge, Sara decided to break her engagement, cancel the wedding, retract the invitations and let Tim move back in with her.

Within a month, Tim informed Sara that he didn't think he needed to stop his drinking after all; a month later, he had decided that they should "wait and see" before getting married. Two years have since passed; Tim and Sara continue to live together exactly as before. He still drinks, there are still no marriage plans, yet Sara is more devoted to Tim than she ever was. She says that being forced to choose taught her that Tim really is number one in her heart. So, after choosing Tim over her other boyfriend, Sara became happier with him, even though the conditions under which she had made her choice have never been fulfilled. Obviously, horse-race bettors are not alone in their willingness to believe in the correctness of a difficult choice once made. Indeed, we all fool ourselves from time to time in order to keep our thoughts and beliefs consistent with what we have already done or decided.

Psychologists have long understood the power of the consistency principle to direct human action. Prominent theorists such as Leon Festinger, Fritz Heider, and Theodore Newcomb have viewed the desire for consistency as a central motivator of our behavior. But is this tendency to be consistent really strong enough to compel us to do what we ordinarily would not want to do? There is no question about it. The drive to be (and look) consistent constitutes a highly potent weapon of social influence, often causing us to act in ways that are clearly contrary to our own best interests.

To understand why consistency is so powerful a motive, it is important to recognize that in most circumstances consistency is valued and adaptive. Inconsistency is commonly thought to be an undesirable personality trait. The woman who changes her mind again and again is considered flighty or scatterbrained. The man whose opinions can be easily influenced is viewed as indecisive and weak-willed. The person whose beliefs, words, and deeds don't match may be seen as confused, two-faced, or even mentally ill. On the other side, a high degree of consistency is normally associated with personal and intellectual strength. It is at the heart of logic, rationality, stability, and honesty.

Certainly, then, good personal consistency is highly valued in our culture. And well it should be. It provides us with a reasonable and gainful orientation to the world. Most of the time we will be better off if our approach to things is well laced with consistency. Without it our lives would be difficult, erratic, and disjointed.

But because it is so typically in our best interests to be consistent, we easily fall into the habit of being automatically so, even in situations where it is not the sensible way to be. When it occurs unthinkingly, consistency can be disastrous. Nonetheless, even blind consistency has its attractions.

First, like most other forms of automatic responding, it offers a shortcut through the density of modern life. Once we have made up our minds about an issue, stubborn consistency allows us a very appealing luxury: We really don't have to think hard about the issue anymore. We don't have to sift through the blizzard of information we encounter every day to identify relevant facts; we don't have to expend the mental energy to weigh the pros and cons; we don't have to make any further tough decisions. Instead, all we have to do when confronted with the issue is to turn on our consistency tape, *whirr,* and we know just what to believe, say, or do. We need only believe, say, or do whatever is consistent with our earlier decision.

The allure of such a luxury is not to be minimized. It allows us a convenient, relatively effortless, and efficient method for dealing with complex daily environments that make severe demands on our mental energies and capacities. It is not hard to understand, then, why automatic consistency is a difficult reaction to curb. It offers us a way to evade the rigors of continuing thought. And as Sir Joshua Reynolds noted, "There is no expedient to which a man will not resort to avoid the real labor of thinking." With our consistency tapes operating, then, we can go about our business happily excused from the toil of having to think too much.

There is a second, more perverse attraction of mechanical consistency as well. Sometimes it is not the effort of hard, cognitive work that makes us shirk thoughtful activity, but the harsh consequences of that activity. Sometimes it is the cursedly clear and unwelcome set of answers provided by straight thinking that makes us mental slackers. There are certain disturbing things we simply would rather not realize. Because it is a preprogrammed and mindless method of responding, automatic consistency can supply a safe hiding place from those troubling realizations. Sealed within the fortress walls of rigid consistency, we can be impervious to the sieges of reason.

One night at an introductory lecture given by the Transcendental Meditation program, I witnessed a nice illustration of how people will hide inside the walls of consistency to protect themselves from the troublesome consequences of thought. The lecture itself was presided over by two earnest young men and was designed to recruit new members into the program. The program claimed it could teach a unique brand of meditation (TM) that would allow us to achieve all manner of desirable things, ranging from simple inner peace to the more spectacular abilities to fly and pass through walls at the program's advanced (and more expensive) stages.

I had decided to attend the meeting to observe the kind of compliance tactics used in recruitment lectures of this sort and had brought along an interested friend, a university professor whose areas of specialization were statistics and symbolic logic. As the meeting progressed and the lectures explained the theory behind TM, I noticed my logician friend becoming increasingly restless. Looking more and more pained and shifting about constantly in his seat, he was finally unable to resist. When the leaders called for questions at the completion of the lecture, he raised his hand and gently but surely demolished the presentation we had just heard. In less than two minutes, he pointed out precisely where and why the lecturers' complex argument was contradictory, illogical, and unsupportable. The effect on the discussion leaders was devastating. After a confused silence, each attempted a weak reply only to halt midway to confer with his partner and finally to admit that my colleague's points were good ones "requiring further study."

More interesting to me, though, was the effect upon the rest of the audience. At the end of the question period, the two recruiters were faced with a crush of audience members submitting their seventy-five-dollar down payments for admission to the TM program. Nudging, shrugging, and chuckling to one another as they took in the payments, the recruiters betrayed signs of giddy bewilderment. After what appeared to have been an embarrassingly clear collapse of their presentation, the meeting had somehow turned into a great success, generating mystifyingly high levels of compliance from the audience. Although more than a bit puzzled, I chalked up the audience response to a failure to understand the logic of my colleague's arguments. As it turned out, however, just the *reverse* was the case.

Outside the lecture room after the meeting, we were approached by three members of the audience, each of whom had given a down payment immediately after the lecture. They wanted to know why we had come to the session. We explained, and we asked the same question of them. One was an aspiring actor who wanted desperately to succeed at his craft and had come to the meeting to learn if TM would allow him to achieve the necessary self-control to master the art; the recruiters had assured him that it would. The second described herself as a severe insomniac who had hopes that TM would provide her with a way to relax and fall asleep easily at night. The third served as unofficial spokesman. He also had a sleep-related problem. He was failing college because there didn't seem to be enough time to study. He had come to the meeting to find out if TM could help by training him to need fewer hours of sleep each night; the additional time could then be used for study. It is interesting to note that the recruiters informed him as well as the insomniac that Transcendental Meditation techniques could solve their respective, though opposite, problems.

Still thinking that the three must have signed up because they hadn't understood the points made by my logician friend, I began to question them about aspects of his argument. To my surprise, I found that they had understood his comments quite well; in fact, all too well. It was precisely the cogency of his argument that drove them to sign up for the program on the spot. The spokesman put it best: "Well, I wasn't going to put down any money tonight because I'm really quite broke right now; I was going to wait until the next meeting. But when your buddy started talking, I knew I'd better give them my money now, or I'd go home and start thinking about what he said and *never* sign up."

All at once, things began to make sense. These were people with real problems; and they were somewhat desperately searching for a way to solve those problems. They were seekers who, if our discussion leaders were to be believed, had found a potential solution in TM. Driven by their needs, they very much wanted to believe that TM was their answer.

Now, in the form of my colleague, intrudes the voice of reason, showing the theory underlying their newfound solution to be unsound. Panic! Something must be done at once before logic takes its toll and leaves them without hope again. Quickly, quickly, walls against reason are needed; and it doesn't matter that the fortress to be erected is a foolish one. "Quick, a hiding place from thought! Here, take this money. Whew, safe in the nick of time. No need to think about the issues any longer. The decision has been made, and from now on the consistency tape can be played whenever necessary: 'TM? Certainly I think it will help me; certainly I expect to continue; certainly I believe in TM. I already put my money down for it, didn't I?' Ah, the comforts of mindless consistency, I'll just rest right here for a while. It's so much nicer than the worry and strain of that hard, hard search."

If, as it appears, automatic consistency functions as a shield against thought, it should not be surprising that such consistency can also be exploited by those who would prefer that we not think too much in response to their requests for our compliance. For the exploiters, whose interest will be served by an unthinking, mechanical reaction to their requests, our tendency for automatic consistency is a gold mine. So clever are they at arranging to have us play our consistency tapes when it profits them that we seldom realize we have been taken. In fine jujitsu fashion, they structure their interactions with us so that our *own* need to be consistent will lead directly to their benefit.

Certain large toy manufacturers use just such an approach to reduce a problem caused by seasonal buying patterns. Of course, the boom time for toy sales occurs before and during the Christmas holiday season. The toy companies make fat profits during this period. Their problem is that toy sales then go into a terrible slump for the next couple of months. Their customers have already spent the amount in their toy budgets and are stiffly resistant to their children's pleas for more. Even those children whose birthdays fall soon after the holidays receive fewer toys because of the recent Christmas spree.

So the toy manufacturers are faced with a dilemma: how to keep sales high during the peak season and, at the same time, retain a healthy demand for toys in the immediately following months. Their difficulty certainly doesn't lie in convincing our naturally insatiable offspring to want a continuous flow of new amusements. A series of flashy television commercials placed among the Saturday morning cartoon shows will produce the usual amounts of begging, whining, and wheedling no matter when it appears during the year. No, the problem is not in motivating kids to want more toys after Christmas.

The problem is in motivating postholiday spent-out parents to reach down for the price of yet another plaything for their already toy-glutted children. What could the toy companies possibly do to produce that unlikely behavior? Some have tried a greatly increased advertising campaign, others have reduced prices during the slack period, but neither of those standard sales devices has proved successful. Not only are both tactics costly but both have also been ineffective in increasing sales to desired levels. Parents are simply not in a toy-buying mood, and the influences of advertising or reduced expense are not enough to shake that stony resistance.

Certain large toy manufacturers, however, think they have found a solution. It's an ingenious one, involving no more than a normal advertising expense and an understanding of the powerful pull of the need for consistency. My first hint of how the toy companies' strategy worked came after I fell for it and then, in true patsy form, fell for it again.

It was January, and I was in the town's largest toy store. After purchasing all too many gifts there for my son a month before, I had sworn not to enter that place or any like it for a long, long time. Yet there I was, not only in the diabolic place but also in the process of buying my son another expensive toy—a big, electric road-race set. In front of the road-race display I happened to meet a former neighbor who was buying his son the same toy. The odd thing was that we almost never saw each other anymore. In fact, the last time was a year earlier in that same store where we were both buying our sons an expensive post-Christmas gift—that time a robot that walked, talked, and laid waste. We laughed about our strange pattern of seeing each other only once a year at the same time, in the same place, while doing the same thing. Later that day, I mentioned the coincidence to a friend who, it turned out, had once worked in the toy business.

"No coincidence," he said knowingly.

"What do you mean, 'No coincidence'?"

"Look," he said, "let me ask you a couple of questions about the road-race set you bought this year. First, did you promise your son that he'd get one for Christmas?"

"Well, yes, I did. Christopher had seen a bunch of ads for them on the Saturday morning cartoon shows and said that was what he wanted for Christmas. I saw a couple of the ads myself and it looked like fun; so I said okay."

"Strike one," he announced. "Now for my second question. When you went to buy one, did you find all the stores sold out?"

"That's right, I did! The stores said they'd ordered some but didn't know when they'd get any more in. So I had to buy Christopher some other toys to make up for the road-race set. But how did you know?"

"Strike two," he said. "Just let me ask one more question. Didn't this same sort of thing happen the year before with the robot toy?"

"Wait a minute . . . you're right. That's just what happened. This is incredible. How did you know?"

"No psychic powers; I just happen to know how several of the big toy companies jack up their January and February sales. They start prior to Christmas with attractive TV ads for certain special toys. The kids, naturally, want what they see and extract Christmas promises for these items from their parents. Now here's where the genius of the companies' plan comes in: They *undersupply* the stores with the toys they've gotten the parents to promise. Most parents find those things sold out and are forced to substitute other toys of equal value. The toy manufacturers, of course, make a point of supplying the stores with plenty of these substitutes. Then, after Christmas, the companies start running the ads again for the other, special toys. That juices up the kids to want those toys more than ever. They go running to their parents whining, 'You promised, you promised,' and the adults go trudging off to the store to live up dutifully to their words."

"Where," I said, beginning to seethe now, "they meet other parents they haven't seen for a year, falling for the same trick, right?"

"Right. Uh, where are you going?"

"I'm going to take that road-race set right back to the store." I was so angry I was nearly shouting.

"Wait. Think for a minute first. Why did you buy it this morning?"

"Because I didn't want to let Christopher down and because I wanted to teach him that promises are to be lived up to."

"Well, has any of that changed? Look, if you take his toy away now, he won't understand why. He'll just know that his father broke a promise to him. Is that what you want?"

"No," I said, sighing, "I guess not. So, you're telling me that they doubled their profit on me for the past two years, and I never even knew it;

and now that I do, I'm still trapped—by my own words. So, what you're really telling me is, 'Strike three.'"

He nodded, "And you're out."

Commitment is the key

Once we realize that the power of consistency is formidable in directing human action, an important practical question immediately arises: How is that force engaged? What produces the *click* that activates the *whirr* of the powerful consistency tape? Social psychologists think they know the answer: commitment. If I can get you to make a commitment (that is, to take a stand, to go on record), I will have set the stage for your automatic and ill-considered consistency with that earlier commitment. Once a stand is taken, there is a natural tendency to behave in ways that are stubbornly consistent with the stand.

As we've already seen, social psychologists are not the only ones who understand the connection between commitment and consistency. Commitment strategies are aimed at us by compliance professionals of nearly every sort. Each of the strategies is intended to get us to take some action or make some statement that will trap us into later compliance through consistency pressures. Procedures designed to create commitment take various forms. Some are fairly straightforward; others are among the most devious compliance tactics we will encounter.

The question of what makes a commitment effective has a number of answers. A variety of factors affect the ability of a commitment to constrain our future behavior. One large-scale program designed to produce compliance illustrates nicely how several of the factors work. The remarkable thing about this program is that it was systematically employing these factors decades ago, well before scientific research had identified them.

During the Korean War many captured American soldiers found themselves in prisoner-of-war camps run by the Chinese Communists. It became clear early in the conflict that the Chinese treated captives quite differently than did their allies, the North Koreans, who favored savagery and harsh punishment to gain compliance. Specifically avoiding the appearance of brutality, the Red Chinese engaged in what they termed their "lenientpolicy," which was in reality a concerted and sophisticated psychological assault on their captives. After the war, American psychologists questioned the returning prisoners intensively to determine what had occurred. The intensive psychological investigation took place, in part, because of the unsettling success of some aspects of the Chinese program. For example, the Chinese were very effective in getting Americans to inform on one another, in striking contrast to the behavior of American POWs in World War II. For this reason, among others, escape plans were quickly uncovered and the escapes themselves almost always unsuccessful.

"When an escape did occur," wrote Dr. Edgar Schein, a principal American investigator of the Chinese indoctrination program in Korea, "the Chinese usually recovered the man easily by offering a bag of rice to anyone turning him in." In fact, nearly all American prisoners in the Chinese camps are said to have collaborated with the enemy in one form or another.[2]

An examination of the Chinese prison-camp program shows that they relied heavily on commitment and consistency pressures to gain the desired compliance from their captives. Of course, the first problem facing the Chinese was how to get any collaboration at all from the Americans. These were men who were trained to provide nothing but name, rank, and serial number. Short of physical brutalization, how could the captors hope to get such men to give military information, turn in fellow prisoners, or publicly denounce their country? The Chinese answer was elementary: Start small and build.

For instance, prisoners were frequently asked to make statements so mildly anti-American or pro-Communist as to seem inconsequential ("The United States is not perfect." "In a Communist country, unemployment is not a problem.") But once these minor requests were complied with, the men found themselves pushed to submit to related yet more substantive requests. A man who had just agreed with his Chinese interrogator that the United States is not perfect might then be asked to indicate some of the ways in which he thought this was the case. Once he had so explained himself, he might be asked to make a list of these "problems with America" and to sign his name to it. Later he might be asked to read his list in a discussion group with other prisoners. "After all, it's what you really believe, isn't it?" Still later he might be asked to write an essay expanding on his list and discussing these problems in greater detail.

The Chinese might then use his name and his essay in an anti-American radio broadcast beamed not only to the entire camp but to other POW camps in North Korea as well as to American forces in South Korea. Suddenly he would find himself a "collaborator," having given aid and comfort to the enemy. Aware that he had written the essay without any strong threats or coercion, many times a man would change his image of himself to be consistent with the deed and with the new "collaborator" label, often resulting in even more extensive acts of collaboration. Thus, while "only a few men were able to avoid collaboration altogether," according to Dr. Schein, "the majority collaborated at one time or another by doing things which seemed to them trivial but which the Chinese were able to turn to

2. It is important to note that the collaboration was not always intentional. The American investigators defined collaboration as "any kind of behavior which helped the enemy" and it thus included such diverse activities as signing peace petitions, running errands, making radio appeals, accepting special favors, making false confessions, informing on fellow prisoners, or divulging military information.

their own advantage. . . . This was particularly effective in eliciting confessions, self-criticism, and information during interrogation."[3]

If the Chinese know about the subtle power of this approach, it should not be surprising that another group of people interested in compliance is also aware of its usefulness. Many business organizations employ it regularly.

For the salesperson, the strategy is to obtain a large purchase by starting with a small one. Almost any small sale will do because the purpose of that small transaction is not profit. It is commitment. Further purchases, even much larger ones, are expected to flow naturally from the commitment. An article in the trade magazine *American Salesman* put it succinctly:

> The general idea is to pave the way for full-line distribution by starting with a small order. . . . Look at it this way—when a person has signed an order for your merchandise, even though the profit is so small it hardly compensates for the time and effort of making the call, he is no longer a prospect—he is a customer.[4]

The tactic of starting with a little request in order to gain eventual compliance with related larger requests has a name: the foot-in-the-door technique. Social scientists first became aware of its effectiveness in the mid-1960s when psychologists Jonathan Freedman and Scott Fraser published an astonishing set of data.[5] They reported the results of an experiment in which a researcher, posing as a volunteer worker, had gone door to door in a residential California neighborhood making a preposterous request of homeowners. The homeowners were asked to allow a public-service billboard to be installed on their front lawns. To get an idea of just how the sign would look, they were shown a photograph depicting an attractive house, the view of which was almost completely obscured by a very large, poorly lettered sign reading DRIVE CAREFULLY. Although the request was normally and understandably refused by the great majority (83 percent) of the other residents in the area, this particular group of people reacted quite favorably. A full 76 percent of them offered the use of their front yards.

The prime reason for their startling compliance has to do with something that had happened to them about two weeks earlier: They had made a small commitment to driver safety. A different volunteer worker had come to their doors and asked them to accept and display a little three-inch-square sign that read BE A SAFE DRIVER. It was such a trifling request that nearly all of them had agreed to it. But the effects of that request were

---

3. The Schein quote comes from his 1956 article "The Chinese Indoctrination Program for Prisoners of War: A Study of Attempted Brainwashing."
4. See Greene (1965) for the source of this advice.
5. Freedman and Fraser published their data in the *Journal of Personality and Social Psychology,* in 1966.

enormous. Because they had innocently complied with a trivial safe-driving request a couple of weeks before, these homeowners became remarkably willing to comply with another such request that was massive in size.

Freedman and Fraser didn't stop there. They tried a slightly different procedure on another sample of homeowners. These people first received a request to sign a petition that favored "keeping California beautiful." Of course, nearly everyone signed since state beauty, like efficiency in government or sound prenatal care, is one of those issues almost no one is against. After waiting about two weeks, Freedman and Fraser sent a new "volunteer worker" to these same homes to ask the residents to allow the big DRIVE CAREFULLY sign to be erected on their lawns. In some ways, their response was the most astounding of any of the homeowners in the study. Approximately half of these people consented to the installation of the DRIVE CAREFULLY billboard, even though the small commitment they had made weeks earlier was not to driver safety but to an entirely different public-service topic, state beautification.

At first, even Freedman and Fraser were bewildered by their findings. Why should the little act of signing a petition supporting state beautification cause people to be so willing to perform a different and much larger favor? After considering and discarding other explanations, Freedman and Fraser came upon one that offered a solution to the puzzle: Signing the beautification petition changed the view these people had of themselves. They saw themselves as public-spirited citizens who acted on their civic principles. When, two weeks later, they were asked to perform another public service by displaying the DRIVE CAREFULLY sign, they complied in order to be consistent with their newly formed self-images. According to Freedman and Fraser,

> What may occur is a change in the person's feelings about getting involved or taking action. Once he has agreed to a request, his attitude may change, he may become, in his own eyes, the kind of person who does this sort of thing, who agrees to requests made by strangers, who takes action on things he believes in, who cooperates with good causes.[6]

What the Freedman and Fraser findings tell us, then, is to be very careful about agreeing to trivial requests. Such an agreement can not only increase our compliance with very similar, much larger requests, it can also make us more willing to perform a variety of larger favors that are only remotely connected to the little one we did earlier. It's this second, general kind of influence concealed within small commitments that scares me.

It scares me enough that I am rarely willing to sign a petition anymore,

6. The quote comes from Freedman and Fraser (1966).

even for a position I support. Such an action has the potential to influence not only my future behavior but also my self-image in ways I may not want. And once a person's self-image is altered, all sorts of subtle advantages become available to someone who wants to exploit that new image.

Who among Freedman and Fraser's homeowners would have thought that the "volunteer worker" who asked them to sign a state beautification petition was really interested in having them display a safe-driving billboard two weeks later? And who among them could have suspected that their decision to display the billboard was largely due to the act of signing the petition? No one, I'd guess. If there were any regrets after the billboard went up, who could they conceivably hold responsible but *themselves* and their own damnably strong civic spirit? They probably never even considered the guy with the "keeping California beautiful" petition and all that knowledge of jujitsu.

Notice that all of the foot-in-the-door experts seem to be excited about the same thing: You can use small commitments to manipulate a person's self-image; you can use them to turn citizens into "public servants," prospects into "customers," prisoners into "collaborators." And once you've got a man's self-image where you want it, he should comply *naturally* with a whole range of your requests that are consistent with this view of himself.

Not all commitments affect self-image, however. There are certain conditions that should be present for a commitment to be effective in this way. To discover what they are, we can once again look to the American experience in the Chinese prison camps of Korea. It is important to understand that the major intent of the Chinese was not simply to extract information from their prisoners. It was to indoctrinate them, to change their attitudes and perceptions of themselves, of their political system, of their country's role in the war, and of communism. And there is evidence that the program often worked alarmingly well.

Dr. Henry Segal, chief of the neuropsychiatric evaluation team that examined returning POWs at the war's end, reported that war-related beliefs had been substantially shifted. The majority of the men believed the Chinese story that the United States had used germ warfare, and many felt that their own forces had been the initial aggressors in starting the war. Similar inroads had been made in the political attitudes of the men:

> Many expressed antipathy toward the Chinese Communists but at the same time praised them for "the fine job they have done in China." Others stated that "although communism won't work in America, I think it's a good thing for Asia." [7]

It appears that the real goal of the Chinese was to modify, at least for a time, the hearts and minds of their captives. If we measure their achieve-

---

7. See Segal (1954) for the article from which this quote originates.

ment in terms of "defection, disloyalty, changed attitudes and beliefs, poor discipline, poor morale, poor *esprit*, and doubts as to America's role," Dr. Segal concluded that "their efforts were highly successful." Because commitment tactics were so much a part of the effective Chinese assault on hearts and minds, it is quite informative to examine the specific features of the tactics they used.

The magic act

Our best evidence of what people truly feel and believe comes less from their words than from their deeds. Observers trying to decide what a man is like look closely at his actions. What the Chinese have discovered is that the man himself uses this same evidence to decide what he is like. His behavior tells him about himself; it is a primary source of information about his beliefs and values and attitudes. Understanding fully this important principle of self-perception, the Chinese set about arranging the prison-camp experience so that their captives would consistently *act* in desired ways. Before long, the Chinese knew, these actions would begin to take their toll, causing the men to change their views of themselves to align with what they had done.

Writing was one sort of confirming action that the Chinese urged incessantly upon the men. It was never enough for the prisoners to listen quietly or even to agree verbally with the Chinese line; they were always pushed to write it down as well. So intent were the Chinese on securing a written statement that if a prisoner was not willing to write a desired response freely, he was prevailed upon to copy it. The American psychologist Edgar Schein describes a standard indoctrination session tactic of the Chinese in these terms:

> A further technique was to have the man write out the question and then the [pro-Communist] answer. If he refused to write it voluntarily, he was asked to copy it from the notebooks, which must have seemed like a harmless enough concession.

But, oh, those "harmless" concessions. We've already seen how apparently trifling commitments can lead to extraordinary further behavior. And the Chinese knew that, as a commitment device, a written declaration has some great advantages. First, it provides physical evidence that the act occurred. Once a man wrote what the Chinese wanted, it was very difficult for him to believe that he had not done so. The opportunities to forget or to deny to himself what he had done were not available, as they are for purely verbal statements. No; there it was in his own handwriting, an irrevocably documented act driving him to make his beliefs and his self-image consistent with what he had undeniably done.

A second advantage of a written testament is that it can be shown to other people. Of course, that means it can be used to persuade those people. It can persuade them to change their own attitudes in the direction of the statement. But more important for the purpose of commitment, it can persuade them that the author genuinely believes what was written. People have a natural tendency to think that a statement reflects the true attitude of the person who made it. What is surprising is that they continue to think so even when they know that the person did not freely choose to make the statement.

Some scientific evidence that this is the case comes from a study by psychologists Edward Jones and James Harris, who showed people an essay that was favorable to Fidel Castro and asked them to guess the true feelings of its author.[8] Jones and Harris told some of these people that the author had chosen to write a pro-Castro essay; and they told the other people that the author had been required to write in favor of Castro. The strange thing was that even those people who knew that the author had been assigned to do a pro-Castro essay guessed that he liked Castro. It seems that a statement of belief produces a *click, whirr* response in those who view it. Unless there is strong evidence to the contrary, observers automatically assume that someone who makes such a statement means it.

Think of the double-barreled effects on the self-image of a prisoner who wrote a pro-Chinese or anti-American statement. Not only was it a lasting personal reminder of his action, it was also likely to persuade those around him that the statement reflected his actual beliefs. And, as we will see in Chapter 4 [not reproduced here], what those around us think is true of us is enormously important in determining what we ourself think is true. For example, one study found that after hearing that they were considered charitable people, New Haven, Connecticut, housewives gave much more money to a canvasser from the Multiple Sclerosis Association.[9] Apparently the mere knowlege that someone viewed them as charitable caused these women to make their actions consistent with another's perception of them.

Once an active commitment is made, then, self-image is squeezed from both sides by consistency pressures. From the inside, there is a pressure to bring self-image into line with action. From the outside, there is a sneakier pressure—a tendency to adjust this image according to the way others perceive us. And because others see us as believing what we have written (even when we've had little choice in the matter), we will once again experience a pull to bring self-image into line with the written statement.

In Korea, several subtle devices were used to get the prisoners to write, without direct coercion, what the Chinese wanted. For example, the Chinese knew that many prisoners were anxious to let their families know that

8. See Jones and Harris (1967).
9. It is noteworthy that the housewives in this study (Kraut, 1973) heard that they were considered charitable at least a full week before they were asked to donate to the Multiple Sclerosis Association.

they were alive. At the same time, the men knew that their captors were censoring the mails and that only some letters were being allowed out of camp. To ensure that their own letters would be released, some prisoners began including in their messages peace appeals, claims of kind treatment, and statements sympathetic to communism. The hope was that the Chinese would want such letters to surface and would, therefore, allow their delivery. Of course, the Chinese were happy to cooperate because those letters served their interests marvelously. First, their worldwide propaganda effort benefited greatly from the appearance of pro-Communist statements by American servicemen. Second, in the service of prisoner indoctrination, they had, without raising a finger of physical force, gotten many men to go on record as supporting the Chinese cause.

A similar technique involved political essay contests that were regularly held in camp. The prizes for winning were invariably small—a few cigarettes or a bit of fruit—but were sufficiently scarce that they generated a lot of interest from the men. Usually the winning essay was one that took a solidly pro-Communist stand . . . but not always. The Chinese were wise enough to realize that most of the prisoners would not enter a contest that they could win only by writing a Communist tract. And the Chinese were clever enough to know how to plant small commitments to communism in the men that could be nurtured into later bloom. So occasionally the prize was given to an essay that generally supported the United States but that bowed once or twice to the Chinese view. The effects of this strategy were exactly what the Chinese wanted. The men continued to participate voluntarily in the contests because they saw that they could win with an essay highly favorable to their own country. But perhaps without realizing it, they began to shade their essays a bit toward communism in order to have a better chance of winning. The Chinese were ready to pounce on any concession to Communist dogma and to bring consistency pressures to bear upon it. In the case of a written declaration within a voluntary essay, they had a perfect commitment from which to build toward collaboration and conversion.

Other compliance professionals also know about the committing power of written statements. The enormously successful Amway Corporation, for instance, has hit upon a way to spur their sales personnel to greater and greater accomplishments. Members of the staff are asked to set individual sales goals and commit themselves to those goals by personally recording them on paper:

One final tip before you get started: Set a goal and *write it down*. Whatever the goal, the important thing is that you set it, so you've got something for which to aim—and that you write it down. There is something magical about writing things down. So set a goal and write it down. When you reach that goal, set another and write that down. You'll be off and running.[10]

If the Amway people have found "something magical about writing things down," so have other business organizations. Some door-to-door sales companies use the magic of written commitments to battle the "cooling-off" laws recently passed in many states. The laws are designed to allow customers a few days after purchasing an item to cancel the sale and receive a full refund. At first this legislation hurt the hard-sell companies deeply. Because they emphasize high-pressure tactics, their customers often buy, not because they want the product but because they are duped or intimidated into the sale. When the new laws went into effect, these customers began canceling in droves.

The companies have since learned a beautifully simple trick that cuts the number of such cancellations drastically. They merely have the customer, rather than the salesman, fill out the sales agreement. According to the sales-training program of a prominent encyclopedia company, that personal commitment alone has proved to be "a very important psychological aid in preventing customers from backing out of their contracts." Like the Amway Corporation, then, these organizations have found that something special happens when people personally put their commitments on paper: They live up to what they have written down.

Another common way for businesses to cash in on the "magic" of written declarations occurs through the use of an innocent-looking promotional device. Before I began to study weapons of social influence, I used to wonder why big companies such as Procter & Gamble and General Foods are always running those "25-, 50-, or 100 words or less" testimonial contests. They all seem to be alike. The contestant is to compose a short personal statement that begins with the words, "Why I like . . . " and goes on to laud the features of whatever cake mix or floor wax happens to be at issue. The company judges the entries and awards some stunningly large prizes to the winners. What had puzzled me was what the companies got out of the deal. Often the contest requires no purchase; anyone submitting an entry is eligible. Yet, the companies appear to be strangely willing to incur the huge costs of contest after contest.

I am no longer puzzled. The purpose behind the testimonial contest is the same as the purpose behind the political essay contests of the Chinese Communists. In both instances, the aim is to get as many people as possible to go on record as liking the product. In Korea, the product was a brand of Chinese communism; in the United States, it might be a brand of cuticle remover. The type of product doesn't matter; the process is the same. Participants voluntarily write essays for attractive prizes that they

10. From "How to begin retailing," Amway Corporation.

have only a small chance to win. But they know that for an essay to have any chance of winning at all, it must include praise for the product. So they find praiseworthy features of the product and describe them in their essays. The result is hundreds of men in Korea or hundreds of thousands of people in America who testify in writing to the product's appeal and who, consequently, experience that "magical" pull to believe what they have written.

The public eye

One reason that written testaments are effective in bringing about genuine personal change is that they can so easily be made public. The prisoner experience in Korea showed the Chinese to be quite aware of an important psychological principle: Public commitments tend to be lasting commitments. The Chinese constantly arranged to have the pro-Communist statements of their captives seen by others. A man who had written a political essay the Chinese liked, for example, might find copies of it posted around camp, or might be asked to read it to a prisoner discussion group, or even to read it on the camp radio broadcast. As far as the Chinese were concerned, the more public the better. Why?

Whenever one takes a stand that is visible to others, there arises a drive to maintain that stand in order to *look* like a consistent person. Remember that earlier in this chapter we described how desirable good personal consistency is as a trait; how someone without it could be judged as fickle, uncertain, pliant, scatterbrained, or unstable; how someone with it is viewed as rational, assured, trustworthy, and sound. Given this context, it is hardly surprising that people try to avoid the look of inconsistency. For appearances' sake, then, the more public a stand, the more reluctant we will be to change it.

An illustration of how public commitments can lead to doggedly consistent further action is provided in a famous experiment performed by a pair of prominent social psychologists, Morton Deutsch and Harold Gerard.[11] The basic procedure was to have college students first estimate in their own minds the length of lines they were shown. At this point, one sample of the students had to commit themselves publicly to their initial judgments by writing them down, signing their names to them, and turning them in to the experimenter. A second sample of students also committed themselves to their first estimates, but they did so privately by putting them on a Magic Writing Pad and then erasing them by lifting the Magic Pad's plastic cover before anyone could see what they had written. A third set of students did not commit themselves to their initial estimates at all; they just kept the estimates in mind privately.

In these ways, Deutsch and Gerard had cleverly arranged for some students to commit themselves publicly, some privately, and some not at all to

11. See Deutsch and Gerard (1955).

their initial decisions. What Deutsch and Gerard wanted to find out was which of the three types of students would be most inclined to stick with their first judgments after receiving information that those judgments were incorrect. So all of the students were given new evidence suggesting that their initial estimates were wrong, and they were then given the chance to change their estimates.

The results were quite clear. The students who had never written down their first choices were the least loyal to those choices. When new evidence was presented that questioned the wisdom of decisions that had never left their heads, these students were the most influenced by the new information to change what they had viewed as the "correct" decision. Compared to these uncommitted students, those who had merely written their decisions for a moment on a Magic Pad were significantly less willing to change their minds when given the chance. Even though they had committed themselves under the most anonymous of circumstances, the act of writing down their first judgments caused them to resist the influence of contradictory new data and to remain consistent with the preliminary choices. But Deutsch and Gerard found that, by far, it was the students who had publicly recorded their initial positions who most resolutely refused to shift from those positions later. Public commitment had hardened them into the most stubborn of all.

The Deutsch and Gerard finding that we are truest to our decisions if we have bound ourselves to them publicly can be put to good use. Consider the organizations dedicated to helping people rid themselves of bad habits. Many weight-reduction clinics, for instance, understand that often a person's private decision to lose weight will be too weak to withstand the blandishments of bakery windows, wafting cooking scents, and late-night Sara Lee commercials. So they see to it that the decision is buttressed by the pillars of public commitment. They require their clients to write down an immediate weight-loss goal and *show* that goal to as many friends, relatives, and neighbors as possible. Clinic operators report that frequently this simple technique works where all else has failed.

Of course, there's no need to pay a special clinic in order to engage a visible commitment as an ally. One San Diego woman described to me how she employed a public promise to help herself finally stop smoking:

> I remember it was after I heard about another scientific study showing that smoking causes cancer. Every time one of those things came out, I used to get determined to quit, but I never could. This time, though, I decided I had to do something. I'm a proud person. It matters to me if other people see me in a bad light. So I thought, "Maybe I can use that pride to help me dump this damn habit." So I made a list of all the people who I really wanted to respect me. Then I went out and got some blank business cards and I wrote on the back of each card, "I promise you that I will never smoke another cigarette."

Within a week, I had given or sent a signed card to everybody on the list—my dad, my brother back East, my boss, my best girlfriend, my ex-husband, everybody but one—the guy I was dating then. I was just crazy about him, and I really wanted him to value me as a person. Believe me, I thought twice about giving him a card because I knew that if I couldn't keep my promise to him I'd die. But one day at the office—he worked in the same building as I did—I just walked up to him, handed him the card, and walked away without saying anything.

Quitting "cold turkey" was the hardest thing I've ever done. There must have been a thousand times when I thought I *had* to have a smoke. But whenever that happened, I'd just picture how all of the people on my list, especially this one guy, would think less of me if I couldn't stick to my guns. And that's all it took. I've never taken another puff.

You know, the interesting thing is the guy turned out to be a real schmuck. I can't figure out what I saw in him back then. But at the time, without knowing it, he helped me get through the toughest part of the toughest thing I've ever had to do. I don't even like him anymore. Still, I do feel grateful in a way because I think he saved my life.

The effort extra

Yet another reason that written commitments are so effective is that they require more work than verbal ones. And the evidence is clear that the more effort that goes into a commitment, the greater is its ability to influence the attitudes of the person who made it. We can find that evidence quite close to home or as far away as the back regions of the primitive world. For example, there is a tribe in southern Africa, the Thonga, that requires each of its boys to go through an elaborate initiation ceremony before he can be counted a man of the tribe. As with many other primitive peoples, a Thonga boy endures a great deal before he is admitted to adult membership in the group. Anthropologists Whiting, Kluckhohn, and Anthony have described this three-month ordeal in brief but vivid terms:

When a boy is somewhere between 10 and 16 years of age, he is sent by his parents to "circumcision school," which is held every 4 or 5 years. Here in company with his age-mates he undergoes severe hazing by the adult males of the society. The initiation begins when each boy runs the gauntlet between two rows of men who beat him with clubs. At the end of this experience he is stripped of his clothes and his hair is cut. He is next met by a man covered with lion manes and is seated upon a stone facing this "lion man." Someone then strikes him from behind and when he turns his head to see who has struck him, his foreskin is seized and in two movements cut off by the "lion man." Afterward he is secluded for three months in the "yard of mysteries," where he can be seen only by the initiated.

During the course of his initiation, the boy undergoes six major trials: beating, exposure to cold, thirst, eating of unsavory foods, punishment, and the threat of death. On the slightest pretext, he may be beaten by one of the newly initiated men, who is assigned to the task by the older men of the tribe. He sleeps without covering and suffers bitterly from the winter cold. He is forbidden to drink a drop of water during the whole three months. Meals are often made nauseating by the half-digested grass from the stomach of an antelope, which is poured over his food. If he is caught breaking any important rule governing the ceremony, he is severely punished. For example, in one of these punishments, sticks are placed between the fingers of the offender, then a strong man closes his hand around that of the novice, practically crushing his fingers. He is frightened into submission by being told that in former times boys who had tried to escape or who had revealed the secrets to women or to the uninitiated were hanged and their bodies burned to ashes.[12]

On the face of it, these rites seem extraordinary and bizarre. Yet, at the same time, they can be seen to be remarkably similar in principle and even in detail to the common initiation ceremonies of school fraternities. During the traditional "Hell Week" held yearly on college campuses, fraternity pledges must persevere through a variety of activities designed by the older members to test the limits of physical exertion, psychological strain, and social embarrassment. At week's end, the boys who have persisted through the ordeal are accepted for full group membership. Mostly their tribulations have left them no more than greatly tired and a bit shaky, although sometimes the negative effects are more serious.

What is interesting is how closely the particular features of Hell Week tasks match those of the tribal initiation rites. Recall that anthropologists identified six major trials to be endured by a Thonga initiate during his stay in the "yard of mysteries." A scan of newspaper reports show that each trial also has its place in the hazing rituals of Greek-letter societies.

Beatings. Fourteen-year-old Michael Kalogris spent three weeks in a Long Island hospital recovering from internal injuries suffered during a Hell Night initiation ceremony of his high-school fraternity, Omega Gamma Delta. He had been administered the "atomic bomb" by his prospective brothers, who told him to hold his hands over his head and keep them there while they gathered around to slam fists into his stomach and back simultaneously and repeatedly.

Exposure to cold. On a winter night, Frederick Bronner, a California junior-college student, was taken three thousand feet up and ten miles into the hills of a national forest by his prospective fraternity brothers. Left to

12. From Whiting, Kluckhohn, and Anthony (1958).

find his way home wearing only a thin sweat shirt and slacks, Fat Freddy, as he was called, shivered in a frigid wind until he tumbled down a steep ravine, fracturing bones and hurting his head. Prevented by his injuries from going on, he huddled there against the cold until he died of exposure.

Thirst. Two Ohio State University freshmen found themselves in the "dungeon" of their prospective fraternity house after breaking the rule requiring all pledges to crawl into the dining area prior to Hell Week meals. Once locked in the house storage closet, they were given only salty foods to eat for nearly two days. Nothing was provided for drinking purposes except a pair of plastic cups in which they could catch their own urine.

Eating of unsavory foods. At Kappa Sigma house on the campus of the University of Southern California, the eyes of eleven pledges bulged when they saw the sickening task before them. Eleven quarter-pound slabs of raw liver lay on a tray. Cut thick and soaked in oil, each was to be swallowed whole, one to a boy. Gagging and choking repeatedly, young Richard Swanson failed three times to down the piece. Determined to succeed, he finally got the oil-soaked meat into his throat where it lodged and, despite all efforts to remove it, killed him.

Punishment. In Wisconsin, a pledge who forgot one section of a ritual incantation to be memorized by all initiates was punished for his error. He was required to keep his feet under the rear legs of a folding chair while the heaviest of his fraternity brothers sat down and drank a beer. Although the pledge did not cry out during the punishment, a bone in each of his feet was broken.

Threats of death. A pledge of Zeta Beta Tau fraternity was taken to a beach area of New Jersey and told to dig his "own grave." Seconds after he complied with orders to lie flat in the finished hole, the sides collapsed, suffocating him before his prospective fraternity brothers could dig him out.

There is another striking similarity between the initiation rites of tribal and fraternal societies: They simply will not die. Resisting all attempts to eliminate or suppress them, such hazing practices have been phenomenally resilient. Authorities, in the form of colonial governments or university administrations, have tried threats, social pressures, legal actions, banishments, bribes, and bans to persuade the groups to remove the hazards and humiliations from their initiation ceremonies. None has been successful. Oh, there may be a change while the authority is watching closely. But this is usually more apparent than real, the harsher trials occurring under more secret circumstances until the pressure is off and they can surface again.

On some college campuses, officials have tried to eliminate dangerous hazing practices by substituting a "Help Week" of civic service or by taking direct control of the initiation rituals. When such attempts are not slyly circumvented by fraternities, they are met with outright physical resistance. For example, in the aftermath of Richard Swanson's choking death at USC, the university president issued new rules requiring that all pledging activities be reviewed by school authorities before going into effect and that adult advisers be present during initiation ceremonies. According to one national magazine, "The new 'code' set off a riot so violent that city police and fire detachments were afraid to enter campus."

Resigning themselves to the inevitable, other college representatives have given up on the possibility of abolishing the degradations of Hell Week. "If hazing is a universal human activity, and every bit of evidence points to this conclusion, you most likely won't be able to ban it effectively. Refuse to allow it openly and it will go underground. You can't ban sex, you can't prohibit alcohol, and you probably can't eliminate hazing!" [13]

What is it about hazing practices that make them so precious to these societies? What could make the groups want to evade, undermine, or contest any effort to ban the degrading and perilous features of their initiation rights? Some have argued that the groups themselves are composed of psychological or social miscreants whose twisted needs demand that others be harmed and humiliated. But the evidence does not support such a view. Studies done on the personality traits of fraternity members, for instance, show them to be, if anything, slightly healthier than other college students in their psychological adjustment. Similarly, fraternities are known for their willingness to engage in beneficial community projects for the general social good. What they are not willing to do, however, is substitute these projects for their initiation ceremonies. One survey at the University of Washington found that, of the fraternity chapters examined, most had a type of Help Week tradition but that this community service was in addition to Hell Week. In only one case was such service directly related to initiation procedures. [14]

The picture that emerges of the perpetrators of hazing practices is of normal individuals who tend to be psychologically stable and socially concerned but who become aberrantly harsh as a group at only one time— immediately before the admission of new members to the society. The evidence, then, points to the ceremony as the culprit. There must be something about its rigors that is vital to the group. There must be some function to its harshness that the group will fight relentlessly to maintain. What?

My own view is that the answer appeared in 1959 in the results of a study little known outside of social psychology. A pair of young researchers, Elliot Aronson and Judson Mills, decided to test their observation that "persons who go through a great deal of trouble or pain to attain something tend to value it more highly than persons who attain the same

13. From Gordon and Gordon (1963).
14. The survey was conducted by Walker (1967).

thing with a minimum of effort." The real stroke of inspiration came in their choice of the initiation ceremony as the best place to examine this possibility. They found that college women who had to endure a severely embarrassing initiation ceremony in order to gain access to a sex discussion group convinced themselves that their new group and its discussions were extremely valuable, even though Aronson and Mills had previously rehearsed the other group members to be as "worthless and uninteresting" as possible. Different coeds, who went through no initiation at all, were decidedly less positive about the "worthless" new group they had joined. Additional research showed the same results when coeds were required to endure pain rather than embarrassment to get into a group. The more electric shock a woman received as part of the initiation ceremony, the more she later persuaded herself that her new group and its activities were interesting, intelligent, and desirable.[15]

Now the harassments, the exertions, even the beatings of initiation rituals begin to make sense. The Thonga tribesman watching, with tears in his eyes, his ten-year-old son tremble through a night on the cold ground of the "year of mysteries," the college sophomore punctuating his Hell Night paddling of his fraternity "little brother" with bursts of nervous laughter, these are not acts of sadism. They are acts of group survival. They function, oddly enough, to spur future society members to find the group more attractive and worthwhile. As long as it is the case that people like and believe in what they have struggled to get, these groups will continue to arrange effortful and troublesome initiation rites. The loyalty and dedication of those who emerge will increase to a great degree the chances of group cohesiveness and survival. Indeed, one study of fifty-four tribal cultures found that those with the most dramatic and stringent initation ceremonies were those with the greatest group solidarity.[16] Given Aronson and Mills' demonstration that the severity of an initiation ceremony significantly heightens the newcomers' *commitment* to the group, it is hardly surprising that groups will oppose all attempts to eliminate this crucial link to their future strength.

The inner choice

Examination of such diverse activities as the indoctrination practices of the Chinese Communists and the initiation rituals of college fraternities has provided some valuable information about commitment. It appears that commitments are most effective in changing a person's self-image and future behavior when they are active, public, and effortful. But there is another property of effective commitment that is more important than the

15. The electric-shock experiment was published seven years after the Aronson and Mills (1959) study by Gerard and Mathewson (1966).

16. Young (1965) conducted this research.

other three combined. To understand what it is, we first need to solve a pair of puzzles in the actions of Communist interrogators and fraternity brothers.

The first puzzle comes from the refusal of fraternity chapters to allow public-service activities to be part of their initiation ceremonies. Recall that one survey showed that community projects, though frequent, were nearly always separated from the membership-induction program. But why? If an effortful commitment is what fraternities are after in their initiation rites, surely they could structure enough distasteful and strenuous civic activities for their pledges; there is plenty of exertion and unpleasantness to be had in the world of old-age-home repairs, mental-health-center yard work, and hospital bedpan duty. Besides, community-spirited endeavors of this sort would do much to improve the highly unfavorable public and media image of fraternity Hell Week rites; a survey showed that for every positive newspaper story concerning Hell Week, there were five negative stories. If only for public-relations reasons, then, fraternities should want to incorporate community-service efforts into their initiation practice. But they don't.

To examine the second puzzle, we need to return to the Chinese prison camps of Korea and the regular political essay contests held for American captives. The Chinese wanted as many Americans as possible to enter these contests so that, in the process, they might write things favorable to the Communist view. If, however, the idea was to attract large numbers of entrants, why were the prizes so small? A few extra cigarettes or a little fresh fruit were often all that a contest winner could expect. In the setting, even these prizes were valuable, but still there were much larger rewards—warm clothing, special mail privileges, increased freedom of movement in camp—that the Chinese could have used to increase the number of essay writers. Yet they specifically chose to employ the smaller rather than the larger, more motivating rewards.

Although the settings are quite different, the surveyed fraternities re-fused to allow civic activities into their initiation ceremonies for the same reason that the Chinese withheld large prizes in favor of less powerful inducements: They wanted the men to *own* what they had done. No excuses, no ways out were allowed. A man who suffered through an arduous hazing could not be given the chance to believe he did so for charitable purposes. A prisoner who salted his political essay with a few anti-American comments could not be permitted to shrug it off as motivated by a big reward. No, the fraternity chapters and Chinese Communists were playing for keeps. It was not enough to wring commitments out of their men; those men had to be made to take inner responsibility for their actions.

Social scientists have determined that we accept inner responsibility for a behavior when we think we have chosen to perform it in the absence of strong outside pressures. A large reward is one such external pressure. It may get us to perform a certain action, but it won't get us to accept inner responsibility for the act. Consequently, we won't feel committed to it. The same is true of a strong threat; it may motivate immediate compliance, but it is unlikely to produce long-term commitment.

All this has important implications for rearing children. It suggests that we should never heavily bribe or threaten our children to do the things we want them truly to believe in. Such pressures will probably produce temporary compliance with our wishes. However, is we want more than just that, if we want the children to believe in the correctness of what they have done, if we want them to continue to perform the desired behavior when we are not present to apply those outside pressures, then we must somehow arrange for them to accept inner responsibility for the actions we want them to take. An experiment by Jonathan Freedman gives us some hints about what to do and what not to do in this regard.

Freedman wanted to see if he could prevent second- to fourth-grade boys from playing with a fascinating toy, just because he had said that it was wrong to do so some six weeks earlier. Anyone familiar with seven-to-nine-year-old boys must realize the enormity of the task. But Freedman had a plan. If he could first get the boys to convince themselves that it was wrong to play with the forbidden toy, perhaps that belief would keep them from playing with it thereafter. The difficult thing was making the boys believe that it was wrong to amuse themselves with the toy—an extremely expensive, battery-controlled robot.

Freedman knew it would be easy enough to have a boy obey temporarily. All he had to do was threaten the boy with severe consequences should he be caught playing with the toy. As long as he was nearby to deal out stiff punishment, Freedman figured that few boys would risk operating the robot. He was right. After showing a boy an array of five toys and warning him, "It is wrong to play with the robot. If you play with the robot, I'll be very angry and will have to do something about it," Freedman left the room for a few minutes. During that time, the boy was observed secretly through a one-way mirror. Freedman tried this threat procedure on twenty-two different boys, and twenty-one of them never touched the robot while he was gone.

So a strong threat was successful while the boys thought they might be caught and punished. But Freedman had already guessed that. He was really interested in the effectiveness of the threat in guiding the boys' behavior later on, when he was no longer around. To find out what would happen then, he sent a young woman back to the boys' school about six weeks after he had been there. She took the boys out of the class one at a time to participate in an experiment. Without ever mentioning any connection with Freedman, she escorted each boy back to the room with the five toys and gave him a drawing test. While she was scoring the test, she told the boy that he was free to play with any toy in the room. Of course, almost all the boys played with a toy. The interesting result was that, of the boys playing with a toy, 77 percent chose to play with the robot that had been forbidden to them earlier. Freedman's severe threat, which had been so successful six weeks before, was almost totally unsuccessful when he was no longer able to back it up with punishment.

But Freedman wasn't finished yet. He changed his procedure slightly with a second sample of boys. These boys, too, were initially shown the array of five toys by Freedman and warned not to play with the robot while he was briefly out of the room because "It is wrong to play with the robot." But this time, Freedman provided no strong threat to frighten a boy into obedience. He simply left the room and observed through the one-way mirror to see if his instruction against playing with the forbidden toy was enough. It was. Just as with the other sample, only one of the twenty-two boys touched the robot during the short time Freedman was gone.

The real difference between the two samples of boys came six weeks later, when they had a chance to play with the toys while Freedman was no longer around. An astonishing thing happened with the boys who had earlier been given no strong threat against playing with the robot: When given the freedom to play with any toy they wished, most avoided the robot, even though it was by far the most attractive of the five toys available (the others were a cheap plastic submarine, a child's baseball glove without a ball, an unloaded toy rifle, and a toy tractor). When these boys played with one of the five toys, only 33 percent chose the robot.

Something dramatic had happened to both groups of boys. For the first group, it was the severe threat they heard from Freedman to back up his statement that playing with the robot was "wrong." It had been quite effective at first, while Freedman could catch them should they violate his rule. Later, though, when he was no longer present to observe the boys' behavior, his threat was impotent and his rule was, consequently, ignored. It seems clear that the threat had not taught the boys that operating the robot was wrong, only that it was unwise to do so when the possibility of punishment existed.

For the other boys, the dramatic event had come from the inside, not the outside. Freedman had instructed them, too, that playing with the robot was wrong, but he had added no threat of punishment should they disobey him. There were two important results. First, Freedman's instruction alone was enough to prevent the boys from operating the robot while he was briefly out of the room. Second, the boys took personal responsibility for their choice to stay away from the robot during that time. They decided that they hadn't played with it because *they* didn't want to. After all, there were no strong punishments associated with the toy to explain their behavior otherwise. Thus, weeks later, when Freedman was nowhere around, they still ignored the robot because they had been changed inside to believe that they did not want to play with it.[17]

---

17. The robot study is reported fully in Freedman (1965).

Adults facing the child-rearing experience can take a cue from the Freed-man study. Suppose a couple wants to impress upon their daughter that lying is wrong. A strong, clear threat ("It's bad to lie, honey; so if I catch you at it, I'll cut your tongue out") might well be effective when the parents are present or when the girl thinks she can be discovered. But it will not achieve the larger goal of convincing her that she does not want to lie because *she* thinks it's wrong. To do that, a much subtler approach is required. A reason must be given that is just strong enough to get her to be truthful most of the time but is not so strong that she sees *it* as the obvious reason for her truthfulness. It's a tricky business because exactly what this barely sufficient reason will be changes from child to child. For one little girl, a simple appeal may be enough ("It's bad to lie, honey; so I hope you won't do it"); for another child, it may be necessary to add a somewhat stronger reason (" . . . because if you do, I'll be disappointed in you"); for a third child, a mild form of warning may be required as well (" . . . and I'll probably have to do something I don't want to do"). Wise parents will know which kind of reason will work on their own children. The important thing is to use a reason that will initially produce the desired behavior and will, at the same time, allow a child to take personal responsibility for that behavior. Thus, the less detectable outside pressure such a reason contains, the better. Selecting just the right reason is not an easy task for parents. But the effort should pay off. It is likely to mean the difference between short-lived compliance and long-term commitment.

For a pair of reasons we have already talked about, compliance professionals love commitments that produce inner change. First, that change is not just specific to the situation where it first occurred; it covers a whole range of related situations, too. Second, the effects of the change are lasting. So, once a man has been induced to take action that shifts his self-image to that of, let's say, a public-spirited citizen, he is likely to be public-spirited in a variety of other circumstances where his compliance may also be desired, and he is likely to continue his public-spirited behavior for as long as his new self-image holds.

There is yet another attraction in commitments that lead to inner change—they grow their own legs. There is no need for the compliance professional to undertake a costly and continuing effort to reinforce the change; the pressure for consistency will take care of all that. After our friend comes to view himself as a public-spirited citizen, he will automatically begin to see things differently. He will convince himself that it is the correct way to be. He will begin to pay attention to facts he hadn't noticed before about the value of community service. He will make himself available to hear arguments he hadn't heard before favoring civic action. And he will find such arguments more persuasive than before. In general, because of the need to be consistent within his system of beliefs, he will assure himself that his choice to take public-spirited action was right. What is important about this process of generating additional reasons to justify the commitment is that the reasons are *new*. Thus, even if the original reason for the civic-minded behavior was taken away, these newly discovered reasons might be enough by themselves to support his perception that he had behaved correctly.

The advantage to an unscrupulous compliance professional is tremendous. Because we build new struts to undergird choices we have committed ourselves to, an exploitative individual can offer us an inducement for making such a choice, and after the decision has been made, can remove that inducement, knowing that our decision will probably stand on its own newly created legs. New-car dealers frequently try to benefit from this process through a trick they call "throwing a low-ball." I first encountered the tactic while posing as a sales trainee at a local Chevrolet dealership. After a week of basic instruction, I was allowed to watch the regular salesmen perform. One practice that caught my attention right away was the low-ball.

For certain customers, a very good price is offered on a car, perhaps as much as four hundred dollars below competitors' prices. The good deal, however, is not genuine; the dealer never intends it to go through. Its only purpose is to cause a prospect to *decide* to buy one of the dealership's cars. Once the decision is made, a number of activities develop the customer's sense of personal commitment to the car—a raft of purchase forms are filled out, extensive financing terms are arranged, sometimes the customer is encouraged to drive the car for a day before signing the contract, "so you can get the feel of it and show it around in the neighborhood and at work." During this time, the dealer knows, customers automatically develop a range of new reasons to support the choice they have now made.

Then something happens. Occasionally an "error" in the calculations is discovered—maybe the salesman forgot to add in the cost of the air conditioner, and if the buyer still requires air conditioning, four hundred dollars must be added to the price. To throw suspicion off themselves, some dealers let the bank handling the financing find the mistake. At other times, the deal is disallowed at the last moment when the salesman checks with his boss, who cancels it because "We'd be losing money." For only another four hundred dollars the car can be had, which, in the context of a multithousand-dollar deal, doesn't seem too steep since, as the salesman emphasizes, the cost is equal to competitors' and "This is the car you chose, right?" Another, even more insidious form of low-balling occurs when the salesman makes an inflated trade-in offer on the prospect's old car as part of the buy/trade package. The customer recognizes the offer as overly generous and jumps at the deal. Later, before the contract is signed, the used-car manager says that the salesman's estimate was four hundred dollars too high and reduces the trade-in allowance to its actual, blue-book level. The customer, realizing that the reduced offer is the fair one, accepts it as appropriate and sometimes feels guilty about trying to take advantage of the salesman's high estimate. I once witnessed a woman provide an embarrassed apology to a salesman who had used the last version of low-balling on her—this while she was signing a new-car contract giving him a huge commission. He looked hurt but managed a forgiving smile.

No matter which variety of low-balling is used, the sequence is the same: An advantage is offered that induces a favorable purchase decision; then, sometime after the decision has been made but before the bargain is sealed, the original purchase advantage is deftly removed. It seems almost incredible that a customer would buy a car under these circumstances. Yet it works—not on everybody, of course, but it is effective enough to be a staple compliance procedure in many, many car showrooms. Automobile dealers have come to understand the ability of a personal commitment to build its own support system, a support system of new justifications for the commitment. Often these justifications provide so many strong legs for the decision to stand on that when the dealer pulls away only one leg, the original one, there is no collapse. The loss can be shrugged off by the customer who is consoled, even made happy, by the array of other good reasons favoring the choice. It never occurs to the buyer that those additional reasons might never have existed had the choice not been made in the first place.[18]

The impressive thing about the low-ball tactic is its ability to make a person feel pleased with a poor choice. Those who have only poor choices to offer us, then, are especially fond of the technique. We can find them throwing low-balls in business, social, and personal situations. For instance, there's my neighbor Tim, a true low-ball aficionado. Recall that he's the one who, by promising to change his ways, got his girlfriend, Sara, to cancel her impending marriage to another and to take him back. Since her decision for Tim, Sara has become more devoted to him than ever, even though he has not fulfilled his promises. She explains this by saying that she has allowed herself to see all sorts of positive qualities in Tim she had never recognized before.

I know full well that Sara is a low-ball victim. Just as sure as I had watched buyers fall for the give-it-and-take-it-away-later strategy in the car showroom, I watched her fall for the same trick with Tim. For his part, Tim remains the guy he has always been. But because the new attractions Sara has discovered (or created) in him are quite real for her, she now seems satisfied with the same arrangement that was unacceptable before her enormous commitment. The decision to choose Tim, poor as it may have been objectively, has grown its own supports and appears to have made Sara genuinely happy. I have never mentioned to Sara what I know about low-balling. The reason for my silence is not that I think her better off in the dark on the issue. As a general guiding principle, more informa-

18. The reader who wishes stronger evidence for the action of the low-ball tactic than my subjective observations in the car showroom may refer to a pair of articles that attest to its effectiveness under controlled, experimental conditions: Cialdini et al. (1978) and Burger and Petty (1981).

tion is always better than less information. It's just that, if I said a word, I am confident she would hate me for it.

Depending on the motives of the person wishing to use them, any of the compliance techniques discussed in this book can be employed for good or for ill. It should not be surprising, then, that the low-ball tactic can be used for more socially beneficial purposes than selling new cars or reestablishing relationships with former lovers. One research project done in Iowa, for example, shows how the low-ball procedure can influence homeowners to conserve energy.[19] The project, headed by Dr. Michael Pallak, began at the start of the Iowa winter when residents who heated their homes with natural gas were contacted by an interviewer. The interviewer gave them some energy-conservation tips and asked them to try to save fuel in the future. Although they all agreed to try, when the researchers examined the utility records of these families after a month and again at winter's end, it was clear that no real savings had occurred. The residents who had promised to make a conservation attempt used just as much natural gas as a random sample of their neighbors who had not been contacted by an interviewer. Just good intentions coupled with information about saving fuel, then, were not enough to change habits.

Even before the project began, Pallak and his research team had recognized that something more would be needed to shift long-standing energy patterns. So they tried a slightly different procedure on a comparable sample of Iowa natural-gas users. These people, too, were contacted by an interviewer, who provided energy-saving hints and asked them to conserve. But for these families, the interviewer offered something else: Those residents agreeing to save energy would have their names publicized in newspaper articles as public-spirited, fuel-conserving citizens. The effect was immediate. One month later, when the utility companies checked their meters, the homeowners in this sample had saved an average of 422 cubic feet of natural gas apiece. The chance to have their names in the paper had motivated these residents to substantial conservation efforts for a period of a month.

Then the rug was pulled out. The researchers extracted the reason that had initially caused these people to save fuel. Each family that had been promised publicity received a letter saying it would not be possible to publicize their names after all.

At the end of the winter, the research team examined the effect that letter had had on the natural-gas usage of the families. Did they return to their old, wasteful habits when the chance to be in the newspaper was removed? Hardly. For each of the remaining winter months, they actually conserved *more* fuel than they had during the time they thought they would be publicly celebrated for it! In terms of percentage of energy savings, they

19. A formal report of the energy-conservation project appears in Pallak et al. (1980).

had managed a 12.2 percent first-month gas savings because they expected to see themselves lauded in the paper. But after the letter arrived informing them to the contrary, they did not return to their previous energy-use levels; instead, they increased their savings to a 15.5 percent level for the rest of the winter.

Although we can never be completely sure of such things, one explanation for their persistent behavior presents itself immediately. These people had been low-balled into a conservation commitment through a promise of newspaper publicity. Once made, that commitment started generating its own support: The homeowners began acquiring new energy habits, began feeling good about their public-spirited efforts, began convincing themselves of the vital need to reduce American dependence on foreign fuel, began appreciating the monetary savings in their utility bills, began feeling proud of their capacity for self-denial, and, most important, began viewing themselves as conservation-minded. With all these new reasons present to justify the commitment to use less energy, it is no wonder that the commitment remained firm even after the original reason, newspaper publicity, had been kicked away.

But strangely enough, when the publicity factor was no longer a possibility, these families did not merely maintain their fuel-saving effort, they heightened it. Any of a number of interpretations could be offered for that still stronger effort, but I have a favorite. In a way, the opportunity to receive newspaper publicity had prevented the homeowners from fully owning their commitment to conservation. Of all the reasons supporting the decision to try to save fuel, it was the only one that had come from the outside; it was the only one preventing the homeowners from thinking that they were conserving gas because they believed in it. So when the letter arrived canceling the publicity agreement, it removed the only impediment to these residents' images of themselves as fully concerned, energy-conscious citizens. This unqualified, new self-image then pushed them to even greater heights of conservation. Whether or not such an explanation is correct, a repeat study done by Pallak indicates that this hidden benefit of the low-ball tactic is no fluke.

The experiment was done in summer on Iowans whose homes were cooled by central air conditioning. Those homeowners who were promised newspaper publicity decreased their electricity use by 27.8 percent during July, as compared to similar homeowners who were not promised any coverage or who were not contacted at all. At the end of July, a letter was sent canceling the publicity promise. Rather than reverting to their old habits, the low-balled residents increased their August energy savings to a stunning 41.6 percent. Much like Sara, they appeared to have become committed to a choice through an initial inducement and were still more dedicated to it after the inducement had been removed.

How to say no

"Consistency is the hobgoblin of little minds." Or, at least, so goes a frequently heard quotation attributed to Ralph Waldo Emerson. But what a very odd thing to say. Looking around, it is obvious that, quite contrary to what Emerson seems to have suggested, internal consistency is a hallmark of logic and intellectual strength, while its lack characterizes the intellectually scattered and limited among us. What, then, could a thinker of Emerson's caliber have meant when he assigned the trait of consistency to the small-minded? I was sufficiently intrigued to go back to the original source of his statement, the essay "Self-Reliance," where it was clear that the problem lay not in Emerson but in the popular version of what he had said. Actually he wrote, "A *foolish* consistency is the hobgoblin of little minds." For some obscure reason, a central distinction had been lost as the years eroded the accurate version of his statement to mean something entirely different and, upon close inspection, entirely silly.[20]

That distinction should not be lost on us, however, because it is vital to the only effective defense I know against the weapons of influence embodied in the combined principles of commitment and consistency. Although consistency is generally good, even vital, there is a foolish, rigid variety to be shunned. It is this tendency to be automatically and unthinkingly consistent that Emerson referred to. And it is this tendency that we must be wary of, for it lays us open to the maneuvers of those who want to exploit the mechanical commitment → consistency sequence for profit.

But since automatic consistency is so useful in allowing us an economical and appropriate way of behaving most of the time, we can't decide merely to eliminate it from our lives altogether. The results would be disastrous. If, rather than whirring along in accordance with our prior decisions and deeds, we stopped to think through the merits of every new action before performing it, we would never have time to accomplish anything significant. We need even that dangerous, mechanical brand of consistency. The only way out of the dilemma is to know when such consistency is likely to lead to a poor choice. There are certain signals—two separate kinds of signals, in fact—to tip us off. We register each type in a different part of our bodies.

The first sort of signal is easy to recognize. It occurs right in the pit of our stomachs when we realize we are trapped into complying with a request we *know* we don't want to perform. It has happened to me a hundred

20. It is not altogether unusual for even some of our most familiar quotations to be truncated by time in ways that greatly modify their character. For example, it is not *money* that the Bible claims as the root of all evil, it is *the love of money*. So as not to be guilty of the same sort of error myself, I should note that the Emerson quote from "Self-reliance" is somewhat longer and substantially more textured than I have reported. In full, it reads, "A foolish consistency is the hobgoblin of little minds adored by little statesmen, and philosophers, and divines."

times. An especially memorable instance, though, took place on a summer evening well before I began to study compliance tactics. I answered my doorbell to find a stunning young woman dressed in shorts and a revealing halter top. I noticed, nonetheless, that she was carrying a clipboard and was asking me to participate in a survey. Wanting to make a favorable impression, I agreed and, I do admit, stretched the truth in my interview answers so as to present myself in the most positive light. Our conversation went as follows:

STUNNING YOUNG WOMAN: Hello, I'm doing a survey on the entertainment habits of city residents, and I wonder if you could answer a few questions for me.

CIALDINI: Do come in.

SYW: Thank you. I'll just sit right here and begin. How many times per week would you say that you go out to dinner?

C: Oh, probably three, maybe four times a week. Whenever I can, really; I love fine restaurants.

SYW: How nice. And do you usually order wine with your dinner?

C: Only if it's imported.

SYW: I see. What about movies? Do you go to the movies much?

C: The cinema? I can't get enough of good films. I especially like the sophisticated kind with the words on the bottom of the screen. How about you? Do you like to see films?

SYW: Uh . . . yes, I do. But let's get back to the interview. Do you go to many concerts?

C: Definitely. The symphonic stuff mostly, of course; but I do enjoy a quality pop group as well.

SYW *(writing rapidly):* Great! Just one more question. What about touring performances by theatrical or ballet companies? Do you see them when they're in town?

C: Ah, the ballet—the movement, the grace, the form—I love it. Mark me down as *loving* the ballet. See it every chance I get.

SYW: Fine. Just let me recheck my figures here for a moment, Mr. Cialdini.

C: Actually, it's Dr. Cialdini. But that sounds so formal; why don't you call me Bob?

SYW: All right, *Bob.* From the information you've already given me, I'm pleased to say that you could save up to twelve hundred dollars a year by joining Clubamerica! A small membership fee entitles you to discounts on most of the activities you've mentioned. Surely someone as socially vigorous as yourself would want to take advantage of the tremendous savings our company can offer on all the things you've already told me you do.

C *(trapped like a rat):* Well . . . uh . . . I . . . uh . . . I guess so.

I remember quite well feeling my stomach tighten as I stammered my agreement. It was a clear call to my brain, "Hey, you're being taken here!" But I couldn't see a way out. I had been cornered by my own words. To decline her offer at that point would have meant facing a pair of distasteful alternatives: If I tried to back out by protesting that I was not actually the man-about-town I had claimed to be during the interview, I would come off a liar; but trying to refuse without that protest would make me come off a fool for not wanting to save twelve hundred dollars. So I bought the entertainment package, even though I knew I had been set up so that the need to be consistent with what I had already said would snare me.

No more, though. I listen to my stomach these days. And I have discovered a way to handle people who try to use the consistency principle on me. I just tell them exactly what they are doing. It works beautifully. Most of the time, they don't understand me; they just become sufficiently confused to want to leave me alone. I think they suspect lunacy in anyone who responds to their requests by explaining what Ralph Waldo Emerson meant in distinguishing between consistency and foolish consistency. Usually they have already begun edging away by the time I have mentioned "hobgoblins of the mind" and are gone long before I have described the *click, whirr* character of commitment and consistency. Occasionally, though, they realize that I am on to their game. I always know when that happens—it's as clear as the egg on their faces. They invariably become flustered, bumble through a hasty exit line, and go for the door.

This tactic has become the perfect counterattack for me. Whenever my stomach tells me I would be a sucker to comply with a request merely because doing so would be consistent with some prior commitment I was tricked into, I relay that message to the requester. I don't try to deny the importance of consistency; I just point out the absurdity of foolish consistency. Whether, in response, the requester shrinks away guiltily or retreats in bewilderment, I am content. I have won; an exploiter has lost.

I sometimes think about how it would be if that stunning young woman of years ago were to try to sell me an entertainment-club membership now. I have it all worked out. The entire interaction would be the same, except for the end:

SYW: . . . Surely someone as socially vigorous as yourself would want to take advantage of the tremendous savings our company can offer on all the things you've already told me you do.

C (*with great self-assurance*): Quite wrong. You see, I recognize what has gone on here. I know that your story about doing a survey was just a pretext for getting people to tell you how often they go out and that, under those circumstances, there is a natural tendency to exaggerate. I also realize that your bosses selected you for this job because of your physical attractiveness and told you to wear clothes showing a lot of your resilient body tissue because a pretty, scantily clad woman is likely to get men to brag about what swingers they are in order to impress her. So I'm not interested in your entertainment club because of what Emerson said about foolish consistency and hobgoblins of the mind.

SYW (*staring blankly*): *Huh?*

C: Look. What I told you during your fake survey doesn't matter. I refuse to allow myself to be locked into a mechanical sequence of commitment and consistency when I know it's wrongheaded. No *click, whirr* for me.

SYW: Huh?

C: Okay, let me put it this way: (1) It would be stupid of me to spend money on something I don't want. (2) I have it on excellent authority, direct from my stomach, that I don't want your entertainment plan. (3) Therefore, if you still believe that I will buy it, you probably also still believe in the Tooth Fairy. Surely, someone as intelligent as yourself would be able to understand that.

SYW (*trapped like a stunning young rat*): Well . . . uh . . . I . . . uh . . . I guess so.

Stomachs are not especially perceptive or subtle organs. Only when it is obvious that we are about to be conned are they likely to register and transmit that message. At other times, when it is not clear that we are being taken, our stomachs may never catch on. Under those circumstances we have to look elsewhere for a clue. The situation of my neighbor Sara provides a good illustration. She made an important commitment to Tim by canceling her prior marriage plans. That commitment has grown its own supports, so that even though the original reasons for the commitment are gone, she remains in harmony with it. She has convinced herself with newly formed reasons that she did the right thing, so she stays with Tim. It is not difficult to see why there would be no tightening in Sara's stomach as a result. Stomachs tell us when we are doing something we think is wrong for us. Sara *thinks* no such thing. To her mind, she has chosen correctly and is behaving consistently with that choice.

Yet, unless I badly miss my guess, there is a part of Sara that recognizes her choice as a mistake and her current living arrangement as a brand of foolish consistency. Where, exactly, that part of Sara is located we can't be sure. But our language does give it a name: heart of hearts. It is, by definition, the one place where we cannot fool ourselves. It is the place where none of our justifications, none of our rationalizations penetrate. Sara has the truth there, although, right now, she can't hear its signal clearly through the noise and static of the new support apparatus she has erected.

If Sara has erred in her choice of Tim, how long could she go without clearly recognizing it, without having a massive heart of hearts attack?

There is no telling. One thing is certain, however: As time passes, the various alternatives to Tim are disappearing. She had better determine soon whether she is making a mistake.

Easier said than done, of course. She must answer an extremely intricate question: "Knowing what I now know, if I could go back in time, would I make the same choice?" The problem lies in the "Knowing what I now know" part of the question. Just what does she now know, accurately, about Tim? How much of what she thinks of him is the result of a desperate attempt to justify the commitment she made? She claims that, since her decision to take him back, he cares for her more, is trying hard to stop his excessive drinking, has learned to make a wonderful omelet, etc. Having tasted a couple of his omelets, I have my doubts. The important issue, though, is whether *she* believes these things, not just intellectually—we can play such mind games on ourselves—but in her heart of hearts.

There may be a little device Sara can use to find out how much of her current satisfaction with Tim is real and how much is foolish consistency. Accumulating psychological evidence indicates that we experience our feelings toward something a split second before we can intellectualize about it.[21] My suspicion is that the message sent by the heart of hearts is a pure, basic feeling. Therefore, if we train ourselves to be attentive, we should register it ever so slightly before our cognitive apparatus engages. According to this approach, were Sara to ask herself the crucial "Would I make the same choice again?" question, she would be well advised to look for and trust the first flash of feeling she experienced in response. It would likely be the signal from her heart of hearts, slipping through undistorted just before the means by which she could kid herself flooded in.[22]

I have begun using the same device myself whenever I even suspect I might be acting in a foolishly consistent manner. One time, for instance, I had stopped at the self-service pump of a filling station advertising a price per gallon a couple of cents below the rate of other stations in the area. But with pump nozzle in hand, I noticed that the price listed on the pump was two cents higher than the display sign price. When I mentioned the difference to a passing attendant, who I later learned was the owner, he mumbled unconvincingly that the rates had changed a few days ago but there hadn't been time to correct the display. I tried to decide what to do. Some reasons for staying came to mind—"I really do need gasoline badly." "This pump is available, and I am in sort of a hurry." "I think I remember that my car runs better on this brand of gas."

21. See Zajonc (1980) for a summary of this evidence.
22. This is not to say that what we feel about an issue is always different from or always to be trusted more than what we think about it. However, the data are clear that our emotions and beliefs often do not point in the same direction. Therefore, in situations involving a decisional commitment likely to have generated supporting rationalizations, feelings may well provide the truer counsel. This would be especially so when, as in the question of Sara's happiness, the fundamental issue at hand concerns an emotion.

I needed to determine whether those reasons were genuine or mere justifications for my decision to stop there. So I asked myself the crucial question, "Knowing what I know about the real price of this gasoline, if I could go back in time, would I make the same choice again?" Concentrating on the first burst of impression I sensed, the answer was clear and unqualified. I would have driven right past. I wouldn't even have slowed down. I knew then that without the price advantage, those other reasons would not have brought me there. They hadn't created the decision; the decision had created them.

That settled, there was another decision to be faced, though. Since I was already there holding the hose, wouldn't it be better to use it than to suffer the inconvenience of going elsewhere to pay the same price? Fortunately, the station attendant-owner came over and helped me make up my mind. He asked why I wasn't pumping the gas. I told him I didn't like the price discrepancy and he said with a snarl, "Listen, nobody's gonna tell me how to run my business. If you think I'm cheating you, just put that hose down *right now* and get off my property as fast as you can do it, bud." Already certain he was a cheat, I was happy to act consistently with my belief and his wishes. I dropped the hose on the spot . . . and drove over it on my way to the closest exit. Sometimes consistency can be a marvelously rewarding thing.

References

Aronson, E., and J. Mills. 1959. The effect of severity of initiation on liking for a group. *Journal of Abnormal and Social Psychology* 59: 177–81.

Burger, J. M., and R. E. Petty. 1981. The low-ball compliance technique: Task or person commitment? *Journal of Personality and Social Psychology* 40:492–500.

Cialdini, R. B., et al. 1978. The low-ball procedure for producing compliance: Commitment, then cost. *Journal of Personality and Social Psychology* 36:463–76.

Deutsch, M., and H. B. Gerard. 1955. A study of normative and informational social influences upon individual judgment. *Journal of Abnormal and Social Psychology* 51:629–36.

Freeman, J. L. 1965. Long-term behavioral effects of cognitive dissonance. *Journal of Experimental Social Psychology* 1:145–55.

Freeman, J. L., and S. C. Fraser. 1966. Compliance without pressure: The foot-in-the-door technique. *Journal of Personality and Social Psychology* 4:195–203.

Gerard, H. B., and G. C. Mathewson. 1966. The effects of severity of initiation and liking for a group: A replication. *Journal of Experimental Social Psychology* 2:278–87.

Gordon, R. E., and K. Gordon. 1963. *The Blight on the Ivy.* Englewood Cliffs, N.J.: Prentice-Hall.

Green, F. 1965. The "foot-in-the-door" technique. *American Salesman* 10:14–16.

Jones, E. E., and V. E. Harris. 1967. The attribution of attitudes. *Journal of Experimental Social Psychology* 3:1–24.

Knox, R. E., and J. A. Inkster. 1968. Postdecisional dissonance at post time. *Journal of Personality and Social Psychology* 8:319–23.

Kraut, R. E. 1973. Effects of social labeling on giving to charity. *Journal of Experimental Social Psychology* 9:551–62.

Pallak, M. S., D. A. Cook, and J. J. Sullivan. 1980. Commitment and energy conservation. *Applied Social Psychology Annual* 1:235–53.

Schein, E. 1956. The Chinese indoctrination program for prisoners of war: A study of attempted "brainwashing." *Psychiatry* 19:149–72.

Segal, H. A. 1954. Initial psychiatric findings of recently repatriated prisoners of war. *American Journal of Psychiatry* 61:358–63.

Walker, M. G. 1967. Organizational type, rites of incorporation, and group solidarity: A study of fraternity Hell Week. University of Washington, Seattle, Ph.D. diss.

Whiting, J. W. M., R. Kluckhohn, and A. Anthony. 1958. The function of male initiation ceremonies at puberty. In *Readings in Social Psychology,* ed. E. E. Maccoby, T. M. Newcomb, and E. L. Hartley. New York: Holt.

Young, F. W. 1965. *Initiation Ceremonies.* New York: Bobbs-Merrill.

Zajonc, R. B. 1980. Feeling and thinking: Preferences need no inferences. *American Psychologist* 35:151–75.

Training the Woman to Know Her Place: The Power of a Nonconscious Ideology

Sandra L. Bem and
Daryl J. Bem

In the beginning God created the heaven and the earth. . . . And God said, Let us make man in our image, after our likeness; and let them have dominion over the fish of the sea, and over the fowl of the air, and over the cattle, and over all the earth. . . . And the rib, which the Lord God had taken from man, made he a woman and brought her unto the man. . . . And the Lord God said unto the woman, What is this that thou has done? And the woman said, The serpent beguiled me, and I did eat. . . . Unto the woman He said, I will greatly multiply thy sorrow and thy conception; in sorrow thou shalt bring forth children; and thy desire shall be to thy husband, and he shall rule over thee. [Gen. 1, 2, 3]

And lest anyone fail to grasp the moral of this story, Saint Paul provides further clarification:

For a man . . . is the image and glory of God; but the woman is the glory of the man. For the man is not of the woman, but the woman of the man. Neither was the man created for the woman, but the woman for the man. [1 Cor. 11]

Let the woman learn in silence with all subjection. But I suffer not a woman to teach, nor to usurp authority over the man, but to be in silence. For Adam was first formed, then Eve. And Adam was not deceived, but the woman, being deceived, was in the transgression. Notwithstanding, she shall be saved in childbearing, if they continue in faith and charity and holiness with sobriety. [1 Tim. 2]

And lest it be thought that only Christians have this rich heritage of ideology about women, consider the morning prayer of the Orthodox Jew:

Adapted from S. L. Bem and D. J. Bem, "Case Study of a Nonconscious Ideology: Training the Woman to Know Her Place," in D. J. Bem, *Beliefs, Attitudes, and Human Affairs,* © 1970 by Wadsworth Publishing Company, Inc. Reprinted by permission of the publisher, Brooks/Cole Publishing Company, Monterey, California.
Order of authorship determined by the flip of a coin.

Blessed art Thou, oh Lord our God, King of the Universe, that I was
not born a gentile.
Blessed art Thou, oh Lord our God, King of the Universe, that I was
not born a slave.
Blessed art Thou, oh Lord our God, King of the Universe, that I was
not born a woman.

Or the Koran, the sacred text of Islam:

Men are superior to women on account of the qualities in which God
has given them preeminence.

Because they think they sense a decline in feminine "faith, charity, and
holiness with sobriety," many people today jump to the conclusion that the
ideology expressed in these passages is a relic of the past. Not so. It has
simply been obscured by an equalitarian veneer, and the ideology has now
become nonconscious. That is, we remain unaware of it because alternative
beliefs and attitudes about women go unimagined. We are like the fish who
is unaware that his environment is wet. After all, what else could it be?
Such is the nature of all nonconscious ideologies. Such is the nature of
America's ideology about women. For even those Americans who agree
that a black skin should not uniquely qualify its owner for janitorial or domestic service continue to act as if the possession of a uterus uniquely
qualifies *its* owner for precisely that.

Consider, for example, the 1968 student rebellion at Columbia University. Students from the radical left took over some administration buildings
in the name of equalitarian principles which they accused the university of
flouting. Here were the most militant spokesmen one could hope to find in
the cause of equalitarian ideals. But no sooner had they occupied the buildings than the male militants blandly turned to their sisters-in-arms and assigned them the task of preparing the food, while they—the menfolk—
would presumably plan further strategy. The reply these males received
was the reply they deserved, and the fact that domestic tasks behind the
barricades were desegregated across the sex line that day is an everlasting
tribute to the class consciousness of the ladies of the left.

But these conscious coeds are not typical, for the nonconscious assumptions about a woman's "natural" talents (or lack of them) are at least as
prevalent among women as they are among men. A psychologist named
Philip Goldberg[1] demonstrated this by asking female college students to
rate a number of professional articles from each of six fields. The articles
were collated into two equal sets of booklets, and the names of the authors
were changed so that the identical article was attributed to a male author
(e.g., John T. McKay) in one set of booklets and to a female author (e.g.,

1. P. Goldberg, "Are Women Prejudiced against Women?" *Transaction* 5 (April 1968):
28–30.

Joan T. McKay) in the other set. Each student was asked to read the articles in her booklet and to rate them for value, competence, persuasiveness, writing style, and so forth.

As he had anticipated, Goldberg found that the identical article received significantly lower ratings when it was attributed to a female author than when it was attributed to a male author. He had predicted this result for articles from professional fields generally considered the province of men, like law and city planning, but to his surprise, these coeds also downgraded articles from the fields of dietetics and elementary school education when they were attributed to female authors. In other words, these students rated the male authors as better at everything, agreeing with Aristotle that "we should regard the female nature as afflicted with a natural defectiveness." We repeated this experiment informally in our own classrooms and discovered that male students show the same implicit prejudice against female authors that Goldberg's female students showed. Such is the nature of a nonconscious ideology!

It is significant that examples like these can be drawn from the college world, for today's students have challenged the established ways of looking at almost every other issue, and they have been quick to reject those practices of our society which conflict explicitly with their major values. But as the above examples suggest, they will find it far more difficult to shed the more subtle aspects of a sex-role ideology which—as we shall now attempt to demonstrate—conflicts just as surely with their existential values as any of the other societal practices to which they have so effectively raised objection. And as we shall see, there is no better way to appreciate the power of a society's nonconscious ideology than to examine it within the framework of values held by that society's avant-garde.

Individuality and self-fulfillment

The dominant values of today's students concern personal growth on the one hand, and interpersonal relationships on the other. The first of these emphasizes individuality and self-fulfillment; the second stresses openness, honesty, and equality in all human relationships.

The values of individuality and self-fulfillment imply that each human being, male or female, is to be encouraged to "do his own thing." Men and women are no longer to be stereotyped by society's definitions. If sensitivity, emotionality, and warmth are desirable human characteristics, then they are desirable for men as well as for women. (John Wayne is no longer an idol of the young, but their pop-art satire). If independence, assertiveness, and serious intellectual commitment are desirable human characteristics, then they are desirable for women as well as for men. The major prescription of this college generation is that each individual should be encouraged to discover and fulfill his own unique potential and identity, unfettered by society's presumptions.

But society's presumptions enter the scene much earlier than most people suspect, for parents begin to raise their children in accord with the popular stereotypes from the very first. Boys are encouraged to be aggressive, competitive, and independent, whereas girls are rewarded for being passive and dependent.[2] In one study, six-month-old infant girls were already being touched and spoken to more by their mothers while they were playing than were infant boys. When they were thirteen months old, these same girls were more reluctant than the boys to leave their mothers; they returned more quickly and more frequently to them; and they remained closer to them throughout the entire play period. When a physical barrier was placed between mother and child, the girls tended to cry and motion for help; the boys made more active attempts to get around the barrier.[3] No one knows to what extent these sex differences at the age of thirteen months can be attributed to the mothers' behavior when the child was six months, but it is hard to believe that the two are unconnected.

As children grow older, more explicit sex-role training is introduced. Boys are encouraged to take more of an interest in mathematics and science. Boys, not girls, are given chemistry sets and microscopes for Christmas. Moreover, all children quickly learn that mommy is proud to be a moron when it comes to mathematics and science, whereas daddy knows all about these things. When a young boy returns from school all excited about biology, he is almost certain to be encouraged to think of becoming a physician. A girl with similar enthusiasm is told that she might want to consider nurse's training later so she can have "an interesting job to fall back upon in case—God forbid—she ever needs to support herself." A very different kind of encouragement. And any girl who doggedly persists in her enthusiasm for science is likely to find her parents as horrified by the prospect of a permanent love affair with physics as they would be by the prospect of an interracial marriage.

These socialization practices quickly take their toll. By nursery school age, for example, boys are already asking more questions about how and why things work.[4] In first and second grade, when asked to suggest ways of improving various toys, boys do better on the fire truck and girls do better on the nurse's kit, but by the third grade, boys do better regardless of the toy presented.[5] By the ninth grade, 25 percent of the boys, but only 3 per-

2. H. Barry III, M. K. Bacon, and I. L. Child, "A Cross-cultural Survey of Some Sex Differences in Socialization," *Journal of Abnormal and Social Psychology* 55 (1957): 327–32; R. R. Sears, E. E. Maccoby, and H. Levin, *Patterns of Child Rearing* (Evanston, Ill.: Row, Peterson, 1957).

3. S. Goldberg and M. Lewis, "Play Behavior in the Year-old Infant: Early Sex Differences," *Child Development* 40 (1969): 21–31.

4. M. E. Smith, "The Influence of Age, Sex, and Situation on the Frequency of Form and Functions of Questions Asked by Preschool Children," *Child Development* 3 (1933): 201–13.

5. E. P. Torrance, *Guiding Creative Talent* (Englewood Cliffs, N.J.: Prentice-Hall, 1962).

cent of the girls, are considering careers in science or engineering.[6] When they apply for college, boys and girls are about equal on verbal aptitude tests, but boys score significantly higher on mathematical aptitude tests—about sixty points higher on the College Board examinations, for example.[7] Moreover, girls improve their mathematical performance if problems are reworded so that they deal with cooking and gardening, even though the abstract reasoning required for their solutions remains the same.[8] Clearly, not just ability, but motivation too, has been affected.

But these effects in mathematics and science are only part of the story. A girl's long training in passivity and dependence appears to exact an even higher toll from her overall motivation to achieve, to search for new and independent ways of doing things, and to welcome the challenge of new and unsolved problems. In one study, for example, elementary school girls were more likely to try solving a puzzle by imitating an adult, whereas the boys were more likely to search for a novel solution not provided by the adult.[9] In another puzzle-solving study, young girls asked for help and approval from adults more frequently than the boys; and, when given the opportunity to return to the puzzles a second time, the girls were more likely to rework those they had already solved, whereas the boys were more likely to try puzzles they had been unable to solve previously.[10] A girl's sigh of relief is almost audible when she marries and retires from the outside world of novel and unsolved problems. This, of course, is the most conspicuous outcome of all: the majority of American women become full-time homemakers. Such are the consequences of a nonconscious ideology.

But why does this process violate the values of individuality and self-fulfillment? It is *not* because some people may regard the role of home-maker as inferior to other roles. That is not the point. Rather, the point is that our society is managing to consign a large segment of its population to the role of homemaker solely on the basis of sex just as inexorably as it has in the past consigned the individual with a black skin to the role of janitor or domestic. It is not the quality of the role itself which is at issue here, but the fact that in spite of their unique identities, the majority of America's women end up in the *same* role.

6. J. C. Flanagan, "Project Talent," unpublished manuscript; cited by J. Kagan, "Acquisition and Significance of Sex Typing and Role Identity," in M. L. Hoffman, ed., *Review of Child Development Research* (New York: Russell Sage Foundation, 1964), 1:137–67.
7. R. Brown, *Social Psychology* (New York: Free Press, 1965), p. 162.
8. G. A. Milton, *Five Studies of the Relation between Sex Role Identification and Achievement in Problem Solving,* Technical Report no. 3, Department of Industrial Administration. Department of Psychology, Yale University, December 1958.
9. J. W. McDavid, "Imitative Behavior in Preschool Children," *Psychological Monographs,* vol. 73, whole no. 486 (1959).
10. V. J. Crandall and A. Rabson, "Children's Repetition Choices in an Intellectual Achievement Situation Following Success and Failure," *Journal of Genetic Psychology* 97 (1960): 161–68.

Even so, however, several arguments are typically advanced to counter the claim that America's homogenization of its women subverts individuality and self-fulfillment. The three most common arguments invoke, respectively, (1) free will, (2) biology, and (3) complementarity.

1. The free will argument proposes that a twenty-one-year-old woman is perfectly free to choose some other role if she cares to do so; no one is standing in her way. But this argument conveniently overlooks the fact that the society which has spent twenty years carefully marking the woman's ballot for her has nothing to lose in that twenty-first year by pretending to let her cast it for the alternative of her choice. Society has controlled not her alternatives, but her motivation to choose any but one of those alternatives. The so-called freedom to choose is illusory and cannot be invoked to justify the society which controls the motivation to choose.

2. The biological argument suggests that there may really be inborn differences between men and women, in, say, independence or mathematical ability. Or that there may be biological factors beyond the fact that women can become pregnant and nurse children which uniquely dictate that they, but not men, should stay home all day and shun serious outside commitment. Maybe female hormones really are responsible somehow. One difficulty with this argument, of course, is that female hormones would have to be different in the Soviet Union, where one-third of the engineers and 75 percent of the physicians are women. In America, women constitute less than 1 percent of the engineers and only 7 percent of the physicians.[11] Female physiology *is* different, and it may account for some of the psychological differences between the sexes, but America's sex-role ideology still seems primarily responsible for the fact that so few women emerge from childhood with the motivation to seek out any role beyond the one that our society dictates.

But even if there really were biological differences between the sexes along these lines, the biological argument would still be irrelevant. The reason can best be illustrated with an analogy.

Suppose that every black American boy were to be socialized to become a jazz musician on the assumption that he has a "natural" talent in that direction, or suppose that his parents should subtly discourage him from other pursuits because it is considered "inappropriate" for black men to become physicians or physicists. Most liberal Americans, we submit, would disapprove. But suppose that it *could* be demonstrated that black Americans, *on the average,* did possess an inborn better sense of rhythm than white Americans. Would *that* justify ignoring the unique characteristics of a *particular* black youngster from the very beginning and specifically socializing him to become a musician? We don't think so. Similarly,

11. N. D. Dodge, *Women in the Soviet Economy* (Baltimore: The Johns Hopkins Press, 1966).

as long as a woman's socialization does not nurture her uniqueness, but treats her only as a member of a group on the basis of some assumed *average* characteristic, she will not be prepared to realize her own potential in the way that the values of individuality and self-fulfillment imply she should.

The irony of the biological argument is that it does not take biological differences seriously enough. That is, it fails to recognize the range of biological differences between individuals of the same sex. Thus, recent research has revealed that biological factors help determine many personality traits. Dominance and submissiveness, for example, have been found to have large inheritable components; in other words, biological factors *do* have the potential for partially determining how dominant or submissive an individual, male or female, will turn out to be. But the effects of this biological potential could be detected only in males.[12] This implies that only the males in our culture are raised with sufficient flexibility, with sufficient latitude given to their biological differences, for their "natural" or biologically determined potential to shine through. Females, on the other hand, are subjected to a socialization which so ignores their unique attributes that even the effects of biology seem to be swamped. In sum, the biological argument for continuing America's homogenization of its women gets hoisted with its own petard.

3. Many people recognize that most women do end up as full-time homemakers because of their socialization and that these women do exemplify the failure of our society to raise girls as unique individuals. But, they point out, the role of the homemaker is not inferior to the role of the professional man: it is complementary but equal.

This argument is usually bolstered by pointing to the joys and importance of taking care of small children. Indeed, mothers *and* fathers find childrearing rewarding, and it is certainly important. But this argument becomes insufficient when one considers that the average American woman now lives to age seventy-four and has her *last* child at about age twenty-six; thus, by the time the woman is thirty-three or so, her children all have more important things to do with their daytime hours than to spend them entertaining an adult woman who has nothing to do during the second half of her life span. As for the other "joys" of homemaking, many writers[13] have persuasively argued that the role of the homemaker has been glamorized far beyond its intrinsic worth. This charge becomes plausible when one considers that the average American homemaker spends the equivalent of a man's working day, 7.1 hours, in preparing meals, cleaning house, laundering, mending, shopping, and doing other household tasks. In other words, 43 percent of her waking time is spent in activity that would com-

12. I. I. Gottesman, "Heritability of Personality: A Demonstration," *Psychological Monographs*, vol. 77, whole no. 572 (1963).
13. B. Friedan, *The Feminine Mystique* (New York: Norton, 1963).

mand an hourly wage on the open market well below the federally set minimum for menial industrial work.

The point is not how little she would earn if she did these things in
someone else's home, but that this use of time is virtually the same for
homemakers with college degrees and for those with less than a grade
school education, for women married to professional men and for women
married to bluecollar workers. Talent, education, ability, interests, motivations: all are irrelevant. In our society, being female uniquely qualifies an
individual for domestic work.

It is true, of course, that the American homemaker has, on the average,
5.1 hours of leisure time per day, and it is here, we are told, that each
woman can express her unique identity. Thus, politically interested women
can join the League of Women Voters; women with humane interests can
become part-time Gray Ladies; women who love music can raise money
for the symphony. Protestant women play canasta; Jewish women play
Mah-Jongg; brighter women of all denominations and faculty wives play
bridge; and so forth.

But politically interested *men* serve in legislatures; *men* with humane
interests become physicians or clinical psychologists; *men* who love music
play in the symphony; and so forth. In other words, why should a woman's
unique identity determine only the periphery of her life rather than its
central core?

Again, the important point is not that the role of homemaker is necessarily inferior, but that the woman's unique identity has been rendered irrelevant. Consider the following "predictability test." When a boy is born, it is
difficult to predict what he will be doing twenty-five years later. We cannot
say whether he will be an artist, a doctor, or a college professor because he
will be permitted to develop and to fulfill his own unique potential, particularly if he is white and middle-class. But if the newborn child is a girl, we
can usually predict with confidence how she will be spending her time
twenty-five years later. Her individuality doesn't have to be considered; it is
irrelevant.

The socialization of the American male has closed off certain options
for him too. Men are discouraged from developing certain desirable traits
such as tenderness and sensitivity just as surely as women are discouraged
from being assertive and, alas, "too bright." Young boys are encouraged
to be incompetent at cooking and child care just as surely as young girls are
urged to be incompetent at mathematics and science.

Indeed, one of the errors of the early feminist movement in this country
was that it assumed that men had all the goodies and that women could
attain self-fulfillment merely by being like men. But that is hardly the utopia implied by the values of individuality and self-fulfillment. Rather, these
values would require society to raise its children so flexibly and with sufficient respect for the integrity of individual uniqueness that some men

might emerge with the motivation, the ability, and the opportunity to stay home and raise children without bearing the stigma of being peculiar. If homemaking is as glamorous as the women's magazines and television commercials portray it, then men, too, should have that option. Even if homemaking isn't all that glamorous, it would probably still be more fulfilling for some men than the jobs in which they now find themselves.

And if biological differences really do exist between men and women in "nurturance," in their inborn motivations to care for children, then this will show up automatically in the final distribution of men and women across the various roles: relatively fewer men will choose to stay at home. The values of individuality and self-fulfillment do not imply that there must be equality of outcome, an equal number of men and women in each role, but that there should be the widest possible variation in outcome consistent with the range of individual differences among people, regardless of sex. At the very least, these values imply that society should raise its males so that they could freely engage in activities that might pay less than those being pursued by their wives without feeling that they were "living off their wives." One rarely hears it said of a woman that she is "living off her husband."

Thus, it is true that a man's options are limited by our society's sex-role ideology, but as the "predictability test" reveals, it is still the woman in our society whose identity is rendered irrelevant by America's socialization practices. In 1954, the United States Supreme Court declared that a fraud and hoax lay behind the slogan "separate but equal." It is unlikely that any court will ever do the same for the more subtle motto that successfully keeps the woman in her place: "complementary but equal."

Interpersonal equality

> Wives, submit yourselves unto your own husbands, as unto the Lord.
> For the husband is the head of the wife, even as Christ is the head
> of the church; and he is the savior of the body. Therefore, as the church
> is subject unto Christ, so let the wives be to their own husbands in
> everything. [Eph. 5]

As this passage reveals, the ideological rationalization that men and women hold complementary but equal positions is a recent invention of our modern "liberal" society, part of the equalitarian veneer which helps to keep today's version of the ideology nonconscious. Certainly those Americans who value open, honest, and equalitarian relationships generally are quick to reject this traditional view of the male-female relationship; and, an increasing number of young people even plan to enter "utopian" marriages very much like the following hypothetical example:

> Both my wife and I earned Ph.D. degrees in our respective disci-
> plines. I turned down a superior academic post in Oregon and

accepted a slightly less desirable position in New York where my wife could obtain a part-time teaching job and do research at one of the several other colleges in the area. Although I would have preferred to live in a suburb, we purchased a home near my wife's college so that she could have an office at home where she would be when the children returned from school. Because my wife earns a good salary, she can easily afford to pay a maid to do her major household chores. My wife and I share all other tasks around the house equally. For example, she cooks the meals, but I do the laundry for her and help her with many of her other household tasks.

Without questioning the basic happiness of such a marriage or its appropriateness for many couples, we can legitimately ask if such a marriage is, in fact, an instance of interpersonal equality. Have all the hidden assumptions about the woman's "natural" role really been eliminated? Has the traditional ideology really been exorcised? There is a very simple test. If the marriage is truly equalitarian, then its description should retain the same flavor and tone even if the roles of the husband and wife were to be reversed:

Both my husband and I earned Ph.D. degrees in our respective disciplines. I turned down a superior academic post in Oregon and accepted a slightly less desirable position in New York where my husband could obtain a part-time teaching job and do research at one of the several other colleges in the area. Although I would have preferred to live in a suburb, we purchased a home near my husband's college so that he could have an office at home where he would be when the children returned from school. Because my husband earns a good salary, he can easily afford to pay a maid to do his major household chores. My husband and I share all other tasks around the house equally. For example, he cooks the meals, but I do the laundry for him and help him with many of his other household tasks.

It seems unlikely that many men or women in our society would mistake the marriage *just* described as either equalitarian or desirable, and thus it becomes apparent that the ideology about the woman's "natural" role nonconsciously permeates the entire fabric of such "utopian" marriages. It is true that the wife gains some measure of equality when her career can influence the final place of residence, but why is it the unquestioned assumption that the husband's career solely determines the initial set of alternatives that are to be considered? Why is it the wife who automatically seeks the part-time position? Why is it *her* maid instead of *their* maid? Why *her* laundry? Why *her* household tasks? And so forth throughout the entire relationship.

The important point here is not that such marriages are bad or that their basic assumptions of inequality produce unhappy, frustrated women.

Quite the contrary. It is the very happiness of the wives in such marriages that reveals society's smashing success in socializing its women. It is a measure of the distance our society must yet traverse toward the goals of self-fulfillment and interpersonal equality that such marriages are widely characterized as utopian and fully equalitarian. It is a mark of how well the woman has been kept in her place that the husband in such a marriage is often idolized by women, including his wife, for "permitting" her to squeeze a career into the interstices of their marriage as long as his own career is not unduly inconvenienced. Thus is the white man blessed for exercising his power benignly while his "natural" right to that power forever remains unquestioned.

Such is the subtlety of a nonconscious ideology!

A truly equalitarian marriage would permit both partners to pursue careers or outside commitments which carry equal weight when all important decisions are to be made. It is here, of course, that the "problem" of children arises. People often assume that the woman who seeks a role beyond home and family would not care to have children. They assume that if she wants a career or serious outside commitment, then children must be unimportant to her. But of course no one makes this assumption about her husband. No one assumes that a father's interest in his career necessarily precludes a deep and abiding affection for his children or a vital interest in their development. Once again America applies a double standard of judgment. Suppose that a father of small children suddenly lost his wife. No matter how much he loved his children, no one would expect him to sacrifice his career in order to stay home with them on a full-time basis—*even if he had an independent source of income.* No one would charge him with selfishness or lack of parental feeling if he sought professional care for his children during the day. An equalitarian marriage simply abolishes this double standard and extends the same freedom to the mother, while also providing the framework for the father to enter more fully into the pleasures and responsibilities of child rearing. In fact, it is the equalitarian marriage which has the most potential for giving children the love and concern of two parents rather than one.

But few women are prepared to make use of this freedom. Even those women who have managed to finesse society's attempt to rob them of their career motivations are likely to find themselves blocked by society's trump card: the feeling that the raising of the children is their unique responsibility and—in time of crisis—ultimately theirs alone. Such is the emotional power of a nonconscious ideology.

In addition to providing this potential for equalized child care, a truly equalitarian marriage embraces a more general division of labor which satisfies what might be called "the roommate test." That is, the labor is divided just as it is when two men or two women room together in college or set up a bachelor apartment together. Errands and domestic chores are assigned by preference, agreement, flipping a coin, given to hired help, or—as is sometimes the case—left undone.

It is significant that today's young people, many of whom live this way prior to marriage, find this kind of arrangement within marriage so foreign to their thinking. Consider an analogy. Suppose that a white male college student decided to room or set up a bachelor apartment with a black male friend. Surely the typical white student would not blithely assume that his black roommate was to handle all the domestic chores. Nor would his conscience allow him to do so even in the unlikely event that his roommate would say: "No, that's okay. I like doing housework. I'd be happy to do it." We suspect that the typical white student would still not be comfortable if he took advantage of this offer, if he took advantage of the fact that his roommate had been socialized to be "happy" with such an arrangement. But change this hypothetical black roommate to a female marriage partner, and somehow the student's conscience goes to sleep. At most it is quickly tranquilized by the thought that "she is happiest when she is ironing for her loved one." Such is the power of a nonconscious ideology.

Of course, it may well be that she *is* happiest when she is ironing for her loved one.

Such, indeed, is the power of a nonconscious ideology!

Self-fulfilling Stereotypes
Mark Snyder

Gordon Allport, the Harvard psychologist who wrote a classic work on the nature of prejudice, told a story about a child who had come to believe that people who lived in Minneapolis were called monopolists. From his father, moreover, he had learned that monopolists were evil folk. It wasn't until many years later, when he discovered his confusion, that his dislike of residents of Minneapolis vanished.

Allport knew, of course, that it was not so easy to wipe out prejudice and erroneous stereotypes. Real prejudice, psychologists like Allport argued, was buried deep in human character, and only a restructuring of education could begin to root it out. Yet many people whom I meet while lecturing seem to believe that stereotypes are simply beliefs or attitudes that change easily with experience. Why do some people express the view that Italians are passionate, blacks are lazy, Jews materialistic, or lesbians mannish in their demeanor? In the popular view, it is because they have not learned enough about the diversity among these groups and have not had enough contact with members of the groups for their stereotypes to be challenged by reality. With more experience, it is presumed, most people of good will are likely to revise their stereotypes.

My research over the past decade convinces me that there is little justification for such optimism—and not only for the reasons given by Allport. While it is true that deep prejudice is often based on the needs of pathological character structure, stereotypes are obviously quite common even among fairly normal individuals. When people first meet others, they cannot help noticing certain highly visible and distinctive characteristics: sex, race, physical appearance, and the like. Despite people's best intentions, their initial impressions of others are shaped by their assumptions about such characteristics.

What is critical, however, is that these assumptions are not merely beliefs or attitudes that exist in a vacuum; they are reinforced by the behavior

Reprinted with permission from *Psychology Today Magazine*, July 1982, © 1982 American Psychological Association.

of both prejudiced people and the targets of their prejudice. In recent years, psychologists have collected considerable laboratory evidence about the processes that strengthen stereotypes and put them beyond the reach of reason and good will.

My own studies initially focused on first encounters between strangers. It did not take long to discover, for example, that people have very different ways of treating those whom they regard as physically attractive and those whom they consider physically unattractive, and that these differences tend to bring out precisely those kinds of behavior that fit with stereotypes about attractiveness.

In an experiment that I conducted with my colleagues Elizabeth Decker Tanke and Ellen Berscheid, pairs of college-age men and women met and became acquainted in telephone conversations. Before the conversations began, each man received a Polaroid snapshot, presumably taken just moments before, of the woman he would soon meet. The photograph, which had actually been prepared before the experiment began, showed either a physically attractive woman or a physically unattractive one. By randomly choosing which picture to use for each conversation, we insured that there was no consistent relationship between the attractiveness of the woman in the picture and the attractiveness of the woman in the conversation.

By questioning the men, we learned that even before the conversations began, stereotypes about physical attractiveness came into play. Men who looked forward to talking with physically attractive women said that they expected to meet decidedly sociable, poised, humorous, and socially adept people, while men who thought that they were about to get acquainted with unattractive women fashioned images of rather unsociable, awkward, serious, and socially inept creatures. Moreover, the men proved to have very different styles of getting acquainted with women whom they thought to be attractive and those whom they believed to be unattractive. Shown a photograph of an attractive woman, they behaved with warmth, friendliness, humor, and animation. However, when the woman in the picture was unattractive, the men were cold, uninteresting, and reserved.

These differences in the men's behavior elicited behavior in the women that was consistent with the men's stereotyped assumptions. Women who were believed (unbeknown to them) to be physically attractive behaved in a friendly, likeable, and sociable manner. In sharp contrast, women who were perceived as physically unattractive adopted a cool, aloof, and distant manner. So striking were the differences in the women's behavior that they could be discerned simply by listening to tape recordings of the women's side of the conversations. Clearly, by acting upon their stereotyped beliefs about the women whom they would be meeting, the men had initiated a chain of events that produced *behavioral confirmation* for their beliefs.

Similarly, Susan Andersen and Sandra Bem have shown in an experiment at Stanford University that when the tables are turned—when it is women who have pictures of men they are to meet on the telephone—many women treat the men according to their presumed physical attractiveness, and by so doing encourage the men to confirm their stereotypes. Little wonder, then, that so many people remain convinced that good looks and appealing personalities go hand in hand.

Sex and race

It is experiments such as these that point to a frequently unnoticed power of stereotypes: the power to influence social relationships in ways that create the illusion of reality. In one study, Berna Skrypnek and I arranged for pairs of previously unacquainted students to interact in a situation that permitted us to control the information that each one received about the apparent sex of the other. The two people were seated in separate rooms so that they could neither see nor hear each other. Using a system of signal lights that they operated with switches, they negotiated a division of labor, deciding which member of the pair would perform each of several tasks that differed in sex-role connotations. The tasks varied along the dimensions of masculinity and femininity: sharpen a hunting knife (masculine), polish a pair of shoes (neutral), iron a shirt (feminine).

One member of the team was led to believe that the other was, in one condition of the experiment, male; in the other, female. As we had predicted, the first member's belief about the sex of the partner influenced the outcome of the pair's negotiations. Women whose partners believed them to be men generally chose stereotypically masculine tasks; in contrast, women whose partners believed that they were women usually chose stereotypically feminine tasks. The experiment thus suggests that much sex-role behavior may be the product of other people's stereotyped and often erroneous beliefs.

In a related study at the University of Waterloo, Carl von Baeyer, Debbie Sherk, and Mark Zanna have shown how stereotypes about sex roles operate in job interviews. The researchers arranged to have men conduct simulated job interviews with women supposedly seeking positions as research assistants. The investigators informed half of the women that the men who would interview them held traditional views about the ideal woman, believing her to be very emotional, deferential to her husband, home-oriented, and passive. The rest of the women were told that their interviewer saw the ideal woman as independent, competitive, ambitious, and dominant. When the women arrived for their interviews, the researchers noticed that most of them had dressed to meet the stereotyped expectations of their prospective interviewers. Women who expected to see a traditional interviewer had chosen very feminine-looking makeup, clothes, and accessories. During the interviews (videotaped through a one-way mirror) these women behaved in traditionally feminine ways and gave traditionally feminine answers to questions such as "Do you have plans to include children and marriage with your career plans?"

Once more, then, we see the self-fulfilling nature of stereotypes. Many sex differences, it appears, may result from the images that people create in their attempts to act out accepted sex roles. The implication is that if stereotyped expectations about sex roles shift, behavior may change, too. In fact, statements by people who have undergone sex-change operations have highlighted the power of such expectations in easing adjustment to a new life. As the writer Jan Morris said in recounting the story of her transition from James to Jan: "The more I was treated as a woman, the more woman I became."

The power of stereotypes to cause people to confirm stereotyped expectations can also be seen in interracial relationships. In the first of two investigations done at Princeton University by Carl Word, Mark Zanna, and Joel Cooper, white undergraduates interviewed both white and black job applicants. The applicants were actually confederates of the experimenters, trained to behave consistently from interview to interview, no matter how the interviewers acted toward them.

To find out whether or not the white interviewers would behave differently toward white and black job applicants, the researchers secretly videotaped each interview and then studied the tapes. From these, it was apparent that there were substantial differences in the treatment accorded blacks and whites. For one thing, the interviewers' speech deteriorated when they talked to blacks, displaying more errors in grammar and pronunciation. For another, the interviewers spent less time with blacks than with whites and showed less "immediacy," as the researchers called it, in their manner. That is, they were less friendly, less outgoing, and more reserved with blacks.

In the second investigation, white confederates were trained to approximate either the immediate or the non-immediate interview styles that had been observed in the first investigation as they interviewed white job applicants. A panel of judges who evaluated the tapes agreed that applicants subjected to the nonimmediate styles performed less adequately and were more nervous than job applicants treated in the immediate style. Apparently, then, the blacks in the first study did not have a chance to display their qualifications to the best advantage. Considered together, the two investigations suggest that in interracial encounters, racial stereotypes may constrain behavior in ways that cause both blacks and whites to behave in accordance with those stereotypes.

Rewriting biography

Having adopted stereotyped ways of thinking about another person, people tend to notice and remember the ways in which that person seems to fit the stereotype, while resisting evidence that contradicts the stereotype. In one investigation that I conducted with Seymour Uranowitz, student subjects read a biography of a fictitious woman named Betty K. We constructed the story of her life so that it would fit the stereotyped images of both lesbians and heterosexuals. Betty, we wrote, never had a steady boyfriend in high school, but did go out on dates. And although we gave her a steady boyfriend in college, we specified that he was more of a close friend than anything else. A week after we had distributed this biography, we gave our subjects some new information about Betty. We told some students that she was now living with another woman in a lesbian relationship; we told others that she was living with her husband.

To see what impact stereotypes about sexuality would have on how people remembered the facts of Betty's life, we asked each student to answer a series of questions about her life history. When we examined their answers, we found that the students had reconstructed the events of Betty's past in ways that supported their own stereotyped beliefs about her sexual orientation. Those who believed that Betty was a lesbian remembered that Betty had never had a steady boyfriend in high school, but tended to neglect the fact that she had gone out on many dates in college. Those who believed that Betty was now a heterosexual tended to remember that she had formed a steady relationship with a man in college, but tended to ignore the fact that this relationship was more of a friendship than a romance.

The students showed not only selective memories but also a striking facility for interpreting what they remembered in ways that added fresh support for their stereotypes. One student who accurately remembered that a supposedly lesbian Betty never had a steady boyfriend in high school confidently pointed to that fact as an early sign of her lack of romantic or sexual interest in men. A student who correctly remembered that a purportedly lesbian Betty often went out on dates in college was sure that these dates were signs of Betty's early attempts to mask her lesbian interests.

Clearly, the students had allowed their preconceptions about lesbians and heterosexuals to dictate the way in which they interpreted and reinterpreted the facts of Betty's life. As long as stereotypes make it easy to bring to mind evidence that supports them and difficult to bring to mind evidence that undermines them, people will cling to erroneous beliefs.

Stereotypes in the classroom and workplace

The power of one person's beliefs to make other people conform to them has been well demonstrated in real life. Back in the 1960s, as most people well remember, Harvard psychologist Robert Rosenthal and his colleague Lenore Jacobson entered elementary-school classrooms and identified one out of every five pupils in each room as a child who could be expected to show dramatic improvement in intellectual achievement during the school year. What the teachers did not know was that the children had been chosen on a random basis. Nevertheless, something happened in the relationships between teachers and their supposedly gifted pupils that led the children to make clear gains in test performance.

It can also do so on the job. Albert King, now a professor of management at Northern Illinois University, told a welding instructor in a vocational training center that five men in his training program had unusually high aptitude. Although these five had been chosen at random and knew nothing of their designation as high-aptitude workers, they showed substantial changes in performance. They were absent less often than were other workers, learned the basics of the welder's trade in about half the usual time, and scored a full 10 points higher than other trainees on a welding test. Their gains were noticed not only by the researcher and by the welding instructor, but also by other trainees, who singled out the five as their preferred co-workers.

Might not other expectations influence the relationships between supervisors and workers? For example, supervisors who believe that men are better suited to some jobs and women to others may treat their workers (wittingly or unwittingly) in ways that encourage them to perform their jobs in accordance with stereotypes about differences between men and woman. These same stereotypes may determine who gets which job in the first place. Perhaps some personnel managers allow stereotypes to influence, subtly or not so subtly, the way in which they interview job candidates, making it likely that candidates who fit the stereotypes show up better than job-seekers who do not fit them.

Unfortunately, problems of this kind are compounded by the fact that members of stigmatized groups often subscribe to stereotypes about themselves. That is what Amerigo Farina and his colleagues at the University of Connecticut found when they measured the impact upon mental patients of believing that others knew their psychiatric history. In Farina's study, each mental patient cooperated with another person in a game requiring teamwork. Half of the patients believed that their partners knew they were patients; the other half believed that their partners thought they were nonpatients. In reality, the nonpatients never knew a thing about anyone's psychiatric history. Nevertheless, simply believing that others were aware of their history led the patients to feel less appreciated, to find the task more difficult, and to perform poorly. In addition, objective observers saw them as more tense, more anxious, and more poorly adjusted than patients who believed that their status was not known. Seemingly, the belief that others perceived them as stigmatized caused them to play the role of stigmatized patients.

Consequences for society

Apparently, good will and education are not sufficient to subvert the power of stereotypes. If people treat others in such a way as to bring out behavior that supports stereotypes, they may never have an opportunity to discover which of their stereotypes are wrong.

I suspect that even if people were to develop doubts about the accuracy of their stereotypes, chances are they would proceed to test them by gathering precisely the evidence that would appear to confirm them.

The experiments I have described help to explain the persistence of stereotypes. But, as is so often the case, solving one puzzle only creates another. If by acting as if false stereotypes were true, people lead others, too, to act as if they were true, why do the stereotypes not come to *be* true? Why, for example, have researchers found so little evidence that attractive people are generally friendly, sociable, and outgoing and that unattractive people are generally shy and aloof?

I think that the explanation goes something like this: Very few among us have the kind of looks that virtually everyone considers either very attractive or very unattractive. Our looks make us rather attractive to some people but somewhat less attractive to other people. When we spend time with those who find us attractive, they will tend to bring out our more sociable sides, but when we are with those who find us less attractive, they will bring out our less sociable sides. Although our actual physical appearance does not change, we present ourselves quite differently to our admirers and to our detractors. For our admirers we become attractive people, and for our detractors we become unattractive. This mixed pattern of behavior will prevent the development of any consistent relationship between physical attractiveness and personality.

Now that I understand some of the powerful forces that work to perpetuate social stereotypes, I can see a new mission for my research. I hope, on the one hand, to find out how to help people see the flaws in their stereotypes. On the other hand, I would like to help the victims of false stereotypes find ways of liberating themselves from the constraints imposed on them by other members of society.

4

Communicating in Organizations: Talk, Talk, Talk

People are talkers. And managers talk even more than most other people. They do most of their managing by talking—talking to persuade, talking to command, talking to sell, talking to teach, talking to give and receive counsel. Managers use talk as their number one tool for communicating up and down and in and out of the organization. This chapter is therefore about the role of talk in the managing process.

The first paper, by Richard Daft and John Wiginton, takes an overall look at the role that talk, and particular uses of talk, play in managerial practice. It proposes, sensibly, that language must fit what it tries to describe and also fit the audience at which it is aimed. Daft argues that plain, "natural" language is frequently much more appropriate than other forms, such as mathematical language, for understanding how organizations work. And he backs his argument with some straightforward observations and examples.

The second paper, Louis Pondy's on leadership, looks at that phenomenon from a talking perspective. He considers the way leaders talk and their uses of language as a tool for getting emotional impact, modifying relationships, or shaping a vision for the organization.

Then we switch to another approach to talk—communicating, mostly by talking, to help, counsel, and build trust among members of our organization. The concern of David Kolb and Richard Boyatzis is with how to set up a helping relationship and how, by communicating, to give effective help to others. Helping requires much more than giving advice or information. It requires communication that enables the "helpee" to *use* the counsel, information, or support that is being given. In effect, Kolb and Boyatzis are looking at methods of non-defense-generating communication.

In the final paper of this section we turn to another very practical use of talk—talking to say no. Dafna Izraeli and Todd Jick consider "The Art of Saying No" and how refusals can be effectively or ineffectively transmitted. Again, the emphasis is on the symbols of language, on the role of talk in affecting attitudes and beliefs. It carries on from our earlier chapter on

202

the human balancing act, showing how balance and imbalance are affected by the ways we talk and are talked to.

Once again the theme is clear: When managers talk, much more than mere factual information is always being communicated. Wise managers, therefore, need to be aware of what they are really talking about.

Language and organization
Richard L. Daft and John C. Wiginton

This paper is concerned with the problem of gaining insight into and making sense of human organizations. The trail of logic begins with six observations about the field of organizations. Then the notion of language is introduced along with three principles from systems theory. These ideas are used to discuss managerial behavior and strategies for insightful organizational research.

Observation 1. Managers do not behave as the analytical writers on management suggest they ought to. For many years management textbooks have stressed the need to plan ahead, organize, and control and coordinate. Managers are supposed to be on top of things, anticipate problems, and use systematic decision processes.

What managers actually do is apparently quite different from this ideal behavior. Based upon his own and others' research, Mintzberg (38) reported that managers spend little time thinking and planning. Instead, managers react to events rather than plan them, and their activities tend to be characterized by brevity, variety, and discontinuity. Decision making involves gossip, unofficial data, informal communications, and intuition. Managers move toward live action, away from reflection, toward personal contact, and away from formal reports and information.

Observation 2. Operations research/management science techniques have had only modest impact within organizations. In the eyes of the consumers of these specialized services, the credibility of OR/MS apparently has been weakening, even while an increasing proportion of managers have received some formal training in these techniques. Leavitt (34, p. 5) contended that "the promise of the computer-assisted management analyst, the operations researcher, the long-range planner has not, in the eyes of many managers, come through to fruition." The disaffection may be widespread.

Reprinted from *Academy of Management Review* 4, no. 2 (1979): 179–91. © 1979 by the Academy of Management.

Grayson (25) reported that in some organizations management science is no longer used for important problems.

Observation 3. Management education does not seem to prepare individuals for management careers beyond a certain level. For example, Livingston (35) found that Harvard MBAs started their careers at high salaries, but seemed to level off after about 15 years, whereas non-MBAs were often more successful at this point in their careers. He concluded that people who get to the top develop skills not taught in management education programs.

Schools of Business and Management have excelled at conveying theory-based, technical knowledge. Thus they train technocrats who can deal with structured problems generally found in initial staff jobs. However, the schools apparently are not able to educate generalists capable of dealing with the unstructured problems faced by most managers (4, 38).

Observation 4. There is a trickle of doubt regarding the value of certain styles of research on organizations. Consider comparative, statistical studies of organizations for example. Child (12) pointed out that the ability to predict variation in organization structures is low, because researchers typically omit qualitative concepts such as goals and strategic choice processes. Argyris (1) argued that comparative statistical studies skim over the complex internal processes of organizations. By using easily-quantified surface variables, researchers fail to test underlying causal explanations for observed structural relationships. Weick (57) urged a strategy of getting into small, everyday organizations and explaining the "why" of observed relationships in preference to doing statistical studies of large organizations.

Observation 5. Organization participants function with severe cognitive limitations. The capacity of the human mind for formulating and solving complex problems is very small compared with the size of the problems whose solution is required for objectively rational behavior in the real world (51). This concept of "bounded rationality" refers to limits on our ability to process information, to think through multiple alternatives in complex situations, and to describe and communicate information regarding ill-defined events. Simon concludes that this leads decision makers to "satisficing" behavior, because managers cannot process sufficient information to permit optimizing behavior.

Observation 6. Organization processes are ambiguous and complex. Many organizational decision situations involve ill-structured, or "wicked" problems (36), because alternatives cannot be clearly identified, meaningful probability estimates are not readily obtained, and outcomes of various actions are inherently unpredictable. In recognition of this, some theorists have attempted to move away from notions of organizations as orderly, predictable systems. For example, one theory has proposed a "garbage can" model to explain decision behavior in organized anarchies (14, 15). Loosely-coupled organizations, apparently pluralistic and seemingly disorderly, have also been described (58). Even the widely held systems conceptualizations of organizations may not represent adequate descriptive models of organizations (56). Current open systems models, for instance, consider the external environment, but fail to capture higher human capacities such as shared meaning and belief systems, self awareness, and human emotion that make human organizations unique (46).

Most of these six observations may already be familiar. But when taken together, they present some curious contradictions. *First,* organization participants work in very complex settings, but appear to resist analytical methods designed to help them overcome inherent cognitive limitations. *Second,* increasing rigor, or at least increasing statistical sophistication, in organization studies does not appear to be associated with increased insight into organizational functioning. *Third,* the technical excellence of management education should be diffusing into organizations. Recently graduated managers could be using sophisticated analytical tools and computer data processing, but apparently they do not. We seek to explain these contradictions.

Understanding organizations

Language

There may be several explanations for the observations and contradictions noted in the last section. A behavioral scientist might suggest improving the relevance of management education by increasing the emphasis on experiential exercises. A management scientist might solve the implementation problem with special training for managers in the use of quantitative techniques. The organizational researcher might propose more careful measurement of variables, and the inclusion of additional variables in regression or more complex models.

These ideas might help. But they are relatively narrow and deal with single issues. There seems to be something deeper—something at the core of these issues which has not yet come to light. We propose that the notion of language as used by organizational participants and as the basis of theory may help us unify these observations and resolve the contradictions.

Language is a system of spoken or written symbols that can communicate ideas, emotions, and experiences (28). Many forms of language may appear in a culture like ours, and these language forms differ widely in their ability to transmit information. If a language has a large pool of symbols which can communicate a wide range of ideas, emotions, and experience, then the language would have high variety and would be considered quite complex. If a language is narrow in scope, however, with few symbols to communicate limited ideas, then the language would be low in variety. Symbols used in a given language also might convey exact, unequivocal meaning to users, and hence the language would be quite precise. On the other hand, symbols might be perceived by users to have a range of meanings, and hence would be somewhat ambiguous.

Language variety and ambiguity tend to be related. For example, what we might call natural language has evolved over a long period. By natural language we mean the ordinary languages such as English, Greek, or Hebrew, rather than the formal or artificial languages which have been designed or invented for special purposes, such as arithmetic, algebra, or FORTRAN (47). Words have come into general use which communicate many of the meanings relevant in our culture. Natural language contains more words than any person can hope or need to assimilate; and further, these words may be combined in countless combinations to communicate concepts. Thus, in many respects, natural language is vast and powerful for transmitting information, but it is also imprecise. Most words have multiple meanings, and users may detect various shades of meaning in a given statement. The imprecision which lends natural language its power also makes it unsuitable for many types of communication. Thus, a subset of natural language—a jargon—may develop to communicate a limited range of concepts with somewhat greater accuracy among people with common interests and experience. For purposes of science, highly specialized languages have evolved or been designed as in mathematics, where syntax and semantics are narrowly constrained and tightly defined. Highly specialized languages provide concepts and related symbols which are precise, unequivocal, and devoid of excess meaning.

We propose that a continuum of language forms which could be used to describe organizational processes might appear as in Figure 1. Variations of natural language make up the center part of the continuum. Special purpose languages (usually mathematically based) tend to be more precise. Other forms of communication (non-verbal) such as music and art tend to be more ambiguous but can communicate ideas and emotions which cannot be verbalized. The arrangement in Figure 1 is tentative and simplified. Distances between the forms of expression in Figure 1 have no meaning because the various forms of language typically blend into the nearest alternatives.

Three principles

Three principles provide the linkage between language and our earlier points about organizations. The *first* is the *principle of incompatibility* (60). The essence of this principle is that as the complexity of a system increases, our ability to make precise yet significant statements about its behavior diminishes. A threshold is reached beyond which precision and

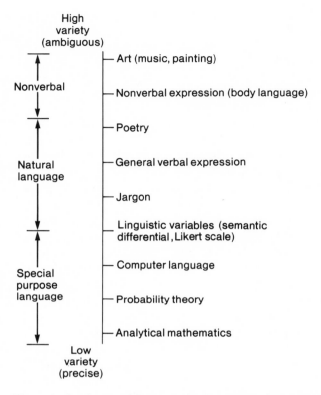

High
variety
(ambiguous)

Nonverbal

Natural
language

Special
purpose
language

Low
variety
(precise)

— Art (music, painting)

— Nonverbal expression (body language)

— Poetry

— General verbal expression

— Jargon

— Linguistic variables (semantic
differential, Likert scale)

— Computer language

— Probability theory

— Analytical mathematics

Figure 1. Continuum of languages for describing organizational reality

significance (or relevance) become almost mutually exclusive characteristics. Significant statements about human systems, or other systems of equal complexity, will necessarily contain some ambiguity and imprecision.

The *second* is the *law of requisite variety* (2), with variety referring to the number of possible states into which a system may enter. The law states that for purposes of control, only variety can neutralize variety. The control mechanism which is employed to control a complex system must have at least as much variety as the system it is intended to control.

The *third* is that of the *Bremermann Limit* (3, 9, 10), which states that there is a limit to the rate at which matter can transmit and process information. As a practical matter, it is difficult to determine when this limit is reached. But since the information required to describe completely any complex system might well exceed the Bremermann Limit, comprehensive, complete descriptions of the real world would then be impossible.

The importance of these principles lies in the implication that when we wish to make a meaningful description or model of a complex system, that description will display certain characteristics. When a system is simple, significant statements can be precise and unequivocal, and mechanisms for control can be simple. Often they are expressed in one of the special purpose languages. When the system is complex, however, significant statements will have to be correspondingly complex, and so will the mechanisms of control. In addition, useful models of complex systems, either descriptive or control, will necessarily deal with general patterns rather than detailed relationships.

Organizational description

We propose that insight into organizational behavior arises from the appropriate fit between the language of description and organizational reality. We also propose that observations about manager behavior and success, quantitative modelling, organizational complexity, and successful and unsuccessful organizational research, can be explained by the choice of language. This is based on the notion that high variety language is needed to make significant statements about complex human organizations. The vastness and complexity of high variety language is what makes it powerful for describing complex systems. Special purpose languages have been constrained by design so that they do *not* contain adequate variety and depth of meaning for this purpose, and thus would appear inadequate.

Figure 2 attempts to describe how language may be related to organizational reality. Cells 2 and 3 represent appropriate matches between language and reality—low variety language with simple phenomena, and high variety language with complex phenomena. In these matches, accurate descriptions will result. Cells 1 and 4 represent mismatches. An example of a cell 1 situation might be a turgidly written, overblown manuscript about a well-known, trivial phenomenon. We do not see many of these because they are weeded out in the editorial process. A cell 4 situation would be the use of a simple, precise mathematical or statistical model to represent organizational processes that are highly complex, amorphous, and intangible.

Most currently published organizational research tends to fall in cells 3 and 4 because researchers tend to work with low variety languages in order to be precise and certain about results. Managers, however, tend to work primarily with high variety forms of language. Managers must function inside their complex organization systems; they must gain insight into the organizational processes in which they are involved. In the next section we examine the use of language by managers, and consider how similar uses of language might benefit organizational researchers.

Organizational management and control

Part of the explanation for the language habits of managers lies in the nature of human thought processes. High variety language, particularly verbal lan-

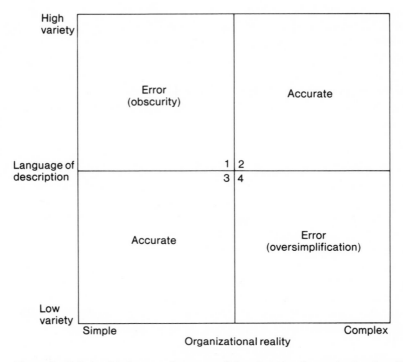

Figure 2. Relationship between language of description and organizational reality

guage, is coextensive with human thinking. Verbal language fits the mind since it is a creation of the mind (13, 53). This compatibility is important because the human mind seeks to understand and manage organizations.

Human cognitive processes are not well understood, but two character-istics are relevant here. *First,* the information processing ability of the hu-man mind is limited. Symbols are processed only a few at a time, and are held in only a few readily accessible memory structures. *Second,* the mind can handle complex, associative concepts (41). The human mind summa-rizes and abstracts information, detects relationships, and organizes pieces of information into coherent wholes. This process is partly accomplished by using high variety language to convey complex ideas. It is the concepts, not the specific words or symbols that describe them, which are apparently retained in the mind. To communicate such concepts to others, words are typically combined in a novel fashion. Thus, while the mind is limited in the number of discrete elements it can process, it nevertheless can handle difficult, ambiguous concepts which can only be communicated with high variety language. By contrast, digital computers are primarily sequential in their mode of operation. Computers can process large numbers of symbols, but they cannot tolerate ambiguity, abstract, interpret, or recognize patterns except to a limited extent.

Part of the manager's task can be viewed as a loose form of organizational control. The manager's control model is typically implicit, and is stored in the individual memory as a set of vague concepts about how the system behaves. The notion of a somewhat vague, yet complex and useful control model is consistent with recent research into "cause-maps," which indicates that organization participants carry highly complex and intelligent means-ends maps about organizational relationships in their memories (7).

Communication to and from the manager will consist mainly of high variety language in order to communicate meaningful statements about the systems which fit the manager's cognitive processes. The manager works with a vague representation of the system because the human mind does not require precision. The manager's mind works with verbal codes which summarize complex events and task relevant information. The use of high variety language and the summarizing process provide an appropriate conceptual model of the subsystem, while reducing the stream of data to and from the manager to the trickle required by the Bremermann Limit.

All models are abstractions, but a simple deterministic model of a complex human system may be an abstraction to such an extent that it fails to satisfy the law of requisite variety. This, we argue, has been recognized intuitively by managers, and may explain why they are unwilling to turn over organizational decision making to mathematical or statistical decision models. It is probably true, however, that data from these decision models may provide useful input to the human decision makers, along with other inputs, in the context of their high variety internal model.

The same reasoning explains why managers often become involved in the current details of their subsystems, which Mintzberg (38) called a preference for live action. Planning, reflection, and control based upon formal information systems implicitly assumes a well understood and stable organizational system. But most human systems, although stable in many respects, tend to be only vaguely understood. Further, destabilizing events can erupt at any time: dissatisfied workers might decide to lead a walk-out; a valued employee may decide to accept an offer from another company; or perhaps delivery of an urgent order for a large customer has fallen behind schedule. Because of this instability, the manager must continually sense various parts of the system, test the implicit model against what is found, incorporate new information, and either revise the cognitive model and/or send signals for system adjustments. The ongoing state of the system and system adjustments are communicated in meetings, telephone conversations, and by rumor and gossip. This high variety information can capture the subtleties and nuances of behavior so that substantial meaning can be conveyed to and from the manager-controller.

There is research evidence that organization participants need and use high variety forms of communication in complex settings. Daft and Macintosh (19) studied the relationship between work-unit technology and information in twenty-four work units. When the nature of the work unit task was poorly understood, participants tended to use high variety, ambiguous information. When the task was well understood and quite routine, participants preferred specific, unequivocal task information such as that contained in procedure manuals or computer output.

Mintzberg (37, 39) discussed the need of top managers for personal information rather than written information from formal channels. We suggest that this type of information provides high variety information necessary for the ill-defined, complex top management job. Managers would prefer spoken to written communication partly because voice pitch, inflection, and pauses convey additional information. In face to face situations, managers could also read gestures, posture, and facial expressions. Keegan (31) reported that executive information sources were largely human rather than documentary. Based upon Keegan's analysis, Pondy and Mitroff (46) observed that information variety was higher as the structure of the manager's situation decreased.

Most information processing by managers thus appears to fall in cell 2 of Figure 2. High variety inputs are used to understand complex situations. Some organizational activities are less complex and better understood, and information in these situations tends to be more precise and lower in variety, similar to cell 3. Thus a variety of language forms are used within organizations, depending on the simplicity-complexity of a given situation.

Organizational research

The logic we have used to explain how managers use language to function within organizations seems also to apply to research on organizations. Researchers develop models of organizations just as managers do, but in explicit rather than implicit forms. To be useful, research models, and the language of the models, should reflect the complexity of the system studied. If organizational models are too simple, or if the language attempts to be too precise, then meaningful statements about organizational functioning appear unlikely. Thus, we argue that high variety language will probably be more appropriate than mathematical and statistical languages for many types of organizational research, and insightful research models will tend to be somewhat ambiguous, vague, and imprecise.

Scientific inquiry traditionally has linked the understanding of a phenomenon with the ability to model it and analyze it in precise, quantitative terms. What has become known as the scientific method in the behavioral sciences is premised on the need to be objective rather than subjective and to avoid imprecision, vagueness, and ambiguity in analysis and measurement (5). Precise measurement and analysis has been largely responsible for research success in the natural sciences (49); but the natural sciences study phenomena suitable to these techniques. It may be a mistake to attempt to apply natural science research techniques in wholesale fashion to many social science problems. Perhaps we should be asking what research methods for organization studies will deliver the greatest understanding. In organization studies, these methods may have to be premised on the need to contain ambiguity and imprecision in order to match the nature of organization processes—to capture their complexity and variety.

Organizational complexity

Pondy and Mitroff (46) recently observed that most organizational research is at Level 1 on Boulding's (8) scale of system complexity. Level 1 systems are simple frameworks, and are reflected in static, cross-sectional studies. This would not be a problem except, as Pondy and Mitroff pointed out, Boulding ranks human organizations at Level 8 (of 9 levels), which ranks them as systems approaching unknowable complexity.

The disparity between research and reality, we argue, is partly explained by language. The research referred to by Pondy and Mitroff is characterized by precisely defined, precisely measured variables so that statistics and mathematics can be used to build models and understand relationships. As Figure 1 illustrates, mathematics and statistics are low in variety, and thus limit the research to simple, quantifiable variables and (generally) linear relationships. In attempting to get at more complex aspects of organizations, investigators may still try to be exact, to quantify, but as a result, this research would tend to fall into cell 4 of Figure 2— oversimplification. Stretched to their utmost limits, statistical models might reach Boulding's Level 3, which is a dynamic control model (29, 17, 30). But the resulting model will still deal with simple, measurable aspects of organizations. In order to capture and deliver insight about the really complex dimensions of organizations, such as those characteristic of Boulding's Levels 4 to 8, richer language which has sufficient variety to communicate these concepts will have to be brought into play. This type of research would fit into cell 2 of Figure 2.

Language helps to determine how we think, and what we see (46, 50). Perhaps those of us in the field of organizations tend to see the stable, tangible characteristics of organizations because those characteristics fit the correlation and regression models we were trained to use for organizational description. It is easy to forget just how messy and ill defined human organizations are.

For one thing, many important variables are intangible. We cannot touch a "norm," for example, or scrape off a piece for microscopic analysis. Human cognition (researcher or participant) is the ultimate source of knowledge and information about these intangibles: to these concepts we assign verbal labels so that we may contemplate and communicate them. In addition, a large number of variables interact even in a simple organizational setting. So many variables can possibly influence behavior that an investigator concerned with complete explanation will be overwhelmed (the Bremermann Limit).

Another source of complexity is that boundaries between some variables are indefinite. In human groups variables may be fused together in varying degrees so that variables do not have clear identities. Moreover, variables are clustered in ways which we do not understand. Rather than a single cause having a single effect, changing one element in such a cluster affects the whole conglomerate.

Given the complex nature of organization systems, how does one conduct effective research? Based upon the ideas presented so far, research into the more complex aspects of organizations would probably have some of the following characteristics: (a) it would focus on general patterns rather than on specific details; (b) it would rely on some type of human observation of the system, and human thought processes would be used to form the observations into a model of the system; (c) many potential explanatory variables would be left unmeasured; (d) imprecision would characterize measured variables and relationships among measured variables; (e) the research process would rely heavily on language of high variety rather than on mathematics or statistics.

Most of the organizational research recognized as major contributions to the field of organization studies also displays some of these characteristics. Key developments in management thought were identified by George (21). The familiar names were included: Mayo, Parsons, Selznick, Likert, Argyris, Simon, Woodward, McGregor, Perrow, Thompson, and Lawrence and Lorsch, along with many others. Most of the research which led to significant insights was loosely done according to traditional scientific criteria. Observations, case examples, and human thinking were the most frequent ingredients. The research outcome in most cases was a general conceptual model which explained some aspect of organizational behavior.

Most of these contributions would fit cell 2 of Figure 2—insight was attained because high variety language described complex processes. Some of these studies have been criticized for lack of scientific rigor (11, 27, 33, 43, 54, 55). One implication of our argument is that too much scientific rigor can in itself be a problem of organization studies. Perhaps if a study such as Lawrence and Lorsch's (32) had been conducted with great scientific rigor, it would have fallen into cell 4, and the insights into organizational functioning which were obtained might have been lost.

Two paradigms

Another way to explain why some publications have widespread influence on the field is that they fall in a paradigm concerned with social definition (46, 48). These studies help shape how we think about organizations because they provide images, metaphors, and concepts with which to understand organizations. An alternate paradigm, perhaps characteristic of cell 3 research, is concerned primarily with fact gathering (46, 48). This paradigm is concerned with facts, accurate measurement, sound methodology, replication, and proof.

Both paradigms are equally necessary to a field of inquiry. On the one hand, as Cummings (16) argued, discipline imposed by the scientific method helps keep the field straight, enabling determination of what we really know about organizations. On the other hand, as Pondy and Boje (45) pointed out, developing fresh insights is a frontier problem in organization theory.

The difficulty is that both approaches to organizations are valuable and important, but they have tended to be mutually exclusive. The concern for precise calculation can inhibit insight. And novel, insightful ideas can be hard to prove in any absolute fashion. In addition, many organization processes are too complex for scientific analysis, at least in the traditional sense. Somehow we may have to encourage a broad base of intellectual activity within organization theory, and perhaps define the scientific method to include a wide range of methods and approaches to organizational analysis.

Research techniques

Organizational research is basically model building (52). If complex organizational behaviors are modelled as if they are simple, well understood, deterministic systems, or even as stochastic systems, then the resulting models will tend to be insignificant. We propose that languages of high variety are useful tools for developing models of organizations because they have sufficient scope and richness of meaning to describe organizational processes.

There is an array of research techniques which are based on high variety language and thus contain requisite variety for organizational analysis. For example, case studies use natural language for both data collection and analysis. Case studies rely on human perceptions, do not treat system elements in a precise, unequivocal manner, and tend to summarize and deal with general patterns rather than with precisely defined elements.

Other examples of data collection techniques which take advantage of natural language are semantic differentials, Likert scales, and open-ended interviews. The resulting variables may be termed "linguistic," because language-based labels are used to classify the various values which the variable may assume. These variables are frequently projected into a numeric scale for quantitative analysis. The structure imposed on the data in this manner, however, may result in too much precision, a reduction of variety, and oversimplification of the underlying model.

The imposition of numeric structure on data is not always necessary. There are rigorous methods of data analysis available which honor data that are linguistic in nature, lending themselves at most to some form of simple classification. Contingency tables treat data in their nominal state, and do not impose any simplifying structural assumptions (61). Recent developments in the analysis of contingency tables by Goodman (22, 23, 24) permit the investigator to interpret the strength of relationships and the amount of variation in a way which is analogous to the analysis of variance in the general linear model.

Techniques also are available that enable investigators to use linguistic variables in formal modelling of complex systems. These techniques are based on the notion of fuzzy sets whose labels are the values of linguistic variables (60). For example, the word "height" denotes a linguistic variable whose values might include "tall," "short," and "not very tall," which are the labels of (fuzzy) sets of individuals whom we would classify as matching those descriptors. Linguistic variables may be used as the arguments of fuzzy algorithms which provide descriptive, deductive, and even normative models of organizational process (40, 59).

Many of these qualitative, natural language-based research techniques seem to be held in low esteem because the absence of precision and quantification does not conform to values of traditional scientific thinking. Nearly all published organizational studies press toward quantification and precision (20). After all, this is how most organization researchers are trained. Furthermore, there is something objective about an F-test statistic. It is unequivocal, and interpretation does not require judgment based upon maturity and experience with organizations. But we may pay a price by imposing narrow requirements on the types of data and analyses which are publishable. Many statistical models, especially those based on the general linear model which most of us have studied, are low in variety and assume particular structure in the data. Thus they are relatively weak for delivering real insight into more complex forms of organizational behavior. Reviewer sentiment against softer, high variety analyses may mean that as a field of inquiry we have been fighting for new knowledge with one arm tied behind our back. The field of organization studies might wish to encourage qualitative research rather than to discriminate against it.

Two caveats

We complete our discussion of organizational research with two caveats. *First,* we do not wish to imply that all number-based, hard research is useless and should be replaced with qualitative studies. Numeric data are suitable to describe organizational phenomena that are simple and quantifiable, such as number of people or hierarchical levels. Moreover, statistical methods enable investigators to summarize data and detect relationships across large numbers of organizations. But getting at deeper, intervening organizational processes requires a different strategy—one whose depth of meaning suitably matches the complexity of the process of interest. For insight into those processes, a single anecdote may communicate more insight than a page full of regression equations.

Second, if organizational research adheres to approaches compatible with traditional scientific thinking, we may expect to find preoccupation with technique, and, consequently, a relative scarcity of new understanding. Organizational researchers may reach the Bremermann Limit or violate the principle of incompatibility without realizing it. Thus, studies striving for completeness and precision will appear to contain some form of methodological shortcoming. Another variable could always be added, a more precise measurement approach could have been used, or some new statistical manipulation tried. The solution is to step back and accept some imprecision. Researchers would thus seek to treat the organizational system more as it really is—a complex, intermingled, blurred and ambiguous whole. To truly understand the system we may have to rely on general patterns rather than on specific variables, on human cognitions rather than on remote, hard data.

Summary

We have argued that recognizing the use of high variety language helps explain observations, and contradictions, about organizational behavior. Managers tend to use high variety forms of communication and resist quantified decision support systems because high variety language can transmit insightful information about highly complex organization systems. Likewise, greater use of quantitative models in organizational research has yielded only limited insight because low variety language can only describe and communicate about simple, tangible, generally linear relationships. In addition, high variety language is coextensive with human cognitive processes because these processes thrive on abstractions, summaries, and conceptual models rather than on discrete symbols, such as numbers. The implications of these ideas are summarized in four propositions that follow. These propositions are not offered as hard conclusions, but as points of departure for further discussion and research.

(a) Managerial behavior characterized by involvement in organizational details, reliance on informal information, and resistance to quantitative decision models is rational.

By "rational" we mean that manager behavior is appropriate to the nature of organizational systems. These systems are complex and combinatorial, and are subject to unpredictable shocks, so managers typically must be in constant touch to understand the system. Informal communication in the form of natural language and visual cues has the variety to communicate significant information about the system, and is also compatible with, and fully utilizes, the managers cognitive processes. Successful managers behave as they do because it seems to work. There is little reason to expect them to change their patterns of behavior toward systematic analysis or formal information.

(b) Decision support systems must be developed to cope with new forms of variety if they are to substantially influence organizational decisions.
Resistance to operations research/management science techniques is probably not explained by resistance to change or lack of training by potential user-managers. OR/MS decision and control models are simply inadequate in their objective functions and detailed specifications to cope with the more difficult dimensions of human organization activity. Thus, OR/MS models can be very useful for measurable, technical problems such as inventory control or maintenance scheduling, but they do not provide assistance for the fuzzy, wicked problems that exist outside the technical domain.

Future developments in models may enable them to play a greater role in organizational decision making. But these developments would require a reversal in direction from precision to vagueness, and from simplifying assumptions to complicating assumptions about organizational processes. Modeling developments based on the theory of fuzzy subsets seem to be in the right direction (60).

(c) Management curricula that encourage the acquisition of natural language skills may be more useful for training successful managers than programs that stress quantitative methods.
Managers play a special language processing role. Managers are control points in organizations, and as such are centers of information networks. They are constantly giving and receiving information about ill-defined events and processes. The ability to understand the nature of these processes based upon high variety language inputs, and the ability to send out accurate images thereof may be a substantial part of the managerial task. Pondy (44) suggested that an effective leader-manager can communicate images to subordinates which enable them to understand their role in an organization. A survey of managers found that top executives had extremely large vocabularies, and perhaps more importantly, were better able to select the more suitable word in a particular context (42). Moreover, vocabulary was strongly related to promotion into executive ranks. Words are the tools of the manager's craft, and a large vocabulary helps the manager to think and communicate more accurately.

However, business schools tend to emphasize quantitative decision skills (4). Business schools excel at the task of immersing students in the technical aspects of psychology, economics, and mathematics. But considering the nature of human organizations, why not also try to give aspiring managers tools which are compatible with the complexity of the situation in which they will be placed? We may wish to reconsider just how far we ought to go in stressing low variety, number-based skills as prerequisites to managerial careers.

(d) Seemingly soft, nonrigorous research techniques are often more rigorous for organizational analysis than traditional research techniques.
In order to make sense of our organizational worlds, we have to use the most powerful, yet suitable, research tools at our disposal. For the processes within organizations, the appropriate research techniques will have to acknowledge complexity and ambiguity. Reliance on high variety forms of language will allow us to identify and interpret events based on the perceptions of humans involved with the system. Linguistic variables could become the focus of analytical techniques rather than numeric data exclusively. And there is no reason to apologize for these procedures. True science will seek the most suitable way to study a particular phenomenon. We are suggesting that softer, qualitative techniques are often better suited to the study of complex human organizations.

Perhaps some movement toward qualitative research is already underway. Case analyses and simple cross-tabulations have recently appeared in the literature (6, 18, 26). If this trend gains momentum, the possibilities are exciting. As organizational researchers shed their bias for traditional quantitative research, we may enter a phase of development in which new knowledge is valued as highly as technical elegance—and understanding ranks equally with method. If these values then find their way into the educational process, natural language skills might be included in research methodology courses. We might find students being encouraged to observe and articulate organizational events rather than simply learning statistical techniques of hypothesis testing. Researchers might be expected to learn to use analogies and metaphors to communicate organizational images.

As the field moves toward richer conceptualizations of organizations, such as that of a social culture which includes higher level human capacities (47), organizational researchers may have to reach out and utilize new forms of expression. The existential, emotional, ephemeral dimensions of organizational life characteristic of Boulding's Levels 7 and 8 may not be fully expressible even with verbal forms of language. Perhaps the only means to capture and communicate such matters will be through language of the highest variety, such as art forms. Art forms can convey meaningful impressions and insights, even if these impressions cannot be "proven." If the richness and breadth of research methodology keeps pace with our conceptualizations about organizations, perhaps in the future a few researchers will publish studies of organizations in poem, or painting, or even in song.

References

1. Argyris, C., *The Applicability of Organizational Sociology* (Cambridge: Cambridge University Press, 1972).

2. Ashby, W. Ross, *An Introduction to Cybernetics* (New York: Wiley, Science Editions, 1956).

3. Ashby, W. Ross, "Analysis of the System to be Modelled," in Ralph

M. Stogdill (Ed.), *The Process of Model Building in the Behavioral Sciences* (Columbus, Ohio: Ohio State University Press, 1970).

4. Badawy, M. K., "The Management Clinic: Meeting the Challenge of Relevancy in Management Education," *Academy of Management Review* 1, no. 4 (1976): 129–33.

5. Berelson, Bernard, and Gary A. Steiner, *Human Behavior* (New York: Harcourt, Brace and World, 1964).

6. Biggart, Nicole W., "The Creative-Destructive Process of Organizational Change: The Case of the Post Office," *Administrative Science Quarterly* 22 (1977): 410–26.

7. Bougon, Michel, Karl Weick, and Din Binkhorst, "Cognitions in Organizations: An Analysis of the Utrecht Jazz Orchestra," *Administrative Science Quarterly* 22 (1977): 606–39.

8. Boulding, Kenneth E., "General Systems Theory: The Skeleton of Science," *Management Science* 2 (1956): 197–207.

9. Bremermann, H. J., "Quantum Noise and Information," in L. M LeCam and J. Neyman (Eds.), *Proceedings of the Fifth Berkeley Symposium on Mathematical Statistics and Probability* (Berkeley and Los Angeles: University of California Press, 1967), 4:15–20.

10. Bremermann, H. J., "Optimization through Evolution and Recombination," in M. C. Yovits, G. T. Jacobi, and G. D. Goldstein (Eds.), *Self-Organizing Systems* (Washington, D.C.: Spartan Books, 1962), pp. 93–106.

11. Carey, Alex, "The Hawthorne Studies: A Radical Criticism," *American Sociological Review* 32 (1967): 403–16.

12. Child, John, "Organizational Structure, Environment and Performance: The Role of Strategic Choice," *Sociology* 6 (1972): 1–22.

13. Chomsky, N., *Language and Mind* (New York: Harcourt, Brace and World, 1968).

14. Cohen, Michael D., James G. March, and Johan P. Olsen, "A Garbage Can Model of Organizational Choice," *Administrative Science Quarterly* 17 (1972): 1–25.

15. Cohen, Michael D., and James G. March, *Leadership and Ambiguity: The American College President* (New York: McGraw-Hill, 1974).

16. Cummings, Larry L., "Towards Organizational Behavior," *Academy of Management Review* 3 (1978): 90–98.

17. Daft, Richard L., and Alexander MacMillan, "Structural Control Models of Organizational Change: A Replication and Caveat," *American Sociological Review* 42 (1977): 667–71.

18. Daft, Richard L., "A Dual-Core Model of Organizational Innovation," *Academy of Management Journal* 21 (1978): 193–210.

19. Daft, Richard L., and Macintosh, Norman B., "A New Approach to the Design and Use of Management Information Systems," *California Management Review* 21, no. 1 (1978): 82–92.

20. Fennell, Mary L., "Trends in Organizational Research: An Interview with Morris Zelditch, Jr., *Seminars on Organizations at Stanford University* 2 (1975): 44–48.

21. George, Claude S., *The History of Management Thought* (Englewood Cliffs, N.J.: Prentice-Hall, 1972).

22. Goodman, Leo A., "The Multivariate Analysis of Qualitative Data: Interactions Among Multiple Classifications," *Journal of the American Statistical Association* 65 (1970): 220–56.

23. Goodman, Leo A., "The Analysis of Multidimensional Contingency Tables: Stepwise Procedures and Direct Estimation Methods for Building Models for Multiple Classifications," *Technometrics* 13 (1971): 33–61.

24. Goodman, Leo A., "Partitioning of Chi-Square, Analysis of Marginal Contingency Tables, and Estimation of Expected Frequencies in Multidimensional Contingency Tables," *Journal of the American Statistical Association* 66 (1971): 339–44.

25. Grayson, C. Jackson, Jr., "Management Science and Business Practice," *Harvard Business Review* (July–August 1973): 41–48.

26. Hall, Roger I., "A System Pathology of an Organization: The Rise and Fall of the Old *Saturday Evening Post*," *Administrative Science Quarterly* 21 (1976): 185–211.

27. Hickson, D. J., D. S. Pugh, and D. C. Pheysey, "Operations Technology and Organization Structure: An Empirical Reappraisal," *Administrative Science Quarterly* 14 (1969): 378–97.

28. Hollander, Edwin P., *Principles and Methods of Social Psychology* (New York: Oxford University Press, 1971).

29. Hummon, Norman P., Patrick Doreian, and Klaus Teuter, "A Structural Control Model of Organizational Change," *American Sociological Review* 40 (1975): 813–24.

30. Hummon, Norman P., and Patrick Doreian, "Reply to Daft and MacMillan," *American Sociological Review* 42 (1977): 672–74.

31. Keegan, W. J., "Multinational Scanning: A Study of Information Sources Utilized by Headquarters Executives in Multinational Companies," *Administrative Science Quarterly* 19 (1974): 411–21.

32. Lawrence, Paul R., and Jay Lorsch, *Organization and Its Environment* (Cambridge, Mass.: Harvard University Press, 1967).

33. Lawrence, Paul R., and Jay Lorsch, "A Reply to Tosi, Aldag, and Storey," *Administrative Science Quarterly* 18 (1973): 397–98.

34. Leavitt, Harold J., "Beyond the Analytic Manager: I, *California Management Review* 17, no. 3 (1975): 5–12.

35. Livingston, J. Sterling, "Myth of the Well-Educated Manager," *Harvard Business Review* (January–February 1971): 79–89.

36. Mason, R. O., and I. I. Mitroff, "A Program for Research on Management Information Systems," *Management Science* 19 (January 1973): 475–86.

37. Mintzberg, Henry. "The Myths of MIS," *California Management Review* 15, no. 1 (1972): 92–97.

38. Mintzberg, Henry, *The Nature of Managerial Work* (New York: Harper and Row, 1973).

39. Mintzberg, Henry, "The Manager's Job: Folklore and Fact, *Harvard Business Review* (July–August 1975): 49–61.

40. Neave, Edwin H., and John C. Wiginton, "Game Theory, Behavior, and the Paradox of the Prisoner's Dilemma: Resolution by Linguistic Variables," Working Paper #77-24, School of Business, Queen's University, October 1977.

41. Newell, Allen, and Herbert A. Simon, *Human Problem Solving* (Englewood Cliffs, N.J.: Prentice-Hall, 1972).

42. Packard, Vance, *The Pyramid Climbers* (New York: McGraw-Hill, 1962).

43. Perrow, Charles, *Complex Organizations: A Critical Essay* (Glenview, Ill.: Scott, Foresman, 1972).

44. Pondy, Louis R., "Leadership is a Language Game," in M. McCall and M. Lombardo (Eds.), *Leadership: Where Else Can We Go?* (Greensboro, N.C.: Center for Creative Leadership, 1976).

45. Pondy, Louis R., and D. M. Boje, "Paradigm Development as a Frontier Problem in Organizational Theory," Unpublished manuscript, University of Illinois, 1976.

46. Pondy, Louis R., and Ian I. Mitroff, "Beyond Open Systems Models of Organization," in B. M. Staw (Ed.), *Research in Organizational Behavior* (Greenwich, Conn.: JAI Press, 1978).

47. Raphael, Bertram, *The Thinking Computer: Mind Inside Matter* (San Francisco: W. H. Freeman, 1976).

48. Ritzer, George, "Sociology: A Multiple Paradigm Science," *The American Sociologist* 10 (1975): 156–67.

49. Snenfield, Arthur, "Scientism and the Study of Society," in F. Machlup (Ed.), *Essays on Hayek* (New York: New York University Press, 1976).

50. Silverman, David, *The Theory of Organizations* (New York: Basic Books, 1971).

51. Simon, Herbert A., *Models of Man* (New York: John Wiley & Sons, 1961).

52. Stogdill, Ralph M. (Ed.), *The Process of Model Building in the Behavioral Sciences* (Columbus, Ohio: Ohio State University Press, 1970).

53. Thomas, L., *The Lives of a Cell: Notes of a Biology Watcher* (New York: Viking Press, 1974).

54. Tosi, H., R. Aldag, and R. Storey, "On the Measurement of Environment: An Assessment of the Lawrence and Lorsch Environmental Assessment Questionnaire," *Administrative Science Quarterly* 18 (1973): 27–36.

55. Tosi, H., R. Aldag, and R. Storey, "Comment on the Lawrence and Lorsch Reply," *Administrative Science Quarterly* 18 (1973): 398–400.

56. Weick, Karl E., "Middle Range Theories of Social Systems," *Behavioral Science* 19 (1974): 357–67.

57. Weick, Karl E., "Amendments to Organizational Theorizing," *Academy of Management Journal* 17, no. 3 (1974): 487–502.

58. Weick, Karl E., "Educational Organizations as Loosely Coupled Systems," *Administrative Science Quarterly* 21 (1976): 1–19.

59. Wenstop, F. E., "Deductive Verbal Models of Organizations," *International Journal of Man-Machine Studies* 8 (1976): 293–311.

60. Zadeh, Lofti A., "Outline of a New Approach to the Analysis of Complex Systems and Decision Processes," *IEEE Transactions on Systems, Man, and Cybernetics,* vol. SMC-3 (1973): 28–44.

61. Ziesel, Hans, *Say It with Figures,* 5th ed. (New York: Harper & Row Publishers, 1968).

Leadership Is a Language Game
Louis R. Pondy

Let me begin by sharing with you some doubts and impressions about the field of leadership.

1. Most people would agree, I think, that leadership is a form of social influence. But then so are most things that involve more than one person (e.g., social facilitation effects, group decision making). So have we solved anything by that categorization? I suppose it does exclude a few things (e.g., leadership as a personality trait), but not much, it seems to me. Perhaps it would help to say that by the term "leadership" we mean social (i.e., interpersonal) influence exercised by a person in some position of superior authority (leaving aside for the time being the source of the authority) over some subordinate.

But, of course, we all recognize that there are "informal" leaders; that is, people who exercise influence over group members without occupying any formally recognized slot. And informal leaders are so common that restricting the term "leadership" to something done by persons in formal leadership positions seems a bit silly. In any case, I entertain doubts as to whether thinking of leadership as a type of social influence is very helpful, although at the present moment I cannot present any viable alternatives.

2. Leadership is applied to a pastiche of behaviors, ranging from that of foreman to that of prophet. It seems unlikely to me that we understand those behaviors well enough to identify the elements common to all. George Graen has mentioned to me that while his Vertical Dyad Linkage model (Dansereau, Graen, & Haga 1975) seemed to fit "administrative supervisors" reasonably well, the Ohio State data on "foremen" fit it much more poorly. And I think of foremen and administrative supervisors as being conceptually adjacent! Have we been misled by the existence of a single term in our language to think that it reflects some uniform reality? Gregory Bateson (1972) has argued that our language is thing-oriented and is impoverished when it comes to thinking about, describing, and talking

Reprinted from *Leadership: Where Else Can We Go?*, edited by M. McCall and M. Lombardo (Durham, N.C.: Duke University Press, 1978).

about relationships. Eskimos have seven different names for snow because they are so familiar with it. Does our insistence on the single term "leadership" say something about our familiarity or experience with it?

3. A closely related point: Our epistemology seems to force us to agree on a conceptual definition of the term "leadership." But Ian Mitroff has been urging on us some alternative inquiring strategies that stress eclecticism and dialecticism in place of agreement (see, for example, Mitroff & Pondy 1974). Now surely there have been a multitude of conceptual schemes for describing leadership, but it seems to me that they have been operating independently with occasional attempts to identify, say, a low LPC score with initiating structure and with a directive leadership style (more on the question of "style" later).

Perhaps what I am suggesting here is that we not only disaggregate leadership conceptually (as suggested in point 2), but that we attempt to fully account for the diversity and divergence of interacting explanations. In other words, the current conceptual schemes are not different enough. They overlap one another too easily. We are getting dense coverage of too limited an area. To one who believes in a consensus epistemology, that would be a signal for celebration, a sure symptom that we are converging on a solution. But is it perhaps a precise solution to the wrong problem? With a style of inquiry that stresses consensus, we have no way of knowing whether we have converged on a local rather than a global optimum—a correct solution to the wrong problem. So, in both this point and the prior one, I am arguing for more variety in the way we think about leadership and in what we think of as leadership.

4. I find the concept of leadership "style" particularly disturbing. It connotes to me superficiality of action, without either sincerity of intent or substantive meaning. My guess is that early researchers on leadership style meant to say something about the whole manner in which the leader approached his task, including his attitudes and values, and that the research on democratic styles of leadership was a reaction on a very fundamental level to the excesses of totalitarian regimes. But somewhere along the line we lost sight of the "deep structure" or meaning of leadership style, and I see it being taught to and practiced by students only at the level of "surface structure," that is, only at the level of superficial expression. The terms deep and surface structure derive from the field of linguistics (e.g., Chomsky 1972), and perhaps it would be worthwhile to take a small detour to explain how they are used there.

Very briefly, grammar is the relation between sound and meaning. In turn, grammar can be decomposed into phonetics, syntactics, and semantics. A phonetic representation (the surface structure of an expression) is what we ordinarily recognize as a string of words comprising a sentence, and phonetics is the study of the relation between sound and its phonetic representation. Semantics studies the relation between meaning and its semantic representation or deep structure, a set of primitive statements or expressions. Syntactics is the study of the relation between phonetic and semantic representations. To speak a language is to be master of all three components of grammar. Now back to leadership.

Suppose we think of leadership as a language. To practice, say, democratic leadership is to understand the set of meanings (values?) to be conveyed, to give them primitive expression, to translate them into stylistic representations, and ultimately to choose sounds and actions that manifest them. My worry is that this overarching process has been truncated, and that we have reduced the grammar of leadership to its phonetics. The syntactics and especially the semantics of leadership have been lost sight of. One particular conjecture about the source of this loss haunts me: Sounds, actions, and surface expressions are observable; they constitute behavior that can be "scientifically" measured in a reproducible way. But deep structures, and especially meanings, are elusive concepts that have no physical, behavioral counterpart. They cannot be observed. But if leadership is to be studied scientifically, attention must therefore be limited to the observable, surface, stylistic components. I reject the epistemology implicit in this conjecture on both scientific and ethical grounds. Perhaps I have overdrawn the parallel between leadership and linguistics, but I do not think so.

5. *Nearly all theories of leadership identify only a small number of strategies to choose from.* You can use either a democratic, autocratic, or laissez-faire style. You can emphasize either consideration or initiating structure. Or if you really want to get fancy, Vroom and Yetton (1973) offer *six* different things you can do. Now there is something profoundly troubling about this. Invariably when I have attempted to teach extant leadership theories, especially to practicing managers, they have bridled under the constraints imposed by so few alternative ways of behaving. I believe that we have sacrificed the creative aspect of leadership for its programmatic aspects. Shouldn't we be trying to document the *variety* of leadership strategies, rather than trying to collapse it into a few constraining categories?

A lesson from linguistics is relevant here again. What is truly remarkable about language is its creative aspect. Virtually all utterances are novel—never before spoken. And even young children and intellectually subnormal people have the capacity to produce creative sentences. Since there is no limit to the length of the longest sentence, there is an unbounded (infinite?) number of possible sentences in a given language. And the problem of linguistics is to describe how this infinite set of sentences is produced and interpreted with our *finite* (!) brain capacities. In fact, Chomsky defines the explanation of this creative aspect as the core problem of the human language:

> Having mastered a language, one is able to understand an indefinite
> number of expressions that are new to one's experience, that bear no

simple resemblance and are in no simple way analogous to the expressions that constitute one's linguistic experience: and one is able, with greater or less facility, to produce such expressions on an appropriate occasion, despite their novelty and independently of detectable stimulus configurations, and to be understood by others who share this still mysterious ability. The normal use of language is, in this sense, a creative activity. This creative aspect of normal language use is one fundamental factor that distinguishes human language from any known system of animal communication. [Chomsky 1972, p. 100].

Chomsky's proposed solution to the problem of finite mind/infinite language is a system of "generative grammar," the heart of which is a relatively small number of transformational rules by which semantic and phonetic representations are mapped into one another. Vroom and Yetton's (1973) decision-tree approach is a step in the right direction of developing a set of rules for deriving the "surface structure" of leadership, but I believe that their procedure still suffers the fundamental flaw of all leadership theories—the failure to recognize the creative unboundedness of leadership acts. In case it is in doubt, I believe the set of leadership acts is of the same order of magnitude as the set of sentences in a natural language. Language is after all one of the key tools of social influence.

6. *For the most part, leadership research has limited itself to looking at social influence that is of the direct, face-to-face variety.* Perhaps this is why there has been so much emphasis on personal style. But some of the most important forms of influence are remote from the behavior being induced. When I start up my car, a buzzer and light on the dashboard instruct me to fasten my seat belt. So I am under the impersonal influence of those devices. But more remotely, I am being influenced by the engineer who designed the devices, by the legislators and bureaucrats who required their use, and by Ralph Nader who caused us to think about auto safety in the first place. Does it make sense to think of these influences as instances of "leadership?"

One of my colleagues at the University of Illinois, Greg Oldham, is trying to broaden the concept of leadership to include any kind of control the leader has over the environment of the group member. (Oldham 1974). I feel very ambivalent about this effort. It accords with my intuition that social influence ought not to be limited to visible, face-to-face interactions. On the other hand, it so diffuses the concept of leadership that it ceases to be an identifiable phenomenon at all, and seems to merge with the whole field of "management." Nevertheless, my inclination is to go with Oldham and broaden the concept to include all of the indirect, remote, and invisible influences of leadership on behavior.

An interesting diversion is suggested by this point. Suppose leadership is a residual category to which we assign the causal responsibility for events we cannot otherwise explain. Several conclusions follow very rapidly. (1) Once the category exists we will try to fill it, so more and more things will be attributed to "leadership," especially in turbulent environments where there are a great number of unique events to make sense of. So we should expect the concept of leadership to expand in high-variety environments and to contract in low-variety environments. Does this suggest a possible study of what people in different settings mean by the term leadership? (2) Leadership results from our assigning *personal* responsibility for events, rather than from the workings of impersonal forces. This assignment is more likely after a success than after a failure. This refines the previous point, to wit, that leadership as an attributional category will expand only upon successful coping with turbulence. (3) Cultures vary in the degree to which personhood is a central concept. It is striking to walk from the Egyptian rooms into the Greek rooms of the British Museum and be hit with the shift in god-forms from animal to human characteristics. (Does this have anything to do with Greece's being the crucible of democracy?) Back from the diversion to the main point—that leadership does (should?) include very remote influences on behavior.

7. *One of the least visible influences on our behavior is the language we use.* "Sharing a language with other persons provides the subtlest and most powerful of all tools for controlling the behavior of these other persons to one's advantage" (Morris 1949, p. 214). This suggests an experimental paradigm that could spawn a hundred fascinating studies: How is a leader's effectiveness related to the language overlap with his subordinates? (It is conceivable that democratic leadership works because it promotes language-sharing? Does that mean that the comparative advantage of democratic leadership will be greatest when language overlap is initially minimal?) My guess is that it should be relatively easy to manipulate language overlap experimentally. But this forces us to ask the question, what does it mean to "share a language"?

One source of not-sharing is having a different lexicon or vocabulary, that is, different words appear in two different languages. This is the less troublesome type of not-sharing (or language-mismatch) because it carries its own signal of mismatch; it generates the question, "What does that mean?" A second and more serious type of language-mismatch is when the lexicons are identical but the "semanticons" differ, that is, when the meanings attached to the words are different. In this case the signal of mismatch is implicit in the way the words are *used,* and thus much more difficult to detect than lexical mismatches. The meaning of a word is the set of ways in which it is used (Parkinson 1968; Wittgenstein 1974). Note that this suggests an operational way of experimentally generating different semanticons for the leaders and their subordinates: Give each of them a different set of uses of certain key items—a sort of word history.

This also says something about how languages come to be shared—by sharing experiences and *talking* about them, that is, by using words and thereby establishing shared meanings. But this suggests that languages evolve when a given lexicon is used to describe new events. That is, meanings change roughly as fast as the enacted environment changes, and the rate of language renewal will need to keep pace if leadership effectiveness is to be sustained. Does this suggest that one of the neglected leadership functions is language renewal? And let me stress a crucial point: It is not sufficient to enact a shared environment; it has to be talked about. Perhaps this is why several studies have shown strong relationships among the number of committees or the frequency of committee meetings and the rates of program change (e.g., Hage, Aiken, & Marrett 1971). What is communicated in a communication is not words, but meanings.[1]

8. *In placing stress on language overlap and meaning creation, we may be missing an obvious point—that the leader's subtle use of the language may also be an important factor in determining his effectiveness, both in enhancing his credibility and in managing the influence process.* Let me give you an example. In Britain, plural verbs are used in certain places where we would use the singular tense, and this inevitably reveals something about the speaker's perception of the relation of group to individual. To be specific, one says, "The government *are* . . ." and "Leeds United *have* defeated West Ham," whereas we would use *is* and *has* and thus reveal our attitude toward the unified action of collectivities. I have no idea how to begin to measure or quantify this notion of subtlety in usage of language, but surely it must be related to the leader's empathy or sensitivity to his colleagues.

9. *What does it mean to be an "effective" leader?* My perception of research in the field is that effectiveness is typically conceptualized as "performance' of the subordinate group"—usually some kind of output measure—or perhaps as compliance or adherence to the leader's directives. In any case, the effectiveness concept and measure is invariably a behavioral one. The "good" leader is one who can get his subordinates to *do* something. What happens if we force ourselves away from this marriage to behavioral concepts? What kind of insights can we get if we say that the effectiveness of a leader lies in his ability to make activity meaningful for those in his role set—not to change behavior but to give others a sense of understanding what they are doing, and especially to articulate it so they can communicate about the meaning of their behavior. Musicians use this kind of terminology to describe their reactions to conductors. Faulkner (1973) quotes musicians as saying of their conductor, "[he] gives us gestures of expression but they're not showing us his meaning," or, "He doesn't communicate with technique or with words. He sort of looks surprised when we play," or they refer to the difference between "playing notes" and "making music." Now some of these expressions refer to an

---

1. See Kurt Back's (1962, pp. 35–48) distinction between a stimulus and a message.

internal, nonarticulated sense of understanding. But the content of the feeling cannot be communicated (except that you may be able to communicate that you have it without describing it). If in addition the leader can *put it into words,* then the meaning of what the group is doing becomes a *social* fact. That is terribly important! The meaning can be exchanged, talked about, modified, amplified, and used for internal processing of information.

The real power of Martin Luther King was not only that he had a dream, but that he could describe it, that it became public, and therefore accessible to millions of people. This dual capacity (surely it is much more than a mere trait) to make sense of things *and* to put them into language meaningful to large numbers of people gives the person who has it enormous leverage. (I must confess to racking my creative insight to the breaking point to find the right phrase to describe this capacity, but the effort was, sad to report, in vain!) One final word: This capacity to go public with sense making involves putting very profound ideas in very simple language. Perhaps that is why it is so rare. But its rarity should not dissuade us from its study.

So far in these notes, I have flirted with language concepts in several different places at two or three different levels. *At one level* I was trying to say that the word "leadership," by its existence, has influenced how we, as social scientists, see the world and how we take an undifferentiated reality and cut it up into one set of chunks rather than another set. Although the uses of a word constitute its meaning, the meaning has at least an instantaneous autonomy and control over the nature of variations in its use. Part of the aim of this conference is to overcome this semantic inertia and to accelerate variations in use of the term leadership. Which of the proposed variations are *selected* for attention by the other participants will depend on how the variations are phrased. But whether these different meanings of the term leadership are *retained* in usage will probably depend on how strong are the participants' vested interests in the current meaning. This process of changing the meaning of a word is an instance of what Wittgenstein has called a "language game." Does this language game (changing the meaning of a word) include processes that we feel comfortable thinking about as "leadership"?

At a second level, I was saying that a leader's understanding of the subtleties of meaning are important to his effectiveness. We can sharpen this point by noting that thought and communication involve a multiplicity of language games in which not only individual words have different meanings, but words in general may have different functions. In part, "understanding the subtleties" requires knowing which language game you are playing. For example, Wittgenstein identifies "reporting an event" and "giving and obeying orders" as distinct language games. The phrase "Five slabs!" in the former game means "There are five slabs," and in the latter game "Bring me five slabs." A more appropriate title for this essay would be "Leadership is a *collection of* language games."

At a third level, how linguistics (and, in particular, Chomsky) has approached the study of language provides a prototype worth imitating. I have already mentioned the creative use of language as an obvious fact that any explanation of language must deal with. No sophisticated data collection procedures and multivariate analyses are needed to establish that fact. Equally important, and I have not yet mentioned this point, is that Chomsky has done two things to make possible a formal, and therefore tractable but still insight-rich, study of language.

First, he distinguished between linguistic competence and performance. By competence he meant those aspects of speech that are person-independent and due only to the formal structure of the language. By performance, he meant how the language is actually spoken, with frequent errors of syntax, stopping and starting over, and so forth. By focusing on language competence, and ignoring issues of performance for the time being, he has been able to formulate solvable problems about the formal structure of language.

Second, by inventing the concepts of phonetic and semantic representations, he has been able to define the field of syntactics, again allowing him to formulate solvable problems, but in a way that the simplifications can be relaxed when a foothold has been established in syntactics.

There is another issue here. Chomsky is interested in understanding the human mind, as opposed to behavior, and he sees language as a way of gaining insight into mind, inasmuch as language is a creation of mind. I have not yet traced the implications of these strategies of inquiry for research on leadership, nor am I certain that they would help leadership research if applied. But they do represent an approach to inquiry that is radically different from that followed by leadership researchers. And thus, if experimented with, they represent a potential source of creative insight.

Although this essay is meant to be an informal set of notes that raises certain issues without necessarily developing them fully, it may be worthwhile to say a few more words about Wittgenstein's concept of language games before concluding. This is a difficult task inasmuch as he nowhere provides a concise definition of either language or language game—and with good reason. To be consistent with his philosophical position, he can establish the meaning of a word only by using it! Just as chess, baseball, and ring-around-the-rosie seem to share no characteristic in common, they still belong to the fuzzy-edged set of things called games. The same with language. Language is used to describe pain and other nonsharable inner sensations, to communicate, to express an idea, and so forth. These are all uses of language, but very different uses, with some overlapping characteristics between some of the uses, but no single attribute common to all. To quote Wittgenstein (1974):

But how many different kinds of sentences are there? Say assertion, question, and command?—There are *countless* kinds, countless different kinds of use of what we call "symbols," "words," "sentences." And this multiplicity is not something fixed, given once and for all; but new types of language, new language-games, as we may say, come into existence, and others become obsolete and get forgotten. . . . Here the term "language-game" is meant to bring into prominence the fact that *speaking* of language is part of an activity, or of a form of life. . . . If you do not keep the multiplicity of language-games in view, you will perhaps be inclined to ask questions like: "What is a question?"—Is it the statement that I do not know such-and-such, or the statement that I wish the other person would tell me . . . ? Or is it the description of my mental state of uncertainty?—And is the cry, "Help!" such a description? [pp. 11–12]

This quote barely begins to give an inkling of Wittgenstein's ideas on language and language games. The significance for us is twofold. First, it suggests that we begin to think of leadership, like language, as a collection of games with *some* similarities, but no single characteristic common to all of them. Second, it begins to map out the philosophical underpinnings of the role of language and meaning in leadership and behavior. At least it has had a profound influence on my own thinking about how meanings are established and what it means to communicate.

Let me conclude with a thought and a poem.

On rereading these notes, there were times when I questioned the sanity of their author. But sanity is the result of a process of social definition. How tolerantly a social system defines sanity has a profound effect on how adaptive that system can be. Marginally sane acts are sources of creativity. Define them to be insane, rather than merely eccentric, and you rob the system of that source of creativity. The fact that this conference may define these ideas to be intriguing rather than insane says something unexpectedly healthy about the field of leadership.

This poem is from Chuang-Tsu (fourth century B.C.):

How shall I talk of the sea to the frog,
    if he has never left his pond?
How shall I talk of the frost to the bird of the summer land,
    if it has never left the land of its birth?
How shall I talk of life with the sage,
    if he is the prisoner of his doctrine?

References

Back, K. W. Can subjects be human and humans be subjects? In J. H. Criswell, H. Solomon, & P. Suppes (Eds.), *Mathematical methods in small group processes.* Stanford, Calif.: Stanford University Press, 1962.

Bateson, G. *Steps to an ecology of mind.* New York: Chandler, 1972.

Chomsky, N. *Language and mind* (enlarged ed.). New York: Harcourt Brace Jovanovich, 1972.

Dansereau, F., Graen, G., & Haga, W. A vertical dyad linkage approach to leadership within formal organizations: A longitudinal investigation of the role making process. *Organizational Behavior and Human Performance,* 1975, 13, 46–78.

Faulkner, R. R. Orchestra interaction: Some features of communication and authority in an artistic organization. *Sociological Quarterly,* 1973, 14, 147–57.

Hage, J., Aiken, M., & Marrett, C. B. Organization structure and communications. *American Sociological Review,* 1971, 36, 860–71.

Mitroff, I. I., & Pondy, L. R. On the organization of inquiry: A comparison of some radically different approaches to policy analysis. *Public Administration Review,* 1974, 34, 471–79.

Morris, C. W. *Signs, language and behavior.* New York: Prentice-Hall, 1949.

Oldham, G. R. Some determinants and consequences of the motivational strategies used by supervisors (Doctoral dissertation, Yale University, 1974). *Dissertation Abstracts International,* 1974, 35, 2477-B. (University Microfilms No. 74-25, 750)

Parkinson, G. H. R. (Ed.). *The theory of meaning.* London: Oxford University Press, 1968.

Vroom, V. H., & Yetton, P. *Leadership and decision making.* Pittsburgh: University of Pittsburgh Press, 1973.

Wittgenstein, L. *Philosophical investigations* (G. E. M. Anscombe, trans.). Oxford: Basil Blackwell, 1974.

On the Dynamics of
the Helping Relationship
David A. Kolb and
Richard E. Boyatzis

Most of us as teachers, managers, parents, or friends find ourselves increasingly involved in giving and receiving help. This process of sharing wealth, knowledge, or skill with one who happens to have less of these valuable commodities is far from being a simple exchange, easily accomplished. Rather we find that the way to an effective helping relationship is fraught with many psychological difficulties that can either sidetrack or destroy the relationship. Carl Rogers, in his classic article, "The Characteristics of a Helping Relationship" defines a helping relationship as one "in which at least one of the parties has the intent of promoting the growth, development, maturity, improved functioning, improved coping with life of the other" (Rogers 1961, pp. 39–40). This definition would include parent and child, teacher and students, manager and subordinates, therapist and patient, consultant and client, and many other less formally defined relationships.

The purpose of this paper and the program of research of which it is a part is to understand more fully the dynamics of helping relationships in order to discover how these relationships may be made more effective. The first part of the paper describes the model that has guided our investigations and the second part reports an experiment which tests some of the propositions implied by the model.

The model of the helping relationship at this point is unfortunately not a precise set of mathematical interrelationships among operationally defined variables, but rather is a preliminary attempt to translate case observations and empirical findings from studies of helping relationships in education, welfare, assistance, and therapy programs into a single theoretical framework which will eventually allow operational definitions of variables and tests of interrelationship. The model itself, depicted in figure 1, emphasizes five key elements in the helping relationship: (1) the task or problem around which the helping relationship develops, (2) the helper with his mo-

Reprinted from Kolb, Rubin, and McIntyre, eds., *Organizational Psychology: A Book of Readings,* © 1974. Reprinted by permission of Prentice-Hall, Inc., Englewood Cliffs, New Jersey.

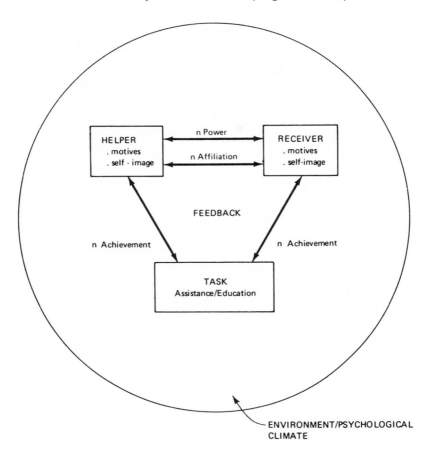

Figure 1. A model for analysis of the helping relationship

tives (achievement motivation, power motivation, and affiliation motivation) and his self-image, (3) the receiver of help and his motives and self-image, (4) the environment and psychological climate in which the helping activities occur, and (5) the information feedback which occurs during the helping process.

The task

The tasks around which helping relationships develop are widely varied—they range from tying a shoe to changing attitudes about birth control to improving the effectiveness of an organization. It is possible to classify all tasks on a single dimension, namely, the extent to which it is required that the receiver of help be capable of accomplishing the task independently when the helper is no longer present. At one end of this dimension are tasks defined as assistance; situations where there is no emphasis on the client's independent task performance. Giving a vagrant a dime for a cup of coffee is a good example of this end of the continuum. Many welfare and foreign aid programs are close to this end of the dimension. The emphasis is on the solution of an immediate problem with no provision for handling recurrences of that problem or similar problems. This type of assistance aimed only at symptom relief is likely to induce a dependency on the helper, making termination of the relationship difficult. When the relationship has been concluded, the client may blame the helper for inadequate help if he cannot replicate a successful result.

The other end of the continuum is education. Here the emphasis is on increasing the client's ecological wisdom, i.e., on developing the client's ability to solve problems like his present problem when they occur by using the resources of his natural environment. The helper avoids using the special knowledge, skills, or other resources he may command to relieve the client's immediate need, but instead works with the client, in the client's frame of reference, to increase his problem-solving ability. The "felt needs" approach to community development is perhaps the purest example of an educational helping relationship.

While the educational approach in most cases holds the greatest potential for the client's long-term benefit, it can cause great frustration to a client with strong needs for symptom relief. In addition the educational approach will in some cases be seen by the client as an intrusion on his privacy and an escalation of his problem. India, for example, was quite willing to receive assistance in the form of surplus food, but grew resentful at U.S. insistence that such assistance be coupled with an educational program to solve their basic problems of food production.

The helper and receiver of help

The personal characteristics of the helper and receiver of help are major factors influencing the process and outcome of the helping relationship. Two types of characteristics are particularly important—the motives and self-image of helper and client. At least three motives seem necessary to understand the dynamics of the helping relationship—power motivation (n Power), affiliation motivation (n Affiliation), and achievement motivation (n Achievement). These motives are important because they determine how the helper and client will orient themselves to one another and to their task.

The helper's and the client's power motivations determine how much they will be concerned about influencing and controlling one another. By asking for and/or receiving help offered, the client places himself in a dependent position, where he often feels weaker than and vulnerable to the source of help. The helper at the same time must deal with tendencies to feel superior, thereby letting the satisfactions of power and control overshadow the sometimes elusive goal of acting in the client's best interest. If the helper and client are unable to resolve power struggles and bring about a situation of power equalization, the relationship can degenerate into rebellion or passivity by the client or rejection by the helper ("He doesn't appreciate what I am trying to do for him"). One empirical example of the detrimental effects of a helper's overconcern with power can be seen in Prakash's (1968) study of effective and ineffective organization change agents. He found that ineffective change agents were more concerned with their own personal goals and with their political position within the organization than were the effective change agents, who were more concerned about task accomplishment.

The helper's and receiver's affiliation motivations determine how much they will be concerned about intimacy and understanding. To be helpful, the helper must know his client and understand how he perceives his problem. The intimacy required for effective understanding is hard to come by in situations where the helper has impossible demands on his time, and yet a lack of intimacy can leave the helper and client in two different worlds speaking two different languages. Too great a concern about affiliation by the helper and his client, on the other hand, can produce pressure toward conformity and mutual sympathy which may cause the helper to lose his perspective on the client's problem and the client to lose his respect for the helper's expertise.

The achievement motivation of the helper and receiver of help determines how concerned they will be about accomplishing their task or solving their problem. A major question here is—How is the goal of the helping relationship defined? Does the helper decide "what's good for" the client or does the client retain the power to decide what help he wants? In the first case the client is likely to have little motivation to accomplish the helper's task and in the second the helper's motivation is likely to be reduced. Only when the interpersonal issues of influence and intimacy have been resolved does it appear possible that the helper and client can agree on a goal to which they are mutually committed. Even if this is accomplished there is still a problem of what are often strong desires to achieve the goal of the helping relationship. Help is often so late in coming that both helper and client feel strong needs to accomplish *something*. The result is usually assistance programs designed to eliminate the client's immediate desperation rather than programs of education designed to help the client diagnose the causes of the problem and learn to solve the problem himself.

There is an interaction among motives in any helping relationship. It is possible for the helper and client to be so highly power motivated that they become preoccupied with controlling one another at the expense of understanding one another and/or accomplishing their task. Similarly, as we have suggested, high achievement motivation can cause the helper and receiver to orient themselves to accomplishing the task without attending to the interpersonal processes of influence and understanding necessary for having the receiver of help learn to solve the problem on his own. In a case like this, the offer of "Here, let me help you," by the helper is often his cue to push the client aside and do the task himself, leaving the client nearly as ignorant about how to solve the problem as before. And finally, high affiliation motivation can lead to concerns about intimacy and understanding that prejudice attempts to influence others and to accomplish tasks.

The implication of this analysis for helping relationships is that moderate levels of achievement, affiliation, and power motivation in the helper and client are optimal for effective help to take place. The dynamics of the helping relationship are such that influence, intimacy and understanding, and a concern for task accomplishment are all necessary for effective help to take place; yet excess concern in any one area can lead to the deterioration of an effective helping relationship.

The self-image and attitudes of the helper and client are also important defining variables in a helping relationship. The client must see himself as capable of improvement and willing to receive help. If this is not so, a major portion of helping activity must center on building self-confidence and optimism before learning can take place. The helper on the other hand must see himself as capable of helping and yet at the same time must not feel himself to be the "know-it-all" expert who has never experienced his own ignorance. This latter point is related to the issues of influence and intimacy discussed earlier. The helper must be willing to influence and at the same time have empathy with the feelings of the person he is helping.

The environment and psychological climate

It is a truism in contemporary social psychology that behavior is a function of both the person and the environment. While one could imagine many environmental variables which could influence the process of helping such as comfort of surroundings, freedom from distraction, etc., we have limited ourselves for the present time to a consideration of those environmental factors which are related to influence, intimacy and understanding, and task accomplishment. Atkinson (1964) and Atkinson and Feather (1966) and Litwin (1961) have argued that the tendency (T) to act in these three ways can be predicted by the strength of the individual's motivation (M) power, affiliation, and achievement; times the individual's perceived probability (P) that action in terms of one or more of these motives will be rewarded; times the amount (I) of power, affiliation, and achievement rewards he expects to get. Thus, the individual acts to maximize his satisfaction following the formula $T = M \times P \times I$ for three motives: power, affiliation, and achievement. While M refers to the individual's motivation, P and I refer to the individual's perception of the environment.

This analysis has important implications for predictions about effective helping, for if the environment tends to reward one motive disproportionately it can alter the behavior of an otherwise moderately motivated helper and client. One example of this occurs in the Peace Corps, where volunteers who might otherwise establish very effective relationships with host country nationals become bogged down in issues of power and control because the host country people (and sometimes the volunteer himself) perceive the Peace Corps to be a political agent of U.S. foreign policy.

Feedback

The last element of the model is the information feedback which occurs during the helping process. Two aspects of information feedback are important here. First, there is the source which controls information. Feedback can be controlled by the task as in the case of programmed instruction, or by the receiver of help as in self-research methods (Kolb et al. 1968; Schwitzgebel 1964) or by the helper as in traditional teaching methods.

The second aspect of information feedback is the characteristic of the information itself, whether it is accurate or distorted, intense or mild, positive or negative, and so on. This second aspect of feedback has been the subject of a great deal of theoretical speculation, especially among students of sensitivity training. For example, Schein and Bennis (1965) suggest the following criteria for valid, helpful feedback: (1) The feedback should be based on publicly observed behavior in the T-group, (2) it should be contiguous in time to the experience it refers to, and (3) it should be modified through all the data sources (i.e., group members) available.

A major question about the characteristics of helpful feedback concerns whether this feedback should be positive (pleasant for the client to hear) or negative (unpleasant). While there are those who feel that negative feedback is sometimes helpful in that it serves to unfreeze the client's self-satisfied concept of himself and increase his motivation to change (cf. Bennis et al., 1964), most learning theorists have concluded that in the long run reward is more effective than punishment. One example of reward-centered feedback is found in the programmed instruction technique of "error-free learning." Rogers, too, places heavy emphasis on the importance of positive feedback to the client in his concept of unconditional positive regard. "I find that the more acceptance and liking I feel toward this individual, the more I will be creating a relationship which he can use. By acceptance I mean a warm regard for him as a person of unconditional self-worth—of value no matter what his condition, or his feelings. . . . This acceptance of each fluctuating aspect of this other person makes it for him a relationship of warmth and safety, and the safety of being liked and prized as a person seems a highly important element in a helping relationship" (Rogers 1961, p. 34). To support his conclusion Rogers cites psychotherapy research by Halkides (1958) which showed that therapists who demonstrated a high degree of unconditional positive regard for their clients were more successful than those who did not.

An experimental study of effective helpers,
ineffective helpers and nonhelpers

To test some of the hypotheses implied in the model presented above we
designed an experiment to study helping as it took place in self-analytic
groups (T-groups, see Schein and Bennis [1965] for full description). We
decided in this study to focus on the characteristics of effective helpers,
leaving aside for the time being questions about the characteristics of effective receivers of help. More specifically we were interested in studying the
motives and self-image of helpers and describing the kind of feedback they
gave to those they were trying to help.

The first step was to define what constituted help in a T-group situation.
*We defined an effective helper as one who, in an environment where giving
help is seen as appropriate (the T-group), attempts to help others while the
others see this help as significant and important to them.* This definition
implies two comparison groups—ineffective helpers who attempt to give
others help but these others do not regard the help as important, and nonhelpers who do not attempt to help. While this definition of help has some
problems in that it is based on the receiver's subjective judgment of how
important the information given by the helper was, it nonetheless seems an
important aspect of any helping process. If the client does not regard the
information that he receives from his helper to be significant it seems unlikely that he will use this information to modify his behavior. Thus this
definition of help can be seen as necessary but possibly not a sufficient aspect of the helping process. What we learn about giving help here can be
considered necessary for effective help in situations where the relationship
is based on information exchange, but other factors may be important in
relationships where the client is required to act on the basis of information
he has received from the helper.

Hypotheses

The following hypotheses were made about differences among effective
helpers, ineffective helpers, and nonhelpers:

> Hypothesis IA: Effective helpers will have moderate scores on power
> affiliation and achievement motivation.
> Hypothesis IB: Ineffective helpers will have high scores on power and
> achievement motivation and low scores on affiliation motivation.
> Hypothesis IC: Nonhelpers will have high scores on affiliation
> motivation and low scores on power and achievement motivation.

Hypothesis IA is an application of the model of the helping relationship
to this experimental situation. Hypothesis IB is based on the notion that
what ineffective helpers had to say was not regarded as significant because
receivers of help felt that the helper was trying to control them (high power

motivation) and that he did not understand them (low affiliation motivation). We also predicted that the ineffective helpers would be less effective because they were overconcerned with the group's task accomplishment (high achievement motivation). We predicted in hypothesis IC that non-helpers would not try to influence others (low power motivation) or try to accomplish the group's task of helping others (low achievement motivation), but would be highly concerned about understanding and empathy with other group members (high affilitation motivation).

Hypothesis II: There will be significant differences in self-image among effective helpers, ineffective helpers, and nonhelpers.

Since so little is known about the relationship between self-image and the process of giving help, no specific hypotheses were made here.

Hypothesis IIIA: Receivers of help will perceive more positive feedback from effective helpers and more negative feedback from ineffective helpers.
Hypothesis IIIB: Receivers of help will perceive more affection-related feedback from effective helpers and more control-related feedback from ineffective helpers.

Due to limitations of the experimental design which will be described next in the procedure section, it was only possible to test differences between the types of feedback given by effective and ineffective helpers since nonhelpers gave very few feedback that was recorded by the receivers of help. In addition, since the type of feedback was described by the receivers of help rather than independent observers, differences between feedback received from effective and ineffective helpers may be due to (1) the type of feedback the helper gave, (2) the type of feedback the receiver heard, or (3) some combination of 1 and 2. Thus, any results concerning hypotheses IIIA and IIIB must be cautiously interpreted with this in mind.

Hypothesis IIIA is based on our earlier reasoning that positive feedback is generally more helpful than negative feedback. Hypothesis IIIB is based on the differential motive patterns that we predicted for helpers and ineffective helpers, i.e., ineffective helpers will be higher in need for power and lower in the need for affiliation than effective helpers. Thus they will give more feedback related to control (power) and less feedback related to affection (affiliation). (No data were collected about feedback related to task accomplishment.)

Procedure

The setting for the experiment was a semester-long course in psychology and human organization, required of master's candidates in management at the M.I.T. Sloan School. As part of the course 111 students participated in 30 hours of T-group training usually divided into two two-hour sessions each week. There were 9 groups of approximately 15 students each. These groups were structured differently from the traditional T-group method (see Schein and Bennis 1965, chapter 3) in that they were focused around a task—helping one another achieve personal change goals. The method used was the self-directed change method developed by Kolb et al. (1968). With this approach students chose, at the beginning of the T-group, individual change goals which they wanted to achieve. They picked goals like having more empathy, being a more effective leader, and talking more; and customarily they shared these goals with other group members, asking them for feedback on their progress. This procedure served to define clearly the group's task as one of helping others achieve their goals.

The students were about half undergraduates and half master's candidates in management. There were two females. About 10% of the students were foreign nationals with varying degrees of fluency in the English language. Subjects ranged in age from 19 to 35, with most in their early twenties.

Data collection

At the beginning of the course students filled out a 60-item semantic differential to describe their self-image and took the standard six-picture Thematic Apperception Test (TAT) described by Atkinson (1958). This test was scored for n Achievement, n Power, and n Affiliation by expert scorers who had demonstrated their scoring reliability according to the procedures specified by Atkinson (1958). The n Power scores were obtained by using Winter's (1967) improved and modified version of Veroff's (Atkinson 1968) power motivation scoring system. The expert scorer demonstrated scoring reliability using practice stories by Winter.

Data feedback on helping was gathered from group members themselves at the end of each session. Each individual at the end of each session filled out the form shown in figure 2. This form asked group members to indicate to whom they had given feedback and from whom they had received feedback during the session. In addition it asked them to describe up to three pieces of feedback which had been most significant to them and to indicate from which group member it had come. The definitions of the feedback description categories are described below as they were given to the group members. The descriptive categories were chosen to represent a wide variety of theoretical notions about what constitutes help and non-helpful feedback.

Name _____ Date _____

I. List below in boxes 1, 2, and 3, the three pieces of feedback from today's session that stand out most in your mind. Do this by recording in these boxes the initials of the giver of the feedback. You may also record here the central theme of the feedback if you wish. Try to put the feedback that stands out most in your mind in box 1, etc. A piece of feedback is defined here as a piece of information from one individual. A giver may be listed as many times as appropriate.

II. Beginning with column 1, go down the column checking those categories which describe the feedback you received. Descriptions of each category appear on the cover sheet. When you have completed column 1, continue in the same fashion in columns 2 and 3.

	1	2	3
Using a −2 to +2 scale, indicate your feelings about the person who gave you the feedback. −2 = dislike very much; −1 = dislike slightly; 0 = neutral to; +1 = like somewhat; +2 = like very much.			
VERBAL (spoken feedback) NON-VERBAL (gestured feedback)			
STRONG (intense, vigorous feedback) WEAK (mild feedback)			
HERE-AND-NOW (feedback about event or behavior in group) THERE-AND-THEN (about event outside of group experience)			
POSITIVE (pleasant to hear) NEGATIVE (unpleasant)			
SUPPORTED (corroborated by others) NON-SUPPORTED (not corroborated)			
OWNED (giver makes it clear that feedback represents his own opinion) NOT OWNED (not clear that feedback represents the giver's own opinion)			
DIRECTED (giver applies remark directly to you) NON-DIRECTED (from general statement, you make application to yourself)			
EVALUATIVE (giver is making value judgment) NON-EVALUATIVE (giver is not making value judgment)			
SOLICITED (you requested feedback) SPONTANEOUS (you did not request feedback)			
Feedback refers to your participation, non-participation, interaction, etc. (INCLUSION)			
Feedback refers to your leadership, influence, lack of influence, etc. (CONTROL)			
Feedback refers to your friendliness, unfriendliness, etc. (AFFECTION)			
Related to your self change project			

III. Check below the names of the people you gave feedback to (G) and received feedback from (R) in today's session.

Name	G	R		Name	G	R

IV. How close are you to your goal today? Rate on a scale 1 to 9 with 1 being farthest from your goal and 9 being closest to it. _____

Figure 2. Feedback form

Description of Feedback Dimensions

Category of Dimension	*Explanation or Description*
Like-Dislike Neutral	Do you like the *person* who gave you this feedback? Do you dislike him? Are you neutral toward him? Rate on scale -2 to $+2$.
Verbal-Nonverbal	Was this feedback *spoken* to you (VERBAL), or was it communicated through gestures, facial expressions, nods, etc. (NONVERBAL)? Check one or the other.
Strong Weak	This dimension refers to the intensity of the feedback. Was it emphatic and vigorous, or was it expressed mildly? Check one or the other.
Here-and-Now	This dimension refers to the content of the feedback. Did it refer to events or behavior taking place now or recently in the group (HERE-AND-NOW), or did it refer to things in the past not shared by other group members (THERE-AND-THEN)? Check one or the other.
Positive-Negative	Did the feedback agree with you or encourage you? Did you like to hear it (POSITIVE)? Or did it disagree with you, discourage you? Was it "painful" to hear (NEGA-TIVE)? Check one or the other.
Supported	This dimension refers to the reaction of other group members to the feedback. Did they corroborate, agree with or support it (SUPPORTED), or did they disagree or remain silent about it (NONSUPPORTED)? Check one or the other.
Owned-Not-Owned	This dimension refers to the person giving you the feedback. Did he attach himself personally to the feedback; did he make it clear that it was his own opinion or feeling (OWNED)? Or was it not clear that the feedback represented the giver's own opinion (NOT OWNED)? *Examples:* Owned—"I think you talk too much." (or) "Nobody in this group listens to me." Not-owned—"Does the group feel that John talks too much?; (or) "Isn't this group supposed to listen to people?" Check one or the other. Hint—not owned feedback is often in question form.
Directed-Nondirected	This dimension refers to *you* as the receiver of feedback. Was the feedback directed or applied to you personally; did it have your "name" on it (DIRECTED)? Or did you have to make the application to yourself from a general statement (NONDIRECTED)? *Examples:* Directed— "John Smith is not sensitive to my feelings." Nondi-rected—"Some people in this group are not sensitive to my feelings." Check one or the other.
Evaluative-Nonevaluative	This dimension applies to the pressure of an implicit or explicit value judgment *in* the feedback. *Example:* Evalua-tive—"I think it's wrong that you should try to control the group." Nonevaluative—"I think you are trying to control the group." Check one or the other. Hint—value judg-ments are often expressed by tone of voice as well as in words.

Spontaneous-Solicited	Solicited feedback is feedback that you specifically asked for. Spontaneous feedback is feedback that someone gives you without being asked. Check one or the other.
Inclusion-Directed	Was the feedback related to any aspect of your participation or nonparticipation in the group, acceptance or rejection by the group, interaction with the group, etc.?
Control-Directed	Did the feedback pertain to any aspect of your influence, lack of influence, leadership, control in the group, etc.?
Affection-Directed	Was the feedback related to your warmth, friendliness, openness, etc.?
Related to Your Self-Change Project	Was the feedback related to the self-change project you have chosen?

Definition of effective, ineffective and nonhelper

The above procedure yielded approximately 15 forms per group session with each group having 11 sessions. With the exception of one group, all of the groups submitted complete data. The group with incomplete data had to be eliminated from our analysis.

The procedure for defining effective, ineffective, and nonhelping was simple. To begin with each group was analyzed separately, since different groups developed somewhat differently due to different trainer styles and member needs. Thus a member was classified as an effective, ineffective, or nonhelper in relation to other group members who shared the same climate as he did, not in relation to the total experimental population. For each member of the group, the investigators totaled the number of times he had been mentioned as a giver of a significant feedback, i.e., his initials had been placed on the top of one of the three columns in figure 2. The investigators also totaled the number of times the member indicated that he had given feedback to other group members, i.e., the number of checks he placed in the "G" box after members' names in figure 2. With these two variables—for each member the number of significant feedbacks members had received from him and the number of feedbacks he reported giving—a matrix of the group members was plotted as shown in figure 3.

Subjects who were above the group median in number of feedbacks given and below the group median in number of significant feedbacks received were classed as ineffective helpers, i.e., they gave a lot of feedback but few people regarded this feedback as significant. Subjects who were below the group median on both variables were classed as nonhelpers. Those who were above both medians were classed as effective helpers, i.e., they gave a lot of feedback and many members reported receiving significant feedback from them. As might be expected few subjects (12 out of 98) fell into the fourth quadrant. Those that did were classed as effective helpers since they in all cases came very close to the median of number of feedbacks given. (We assumed that many of those who fell in this quadrant

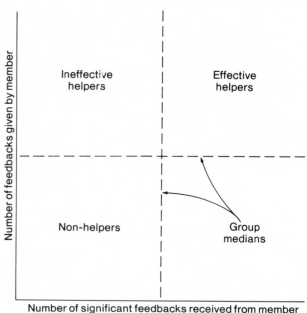

Figure 3. Definition of effective, ineffective, and non-helpers

did so because they failed to check the names of all of the people to whom they had given feedback.) The effective, ineffective, and nonhelpers from each group were then combined to form a total sample of 98 subjects—47 effective helpers, 24 ineffective helpers, and 27 nonhelpers.

Results and discussion

Motivation

The n Achievement, n Power, and n Affiliation scores for the three groups are shown in table 1, and portrayed graphically in figure 4. As figure 4 indicates, the results for all three motives were in the direction predicted, although in several cases difference did not reach the .05 level of significance. The most clearcut differences were shown on n Affiliation and n Power. Ineffective helpers scored much lower on n Affiliation than did effective helpers or nonhelpers. The difference in n Affiliation scores between nonhelpers and effective helpers, however, was not significant. Ineffective helpers scored much higher on n Power than did effective helpers or nonhelpers. There was no significant difference between the n Power scores of effective helpers and nonhelpers. The n Achievement scores were significantly higher for ineffective helpers than for effective helpers, but again the difference between effective helpers and nonhelpers was not statistically meaningful.

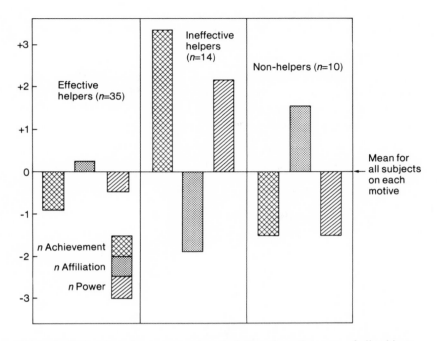

Figure 4. Helpers' motives expressed as deviations from the mean of all subjects

Table 1. Motive scores of effective helpers, ineffective helpers, and nonhelpers

Gp Motive	A n=35 Effective helpers	B n=14 Ineffective helpers	C n=10 Non- helpers	p value[a] A v. B	A v. C	B v. C
n Achievement	9.20	13.50	8.64	.04	NS	.09
n Power	4.51	7.14	3.50	.01	NS	.001
n Affiliation	5.37	3.29	6.64	.03	NS	.02

[a]Mann-Whitney U-test 1-tail, NS = $p > .10$.

Viewed overall, these results can generally be seen as supporting the hypothesis that effective helpers are moderately motivated in *n* Achievement, *n* Power, and *n* Affiliation, while ineffective helpers are high in the need for power and achievement and low on *n* Affiliation, and nonhelpers are low in needs for power and achievement and high on *n* Affiliation. However, a more cautious conclusion based only on statistically significant differences would suggest that ineffective helpers are differentiated from effective helpers and nonhelpers by very high *n* Achievement and *n* Power scores and very low *n* Affiliation scores. In this experiment none of the three motives significantly differentiates effective helpers and nonhelpers.

Self image

The semantic differential data on the self-image of effective, ineffective, and nonhelpers is shown in table 2. Only those adjective pairs which differentiated at least two of the three groups beyond the .05 level (2-tail) are shown in the table. While no specific hypotheses were made about self-

Table 2. Self-image of effective helpers, ineffective helpers, and non-helpers

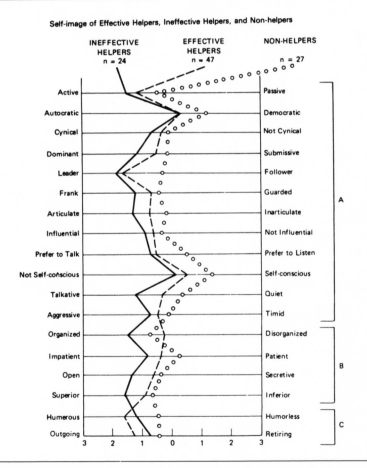

Note: A = adjectives differentiating non-helpers from both effective and ineffective helpers (Mann-Whitney U-test $p < .05$ 2-tail); B = adjectives differentiating non-helpers from ineffective helpers ($p < .05$ 2-tail) and effective helpers from ineffective helpers ($p < .10$ 2-tail); C = adjectives differentiating effective from ineffective helpers only ($p < .05$). No adjectives differentiate effective from ineffective helpers at the .05 level 2-tail.

image, these data are interesting in that they seem to support the conception of effective helpers, ineffective helpers, and nonhelpers suggested by the motivation results. The nonhelpers are different from both the effective and ineffective helpers in that they describe themselves as more passive, democratic, not cynical, submissive, followers, guarded, quiet, timid, not influential, inarticulate, self-conscious, and preferring to listen. The general picture that emerges from these adjectives is that of an accepting, democratic person who lacks the self-confidence to influence others.

Ineffective helpers, on the other hand, describe themselves differently from nonhelpers ($p < .05$, 2-tail) and effective helpers ($p < .10$, 2-tail)— seeing themselves as organized, impatient, open, and superior. These adjectives seem to portray an extreme self-confidence with impatience and lack of interest in others.

The most interesting part of table 2 is that the effective helpers consistently (with three exceptions) place themselves between the ineffective and nonhelpers. They are, it appears, self-confident without being overbearing—a moderation which is suggested by their moderate motive scores in achievement, affiliation, and power.

The above results, while only suggestive, are extremely useful in that they help to sharpen our mental image of two types of help that are doomed to failure—the brash, overconfident, superior approach which places the client on the defensive, and the timid, hesitant, passive approach which may raise questions about the helper's qualifications and lead to a lack of confidence in the helper. The description of the successful helper is somewhat vague from the self-descriptions in table 2 because no adjectives significantly differentiate effective helpers from the other two groups.

Feedback

The types of feedback given by effective and ineffective helpers is shown in table 3. The figures after each category represent the percent of the total number of significant feedbacks received from each group. Totals equal greater than 100% because more than one characteristic was checked on each piece of feedback. The hypothesis that receivers would report more control feedback from ineffective helpers was supported (33% vs. 26%, $p < .03$, 1-tail). The hypothesis that less affection feedback would be received from them was not supported, however.

The hypothesis that effective helpers would give more positive feedback and ineffective helpers more negative feedback was also supported by the data. It is difficult, however, to assess the implication of this result. We cannot say conclusively that effective helpers *gave* more positive than negative feedback—we can only say that more positive feedback was heard from effective helpers. This can either be due to the fact that effective helpers did give more positive feedback or due to the fact that negative feedback given by effective helpers was ignored by receivers of help.

The other unpredicted results are difficult to explain. A greater percent-

Table 3. Comparison of types of feedback given by effective ($n = 47$)
and ineffective helpers ($n = 24$)

Feedback Category	Effective Helpers[a]	Ineffective Helpers[a]	p of Difference[b]
Verbal	92	96	.007
Nonverbal	6	3	.008
Strong	63	59	NS
Weak	34	40	NS
Here-and-Now	87	86	NS
There-and-Then	10	13	NS
Positive	55	45	.04 1-tail
Negative	42	54	.04 1-tail
Supported	64	66	NS
Nonsupported	33	33	NS
Owned	90	96	.002
Not Owned	8	3	.002
Directed	83	86	NS
Nondirected	14	13	NS
Evaluative	71	71	NS
Nonevaluative	26	27	NS
Solicited	27	33	NS
Spontaneous	70	65	NS
Inclusion	47	44	NS
Control	26	33	.03 1-tail
Affection	22	20	.12 1-tail
Related to Self-Change Project	52	52	NS

[a]Figures represent % of total significant feedback received from each group. These total greater than 100% because more than one characteristic was checked on each piece of feedback.

[b]Probabilities marked 1-tail were predicted in advance, all others are 2-tail. (NS = 7.10)

age of nonverbal feedback (6% vs. 3%) and not-owned feedback (8% vs. 3%) was received from effective helpers than from ineffective helpers. The most plausible explanation seems to be that the ineffective helpers were unable to communicate so subtly—using nonverbal expressions or opinions they did not clearly identify as their own—because they lacked the empathy to time such or because their controlling behavior caused receivers defensively to block out such communications.

Summary

The results of this experiment suggest that the helping relationship is best viewed as one involving a complex interaction of at least three motives—n Achievement, n Affiliation, and n Power. Effective helpers appear to be those individuals who score moderately on these three motives. A similar moderation appears in the self-image of effective helpers. They are not as brash and overconfident as ineffective helpers nor as timid and self-conscious as nonhelpers. The feedback that is received from effective helpers tends to be more positive and less related to control issues than feedback from ineffective helpers. Also, receivers of help get more nonverbal and not-owned feedback from effective helpers.

In future research, other implications of the model of the helping relationship should be explored. We are currently involved in investigating the characteristics of effective receivers of help following the same research paradigm described here. The generality of the model should at some point be tested by research in a situation where the task is not an interpersonal one. Also, the impact of different psychological climates on the helping process should be investigated.

Bibliography

Atkinson, J. (ed.) *Motives in fantasy, action and society.* Princeton, New Jersey: Van Nostrand, 1958.

Atkinson, J. *An introduction to motivation.* Princeton, New Jersey: Van Nostrand, 1964.

Atkinson, J., and Feather, N. T. *A theory of achievement motivation.* New York: John Wiley and Sons, 1966.

Bennis, W.; Schein, E.; Berlew, D.; and Steele, F. *Interpersonal dynamics.* Homewood, Illinois: Dorsey Press, 1964.

Halkides, G. *An experimental study of four conditions necessary for therapeutic change.* Unpublished doctoral dissertation, University of Chicago, 1958.

Kolb, D.; Winter, S; and Berlew, D. Self-directed change: Two studies. *Journal of Applied Behavioral Science,* 1968, vol. 4, 453–73.

Prakash, S. *Some characteristics of an effective organization development agent.* Unpublished master's thesis, Sloan School of Management, Massachusetts Institute of Technology, 1968.

Rogers, C. *On becoming a person.* Cambridge, Massachusetts: Riverside Press, 1961.

Schein, E., and Bennis, W. *Personal and organizational change through group methods.* New York: John Wiley and Sons, 1965.

Schwitzgebel, R. *A simple behavioral system for recording and implementing change in natural settings.* Unpublished doctoral thesis, Harvard University, 1964.

Winter, David G. *Power motivation in thought and action.* Unpublished doctoral thesis, Harvard University, 1967.

The Art of Saying No:
Linking Power to Culture
Dafna M. Izraeli
and Todd D. Jick

Introduction

A Chinese rejection letter

The SWSers who visited China last spring learned that it is not only what the Chinese say but how they say it that reveals their unique perspective on life. Imagine how different it might feel to receive in place of the familiar "we regret . . ." letter, a rejection like the following sent to a British author of a paper on the economy submitted to a Chinese journal:

> We have read your manuscript with boundless delight. If we were to publish your paper it would be impossible for us to publish any work of a lower standard. And as it is unthinkable that, in the next thousand years we shall see its equal, we are, to our regret, compelled to return your divine composition, and beg you a thousand times to overlook our short sight and timidity. (*Source:* Sociologists for Women in Society [SWS] Network, 1982.)

If you had received this eloquent rejection letter, what might you have learned or understood? First and foremost, your article has undeniably been rejected. Thus, on one level, this letter conveys straightforward technical or instrumental information. At another level, you might have learned something about how bad news is delivered in Chinese culture in light of the (humorous?) rationale for the rejection. But you might also have recognized how, in a more subtle way, the submission and rejection "ritual" reaffirms the journal's authority and power to define what is an acceptable standard, and who is entitled to have their work published in it. In other words, this exchange can also be understood on a more ceremonial or symbolic level (Allaire and Firsirotu 1984) that primarily "says things" rather than does things (Leach 1968).

Reproduced from *Organization Studies* 7, no. 2 (1986): 171–92, © 1986 EGOS.
The authors would like to thank Diane Margolis, Judy Lorber, Arie Shirom, Gareth Morgan, and Adrian McLean for discussing ideas in the paper with them.

This paper examines how a commonly experienced occurrence in organizations is managed, namely, the denial or refusal of a request. Systematic evidence will be presented of how those in authority manage encounters with subordinates whose requests for some organizational resource have been denied and who, in so doing, also attempt to articulate and reaffirm the values and legitimacy of the powerholders.

There are always some people in an organization receiving less than they expect or less than they deem themselves entitled to. In recent years, though, it seems that refusals have indeed become more prevalent in organizations and more problematic to handle for managers. Two recent trends seem to be responsible: a shift from economically good times to times of relative economic scarcity requiring organizational retrenchment, and an expansion of perceived entitlement as reflected in the growth of participative management. Both conditions lead to a negative shift in the ratio of those to whom the organization says "yes" to those to whom it says "no." In the first case, an ethos of expansiveness must give way to an ethos of frugality, restraint, and sacrifice (Jick and Murray 1982). In the second case, beliefs about entitlement must be redefined.

Unless organizations can legitimize such "deprivations" and help members accept failure, they run the risk of resentment and disengagement among their labour force (Kanter 1977). Procedures and collective actions for "cooling out" disappointments, or at least for controlling the damage these may cause, become essential for the continuity and integrity of existing social arrangements (Goffman 1952; Clark 1960). Members must be helped to see how things are different from what they have perceived and to shift their behaviour accordingly. Organizations thus may attempt to influence members to want less, to delay their gratification and, in any case, to view the refusal as rational and equitable.

Refusals as political and cultural ritual

The event in which the refusal is conveyed has many of the elements of a secular ritual (Moor and Myerhoff 1977). It is a regularly repeated event, "a standardized form of behaviour/custom" (Goody 1961, 159) incorporating "symbolic expressions of sentiments" (Radcliffe Brown 1977, 105) and constituting affirmations of values, world views, and social organizations which sustain and are legitimated by them (Simmel 1971). Like rituals, refusals provide socially constructed responses to confront problematic situations (Goffman 1967) by providing participants with a series of rationalizations which enable them to cope with the tension and even anxiety generated by the denial and the need to convey it.

Studies of organizational culture have only recently begun to consider political interpretations of routine, ritualized activity and discourse in organizations (Riley 1983; Gronn 1983; Abravanel 1983; Wilkins 1983; Moch 1980).

Culture-building mechanisms such as symbols, language, accounts, ideologies, ceremonies, and myths have become increasingly subject to political analysis relative to their role in sustaining and legitimating authority and in securing or preserving a semblance of order, harmony and consensus in organizations (Abravanel 1983; Riley 1983; Smircich and Morgan 1982). From this perspective, accounts and explanations are not mere descriptions of how decisions were arrived at, but are rather retrospective rationalizations couched in culturally acceptable rhetoric.

Such would then be the case with refusal instances. They are ideological devices that function to impose the "managers' definition of reality upon discourse and conduct within and around the organization" (Brown 1978, 360). Thus, words, accounts and symbols often cloak power (Gronn 1983). Linking the power analysis of Marx with the concern for consciousness of Simmel, Brown (1978, 376) observes that in hierarchical organizations "there comes to be not only a concentration of control over the contents of reality (the means of production) but also over the definition of reality (i.e., foundational assumptions concerning what constitutes 'property,' 'rights,' 'obligations,' 'legitimacy' and so on)."

Management does not have a monopoly over the definitional process. The framing of organizational problems, the interpretive schemes, and the definition of reality are rarely uncontroversial (Izraeli 1977; Brown 1978; Morgan 1984). Organizations, as "culture-bearing milieu," provide an arena for the potential expression and enactment of "multiple nested and/or overlapping cultures" (Louis 1983). Anthropological studies of life on the shop floor are rich in their documentation of the world of workers who operate with a different set of skills, perspectives and interests and whose versions of "what is going on here" is frequently very different from that of management (Roethlisberger and Dickson 1939; Lupton 1963; Crozier 1964; Cunnison 1966; Izraeli 1980).

In the face of such tensions and conflicts, management typically seeks to build and sustain consensus while reinforcing its control (Abravanel 1983). How is this done? Traditional tools of management include selective recruitment, training and promotion, role modelling, organizational and physical design, and direct communication of desired norms and values (Baker 1980). Smircich and Morgan (1982) argue that effective leadership relies on the more subtle management of meaning whereby the leader's definition of the situation serves as a basis for action by others—actions oriented to the achievement of ends desirable from the leader's viewpoint. Thus, the manager's role is portrayed as "framer of contexts, a maker and shaper of interpretive schemes (who) must deal with multiple realities" (Smircich 1983). If effectively carried out, the control structure remains invisible and achieves compliance on the basis of value premises. If ineffective, however, then the power dimension of hierarchical relations becomes more transparent and may lead to resistance.

Refusals as the delivery of bad news

Refusal events in organizations may be classified as a specific case of the accumulating literature on the generic situation of the delivery of bad news. Findings show that people are generally reluctant to communicate bad news, that bad news is perceived to be more important than good news (Tesser, Rosen and Batchelor 1972; Tesser and Rosen 1975), and that people prefer to deliver bad news in face-to-face conditions rather than through the impersonal medium of a written notice (Lengel and Daft 1984; Griffin, Bateman and Head 1984). Bies (1982) found that the defining core of bad news is itself variable in meaning. The degree of its "badness" is a function of the context and is influenced by whether or not an explanation is provided, whether the explanation focusses on the individual or on factors external to him/her and on the time perspective. What is defined as good or bad is thus socially mediated.

The classic work in this field is by Goffman (1952) who focussed on the need to placate victims of disappointed expectations and to prevent those who feel they have been cheated of their entitlements from "squawking." This theme is developed by Clark in his study of Blacks in higher education (1960). The delivery of bad news, however, has been studied most extensively by sociologists in medical settings (Glaser and Strauss 1965, 1968; Sudnow 1967) where communicating bad news to patients and/or their kin is part of the doctor's role. McClenahen and Lofland (1976) examined the tactics used by U.S. deputy marshals when bearing bad news such as delivering summons/complaints, taking federally accused into custody, and delivering the convicted to prison. They distinguish between two kinds of bearers of bad news: those who enact the role in their private lives (amateurs) and those who perform it as part of their work or occupation:

> Amateur bearers seem more likely to be concerned with the trauma their news may cause the recipient; occupational bearers tend to be more concerned with avoiding "scenes" initiated by emotionally disturbed recipients. Amateur bearers worry about the impact the news will have upon its target; occupational bearers worry about the impact the news will have upon themselves. (1976, 252)

Managers who convey refusals are occupational bearers of bad news. Their situation, however, differs from that of the deputy marshal in that the bad news is delivered between individuals who know each other and not between total strangers. It also differs from that of both the doctors and the deputy marshal in that the delivery of bad news is between persons who are engaged in an ongoing relationship in the same organization and who are mutually dependent on each other for goodwill and cooperation, albeit not to the same extent. In addition, unlike the marshal, but similar to the doctor, managers may on other occasions deliver good news to the same recipient. Subsequently, although the manager is an occupational and not an amateur bearer of bad news, the continuity and interdependence of the relationship enhances the manager's concern for the impact the news has on the target and particularly on the target's attitudes and consequent behaviour towards his or her work in the organization. This exploratory study will define and classify the strategies used by managers in delivering bad news and will lay the groundwork for future empirical research on individual and organizational variations.

Methodology

The methodology employed was designed to meet the needs of an exploratory study. A variety of samples and instruments were utilized to examine refusals as experienced by organizational participants. First, a critical incident technique was utilized to collect actual refusal experiences as recalled by respondents. Three samples of refusees (those whose request had been refused) were taken: in the U.S. (N = 48); Canada (N = 90); and Israel (N = 31). Most comprised part-time graduate business students and 80 percent were currently employed. All had had some previous work experience and represented a large cross-section of organizations. Although there was some small variation across samples, the average age of respondents was approximately 30 and the samples were generally half female and half male. The great majority of respondents may be classified as lower participants since 79 percent characterized themselves as non-managerial employees or first-level supervisors. The data were collected anonymously.

A fourth sample of respondents represented a cross-section of Israeli managers (N = 43) participating in two university-sponsored training programmes for managers. All but four were males and the average age was 38. Unlike the previous three samples, these more senior managers were asked to recall an actual incident of a refusal experience as a "refusor." This sample, while not matched with the other sample of Israeli "requestors," was intended to explore possible differences between the perceptions of requestors and refusors.

Respondents in all four samples were asked to recall an actual incident in which a request for resources was denied. The specific instructions were as follows:

> Organizations never have enough resources to provide everyone with what they request: In order to understand more about how organizations behave under such conditions, please refer back to your own experiences. Please recall an episode in your experience working in an organization which reflects the following:
> *Refusee:* You've asked for, or let it be known, you'd like something

such as a budget increase, an additional secretary, larger office space, assignment of a new project, salary hike, etc. However, you found that it would not be granted.

Refusor: You have notified someone in your organization that a request they had made, such as for a budget increase, an additional secretary, larger office space, promotion, assignment to a new project and the like, had been refused.

Please describe: (a) the nature of the request; (b) what was said regarding the refusal; (c) how it was said, (e.g. . . . verbally, in memo form, grapevine), and, (d)—for refusees—your reactions and feelings; or (d)—for refusors—who was the person making the request—his/her job, position and relationship to you.

Please be as specific as possible about the chronology of events, the communications and/or dialogue between you and the other person, and the resolution.

All but one of the respondents were willing or able to recall a refusal incident. Categories of strategies and techniques with which "organizations say no" were then identified. The categories were constructed in a two-stage process. An initial set was generated inductively from descriptions of case incidents collected from a convenience sample of authors' acquaintances. Then, the responses to the above questionnaire were content analysed by two independent judges whose mandate was to sort the cases into these categories. The procedure was repeated in Israel. Consensus between the coders was used as the criterion to assign a given strategy to a category. Problems in classification were used as an opportunity to refine categories. The categories are by no means exhaustive, and for many responses more than one category was activated.

Finally, in-depth interviews of 1½–2 hours in length were conducted with nine Israeli school principals (four primary, one junior high and four high school; six males and three females) to probe the effects of context on refusal strategy and style refusal. Additional informal, open-ended interviews were conducted with 25 managers and colleagues. The open- and closed-ended interviews, combined with the critical incident data, were designed to build grounded theory by means of triangulation (Jick 1979).

Results

Analysis of our data suggests four types of explanations are offered to convey refusals: normative invocation, entitlement denial, equity, and benevolence. In addition, there are explicit refusals without any explanation and attrition techniques of avoidance or stalling. Our typology of refusal modes is summarized in Table 1.

Table 1. A classification of refusal tactics

Explanation
1. NORMATIVE INVOCATION = An appeal to substantial and/or procedural rationality.
2. EQUITY = An appeal to individual or collective fairness.
3. ENTITLEMENT DENIAL = Disclamation of definition of entitlements according to technical skills, seniority, age, or less formalized criteria such as sex, race, and personal connections.
4. BENEVOLENCE = Refusal explained in terms of the "real" interests of the refusee and/or generosity of the organization.

No Explanation
1. EXPLICIT REFUSAL, BUT NO EXPLANATION = Clear refusal but no espoused rationale (e.g. "No you can't have it.")
2. ATTRITION (AVOIDANCE AND STALLING), IMPLICIT REFUSAL = No clear refusal but through avoidance and stalling, no action is taken.

Normative invocation

The most frequently used refusal strategy was that of a normative invocation in which the denial was explained and justified in terms of higher order values and their structural manifestations. Following Simon (1976) we may distinguish between two types of normative invocations: "substantial rationality," which refers to refusals justified on the basis of maximizing the organization's profit or service goals and "procedural rationality" which refers to refusals justified on the basis of complying with bureaucratic rules and procedures. Functional rationality and technical efficiency are aspects of organizational ideology which legitimate the division of labour and the structure of authority (Kanter 1977). Consequently, decisions professed to have been taken on those grounds are made legitimate and, by implication, correct. "We can't afford to increase your budget this year," "It's against company policy," "It's the rule here," "The interests of the organization require that," are examples of statements tendered as reasons for not granting a request.

Normative invocations are occasions for the superior to explicate "the organization's point of view" and in so doing, to reaffirm management's right to define what the prevailing point of view is in the situation. The following examples are taken from our data:

Refusee 1: "It's not in the budget."
Request to hire an additional manager to cover afternoon shift operations. Was told could not afford to add to head count during decline in sales. *Response:* Frustrated because I was convinced of the need and felt that the expense could be justified.

Refusee 2: "The needs of the organization."
Requested a subordinate be transferred for his and the company's benefit. Was told no, not now. Needs of my boss's organization too

great at this time to release him, perhaps later. *Response:* Felt as if I had been out of line in making the request (which I wasn't) and felt hesitant about any future requests.

Refusee 3: "We can't afford it."
Requested a pay raise. Was told not possible due to budget constraints. *Response:* Did not believe my bureau chief. I knew there was money available for raises and that it was his discretion solely that determined that distribution.

Refusor 1: "For the client's welfare."
A teacher of English wished to concentrate her teaching schedule so as to be at school only two days a week. Technically this was possible, but I adamantly refused saying it would make things more difficult for the students and their welfare always stood before my eyes as a top priority.

Differences among the various types of organization in terms of the rhetoric of normative justification naturally varied somewhat. Business organizations tended to use rational-financial explanations while government administrators relied more on rules and procedural rationality. Service organizations were more typified by client or service goals. For example, the school principals reported frequent emphasis on "the good of the child." Disagreements, however, may emerge in terms of whose definition of the child's best interests should prevail.

In the above illustrations, the refusal is rationalized in terms of the rules of behaviour generally followed. In some cases the rationality of the decision was openly questioned, even the wisdom of the criterion used for making the decision was criticized (e.g., Refusee 2). In no case, however, was the right of the superior to make the decision, and impose it upon the subordinate, questioned. Subordinate and superior share an understanding of how the organization works. That understanding includes the belief that each holds about his/her relative authority and power in the situation. The ceremonies of refusal are micro-events in which these beliefs are tested against the reality and then either validated and reinforced, or weakened and perhaps transformed.

There are a number of reasons why normative invocations are the most frequently used rhetoric for conveying refusals. First, as already noted, they have high legitimacy in the organizational culture and form the basis for that culture. Furthermore, reference to rational considerations impersonalizes the refusal and veils the power dimension in the interaction between subordinate and superior (Gouldner 1954). They are, in addition, difficult to refute since lower participants are usually less knowledgeable about rules and budget allocations than their superiors. However, even when the subordinate believes that the explanation does not represent the "real" basis for the decision, as in the case of Refusee 3, few are ready to challenge and declare that "the king has no clothes."

Entitlement denial

Organizational cultures define what kind of people are entitled to what sort of treatment. People are sorted for entitlements according to their technical skills, seniority, as well as many other less formalized criteria, such as class, race, sex, age, and personal connections. The subordinate who initiates a request is frequently making a claim to being a certain kind of person or to having a certain status which entitles him/her to make the request and expect that it be granted.[1]

Organizations differ in the specificity, universality and stability of the requisites for entitlements. Where these are highly specific (such as words per minute for getting a typing job), universally applied, and stable over time, individuals making requests are more likely to know the requirements and be able to assess whether they are entitled to that which they claim. Requisites, however, may also be diffuse as when quality is stressed, and particularistic as when each request is treated as unique and changing. Such is often the situation in cases of university tenure and promotion. Entitlement denial is more likely to be used as the basis for refusals where requisites are diffuse and more subjective, since the refusee is less likely to be in a position to appeal.

An entitlement denial is an occasion when the rejection of the claim forms the basis for the refusal. The message conveyed is that "you are not what you present yourself to be." This strategy shifts the responsibility for the refusal from the organization to the individual. If effective, the subordinate will perceive the organization as acting equitably and him/herself as inadequate. When the inadequacy is defined as remediable, and the subordinate is led to believe that she/he may become what she/he has professed to be (provided she/he publishes more articles, gets more experience, etc.) then fervor of effort is likely to ensue.

> *Refusee 4: "You will get what you deserve."*
> A better rating on my annual evaluation was requested. I was told it would not be granted because I did not "stand out in the crowd." I had a verbal interview. I was very angry. I requested and obtained a second verbal interview. I requested a full explanation of the evaluation process and criteria. I presented my case based on the criteria. At a third interview I was informed my rating had been improved as I had requested. I was informed that the improved rating was not due to my efforts but because my manager's superior thought I deserved the rating.

In the above case the refusee negotiated a redefinition of the quality of his contribution which led to a reassessment of his entitlement.

Another form of entitlement denial is to insist that the subordinate has

---

1. We are grateful to Diane Margolis for this interpretation.

not met the time requirements for that which she/he requests, as in the following examples:

> *Refusee 5: "You are not senior enough."*
> On a part-time job, I requested more hours of work for the summer. The request was refused as management replied that the number of hours allocated was based on seniority and individuals who had been with the firm longer than myself were able to obtain more hours of work. *Response:* I felt that work performance is a more important criterion than seniority; however, since the company places more importance on seniority, I accepted the explanation with reluctance.

> *Refusee 6: "You're not old enough."*
> I worked in a commercial bank. Asked to be promoted to commercial banking officer from division assistant. I was told that I was too young and not ready for the position (I was only 22 years old).

Merton (1982) referred to such time considerations as "socially expected durations"; namely, culturally prescribed and socially patterned expectations about the amount of time something will or should take. They are not the same as actual durations. The enactment of a socially expected duration as a justification for refusal may reflect the belief that during a specified time something will occur which is not likely to occur in less (or more) time. Time then becomes the measurable substitute for whatever process is supposed to occur.

Entitlement denial may also take the form of discrediting the subordinate's presentation of self and accrediting him/her with a less attractive identity. The superior may select from a variety of labels (too aggressive, too impatient, uncooperative, poor team worker), any or all of which might serve to disqualify the subordinate for the very benefits being sought. None of our respondents reported using a discrediting tactic and few reported being the object of one. This may reflect the exclusion of socially undesirable behaviour in the accounts of refusors and of experiences of degradation in the accounts of requestors.

In sum, entitlement denial shifts responsibility for the refusal to the individual and reinforces the sanctity and impenetrability of organizational rules, values, and stature.

Equity

Equity explanations are justifications in which an explicit or implicit reference is made to a standard of social or collective fairness. We include in this category only refusals in which some comparison was made between the refusee and other members in the organization. Refusals in which deservedness was determined on the basis of the individual's inputs/outputs were classified as entitlement denial. Equity is essentially an externally based value principle about how resources should be allocated. The predominant type of refusals in this category related to the rules of allocation and conveyed the message that "if you get what you ask for, others in the organization will deem it not fair they do not get the same." For example:

> *Refusee 7: "Have you gone mad?"*
> A public health nurse asked that a car be made available to her for her house calls to chronically ill patients. The response from her superior was "Have you gone mad? I am not even prepared to consider it. If you get a car everyone else will demand one."

> *Refusee 8: "It will create a precedent."*
> A subordinate asked to work shorter hours in an organization where there were no part-time workers. The reply was that granting the request would create an undesirable precedent.

In both illustrations, the person requesting is not told she/he is not entitled to what is being asked for or that it was not in the substantial interest of the organization that the request be granted. The refusal was based on the superiors' perceptions of the beliefs about fairness current in the organization and the consequent entitlements that would be generated among other members as a consequence of granting this request. The apparently moral concern thus becomes a rational consideration since to infringe upon workers' beliefs of what was fair could result in unrest and increased demands on the organization for resources.

A second type of fairness explanation was based on the premise that the amount of resources available is fixed and if the refusee is granted his/her request others will have to be deprived of some resource to which they are entitled. For example:

> *Refusee 9: "Are you willing to spoil the family relations?"*
> An efficiency expert in a consulting department of a productivity institute requested additional mileage allowance since her clients were located farther from headquarters than were the clients of other members of the department. At the time all department members received an equal mileage allowance. Her superior refused explaining that if he gave her more he would have to reduce the allowance of other members. That would spoil the family relations in the department. He asked her if she wished to do so and was she willing that he cut back on the allowance of the others. She deferred.

> *Refusee 10: "This time you will change your vacation."*
> A manager reported that one of his subordinates asked to take his vacation during the summer months, a time preferred by most employees in the organization. "I first got all the facts together and then explained to the employee that he had had his vacation during the summer months during the past two years while others had to either advance or postpone theirs. This year he would have to choose another time."

In the first example, the woman posed what appeared to be an equitable request—namely that her mileage payment relative to the miles driven should be equal to the payment to others relative to the miles they drove. The superior, however, defined the situation in terms of an alternative principle of fairness—depriving others of what they had already been promised they would receive and presumably also believed they were entitled to. In this example, the victim is coopted to participate in affirming the wisdom of her own refusal. To do otherwise would make her responsible for any negative outcomes that might ensue.

It is interesting to note that the majority of cases of equity refusals were from the Israeli sample which may suggest that differences in societal culture (as different from organizational culture) are at play. Cross-cultural studies of managerial and work culture indicate that Israel is more collectively oriented and the U.S. a more individually oriented society (Hofstede 1984). In collective societies, the range of persons who may become reference points for comparison and determining entitlements is greater than in individualistic societies.

Benevolence

A benevolent justification is one in which the refusal is explained in terms of the "real" interests of the refusee—a case of "for your own good" (FYOG). In FYOG the meaning of the refusal is inverted and redefined as "good news" even if not immediately recognized as such by the refusee.

In FYOG rituals the benevolence may be directed to the subordinate either as a member of the organization (the public career) or as a person and member of a family (the private career). In both, the primacy of the superior's concern for the subordinate's welfare is the dominant posture and the presumption is that the superior's understanding of the subordinate's goals and the means for their achievement is greater than that of the subordinate. In relation to the public career, typical statements are "the job is not right for you," "you think you'll like it but you won't," "a pay increase now will arouse a lot of hostility." In the private career, typical statements employed particularly with women are: "If you become a manager how will you take care of your kids" or "how will your husband feel." When the benevolence is strongly paternalistic scratching the surface reveals hints of "intimidation": statements like "If I raise this with the board, they'll think you're a trouble maker" or "I'm willing to do this for you but you will have to bear the consequences."

While a number of colleagues and acquaintances in informal conversations reported receiving benevolent explanations for refusals, none were reported by the refusee samples. Refusors, however, did describe benevolent refusal strategies. The following are some examples:

Refusor 2: A senior secretary in a department with four years' seniority asked to be moved to another department as a result of a conflict with her immediate superior. The secretary does her work well and is in the job that is best suited to her. In my opinion the conflict was the result of a misunderstanding and her request for a transfer only the reflection of momentary anger. I explained my view to her and told her I thought her job ideal for her and pressing her request for a transfer would damage her position in the organization.

Refusor 3: A service technician asked for permission to do similar work as a technician after hours on his "free time." I refused and explained to him that such work could create conflicts of loyalty for him. In addition his free time was intended for him to rest and if he failed to do so, his accumulated fatigue would not be good for him or for the company.

In the first case, benevolence masks a patriarchal-power position. The refusee is not made party to the decision of what is in her best interests—even the manager whom one would expect would wish to present himself in a favourable light, does not report presenting the subordinate with an option. In the second case, benevolence is used instead of normative invocation since there is apparently a policy against technicians moonlighting which is why the technician sought special permission. One can only conjecture why the benevolence explanation was stressed over the policy one.

One may speculate that the incongruence between a refusal decision to which the refusee is not a party and a benevolent explanation strains the credibility of the explanation. This may be the reason why none of our sample reported benevolence as the tactics used for justifying the denial.

"See how fair we are"

A number of other techniques were used which we classified as being of a benevolent character. These include "booby prize," "delayed gratification" and "recycling." "See how fair we are" is the implicit message when the subordinate is offered an alternative, one less costly to the organization. "Booby prize" is given as consolation and includes change in job title instead of in job responsibility, a trip to a conference, or a portion of whatever was asked for, whether time, money or some other resource. The prize may have greater symbolic than substantial value, as when the refusal is redefined as a compliment in the following example of meaning inversal.

Refusee 11: "You're too good for a better job."
Perhaps one year ago I requested of my boss to be placed on a new project. My boss himself explained to me that I was in a sort of Catch-22 situation. I had done so well at my job in terms of defining my role and my interrelationships with the other disciplines that I was irreplaceable. I was told that I would have to follow the project through to completion. I was given extra responsibility which only took *one day every three weeks* (our emphasis). It gave me the diver-

sification I desired. The way my boss posed the explanation was very flattering.

"Delayed gratification" was found to be a more common technique than booby prize, perhaps because it is less costly to the organization, at least in the short run. It refers to the technique of following the refusal with a suggestion that the person try again in the future—whether the time period be specified or left vague. This is consistent with Bies' (1982) laboratory findings that explanations oriented to future promises rather than to past achievements reduced the perceived "badness" of the bad news.

"Recycling" refers to the process by which individuals are helped to adopt a new identity in cases where the refusal has damaged the original one. It is a face-saving technique which takes a number of forms. One executive reported that when a vice president had been denied promotion, he was encouraged to move to another plant where this biographical scar would not be detected. People who are denied positions may be given generous letters of recommendation to help them move elsewhere. A provost of a university reported that when individuals make requests on behalf of groups or constituencies, they need to be helped to save face with those who sent them. In such cases, after discussing the refusal with the person, he sends him a letter confirming that he had put up a tough fight and had made a strong case for his request on behalf of his constituency, but, despite his great efforts, the request could not be met. Techniques such as "recycling" and "booby prize" often have greater value for the effect they have on the refusee's peers and their regard for him or her than they have for the refusee directly.

No explanation

There were also instances reported in which no explanation was proferred. In a minority of cases, the refusals were tersely to the point: "No you cannot have it." But the most common type of non-explanation was some form of attrition. Attrition behaviours are a form of "non-violent" resistance in which refusal is frequently implicit but not openly voiced. If successful they produce motivational fatigue as the subordinate gets used to his/her condition and comes to accept it. Attrition takes two forms: avoidance and stalling.

"Avoidance" takes place when the subordinate's initiatives are disattended (Goffman 1959). Telephone messages are not responded to, letters are not answered. After one or two attempts, the subordinate may either get discouraged or get the message and withdraw from further initiatives. This response was very rare in our study.

"Avoidance" is more likely to take this form in large organizations where relations are relatively formalized and the person to whom the communication is directed is not the immediate superior or at least not personally known to the subordinate. These conditions make more difficult the use of informal modes of access to those in authority. Such inaccessibility may be specifically fostered for that purpose. "Avoidance," however, may also occur in face-to-face encounters as in the following example related by a newly tenured associate professor:

> I wrote my dean asking for an extended leave. He didn't reply. I met
> him several times after that at faculty meetings but each time he
> avoided raising the issue. I was forced to be the one to raise it. I began
> to feel like a nag. Last time he walked right by me as if I weren't
> there. I knew I had better not raise the issue there.

"Avoidance" is most likely to deter only the more timid and those whose position in the organization is precarious. When the subordinate persists, the superior may be persuaded to shift to another tactic.

"My hands are tied" or "It's not up to me" is another type of avoidance ritual in which the superior denies responsibility for the decision and avoids dealing with the issue by pointing to others who may be credibly presented as constraining action on the part of the superior. Organizations that generate a large number of committees provide fertile ground for the use of this ritual.

"Stalling" refers to tactics used to gain time, such as "I'll look into it," or "You look into it." As different from "avoidance," stalling tactics convey the message that something is being done to remedy the situation. "Stalling" may also have an attritional effect but successful stalling rites sustain the subordinate's belief in the organization's good will toward him/her and the hope that at some time in the future the matter will be resolved to the subordinate's satisfaction, as in the following example:

> *Refusee 12: "I'll get back to you."*
> Requested an increase in salary. The initial response was positive with
> the supervisor saying he would get back to me. A few weeks passed
> with no response so I approached him. Again a few weeks passed and
> then I was told it would come in the form of a bonus and pay increase
> at the end of the year. It's been six months since my request and al-
> though they haven't said no, I haven't seen any increase or been
> informed of the amount.

In "I'll look into it" the manager presumably takes it upon him/herself to pursue the matter further after the subordinate leaves. This expression of intent and goodwill may be lent greater credibility by a jotting down of a note as if once recorded, "I'll look into it" takes on an "as good as done" quality. Two school principals reported that they generally refrained from immediately saying "no" even if they had already decided to refuse the request in order to impress upon the teacher that they had made an effort on her or his behalf.

"You look into it" transfers responsibility for the next step to the subordinate. S/he is asked to do something which is presented as necessary before anything else can be done. This may require preparing a report explaining his/her position on the issue or collecting data which may be difficult to obtain:

> *Refusee 13: "Bring me proof."*
> I requested additional office help (one person) for duties the junior marketing assistant had in addition to her researching and analyzing functions; since when her work load backs up, so does mine. (I am the senior marketing research assistant.) The refusal was based on the overall all-corporate freeze, in addition to the lack of long-term history regarding the amount of work that such an extra person would have— in other words, I couldn't prove that there would always be 40 hours of work per week for a secretary.

Successful stalling may be extended for a relatively long time until either the superior is replaced or circumstances change so as to make the initial request no longer relevant. The following incident reveals how the first supervisor was spared the refusal while her replacement shifts responsibility for solving the problem to the subordinate, an implicit discrediting ritual:

> *Refusee 14: "Wait till things settle down."*
> I requested an exchange of offices, to be nearer my boss and co-workers. My boss said to wait until "things settled down," then, until the organizational development project was finished. I waited 12 months. My boss moved up to the executive director, reporting to the vice-president, and my new boss told me (two weeks ago) that no change would be made; I was also told that it was up to me to overcome the obstacle of distance and to find ways to integrate myself into the activities of my co-workers.

Stalling ceremonies are successful when they convey a message of goodwill and get the manager off the hook, if only temporarily. The general cultural norm according to which it is not nice to refuse a request, makes it generally more difficult to say "no" than to say "yes."

Summary

Table 2 summarizes the distribution of refusal tactics across all four samples and points to three major observations. First, in terms of general patterns of tactic types (those with explanation and those without), refusals were accompanied by explanations in the large majority of cases. The explanation most typically offered was the normative invocation type while benevolent rationales were least often reported. Second, refusors reported that they rarely "brushed off" a request without explanation, whereas 20 percent of the refusees reported instances of no explanation. This is consistent with traditional findings indicating wide perceptual gaps between sub-

Table 2. Refusal strategy used as perceived by lower-level refusees and middle-/upper-level refusors

Espoused Refusal Strategy	Refusee Sample (Lower Level)			Refusor Sample (Middle/ Upper Level)
	U.S. (N = 48)	Canada (N = 90)	Israel (N = 31)	Israel (N = 43)
Explanation				
Normative Invocation	50%	76%	46%	52%
Equity	4	0	14	15
Benevolence	0	0	0	10
Entitlement Denial	20	2	14	18
Miscellaneous	4	2	3	2
Subtotal	78	80	77	97
No Explanation				
Explicit Refusal	5%	6%	5%	0%
Attrition	17	14	18	3
Subtotal	22	20	23	3
TOTAL	100%	100%	100%	100%

ordinates and superiors (although this study was not a paired sample). Finally, there appear to be cross-cultural differences in the use of tactics, and although not tested here, there were indications as well of differences across organizations. According to the data, Canadians tend to be more oriented to organization rationality than either Americans or Israelis. Israelis, however, were more equity-oriented than either other nationality while Americans were the most "heavy-handed" in terms of entitlement denial. Linkages to national values and a national ethos are suggestive but speculative.

In approximately 20 percent of the cases the enactment of more than one refusal mode was reported. In almost every case, the refusal was conveyed in a face-to-face encounter; only rarely was it delivered by telephone or in a letter. This finding supports those of Lengel and Daft (1984) and Griffin, Bateman and Head (1984) who found that bad news tends to be delivered in person. A possible explanation may be that the refusor's presence enhances his or her ability to exert damage control, should this be necessary.

Discussion

Goffman (1952) argued that the individual (the mark) needs to be cooled out so that she/he does not "squawk," create a row, or be an embarrassment to the organization in some other way. The refused member, however, must not only be "cooled out" but then also "cooled in" to the culture so that his/her commitments are reharnessed to the purposes of the organization (as defined by managers). In this sense, the refusal process can be characterized in ritualized terms because, as pointed out by Benford and Kurtz (1984), rituals both provide solutions to problems concerning difficult situations *and* serve to reify social processes and reinforce social structure.

The refusal ritual first helps solve a problem of inadequate information. On this level, the refusal process can convey explicit guidelines and information about "the way things are done around here." On another level, refusals reinforce the social structure in that they define realities, personal status and entitlements, and what influence people can exercise. The symbolic sphere is intertwined with the power sphere. Smircich and Morgan (1982) characterized this type of process as "power-based reality construction." Refusal rituals contribute to the reaffirmation of the values, norms, beliefs (i.e., culture) of the organization as defined by managers, and sustain institutional order. As such, Pfeffer (1981, 299) argued that the distribution of power ". . . is perpetuated because people come to believe that this is how things always were, always will be and always should be."

Refusals, however, also arouse resentment and create tensions—which may indeed test the strength of the dominant culture. Many of the refused subordinates in this study reported feeling frustrated, resentful, angry, and alienated. While part of the message of the refusal process underscores the relative unimportance or powerlessness of the subordinates, it may create unintended consequences as well. In some few cases, the employee actually resigned. In others, employees tried to resist the refusal—albeit within the ground rules of "evidence" defined by management. Some persisted until the refusal decision was overturned. For many, the disgruntlement appears to have resulted at least temporarily in demoralization, discouragement, and even some questioning of the fairness or wisdom of policies, and persons in authority. It was not always clear that these people were indeed appeased and ready to do what was expected of them, willingly.

Although the perception of the ground rules may be shared and the distribution of power generally accepted, subordinates clearly had not bought all the values. One group in the organization "produces" culture but it is not necessarily consumed isomorphically by other groups. That is, being "in" the culture and enacting behaviour within its terms is distinct from being "of" the culture, internalizing the dominant values and definitions of reality. The subordinate is typically not an equal partner in the determination of the culture nor, however, is he or she without power. Thus the dialectic tension: the more the culture is reaffirmed, the more the potential exists for resentment and opposition.

In this respect, the refusal process represents a delicate and difficult dilemma for organizations to manage. An abundance of refusals would presumably drain the reservoir of organizational goodwill and create uncomfortable tensions. It is thus in the interests of managers to institutionalize refusal reduction mechanisms which mitigate the need to say no. A number of such mechanisms were identified in the course of our interviews.

One technique is the *explication of rules*. When organizational values are communicated at the outset and the policies regarding the allocation of resources are routinized, explicit and widely known, the need for refusals could be preempted. The assumption underlying this argument is that requests are prompted by a lack of information concerning the rules and regulations and once these are known, and thus the ignorance eradicated, the number of unrequitable requests would decline.

A second technique is through the *avoidance of entitlement creation*. The allocation of salaries and other benefits at regular and specified intervals of time create expectations and potential requests. Those to whom management does not want to give benefits must then be explicitly refused. Organizations, therefore, may seek to prevent the routinization of resource distributions as a means for avoiding the establishment of entitlements. In place of a yearly salary hiking ritual, for example, individuals are invited into management from time to time as determined by management. While bureaucratic rules limit the freedom of management—the avoidance of routinization preserves its control (Crozier 1964).

The *norm of secrecy* facilitates the avoidance of entitlements. Where the culture defines it as "inappropriate" to share information about salaries and other benefits, those who are denied the benefits lack the information to assess their loss and the motivation to squawk.

In addition to their official function of jointly assessing worker performance, *performance evaluation sessions* also serve to transmit information in both directions concerning expectations and perceived entitlements. It becomes an occasion for encouraging the worker to make interpretations of his/her condition which would discourage unsolicited requests. At the same time, the evaluator is also gathering information about the worker's anticipated rewards and assessing the probabilities of his/her squawking if disappointed. In other words, performance evaluation is a political event in which both the evaluator and the evaluee gauge each other's intentions and attempt to manipulate and monitor future possible requests and refusals.

Finally, there are many ways in which the *psychological or other costs* of making a request can be heightened particularly since every request involves some measure of uncertainty and risk for the requestor.

Directions for future research

The identification of "refusals" as a domain for research stimulates a large number of questions for organizational research. A few are listed here with some preliminary directions for investigation suggested by our data:

First, in what ways do organizations or subunits differ in the patterned use of refusal tactics? What are the correlates of refusal tactic choice? Given the interest today in the description of corporate cultures, it is plausible to assume, for example, that participative-type cultures would evidence different patterns of refusal frequency and mode than autocratic style cultures.

In the Israeli refusor sample, use of the entitlement denial tactic was reported considerably more often among the more powerful than among the less powerful managers. Relative to their proportion in the sample, a larger percentage of older, more senior, and higher level managers reported using entitlemental denial than young, low seniority and junior level managers. School principals, in addition, explicitly emphasized that they avoid explanations which put responsibility on the teacher and prefer to emphasize the welfare of the students or the rules of the ministry of education as explanations for refusals. The schools studied all had relatively flat hierarchies, and salaries were determined by nationwide contracts. It appears that the entitlement denial tactic involves a greater use of power, and those who feel relatively powerless are less likely to resort to it. Future research needs to explore other individual and organizational factors that may influence choice of tactic.

Second, is there a relationship between choice of refusal tactic or frequency of refusal rituals and some measure of organizational effectiveness? Peters and Waterman (1982) contend that excellent companies are those in which people do more and ask less for permission—that is, companies in which there are fewer refusals. The relationship between excellence and rate of refusals is probably mediated by rate of growth, availability of slack resources and other such factors which contribute both to excellence and the need to refuse requests.

Third, what are the patterned responses of refusees to their conditions and what are the determinants of these patterns? We were struck by the large number of subordinates who reported feeling angry or cheated. This finding may be an artifact of the method which asked respondents to recall an incident and perhaps incidents involving strong feelings were aroused. Yet Faulkner (1974, 135) observed that most studies "beg the sociological question: how do people in highly competitive work structure design and organize their careers so as to handle issues of denial and failure." Despite some few contributions since (e.g., Kanter 1977), there is still a lack of sociological studies on the demise of mobility aspirations in the light of blocked opportunities. We have suggested that refusals may become an occasion for negotiation and power dynamics in which refusees are not merely passive recipients of bad news but active protagonists for a redefinition of the outcome. How and under what conditions this occurs needs to be studied.

Fourth, all other things being equal, who is more likely to get refused? What are the characteristics of the refusee, of the situation, or of his/her relationship to the refusor that affect the probability of his/her being refused—his/her "refusal quotient?"

Fifth, what are the more effective and less effective ways of conveying refusal? The personnel literature, for example, provides little to no guidance in instructing managers on how to deal with denial of requests or related issues. Clearly, based on the results of this study, refusees rarely reported being helped by the refusor to find alternative solutions to the problems which the request was intended to resolve. Is this behaviour rewarded in organizations?

Finally, what are the similarities and differences in contrasting refusal rituals with acceptance instances? Do they follow a similar logic? Recent work on compliance (Cialdini 1984) offers a useful opportunity for comparing the two social processes.

This paper has taken a micro-political perspective in examining the surface and underlying interpretation of a rather routine event in daily working life—the art of saying no. We have identified and classified a variety of refusal tactics and have suggested ways in which organizations try to protect themselves from having to say "I regret that . . ." The management and understanding of refusal rituals represents a microcosm of power and culture issues and offers a domain rich in research possibilities and application. Remarkable throughout this research was the finding that there is no shortage of refusal experiences from which to draw.

References

(1983) "Mediatory myths in the service of organizational ideology" in *Organizational symbolism*. L. R. Pondy, P. Frost, G. Morgan, and T. Dandridge (eds.), 273–294. Greenwich, Conn.: JAI Press.

Allaire, Y., and M. E. Firsirotu (1984), "Theories of organizational culture." *Organization Studies* 3: 193–226.

Baker, E. L. (1980), "Managing organizational culture." *Management Review,* July: 8–13.

Benford, R., and L. R. Kurtz (1984), "Performing the nuclear ceremony: the arms race as a ritual." Paper presented at the annual meeting of the Society for Sociological Study of Social Problems. San Antonio, Texas, August 22.

Bies, R. J. (1982), "The delivery of bad news in organizations: a social information perspective." Paper presented at the Academy of Management Meeting, New York City.

Brown, R. H. (1978), "Bureaucracy as praxis: toward a political phenomenology of formal organizations." *Administrative Science Quarterly* 23: 365–382.

Cialdini, R. B. (1984), *Influence: how and why people agree to things.* New York: William Morrow.

Clark, Burton R. (1960), "The cooling out function in higher education." *The American Journal of Sociology* 65: 569–575.

Clark, P. B., and J. Q. Wilson (1961), "Incentive systems: a theory of organizations." *Administrative Science Quarterly* 6: 129–166.

Crozier, M. (1964), *The bureaucratic phenomenon.* Chicago: University of Chicago Press.

Cunnison, S. (1966), *Wages and work allocation.* London: Tavistock.

Faulkner, R. R. (1974), "Coming of age in organizations: a comparative study of career contingencies and adult socialization." *Sociology of Work and Occupation* 1: 131–173.

Glaser, B. G., and A. L. Strauss (1965), *Awareness of dying*. Chicago: Aldine.

Glaser, B. G., and A. L. Strauss (1968), *Time for dying*. Chicago: Aldine.

Goffman, E. (1952), "On cooling the mark out." *Psychiatry,* November 15: 451–463.

Goffman, E. (1959), *The presentation of self in everyday life*. Garden City, New York: Doubleday.

Goffman, E. (1967), *Interaction ritual: essays in face-to-face behavior*. Chicago: Aldine.

Goody, J. (1961), "Religion and ritual: the definitional problem." *British Journal of Sociology* 12: 142–164.

Gouldner, A. (1954), *Patterns of industrial democracy*. London: Routledge and Kegan Paul.

Griffin, R., T. Bateman, and T. Head (1984), "Managerial media selection of the delivery of good and bad news: a laboratory experiment." Paper presented at the Academy of Management Meetings, Boston.

Gronn, P. (1983), "Talk as the work: the accomplishment of school administration." *Administrative Science Quarterly* 28/1: 1–21.

Hofstede, G. (1984), "The cultural relativity of the quality of life concept." *Academy of Management Review* 9/3: 389–398.

Izraeli, D. N. (1977), "Settling in: an interactionist perspective on the entry of the new manager." *Pacific Sociological Review* 20/1: 135–160.

Izraeli, D. N. (1980), "The shifting boundaries of a television assembly department" in *A composite portrait of Israel*. E. Marx (ed.), 113–135. London: Academic Press.

Jick, T. D. (1979), "Mixing qualitative and quantitative methods: triangulation in action." *Administrative Science Quarterly* 24/4: 602–611.

Jick, T. D., and V. V. Murray (1982), "The management of hard times: budget cutbacks in public sector organizations." *Organization Studies* 3/2: 141–169.

Kanter, R. M. (1977), *Men and women of the corporation*. New York: Basic Books.

Leach, E. R. (1968), "Ritual" in *International encyclopedia of social sciences* 13: 520–526. New York: Macmillan.

Lengel, R., and R. Daft (1984), "Richness match: a contingency model of managerial information source preferences." Paper presented at the Academy of Management Meetings, Boston.

Louis, M. R. (1983), "Organizations as culture-bearing milieu" in *Organizational symbolism*. L. R. Pondy, P. Frost, G. Morgan, and T. Dandridge (eds.), 39–54. Greenwich, Conn.: JAI Press.

Lupton, T. (1963), *On the shop floor*. London: Pergamon Press.

McClenahen, L., and J. Lofland (1976), "Bearing bad news: tactics of the deputy U.S. marshal." *Sociology of Work and Occupations* 3/3: 251–272.

Merton, R. (1982), "Socially expected durations." Paper presented at Annual Meeting of the American Sociological Association, San Francisco.

Moch, M. (1980), "Chewing ass out: the enactment of power relationships through language and ritual." Paper presented at the Academy of Management Meetings, Detroit, August.

Moore, S. F., and B. G. Myerhoff, eds. (1977), *Secular ritual.* Assen: Van Gorcum.

Morgan, G. (1984), "Creating social reality: organizations as cultures." Unpublished manuscript, York University.

Peters, T., and R. H. Waterman (1982), *In search of excellence.* New York: Harper and Row.

Pettigrew, A. M. (1979), "On studying organization cultures." *Administrative Science Quarterly* 24: 570–581.

Pfeffer, J. (1981), *Power in organizations.* Boston: Pitman.

Radcliffe-Brown, A. R. (1977), "Religion and society" in *The social anthropology of Radcliffe-Brown,* 103–128. London: Routledge and Kegan Paul.

Riley, P. (1983), "A structurationist account of political cultures." *Administrative Science Quarterly* 28/3: 414–437.

Roethlisberger, R. J., and W. J. Dickson (1939), *Management and the worker.* Cambridge, Massachusetts: Harvard University Press.

Simmel, G. (1971), *On individuality and social forms: selected writings.* Donald N. Levine (ed.), 6–22. Chicago: University of Chicago Press.

Simon, Herbert A. (1976), *Administrative behavior* (3rd Ed.). New York: Macmillan.

Smircich, L. (1983), "Organizations and shared meanings" in *Organizational symbolism.* L. R. Pondy, P. Frost, G. Morgan and T. Dandridge (eds.), 55–65. Greenwich, Conn.: JAI Press.

Smircich, L., and G. Morgan (1982), "Leadership: the management of meaning." *Journal of Applied Behavioral Science* 18/3: 257–273.

Sudnow, D. (1967), *Passing on.* Englewood Cliffs, New Jersey: Prentice-Hall.

Tesser, A., and S. Rosen (1975), "The reluctance to transmit bad news" in *Advances in experimental social psychology,* Vol. 8. L. Berkowitz (ed.), 294–323. New York: Academic Press.

Tesser, A., S. Rosen, and T. R. Batchelor (1972), "On the reluctance to communicate bad news (the MUM effect): a role play extension." *Journal of Personality* 40: 88–103.

Wilkins, A. L. (1983), "Organizational stories as symbols which control the organization" in *Organizational symbolism.* L. R. Pondy, P. Frost, G. Morgan, and T. Dandridge (eds.), 81–92. Greenwich, Conn.: JAI Press.

5 Leading: Inspiration and Direction

Leadership, personal leadership, has become important again. We say "again" because in the 1950s, 1960s, and even the 1970s we didn't hear much about personal leadership on the management scene. We heard a lot about leadership as a set of functions, with the leader as someone who made sure that those functions were performed and consensus achieved.

But the idea of the "transformational" leader, of the visionary and missionary leader, is back and alive and well, *along with* (*not* instead of) the humanistic, team-building leader.

So this section starts with Edgar Schein's paper on the role of the founder as leader and culture builder. It reasserts the importance, for decades ahead, of the founder's leadership role in new organizations, showing how founders' visions and determination can shape organizations' long-term culture.

Then we go to Abraham Zaleznik's argument that managers and leaders need not be the same thing. Some managers are leaders, but some aren't. Again, the emphasis is on personal attributes and attitudes as determinants of effective leadership.

The third paper, by Douglas McGregor, is, as many readers know, one of the all-time classics of organizational behavior. McGregor was himself a leader, an influencer of American, and indeed world, attitudes toward the managing of human beings. The McGregor paper is aimed at the beliefs held by people in leadership positions. He makes the now-famous distinction between two such sets of beliefs, which he labels Theory X and Theory Y. And he argues that Theory X assumptions (assumptions that humans are fundamentally lazy organisms, motivated only by states of deprivation) push one toward an authoritarian and perhaps punitive view of the managing process. However, Theory Y assumptions (steeped in the notion that humans are knowing, growing, and searching organisms) drive one toward much more participative practices in the leading of organizations.

The fourth paper in this section switches to still another problem—the movement of women into leadership roles in management. In her paper,

Jean Lipman-Blumen argues that access to key information and key people is a necessary condition for achieving power in organizations, and that access to such resources is often very difficult for women to attain in men's organizations. Even if the formal organizational network officially permits such access, the informal (what she calls the "homosocial") male network is often impenetrable for people who are not members of the in group. Lipman-Blumen then goes on to offer some tips for women (or for anyone on the outside looking in at the old boy network) on ways of breaking through to gain positions of leadership and power in organizational hierarchies.

The Role of the Founder in Creating Organizational Culture

Edgar H. Schein

How do the entrepreneur/founders of organizations create organizational cultures? And how can such cultures be analyzed? These questions are central to this article. First I will examine what organizational culture is, how the founder creates and embeds cultural elements, why it is likely that first-generation companies develop distinctive cultures, and what the implications are in making the transition from founders or owning families to "professional" managers.

The level of confusion over the term *organizational culture* requires some definitions of terms at the outset. An organizational cuture depends for its existence on a definable organization, in the sense of a number of people interacting with each other for the purpose of accomplishing some goal in their defined environment. An organization's founder simultaneously creates such a group and, by force of his or her personality, begins to shape the group's culture. But that new group's culture does not develop until it has overcome various crises of growth and survival, and has worked out solutions for coping with its external problems of adaptation and its internal problems of creating a workable set of relationship rules.

Organizational culture, then, is the pattern of basic assumptions that a given group has invented, discovered, or developed in learning to cope with its problems of external adaptation and internal integration—a pattern of assumptions that has worked well enough to be considered valid and, therefore, to be taught to new members as the correct way to perceive, think, and feel in relation to those problems.

In terms of external survival problems, for example, I have heard these kinds of assumptions in first-generation companies:

The way to decide on what products we will build is to see whether we ourselves like the product; if *we* like it, our customers will like it.

The only way to build a successful business is to invest no more than 5 percent of your own money in it.

The customer is the key to our success, so we must be totally dedicated to total customer service.

In terms of problems of internal integration the following examples apply:

Ideas can come from anywhere in this organization, so we must maintain a climate of total openness.

The only way to manage a growing business is to supervise every detail on a daily basis.

The only way to manage a growing business is to hire good people, give them clear responsibility, tell them how they will be measured, and then leave them alone.

Several points should be noted about the definition and the examples. First, culture is not the overt behavior or visible artifacts one might observe on a visit to the company. It is not even the philosophy or value system that the founder may articulate or write down in various "charters." Rather, it is the assumptions that underlie the values and determine not only behavior patterns, but also such visible artifacts as architecture, office layout, dress codes, and so on. This distinction is important because founders bring many of these assumptions with them when the organization begins; their problem is how to articulate, teach, embed, and in other ways get their own assumptions across and working in the system.

Founders often start with a theory of how to succeed; they have a cultural paradigm in their heads, based on their experience in the culture in which they grew up. In the case of a founding *group,* the theory and paradigm arise from the way that group reaches consensus on their assumptions about how to view things. Here, the evolution of the culture is a multi-stage process reflecting the several stages of group formation. The ultimate organizational culture will always reflect the complex interaction between (1) the assumptions and theories that founders bring to the group initially and (2) what the group learns subsequently from its own experiences.

What is organizational culture about?

Any new group has the problem of developing shared assumptions about the nature of the world in which it exists, how to survive in it, and how to manage and integrate internal relationships so that it can operate effectively and make life livable and comfortable for its members. These external and internal problems can be categorized as shown in Figure 1.

The external and internal problems are always intertwined and acting

PROBLEMS OF EXTERNAL ADAPTATION AND SURVIVAL

1. Developing consensus on the *primary task, core mission,* or *manifest and latent functions of the group*—for example, strategy.

2. Consensus on *goals,* such goals being the concrete reflection of the core mission.

3. Developing consensus on the *means to be used* in accomplishing the goals—for example, division of labor, organization structure, reward system, and so forth.

4. Developing consensus on the *criteria to be used in measuring how well the group is doing against its goals and targets*—for example, information and control systems.

5. Developing consensus on *remedial or repair strategies* as needed when the group is not accomplishing its goals.

PROBLEMS OF INTERNAL INTEGRATION

1. *Common language and conceptual categories.* If members cannot communicate with and understand each other, a group is impossible by definition.

2. Consensus on *group boundaries and criteria for inclusion and exclusion.* One of the most important areas of culture is the shared consensus on who is in, who is out, and by what criteria one determines membership.

3. Consensus on *criteria for the allocation of power and status.* Every organization must work out its pecking order and its rules for how one gets, maintains, and loses power. This area of consensus is crucial in helping members manage their own feelings of aggression.

4. Consensus on *criteria for intimacy, friendship, and love.* Every organization must work out its rules of the game for peer relationships, for relationships between the sexes, and for the manner in which openness and intimacy are to be handled in the context of managing the organization's tasks.

5. Consensus on *criteria for allocation of rewards and punishments.* Every group must know what its heroic and sinful behaviors are: what gets rewarded with property, status, and power; and what gets punished through the withdrawal of rewards and, ultimately, excommunication.

6. Consensus on *ideology and "religion."* Every organization, like every society, faces unexplainable events that must be given meaning so that menbers can respond to them and avoid the anxiety of dealing with the unexplainable and uncontrollable.

Figure 1. External and internal problems

simultaneously. A group cannot solve its external survival problem without being integrated to some degree to permit concerted action, and it cannot integrate itself without some successful task accomplishment vis-à-vis its survival problem or primary task.

The model of organizational culture that then emerges is one of shared solutions to problems which work well enough to begin to be taken for granted—to the point where they drop out of awareness, become unconscious assumptions, and are taught to new members as a reality and as the correct way to view things. If one wants to identify the elements of a given culture, one can go down the list of issues and ask how the group views itself in relation to each of them: What does it see to be its core mission, its goals, the way to accomplish those goals, the measurement systems and procedures it uses, the way it remedies actions, its particular jargon and

---

1. *The organization's relationship to its environment.* Reflecting even more basic assumptions about the relationship of humanity to nature, one can assess whether the key members of the organization view the relationship as one of dominance, submission, harmonizing, finding an appropriate niche, and so on.

2. *The nature of reality and truth.* Here are the linguistic and behavioral rules that define what is real and what is not, what is a "fact," how truth is ultimately to be determined, and whether truth is "revealed" or "discovered"; basic concepts of time as linear or cyclical, monochronic or polychronic; basic concepts such as space as limited or infinite and property as communal or individual; and so forth.

3. *The nature of human nature.* What does it mean to be "human," and what attributes are considered intrinsic or ultimate? Is human nature good, evil, or neutral? Are human beings perfectible or not? Which is better, Theory X or Theory Y?

4. *The nature of human activity.* What is the "right" thing for human beings to do, on the basis of the above assumptions about reality, the environment, and human nature: to be active, passive, self-developmental, fatalistic, or what? What is work and what is play?

5. *The nature of human relationships.* What is considered to be the "right" way for people to relate to each other, to distribute power and love? Is life cooperative or competitive; individualistic, group collaborative, or communal; based on traditional lineal authority, law, or charisma; or what?

Figure 2. Basic underlying assumptions around which paradigms form

meaning system, the authority system, peer system, reward system, and ideology? One will find, when one does this, that there is in most cultures a deeper level of assumptions which ties together the various solutions to the various problems, and this deeper level deals with more ultimate questions. The real cultural essence, then, is what members of the organization assume about the issues shown in Figure 2.

In a fairly "mature" culture—that is, in a group that has a long and rich history—one will find that these assumptions are patterned and interrelated into a "cultural paradigm" that is the key to understanding how members of the group view the world. In an organization that is in the process of formation, the paradigm is more likely to be found only in the founder's head, but it is important to try to decipher it in order to understand the biases or directions in which the founder "pushes" or "pulls" the organization.

How do organizational cultures begin?

The role of the founder

Groups and organizations do not form accidentally or spontaneously. They are usually created because someone takes a leadership role in seeing how the concerted action of a number of people could accomplish something that would be impossible through individual action alone. In the case of social movements or new religions, we have prophets, messiahs, and other kinds of charismatic leaders. Political groups or movements are started by leaders who sell new visions and new solutions. Firms are created by entrepreneurs who have a vision of how a concerted effort could create a new product or service in the marketplace. The process of culture formation in the organization begins with the founding of the group. How does this happen?

In any given firm the history will be somewhat different, but the essential steps are functionally equivalent:

1. A single person (founder) has an idea for a new enterprise.

2. A founding group is created on the basis of initial consensus that the idea is a good one: workable and worth running some risks for.

3. The founding group begins to act in concert to create the organization by raising funds, obtaining patents, incorporating, and so forth.

4. Others are brought into the group according to what the founder or founding group considers necessary, and the group begins to function, developing its own history.

In this process the founder will have a major impact on how the group solves its external survival and internal integration problems. Because the founder had the original idea, he or she will typically have biases on how to get the idea fulfilled—biases based on previous cultural experiences and personality traits. In my observation, entrepreneurs are very strong-minded about what to do and how to do it. Typically they already have strong assumptions about the nature of the world, the role their organization will play in that world, the nature of human nature, truth, relationships, time, and space.

Three examples

Founder A, who built a large chain of supermarkets and department stores, was the dominant ideological force in the company until he died in his seventies. He assumed that his organization could be dominant in the market and that his primary mission was to supply his customers with a quality, reliable product. When A was operating only a corner store with his wife, he built customer relations through a credit policy that displayed trust in the customer, and he always took products back if the customer was not satisfied. Further, he assumed that stores had to be attractive and spotless, and that the only way to ensure this was by close personal supervision. He would frequently show up at all his stores to check into small details. Since he assumed that only close supervision would teach subordinates the right skills, he expected all his store managers to be very visible and very much on top of their jobs.

A's theory about how to grow and win against his competition was to be innovative, so he encouraged his managers to try new approaches, to bring in consulting help, to engage in extensive training, and to feel free to experiment with new technologies. His view of truth and reality was to find it wherever one could and, therefore, to be open to one's environment and never take it for granted that one had all the answers. If new things worked, A encouraged their adoption.

Measuring results and fixing problems was, for A, an intensely personal matter. In addition to using traditional business measures, he went to the stores and, if he saw things not to his liking, immediately insisted that they be corrected. He trusted managers who operated on the basis of similar kinds of assumptions and clearly had favorites to whom he delegated more.

Authority in this organization remained very centralized; the ultimate source of power, the voting shares of stock, remained entirely in the family. A was interested in developing good managers throughout the organization, but he never assumed that sharing ownership through some kind of stock option plan would help in that process. In fact, he did not even share ownership with several key "lieutenants" who had been with the company through most of its life but were not in the family. They were well paid, but received no stock. As a result, peer relationships were officially defined as competitive. A liked managers to compete for slots and felt free to get rid of "losers."

A also introduced into the firm a number of family members who received favored treatment in the form of good developmental jobs that would test them for ultimate management potential. As the firm diversified, family members were made division heads even though they often had relatively little general management experience. Thus peer relationships were highly politicized. One had to know how to stay in favor, how to deal with family members, and how to maintain trust with nonfamily peers in the highly competitive environment.

A wanted open communication and high trust levels, but his own assumptions about the role of the family, the effect of ownership, and the correct way to manage were, to some degree, in conflict with each other, leading many of the members of the organization to deal with the conflicting signals by banding together to form a kind of counter-culture within the founding culture. They were more loyal to each other than to the company.

Without going into further detail, I want to note several points about the "formation" of this organization and its emerging culture. By definition, something can become part of the culture only if it works. A's theory and assumptions about how things "should be" worked, since his company grew and prospered. He personally received a great deal of reinforcement for his own assumptions, which undoubtedly gave him increased confidence that he had a correct view of the world. Throughout his lifetime he steadfastly adhered to the principles with which he started, and did everything in his power to get others to accept them as well. At the same time, however, A had to share concepts and assumptions with a great many other people. So as his company grew and learned from its own experience, A's assumptions gradually had to be modified, or A had to withdraw from certain areas of running the business. For example, in their diversification efforts, the management bought several production units that would permit backward integration in a number of areas—but, because they recognized that they knew little about running factories, they brought in fairly strong, autonomous managers and left them alone.

A also had to learn that his assumptions did not always lead to clear signals. He thought he was adequately rewarding his best young general managers, but could not see that for some of them the political climate, the absence of stock options, and the arbitrary rewarding of family members made their own career progress too uncertain. Consequently, some of his best people left the company—a phenomenon that left A perplexed but unwilling to change his own assumptions in this area. As the company matured, many of these conflicts remained and many subcultures formed around groups of younger managers who were functionally or geographically insulated from the founder.

Founder B built a chain of financial service organizations using sophisticated financial analysis techniques in an urban area where insurance companies, mutual funds, and banks were only beginning to use these techniques. He was the conceptualizer and the salesman in putting together the ideas for these new organizations, but he put only a small percentage of the money up himself, working from a theory that if he could not convince investors that there was a market, then the idea was not sound. His initial assumption was that he did not know enough about the market to gamble with his own money—an assumption based on experience, according to a story he told about the one enterprise in which he had failed miserably. With this enterprise, he had trusted his own judgment on what customers would want, only to be proven totally wrong the hard way.

B did not want to invest himself heavily in his organizations, either financially or personally. Once he had put together a package, he tried to find people whom he trusted to administer it. These were usually people who, like himself, were fairly open in their approach to business and not too hung up on previous assumptions about how things should be done. One can infer that B's assumptions about concrete goals, the means to be used to achieve them, measurement criteria, and repair strategies were pragmatic: Have a clear concept of the mission, test it by selling it to investors, bring in good people who understand what the mission is, and then leave them alone to implement and run the organization, using only ultimate financial performance as a criterion.

B's assumptions about how to integrate a group were, in a sense, irrelevant since he did not inject himself very much into any of his enterprises. To determine the cultures of those enterprises, one had to study the managers put into key positions by B—matters that varied dramatically from one enterprise to the next. This short example illustrates that there is nothing automatic about an entrepreneur's process of inserting personal vision or style into his or her organization. The process depends very much on whether and how much that person wants to impose himself or herself.

Founder C, like A, was a much more dominant personality with a clear idea of how things should be. He and four others founded a manufacturing concern several years ago, one based on the founder's product idea along with a strong intuition that the market was ready for such a product. In this case, the founding group got together because they shared a concept of the core mission, but they found after a few years that the different members held very different assumptions about how to build an organization. These differences were sufficient to split the group apart and leave C in control of the young, rapidly growing company.

C held strong assumptions about the nature of the world—how one discovers truth and solves problems—and they were reflected in his management style. He believed that good ideas could come from any source; in particular, he believed that he himself was not wise enough to know what was true and right, but that if he heard an intelligent group of people debate an idea and examine it from all sides, he could judge accurately whether it was sound or not. He also knew that he could solve problems best in a group where many ideas were batted around and where there was a high level of mutual confrontation around those ideas. Ideas came from individuals, but the testing of ideas had to be done in a group.

C also believed very strongly that even if he knew what the correct course of action was, unless the parties whose support was critical to implementation were completely sold on the idea, they would either misunderstand or unwittingly sabotage the idea. Therefore, on any important decision, C insisted on wide debate, many group meetings, and selling the idea down and laterally in the organization; only when it appeared that everyone understood and was committed would he agree to going ahead. C felt so strongly about this that he often held up important decisions even when he personally was already convinced of the course of action to take. He said that he did not want to be out there leading all by himself if he could not count on support from the troops; he cited past cases in which, thinking he had group support, he made a decision and, when it failed, found his key subordinates claiming that he had been alone in the decision. These experiences, he said, taught him to ensure commitment before going ahead on anything, even if doing so was time-consuming and frustrating.

While C's assumptions about how to make decisions led to a very group-oriented organization, his theory about how to manage led to a strong individuation process. C was convinced that the only way to manage was to give clear and simple individual responsibility and then to measure the person strictly on those responsibilities. Groups could help make decisions and obtain commitment, but they could not under any circumstance be responsible or accountable. So once a decision was made, it had to be carried out by individuals; if the decision was complex, involving a reorganization of functions, C always insisted that the new organization had to be clear and simple enough to permit the assignment of individual accountabilities.

C believed completely in a proactive model of man and in man's capacity to master nature; hence he expected of his subordinates that they would always be on top of their jobs. If a budget had been negotiated for a year, and if after three months the subordinate recognized that he would overrun the budget, C insisted that the subordinate make a clear decision either to find a way to stay within the budget or to renegotiate a larger budget. It was not acceptable to allow the overrun to occur without informing others and renegotiating, and it was not acceptable to be ignorant of the likelihood that there would be an overrun. The correct way to behave was always to know what was happening, always to be responsible for what was happening, and always to feel free to renegotiate previous agreements if they no longer made sense. C believed completely in open communications and the ability of people to reach reasonable decisions and compromises if they confronted their problems, figured out what they wanted to do, were willing to marshal arguments for their solution, and scrupulously honored any commitments they made.

On the interpersonal level, C assumed "constructive intent" on the part of all members of the organization, a kind of rational loyalty to organizational goals and to shared commitments. This did not prevent people from competitively trying to get ahead—but playing politics, hiding information, blaming others, or failing to cooperate on agreed-upon plans were defined as sins. However, C's assumptions about the nature of truth and the need for every individual to keep thinking out what he or she thought was the correct thing to do in any given situation led to frequent interpersonal tension. In other words, the rule of honoring commitments and following through on consensually reached decisions was superseded by the rule of doing only what you believed sincerely to be the best thing to do in any given situation. Ideally, there would be time to challenge the original decision and renegotiate, but in practice time pressure was such that the subordinate, in doing what was believed to be best, often had to be insubordinate. Thus people in the organization frequently complained that decisions did not "stick," yet had to acknowledge that the reason they did not stick was that the assumption that one had to do the correct thing was even more important. Subordinates learned that insubordination was much less likely to be punished than doing something that the person knew to be wrong or stupid.

C clearly believed in the necessity of organization and hierarchy, but he did not trust the authority of position nearly so much as the authority of reason. Hence bosses were granted authority only to the extent that they could sell their decisions; as indicated above, insubordination was not only tolerated, but actively rewarded if it led to better outcomes. One could infer from watching this organization that it thrived on intelligent, assertive, individualistic people—and, indeed, the hiring policies reflected this bias.

So, over the years, the organization C headed had a tendency to hire and keep the people who fit into the kind of management system I am describing. And those people who fit the founder's assumptions found themselves feeling increasingly like family members in that strong bonds of mutual support grew up among them, with C functioning symbolically as a kind of benign but demanding father figure. These familial feelings were very important, though quite implicit, because they gave subordinates a feeling of security that was needed to challenge each other and C when a course of action did not make sense.

The architecture and office layout in C's company reflected his assumptions about problem solving and human relationships. He insisted on open office landscaping; minimum status differentiation in terms of office size, location, and furnishings (in fact, people were free to decorate their offices any way they liked); open cafeterias instead of executive dining rooms; informal dress codes; first-come, first-serve systems for getting parking spaces; many conference rooms with attached kitchens to facilitate meetings and to keep people interacting with each other instead of going off for meals; and so forth.

In summary, C represents a case of an entrepreneur with a clear set of assumptions about how things should be, both in terms of the formal business arrangements and in terms of internal relationships in the organization—and these assumptions still reflect themselves clearly in the organization some years later.

Let us turn next to the question of how a strong founder goes about embedding his assumptions in the organization.

How are cultural elements embedded?

The basic process of embedding a cultural element—a given belief or assumption—is a "teaching" process, but not necessarily an explicit one. The basic model of culture formation, it will be remembered, is that someone must propose a solution to a problem the group faces. Only if the group shares the perception that the solution is working will that element be adopted, and only if it continues to work will it come to be taken for granted and taught to newcomers. It goes without saying, therefore, that only elements that solve group problems will survive, but the previous issue of "embedding" is how a founder or leader gets the group to do things in a certain way in the first place, so that the question of whether it will work can be settled. In other words, embedding a cultural element in this context means only that the founder/leader has ways of getting the group to try out certain responses. There is no guarantee that those responses will, in fact, succeed in solving the group's ultimate problem. How do founder/leaders do this? I will describe a number of mechanisms ranging from very explicit teaching to very implicit messages of which even the founder may be unaware. These mechanisms are shown in Figure 3.

Each of the mechanisms listed below is used by founders and key leaders to embed a value or assumption they hold, though the message may be very implicit in the sense that the leader is not aware of sending it. Leaders also may be conflicted, which leads to conflicting messages. A given mechanism may convey the message very explicitly, ambiguously, or totally implicitly. The mechanisms are listed below from more or less explicit to more or less implicit ones.

1. *Formal statements of organizational philosophy, charters, creeds, materials used for recruitment and selection, and socialization.*

2. *Design of physical spaces, facades, buildings.*

3. *Deliberate role modeling, teaching, and coaching by leaders.*

4. *Explicit reward and status system, promotion criteria.*

5. *Stories, legends, myths, and parables about key people and events.*

6. *What leaders pay attention to, measure, and control.*

7. *Leader reactions to critical incidents and organizational crises* (times when organizational survival is threatened, norms are unclear or are challenged, insubordination occurs, threatening or meaningless events occur, and so forth).

8. *How the organization is designed and structured.* (The design of work, who reports to whom, degree of decentralization, functional or other criteria for differentiation, and mechanisms used for integration carry implicit messages of what leaders assume and value.)

9. *Organizational systems and procedures.* (The types of information, control, and decision support systems in terms of categories of information, time cycles, who gets what information, and when and how performance appraisal and other review processes are conducted carry implicit messages of what leaders assume and value.)

10. *Criteria used for recruitment, selection, promotion, leveling off, retirement, and "excommunication" of people.* (The implicit and possibly unconscious criteria that leaders use to determine who "fits" and who doesn't "fit" membership roles and key slots in the organization).

Figure 3. How is culture embedded and transmitted?

As the above case examples tried to show, the initial thrust of the messages sent is very much a function of the personality of the founder; some founders deliberately choose to build an organization that reflects their own personal biases while others create the basic organization but then turn it over to subordinates as soon as it has a life of its own. In both cases, the process of culture formation is complicated by the possibility that the founder is "conflicted," in the sense of having in his or her own personality several mutually contradictory assumptions.

The commonest case is probably that of the founder who states a philosophy of delegation but who retains tight control by feeling free to intervene, even in the smallest and most trivial decisions, as A did. Because the owner is granted the "right" to run his or her own company, subordinates will tolerate this kind of contradictory behavior and the organization's culture will develop complex assumptions about how one runs the organization "in spite of" or "around" the founder. If the founder's conflicts are severe to the point of interfering with the running of the organization, buffering layers of management may be built in or, in the extreme, the board of directors may have to find a way to move the founder out altogether.

The mechanisms listed in Figure 3 are not equally potent in practice, but they can reinforce each other to make the total message more potent than individual components. In my observation the most important or potent messages are role modeling by leaders (item 3), what leaders pay attention to (item 6), and leader reactions to critical events (item 7). Only if we observe these leader actions can we begin to decipher how members of the organization "learned" the right and proper things to do, and what model of reality they were to adopt.

To give a few examples, A demonstrated his need to be involved in everything at a detailed level by frequent visits to stores and detailed inspections of what was going on in them. When he went on vacation, he called the office every single day at a set time and wanted to know in great detail what was going on. This behavior persisted into his period of semi-retirement, when he would still call *daily* from his retirement home, where he spent three winter months.

A's loyalty to his family was quite evident: He ignored bad business results if a family member was responsible, yet punished a non-family member involved in such results. If the family member was seriously damaging the business, A put a competent manager in under him, but did not always give that manager credit for subsequent good results. If things continued to go badly, A would finally remove the family member, but always with elaborate rationalizations to protect the family image. If challenged on this kind of blind loyalty, A would assert that owners had certain rights that could not be challenged. Insubordination from a family member was tolerated and excused, but the same kind of insubordination from a non-family member was severely punished.

In complete contrast, B tried to find competent general managers and turn a business over to them as quickly as he could. He involved himself only if he absolutely had to in order to save the business, and he pulled out of businesses as soon as they were stable and successful. B separated his family life completely from his business and had no assumptions about the rights of a family in a business. He wanted a good financial return so that he could make his family economically secure, but he seemed not to want his family involved in the businesses.

C, like B, was not interested in building the business on behalf of the family; his preoccupation with making sound decisions overrode all other concerns. Hence C set out to find the right kinds of managers and then "trained" them through the manner in which he reacted to situations. If managers displayed ignorance or lack of control of an area for which they were responsible, C would get publicly angry at them and accuse them of incompetence. If managers overran a budget or had too much inventory and did not inform C when this was first noticed, they would be publicly chided, whatever the reason was for the condition. If the manager tried to defend the situation by noting that it developed because of actions in another part of the same company, actions which C and others had agreed to, C would point out strongly that the manager should have brought that issue up much earlier and forced a rethinking or renegotiation right away. Thus C made it clear through his reactions that poor ultimate results could be excused, but not being on top of one's situation could never be excused.

C taught subordinates his theory about building commitment to a decision by systematically refusing to go along with something until he felt the commitment was there, and by punishing managers who acted impulsively or prematurely in areas where the support of others was critical. He thus set up a very complex situation for his subordinates by demanding on the one hand a strong individualistic orientation (embodied in official company creeds and public relations literature) and, on the other, strong rules of consensus and mutual commitment (embodied in organizational stories, the organization's design, and many of its systems and procedures).

The above examples highlighted the differences among the three founders to show the biases and unique features of the culture in their respective companies, but there were some common elements as well that need to be mentioned. All three founders assumed that the success of their business(es) hinged on meeting customer needs: their most severe outbursts at subordinates occurred when they learned that a customer had not been well treated. All of the official messages highlighted customer concern, and the reward and control systems focused heavily on such concerns. In the case of A, customer needs were even put ahead of the needs of the family; one way a family member could really get into trouble was to mess up a customer relationship.

All three founders, obsessed with product quality, had a hard time seeing how some of their own managerial demands could undermine quality by forcing compromises. This point is important because in all the official messages, commitment to customers and product quality were uniformly emphasized—making one assume that this value was a clear priority. It was only when one looked at the inner workings of A's and C's organizations that one could see that other assumptions which they held created internal conflicts that were difficult to overcome—conflicts that introduced new cultural themes into the organizations.

In C's organization, for example, there was simultaneously a concern for customers and an arrogance toward customers. Many of the engineers involved in the original product designs had been successful in estimating what customers would really want—a success leading to their assumption that they understood customers well enough to continue to make product designs without having to pay too much attention to what sales and marketing were trying to tell them. C officially supported marketing as a concept, but his underlying assumption was similar to that of his engineers, that he really understood what his customers wanted; this led to a systematic ignoring of some inputs from sales and marketing.

As the company's operating environment changed, old assumptions about the company's role in that environment were no longer working. But neither C nor many of his original group had a paradigm that was clearly workable in the new situation, so a period of painful conflict and new learning arose. More and more customers and marketing people began to complain, yet some parts of the organization literally could not hear or deal with these complaints because of their belief in the superiority of their products and their own previous assumptions that they knew what customers wanted.

In summary, the mechanisms shown in Figure 3 represent *all* of the possible ways in which founder messages get communicated and embedded, but they vary in potency. Indeed, they may often be found to conflict with each other—either because the founder is internally conflicted or because the environment is forcing changes in the original paradigm that lead different parts of the organization to have different assumptions about how to view things. Such conflicts often result because new, strong managers who are not part of the founding group begin to impose their own assumptions and theories. Let us look next at how these people may differ and the implications of such differences.

Founder/owners vs. "professional managers"

Distinctive characteristics or "biases" introduced by the founder's assumptions are found in first-generation firms that are still heavily influenced by founders and in companies that continue to be run by family members. As noted above, such biases give the first-generation firm its distinctive character, and such biases are usually highly valued by first-generation employees because they are associated with the success of the enterprise. As the organization grows, as family members or non-family managers begin to introduce new assumptions, as environmental changes force new responses from the organization, the original assumptions begin to be strained. Employees begin to express concern that some of their "key" values will be lost or that the characteristics that made the company an exciting place to work are gradually disappearing.

Clear distinctions begin to be drawn between the founding family and the "professional" managers who begin to be brought into key positions. Such "professional" managers are usually identified as non-family and as non-owners and, therefore, as less "invested" in the company. Often they have been specifically educated to be managers rather than experts in whatever is the company's particular product or market. They are perceived, by virtue of these facts, as being less loyal to the original values and assumptions that guided the company, and as being more concerned with short-run financial performance. They are typically welcomed for bringing in much-needed organizational and functional skills, but they are often mistrusted because they are not loyal to the founding assumptions.

Though these perceptions have strong stereotypic components, it's possible to see that much of the stereotype is firmly based in reality if one examines a number of first-generation and family-owned companies. Founders and owners do have distinctive characteristics that derive partly from their personalities and partly from their structural position as owners. It is important to understand these characteristics if one is to explain how strongly held many of the values and assumptions of first-generation or family-owned companies are. Figure 4 examines the "stereotype" by polarizing the founder/owner and "professional" manager along a number of motivational, analytical, interpersonal, and structural dimensions.

The main thrust of the differences noted is that the founder/owner is seen as being more self-oriented, more willing to take risks and pursue non-economic objectives and, by virtue of being the founder/owner, more *able* to take risks and to pursue such objectives. Founder/owners are more often intuitive and holistic in their thinking, and they are able to take a long-range point of view because they are building their own identities through their enterprises. They are often more particularistic in their orientation, a characteristic that results in the building of more of a community in the early organizational stages. That is, the initial founding group and the first generation of employees will know each other well and will operate more on personal acquaintance and trust than on formal principles, job descriptions, and rules.

The environment will often be more political than bureaucratic, and founder-value biases will be staunchly defended because they will form the basis for the group's initial identity. New members who don't fit this set of assumptions and values are likely to leave because they will be uncomfortable, or they will be ejected because their failure to confirm accepted patterns is seen as disruptive.

Founder/owners, by virtue of their position and personality, also tend to fulfill some *unique functions* in the early history of their organizations:

1. *Containing and absorbing anxiety and risk.* Because they are positionally more secure and personally more confident, owners more than managers absorb and contain the anxieties and risks that are inherent in creating, developing, and enlarging an organization. Thus in times of stress, owners play a special role in reassuring the organization that it will survive. They are the stakeholders; hence they do have the ultimate risk.

2. *Embedding non-economic assumptions and values.* Because of their willingness to absorb risk and their position as primary stakeholders, founder/owners are in a position to insist on doing things which may not be optimally efficient from a short-run point of view, but which reflect their own values and biases on how to build an effective organization and/or how

MOTIVATION AND EMOTIONAL ORIENTATION	
Entrepreneurs/founders/owners are . . .	*Professional managers are . . .*
Oriented toward creating, building.	Oriented toward consolidating, surviving, growing.
Achievement-oriented.	Power- and influence-oriented.
Self-oriented, worried about own image; need for "glory" high.	Organization-oriented, worried about company image.
Jealous of own prerogatives, need for autonomy high.	Interested in developing the organization and subordinates.
Loyal to own company, "local."	Loyal to profession of management, "cosmopolitan."
Willing and able to take moderate risks on own authority.	Able to take risks, but more cautious and in need of support.
ANALYTICAL ORIENTATION	
Primarily intuitive, trusting of own intuitions.	Primarily analytical, more cautious about intuitions.
Long-range time horizon.	Short-range time horizon.
Holistic; able to see total picture, patterns.	Specific; able to see details and their consequences.
INTERPERSONAL ORIENTATION	
"Particularistic," in the sense of seeing individuals as individuals.	"Universalistic," in the sense of seeing individuals as members of categories like employees, customers, suppliers, and so on.
Personal, political, involved.	Impersonal, rational, uninvolved.
Centralist, autocratic.	Participative, delegation-oriented.
Family ties count.	Family ties are irrelevant.
Emotional, impatient, easily bored.	Unemotional, patient, persistent.
STRUCTURAL/POSITIONAL DIFFERENCES	
Have the privileges and risks of ownership.	Have minimal ownership, hence fewer privileges and risks.
Have secure position by virtue of ownership.	Have less secure position, must constantly prove themselves.
Are generally highly visible and get close attention.	Are often invisible and do not get much attention.
Have the support of family members in the business.	Function alone or with the support of non-family members.
Have the obligation of dealing with family members and deciding on the priorities family issues should have relative to company issues.	Do not have to worry about family issues at all, which are by definition irrelevant.
Have weak bosses, Boards that are under their own control.	Have strong bosses, Boards that are not under their own control.

Figure 4. How do founder/owners differ from professional managers?

to maximize the benefits to themselves and their families. Thus founder/ owners often start with humanistic and social concerns that become reflected in organizational structure and process. Even when "participation," or "no layoffs," or other personnel practices such as putting marginally competent family members into key slots are "inefficient," owners can insist that this is the only way to run the business and make that decision stick in ways that professional managers cannot.

3. *Stimulating innovation.* Because of their personal orientation and their secure position, owners are uniquely willing and able to try new innovations that are risky, often with no more than an intuition that things will improve. Because managers must document, justify, and plan much more carefully, they have less freedom to innovate.

As the organization ages and the founder becomes less of a personal force, there is a trend away from this community feeling toward more of a rational, bureaucratic type of organization dominated by general managers who may care less about the original assumptions and values, and who are not in a position to fulfill the unique functions mentioned above. This trend is often feared and lamented by first- and second-generation employees. If the founder introduces his or her own family into the organization, and if the family assumptions and values perpetuate those of the founder, the original community feeling may be successfully perpetuated. The original culture may then survive. But at some point there will be a complete transition to general management, and at that point it is not clear whether the founding assumptions survive, are metamorphosed into a new hybrid, or are displaced entirely by other assumptions more congruent with what general managers as an occupational group bring with them.

4. *Originating evolution through hybridization.* The founder is able to impose his or her assumptions on the first-generation employees, but these employees will, as they move up in the organization and become experienced managers, develop a range of new assumptions based on their own experience. These new assumptions will be congruent with some of the core assumptions of the original cultural paradigm, but will add new elements learned from experience. Some of these new elements or new assumptions will solve problems better than the original ones because external and internal problems will have changed as the organization matured and grew. The founder often recognizes that these new assumptions are better solutions, and will delegate increasing amounts of authority to those managers who are the best "hybrids": those who maintain key old assumptions yet add relevant new ones.

The best example of such hybrid evolution comes from a company that was founded by a very free-wheeling, intuitive, pragmatic entrepreneur: "D" who, like C in the example above, believed strongly in individual creativity, a high degree of decentralization, high autonomy for each organizational unit, high internal competition for resources, and self-control mechanisms rather than tight, centralized organizational controls. As this company grew and prospered, coordinating so many autonomous units became increasingly difficult, and the frustration that resulted from internal competition made it increasingly expensive to maintain this form of organization.

Some managers in this company, notably those coming out of manufacturing, had always operated in a more disciplined, centralized manner—without, however, disagreeing with core assumptions about the need to maximize individual autonomy. But they had learned that in order to do certain kinds of manufacturing tasks, one had to impose some discipline and tight controls. As the price of autonomy and decentralization increased, D began to look increasingly to these manufacturing managers as potential occupants of key general management positions. Whether he was conscious of it or not, what he needed was senior general managers who still believed in the old system but who had, in addition, a new set of assumptions about how to run things that were more in line with what the organization now needed. Some of the first-generation managers were quite nervous at seeing what they considered to be their "hardnosed" colleagues groomed as heirs apparent. Yet they were relieved that these potential successors were part of the original group rather than complete outsiders.

From a theoretical standpoint, evolution through hybrids is probably the only model of culture change that can work, because the original culture is based so heavily on community assumptions and values. Outsiders coming into such a community with new assumptions are likely to find the culture too strong to budge, so they either give up in frustration or find themselves ejected by the organization as being too foreign in orientation. What makes this scenario especially likely is the fact that the *distinctive* parts of the founding culture are often based on biases that are not economically justifiable in the short run.

As noted earlier, founders are especially likely to introduce humanistic, social service, and other non-economic assumptions into their paradigm of how an organization should look, and the general manager who is introduced from the outside often finds these assumptions to be the very thing that he or she wants to change in the attempt to "rationalize" the organization and make it more efficient. Indeed, that is often the reason the outsider is brought in. But if the current owners do not recognize the positive functions their culture plays, they run the risk of throwing out the baby with the bath water or, if the culture is strong, wasting their time because the outsider will not be able to change things anyway.

The ultimate dilemma for the first-generation organization with a strong founder-generated culture is how to make the transition to subsequent generations in such a manner that the organization remains adaptive to its changing external environment without destroying cultural elements that have given it its uniqueness, and that have made life fulfilling in the internal environment. Such a transition cannot be made effectively if the succession problem is seen only in power or political terms. The thrust of this analysis is that the *culture* must be analyzed and understood, and that the founder/owners must have sufficient insight into their own culture to make an intelligent transition process possible.

Acknowledgments and selected bibliography

The research on which this paper is based was partly sponsored by the Project on the Family Firm, Sloan School of Management, M.I.T., and by the Office of Naval Research, Organizational Effectiveness Research Programs, under Contract No. N00014–80–C–0905, NR 170–911.

The ideas explored here have been especially influenced by my colleague Richard Beckhard and by the various entrepreneurs with whom I have worked for many years in a consulting relationship. Their observations of themselves and their colleagues have proved to be an invaluable source of ideas and insights.

Earlier work along these lines has been incorporated into my book *Career Dynamics* (Addison-Wesley, 1978). Further explication of the ideas of an organizational culture can be found in Andrew M. Pettigrew's article "On Studying Organizational Cultures" (*Administrative Science Quarterly,* December 1979), Meryl Louis's article "A Cultural Perspective on Organizations" (*Human Systems Management,* 1981, 2, 246–258), and in H. Schwartz and S. M. Davis's "Matching Corporate Culture and Business Strategy" (*Organizational Dynamics,* Summer 1981).

The specific model of culture that I use was first published in my article "Does Japanese Management Style Have a Message for American Managers?" (*Sloan Management Review,* Fall 1981) and is currently being elaborated into a book on organizational culture.

Managers and Leaders: Are They Different?

Abraham Zaleznik

What is the ideal way to develop leadership? Every society provides its own answer to this question, and each, in groping for answers, defines its deepest concerns about the purposes, distributions, and uses of power. Business has contributed its answer to the leadership question by evolving a new breed called the manager. Simultaneously, business has established a new power ethic that favors collective over individual leadership, the cult of the group over that of personality. While ensuring the competence, control, and the balance of power relations among groups with the potential for rivalry, managerial leadership unfortunately does not necessarily ensure imagination, creativity, or ethical behavior in guiding the destinies of corporate enterprises.

Leadership inevitably requires using power to influence the thoughts and actions of other people. Power in the hands of an individual entails human risks: first, the risk of equating power with the ability to get immediate results; second, the risk of ignoring the many different ways people can legitimately accumulate power; and third, the risk of losing self-control in the desire for power. The need to hedge these risks accounts in part for the development of collective leadership and the managerial ethic. Consequently, an inherent conservatism dominates the culture of large organizations. In *The Second American Revolution,* John D. Rockefeller, 3rd. describes the conservatism of organizations: "An organization is a system, with a logic of its own, and all the weight of tradition and inertia. The deck is stacked in favor of the tried and proven way of doing things and against the taking of risks and striking out in new directions." [1]

Out of this conservatism and inertia organizations provide succession to power through the development of managers rather than individual leaders. And the irony of the managerial ethic is that it fosters a bureaucratic culture

1. John D. Rockefeller, 3d., *The Second American Revolution* (New York: Harper-Row, 1973), p. 72.

in business, supposedly the last bastion protecting us from the encroach-
ments and controls of bureaucracy in government and education. Perhaps
the risks associated with power in the hands of an individual may be necessary ones for business to take if organizations are to break free of their
inertia and bureaucratic conservatism.

Manager vs. leader personality

Theodore Levitt has described the essential features of a managerial culture
with its emphasis on rationality and control:

> Management consists of the rational assessment of a situation and the
> systematic selection of goals and purposes (what is to be done?); the
> systematic development of strategies to achieve these goals; the
> marshalling of the required resources; the rational design, organiza-
> tion, direction, and control of the activities required to attain the
> selected purposes; and, finally, the motivating and rewarding of people
> to do the work.[2]

In other words, whether his or her energies are directed toward goals,
resources, organization structures, or people, a manager is a problem
solver. The manager asks himself, "What problems have to be solved, and
what are the best ways to achieve results so that people will continue to
contribute to this organization?" In this conception, leadership is a practical effort to direct affairs; and to fulfill his task, a manager requires that
many people operate at different levels of status and responsibility. Our
democratic society is, in fact, unique in having solved the problem of providing well-trained managers for business. The same solution stands ready
to be applied to government, education, health care, and other institutions.
It takes neither genius nor heroism to be a manager, but rather persistence,
tough-mindedness, hard work, intelligence, analytical ability and, perhaps
most important, tolerance and good will.

Another conception, however, attaches almost mystical beliefs to what
leadership is and assumes that only great people are worthy of the drama of
power and politics. Here, leadership is a psychodrama in which, as precon-
dition for control of a political structure, a lonely person must gain control
of him or herself. Such an expectation of leadership contrasts sharply with
the mundane, practical, and yet important conception that leadership is
really managing work that other people do.

Two questions come to mind. Is this mystique of leadership merely a
holdover from our collective childhood of dependency and our longing for
good and heroic parents? Or, is there a basic truth lurking behind the need
for leaders that no matter how competent managers are, their leadership

---

2. Theodore Levitt, "Management and the Post Industrial Society," *The Public Interest*,
Summer 1976, p. 73.

stagnates because of their limitations in visualizing purposes and generating value in work? Without this imaginative capacity and the ability to communicate, managers, driven by their narrow purposes, perpetuate group conflicts instead of reforming them into broader desires and goals.

If indeed problems demand greatness, then, judging by past performance, the selection and development of leaders leave a great deal to chance. There are no known ways to train "great" leaders. Furthermore, beyond what we leave to chance, there is a deeper issue in the relationship between the need for competent managers and the longing for great leaders.

What it takes to ensure the supply of people who will assume practical responsibility may inhibit the development of great leaders. Conversely, the presence of great leaders may undermine the development of managers who become very anxious in the relative disorder that leaders seem to generate. The antagonism in aim (to have many competent managers as well as great leaders) often remains obscure in stable and well-developed societies. But the antagonism surfaces during periods of stress and change, as it did in the Western countries during both the Great Depression and World War II. The tension also appears in the struggle for power between theorists and professional managers in revolutionary societies.

It is easy enough to dismiss the dilemma I pose (of training managers while we may need new leaders, or leaders at the expense of managers) by saying that the need is for people who can be *both* managers and leaders. The truth of the matter as I see it, however, is that just as a managerial culture is different from the entrepreneurial culture that develops when leaders appear in organizations, managers and leaders are very different kinds of people. They differ in motivation, personal history, and in how they think and act.

A technologically oriented and economically successful society tends to depreciate the need for great leaders. Such societies hold a deep and abiding faith in rational methods of solving problems, including problems of value, economics, and justice. Once rational methods of solving problems are broken down into elements, organized, and taught as skills, then society's faith in technique over personal qualities in leadership remains the guiding conception for a democratic society contemplating its leadership requirements. But there are times when tinkering and trial and error prove inadequate to the emerging problems of selecting goals, allocating resources, and distributing wealth and opportunity. During such times, the democratic society needs to find leaders who use themselves as the instruments of learning and acting, instead of managers who use their accumulation of collective experience to get where they are going.

The most impressive spokesman, as well as exemplar of the managerial viewpoint, was Alfred P. Sloan, Jr. who, along with Pierre du Pont, designed the modern corporate structure. Reflecting on what makes one management successful while another fails, Sloan suggested that "good management rests on a reconciliation of centralization and decentralization, or 'decentralization with coordinated control.' " [3]

Sloan's conception of management, as well as his practice, developed by trial and error, and by the accumulation of experience. Sloan wrote:

> There is no hard and fast rule for sorting out the various responsibilities and the best way to assign them. The balance which is struck . . . varies according to what is being decided, the circumstances of the time, past experience, and the temperaments and skills of the executive involved.[4]

In other words, in much the same way that the inventors of the late nineteenth century tried, failed, and fitted until they hit on a product or method, managers who innovate in developing organizations are "tinkerers." They do not have a grand design or experience the intuitive flash of insight that, borrowing from modern science, we have come to call the "breakthrough."

Managers and leaders differ fundamentally in their world views. The dimensions for assessing these differences include managers' and leaders' orientations toward their goals, their work, their human relations, and their selves.

Attitudes toward goals

Managers tend to adopt impersonal, if not passive, attitudes toward goals. Managerial goals arise out of necessities rather than desires, and, therefore, are deeply embedded in the history and culture of the organization.

Frederic G. Donner, chairman and chief executive officer of General Motors from 1958 to 1967, expressed this impersonal and passive attitude toward goals in defining GM's position on product development:

> To meet the challenge of the marketplace, we must recognize changes in customer needs and desires far enough ahead to have the right products in the right places at the right time and in the right quantity.

> We must balance trends in preference against the many compromises that are necessary to make a final product that is both reliable and good looking, that performs well and that sells at a competitive price in the necessary volume. We must design, not just the cars we would like to build, but more importantly, the cars that our customers want to buy.[5]

Nowhere in this formulation of how a product comes into being is there a notion that consumer tastes and preferences arise in part as a result of what manufacturers do. In reality, through product design, advertising, and pro-

3. Alfred P. Sloan, Jr., *My Years with General Motors* (New York: Doubleday & Co. 1964), p. 429.
4. Ibid., p. 429.
5. Ibid., p. 440.

motion, consumers learn to like what they then say they need. Few would argue that people who enjoy taking snapshots *need* a camera that also develops pictures. But in response to novelty, convenience, a shorter interval between acting (taking the snap) and gaining pleasure (seeing the shot), the Polaroid camera succeeded in the marketplace. But it is inconceivable that Edwin Land responded to impressions of consumer need. Instead, he translated a technology (polarization of light) into a product, which proliferated and stimulated consumers' desires.

The example of Polaroid and Land suggests how leaders think about goals. They are active instead of reactive, shaping ideas instead of responding to them. Leaders adopt a personal and active attitude toward goals. The influence a leader exerts in altering moods, evoking images and expectations, and in establishing specific desires and objectives determines the direction a business takes. The net result of this influence is to change the way people think about what is desirable, possible, and necessary.

Conceptions of work

What do managers and leaders do? What is the nature of their respective work?

Leaders and managers differ in their conceptions. Managers tend to view work as an enabling process involving some combination of people and ideas interacting to establish strategies and make decisions. Managers help the process along by a range of skills, including calculating the interests in opposition, staging and timing the surfacing of controversial issues, and reducing tensions. In this enabling process, managers appear flexible in the use of tactics: they negotiate and bargain, on the one hand, and use rewards and punishments, and other forms of coercion, on the other. Machiavelli wrote for managers and not necessarily for leaders.

Alfred Sloan illustrated how this enabling process works in situations of conflict. The time was the early 1920s when the Ford Motor Co. still dominated the automobile industry using, as did General Motors, the conventional water-cooled engine. With the full backing of Pierre du Pont, Charles Kettering dedicated himself to the design of an air-cooled engine, which, if successful, would have been a great technical and market coup for GM. Kettering believed in his product, but the manufacturing division heads at GM remained skeptical and later opposed the new design on two grounds: first, that it was technically unreliable, and second, that the corporation was putting all its eggs in one basket by investing in a new product instead of attending to the current marketing situation.

In the summer of 1923 after a series of false starts and after its decision to recall the copper-cooled Chevrolets from dealers and customers, GM management reorganized and finally scrapped the project. When it dawned on Kettering that the company had rejected the engine, he was deeply discouraged and wrote to Sloan that without the "organized resistance" against the project it would succeed and that unless the project were saved, he would leave the company.

Alfred Sloan was all too aware of the fact that Kettering was unhappy and indeed intended to leave General Motors. Sloan was also aware of the fact that, while the manufacturing divisions strongly opposed the new engine, Pierre du Pont supported Kettering. Furthermore, Sloan had himself gone on record in a letter to Kettering less than two years earlier expressing full confidence in him. The problem Sloan now had was to make his decision stick, keep Kettering in the organization (he was much too valuable to lose), avoid alienating du Pont, and encourage the division heads to move speedily in developing product lines using conventional water-cooled engines.

The actions that Sloan took in the face of this conflict reveal much about how managers work. First, he tried to reassure Kettering by presenting the problem in a very ambiguous fashion, suggesting that he and the Executive Committee sided with Kettering, but that it would not be practical to force the divisions to do what they were opposed to. He presented the problem as being a question of the people, not the product. Second, he proposed to reorganize around the problem by consolidating all functions in a new division that would be responsible for the design, production, and marketing of the new car. This solution, however, appeared as ambiguous as his efforts to placate and keep Kettering in General Motors. Sloan wrote: "My plan was to create an independent pilot operation under the sole jurisdiction of Mr. Kettering, a kind of copper-cooled-car division. Mr. Kettering would designate his own chief engineer and his production staff to solve the technical problems of manufacture." [6]

While Sloan did not discuss the practical value of this solution, which included saddling an inventor with management responsibility, he in effect used this plan to limit his conflict with Pierre du Pont.

In effect, the managerial solution that Sloan arranged and pressed for adoption limited the options available to others. The structural solution narrowed choices, even limiting emotional reactions to the point where the key people could do nothing but go along, and even allowed Sloan to say in his memorandum to du Pont, "We have discussed the matter with Mr. Kettering at some length this morning and he agrees with us absolutely on every point we made. He appears to receive the suggestion enthusiastically and has every confidence that it can be put across along these lines." [7]

Having placated people who opposed his views by developing a structural solution that appeared to give something but in reality only limited options, Sloan could then authorize the car division's general manager, with whom he basically agreed, to move quickly in designing water-cooled cars for the immediate market demand.

6. Ibid., p. 91.
7. Ibid., p. 91.

Years later Sloan wrote, evidently with tongue in cheek, "The copper-cooled car never came up again in a big way. It just died out, I don't know why." [8]

In order to get people to accept solutions to problems, managers need to coordinate and balance continually. Interestingly enough, this managerial work has much in common with what diplomats and mediators do, with Henry Kissinger apparently an outstanding practitioner. The manager aims at shifting balances of power toward solutions acceptable as a compromise among conflicting values.

What about leaders, what do they do? Where managers act to limit choices, leaders work in the opposite direction, to develop fresh approaches to longstanding problems and to open issues for new options. Stanley and Inge Hoffmann, the political scientists, liken the leader's work to that of the artist. But unlike most artists, the leader himself is an integral part of the aesthetic product. One cannot look at a leader's art without looking at the artist. On Charles de Gaulle as a political artist, they wrote: "And each of his major political acts, however tortuous the means or the details, has been whole, indivisible and unmistakably his own, like an artistic act." [9]

The closest one can get to a product apart from the artist is the ideas that occupy, indeed at times obsess, the leader's mental life. To be effective, however, the leader needs to project his ideas into images that excite people, and only then develop choices that give the projected images substance. Consequently, leaders create excitement in work.

John F. Kennedy's brief presidency shows both the strengths and weaknesses connected with the excitement leaders generate in their work. In his inaugural address he said, "Let every nation know, whether it wishes us well or ill, that we shall pay any price, bear any burden, meet any hardship, support any friend, oppose any foe, in order to assure the survival and the success of liberty."

This much-quoted statement forced people to react beyond immediate concerns and to identify with Kennedy and with important shared ideals. But upon closer scrutiny the statement must be seen as absurd because it promises a position which if in fact adopted, as in the Viet Nam War, could produce disastrous results. Yet unless expectations are aroused and mobilized, with all the dangers of frustration inherent in heightened desire, new thinking and new choice can never come to light.

Leaders work from high-risk positions, indeed often are temperamentally disposed to seek out risk and danger, especially where opportunity and reward appear high. From my observations, why one individual seeks risks while another approaches problems conservatively depends more on his or her personality and less on conscious choice. For some, especially

---

8. Ibid., p. 93.
9. Stanley and Inge Hoffmann, "The Will for Grandeur: de Gaulle as Political Artist," *Daedalus,* Summer 1968, p. 849.

those who become managers, the instinct for survival dominates their need for risk, and their ability to tolerate mundane, practical work assists their survival. The same cannot be said for leaders who sometimes react to mundane work as to an affliction.

Relations with others

Managers prefer to work with people; they avoid solitary activity because it makes them anxious. Several years ago, I directed studies on the psychological aspects of career. The need to seek out others with whom to work and collaborate seemed to stand out as important characteristics of managers. When asked, for example, to write imaginative stories in response to a picture showing a single figure (a boy contemplating a violin, or a man silhouetted in a state of reflection), managers populated their stories with people. The following is an example of a manager's imaginative story about the young boy contemplating a violin:

> "Mom and Dad insisted that junior take music lessons so that someday he can become a concert musician. His instrument was ordered and had just arrived. Junior is weighing the alternatives of playing football with the other kids or playing with the squeak box. He can't understand how his parents could think a violin is better than a touchdown.
>
> After four months of practicing the violin, junior has had more than enough, Daddy is going out of his mind, and Mommy is willing to give in reluctantly to the men's wishes. Football season is now over, but a good third baseman will take the field next spring.[10]

This story illustrates two themes that clarify managerial attitudes toward human relations. The first, as I have suggested, is to seek out activity with other people (i.e. the football team), and the second is to maintain a low level of emotional involvement in these relationships. The low emotional involvement appears in the writer's use of conventional metaphors, even clichés, and in the depiction of the ready transformation of potential conflict into harmonious decisions. In this case, Junior, Mommy, and Daddy agree to give up the violin for manly sports.

These two themes may seem paradoxical, but their coexistence supports what a manager does, including reconciling differences, seeking compromises, and establishing a balance of power. A further idea demonstrated by how the manager wrote the story is that managers may lack empathy, or the capacity to sense intuitively the thoughts and feelings of others. To illustrate attempts to be empathic, here is another story written to the same stimulus picture by someone considered by his peers to be a leader:

10. Abraham Zaleznik, Gene W. Dalton, and Louis B. Barnes, *Orientation and Conflict in Career* (Boston: Division of Research, Harvard Business School, 1970), p. 316.

> This little boy has the appearance of being a sincere artist, one who is deeply affected by the violin, and has an intense desire to master the instrument.
>
> He seems to have just completed his normal practice session and appears to be somewhat crestfallen at his inability to produce the sounds which he is sure lie within the violin.
>
> He appears to be in the process of making a vow to himself to expend the necessary time and effort to play this instrument until he satisfies himself that he is able to bring forth the qualities of music which he feels within himself.
>
> With this type of determination and carry through, this boy became one of the great violinists of his day.[11]

Empathy is not simply a matter of paying attention to other people. It is also the capacity to take in emotional signals and to make them mean something in a relationship with an individual. People who describe another person as "deeply affected" with "intense desire," as capable of feeling "crestfallen" and as one who can "vow to himself," would seem to have an inner perceptiveness that they can use in their relationships with others.

Managers relate to people according to the role they play in a sequence of events or in a decision-making *process,* while leaders, who are concerned with ideas, relate in more intuitive and empathetic ways. The manager's orientation to people, as actors in a sequence of events, deflects his or her attention away from the substance of people's concerns and toward their roles in a process. The distinction is simply between a manager's attention to *how* things get done and a leader's to *what* the events and decisions mean to participants.

In recent years, managers have taken over from game theory the notion that decision-making events can be one of two types: the win-lose situation (or zero-sum game) or the win-win situation in which everybody in the action comes out ahead. As part of the process of reconciling differences among people and maintaining balances of power, managers strive to convert win-lose into win-win situations.

As an illustration, take the decision of how to allocate capital resources among operating divisions in a large, decentralized organization. On the face of it, the dollars available for distribution are limited at any given time. Presumably, therefore, the more one division gets, the less is available for other divisions.

Managers tend to view this situation (as it affects human relations) as a conversion issue: how to make what seems like a win-lose problem into a win-win problem. Several solutions to this situation come to mind. First,

11. Ibid., p. 294.

the manager focuses others' attention on procedure and not on substance. Here the actors become engrossed in the bigger problem of *how* to make decisions, not *what* decisions to make. Once committed to the bigger problem, the actors have to support the outcome since they were involved in formulating decision rules. Because the actors believe in the rules they formulated, they will accept present losses in the expectation that next time they will win.

Second, the manager communicates to his subordinates indirectly, using "signals" instead of "messages." A signal has a number of possible implicit positions in it while a message clearly states a position. Signals are inconclusive and subject to reinterpretation should people become upset and angry, while messages involve the direct consequence that some people will indeed not like what they hear. The nature of messages heightens emotional response, and, as I have indicated, emotionally makes managers anxious. With signals, the question of who wins and who loses often becomes obscured.

Third, the manager plays for time. Managers seem to recognize that with the passage of time and the delay of major decisions, compromises emerge that take the sting out of win-lose situations; and the original "game" will be superseded by additional ones. Therefore, compromises may mean that one wins and loses simultaneously, depending on which of the games one evaluates.

There are undoubtedly many other tactical moves managers use to change human situations from win-lose to win-win. But the point to be made is that such tactics focus on the decision-making process itself and interest managers rather than leaders. The interest in tactics involves costs as well as benefits, including making organizations fatter in bureaucratic and political intrigue and leaner in direct, hard activity and warm human relationships. Consequently, one often hears subordinates characterize managers as inscrutable, detached, and manipulative. These adjectives arise from the subordinates' perception that they are linked together in a process whose purpose, beyond simply making decisions, is to maintain a controlled as well as rational and equitable structure. These adjectives suggest that managers need order in the face of the potential chaos that many fear in human relationships.

In contrast, one often hears leaders referred to in adjectives rich in emotional content. Leaders attract strong feelings of identity and difference, or of love and hate. Human relations in leader-dominated structures often appear turbulent, intense, and at times even disorganized. Such an atmosphere intensifies individual motivation and often produces unanticipated outcomes. Does this intense motivation lead to innovation and high performance, or does it represent wasted energy?

Senses of self

In *The Varieties of Religious Experience,* William James describes two basic personality types, "once-born" and "twice-born." [12] People of the former personality type are those for whom adjustments to life have been straightforward and whose lives have been more or less a peaceful flow from the moment of their births. The twice-borns, on the other hand, have not had an easy time of it. Their lives are marked by a continual struggle to attain some sense of order. Unlike the once-borns they cannot take things for granted. According to James, these personalities have equally different world views. For a once-born personality, the sense of self, as a guide to conduct and attitude, derives from a feeling of being at home and in harmony with one's environment. For a twice-born, the sense of self derives from a feeling of profound separateness.

A sense of belonging or of being separate has a practical significance for the kinds of investments managers and leaders make in their careers. Managers see themselves as conservators and regulators of an existing order of affairs with which they personally identify and from which they gain rewards. Perpetuating and strengthening existing institutions enhances a manager's sense of self-worth: he or she is performing in a role that harmonizes with the ideals of duty and responsibility. William James had this harmony in mind—this sense of self as flowing easily to and from the outer world—in defining a once-born personality. If one feels oneself as a member of institutions, contributing to their well-being, then one fulfills a mission in life and feels rewarded for having measured up to ideals. This reward transcends material gains and answers the more fundamental desire for personal integrity which is achieved by identifying with existing institutions.

Leaders tend to be twice-born personalities, people who feel separate from their environment, including other people. They may work in organizations, but they never belong to them. Their sense of who they are does not depend upon memberships, work roles, or other social indicators of identity. What seems to follow from this idea about separateness is some theoretical basis for explaining why certain individuals search out opportunities for change. The methods to bring about change may be technological, political, or ideological, but the object is the same: to profoundly alter human, economic, and political relationships.

Sociologists refer to the preparation individuals undergo to perform in roles as the socialization process. Where individuals experience themselves as an integral part of the social structure (their self-esteem gains strength through participation and conformity), social standards exert

12. William James, *Varieties of Religious Experience* (New York: Mentor Books, 1958).

powerful effects in maintaining the individual's personal sense of continuity, even beyond the early years in the family. The line of development from the family to schools, then to career is cumulative and reinforcing. When the line of development is not reinforcing because of significant disruptions in relationships or other problems experienced in the family or other social institutions, the individual turns inward and struggles to establish self-esteem, identity, and order. Here the psychological dynamics center on the experience with loss and the efforts at recovery.

In considering the development of leadership, we have to examine two different courses of life history: (1) development through socialization, which prepares the individual to guide institutions and to maintain the existing balance of social relations; and (2) development through personal mastery, which impels an individual to struggle for psychological and social change. Society produces its managerial talent through the first line of development, while through the second leaders emerge.

Development of leadership

The development of every person begins in the family. Each person experiences the traumas associated with separating from his or her parents, as well as the pain that follows such frustration. In the same vein, all individuals face the difficulties of achieving self-regulation and self-control. But for some, perhaps a majority, the fortunes of childhood provide adequate gratifications and sufficient opportunities to find substitutes for rewards no longer available. Such individuals, the "once-borns," make moderate identifications with parents and find a harmony between what they expect and what they are able to realize from life.

But suppose the pains of separation are amplified by a combination of parental demands and the individual's needs to the degree that a sense of isolation, of being special, and of wariness disrupts the bonds that attach children to parents and other authority figures? Under such conditions, and given a special aptitude, the origins of which remain mysterious, the person becomes deeply involved in his or her inner world at the expense of interest in the outer world. For such a person, self-esteem no longer depends solely upon positive attachments and real rewards. A form a self-reliance takes hold along with expectations of performance and achievement, and perhaps even the desire to do great works.

Such self-perceptions can come to nothing if the individual's talents are negligible. Even with strong talents, there are no guarantees that achievement will follow, let alone that the end result will be for good rather than evil. Other factors enter into development. For one thing, leaders are like artists and other gifted people who often struggle with neuroses; their ability to function varies considerably even over the short run, and some potential leaders may lose the struggle altogether. Also, beyond early childhood, the patterns of development that affect managers and leaders involve the selective influence of particular people. Just as they appear flexible and evenly distributed in the types of talents available for development, managers form moderate and widely distributed attachments. Leaders, on the other hand, establish, and also break off, intensive one-to-one relationships.

It is a common observation that people with great talents are often only indifferent students. No one, for example, could have predicted Einstein's great achievements on the basis of his mediocre record in school. The reason for mediocrity is obviously not the absence of ability. It may result, instead, from self-absorption and the inability to pay attention to the ordinary tasks at hand. The only sure way an individual can interrupt reverie-like preoccupation and self-absorption is to form a deep attachment to a great teacher or other benevolent person who understands and has the ability to communicate with the gifted individual.

Whether gifted individuals find what they need in one-to-one relationships depends on the availability of sensitive and intuitive mentors who have a vocation in cultivating talent. Fortunately, when the generations do meet and the self-selections occur, we learn more about how to develop leaders and how talented people of different generations influence each other.

While apparently destined for a mediocre career, people who form important one-to-one relationships are able to accelerate and intensify their development through an apprenticeship. The background for such apprenticeships, or the psychological readiness of an individual to benefit from an intensive relationship, depends upon some experience in life that forces the individual to turn inward. A case example will make this point clearer. This example comes from the life of Dwight David Eisenhower, and illustrates the transformation of a career from competent to outstanding.[13]

Dwight Eisenhower's early career in the Army foreshadowed very little about his future development. During World War I, while some of his West Point classmates were already experiencing the war firsthand in France, Eisenhower felt "embedded in the monotony and unsought safety of the Zone of the Interior . . . that was intolerable punishment."[14]

Shortly after World War I, Eisenhower, then a young officer somewhat pessimistic about his career chances, asked for a transfer to Panama to work under General Fox Connor, a senior officer whom Eisenhower admired. The army turned down Eisenhower's request. This setback was very much on Eisenhower's mind when Ikey, his first-born son, succumbed to influenza. By some sense of responsibility for its own, the army transferred Eisenhower to Panama, where he took up his duties under General Connor with the shadow of his lost son very much upon him.

13. This example is included in Abraham Zaleznik and Manfred F. R. Kets de Vries, *Power and the Corporate Mind* (Boston: Houghton Mifflin, 1975).

14. Dwight D. Eisenhower, *At Ease: Stories I Tell to Friends* (New York: Doubleday, 1967), p. 136.

In a relationship with the kind of father he would have wanted to be, Eisenhower reverted to being the son he lost. In this highly charged situation, Eisenhower began to learn from his mentor. General Connor offered, and Eisenhower gladly took, a magnificent tutorial on the military. The effects of this relationship on Eisenhower cannot be measured quantitatively, but, in Eisenhower's own reflections and the unfolding of his career, one cannot overestimate its significance in the reintegration of a person shattered by grief.

As Eisenhower wrote later about Connor, "Life with General Connor was a sort of graduate school in military affairs and the humanities, leavened by a man who was experienced in his knowledge of men and their conduct. I can never adequately express my gratitude to this one gentleman. . . . In a lifetime of association with great and good men, he is the one more or less invisible figure to whom I owe an incalculable debt." [15]

Some time after his tour of duty with General Connor, Eisenhower's breakthrough occurred. He received orders to attend the Command and General Staff School at Fort Leavenworth, one of the most competitive schools in the army. It was a coveted appointment, and Eisenhower took advantage of the opportunity. Unlike his performance in high school and West Point, his work at the Command School was excellent; he was graduated first in his class.

Psychological biographies of gifted people repeatedly demonstrate the important part a mentor plays in developing an individual. Andrew Carnegie owed much to his senior, Thomas A. Scott. As head of the Western Division of the Pennsylvania Railroad, Scott recognized talent and the desire to learn in the young telegrapher assigned to him. By giving Carnegie increasing responsibility and by providing him with the opportunity to learn through close personal observation, Scott added to Carnegie's self-confidence and sense of achievement. Because of his own personal strength and achievement, Scott did not fear Carnegie's aggressiveness. Rather, he gave it full play in encouraging Carnegie's initiative.

Mentors take risks with people. They bet initially on talent they perceive in younger people. Mentors also risk emotional involvement in working closely with their juniors. The risks do not always pay off, but the willingness to take them appears crucial in developing leaders.

Can organizations develop leaders?

The examples I have given of how leaders develop suggest the importance of personal influence and the one-to-one relationship. For organizations to encourage consciously the development of leaders as compared with managers would mean developing one-to-one relationships between junior and senior executives and, more important, fostering a culture of individualism

15. Ibid., p. 187.

and possibly elitism. The elitism arises out of the desire to identify talent and other qualities suggestive of the ability to lead and not simply to manage.

The Jewel Companies Inc. enjoy a reputation for developing talented people. The chairman and chief executive officer, Donald S. Perkins, is perhaps a good example of a person brought along through the mentor approach. Franklin J. Lunding, who was Perkins's mentor, expressed the philosophy of taking risks with young people this way: "Young people today want in on the action. They don't want to sit around for six months trimming lettuce." [16]

This statement runs counter to the culture that attaches primary importance to slow progression based on experience and proved competence. It is a high-risk philosophy, one that requires time for the attachment between senior and junior people to grow and be meaningful, and one that is bound to produce more failures than successes.

The elitism is an especially sensitive issue. At Jewel the MBA degree symbolized the elite. Lunding attracted Perkins to Jewel at a time when business school graduates had little interest in retailing in general, and food distribution in particular. Yet the elitism seemed to pay off: not only did Perkins become the president at age 37, but also under the leadership of young executives recruited into Jewel with the promise of opportunity for growth and advancement, Jewel managed to diversify into discount and drug chains and still remain strong in food retailing. By assigning each recruit to a vice president who acted as a sponsor, Jewel evidently tried to build a structure around the mentor approach to developing leaders. To counteract the elitism implied in such an approach, the company also introduced an "equalizer" in what Perkins described as "the first assistant philosophy." Perkins stated:

> Being a good first assistant means that each management person thinks of himself not as the order-giving, domineering boss, but as the first assistant to those who "report" to him in a more typical organizational sense. Thus we mentally turn our organizational charts upside-down and challenge ourselves to seek ways in which we can lead . . . by helping . . . by teaching . . . by listening . . . and by managing in the true democratic sense . . . that is, with the consent of the managed. Thus the satisfactions of leadership come from helping others to get things done and changed—and not from getting credit for doing and changing things ourselves. [17]

While this statement would seem to be more egalitarian than elitist, it does reinforce a youth-oriented culture since it defines the senior officer's job as primarily helping the junior person.

16. "Jewel Lets Young Men Make Mistakes," *Business Week,* January 17, 1970, p. 90.
17. "What Makes Jewel Shine So Bright," *Progressive Grocer,* September 1973, p. 76.

A myth about how people learn and develop that seems to have taken hold in the American culture also dominates thinking in business. The myth is that people learn best from their peers. Supposedly, the threat of evaluation and even humiliation recedes in peer relations because of the tendency for mutual identification and the social restraints on authoritarian behavior among equals. Peer training in organizations occurs in various forms. The use, for example, of task forces made up of peers from several interested occupational groups (sales, production, research, and finance) supposedly removes the restraints of authority on the individual's willingness to assert and exchange ideas. As a result, so the theory goes, people interact more freely, listen more objectively to criticism and other points of view and, finally, learn from this healthy interchange.

Another application of peer training exists in some large corporations, such as Philips, N.V. in Holland, where organization structure is built on the principle of joint responsibility of two peers, one representing the commercial end of the business and the other the technical. Formally, both hold equal responsibility for geographic operations or product groups, as the case may be. As a practical matter, it may turn out that one or the other of the peers dominates the management. Nevertheless, the main interaction is between two or more equals.

The principal question I would raise about such arrangements is whether they perpetuate the managerial orientation, and preclude the formation of one-to-one relationships between senior people and potential leaders.

Aware of the possible stifling effects of peer relationships on aggressiveness and individual initiative, another company, much smaller than Philips, utilizes joint responsibility of peers for operating units, with one important difference. The chief executive of this company encourages competition and rivalry among peers, ultimately appointing the one who comes out on top for increased responsibility. These hybrid arrangements produce some unintended consequences that can be disastrous. There is no easy way to limit rivalry. Instead, it permeates all levels of the operation and opens the way for the formation of cliques in an atmosphere of intrigue.

A large, integrated oil company has accepted the importance of developing leaders through the direct influence of senior on junior executives. One chairman and chief executive officer regularly selected one talented university graduate whom he appointed his special assistant, and with whom he would work closely for a year. At the end of the year, the junior executive would become available for assignment to one of the operating divisions, where he would be assigned to a responsible post rather than a training position. The mentor relationship had acquainted the junior executive firsthand with the use of power, and with the important antidotes to the power disease called *hubris*—performance and integrity.

Working in one-to-one relationships, where there is a formal and recognized difference in the power of the actors, takes a great deal of tolerance for emotional interchange. This interchange, inevitable in close working arrangements, probably accounts for the reluctance of many executives to become involved in such relationships. *Fortune* carried an interesting story on the departure of a key executive, John W. Hanley, from the top management of Procter & Gamble, for the chief executive officer position at Monsanto.[18] According to this account, the chief executive and chairman of P&G passed over Hanley for appointment to the presidency and named another executive vice president to this post instead.

The chairman evidently felt he could not work well with Hanley who, by his own acknowledgement, was aggressive, eager to experiment and change practices, and constantly challenged his superior. A chief executive officer naturally has the right to select people with whom he feels congenial. But I wonder whether a greater capacity on the part of senior officers to tolerate the competitive impulses and behavior of their subordinates might not be healthy for corporations. At least a greater tolerance for interchange would not favor the managerial team player at the expense of the individual who might become a leader.

I am constantly surprised at the frequency with which chief executives feel threatened by open challenges to their ideas, as though the source of their authority, rather than their specific ideas, were at issue. In one case a chief executive officer, who was troubled by the aggressiveness and sometimes outright rudeness of one of his talented vice presidents, used various indirect methods such as group meetings and hints from outside directors to avoid dealing with his subordinate. I advised the executive to deal head-on with what irritated him. I suggested that by direct, face-to-face confrontation, both he and his subordinate would learn to validate the distinction between the authority to be preserved and the issues to be debated.

To confront is also to tolerate aggressive interchange, and has the net effect of stripping away the veils of ambiguity and signaling so characteristic of managerial cultures, as well as encouraging the emotional relationship leaders need if they are to survive.

18. "Jack Hanley Got There by Selling Harder," *Fortune*, November 1976.

The Human Side of Enterprise
Douglas M. McGregor

It has become trite to say that the most significant developments of the next quarter-century will take place not in the physical but in the social sciences, that industry—the economic organ of society—has the fundamental know-how to utilize physical science and technology for the material benefit of mankind, and that we must now learn how to utilize the social sciences to make our human organizations truly effective.

Many people agree in principle with such statements; but so far they represent a pious hope—and little else. Consider with me, if you will, something of what may be involved when we attempt to transform the hope into reality.

Problems and opportunities facing management

Let me begin with an analogy. A quarter-century ago basic conceptions of the nature of matter and energy had changed profoundly from what they had been since Newton's time. The physical scientists were persuaded that under proper conditions new and hitherto unimagined sources of energy could be made available to mankind.

We know what has happened since then. First came the bomb. Then, during the past decade, have come many other attempts to exploit these scientific discoveries—some successful, some not.

The point of my analogy, however, is that the application of theory in this field is a slow and costly matter. We expect it always to be thus. No one is impatient with the scientist because he cannot tell industry how to build a simple, cheap, all-purpose source of atomic energy today. That it will take at least another decade and the investment of billions of dollars to achieve results which are economically competitive with present sources of power is understood and accepted.

It is transparently pretentious to suggest any *direct* similarity between the developments in the physical sciences leading to the harnessing of

Reprinted from *Leadership and Motivation* by Douglas McGregor by permission of The M.I.T. Press, Cambridge, Massachusetts, © 1966, 1968, The M.I.T. Press.

atomic energy and potential developments in the social sciences. Neverthe-less, the analogy is not as absurd as it might appear to be at first glance.

To a lesser degree, and in a much more tentative fashion, we are in a position in the social sciences today like that of the physical sciences with respect to atomic energy in the thirties. We know that past conceptions of the nature of man are inadequate and in many ways incorrect. We are be-coming quite certain that, under proper conditions, unimagined resources of creative human energy could become available within the organizational setting.

We cannot tell industrial management how to apply this new knowledge in simple, economic ways. We know it will require years of exploration, much costly development research, and a substantial amount of creative imagination on the part of management to discover how to apply this grow-ing knowledge to the organization of human effort in industry.

May I ask that you keep this analogy in mind—overdrawn and preten-tious though it may be—as a framework for what I have to say.

Management's task: Conventional view

The conventional conception of management's task in harnessing human energy to organizational requirements can be stated broadly in terms of three propositions. In order to avoid the complications introduced by a la-bel, I shall call this set of propositions "Theory X":

1. Management is responsible for organizing the elements of produc-tive enterprise—money, materials, equipment, people—in the interest of economic ends.

2. With respect to people, this is a process of directing their efforts, motivating them, controlling their actions, modifying their behavior to fit the needs of the organization.

3. Without this active intervention by management, people would be passive—even resistant—to organizational needs. They must therefore be persuaded, rewarded, punished, controlled—their activities must be di-rected. This is management's task—in managing subordinate managers or workers. We often sum it up by saying that management consists of getting things done through other people.

Behind this conventional theory there are several additional beliefs—less explicit, but widespread:

4. The average man is by nature indolent—he works as little as possible.

5. He lacks ambition, dislikes responsibility, prefers to be led.

6. He is inherently self-centered, indifferent to organizational needs.

7. He is by nature resistant to change.

8. He is gullible, not very bright, the ready dupe of the charlatan and the demagogue.

The human side of economic enterprise today is fashioned from propositions and beliefs such as these. Conventional organization structures, managerial policies, practices, and programs reflect these assumptions.

In accomplishing its task—with these assumptions as guides—management has conceived of a range of possibilities between two extremes.

The hard or the soft approach?

At one extreme, management can be "hard" or "strong." The methods for directing behavior involve coercion and threat (usually disguised), close supervision, tight controls over behavior. At the other extreme, management can be "soft" or "weak." The methods for directing behavior involve being permissive, satisfying people's demands, achieving harmony. Then they will be tractable, accept direction.

This range has been fairly completely explored during the past half-century, and management has learned some things from the exploration. There are difficulties in the "hard" approach. Force breeds counterforces: restriction of output, antagonism, militant unionism, subtle but effective sabotage of management objectives. This approach is especially difficult during times of full employment.

There are also difficulties in the "soft" approach. It leads frequently to the abdication of management—to harmony, perhaps, but to indifferent performance. People take advantage of the soft approach. They continually expect more, but they give less and less.

Currently, the popular theme is "firm but fair." This is an attempt to gain the advantages of both the hard and soft approaches. It is reminiscent of Teddy Roosevelt's "speak softly and carry a big stick."

Is the conventional view correct?

The findings which are beginning to emerge from the social sciences challenge this whole set of beliefs about man and human nature and about the task of management. The evidence is far from conclusive, certainly, but it is suggestive. It comes from the laboratory, the clinic, the schoolroom, the home, and even to a limited extent from industry itself.

The social scientist does not deny that human behavior in industrial organization today is approximately what management perceives it to be. He has, in fact, observed it and studied it fairly extensively. But he is pretty sure that this behavior is not consequence of man's inherent nature. It is a consequence rather of the nature of industrial organizations, of management philosophy, policy, and practice. The conventional approach of Theory X is based on mistaken notions of what is cause and what is effect.

"Well," you ask, "what then is the *true* nature of man? What evidence leads the social scientist to deny what is obvious?" And, if I am not mistaken, you are also thinking, "Tell me—simply, and without a lot of scientific verbiage—what you think you know that is so unusual. Give me—without a lot of intellectual claptrap and theoretical nonsense—some practical ideas which will enable me to improve the situation in my organization. And remember, I'm faced with increasing costs and narrowing profit margins. I want proof that such ideas won't result simply in new and costly human relations frills. I want practical results, and I want them now."

If these are your wishes, you are going to be disappointed. Such requests can no more be met by the social scientist today than could comparable ones with respect to atomic energy be met by the physicist fifteen years ago. I can, however, indicate a few of the reasons for asserting that conventional assumptions about the human side of enterprise are inadequate. And I can suggest—tentatively—some of the propositions that will comprise a more adequate theory of the management of people. The magnitude of the task that confronts us will then, I think, be apparent.

Man as a wanting animal

Perhaps the best way to indicate why the conventional approach of management is inadequate is to consider the subject of motivation. In discussing this subject I will draw heavily on the work of my colleague, Abraham Maslow of Brandeis University. His is the most fruitful approach I know. Naturally, what I have to say will be overgeneralized and will ignore important qualifications. In the time at our disposal, this is inevitable.

Physiological and safety needs

Man is a wanting animal—as soon as one of his needs is satisfied, another appears in its place. This process is unending. It continues from birth to death.

Man's needs are organized in a series of levels—a hierarchy of importance. At the lowest level, but preeminent in importance when they are thwarted, are his physiological needs. Man lives by bread alone, when there is no bread. Unless the circumstances are unusual, his needs for love, for status, for recognition are inoperative when his stomach has been empty for a while. But when he eats regularly and adequately, hunger ceases to be an important need. The sated man has hunger only in the sense that a full bottle has emptiness. The same is true of the other physiological needs of man—for rest, exercise, shelter, protection from the elements.

A satisfied need is not a motivator of behavior! This is a fact of profound significance. It is a fact which is regularly ignored in the conventional approach to the management of people. I shall return to it later. For the moment, one example will make my point. Consider your own need for air. Except as you are deprived of it, it has no appreciable motivating effect upon your behavior.

When the physiological needs are reasonably satisfied, needs at the next higher level begin to dominate man's behavior—to motivate him. These are called safety needs. They are needs for protection against danger, threat, deprivation. Some people mistakenly refer to these as needs for security.

However, unless man is in a dependent relationship where he fears arbitrary deprivation, he does not demand security. The need is for the "fairest possible break." When he is confident of this, he is more than willing to take risks. But when he feels threatened or dependent, his greatest need is for guarantees, for protection, for security.

The fact needs little emphasis that since every industrial employee is in a dependent relationship, safety needs may assume considerable importance. Arbitrary management actions, behavior which arouses uncertainty with respect to continued employment or which reflects favoritism or discrimination, unpredictable administration or policy—these can be powerful motivators of the safety needs in the employment relationship *at every level* from worker to vice-president.

Social needs

When man's physiological needs are satisfied and he is no longer fearful about his physical welfare, his social needs become important motivators of his behavior—for belonging, for association, for acceptance by his fellows, for giving and receiving friendship and love.

Management knows today of the existence of these needs, but it often assumes quite wrongly that they represent a threat to the organization. Many studies have demonstrated that the tightly knit, cohesive work group may, under proper conditions, be far more effective than an equal number of separate individuals in achieving organizational goals.

Yet management, fearing group hostility to its own objectives, often goes to considerable lengths to control and direct human efforts in ways that are inimical to the natural "groupiness" of human beings. When man's social needs—and perhaps his safety needs, too—are thus thwarted, he behaves in ways which tend to defeat organizational objectives. He becomes resistant, antagonistic, uncooperative. But this behavior is a consequence, not a cause.

Ego needs

Above the social needs—in the sense that they do not become motivators until lower needs are reasonably satisfied—are the needs of greatest significance to management and to man himself. They are the egoistic needs, and they are of two kinds:

1. Those needs that relate to one's self-esteem—needs for self-confidence, for independence, for achievement, for competence, for knowledge.

2. Those needs that relate to one's reputation—needs for status, for recognition, for appreciation, for the deserved respect of one's fellows.

Unlike the lower needs, these are rarely satisfied; man seeks indefinitely for more satisfaction of these needs once they have become important to him. But they do not appear in any significant way until physiological, safety, and social needs are all reasonably satisfied.

The typical industrial organization offers few opportunities for the satisfaction of these egoistic needs to people at lower levels in the hierarchy. The conventional methods of organizing work, particularly in mass production industries, give little heed to these aspects of human motivation. If the practices of scientific management were deliberately calculated to thwart these needs—which, of course, they are not—they could hardly accomplish this purpose better than they do.

Self-fulfillment needs

Finally—a capstone, as it were, on the hierarchy of man's needs—there are what we may call the needs for self-fulfillment. These are the needs for realizing one's own potentialities, for continued self-development, for being creative in the broadest sense of that term.

It is clear that the conditions of modern life give only limited opportunity for these relatively weak needs to obtain expression. The deprivation most people experience with respect to other lower-level needs diverts their energies into the struggle to satisfy *those* needs, and the needs for self-fulfillment remain dormant.

The dynamics of motivation

Now, briefly, a few general comments about motivation:

We recognize readily enough that a man suffering from a severe dietary deficiency is sick. The deprivation of physiological needs has behavioral consequences. The same is true—although less well recognized—of deprivation of higher-level needs. The man whose needs for safety, association, independence, or status are thwarted is sick just as surely as is he who has rickets. And his sickness will have behavioral consequences. We will be mistaken if we attribute his resultant passivity, his hostility, his refusal to accept responsibility to his inherent "human nature." These forms of behavior are *symptoms* of illness—of deprivation of his social and egoistic needs.

The man whose lower-level needs are satisfied is not motivated to satisfy those needs any longer. For practical purposes they exist no longer. (Remember my point about your need for air.) Management often asks, "Why aren't people more productive? We pay good wages, provide good working conditions, have excellent fringe benefits, and steady employment. Yet people do not seem to be willing to put forth more than minimum effort."

The fact that management has provided for these physiological and safety needs has shifted the motivational emphasis to the social and perhaps to the egoistic needs. Unless there are opportunities *at work* to satisfy these higher-level needs, people will be deprived; and their behavior will reflect this deprivation. Under such conditions, if management continues to focus its attention on physiological needs, its efforts are bound to be ineffective.

People *will* make insistent demands for more money under these conditions. It becomes more important than ever to buy the material goods and services which can provide limited satisfaction of the thwarted needs. Although money has only limited value in satisfying many higher-level needs, it can become the focus of interest if it is the *only* means available.

The carrot and stick approach

The carrot and stick theory of motivation (like Newtonian physical theory) works reasonably well under certain circumstances. The *means* for satisfying man's physiological and (within limits) his safety needs can be provided or withheld by management. Employment itself is such a means, and so are wages, working conditions, and benefits. By these means the individual can be controlled so long as he is struggling for subsistence. Man lives for bread alone when there is no bread.

But the carrot and stick theory does not work at all once man has reached an adequate subsistence level and is motivated primarily by higher needs. Management cannot provide a man with self-respect, or with the respect of his fellows, or with the satisfaction of needs for self-fulfillment. It can create conditions such that he is encouraged and enabled to seek such satisfactions *for himself,* or it can thwart him by failing to create those conditions.

But this creation of conditions is not "control." It is not a good device for directing behavior. And so management finds itself in an odd position. The high standard of living created by our modern technological know-how provides quite adequately for the satisfaction of physiological and safety needs. The only significant exception is where management practices have not created confidence in a "fair break"—and thus where safety needs are thwarted. But by making possible the satisfaction of low-level needs, management has deprived itself of the ability to use as motivators the devices on which conventional theory has taught it to rely—rewards, promises, incentives, or threats and other coercive devices.

Neither hard nor soft

The philosophy of management by direction and control—*regardless of whether it is hard or soft*—is inadequate to motivate because the human needs on which this approach relies are today unimportant motivators of behavior. Direction and control are essentially useless in motivating people whose important needs are social and egoistic. Both the hard and the soft approach fail today because they are simply irrelevant to the situation.

People, deprived of opportunities to satisfy at work the needs which are now important to them, behave exactly as we might predict—with indolence, passivity, resistance to change, lack of responsibility, willingness to follow the demagogue, unreasonable demands for economic benefits. It would seem that we are caught in a web of our own weaving.

In summary, then, of these comments about motivation: Management by direction and control—whether implemented with the hard, the soft, or the firm but fair approach—fails under today's conditions to provide effective motivation of human effort toward organizational objectives. It fails because direction and control are useless methods of motivating people whose physiological and safety needs are reasonably satisfied and whose social, egoistic, and self-fulfillment needs are predominant.

A new perspective

For these and many other reasons, we require a different theory of the task of managing people based on more adequate assumptions about human nature and human motivation. I am going to be so bold as to suggest the broad dimensions of such a theory. Call it "Theory Y," if you will:

1. Management is responsible for organizing the elements of productive enterprise—money, materials, equipment, people—in the interest of economic ends.

2. People are *not* by nature passive or resistant to organizational needs. They have become so as a result of experience in organizations.

3. The motivation, the potential for development, the capacity for assuming responsibility, the readiness to direct behavior toward organizational goals are all present in people. Management does not put them there. It is a responsibility of management to make it possible for people to recognize and develop these human characteristics for themselves.

4. The essential task of management is to arrange organizational conditions and methods of operation so that people can achieve their own goals *best* by directing *their* own efforts toward organizational objectives.

This is a process primarily of creating opportunities, releasing potential, removing obstacles, encouraging growth, providing guidance. It is what Peter Drucker has called "management by objectives" in contrast to "management by control."

And I hasten to add that it does *not* involve the abdication of management, the absence of leadership, the lowering of standards, or the other characteristics usually associated with the "soft" approach under Theory X. Much to the contrary. It is no more possible to create an organization today which will be a fully effective application of this theory than it was to build an atomic power plant in 1945. There are many formidable obstacles to overcome.

Some difficulties

The conditions imposed by conventional organization theory and by the approach of scientific management for the past half-century have tied men to limited jobs which do not utilize their capabilities, have discouraged the acceptance of responsibility, have encouraged passivity, have eliminated meaning from work. Man's habits, attitudes, expectations—his whole conception of membership in an industrial organization—have been conditioned by his experience under these circumstances. Change in the direction of Theory Y will be slow, and it will require extensive modification of the attitudes of management and workers alike.

People today are accustomed to being directed, manipulated, controlled in industrial organizations and to finding satisfaction for their social, egoistic, and self-fulfillment needs away from the job. This is true of much of management as well as of workers. Genuine "industrial citizenship"—to borrow again a term from Drucker—is a remote and unrealistic idea, the meaning of which has not even been considered by most members of industrial organizations.

Another way of saying this is that Theory X places exclusive reliance upon external control of human behavior, while Theory Y relies heavily on self-control and self-direction. It is worth noting that this difference is the difference between treating people as children and treating them as mature adults. After generations of the former, we cannot expect to shift to the latter overnight.

Applications of the theory

Before we are overwhelmed by the obstacles, let us remember that the application of theory is always slow. Progress is usually achieved in small steps.

Consider with me a few innovative ideas which are entirely consistent with Theory Y and which are today being applied with some success:

Decentralization and delegation

These are ways of freeing people from the too-close control of conventional organization, giving them a degree of freedom to direct their own activities, to assume responsibility, and, importantly, to satisfy their egoistic needs. In this connection, the flat organization of Sears, Roebuck and Company provides an interesting example. It forces "management by objectives" since it enlarges the number of people reporting to a manager until he cannot direct and control them in the conventional manner.

Job enlargement

This concept, pioneered by I.B.M. and Detroit Edison, is quite consistent with Theory Y. It encourages the acceptance of responsibility at the bottom of the organization; it provides opportunities for satisfying social and egoistic needs. In fact, the reorganization of work at the factory level offers one of the more challenging opportunities for innovation consistent with Theory Y. The studies by A. T. M. Wilson and his associates of British coal mining and Indian textile manufacture have added appreciably to our understanding of work organization. Moreover, the economic and psychological results achieved by this work have been substantial.

Participation and consultative management

Under proper conditions these results provide encouragement to people to direct their creative energies toward organizational objectives, give them some voice in decisions that affect them, provide significant opportunities for the satisfaction of social and egoistic needs. I need only mention the Scanlon Plan as the outstanding embodiment of these ideas in practice.

The not infrequent failure of such ideas as these to work as well as expected is often attributable to the fact that a management has "bought the idea" but applied it within the framework of Theory X and its assumptions. . Delegation is not an effective way of exercising management by control. Participation becomes a farce when it is applied as a sales gimmick or a device for kidding people into thinking they are important. Only the management that has confidence in human capacities and is itself directed toward organizational objectives rather than toward the preservation of personal power can grasp the implications of this emerging theory. Such management will find and apply successfully other innovative ideas as we move slowly toward the full implementation of a theory like Y.

Performance appraisal

Before I stop, let me mention one other practical application of Theory Y which—while still highly tentative—may well have important consequences. This has to do with performance appraisal within the ranks of management. Even a cursory examination of conventional programs of performance appraisal will reveal how completely consistent they are with Theory X. In fact, most such programs tend to treat the individual as though he were a product under inspection on the assembly line.

Take the typical plan: substitute "product" for "subordinate being appraised," substitute "inspector" for "superior making the appraisal," substitute "rework" for "training or development," and, except for the attributes being judged, the human appraisal process will be virtually indistinguishable from the product inspection process.

A few companies—among them General Mills, Ansul Chemical, and General Electric—have been experimenting with approaches which involve the individual in setting "targets" or objectives *for himself* and in a *self*-evaluation of performance semiannually or annually. Of course, the superior plays an important leadership role in this process—one, in fact, which demands substantially more competence than the conventional approach. The role is, however, considerably more congenial to many managers than the role of "judge" or "inspector" which is forced upon them by conventional performance. Above all, the individual is encouraged to take a greater responsibility for planning and appraising his own contribution to organizational objectives; and the accompanying effects on egoistic and self-fulfillment needs are substantial. This approach to performance appraisal represents one more innovative idea being explored by a few managements who are moving toward the implementation of Theory Y.

Conclusion

And now I am back where I began. I share the belief that we could realize substantial improvements in the effectiveness of industrial organizations during the next decade or two. Moreover, I believe the social sciences can contribute much to such developments. We are only beginning to grasp the implications of the growing body of knowledge in these fields. But if this conviction is to become a reality instead of a pious hope, we will need to view the process much as we view the process of releasing the energy of the atom for constructive human ends—as a slow, costly, sometimes discouraging approach toward a goal which would seem to many to be quite unrealistic.

The ingenuity and the perseverance of industrial management in the pursuit of economic ends have changed many scientific and technological dreams into commonplace realities. It is now becoming clear that the application of these same talents to the human side of enterprise will not only enhance substantially these materialistic achievements but will bring us one step closer to "the good society." Shall we get on with the job?

Female Leadership
In Formal Organizations:
Must the Female Leader
Go Formal?
Jean Lipman-Blumen

From Machiavelli to modern times, the conundrum of leadership has tantalized the human intellect. Since the general issue of leadership is so problematical, it is hardly surprising that the conditions of female leadership are even more ambiguous (particularly since most leadership studies have focused on male subjects). And, as with other poorly understood phenomena, female leadership is overgrown with mythology. Accepted myths, as well as some research (when it is even possible to distinguish between the two), suggest that women make poor leaders, and, in recognition of this "fact," subordinates dislike working for them (Ellman 1963; Bowman et al. 1965; and Bass et al. 1971).[1] That women have not had a major share in leadership roles is seen as further proof of their shortcomings—another case of "blaming the victim." Moreover, those women who are acknowledged leaders are perceived, in a peculiar combination of denigration and praise, as masculine. The first prime minister of Israel, Ben-Gurion, allegedly described Golda Meir as the only real man in his Cabinet.

These myths are difficult to shatter, particularly since "evidence" marshalled to support them rests upon the relatively small numbers of women leaders in both the public and private sector. Despite recent harbingers of change, the last two centuries have been a virtual wasteland for American women in the important leadership arena of public life.[2] Even in the 1970s, within the private sector, women only rarely are found in key leadership

This paper has been abridged, with permission. It appears in full in M. Horner, C. Nadelson, and M. Notman, eds. *The Challenge of Change* (New York: Plenum, 1983).

1. More recent evidence (Handley and Sedlacek 1977) suggests that women who work for a female supervisor are more likely to report greater job satisfaction and less sex bias than women working for male managers.

2. Between 1776 and 1976, the federal government has included 11 women vs. 1,715 men in the U.S. Senate, 87 women vs. 9,591 men in the U.S. House of Representatives, no women and 101 men in the Supreme Court, and 5 women vs. 507 men in the president's Cabinet. At the present time (1978), two women serve in the U.S. Senate (both through widow's inheritance), and 18 of the 435 U.S. Representatives are women, constituting 3.6% of the total Congressional membership (Center for American Women and Politics 1978).

positions.³ But the winds of change are slowly beginning to blow.⁴ Rising concern about women as leaders in the private and public sectors has been presaged by the emergence of groups specifically designed to promote female leadership.⁵ At the same time, industry, government, and academia have felt the growing pressures to bring women into leadership positions.

With increasing attention focused on women as leaders in public and private arenas, it seems appropriate to reconsider the nature of female leadership. This paper addresses that question in the context of male-female relationships in contemporary organizations.

The purpose of this paper is not to present a systematic review of leadership theories, achievement literature, or even female leadership and achievement research. Rather, its aim is to examine a group of ideas related to female leadership, most of which, we shall contend, have contributed to its current condition. To that end, we shall be concerned with (*a*) female and male leadership in mixed-sex groups; (*b*) communication as authority and the homosociality of the informal structure; (*c*) male-female socialization as it affects formal organizations; (*d*) the informal organizational structure as a resource-allocation device; (*e*) male-female predilections for different achievement styles; and finally (*f*) some possibilities for change.

Female and male leadership in mixed-sex groups

The growing literature on leadership behavior in mixed-sex groups has distilled three major generalizations about the differences between male and female behavior (Hall 1972; Lockheed and Hall 1976; Lockheed 1976):

First, *men talk more than women;* that is they "initiate more verbal acts" (Lockheed and Hall 1976). The evidence contradicts the mythology which would have us believe that women talk more than men. Talking or communicating, as we shall argue later, is an important aspect of leadership, and women, in the company of men, often apparently feel inhibited about talking. Negative attitudes toward female communication have not

---

3. Among the Fortune 500 companies, only 1 (.2%) has a woman as chief executive officer, and women constitute only 1.1% of the presidents of national unions. Among four-year institutions of higher learning, 3.6% have women presidents, and 2.4% have women vice-presidents. In two-year colleges, women comprise 0.6% of the chief executive officers (Estler and Davis 1977).

4. In state legislatures, women are winning an increasing number of seats, with a 1.3% gain (8% to 9.3%) in the three-year period 1975–78. While women are gaining in areas of elective office, their record in appointed managerial or administrative roles is somewhat less vigorous. Between 1959 and 1974, among managerial and administrative workers, women increased only 3.1%, from 15.5% to 18.6%, respectively (U.S. Department of Labor 1975). Nonetheless, the number of women applying to and graduating from law and business schools is on the rise, and the percentage of women seeking ordination degrees in divinity schools has increased 180.9% since 1970, offering some slight basis for optimism about their future corner on the leadership market.

5. For example, the National Women's Political Caucus was formed to assist women political candidates, and a presidential task force was appointed to consider the factors inhibiting women business owners.

changed much since Aristotle wrote, ". . . a woman would be thought lo-
quacious if she imposed no more restraint on her conversation than a good
man" (Jowett 1943, p. 294).

Other research on the relationship between activity levels and perceived
leadership reports that those group members who are the most active—
including verbally active—are most likely to be perceived as leaders by
other group members (Lana et al. 1960; Marsk 1964; Zdep and Oakes
1967; Zdep 1969; Morris and Hackman 1969). The "Catch-22" situation
that women face in trying to balance group behavior, verbal activity, and
leadership is classic.

The second generalization that emerges from the research on leadership
in mixed-sex groups is that *men's opinions are more likely than women's to
influence the opinions of both male and female group members*. Testing for
the extent to which subjects would acquiesce to a distorted norm, Tuddenham et al. (1958) found that in mixed-sex groups men were less likely
to acquiesce than in all-male groups, while women tended to acquiesce
more than they had in all-female groups. Whittaker's (1965) experiments
with judgments about autokinetic lights revealed that male opinion leaders
were more readily followed by both male and female subjects, but that female opinion leaders evoked considerable resistance from subjects of both
sexes. Again, the works of Strodtbeck et al. (1957), Kenkel (1957), and
Zander and Van Egmond (1958) all seem to offer supportive evidence. The
resistance women encounter when offering their analyses of problems
presents a serious obstacle to female leadership.

The third generalization centers around Parsons' (1955) formulation
that *males are more task-oriented, while females are more socio-emotion-
ally oriented*. According to Borgatta and Stimson (1963), as well as Strodtbeck and Mann (1956) and Heiss (1962), men are more likely than women
to offer task-related suggestions in a group decision-making situation,
while women are more likely than men to provide encouragement and support to other group members.

More recent work by Lockheed and Hall (1976) suggests that men are
not necessarily more active and task-oriented than women, but that male-
ness represents a more highly valued status characteristic which is translated into increased opportunities for action and, therefore, leadership,
within a group setting. Their research offers the possibility that intervention techniques—such as training and demonstrating competence specific
to the task at hand—may offset the initial leadership advantage that males
bring to groups simply on the basis of their sex.

To confound the problem, Bartol and Wortman (1975) present data that
cast doubt upon the notion that the leader's sex inevitably influences the
subordinates' perception of the leader's behavior or the subordinates' job
satisfaction. Their findings reveal that, from the subordinates' perspective,
the sex of the leader bears no relationship to the association between

perceived leader behavior and satisfaction with supervision. Moreover, Bartol and Wortman's findings call attention to sex of the subordinates as a powerful variable in predicting the satisfaction levels of subordinates. Male subordinates are more likely than females to express lower levels of satisfaction, regardless of the leader's sex.

Despite the many areas of conflict among the research results to date, some useful insights still may be gained from juxtaposing certain findings that have emerged:

If, in mixed-sex situations (as in day-to-day organizational life), the more active members are seen as leaders;

men are given more opportunities to talk and act; men actually do talk more than women;

men's opinions are more likely to influence the group positively and women's opinions are more likely to evoke negative or resistant reactions;

male subordinates are more likely than female subordinates to express dissatisfaction with their leader, regardless of the leader's sex; and

the most important informal groups consist of men (as we shall discuss below),

then the current structure of organizations serves as a serious barrier to the acceptance of female leadership.

Communication as authority and the homosociality of the informal structure

The Bartol and Wortman (1975) study is important because it begins to shift the focus beyond the behavior and characteristics of women as leaders. Much of the recent leadership and management literature has placed a disproportionate emphasis upon the personal characteristics of the leader (Hennig and Jardim 1977; Bayes and Newton 1978). Other organizational literature, however, makes it clear that the authority of position most commonly held by men is buttressed by the symbols (e.g., corner offices, chauffered limousines) that authenticate authority.

More importantly, the decision that an act of leadership has authority "lies with the persons to whom it is addressed and does not reside in 'persons of authority' or those who issue these orders" (Barnard 1968, p. 163). The question of female leadership (or nonleadership), therefore, should be considered in terms of its acceptance or legitimation by those to whom it is directed. This is not to deny that the character of the communication (to which we shall return later) has some weight, but more to emphasize the importance of the attitudes of the subordinate group members. If (1) authority is indeed a characteristic of communication and "rests upon . . . acceptance or consent" (Barnard 1968, p. 164), and (2) the subordinate group has a high proportion of men, then women who attempt leadership, or more modestly managerial, roles in formal organizations (other than all-female organizations) are in serious trouble.

If we recall, first, that the mixed-sex group research indicates that women talk less than men, it is clear that the issue of establishing communication, and thereby authority, is more problematical for women. One function of the myth of women's loquaciousness becomes apparent: it serves as a control mechanism for limiting women's communication in the presence of men. By inhibiting women's communications in the presence of men for fear of fulfilling a negative female stereotype, the women's leadership behavior in mixed-sex groups also is conveniently limited.

Second, mixed-group research tells us that even when women do talk, their contributions tend to have a negative effect upon group opinion. But the formal and (perhaps even more importantly) the informal systems are areas which separately generate the group opinions by which one's authority is maintained.

The individual builds a credibility base within each sphere on somewhat different grounds: official rank in the formal system; sentiment and personalities in the informal system. The personal credibility generated in the informal system influences one's authority in the formal structure, and often vice versa. From a slightly different vantage point, the leader who also is a member of the informal system (i.e., "the old boy network") is allowed an extra margin of credibility. All other things being equal, in official settings, that leader's co-workers are prepared to be receptive to his ideas. (Compare this to the common experience of high-level organizational women, excluded from the informal male system, who point out that their comments in official situations often are ignored altogether or attributed to a male member of the group.)

To add to the complexity of life in organizations, credibility associated with formal rank marks the individual as a desirable recruit for the informal structure. It is easy to see that the connection between the formal and informal bases of credibility has a Catch-22 circularity. If you're "in" in one system, you're likely to be "in" in the other system, which in turn makes you more "in" in the first. Of course, it follows that if you're "out" in one, you're more likely to be "out" in the other, and so on. Thus, for the formal and informal bases of credibility to potentiate one another, the individual must have access to both the formal and the informal. External pressures rather recently have created opening wedges for women in formal structures. Nevertheless, women in leadership positions still confront the formidable problem of gaining access to the informal structure, the greenhouse milieu for growing not only sentiment and affection so critical to public opinion, but also decisions and transactions that ultimately move the formal structure.

In addition to building supportive sentiment and affection within the informal structure, a leader must sharpen communication by an accurate assessment of events, conditions, and people. Again, there is a troublesome circularity to such information flows. To be credible, information from leaders to followers must be informed by the culture and currency of the followers' group. The leader gains credibility when s/he seems to know more than the followers know. A leader who transmits information which subordinates perceive as naive soon loses credibility. Formal information is augmented by intelligence that flows from the informal network. Such intelligence is, itself, a valuable resource.

This is not to deny that women in leadership positions receive the usual official information through formal channels, such as staff meetings, briefings, memoranda, and the like. Rather, we are suggesting that the "insider's" knowledge—offering the insider strategic advantages—is not readily available to women, who are blocked from executive level, all-male groups.

Women's exclusion from the informal network prevents them from developing an "intelligence or communication base," which then could spread a mantle of authority over their communications in the formal structure. The resulting handicap activates a vicious cycle which women managers or leaders rarely have the resources to break. The parallel all-female informal networks that ordinarily arise do not transmit executive and policy level information. This is partly the result of the sex segregation of formal organizations (Blaxall and Reagan 1976) and the long-standing tendency for women to be confined within the lowest strata of such structures. Rarely are there sufficient numbers of executive-level women within any single formal organization to constitute an informal network. Only recently have women begun to develop interorganizational networks to offset the information barrier.[6]

Although informal networks, in general, are sex segregated, social relationships between individual men and women provide conduits for resource exchange between these structures. For example, the secretary-executive relationship historically has been the channel through which the male executives tapped into the female informal network, thereby acquiring valuable information about their male co-workers. Similarly, females

6. Some recent exceptions have begun to emerge in the world of women's issues, within the public and private sectors, where strong informal networks have developed. Since women's programs commonly involve small, all-female staff within large mostly male (except for support staff) organizations, the feminist networks that have developed often cross organizational lines. These informal structures serve as avenues for policy level and other information, support, decision-making and strategy development across organizational boundaries. Thus, women managers in unrelated subdivisions of a large-scale organization, in separate but similar private institutions, and within different agencies in government have created effective feminist homosocial networks. These networks have involved coalitions not only among "insiders" in different divisions, but also between "insiders" and "outsiders." Nonetheless, because of the common segregation of women professionals within their own organizations, women leaders still have difficulty penetrating the informal male homosocial structures within their parent organizations.

in organizational settings often have had to rely on their individual relationships with male co-workers to gain access to important organizational information.

Male-female socialization and formal organizations

Male homosociality[7] has been described elsewhere as a powerful factor in the sex segregation of American social institutions (Lipman-Blumen 1976). The male homosocial ethic focuses on competition and winning—often in team settings—and operates within a context replete with complex role networks and clearly articulated hierarchies.

The team, with its formal structure of interlocking task-oriented roles, is a depersonalized world. Specialized skill is the primary, if not the only, criterion for entry into team roles; while feelings, sensitivities, understanding, and other interpersonal skills are far less relevant. No soccer team is complete without a goalie, and the goalie position is filled by the individual most adept at defending the goal, without regard to that individual's interpersonal skills.

Males learn early on that winning the game often means playing with teammates they may not like. Team spirit is the recognition of the superordinate importance of the group over the individual. Personal relationships among role occupants become the domain of the informal, not the formal, structure. The informal structure provides a necessary cushion against the impersonality of the formal structure (i.e., the team) and arises in the service of the formal structure.

The informal structure fulfills the personal needs frustrated by the formal structure. In his recent autobiography, Roethlisberger (1977), the dean of the early human relations movement in management, lucidly underscores this distinction:

> These relations of interconnectedness among persons . . . I call the strong, close, and warm relationships. They make the cheese more binding. The (formal) ones in contrast are weak, distant, and cold. . . . It seemed to me that in most organizations the employees found these informal relationships rewarding. Whenever and wherever it was possible, they generated them like crazy. . . . The two kinds of relations were in sharp contrast. Among members of (formal) relations, there were few interactions, few close friendships and seldom any small, warm, cozy groups. There was sometimes "respect" but quite often distrust, apprehension, and suspicion. Interaction was limited to what the task required. It looked as if the logic of rational management generated weak, distant, and cold relations, whereas the employees as persons generated strong, close, and warm relations.

7. Homosociality is defined as the "seeking, enjoyment, and/or preference for the company of the same sex."

The outcome, which was often conflict, was not because anyone was deliberately trying to throw a monkey wrench in the machinery. The logic of management could do only what it was supposed to do, its business, so to speak. It could only produce those relations in which rational order existed. To ask it to produce strong, close, cozy and comfortable relations would be like asking an icicle to produce warmth for man. However, that man as man sought for these warm relations was also not being just ornery. He also was doing what his nature as man and the itch-ouch balance compelled him to do. [pp. 165–66]

Given the offsetting warmth of the informal structure, the team members can tolerate more readily the coolness of the formal structure. This formal-informal counterpoint provides the milieu for male socialization. Men learn early in childhood to distinguish and move easily between formal and informal structures.

Women grow up outside the world of large, complexly structured teams. They are socialized in small play groups of two or three individuals (Maccoby and Jacklin 1974), in which the formal is not differentiated from the informal structure. The focus is upon individual personalities and the relationships among them. Winning is not highly emphasized, relating is.

Thus socialized, women often see the formal and informal worlds as one and treat even formal roles informally. Given the emotionally positive aspects of the informal structure, as Roethlisberger has described it, the choice is a natural one, one that men, too, probably would take if the structure of their world permitted.

But women's inexperience in separating the formal from the informal structure becomes a liability. The effects can be particularly destructive when, as adults, they enter leadership roles requiring differentiation of formal and informal structures. And it is not simply a question of inexperience. Women learn to *value* personal relationships, to rank their importance above simple task-orientation and winning. The more adept females become in interpersonal relationships, the more they value this modus vivendi, and the more likely they are to incorporate this value in their managerial style (Reif et al. 1975).

Raphaela Best (in progress), in the ethnographic study of third-graders at play, describes how little girls happily let their female friends win a race in the name of friendship. The playtime role structures of young females are not depersonalized. Personality counts. It is the individual, not the role, who has salience. An individual who does not have certain personal characteristics will not be accepted in the playmate role, even if the role remains vacant. The emphasis is upon people as personalities and upon relationships, rather than upon the structure and coordination of goal-oriented roles. The goal *is* the relationship; the external task may even be the means. The focus is on relating, not on winning.

If it is important to women to like the person in the related role, it is equally (perhaps too) critical for them to feel that *they* are liked.[8] In fact, the early achievement studies of McClelland et al. (1953) suggested that social acceptability cues were the only cues likely to stimulate need for achievement in female subjects. The need to be liked, thus, may impede women in organizational situations which require competence and task-orientation, unallowed with personal popularity.

Homosociality as a resource-allocation device

Like the formal structure, the informal structure is composed of numerous, segmented, and unequal parts. It reflects the hierarchy and sex segregation of the formal structure. Indeed, sex segregation in the informal structure is often more severe than in the formal one. This homosociality that characterized the informal structure provides a mechanism for the control and distribution of resources. Both tangible and intangible resources flow along the informal network. Personal *autonomy,* for example, is often dispersed through its tributaries. That is, the ordinary bureaucratic controls are not applied very rigidly to those who are solid members of the informal network. Another vital resource, time, is also allocated through informal channels. Personal time, as well as official deadlines, are granted a measure of flexibility from members of the informal network. For example, such members are less likely to have their comings and going carefully scrutinized. Their organizational tethers are longer, providing greater latitude for action before being called to account. Their time, autonomy, personal and organizational freedom are thereby enlarged.

These important resources are building blocks of power which create leverage in the formal system. The leader who accrues autonomy and time can in turn provide special treatment for staff, colleagues, and clients, which eventually yields loyalty, reciprocal help, profits, and promotions.

The informal structure also distributes *loopholes,* ways around the formal requirements of the system. *Special perquisites* are distributed, as well. For example, in times of tight budgets, when travel funds supposedly are restricted, favored members of the informal network usually can manage to have their travel orders approved.

Still another resource available through the informal network is *accessibility* to people and services. While formal availability of co-workers and services is a legitimate part of every formal organizational role, approachability is enhanced or inhibited by the informal system. Thus, while the division manager has some legitimate claim on the time and help of his/her supervisor, that claim is processed quickly or lackadaisically according to the manager's informal standing. The co-member of the informal group does not "cool his heels" waiting for an appointment. Both the quality and

---

8. The reciprocal need to be liked was suggested to me in personal communication by Professor Constantiana Safilios-Rothschild in 1978.

quantity of entrée and service are influenced by the informal system. Even official resources, such as staff and budget, are influenced by the informal structure. Any seasoned observer of the organizational scene has witnessed how favored members of the informal system somehow manage to secure additional staff and increased budgets beyond whatever official allocations have been set.

Political, financial, legal, professional, and other extraorganizational help are still other resources that flow along the informal waters. The easy accessibility of the informal group allows the insiders to develop a sixth sense within the organization. They know one another well enough to sense when it is the appropriate moment to ask for or offer help. This easy access provides the context within which "understanding" about goals, values, and sentiments develops, reducing the probability of serious political or interpersonal errors that could jeopardize leadership. All these valuable resources—autonomy, freedom, time, loopholes, perquisites, accessibility to people and services, political, professional, financial, and legal help (not to mention valuable "insider's" information discussed earlier)—are distributed by the all-male executive informal system.

Of course, homosocial enclaves of women also exist and serve as control and distribution mechanisms. But the resources that flow along the channels of the women's network are likely to be interpersonal and relational in nature. The access of women to crucial organizational resources is more limited, and, thus, the largesse that can be distributed to other women often is not keyed to organizational or professional goals.

Because women rarely have access to the informal male structure, they commonly lack the resources necessary for negotiating their way through the higher levels of the formal structure. They do not participate in the transactions which allocate vital organizational resources. As a result, they have less access to executive power and limited maneuverability within the organization.

Those women who enter the formal organization with significant resources of their own (e.g., family fortunes, prior connections to powerful members of the organization, or political or professional networks) usually are better able to counter the informal male network. If such women can maintain their resources, their authority may be sustained and even acknowledged by their male colleagues.

Occasionally women with male mentors develop indirect routes to information and other key resources from the informal system. Mentors who are privy to the power centers within the organization are able to confer an impressive array of largesse, including status and support, upon their proteges. Although young, ambitious men in organizations rather easily attach themselves to successful male mentors, such a process poses greater difficulties for women and may be fraught with sexual overtones (Rowe 1977; Shapiro et al. 1978).

Male and female achievement styles

While the nature of the structures within which one seeks goals are undeniably important, how one goes about attaining those goals is probably just as crucial. Both men and women develop characteristic ways of achieving whatever goals they set for themselves. The more adept one becomes at certain achievement "styles" the more likely one is to continue to use them.

Men raised in the world of competitive teams easily focus on *direct* achievement styles, on getting things done, on winning. The early male world encourages pitting oneself against one's environment, acting directly in one's behalf, achieving through one's own efforts. Each team player has a specific piece of direct action to contribute to the general task of winning. The reward of winning is shared among all, even though the quarterback may be seen as the key player.

Another factor contributing to this direct achievement style is the early understanding that adult men are expected to support themselves and possibly others. Men are socialized to act in their own behalf. For adult males, there are only two "escapes" from responsibility for direct action: either recurrently demonstrated failure to perform or its opposite, a substantial history of successful performance. Either of these two histories may let men off the hook. But there are many legitimate loopholes—including marriage—to channel females away from frontline responsibility.

The difference between the early socialization of boys and girls is great on this issue of self-reliance. Little boys traditionally are asked what they want to be when they grow up; little girls, whom they want to marry. Hennig and Jardim (1977) remind us of the enormity of the resulting differences in mind set (p. 15). From early socialization, males expect to protect and support women; and women traditionally have accepted this arrangement without recognizing that such protection is tantamount to control.

While men are pushed into a direct achievement world, women are encouraged to become relational achievers (Lipman-Blumen and Leavitt 1976, 1978a, 1978b). For women, the relationship itself often becomes the goal. And acts that contribute to building relationships become valued means of achieving. *Relational* achievement styles are translated into certain occupational roles, often the traditional "feminine occupations" such as teaching, social work, and nursing. But other, less specific roles also include large relational components, coaching and managing. And here we begin to see the importance of such roles for organizations.

It is an interesting characteristic of formal organizations that the common reward for competent task performance as a nonsupervisor is promotion to supervisor. But supervision usually requires a large relational component. Supervisors, that is, are not just doers, but coaches, mentors, developers of their people. The shift from direct bench to supervisory work may thus be difficult for both company and supervisor. But it appears that it is precisely in this area that women can offer very strong skills. Yet present organizational reward systems frustrate the match of women to managerial roles. Nonetheless, it is clear that technical expertise without such relational skills rarely sends one to the head of the leadership line.[9]

Some possibilities for change

While many changes to ease some of these problems are possible, few are simple and feasible. For example, decentralization of large organizations into much smaller units would increase local autonomy of leaders and enhance interpersonal bonds. But few organizations are likely to pay the costs of a major decentralization program solely to gain the advantages outlined here. Similarly, rotating leadership positions could yield salutary effects. But leader rotation would also entail (or so the myth suggests) such costs that few organizations are likely to do it just to open pathways for women.

On the other hand, organizations can, as they debate structural and operational change, factor in the likely impact of proposed changes on subsequent leadership patterns. And further, women, as they search the job market, would do well to evaluate potential employers against criteria like the degree of decentralization of leadership power, the extent to which interpersonal skills are *explicitly* weighed and rewarded in personnel evaluations, and the extent to which the organization has demonstrated flexibility in the promotional policies, as well as the degree to which it *demonstrably* values employee behaviors that glue the organization together into a solid social unit.

Some other changes that organizations can make are far less costly than such major structural changes, and far more feasible. Here are some possibilities:

— Women leaders can be brought into the organizations at *high enough levels* so their positions carry adequate and unequivocal formal credibility. Unlike men, women have special difficulty in establishing credibility when they enter at lower ranks.

— The domains women leaders are asked to supervise can be made more *central* to the goals of the organization.

— Women leaders can be anointed with both *symbols of power* and the *reality of resources*. Corner offices and large budgets will lend clout to women leaders, just as they always have to men. Adequate resources and the symbols of clout will encourage male co-workers to seek the help, and even the sponsorship, of women leaders.

— Two other obvious possibilities: encourage women (1) to create their *own informal groups* and (2) to find ways of entering men's. The former may be easier than the latter.

9. Japanese organizational structures tend to assign higher priority to interpersonal or relational skills than to technical expertise (Abegglen 1958; Johnson and Ouchi 1974; Okamoto; Vogel 1968; Lipman-Blumen and Leavitt 1978).

— If a *cadre* of high-level women is brought into the organization in positions that minimize potential competition among them, they can build their own informal network, providing each other with executive-level information and other resources, as well as interpersonal support. Where there are too few top-level women in an organization, women leaders can construct (and in many places they are doing so) an *interorganizational* informal network composed of top-level women in analogous positions.

— Even if the woman leader cannot enter as a bona fide member of the male informal network, she still may develop access to information transmitted through the informal system. Not only will individual ties to one or more members of the male informal network help, but particular male co-workers may be more helpful than others. For example, a *male* member of the informal system to whom the woman leader reports in the formal structure is a key linkpin to the informal structure. *Enlisting* that *male supervisor's help,* in fact, making it his *quasi-legitimate* responsibility to keep the female leader posted, is an important method for sustaining her information level (and therefore her credibility in the formal group). Obviously, this tactic must be used with special care to avoid jeopardizing the male informant's status as a trustworthy member of the informal group.

— So much has been written recently about the role of *mentors* in individual careers that it is unnecessary to dwell at length on that strategy. Nonetheless, the male supervisor just mentioned is one possible mentor. But other *high-status males* both in and sometimes outside the organization are likely candidates as mentors for nascent women leaders.

— Another structural possibility for enhancing women's credibility as group leaders is to pay serious attention to the *sex* and *status* composition of the ingroups. If, as the literature tells us, male subordinates are more likely than females to express dissatisfaction regardless of the leader's sex, then initially women leaders should be given groups in which there is a *slight preponderance of women*. Once their reputations and confidence are established, they can move on to groups with higher proportions of men. It is also useful, if possible, to include at least one high-status male group member who is clearly perceived as (and, in fact, is) her ally.

— Credibility in groups, we have seen, is enhanced by active participation. Roles such as team leader, expert on a given issue, liaison person to other important groups all offer structured possibilities for unequivocal contribution to goals. As we noted earlier, individuals who contribute to group tasks, rather than to the socioemotional climate of the group, are more likely to be seen as leaders, given our current value system. As group leaders, women, at least initially, should *downplay* expressions of nurturance and emotional support, concentrating instead on task-related directions, reinforcements, and advice. The reciprocal of this strategy is to train males (1) to *listen* when women talk and (2) to offer *emotional and social support* to other group members.

— Training women as specialists in *short-term* tasks is an important means of refocussing the group's perceptions of her value to goal attainment. For example, a consulting group which plans to bid on a contract in a new substantive area could give a woman leader special training in that subject to ensure her claim to unique leadership eligibility.

An important caveat: specialist roles often prove to be dead-end. So if women enter organizations as specialists, clear pathways toward the "generalist" ranks of leadership have to be carefully kept open. Urging women to enter organizations as specialists runs counter to the current trend in leading business schools, where managers are advised to become "generalists!" Nonetheless, entering the group as a specialist can be a useful *short-term* strategy by which women at the outset establish their leadership credibility before moving on to generalist roles.

Although women's comments often are ignored in group discussions, research findings suggest that leadership is attributed to the group members who talk frequently. *Structured opportunities* to encourage women to talk more in groups therefore make sense. For example, women can be given frequent opportunities (and should welcome them!) to make oral presentations. Placing women in roles like team leader, presenter, or discussion leader, offers structured opportunities for women to talk. If men's subsequent performance is partially dependent on information gleaned from a woman leader's presentation, this "*structured talking*" by women could be a valuable way of encouraging males' "*structured listening*."

— "Anointed analysis," in which a woman's opinions are validated by the *explicit approval* of a high-status male leader, is another means of motivating women to talk and men to listen. In official meetings, the top executive can solicit a woman executive's opinion, listen deferentially and attentively, and thus set the example for other males in the organization.

— *Closing* some of the *escape hatches* from responsibility for women, including their socially approved avoidance of mathematics and science (Aiken 1970, 1976; Fenema 1976; Sells 1973; Tobias 1978), will facilitate the development of direct achievement styles in women. Males are raised with the societal expectation that they must do for themselves; they must *directly* encounter their environment. Females are socialized to the expectation that they will *not* be directly responsible for themselves. In fact, by helping others to achieve or by providing encouragement and emotional support, they can achieve *indirectly*. As more women recognize and accept the inevitability of labor force participation, just as men do, they will value more the benefits derived from moving flexibly between direct and relational achievement styles and roles.

At the same time that we are closing some of the *escape hatches* for women, it is reasonable to think about *opening* a few for *men*. Offering men opportunities to follow less rigid career paths, to take nonorganizational roles, to feel freer to enter and leave the labor force at different points can ease the tensions many men currently feel in their occupational lives. Developing the flexibility to shift from direct to relational achievement styles may be a decided asset in this process.

— As we noted earlier, the barriers against women entering the male homosocial network have been impervious. What, if any, tactics might be useful in that realm? Some possibilities: selection of people already like present group members; training new members to be more like group members in relevant ways; training old group members to be more like the new entrants; promoting the entry of women who are *similar* to the male homosocial group in terms of education, political outlook, and professional interests. But it is clear that these approaches also carry serious limitations: (1) they downplay the special skills, qualities, and orientations that women can bring to organizations and limit the potential strength and richness that diversity brings to any group; and (2) they ignore the important imperative of affirmative action.

Conclusions

The approaches to change listed in this section cover a broad range— small, large, short-term, long-term, individual, organizational, and societal. Implementation of change is the subject of an impressive literature (Leavitt and Webb 1978) whose distillation is not possible in a few paragraphs. And clearly, the vast societal changes that are called for are beyond the scope of this chapter. But perhaps a few last cautionary words are in order.

We are *not* proposing that women should become pseudomen and men pseudowomen. The need is for greater balance and freedom for both sexes. Sex role stereotypes of active males and passive, helpful females contribute to the rigidity with which the sexes are pressed into sex-segregated organizational roles. While changing such stereotypes in the whole society is a longer and more arduous endeavor, altering values and perceptions inside organizations is a far more attainable goal. The linkages among competition, aggression, and masculinity can be loosened. Women can work aggressively and compete without being perceived as "defeminized." And men can, if we permit and encourage it, behave more supportively without fearing "demasculinization." The separation of masculinity and femininity from competition and aggressiveness on the one hand, and helpfulness and passivity on the other, is a task which both the present managers of organizations and women who aspire to management roles can begin to address immediately.

Bibliography

Abegglen, J. G. *The Japanese factory.* Glencoe, Ill.: The Free Press, 1958.

Aiken, L. R. Update on attitudes and other affective variables in learning mathematics. *Review of Educational Research,* 1976, 46:293–311.

————. Attitudes toward mathematics. *Review of Educational Research,* 1970, *40*:551–96.

Argyris, C. *Understanding organizational behavior.* Homewood, Ill.: Dorsey Press, 1960.

Askinas, B. E. The impact of coeducational living on peer interaction. (Doctoral dissertation, Stanford University, 1971.) *Dissertation Abstracts International,* 1971, *32,* 1634–A.

Barnard, C. I. *Functions of the executive.* Cambridge, Mass.: Harvard University Press, 1968.

Bartol, K. M., & Wortman, Jr., M. S. Male versus female leaders: Effects on perceived leader behavior and satisfaction in a hospital. *Personnel Psychology,* 1975, *28*:533–47.

Bass, B. M., Krusell, J., & Alexander, R. A. Male managers' attitudes toward working women. *American Behavioral Scientist,* 1971, *15*: 221–36.

Bayes, M., & Newton, P. M. Women in authority: A sociopsychological analysis. *The Journal of Applied Behavioral Science,* 1978, *14* (1): 7–25.

Bernard, J. *The female world.* New York: Free Press, 1981.

Best, R. *The group, sex and learning in the primary grades,* in progress.

Blake, R. R., & Mouton, J. S. *Grid organization development.* Houston, Texas: Gulf Publishing Co., 1968.

Blaxall, M., & Reagen, B., Eds. *Women and the workplace: The implications of occupational segregation.* Chicago, Ill.: The University of Chicago Press, 1976.

Borgatta, E. F., & Stimson, J. Sex differences in interaction characteristics. *Journal of Social Psychology,* 1963, *60*:89–100.

Bowman, C. W., Worthy, N. B., & Greyser, S. A. Are women executives people? *Harvard Business Review,* July-August 1965, *43*:14–17+.

Bradford, D. L., Sargent, A. C., Sprague, M. S. The executive man and woman: The issue of sexuality. Chapter 3 in *Bringing women into management,* Eds. Gordon, F. E., & Strober, M. H. New York: McGraw-Hill, 1975, 39–58.

Couch, A. S., & Carter, L. A factorial study of the rated behavior of group members. Paper presented at Eastern Psychological Association, Atlantic City, April 1952.

Ellman, E. S. *Managing women in business.* Waterford, Conn.: Prentice-Hall, Inc., 1963.

Estler, S., & Davis, C. *Women in decision-making.* Stanford University Center for Research on Women, 1977 (April).

Fenema, E. *Influences of selected cognitive, effective and educational variables in sex-related differences in mathematics learning and studying.* National Institute of Education, Grant No. P–76–0274, 1976.

Gibb, C. A. Leadership. Chapter 24 in *Handbook of social psychology,* Vol. II, Ed. Lindzey, G. Reading, Mass.: Addison-Wesley Publishing Co., Inc., 877–920.

Hall, K. P. Sex differences in initiation and influence in decision-making among prospective teachers. (Doctoral dissertation, Stanford University, 1972.) *Dissertation Abstracts International,* 1972, *33* (8), 3952–A.

Halpin, A. W., & Winer, B. J., A factorial study in the leader-behavior descriptions. In *Leader behavior: Its description and measurement,* Eds. Stogdill, R. M., & Coons, A. E., 1957, 39–51. Columbus: Ohio State University, Bureau of Business Research, Research Monograph #88.

Handley, A., & Sedlacek, W. Characteristics and work attitudes of women working on campus. *National Association of Women Deans, Administrators, and Counselors,* 1977, *40*(4).

Heiss, J. Degree of intimacy and male-female interaction. *Sociometry,* 1962, *25*:197–208.

Hennig, M., & Jardim, A. *The managerial woman.* Garden City, N.Y.: Anchor Press/Doubleday & Co., Inc., 1977.

Hoffman, L. W. Early childhood experiences and women's achievement motives. *Journal of Social Issues,* 1972, *28*(2), 129–55.

Johnson, R. T., & Ouchi, W. G. Made in America (under Japanese management). *Harvard Business Review,* Sept.-Oct., 1974:61–69.

Jowett, B. Trans. *Aristotle's politics.* New York, N.Y.: Modern Library, 1943.

Kanter, R. M. *Men and women of the corporation.* New York, N.Y.: Basic Books, Inc., 1977.

Kenkel, W. F. Differentiation in family decision making. *Sociology and Social Research,* 1957, *42*:18–25.

Lana, R. E., Vaughan, W., & McGinnies, E. Leadership and friendship status as factors in discussion group interaction. *Journal of Social Psychology,* 1960, *52*:127–34.

Leavitt, H. J. Beyond the analytic manager. *California Management Review,* spring 1975, *17*(3):5–12; and summer 1975, *17*(4):11–21.

———. Applied organization change in industry: Structural, Technical, and human approaches. Chapter 4 in *New perspectives in organization research,* Eds. W. W. Cooper, H. J. Leavitt, M. W. Shelly, 2. New York, N.Y.: John Wiley & Sons, Inc., 1964, 55–71.

Leavitt, H. J., & Lipman-Blumen, J. Achievement styles and managerial behavior: The case for the relational manager. Unpublished manuscript, 1978.

Leavitt, H. J., & Webb, E. Implementing: Two approaches. Research Paper #440, May 1978, Research Paper Series, Graduate School of Business, Stanford University.

Lipman-Bluman, J. A paradigm for the entrance of women into new occupational roles. In *Women organizing,* Eds., Cummings, B., & Schuck, V. Garden City, N.Y.: Adelphi University Press, 1979.

————. A crisis perspective on divorce and role change. Chapter 10 in *Women into wives: The legal and economic impact of marriage.* Sage Yearbooks in Women's Policy Studies, Vol. 2, Eds., Chapman, J. R., & Gates, M. Beverly Hills, Calif.: Sage Publications, 1977.

————. Toward a homosocial theory of sex roles: An explanation of the sex segregation of social institutions. *Signs,* spring 1976, *1*(3), Part 2, 15–31. (Reprinted in *Women and the workplace,* Eds., Blaxall, M., & Reagan, B. Chicago, Ill.: University of Chicago Press, 1976.)

————. A crisis framework applied to macro-sociological family changes: Marriage, divorce, and occupational trends associated with World War II. *Journal of Marriage and the Family,* November, 1975, 889–902.

————. Role de-differentiation as a system response to crisis: Occupational and political roles of women. *Sociological Inquiry,* 1973, *43*(2): 105–29.

Lipman-Blumen, J., & Leavitt, H. J. Socialization and achievement patterns in cross-cultural perspective: Japanese and American family and work roles. Presented at the Ninth World Congress of Sociology, Uppsala, Sweden, August 14–19, 1978.

————. Sexual behavior as an expression of achievement orientation. In *Human sexual development: Alternative perspectives,* Ed. Katchadourian, H. Berkeley, Calif.: University of California Press, 1978.

————. Vicarious and direct achievement patterns in adulthood. *The Counseling Psychologist,* 1976, *6*(1):26–32. (Reprinted in *Career development and counseling of women,* Eds., Hansen, J. S., & Rapoza-Blocher, R. S., Springfield, Ill.: Charles C. Thomas Publishing Co., 1977.)

Lockheed, M. E. Cognitive style effects on sex status in student work groups. *Journal of Educational Psychology,* 1977, *69*(2):158–65.

————. The modification of female leadership behavior in the presence of males. Educational Testing Service, Princeton, New Jersey. N.I.E. Grant No. NE–G–00–3–0130, October 1976.

Lockheed, M. E., & Hall, K. P. Conceptualizing sex as a status characteristic: Applications to leadership training strategies. *Journal of Social Issues,* 1976, *32*(3):111–23.

Maccoby, E. M., & Jacklin, C. N. *The psychology of sex differences.* Stanford, Calif.: Stanford University Press, 1974.

Marak, G. E. The evolution of leadership structure. *Sociometry,* 1964, *27*:174–82.

McClelland, D. C., Atkinson, J. W., Clark, R. A., & Lowell, E. L. *The achievement motive.* New York: Irvington Publishers, 1953.

Michels, R. Authority. In *The encyclopedia of the social sciences,* Eds. Seligman, R. A., & Johnson, A. New York, N.Y.: Macmillan, 1937.

Morris, C. G., & Hackman, J. R. Behavioral correlates of perceived leadership. *Journal of Personality and Social Psychology,* 1969, *13*:350–61.

Okamoto, Y. Japanese business behavior and the management based on groupism. Mimeographed ms., Faculty of Economics, University of Tokyo, no date.

Parsons, T. Family structure and the socialization of the child. In *Family socialization and interaction process,* Eds. Parsons, T., Bales, R. F. Glencoe, Ill.: The Free Press, 1955.

⸻. *Essays in sociological theory pure and applied.* Glencoe, Ill.: The Free Press, 1949.

Reif, W. E., Newstrom, J. W., & Monezka, R. M. Exploding some myths about women managers. *California Management Review,* summer, 1975, *7*(4):72–79.

Roethlisberger, F. J. *The elusive phenomena: An autobiographical account of my work in the field of organizational behavior at the Harvard Business School.* Ed. Lombard, G. F. F. Boston, Mass.: Division of Research, Graduate School of Business Administration, Harvard University, 1977.

Rowe, M. P. Go hire yourself a mentor. In Proceedings of the Conference on Women's Leadership and Authority in the Health Professions, U.C. Santa Cruz, June 19–21, 1977, sponsored by Program for Women in Health Sciences, University of California, San Francisco, pp. 40–42.

Safilios-Rothschild, C. Theoretical model of sex discrimination in education. April 25, 1977, Final Report, Unpublished, Wayne State University.

⸻. Sex role socialization patterns in selected societies. Paper presented at the American Educational Research Association Annual Meetings, April 2, 1975, Washington, D.C.

Sells, L. High school mathematics as the critical filter in the job market. In *Developing opportunities for minorities in graduate education.* Proceedings of the Conference on Minority Graduate Education at the University of California, Berkeley, May 1973, pp. 47–59.

Shapiro, E., Haseltine, F., & Rowe, M. P. Moving up: Role models, mentors, and the 'patron system.' *Sloan Management Review,* spring 1978, *19*:51–58.

Shaw, M. E., & Sadler, O. W. Interaction patterns in heterosexual dyads varying in degree of intimacy. *Journal of Social Psychology,* 1965, *66*:345–51.

Strodtbeck, F. L., James, R. M., & Hawkins, C. Social status in jury deliberations. *American Sociological Review,* 1957, *22*:713–19.

Strodtbeck, F. L., & Mann, R. D. Sex role differentiation in jury deliberations. *Sociometry,* 1956, *19*:3–11.

Tannenbaum, A., Kavcic, B., Rosner, M., Vianello, M., & Wieser, G. *Hierarchy in organizations: An international comparison.* San Francisco, Cal.: Jossey Bass, 1974.

Tobias, S. *Overcoming math anxiety,* 1st ed. New York, N.Y.: Norton & Co., 1978.

Tuddenham, R. D., MacBride, P., & Zahn, V. The influence of the sex composition of the groups upon yielding to a distorted group norm. *Journal of Psychology*, 1958, *46*:243–51.

U.S. Department of Labor, Women's Bureau. *1975 Handbook on women workers*. Washington, D.C.: Government Printing Office, 1975, Bulletin 297.

Vogel, E. F. *Japan's new middle class: The salary man and his family in a Tokyo suburb*. Berkeley, Calif.: University of California Press, 1968.

Vroom, V., & Yetton, P. W. *Leadership and decision-making*. Pittsburgh, Pa.: University of Pittsburgh, 1973.

Weber, Max. *The theory of social and economic organization*. (Translated by Henderson, A. M., & Parsons, T.) Glencoe, Ill.: The Free Press, 1947.

Whittaker, J. O. Sex differences and susceptibility to interpersonal persuasion. *Journal of Social Psychology*, 1965, *66*:91–92.

Zander, A., & Van Egmond, E. Relationship of intelligence and social power to the interpersonal behavior of children. *Journal of Educational Psychology*, 1958, *49*:257–68.

Zdep, S. M. Intragroup reinforcement and its effects on leadership behavior. *Organizational Behavior and Human Performance*, 1969, *4*:284–98.

Zdep, S. M., & Oakes, W. F. Reinforcement of leadership behavior in group discussion. *Journal of Experimental Social Psychology*, 1967, *3*:310–20.

6

Power: Over and
Under the Table

In the world of organizational behavior, *power* used to be a dirty word. It carried connotations of authoritarianism and manipulation. In the last few years, however, *power* is back, alive and well. There are good reasons. One reason is that power is a reality; some people simply control more valued resources than others. Another reason is that power is a motive. The search for it drives some people more than it drives others, with important managerial consequences. And a third reason is that power—control over means and resources—is necessary in the managing of organizations. Managers need it and need to be able to use it in order to negotiate, trade, and persuade.

But the word *power* these days connotes much different ideas than the dictatorial image of the past. In the four papers in this section, we look at power from four important but different angles. First, Gerald Salancik and Jeffrey Pfeffer show us a model describing how power is attained in an organization and by whom, and how those people hang on to it.

The Michael Moch and Anne Huff piece looks at how power is implemented, especially through somewhat subtle devices such as language and ritual.

The third article, by Norman Martin and John Howard Sims, is an old and challenging one. It looks at power from the perspective of the user, the manager, and offers debatable and controversial advice on what clever managers should and should not do to build and maintain their power position. Our advice: Read it, but think about it a good deal, before you decide to follow its dicta.

And the last paper in this section, taken from Jean Lipman-Blumen's book *Gender Roles and Power,* raises some challenging hypotheses about the underside of power. How come people who don't have it don't always go after it? Why have women, for example, stayed in their "place," the less powerful place, for so long?

Managers, the theme of this section proposes, need power and need to use it. But how they get it, how they use it, and to what ends they use it are all issues that raise not only important ethical questions but pragmatic questions bearing on the health of the manager's organization.

345

Who Gets Power—and How They Hold on to It: A Strategic-Contingency Model of Power

Gerald R. Salancik and
Jeffrey Pfeffer

Power is held by many people to be a dirty word or, as Warren Bennis has said, "It is the organization's last dirty secret."

This article will argue that traditional "political" power, far from being a dirty business, is, in its most naked form, one of the few mechanisms available for aligning an organization with its own reality. However, institutionalized forms of power—what we prefer to call the cleaner forms of power: authority, legitimization, centralized control, regulations, and the more modern "management information systems"—tend to buffer the organization from reality and obscure the demands of its environment. Most great states and institutions declined, not because they played politics, but because they failed to accommodate to the political realities they faced. Political processes, rather than being mechanisms for unfair and unjust allocations and appointments, tend toward the realistic resolution of conflicts among interests. And power, while it eludes definition, is easy enough to recognize by its consequences—the ability of those who possess power to bring about the outcomes they desire.

The model of power we advance is an elaboration of what has been called strategic-contingency theory, a view that sees power as something that accrues to organizational subunits (individuals, departments) that cope with critical organizational problems. Power is used by subunits, indeed, used by all who have it, to enhance their own survival through control of scarce critical resources, through the placement of allies in key positions, and through the definition of organizational problems and policies. Because of the processes by which power develops and is used, organizations become both more aligned and more misaligned with their environments. This contradiction is the most interesting aspect of organizational power, and one that makes administration one of the most precarious of occupations.

Reprinted, by permission of the publisher, from *Organizational Dynamics,* Winter 1977, © 1977 by American Management Association, New York. All rights reserved.

What is organizational power?

You can walk into most organizations and ask without fear of being misunderstood, "Which are the powerful groups or people in this organization?" Although many organizational informants may be *unwilling* to tell you, it is unlikely they will be *unable* to tell you. Most people do not require explicit definitions to know what power is.

Power is simply the ability to get things done the way one wants them to be done. For a manager who wants an increased budget to launch a project that he thinks is important, his power is measured by his ability to get that budget. For an executive vice-president who wants to be chairman, his power is evidenced by his advancement toward his goal.

People in organizations not only know what you are talking about when you ask who is influential but they are likely to agree with one another to an amazing extent. Recently, we had a chance to observe this in a regional office of an insurance company. The office had 21 department managers; we asked ten of these managers to rank all 21 according to the influence each one had in the organization. Despite the fact that ranking 21 things is a difficult task, the managers sat down and began arranging the names of their colleagues and themselves in a column. Only one person bothered to ask, "What do you mean by influence?" When told "power," he responded, "Oh," and went on. We compared the rankings of all ten managers and found virtually no disagreement among them in the managers ranked among the top five or the bottom five. Differences in the rankings came from department heads claiming more influence for themselves than their colleagues attributed to them.

Such agreement on those who have influence, and those who do not, was not unique to this insurance company. So far we have studied over 20 very different organizations—universities, research firms, factories, banks, retailers, to name a few. In each one we found individuals able to rate themselves and their peers on a scale of influence or power. We have done this both for specific decisions and for general impact on organizational policies. Their agreement was unusually high, which suggests that distributions of influence exist well enough in everyone's mind to be referred to with ease—and, we assume, with accuracy.

Where does organizational power come from?

Earlier we stated that power helps organizations become aligned with their realities. This hopeful prospect follows from what we have dubbed the strategic-contingencies theory of organizational power. Briefly, those subunits most able to cope with the organization's critical problems and uncertainties acquire power. In its simplest form, the strategic-contingencies theory implies that when an organization faces a number of lawsuits that threaten its existence, the legal department will gain power and influence over organizational decisions. Somehow other organizational interest groups will recognize its critical importance and confer upon it a status and power never before enjoyed. This influence may extend beyond handling legal matters and into decisions about product design, advertising production, and so on. Such extensions undoubtedly would be accompanied by appropriate, or acceptable, verbal justifications. In time, the head of the legal department may become the head of the corporation, just as in times past the vice-president for marketing had become the president when market shares were a worrisome problem and, before him, the chief engineer, who had made the production line run as smooth as silk.

Stated in this way, the strategic-contingencies theory of power paints an appealing picture of power. To the extent that power is determined by the critical uncertainties and problems facing the organization and, in turn, influences decisions in the organization, the organization is aligned with the realities it faces. In short, power facilitates the organization's adaptation to its environment—or its problems.

We can cite many illustrations of how influence derives from a subunit's ability to deal with critical contingencies. Michael Crozier described a French cigarette factory in which the maintenance engineers had a considerable say in the plantwide operation. After some probing he discovered that the group possessed the solution to one of the major problems faced by the company, that of troubleshooting the elaborate, expensive, and irrascible automated machines that kept breaking down and dumbfounding everyone else. It was the one problem that the plant manager could in no way control.

The production workers, while troublesome from time to time, created no insurmountable problems; the manager could reasonably predict their absenteeism or replace them when necessary. Production scheduling was something he could deal with since, by watching inventories and sales, the demand for cigarettes was known long in advance. Changes in demand could be accommodated by slowing down or speeding up the line. Supplies of tobacco and paper were also easily dealt with through stockpiles and advance orders.

The one thing that management could neither control nor accommodate to, however, was the seemingly happenstance breakdowns. And the foremen couldn't instruct the workers what to do when emergencies developed since the maintenance department kept its records of problems and solutions locked up in a cabinet or in its members' heads. The breakdowns were, in truth, a critical source of uncertainty for the organization, and the maintenance engineers were the only ones who could cope with the problem.

The engineers' strategic role in copng with breakdowns afforded them a considerable say on plant decisions. Schedules and production quotas were set in consultation with them. And the plant manager, while formally their boss, accepted their decisions about personnel in their operation. His submission was to his credit, for without their cooperation he would have had an even more difficult time in running the plant.

Ignoring critical consequences

In this cigarette factory, sharing influence with the maintenance workers reflected the plant manager's awareness of the critical contingencies. However, when organizational members are not aware of the critical contingencies they face, and do not share influence accordingly, the failure to do so can create havoc. In one case, an insurance company's regional office was having problems with the performance of one of its departments, the coding department. From the outside, the department looked like a disaster area. The clerks who worked in it were somewhat dissatisfied; their supervisors paid little attention to them, and they resented the hard work. Several other departments were critical of this manager, claiming that she was inconsistent in meeting deadlines. The person most critical was the claims manager. He resented having to wait for work that was handled by her department, claiming that it held up his claims adjusters. Having heard the rumors about dissatisfaction among her subordinates, he attributed the situation to poor supervision. He was second in command in the office and therefore took up the issue with her immediate boss, the head of administrative services. They consulted with the personnel manager and the three of them concluded that the manager needed leadership training to improve her relations with her subordinates. The coding manager objected, saying it was a waste of time, but agreed to go along with the training and also agreed to give more priority to the claims department's work. Within a week after the training, the results showed that her workers were happier but that the performance of her department had decreased, save for the people serving the claims department.

About this time, we began, quite independently, a study of influence in this organization. We asked the administrative services director to draw up flow charts of how the work of one department moved on to the next department. In the course of the interview, we noticed that the coding department began or interceded in the work flow of most of the other departments and casually mentioned to him, "The coding manager must be very influential." He said "No, not really. Why would you think so?" Before we could reply he recounted the story of her leadership training and the fact that things were worse. We then told him that it seemed obvious that the coding department would be influential from the fact that all the other departments depended on it. It was also clear why productivity had fallen. The coding manager took the training seriously and began spending more time raising her workers' spirits than she did worrying about the problems of all the departments that depended on her. Giving priority to the claims area only exaggerated the problem, for their work was getting done at the expense of the work of the other departments. Eventually the company hired a few more clerks to relieve the pressure in the coding department and performance returned to a more satisfactory level.

Originally we got involved with this insurance company to examine how the influence of each manager evolved from his or her department's handling of critical organizational contingencies. We reasoned that one of the most important contingencies faced by all profit-making organizations was that of generating income. Thus we expected managers would be influential to the extent to which they contributed to this function. Such was the case. The underwriting managers, who wrote the policies that committed the premiums, were the most influential; the claims managers, who kept a lid on the funds flowing out, were a close second. Least influential were the managers of functions unrelated to revenue, such as mailroom and payroll managers. And contrary to what the administrative services manager believed, the third most powerful department head (out of 21) was the woman in charge of the coding function, which consisted of rating, recording, and keeping track of the codes of all policy applications and contracts. Her peers attributed more influence to her than could have been inferred from her place on the organization chart. And it was not surprising, since they all depended on her department. The coding department's records, their accuracy and the speed with which they could be retrieved, affected virtually every other operating department in the insurance office. The underwriters depended on them in getting the contracts straight; the typing department depended on them in preparing the formal contract document; the claims department depended on them in adjusting claims; and accounting depended on them for billing. Unfortunately, the "bosses" were not aware of these dependencies, for unlike the cigarette factory, there were no massive breakdowns that made them obvious, while the coding manager, who was a hard-working but quiet person, did little to announce her importance.

The cases of this plant and office illustrate nicely a basic point about the source of power in organizations. The basis for power in an organization derives from the ability of a person or subunit to take or not take actions that are desired by others. The coding manager was seen as influential by those who depended on her department, but not by the people at the top. The engineers were influential because of their role in keeping the plant operating. The two cases differ in these respects: The coding supervisor's source of power was not as widely recognized as that of the maintenance engineers, and she did not use her source of power to influence decisions; the maintenance engineers did. Whether power is used to influence anything is a separate issue. We should not confuse this issue with the fact that power derives from a social situation in which one person has a capacity to do something and another person does not, but wants it done.

Power sharing in organizations

Power is shared in organizations; and it is shared out of necessity more than out of concern for principles of organizational development or participatory democracy. Power is shared because no one person controls all the desired activities in the organization. While the factory owner may hire people to operate his noisy machines, once hired they have some control over the use of the machinery. And thus they have power over him in the same way he has power over them. Who has more power over whom is a mooter point than that of recognizing the inherent nature of organizing as a sharing of power.

Let's expand on the concept that power derives from the activities desired in an organization. A major way of managing influence in organizations is through the designation of activities. In a bank we studied, we saw this principle in action. This bank was planning to install a computer system for routine credit evaluation. The bank, rather progressive-minded, was concerned that the change would have adverse effects on employees and therefore surveyed their attitudes.

The principal opposition to the new system came, interestingly, not from the employees who performed the routine credit checks, some of whom would be relocated because of the change, but from the manager of the credit department. His reason was quite simple. The manager's primary function was to give official approval to the applications, catch any employee mistakes before giving approval, and arbitrate any difficulties the clerks had in deciding what to do. As a consequence of his role, others in the organization, including his superiors, subordinates, and colleagues, attributed considerable importance to him. He, in turn, for example, could point to the low proportion of credit approvals, compared with other financial institutions, that resulted in bad debts. Now, to his mind, a wretched machine threatened to transfer his role to a computer programmer, a man who knew nothing of finance and who, in addition, had ten years less seniority. The credit manager eventually quit for a position at a smaller firm with lower pay, but one in which he would have more influence than his redefined job would have left him with.

Because power derives from activities rather than individuals, an individual's or subgroup's power is never absolute and derives ultimately from the context of the situation. The amount of power an individual has at any one time depends, not only on the activities he or she controls, but also on the existence of other persons or means by which the activities can be achieved and on those who determine what ends are desired and, hence, on what activities are desired and critical for the organization. One's own power always depends on other people for these two reasons. Other people, or groups or organizations, can determine the definition of what is a critical contingency for the organization and can also undercut the uniqueness of the individual's personal contribution to the critical contingencies of the organization.

Perhaps one can best appreciate how situationally dependent power is by examining how it is distributed. In most societies, power organizes around scarce and critical resources. Rarely does power organize around abundant resources. In the United States, a person doesn't become powerful because he or she can drive a car. There are simply too many others who can drive with equal facility. In certain villages in Mexico, on the other hand, a person with a car is accredited with enormous social status and plays a key role in the community. In addition to scarcity, power is also limited by the need for one's capacities in a social system. While a racer's ability to drive a car around a 90° turn at 80 mph may be sparsely distributed in a society, it is not likely to lend the driver much power in the society. The ability simply does not play a central role in the activities of the society.

The fact that power revolves around scarce and critical activities, of course, makes the control and organization of those activities a major battleground in struggles for power. Even relatively abundant or trivial resources can become the bases for power if one can organize and control their allocation and the definition of what is critical. Many occupational and professional groups attempt to do just this in modern economies. Lawyers organize themselves into associations, regulate the entrance requirements for novitiates, and then get laws passed specifying situations that require the services of an attorney. Workers had little power in the conduct of industrial affairs until they organized themselves into closed and controlled systems. In recent years, women and blacks have tried to define themselves as important and critical to the social system, using law to reify their status.

In organizations there are obviously opportunities for defining certain activities as more critical than others. Indeed, the growth of managerial thinking to include defining organizational objectives and goals has done much to foster these opportunities. One sure way to liquidate the power of groups in the organization is to define the need for their services out of existence. David Halberstam presents a description of how just such a thing happened to the group of correspondents that evolved around Edward R. Murrow, the brilliant journalist, interviewer, and war correspondent of CBS News. A close friend of CBS chairman and controlling stockholder William S. Paley, Murrow, and the news department he directed, were endowed with freedom to do what they felt was right. He used it to create some of the best documentaries and commentaries ever seen on television. Unfortunately, television became too large, too powerful, and too suspect in the eyes of the federal government that licensed it. It thus became, or at least the top executives believed it had become, too dangerous to have in-depth, probing commentary on the news. Crisp, dry uneditorializing head-liners were considered safer. Murrow was out and Walter Cronkite was in.

The power to define what is critical in an organization is no small power. Moreover, it is the key to understanding why organizations are either aligned with their environments or misaligned. If an organization defines certain activities as critical when in fact they are not critical, given the flow of resources coming into the organization, it is not likely to survive, at least in its present form.

Most organizations manage to evolve a distribution of power and influence that is aligned with the critical realities they face in the environment. The environment, in turn, includes both the internal environment, the shifting situational contexts in which particular decisions get made, and the external environment that it can hope to influence but is unlikely to control.

The critical contingencies

The critical contingencies facing most organizations derive from the environmental context within which they operate. This determines the available needed resources and thus determines the problems to be dealt with. That power organizes around handling these problems suggests an important mechanism by which organizations keep in tune with their external environments. The strategic-contingencies model implies that subunits that contribute to the critical resources of the organization will gain influence in the organization. Their influence presumably is then used to bend the organization's activities to the contingencies that determine its resources. This idea may strike one as obvious. But its obviousness in no way diminishes its importance. Indeed, despite its obviousness, it escapes the notice of many organizational analysts and managers, who all too frequently think of the organization in terms of a descending pyramid, in which all the departments in one tier hold equal power and status. This presumption denies the reality that departments differ in the contributions they are believed to make to the overall organization's resources, as well as to the fact that some are more equal than others.

Because of the importance of this idea to organizational effectiveness, we decided to examine it carefully in a large midwestern university. A university offers an excellent site for studying power. It is composed of departments with nominally equal power and is administered by a central executive structure much like other bureaucracies. However, at the same time it is a situation in which the departments have clearly defined identities and face diverse external environments. Each department has its own bodies of knowledge, its own institutions, its own sources of prestige and resources. Because the departments operate in different external environments, they are likely to contribute differentially to the resources of the overall organization. Thus a physics department with close ties to NASA may contribute substantially to the funds of the university; and a history department with a renowned historian in residence may contribute to the intellectual credibility or prestige of the whole university. Such variations permit one to examine how these various contributions lead to obtaining power within the university.

We analyzed the influence of 29 university departments throughout an 18-month period in their history. Our chief interest was to determine whether departments that brought more critical resources to the university would be more powerful than departments that contributed fewer or less critical resources.

To identify the critical resources each department contributed, the heads of all departments were interviewed about the importance of seven different resources to the university's success. The seven included undergraduate students (the factor determining size of the state allocations by the university), national prestige, administrative expertise, and so on. The most critical resource was found to be contract and grant monies received by a department's faculty for research or consulting services. At this university, contract and grants contributed somewhat less than 50 percent of the overall budget, with the remainder primarily coming from state appropriations. The importance attributed to contract and grant monies, and the rather minor importance of undergraduate students, was not surprising for this particular university. The university was a major center for graduate education; many of its departments ranked in the top ten of their respective fields. Grant and contract monies were the primary source of discretionary funding available for maintaining these programs of graduate education, and hence for maintaining the university's prestige. The prestige of the university itself was critical both in recruiting able students and attracting top-notch faculty.

From university records it was determined what relative contributions each of the 29 departments made to the various needs of the university (national prestige, outside grants, teaching). Thus, for instance, one department may have contributed to the university by teaching 7 percent of the instructional units, bringing in 2 percent of the outside contracts and grants, and having a national ranking of 20. Another department, on the other hand, may have taught 1 percent of the instructional units, contributed 12 percent to the grants, and be ranked the third best department in its field within the country.

The question was: Do these different contributions determine the relative power of the departments within the university? Power was measured in several ways; but regardless of how measured, the answer was Yes. Those three resources together accounted for about 70 percent of the variance in subunit power in the university.

But the most important predictor of departmental power was the department's contribution to the contracts and grants of the university. Sixty percent of the variance in power was due to this one factor, suggesting that the power of departments derived primarily from the dollars they provided for graduate education, the activity believed to be the most important for the organization.

The impact of organizational power on decision making

The measure of power we used in studying this university was an analysis of the responses of the department heads we interviewed. While such perceptions of power might be of interest in their own right, they contribute little to our understanding of how the distribution of power might serve to align an organization with its critical realities. For this we must look to how power actually influences the decisions and policies of organizations.

While it is perhaps not absolutely valid, we can generally gauge the relative importance of a department of an organization by the size of the budget allocated to it relative to other departments. Clearly it is of importance to the administrators of those departments whether they get squeezed in a budget crunch or are given more funds to strike out after new opportunities. And it should also be clear that when those decisions are made and one department can go ahead and try new approaches while another must cut back on the old, then the deployment of the resources of the organization in meeting its problem is most directly affected.

Thus our study of the university led us to ask the following question: Does power lead to influence in the organization? To answer this question, we found it useful first to ask another one, namely: Why should department heads try to influence organizational decisions to favor their own departments to the exclusion of other departments? While this second question may seem a bit naive to anyone who has witnessed the political realities of organizations, we posed it in a context of research on organizations that sees power as an illegitimate threat to the neater rational authority of modern bureaucracies. In this context, decisions are not believed to be made because of the dirty business of politics but because of the overall goals and purposes of the organization. In a university, one reasonable basis for decision making is the teaching workload of departments and the demands that follow from that workload. We would expect, therefore, that departments with heavy student demands for courses would be able to obtain funds for teaching. Another reasonable basis for decision making is quality. We would expect, for that reason, that departments with esteemed reputations would be able to obtain funds both because their quality suggests they might use such funds effectively and because such funds would allow them to maintain their quality. A rational model of bureaucracy intimates, then, that the organizational decisions taken would favor those who perform the stated purposes of the organization—teaching undergraduates and training professional and scientific talent—well.

The problem with rational models of decision making, however, is that what is rational to one person may strike another as irrational. For most departments, resources are a question of survival. While teaching undergraduates may seem to be a major goal for some members of the university, developing knowledge may seem so to others; and to still others, advising governments and other institutions about policies may seem to be the crucial business. Everyone has his own idea of the proper priorities in a just world. Thus goals rather than being clearly defined and universally agreed upon are blurred and contested throughout the organization. If such is the case, then the decisions taken on behalf of the organization as a whole are likely to reflect the goals of those who prevail in political contests, namely, those with power in the organization.

Will organizational decisions always reflect the distribution of power in the organization? Probably not. Using power for influence requires a certain expenditure of effort, time, and resources. Prudent and judicious persons are not likely to use their power needlessly or wastefully. And it is likely that power will be used to influence organizational decisions primarily under circumstances that both require and favor its use. We have examined three conditions that are likely to affect the use of power in organizations: scarcity, criticality, and uncertainty. The first suggests that subunits will try to exert influence when the resources of the organization are scarce. If there is an abundance of resources, then a particular department or a particular individual has little need to attempt influence. With little effort, he can get all he wants anyway.

The second condition, criticality, suggests that a subunit will attempt to influence decisions to obtain resources that are critical to its own survival and activities. Criticality implies that one would not waste effort, or risk being labeled obstinate, by fighting over trivial decisions affecting one's operations.

An office manager would probably balk less about a threatened cutback in copying machine usage than about a reduction in typing staff. An advertising department head would probably worry less about losing his lettering artist than his illustrator. Criticality is difficult to define because what is critical depends on people's beliefs about what is critical. Such beliefs may or may not be based on experience and knowledge and may or may not be agreed upon by all. Scarcity, for instance, may itself affect conceptions of criticality. When slack resources drop off, cutbacks have to be made—those "hard decisions," as congressmen and resplendent administrators like to call them. Managers then find themselves scrapping projects they once held dear.

The third condition that we believe affects the use of power is uncertainty: When individuals do not agree about what the organization should do or how to do it, power and other social processes will affect decisions. The reason for this is simply that, if there are no clear-cut criteria available for resolving conflicts of interest, then the only means for resolution is some form of social process, including power, status, social ties, or some arbitrary process like flipping a coin or drawing straws. Under conditions of uncertainty, the powerful manager can argue his case on any grounds and usually win it. Since there is no real consensus, other contestants are not likely to develop counter arguments or amass sufficient opposition. Moreover, because of his power and their need for access to the resources he controls, they are more likely to defer to his arguments.

Although the evidence is slight, we have found that power will influence the allocations of scarce and critical resources. In the analysis of power in the university, for instance, one of the most critical resources needed by departments is the general budget. First granted by the state legislature, the general budget is later allocated to individual departments by the university administration in response to requests from the department heads. Our analysis of the factors that contribute to a department getting more or less of this budget indicated that subunit power was the major predictor, overriding such factors as student demand for courses, national reputations of departments, or even the size of a department's faculty. Moreover, other research has shown that when the general budget has been cut back or held below previous uninflated levels, leading to monies becoming more scarce, budget allocations mirror departmental powers even more closely.

Student enrollment and faculty size, of course, do themselves relate to budget allocations, as we would expect since they determine a department's need for resources, or at least offer visible testimony of needs. But departments are not always able to get what they need by the mere fact of needing. In one analysis it was found that high-power departments were able to obtain budget without regard to their teaching loads and, in some cases, actually in inverse relation to their teaching loads. In contrast, low-power departments could get increases in budget only when they could justify the increases by a recent growth in teaching load, and then only when it was far in excess of norms for other departments.

General budget is only one form of resource that is allocated to departments. There are others such as special grants for student fellowships or faculty research. These are critical to departments because they affect the ability to attract other resources, such as outstanding faculty or students. We examined how power influenced the allocations of four resources department heads had described as critical and scarce.

When the four resources were arrayed from the most to the least critical and scarce, we found that departmental power best predicted the allocations of the most critical and scarce resources. In other words, the analysis of how power influences organizational allocations leads to this conclusion: Those subunits most likely to survive in times of strife are those that are most critical to the organization. Their importance to the organization gives them power to influence resource allocations that enhance their own survival.

How external environment influences executive selection

Power not only influences the survival of key groups in an organization, it also influences the selection of individuals to key leadership positions, and by such a process further aligns the organization with its environmental context.

We can illustrate this with a recent study of the selection and tenure of chief administrators in 57 hospitals in Illinois. We assumed that since the critical problems facing the organization would enhance the power of certain groups at the expense of others, then the leaders to emerge should be those most relevant to the context of the hospitals. To assess this we asked each chief administrator about his professional background and how long he had been in office. The replies were then related to the hospital's funding, ownership, and competitive conditions for patients and staff.

One aspect of a hospital's context is the source of its budget. Some hospitals, for instance, are run much like other businesses. They sell bed space, patient care, and treatment services. They charge fees sufficient both to cover their costs and to provide capital for expansion. The main source of both their operating and capital funds is patient billings. Increasingly, patient billings are paid for, not by patients, but by private insurance companies. Insurers like Blue Cross dominate and represent a potent interest group outside a hospital's control but critical to its income. The insurance companies, in order to limit their own costs, attempt to hold down the fees allowable to hospitals, which they do effectively from their positions on state rate boards. The squeeze on hospitals that results from fees increasing slowly while costs climb rapidly more and more demands the talents of cost accountants or people trained in the technical expertise of hospital administration.

By contrast, other hospitals operate more like social service institutions, either as government health-care units (Bellevue Hospital in New York City and Cook County Hospital in Chicago, for example) or as charitable institutions. These hospitals obtain a large proportion of their operating and capital funds, not from privately insured patients, but from government subsidies or private donations. Such institutions rather than requiring the talents of a technically efficient administrator are likely to require the savvy of someone who is well integrated into the social and political power structure of the community.

Not surprisingly, the characteristics of administrators predictably reflect the funding context of the hospitals with which they are associated. Those hospitals with larger proportions of their budget obtained from private insurance companies were most likely to have administrators with backgrounds in accounting and least likely to have administrators whose professions were business or medicine. In contrast, those hospitals with larger proportions of their budget derived from private donations and local governments were most likely to have administrators with business or professional back-grounds and least likely to have accountants. The same held for formal training in hospital management. Professional hospital administrators could easily be found in hospitals drawing their incomes from private insurance and rarely in hospitals dependent on donations or legislative appropriations.

As with the selection of administrators, the context of organizations has also been found to affect the removal of executives. The environment, as a source of organizational problems, can make it more or less difficult for executives to demonstrate their value to the organization. In the hospitals we studied, long-term administrators came from hospitals with few prob-lems. They enjoyed amicable and stable relations with their local business and social communities and suffered little competition for funding and staff. The small city hospital director who attended civic and Elks meetings while running the only hospital within a 100-mile radius, for example, had little difficulty holding on to his job. Turnover was highest in hospitals with the most problems, a phenomenon similar to that observed in a study of industrial organizations in which turnover was highest among executives in industries with competitive environments and unstable market conditions. The interesting thing is that instability characterized the industries rather than the individual firms in them. The troublesome conditions in the indi-vidual firms were attributed, or rather misattributed, to the executives themselves.

It takes more than problems, however, to terminate a manager's leader-ship. The problems themselves must be relevant and critical. This is clear from the way in which an administrator's tenure is affected by the status of the hospital's operating budget. Naively we might assume that all admin-istrators would need to show a surplus. Not necessarily so. Again, we must distinguish between those hospitals that depend on private donations for funds and those that do not. Whether an endowed budget shows a surplus or deficit is less important than the hospital's relations with benefactors. On the other hand, with a budget dependent on patient billing, a surplus is al-most essential; monies for new equipment or expansion must be drawn from it, and without them quality care becomes more difficult and patients scarcer. An administrator's tenure reflected just these considerations. For those hospitals dependent upon private donations, the length of an admin-istrator's term depended not at all on the status of the operating budget but was fairly predictable from the hospital's relations with the business com-munity. On the other hand, in hospitals dependent on the operating budget for capital financing, the greater the deficit the shorter was the tenure of the hospital's principal administrators.

Changing contingencies and eroding power bases

The critical contingencies facing the organization may change. When they do, it is reasonable to expect that the power of individuals and subgroups will change in turn. At times the shift can be swift and shattering, as it was recently for powerholders in New York City. A few years ago it was believed that David Rockefeller was one of the ten most powerful people in the city, as tallied by *New York* magazine, which annually sniffs out power for the delectation of its readers. But that was before it was revealed that the city was in financial trouble, before Rockefeller's Chase Manhattan Bank lost some of its own financial luster, and before brother Nelson lost some of his political influence in Washington. Obviously David Rockefeller was no longer as well positioned to help bail the city out. Another loser was an attorney with considerable personal connections to the political and religious leaders of the city. His talents were no longer in much demand. The persons with more influence were the bankers and union pension fund executors who fed money to the city; community leaders who represent blacks and Spanish-Americans, in contrast, witnessed the erosion of their power bases.

One implication of the idea that power shifts with changes in organizational environments is that the dominant coalition will tend to be that group that is most appropriate for the organization's environment, as also will the leaders of an organization. One can observe this historically in the top executives of industrial firms in the United States. Up until the early 1950s, many top corporations were headed by former production line managers or engineers who gained prominence because of their abilities to cope with the problems of production. Their success, however, only spelled their demise. As production became routinized and mechanized, the problem of most firms became one of selling all those goods they so efficiently produced. Marketing executives were more frequently found in corporate boardrooms. Success outdid itself again, for keeping markets and production steady and stable requires the kind of control that can only come from acquiring competitors and suppliers or the invention of more and more appealing products—ventures that typically require enormous amounts of capital. During the 1960s, financial executives assumed the seats of power. And they, too, will give way to others. Edging over the horizon are legal experts, as regulation and antitrust suits are becoming more and more frequent in the 1970s, suits that had their beginnings in the success of the expansion generated by prior executives. The more distant future, which is likely to be dominated by multinational corporations, may see former secretaries of state and their minions increasingly serving as corporate figureheads.

The nonadaptive consequences of adaptation

From what we have said thus far about power aligning the organization with its own realities, an intelligent person might react with a resounding ho-hum, for it all seems too obvious: Those with the ability to get the job done are given the job to do.

However, there are two aspects of power that make it more useful for understanding organizations and their effectiveness. First, the "job" to be done has a way of expanding itself until it becomes less and less clear what the job is. Napoleon began by doing a job for France in the war with Austria and ended up emperor, convincing many that only he could keep the peace. Hitler began by promising an end to Germany's troubling postwar depression and ended up convincing more people than is comfortable to remember that he was destined to be the savior of the world. In short, power is a capacity for influence that extends far beyond the original bases that created it. Second, power tends to take on institutionalized forms that enable it to endure well beyond its usefulness to an organization.

There is an important contradiction in what we have observed about organizational power. On the one hand we have said that power derives from the contingencies facing an organization and that when those contingencies change so do the bases for power. On the other hand we have asserted that subunits will tend to use their power to influence organizational decisions in their own favor, particularly when their own survival is threatened by the scarcity of critical resources. The first statement implies that an organization will tend to be aligned with its environment since power will tend to bring to key positions those with capabilities relevant to the context. The second implies that those in power will not give up their positions so easily; they will pursue policies that guarantee their continued domination. In short, change and stability operate through the same mechanism, and, as a result, the organization will never be completed in phase with its environment or its needs.

The study of hospital administrators illustrates how leadership can be out of phase with reality. We argued that privately funded hospitals needed trained technical administrators more so than did hospitals funded by donations. The need as we perceived it was matched in most hospitals, but by no means in all. Some organizations did not conform with our predictions. These deviations imply that some administrators were able to maintain their positions independent of their suitability for those positions. By dividing administrators into those with long and short terms of office, one finds that the characteristics of longer-termed administrators were virtually unrelated to the hospital's context. The shorter-termed chiefs, on the other hand, had characteristics more appropriate for the hospital's problems. For a hospital to have a recently appointed head implies that the previous administrator had been unable to endure by institutionalizing himself.

One obvious feature of hospitals that allowed some administrators to enjoy a long tenure was a hospital's ownership. Administrators were less entrenched when their hospitals were affiliated with and dependent upon larger organizations, such as governments or churches. Private hospitals offered more secure positions for administrators. Like private corporations, they tend to have more diffused ownership, leaving the administrator unopposed as he institutionalizes his reign. Thus he endures, sometimes at the expense of the performance of the organization. Other research has demonstrated that corporations with diffuse ownership have poorer earnings than those in which the control of the manager is checked by a dominant shareholder. Firms that overload their boardrooms with more insiders than are appropriate for their context have also been found to be less profitable.

A word of caution is required about our judgment of "appropriateness." When we argue some capabilities are more appropriate for one context than another, we do so from the perspective of an outsider and on the basis of reasonable assumptions as to the problems the organization will face and the capabilities they will need. The fact that we have been able to predict the distribution of influence and the characteristics of leaders suggest that our reasoning is not incorrect. However, we do not think that all organizations follow the same pattern. The fact that we have not been able to predict outcomes with 100 percent accuracy indicates they do not.

Mistaking critical contingencies

One thing that allows subunits to retain their power is their ability to name their functions as critical to the organization when they may not be. Consider again our discussion of power in the university. One might wonder why the most critical tasks were defined as graduate education and scholarly research, the effect of which was to lend power to those who brought in grants and contracts. Why not something else? The reason is that the most powerful departments argued for those criteria and won their case, partly because they were more powerful.

In another analysis of this university, we found that all departments advocate self-serving criteria for budget allocation. Thus a department with large undergraduate enrollments argued that enrollments should determine budget allocations, a department with a strong national reputation saw prestige as the most reasonable basis for distributing funds, and so on. We further found that advocating such self-serving criteria actually benefited a department's budget allotments but, also, it paid off more for departments that were already powerful.

Organizational needs are consistent with a current distribution of power also because of a human tendency to categorize problems in familiar ways. An accountant sees problems with organizational performance as cost accountancy problems or inventory flow problems. A sales manager sees them as problems with markets, promotional strategies, or just unaggressive salespeople. But what is the truth? Since it does not automatically announce itself, it is likely that those with prior credibility, or those with power, will be favored as the enlightened. This bias, while not intentionally self-serving, further concentrates power among those who already possess it, independent of changes in the organization's context.

Institutionalizing power

A third reason for expecting organizational contingencies to be defined in familiar ways is that the current holders of power can structure the organization in ways that institutionalize themselves. By institutionalization we mean the establishment of relatively permanent structures and policies that favor the influence of a particular subunit. While in power, a dominant coalition has the ability to institute constitutions, rules, procedures, and information systems that limit the potential power of others while continuing their own.

The key to institutionalizing power always is to create a device that legitimates one's own authority and diminishes the legitimacy of others. When the "Divine Right of Kings" was envisioned centuries ago it was to provide an unquestionable foundation for the supremacy of royal authority. There is generally a need to root the exercise of authority in some higher power. Modern leaders are no less affected by this need. Richard Nixon, with the aid of John Dean, reified the concept of executive privilege, which meant in effect that what the president wished not to be discussed need not be discussed.

In its simpler form, institutionalization is achieved by designating positions or roles for organizational activities. The creation of a new post legitimizes a function and forces organization members to orient to it. By designating how this new post relates to older, more established posts, moreover, one can structure an organization to enhance the importance of the function in the organization. Equally, one can diminish the importance of traditional functions. This is what happened in the end with the insurance company we mentioned that was having trouble with its coding department. As the situation unfolded, the claims director continued to feel dissatisfied about the dependency of his functions on the coding manager. Thus he instituted a reorganization that resulted in two coding departments. In so doing, of course, he placed activities that affected his department under his direct control, presumably to make the operation more effective. Similarly, consumer-product firms enhance the power of marketing by setting up a coordinating role to interface production and marketing functions and then appoint a marketing manager to fill the role.

The structures created by dominant powers sooner or later become fixed and unquestioned features of the organization. Eventually, this can be devastating. It is said that the battle of Jena in 1806 was lost by Frederick the Great, who died in 1786. Though the great Prussian leader had no direct hand in the disaster, his imprint on the army was so thorough, so embedded in its skeletal underpinnings, that the organization was inappropriate for others to lead in different times.

Another important source of institutionalized power lies in the ability to structure information systems. Setting up committees to investigate particular organizational issues and having them report only to particular individuals or groups facilitates their awareness of problems by members of those groups while limiting the awareness of problems by the members of other groups. Obviously, those who have information are in a better position to interpret the problems of an organization, regardless of how realistically they may, in fact, do so.

Still another way to institutionalize power is to distribute rewards and resources. The dominant group may quiet competing interest groups with small favors and rewards. The credit for this artful form of cooptation belongs to Louis XIV. To avoid usurpation of his power by the nobles of France and the Fronde that had so troubled his father's reign, he built the palace at Versailles to occupy them with hunting and gossip. Awed, the courtiers basked in the reflected glories of the "Sun King" and the overwhelming setting he had created for his court.

At this point, we have not systematically studied the institutionalization of power. But we suspect it is an important condition that mediates between the environment of the organization and the capabilities of the organization for dealing with that environment. The more institutionalized power is within an organization, the more likely an organization will be out of phase with the realities it faces. President Richard Nixon's structuring of his White House is one of the better documented illustrations. If we go back to newspaper and magazine descriptions of how he organized his office from the beginning in 1968, most of what occurred subsequently follows almost as an afterthought. Decisions flowed through virtually only the small White House staff; rewards, small presidential favors of recognition, and perquisites were distributed by this staff to the loyal; and information from the outside world—the press, Congress, the people on the streets—was filtered by the staff and passed along only if initialed "bh." Thus it was not surprising that when Nixon met war protestors in the early dawn, the only thing he could think to talk about was the latest football game, so insulated had he become from their grief and anger.

One of the more interesting implications of institutionalized power is that executive turnover among the executives who have structured the organization is likely to be a rare event that occurs only under the most pressing crisis. If a dominant coalition is able to structure the organization and interpret the meaning of ambiguous events like declining sales and profits or lawsuits, then the "real" problems to emerge will easily be incorporated into traditional modes of thinking and acting. If opposition is designed out of the organization, the interpretations will go unquestioned. Conditions will remain stable until a crisis develops, so overwhelming and visible that even the most adroit rhetorician would be silenced.

Implications for the management of power in organizations

While we could derive numerous implications from this discussion of power, our selection would have to depend largely on whether one wanted to increase one's power, decrease the power of others, or merely maintain one's position. More important, the real implications depend on the particulars of an organizational situation. To understand power in an organization one must begin by looking outside it—into the environment—for those groups that mediate the organization's outcomes but are not themselves within its control.

Instead of ending with homilies, we will end with a reversal of where we began. Power, rather than being the dirty business it is often made out to be, is probably one of the few mechanisms for reality testing in organizations. And the cleaner forms of power, the institutional forms, rather than having the virtues they are often credited with, can lead the organization to become out of touch. The real trick to managing power in organizations is to ensure somehow that leaders cannot be unaware of the realities of their environments and cannot avoid changing to deal with those realities. That, however, would be like designing the "self-liquidating organization," an unlikely event since anyone capable of designing such an instrument would be obviously in control of the liquidations.

Management would do well to devote more attention to determining the critical contingencies of their environments. For if you conclude, as we do, that the environment sets most of the structure influencing organizational outcomes and problems, and that power derives from the organization's activities that deal with those contingencies, then it is the environment that needs managing, not power. The first step is to construct an accurate model of the environment, a process that is quite difficult for most organizations. We have recently started a project to aid administrators in systematically understanding their environments. From this experience, we have learned that the most critical blockage to perceiving an organization's reality accurately is a failure to incorporate those with the relevant expertise into the process. Most organizations have the requisite experts on hand but they are positioned so that they can be comfortably ignored.

One conclusion you can, and probably should, derive from our discussion is that power—because of the way it develops and the way it is used—will always result in the organization suboptimizing its performance. However, to this grim absolute, we add a comforting caveat: If any criteria other than power were the basis for determining an organization's decisions, the results would be even worse.

Selected bibliography

The literature on power is at once both voluminous and frequently empty of content. Some is philosophical musing about the concept of power, while other writing contains popularized palliatives for acquiring and exercising influence. Machiavelli's *The Prince*, if read carefully, remains the single best prescriptive treatment of power and its use. Most social scientists have approached power descriptively, attempting to understand how it is acquired, how it is used, and what its effects are. Mayer Zald's edited collection *Power in Organizations* (Vanderbilt University Press, 1970), is one of the more useful sets of thoughts about power from a sociological perspective, while James Tedeschi's edited book *The Social Influence Processes* (Aldine-Atherton, 1972) represents the social psychological approach to understanding power and influence. The strategic contingencies approach, with its emphasis on the importance of uncertainty for understanding power in organizations, is described by David Hickson and his colleagues in "A Strategic Contingencies Theory of Intraorganizational Power" (*Administrative Science Quarterly,* December 1971, pp. 216–229).

Unfortunately, while many have written about power theoretically, there have been few empirical examinations of power and its use. Most of the work has taken the form of case studies. Michel Crozier's *The Bureaucratic Phenomenon* (University of Chicago Press, 1964) is important because it describes a group's source of power as control over critical activities and illustrates how power is not strictly derived from hierarchical position. J. Victor Baldridge's *Power and Conflict in the University* (John Wiley & Sons, 1971) and Andrew Pettigrew's study of computer purchase decisions in one English firm (*Politics of Organizational Decision-Making,* Tavistock, 1973) both present insights into the acquisition and use of power in specific instances. Our work has been more empirical and comparative, testing more explicitly the ideas presented in this article. The study of university decision making is reported in articles in the June 1974, pp. 135–151, and December 1974, pp. 453–473, issues of the *Administrative Science Quarterly,* the insurance firm study in J. G. Hunt and L. L. Larson's collection, *Leadership Frontiers* (Kent State University Press, 1975), and the study of hospital administrator succession will appear in 1977 in the *Academy of Management Journal.*

Power Enactment through Language and Ritual

Michael Moch and
Anne S. Huff

Studies of organization structure tend to avoid the question of how structure is generated and elaborated. Designers usually implicitly presume that structural change can be imposed . . . that relationships are, somehow, *demergent:* they are in place when incumbents move into them and can be changed through a combination of design staff expertise and organizational development tactics. A few theorists, like Whyte (19) and Bittner (3), have urged that structure is also *emergent* and that structural relationships must be studied over time as they occur and change. Without knowledge of how structure emerges, these pioneers suggested, we won't be able to effectively design organizations or—perhaps more correctly—we won't be able to implement the designs we make.

With the publication of Weick's *The Social Psychology of Organizing* (18) and Silverman's *Theory of Organizations* (17), wider attention has been drawn to dynamic approaches to structure. Most recently Ranson, Hinings, and Greenwood (16) argue that "the traditional perspective which views structure as a function of environmental and contextual constraints must be complimented with a perspective which acknowledges the creativity of organization members to establish/generate structures within these contextual constraints." Organizations are to some extent self-designing. What is needed, therefore, are studies of the generation of structure—studies which identify patterns and processes characterizing the emergent qualities of structural relationships.

This paper discusses one of the many aspects of structure which arise in organizations—the generation of power relationships. Power is defined as a relational concept: power is exhibited when one person gets another to do something despite resistance; or, alternatively, when one person gets another not to do something he or she wants to do (see [7]). Much has been written about the bases of such power. There is, for example, expert power, referent power, and power legitimated by position. Yet we know little about

Reprinted by permission of the publisher from *Journal of Business Research* 11:293–316, © 1983 by Elsevier Science Publishing Co., Inc.

how these possible sources of control over others are converted into on-going power relationships. And surely this translation is sometimes problematic, for we have all seen powerless experts, and powerless bosses.

Those who study organizations have reason to be particularly interested in the emergence and/or generation of power relationships from a legitimate organizational base, or position, in an established hierarchy. Simply put, how do bosses acquire and maintain power? How do they get their subordinates to act (or not act) against their inclinations?

Perhaps the most compelling theoretical answer to these questions to date is offered by Blau (4) and other exchange theorists. The exchange perspective suggests that hierarchical position provides bosses with resources which can be spent to secure behavior advantageous to the boss, the organization, or both. While this perspective is persuasive, it presumes that position power must be based upon access to resources in order to be effective. This is not always the case; potential position power can be translated into actual power through the use of language and ritual.

The intelligent use of resources for exchange purposes is often explicit. Rituals, however, are often understandable to only a few—those who have been indoctrinated or socialized into a culture specific viewpoint. It therefore can be very difficult for an outsider to observe and understand what is taking place. We have, however, formulated a broad picture of one way ritual can engender and support hierarchically-based power. A person occupying a superior position in a hierarchy can enhance their control by using the "right" to define problems and diagnose their causes. The exact nature of organizational problems is often ambiguous and therefore open to social definition (14). Ambiguity arises especially from incompatibilities between requirements for task efficiency and culturally derived requirements for performance, as noted by Meyer and Rowan (13). A boss can often use such ambiguity to create a definition of the situation which mandates certain behaviors.

When individuals are insufficiently socialized or, for other reasons, fail to conform to this definition of the situation, the boss may use language and/or ritual to help further define the situation. He/she can *identify the individual or individuals who are resisting as the problem*. The diagnosis often takes the form of tying blame to personal attributes: subordinates are not conforming to desired behavior, for example, because they are lazy or incompetent. Those who use blaming strategies and those who are its recipients have several labels for it. While among academics what we are talking about is often called "degradation" (8), in organizations it's called dumping, shitting, reaming, and screwing. A particularly colorful label, one used by both blamers and blamees in the organization we have studied, is "chewing ass out".

"Chewing ass out" is called upon when other methods fail—when the boss cannot or has not been able to use exchanges to generate power, when the situation can not be defined in less confrontive or abusive ways, when resistance occurs or appears to be imminent despite the use of other bases of power. Yet blaming rituals are not the procedures of last resort. They often precede the invocation of official sanctions such as suspension, docking, or termination. The latter reflect *failure* to exercise power and are costly both in terms of training and other replacement costs and in terms of the impact of such sanctions on the remaining employees. They damage the use of exchange, for example, by exposing the often involuntary nature of compliance. This is particularly costly in "democratic" organizations in which members value freedom of choice and believe that voluntary activity is the most effective means for securing efficiency and productivity. As the boss we will describe told his immediate subordinates in a staff meeting: "It's the easiest thing in the world to fire someone. What you need is cooperation."

This manager was obliged by his superiors to cooperate with a clear-cut institutional embodiment of a democratic-voluntaristic belief system: a quality of work experiment conducted in his plant. The presence of this program, its acceptance by his superiors, and the ever-present outsiders implementing and evaluating the experiment, made the overt application of coercive tactics extremely costly.

Although he was the plant manager, he was relatively new to the plant and did not have much of an expertise-oriented power base. The plant organization was very centralized at corporate headquarters, so the manager had few discretionary resources with which to engage in exchange relations. Despite all of these constraints, the manager (perhaps properly) felt he *had* to get employees to do his bidding in order to meet very rigid production schedules, schedules which were compromised by the amount of employee time the quality of work experiment consumed without providing (at least in the short run) direct return. As we will see, his response provided documentation for Ranson et al.'s (16) contention that establishing power relationships can be a creative act. In this case, the plant manager forged and maintained considerable control even as external designers and change agents tried to tip the balance toward greater worker involvement.

Discourse analysis

People don't always mean what they say or say what they mean. In this case, the specific words used by the plant manager almost always allowed for a defense which could begin with "but I was only . . ." (e.g., but I was only explaining our way of doing things, but I was only trying to make sure it didn't happen again.) However, the visible impact of the manager's words, in what we identify as blaming rituals which enact power relationships, were often at odds with this benign interpretation. A method is needed for getting at meaning without having to consider *only* words, tones, and their sequencing.

In *Introduction to Discourse Analysis* Coulthard (6) reviews a good deal of recent work in linguistics, philosophy, sociology, and anthropology designed to deal with precisely this problem. The key concern of Coulthard's analysis of this literature is with "the rules of *use* which describe how *utterances* perform social acts" ([6, p. 9], author's emphasis). The researchers reviewed argue strongly that one cannot fully understand the meaning of a statement without reference to implicit assumptions being made by the participants in the discourse—speakers *and* listeners. Lakoff, for example, says that:

> in order to predict correctly the applicability of many rules one must be able to refer to assumptions about the social context of an utterance, as well as to other implicit assumptions made by the participants in a discourse (9).

There are, therefore, nonlinguistic (social) components of speech, components beyond simply phonology, grammar, and discourse. These components have to do, among other things, with intention and the interpretation of intention.

Discourse analysts and sociolinguists have developed different schemes for classifying linguistic and nonlinguistic parts of speech. These schemes often overlap and can be confusing. They also tend to focus on the speaker and fail to adequately distinguish between intentions and interpretations of speakers and listeners (e.g., Austin [1]). We have therefore developed a classification scheme which, while based upon earlier efforts (especially Austin [1] and Coulthard [6]), makes more of the distinction between intent and response. The categories are:

> *locutionary act:* the act of verbalizing
> *illocutionary act:* nonlinguistic acts which carry meaning, often used in conjunction with a locutionary act
> *perlocutionary intention:* what the speaker *intends to do* through speaking
> *perlocutionary response:* the listener's interpretation of perlocutionary intent.

The locutionary act is the act of saying something. Illocutionary acts, such as ritual gestures and the display of symbols, help define the context of the utterance and thereby provide clues as to the meaning. Perlocutionary intent defines what the speaker intends to *do* through the combination of locutionary and illocutionary acts.

The concern here is not with simple descriptions or statements of fact. Rather, utterances which have the potential of doing something through the saying of them are the concern, what discourse analysts call "performatives" or "speech acts." For example, a minister pronounces a couple man and wife. The pronouncement does the thing that's said. Similarly, a referee declares a foul. Weick's description of Simon's story of the umpires is useful here:

> The story goes that three umpires disagreed about the task of calling balls and strikes. The first one said, "I calls them as they is." The second one said "I calls them as I sees them." The third and cleverest umpire said, "They ain't nothin' till I calls them" (18, p. 1).

Weick properly credits the third umpire with recognizing a "key element in organizational life: the important role that people play in creating the environments that impose on them" (18, p. 5). The "reality of the foul, the ball, or the strike is as much created by the referee or the umpire as it is by the "facts" or even by "perceptions" of facts.

Utterances, then, by interpreting events can create reality. They define reality and are particularly important when there is little consensus about the facts or when there are divergent perceptions; in short, when the cues are equivocal. But the import of performatives goes deeper than this. Locution may qualify as performative by affecting individuals' perceptions of themselves as well as their relationships with others. Take the jury whose members declare a defendant guilty. The defendant then can *become* guilty, in the mind of the public and even in her/his own eyes. Likewise, consider students who hear from their professor that they do not have what it takes to be creative thinkers. The student can *become* mundane. In the case of power rituals, people can *become* powerful or powerless. The speech act or performative creates through saying.

Perlocutionary response refers to the actual impact of the speaker's remarks on the listener or listeners. It is that which gets created. This response may not match the speaker's intention. Locutionary acts are often more ambiguous than those uttered by umpires, by ministers, or judges in the process of performing their formal duties. For example, saying "I promise," "I apologize," or "I warn you" performs the act uttered; however, there are few formal conventions governing their use, and it is not always clear what the speaker is trying to *do* (6, 14).

Listeners therefore may misunderstand and misrespond to locutionary acts. The intrinsic ambiguity of language and situation also allows the listener to *intentionally* misread such acts, especially if he or she wants to resist the implications of the utterance. The speaker, likewise, may *intentionally* disguise her/his perlocutionary intention, especially if it is not congruent with the prevailing cultural values or beliefs. For example, a supervisor may want to order a subordinate to do something but, in the face of values associated with democracy and voluntarism, may begin the locution with something like "would you please . . ." or "can you . . .". The speaker's perlocutionary intention would be less ambiguously conveyed if

Table 1. Alternative constructions of a locution

Boss' locutionary act	Boss' perlocutionary intention (1)	Subordinate's perlocutionary response (2)
Excuuuuuuuuse me!	You *are* a Jerk	I'm being apologized to
I am shocked	I am surprised	I have done something awful
You don't know your job	You are an ignoramus	I've been poorly trained
You fail this exam	You do not know this material	I'm a failure
You have not done your homework	You are a lazy bum	I did not study

the superior were to say "I order you to do X." Listeners who misread the boss's perlocutionary intent, however, and choose not to follow a "suggestion," do so at their peril.

While many orders phrased as requests are clearly and properly interpreted in organizations, there are also many possibilities for confusion—on the part of both speaker and listener. Consider the alternatives in Table 1. If column 1 identifies intention of the speaker, a response from column 2 misfires (from the boss's perspective), and can make trouble for the "recalcitrant" subordinate.

Misreadings of this sort can lead to "communication problems." These problems arise from a gap between perlocutionary intention and perlocutionary response. But ambiguity can also be put to use. When the organization requires directed action and cannot, if only for resource limitations, conform to prevailing values, the speaker must disguise his or her perlocutionary intent. This increases equivocality. Listeners who misread intent—for example, those who focus attention on culture—conforming or ceremonial statements such as "I would appreciate it if you . . .", feel they've experienced a communication problem when the manager expresses displeasure or anger at a response which does not closely match what was intended to be an order. Even then, however, the manager may not be able to explain directly why she/he is angry, if such an expression would violate socially accepted values and norms.

One way speakers can communicate their perlocutionary intent without directly confronting incompatible social values or beliefs is to emphasize the illocutionary aspects of speech. Tones, gestures, rituals, and symbols tend to be more ambiguous than sentences, particularly to the uninitiated. By engaging others in a guessing game, analogous to Weick's description of the enactment of charades (18, p. 152), a speaker can reward or punish acceptable and unacceptable interpretation of his or her utterance until the listeners converge on a solution congruent with the speaker's perlocutionary intent. With a sufficient number of iterations, the enactment process can become a social ritual which creates and maintains the intended results without requiring the guessing game. Ambiguous utterances, then, can realize the speaker's perlocutionary intention and elicit the desired perlocutionary response through a careful and consistent use of illocutionary acts associated with the utterance. Such rituals will have evolved through a process of reinforcement over time and therefore rituals are likely to be unique to particular cultures. The uninitiated and those who are not helped to "see" will miss the real importance of the locution, often intendedly so.

Borrowing again from Austin (1), more can be said about how perlocutionary intent and response are brought together. So long as there is

1. A conventional procedure (ritual),
2. Particular persons and circumstances (e.g., one in the correct hierarchical position, speaking at the right time, in the right way, in the right place),
3. Correct performance by all,
4. Complete performance by all,

a speech act is likely to elicit the intended response. Without all four of these components, however, the performance often misfires, and the intended reality is not enacted. For example: the guilty verdict doesn't work if there is procedural error which, via another (properly performed) combination of locutionary and illocutionary acts, is judged to cause a mistrial. The umpire who hesitates implicitly acknowledges that his act is not intended as a performative, but rather a statement of perception which can be judged by others as well as by himself . . . boos, hoots, and opposition often follow. The supervisor who exhibits technical ignorance while blaming others for errors similarly may succeed only in making a fool of himself. When all four characteristics are in place, however, the illocutionary act *does* what it says. It elicits the intended response and thereby creates a social reality, even—and perhaps especially—when it is not possible or feasible to conduct the construction process explicitly.

Background on the site

To understand meanings associated with statements, it is essential to know something about the historical/cultural context in which locutionary acts occur. This article analyzes data from one plant in a large, billion dollar division of an even larger organization. This division was formed around the turn of the century when advances in food preserving technology and transportation made a nation-wide food processing firm feasible. Food production moved quickly from small-shop production to mass production, and the production function gave way in importance to the preserving and marketing functions. Almost anyone could produce the goods; the competitive advantage came to those who could preserve it and achieve brand recognition.

The plant was built in 1948. It is located in the south and primarily employs unskilled labor. The work itself is often difficult work done under conditions involving heat, high humidity, and noisy machinery. The production process is patterned after an almost classic industrial engineering paradigm: assembly line, with a functional division of labor. A lack of direct job related amenities is felt to be compensated for by relatively high wages and fringe benefits.

According to the union business agent, who was there at the time, the first plant manager ". . . operated (the) plant like it was his home . . . very firm . . . very fair in policing what he did." The first personnel manager was an emotionally "tough" sort of man, but the plant manager was able to tone him down through ". . . a fatherly advice-type thing." Following the first manager were several others. The manager immediately preceding the one described in this study, again according to the business agent, was ". . . the best organizer of the whole bunch . . . argumentative [but] . . . always trying to find ways to resolve things."

The present plant manager had been in place only a year prior to the initiation of the quality of work program which led to our observation. He had been assistant manager for the preceding twenty years in the largest plant owned by the division. It is important that the "best organizer of the whole bunch" was promoted to manage this large plant while the present manager was "promoted" to manage our smaller study site. He was about 62 years old and apparently holding his last position with the company.

Family imagery was used by more than the union business agent to describe the plant and its employees. People spoke of the current plant manager as acting "like a father." One said "we're like a family," another complained that "we're treated like children," a third indicated "we fight, but we stick together against others."

There was some sense that the family atmosphere was deteriorating: "This plant has lost the family atmosphere it used to have . . . my wife . . . she's been out there 28 years . . . if a woman got pregnant [it used to be] you couldn't carry the gifts out the door." But the control implications of the family metaphor were still strong—even for the speaker above. In describing how to get people to change, for example, he felt: "It's gotta be done on a gradual, firm, constructive approach . . . just like you would raise your child . . . you gotta police it like they were children." Paternalistic discipline often was intertwined with support in this pervasive family imagery, however, as one of the top managers indicated in an interview:

MANAGER: We make hundreds of decisions every day, and people don't know it, but we make them for them.

INTERVIEWER: Would it help if more people knew the kinds of decisions you were making and the reasons why you make them as you do?

MANAGER: No. Some people, not very many, will use that kind of information against you. A little knowledge is a bad thing. One bad apple spoils the bunch: this is never truer than on a packing line. When I walk out on the floor, I hear "buzz, buzz." That is what I call singing. When there's no singing, then something's wrong and I have to decide whether to look into it to find out what's up. One person on a line can hurt us very badly.

INTERVIEWER: Would it help if the (quality of work program) could find a way to increase trust and cooperation so that this sort of problem would be minimized?

MANAGER: Wait a minute! We have the most cooperative people in the company. I'll put my people against any others from any other plant. We have great cooperation and people are eager workers. It's just that some people would like nothing better than to stick it up my ass (pause) or your ass.

Varieties of power rituals

Staff meetings were held in a relatively small conference room adjoining the plant manager's office. The manager's office was panelled and carpeted. The conference room had a linoleum tile floor and light green unadorned walls. Prior to each meeting, the manager generally waited in his relatively larger office until his subordinates had entered and taken their positions around a long narrow table, leaving the head position open. The manager would then enter through the separate door from his office, usually with a pile of documents, and begin the meeting, often with a prefatory "gentlemen . . .".

Rituals enacting power relations (and thus controlling subordinates) were frequent occurrences during staff meetings. One type of ritual enacted differential expertise. For example, one common ploy placed the plant manager in the role of teacher. At the beginning of the meeting, the plant manager sometimes introduced a copy of an article from a popular magazine. He once presented an article from *Reader's Digest* titled "The Businessman," for example, and asked each subordinate in turn to read a paragraph out loud and pass it on until the article had been read in its entirety. The manager frequently presented such material as his subordinates' "assignment."

Many staff meeting rituals were less benign and may be fully understood only as a special class of performatives—speech acts which created subordination by degrading the subordinates. These rituals frequently began with a challenge to the group and ended by the manager expressing disappointment or disdain when a particular individual failed to demonstrate an adequate level of competence. The requisite competence, however, was left to the judgement of the plant manager, and the demonstrations often were contrived to exhibit the subordinate's ignorance, lack of dedication, and so on.

Dale F. (a disguised name), the newest member to the senior staff, was the most frequent recipient of blame. He had become superintendent of the assembly operation after serving in the research department at corporate headquarters. He had had no previous experience in assembly operations, and this lack of experience frequently resulted in production errors. In addition to his primary duties as assembly supervisor, Dale was also the co-chairman of the quality of work committee formed by plant employees and was personally very committed to finding new ways to involve employees in making important decisions for plant operations.

The following accounts, generated from notes taken by an outside observer, indicate the variety of ways in which Dale was "chewed out" in staff meetings:

March 16: Discussion in the staff meeting turned to the problem of who should pick up samples for quality control checks. The head of quality control felt that samples should be delivered to his office by employees from the assembly operation. Dale (as head of assembly) felt that quality control employees had fewer time constraints, as they did not have to keep pace with continuously flowing product. (The plant manager) after listening to the discussion for a while, noted, using a semiangry tone, that "problems start in the assembly area with an improper mixture or temperature. You [looking at Dale] should be the *most* concerned that rechecks are picked up, tested, and the proper adjustments made." This ended the discussion; however, Dale expressed considerable anger after the meeting, feeling that he had been publicly chastized.

April 20: (It was generally known that Dale had been having marital problems, although he had taken considerable care to keep this information secret.) After a brief statement about how everyone has to learn to balance the demands of work life and family life, the plant manager said, "My door is always open to discuss family problems people are having. I do not want to see outside problems causing a slowdown in the plant."

May 2: (During the previous week, the plant failed to pass a company inspection.) Responsibility for the failure was placed on Dale and John W., the superintendent of the department responsible for sanitation. John had been planning a vacation trip to Colorado. The plant manager concluded his review of the failed inspection by saying, "I can't understand how some people can plan vacations when these sorts of things are going on." After the meeting, John said he felt that his commitment to the plant had been called into question.

May 4: (Plant efficiency ratings had dropped.) As the plant manager entered the room, the assistant manager looked around and said: "does everyone have their seatbelts on?" Blame for the falling ratings was placed squarely on Dale's shoulders. After the meeting Dale said he failed to understand why the others were asked to be present, since "I was the only one who had to be there."

June 8:

MNGR: Gentlemen, I want each of you to tell me your efficiency objective for the month. (followed by silence, no volunteers) Mr. F., what is *your* efficiency objective for the month?

DALE: (Considerable pause) I don't have one, sir.

MNGR: (disgustedly) Any superintendent worth his salt has an efficiency objective.

The topic then was dropped. No others were asked to report their efficiency objective.

July 13:

MNGR: Gentlemen, I want to recommend you on the wonderful party for Don G.'s retirement. (Dale had failed to attend Don's retirement party.) Not everyone attended, though, and some were department heads . . . they sure are willing to socialize at quality of work committee meetings.

Not all control rituals ended in Dale's degradation. For example, the plant manager opened one staff meeting with, "Gentlemen, what are our four objectives?" These objectives (community, attitude, energy, and safety) had been announced at corporate headquarters, but it is not known whether anyone at the plant knew what they were. No one responded to the manager's question, and he simply ended the discussion with "I'm disappointed in you."

The lack of response to the manager's questions was typical; there seemed to be a norm against responding. At one point, for example, the superintendent of the maintenance department was replaced. The new superintendent had not been socialized into staff meeting norms, and tended to try to answer the plant manager's questions. He received noticeable scowls from his counterparts and soon became as mute as they.

The contrived nature of these rituals, set up so that there often were no adequate answers, is especially clear in the following sequence:

MNGR: Gentlemen, what are the five E's? [silence] Mr. F., what are the five E's?

DALE: Uh . . . uh . . . (slouching) . . . the environment.

MNGR: Yes. . . .

DALE: Uh . . . energy.

MNGR: That's two. . . .

DALE: Uh . . . uh . . . I don't know. . . .

MNGR: (standing and becoming red in the face . . . clenching his fists) I am disgruntled, distended, and filled with disgruntment!!!!

Prior to the meeting, few, if any, had ever heard of the five E's. The perlocutionary intention, it seems to us, was neither to inform nor to test subordinates, since the rest of the five E's were not discussed, but rather to enact subordination. In addition, the ritual was so common, such an integral part of the staff meetings, that there was a very good match between the perlocutionary intent and the perlocutionary response. Even when the manager mishandled his expression of anger ("I am disgrunted, distended and filled with disgruntment"), no one laughed. Everyone knew what was being done. After the meeting, Dale took great delight in the manager's "disgruntment." During the meeting, however, he was quite serious and embarrassed.

Power rituals were not restricted to staff meetings. They were part of daily routine in the plant. One of the mechanics described a typical situation as follows:

> When there's a machine broken down in the assembly shop, they call me down there to work on it. I get there and there's a crowd of people standing around it. So I can't get to it to work on it. It's all the foremen standing around trying to decide who is to blame for the breakdown. After they find somebody, then they let me get to work.

In another incident, a supervisor in the packaging department expressed sincere surprise that the people associated with the quality of work program expected him to get his subordinates to work but "won't let me be mean."

An employee survey was conducted as part of the quality of work program. Results of this survey were fed back to employees in small work groups, and the resulting discussions provided additional insight into the use of control rituals. When the discussion revolved around "communication problems" (only 38% of the employees agreed that "At work communication is good."), it was frequently noted, that as one employee put it, "You don't find out things until your ass gets chewed out."

What gets "found out" in such blaming rituals is the existence of a gap between perlocutionary intentions and listeners' interpretations. Anger at attributions of personal characteristics as sources of these problems were common in these discussions.

BEATRICE: Once I said the line was goin' too fast. The supervisor said, "you're nuthin but a gripe." I'm an individual!

REBECCA: When I express myself, they say "there goes Rebecca again. Always griping."

TODD: Before work begins, we gripe. When it comes to talking to supervisors, no one speaks up . . . if you do, you're labeled as a trouble-maker.

BEATRICE: We get hollered at. Eleanor and I are in trouble all the time! If you get a reputation, you never outlive it. Take me. I'm always late, even if I get here at 7 (on time). Eleanor too . . . she's a "trouble-maker" and has a problem with "absenteeism." Supervisors sit there and hold kangaroo court on people.

An interesting sequence occurred when one group was shown that 43% of the employees agreed with the statement "my co-workers are afraid to express their real views." A supervisor in the group took up the defense.

SUPERVISOR: I like to argue, but I don't lose respect when people speak up . . .
SUBORDINATE: You get damn mad at 'em though.
SUPERVISOR: When people argue with me, do I tell 'em they're no good?
MAINTENANCE PERSON: Let's change the subject (general laughter).

(Forty percent of the employees agreed with the statement, "my supervisor looks for someone to blame when something goes wrong.")

It is our contention that blaming rituals, whether intended or not, can function as performatives. The judgements rendered can create the facts they are attributing just as jury decisions function to enact guilt or innocence. The impact of such performatives on the recipients of the blaming ritual can be substantial. As one lower-level supervisor said:

If you bring anything up, (the plant manager) directs rage at you, so you don't say anything. I feel he should let us know that if we have anything on our mind we can talk about it without him getting in a rage and embarrassing you in front of the committee . . . nobody has calmed him down or called a halt. But he just goes on and on, and you're sitting there like a little fool. He doesn't say anything till things don't go his way. Then he stands and lets you have it . . . he sits there like a jailer.

INTERVIEWER: It sounds like he has you in prison.
SUPERVISOR: Especially your words, the things on your mind . . .

Ritual and control

The incidents described above, especially those observed in staff meetings, fulfill all four of the requirements which allow an otherwise ambiguous statement to make something so by saying it. They follow a conventional procedure (e.g., established seating pattern, the manager entering last by a separate door, the stack of materials placed on the table) in well established circumstances (e.g., the weekly staff meeting itself). They also involve correct and complete performance. Each instance that we identified had the following commonalities:

an utterance performed by the manager,
"cues" of anger, including red face, increase in volume, from the manager,

silence on the part of the audience,
silence, or occasional limited response, on the part of the direct recipient.

Understanding of the ritualistic nature of these events seemed to be complete on all sides. When the boss declared he was "disgrunted, distended, and filled with disgruntment!" nobody laughed. And, when a new supervisor joined the meetings from the maintenance group, and attempted to respond to the apparent "objective" meaning of the statements, he was quickly informed by the veterans not to become involved.

There are two main types of ritual enactments of power relations in the setting we studied. Both were touched upon earlier but can now be distinguished more explicitly. First, there are rituals which evoke images familiar to employees, such as the image of the teacher or a father. These images have clear implications for power relations, since it generally is clear the boss is assuming the role of a teacher, a father, or other relatively powerful figure. There are probably a limited number of images which can be useful in thus supporting hierarchy, and different images are probably evoked with different frequencies in different subcultures. A complete typology, however, must await future research.

The second type of ritual enactment of power relations involved what participants called "chewing ass out." Generally, the stage has been set. The manager had assumed the mantle of father, or teacher, and was not getting the degree of deference he desired. He then would make statements which implied that some personal characteristic of the person(s) he was seeking to subordinate was responsible for lack of conformity. Sometimes the employee's commitment was questioned. At other times skill or knowledge was called into question. As there are probably a finite number of control images, there are probably a finite number of such attributions, but again, the attributions used might be expected to vary considerably across subcultures. Our present data do not permit an exhaustive, or even a thorough classification. The key point, however, is that *some* individual characteristic or set of characteristics is identified as being responsible for failure in this kind of power-enacting ritual. The person becomes the problem.

The effectiveness of the chewing ass out rituals we were able to gather as one kind of blaming ritual seemed to depend primarily on two features:

1. *Surprise*. Although the setting was a well recognized stage for these events, the exact nature of the blame was almost always completely unpredictable.

2. *Unanswerable logic*. In addition, each situation involved a question or accusation for which there could be no correct answer. The plant manager's response to the problem of who should pick up samples was to attribute lack of concern to Dale. Should Dale challenge such a subtly applied attribution and make it explicit by so doing, or should he demonstrate his concern by agreeing to pick up the samples? Either way he loses and he ends up being forced to do what he did not want to do.

Surprise and the double-bind nature of the ritual appear to confuse the person being chewed out. This may partially explain why employees tended to accept or at least not resist the implication that *they* are the problem.

In fact, perhaps both types of power rituals, those which evoke images of analogous superior-subordinate relationships and those which enact subordination through degradation, are similarly based on the definition of subordinate fault. Each ritual starts when the manager defines the problem. The manager decides to take time to "educate" his subordinates, for example. The problem, by implication, is lack of knowledge. If the lesson is not performed satisfactorily, the further problem is stupidity, laziness, and so on. Or the manager tells subordinates that his door is always open to discuss family relations. The problem, by implication, is family pressures affecting production efficiency.

Once the problem is defined, the solution is clear. Ignorant subordinates should ask their superiors for help, which enacts a power relationship based on differential expertise. Subordinates having family problems should come to the manager for counseling. Such imagery again helps enact a power relationship based on differential experience. Whether the ritual simply evokes images or degrades the subordinate, therefore, the underlying mechanism is the same. The person in a higher position uses his or her "right" to define the problem. This definition must conform to overtly rational criteria. However, it also implies solutions which, if carried out, enact power relations.

A successful ritual, however, by definition requires the *mutual* production of the boss, the recipient and the audience. If the only participant to enhance their power is the boss—why does the ritual continue? Somewhat contradictory answers can be given to this question. On the one hand, once the pattern becomes established, rituals may take a great deal of energy to change. Established behavior is the path of least resistance. Many encounters within an organization continue for this reason alone. There is, however, probably much more than habit involved in the production of the rituals we have described. The chewing-out ritual is useful from the boss's perspective because it intensifies the message—the perlocutionary intent. Especially when direct heavy-handed control is discouraged, the chewing-ass-out ritual provides one way of making a control event and insuring that subordinates will be careful to do as they are "asked." Should any of the participants resist, they are likely to get "chewed out." This has considerable social cost within the immediate group and is a further tool for insuring conformity.

In opposition to this explanation, it may be that power rituals, including chewing ass out, also *contain* the boss's attempts at control. Subordinates are thus motivated to play the part—and make sure their fellows play theirs. The course of the performance and the end of the performance is known. The ritual in itself "cools" the boss and perhaps allows him to vent on relatively unimportant matters. Should the ritual be resisted, subordinates might gain power. They also stand to lose what little they have. The prudent response may be to opt for the status quo.

Scatological and sexual language and control

From the start our curiosity was piqued by the frequent use of sexual and scatological language in describing blaming rituals at this site. Many incidents echo the overall reference to these events as "chewing ass out"—the label used both by the manager and by employees. For example, the superintendent warned that "some people would like nothing better than to stick it up my ass—or your ass." Employees often expressed concern that "somebody is going to get fucked" because of the quality of work program.

The many examples of scatological and sexual language we heard at the site are certainly not unique to this organization. They also reflect conventional informal language broadly used in society today. We suggest, however, that such language should be taken seriously by those who want to understand the implications of control.

It is interesting, for example, that euphemisms are *not* used in this situation as they are in many other superior-subordinate encounters. Bosmajian's work on *The Language of Oppression* (5) gives many examples of the way in which the structure of power and control is often veiled from view through the use of euphemisms. The underlying analysis is that "when a word acquires a bad connotation by association with something people find unpleasant or embarrassing to think of, people will reach for substitutes for that word that do not have this uncomfortable effect" (9, p. 57). Lakoff's discussion of job terminology, for example, notes that

> For at least some speakers, the more demeaning the job, the more the person holding it (if female) is likely to be described as a *lady*. Thus *cleaning lady* is at least as common as *cleaning woman, saleslady* as *saleswoman*. But one says, normally, *woman doctor*. To say *lady doctor* is to be very condescending; it constitutes an insult (10, pp. 59–60).

Compare this with Bosmajian's discussion of the language used by participants in the Vietnam war (5, pp. 125–28). "Pacification" of villages involved forced relocation, burning all household possessions, and shooting resistors. An air raid was known as a "routine limited duration protection reaction." One crewman described his participation in such raids as "delivering the mail."

Why, then, do *all* participants (the boss and his subordinates) retain the title "chewing ass out," and its relatives, rather than reaching for more palatable substitutes in the setting we've studied? We take this language as graphically describing a sense of personal abuse—the extension of control beyond the range of "you do not understand this job" to "you are personally deficient; you are the problem." This language expresses the intensity of the boss's intent and the intensity of the subordinate's response. The fact that chewing ass out moves beyond ordinary control mechanisms is recognized through the use of nonacceptable language.

On the other hand, just as ritual contains the blame, so does the use of sexual and scatological language. It keeps the more extensive forms of control at the informal level—where they rarely get into formal meetings or formal records. Calling these events instances of chewing ass out decouples them from other control efforts—a separation of potential benefit to the boss who could get called on the carpet by his own superiors for going beyond the cultural norms, and by the subordinate who does not want to be public about a definition of the situation which makes his/her personal attributes part of the problem. This point must be underscored. Just as "chewing ass out" is a topic on the fringes of academic acceptability, so too it is on the outskirts of organizational acceptability. The language itself pushes the rituals we have described away from public, acceptable, and more ceremonial discussions of control.

Finally, the language of chewing ass out is useful for effect. Swearing at one level may be a genuine emotional release while on another level it can be uttered with the prelocutionary intent of getting *others* to see the speech event so marked as one of great emotion. Thus the boss may retain sexual/scatological language to focus and intensify the response of the person chastised. Similarly, employees may retain the language to help convince the boss that the event is taken seriously, even while it is the subject of some joking among themselves.

Task efficiency and control

Democratic societal values seem to have increasingly emphasized freedom of choice and supported a search for new strategies of coordination and control—strategies which rely on cooperation rather than coercion. The human relations movement and, more recently, the quality of work movement reflect the impact of these changing values on organizations. From Barnard (2) to Mills (14), the argument has been made that organizational effectiveness and efficiency require *voluntary* cooperation and that more traditional methods based upon formal control and managerial decrees are likely to be less and less effective.

The quality of work experiment introduced in the plant studied here can be seen as a part of this social movement imposed upon a system which had a long tradition of hierarchical control. Initial support for the experiment came from the division president, a Harvard MBA with a strong commitment to contemporary management techniques designed to instill employee commitment and cooperation. He had risen to the presidency from a staff position and had little production experience. Nevertheless, he was insistent. In a meeting with national-level production people, including the plant manager at the site described, the president said, adding emphasis by hitting the table, "This is a good program. It's got (my) name on it, so it's going to succeed!"

The production managers were considerably less sanguine. The national level head of production had once been an assembler in the very plant we studied. The regional manager had once been the plant's manager. They seemed to feel that they were being pressed between an existing structure of control which had a long successful tradition in the organization and a newer set of values and beliefs which bore little resemblance to—and in fact contradicted—what they believed were deepseated organizational realities. They presumed that participative management would undermine discipline and lead to a decline in productivity.

This dilemma—between the organization's established, task-related control structure and an alternative generally considered to be more legitimate by the surrounding culture—has been described by Meyer and Rowan (13). They note that the links between effectiveness and various structures designed to achieve coordination and control are often ambiguous. It is not always clear that one structure or another will promote effectiveness. The choice of structures, therefore, rests upon beliefs and values operating in the organization's environment. In the absence of clear-cut tests, structures are accorded legitimacy on the basis of their isomorphism with beliefs and values operating in the society-at-large.

Meyer and Rowan emphasize the fact that "technical activities and demands for efficiency create conflicts and inconsistencies in an . . . organization's efforts to conform to the (culturally determined) ceremonial rules of production . . . these inconsistencies make a concern for efficiency and tight coordination and control problematic" (13, p. 355). An organization opting only for what insiders believe to be the most effective structures, in fact, may do so at its peril. In the plant studied here, holding to traditional patterns might result in maintaining current production levels; however, it would also result in the social judgment (by the president of the company, as well as by outsiders) of ineffectively maintaining an authoritarian structure in an increasingly democratic society. Therefore, in Meyer and Rowan's words, ". . . the organization must struggle and link the requirements of ceremonial elements to technical activities" (13, p. 356) despite the fact that "categorical (ceremonial) rules conflict with the logic of efficiency" (13, p. 355).

This linking may be done in several ways. Meyer and Rowan describe three possibilities—decoupling, minimized external evaluation, and the "logic of confidence and good faith." All of these mechanisms were employed by the firm studied to help manage discontinuities introduced by the quality of work program. In addition, however, the case data we have examined suggests that a "logic of blame" may provide a fourth way in which organizations reconcile demands for task efficiency with ceremonial, culturally derived demands. This fourth means of reconciliation is particularly interesting because it reverses many of the assumptions made by Meyer and Rowan in their discussion of the logic of faith and confidence—while having at its core the collaboration required for successful performatives.

First, however, there is evidence of decoupling, in which "elements of structure are decoupled from activities and from each other" (13, p. 357). Decoupling was useful in the plant we studied to separate societal and upper management values supporting participation from an authoritarian control style at the plant site. The decoupling was performed, in part, linguistically. The plant manager, caught between superiors who insisted on participation and subordinate supervisors who held to authoritarian styles, engaged in locutionary acts with equivocal meaning. His statements could be read either as helpful or as authoritarian, as in the case where he said to his staff (but was referring to Dale) that his door was always open but family problems should not interfere with work performance.

The tension between social, ceremonial requirements for performance, and the presumed requirements of efficiency, in short, appear to be (partially) managed if attributions of blame are made informally through isolated blaming rituals which can be understood by those to whom they are directed *and* defended on other grounds against those who would find them abhorrent. The language itself, we have argued, precludes wide usage and isolates incidents. It also has meaning which can be opaque to outsiders, thus accomplishing the separation Meyer and Rowan suggest is necessary.

We also found efforts to minimize external evaluation (14, p. 359). Managers resisted plant-wide employee surveys which were part of the quality of work experiment. The first survey was scheduled only after the division president overruled production management. Feedback of results from the second survey to employees was postponed several times and then cancelled. The day-to-day activities of the outsiders associated with the quality of work experiment were often made very difficult. For example, it took the observation staff several months to arrange an interview with the assistant manager and then the interview was cut short. The assistant manager felt that the quality of work staff was trying to drive a wedge between himself and the plant manager: "It's divide and conquer. I've seen it before." He was particularly adverse to talking with one of the outside consultants brought in to help the quality of work committee. The plant manager eventually ruled that this consultant could not speak with the assistant manager unless he, the plant manager, were present. Eventually, the entire observation/evaluation component of the quality of work experiment was prematurely cancelled.

Finally, we have an interesting case of "the logic of confidence and good faith." We suspect that confidence and good faith in the plant we studied arose especially from the images of school and family—images which pervaded employees' speech and action. Father figures and teachers, in this stereotype, know more than other family members. *They* will be able to understand and deal with discontinuities and other problems. They also can chew out subordinates "for their own good," thus reconciling good faith with what otherwise may be viewed only as personal abuse.

On the other hand, an alternative to good faith and confidence is a logic of bad faith. Parties assuming the worst of each other as individuals are also able to gloss over more deep seated tensions between ceremonial requirements for performance and technical requirements. To paraphrase the mechanic quoted earlier: "When something goes wrong . . . decide who's to blame . . . then let me get back to work." Even the possibility of finding someone to blame may be sufficient to allow the organization to continue relatively undisturbed by the deep-seated discontinuities Meyer and Rowan describe.

Conclusion

The patterns observed in our plant are unlikely to be unique. Nor are they isolated at lower levels in organizations. Consider these excerpts from John DeLorean's description of behavior of top management at General Motors:

> Intimidation is a favorite tool, and once again the art of management by intimidation as I know it at GM began with Frederic Donner. He was the master intimidator and often reverted to gimmicks to show his power.
>
> One time in an Administrative Committee meeting he asked the head of GM Truck and Coach Division, "How many buses did you build last month?"
>
> The executive replied, "Approximately three thousand" or a rounded figure like that. It was an approximation.
>
> Donner scowled and snapped back something like, "Last month you built three thousand, one hundred and eighty-seven vehicles." Whatever the figure was, it was precise.
>
> It was obvious to most of us in the meeting that Donner had just looked it up since the precise figure wasn't all that important. But the fact that he would rattle off the exact production figure in such an authoritarian, arrogant manner told us just one thing, that Donner was trying to make the point, "Look how I know this goddam business, people! Look what a mind I have!" (20, p. 44).

This incident closely follows the form of the "5 E's" and the "4 objectives" episodes we report above, and DeLorean's analysis is very close to ours. There is also evidence from this controversial book of labeling behavior similar to our reports of employees becoming "gripes," "troublemakers," and prone to "absenteeism" in the eyes of management.

> One of [Keyes'] duties was to tell has-been executives that they were going to take an early retirement . . . If one rebelled, he'd gather a

case against the executive, break the results to him, and then give him the option of being fired or taking early retirement. On one occasion, he built up a case against an executive charging that "he did not travel enough to keep in touch with his operations." Then Keyes turned around and charged another executive whose "time was at hand" with traveling too much. "You're never home minding the store," he told him. In some cases, it was publicly announced that this or that executive was taking early retirement for health reasons. The word around the corporation was "When Keyes tells you that you're sick, you're sick" (20, pp. 46, 47).

Such practices are deeply rooted in basic organizational and social realities. Yet, as Meyer and Rowan note, external evaluation will inevitably uncover inconsistencies and behaviors which are socially deemed to be inefficient (13). We must be careful, therefore, not to render quick judgment. "Bad management" is a relative term and is at least as much a function of the values of the judge as it is of the behavior observed. We also must view the issue of control—and the use of language and ritual to coerce and control—in context. Language and ritual were among the few tools available to a manager who could not always claim control on the basis of expertise, past exchanges, or other more acceptable foundations. Yet he had responsibility for getting the product out the door and was evaluated on this basis by his immediate superiors. All he had was his formal position, and using his right to define problems, he tried to make do.

On our last day in the plant, we were coding data in the staff room next to the manager's office. They were remodeling the offices and a craftsman asked the plant manager where he wanted the air intake vent to be placed.

I want it right above my desk, and I want it to run above the ceiling and come out over (the assistant manager's) desk, so that when I get really mad and jump up and down on my desk, I'll go up into the vent and come out on (the assistant manager's) desk and give him *Hell*.

He said this lightly and, although we couldn't see him, he undoubtedly was smiling. But what was his perlocutionary intention? What might have been the craftsman's immediate perlocutionary response? What might be the response of others in the organization, not least the assistant manager, as this story gets repeated?

References

1. Austin, J. L., *How to Do Things with Words*. Cambridge, Mass.: Harvard University Press, 1962.

2. Bernard, Chester I., *The Functions of the Executive*. Cambridge, Mass.: Harvard University Press, 1938.

3. Bittner, Egon, The Concept of Organization, *Soc. Res.* 32 (1965): 239–255.

4. Blau, Peter M., *Exchange and Power in Social Life*. New York: Wiley, 1964.

5. Bosmajian, Haig, *The Language of Oppression*. Washington, D.C.: Public Affairs Press, 1974.

6. Coulthard, Malcolm, *An Introduction to Discourse Analysis*. London: Longman, 1977.

7. Emerson, Richard, Power-dependence Relations, *Amer. Sociol. Rev.* 27 (1962): 31–41.

8. Gephart, Robert P. Jr., Status Degradation and Organizational Succession: An Ethnomethodological Approach, *Admin. Sci. Quart.* 23 (1978): 553–581.

9. Lakoff, Robin, Language in Context, *Language* 48 (1972): 907–927.

10. Lakoff, Robin, Language and Woman's Place, *Language in Society* 2 (1973): 45–80.

11. Likert, Rensis, *New Patterns of Management*, New York: McGraw-Hill, 1961.

12. Likert, Rensis, *The Human Organization: It's Management and Value*. New York: McGraw-Hill, 1967.

13. Meyer, John, and Brian Rowan, Institutionalized Organizations: Formal Structure as Myth and Ceremony, *Amer. J. Sociol.* 83 (1977): 240–263.

14. Mills, Ted, Human Resources—Why the New Concern, *Harvard Bus. Rev.* 53 (1975): 120–134.

15. Pondy, Louis, Leadership is a Language Game, in *Leadership: Where Else Can We Go?*, M. McCall and M. Lombardo (eds.). Durham, N.C.: Duke University Press, 1978.

16. Ranson, Stewart, Hinings, Bob, and Greenwood, Royston, The Structuring of Organizational Structures, *Admin. Sci. Quart.* 25 (1980): 1–17.

17. Silverman, David, *The Theory of Organizations*, New York: Basic Books, 1970.

18. Weick, Karl E., *The Social Psychology of Organizing*. Reading, Mass.: Addison-Wesley, 1969, revised 1979.

19. Whyte, William Foote, *Organizational Behavior: Theory and Application*. Homewood, Ill.: Irwin-Dorsey, 1969.

20. Wright, Patrick J., *On A Clear Day You Can See General Motors*. Grosse Point, Mich.: Wright, 1979.

Power Tactics

Norman H. Martin and
John Howard Sims

Executives—whether in business, government, education, or the church—
have power and use it. They maneuver and manipulate in order to get a job
done and, in many cases, to strengthen and enhance their own position.
Although they would hate the thought and deny the allegation, the fact is
that they are politicians. "Politics," according to one of the leading authorities in this complex and fascinating field, "is . . . concerned with relationships of control or of influence. To phrase the idea differently, politics
deals with human relationships of superordination and subordination, of
dominance and submission, of the governors and the governed."[1] In this
sense, everyone who exercises power must be a politician.

It is true, as many others have pointed out in different connections, that
we in this country have an instinctive revulsion against the term "power."
It carries immoral connotations for us, despite the definitions of men like
R. H. Tawney, the economic historian, who divorces it from any ethical
attributes by calling it simply "the capacity of an individual or group of
individuals to modify the conduct of other individuals or groups in the
manner which he desires, and to prevent his own conduct from being modified in the manner which he does not."[2]

Furthermore, though we glorify ambition in the abstract, we frown on
its practice and are distressed at the steps which must be taken if ambition
is to be translated into actual advancement. Thus when power is coupled
with ambition, we shy away and try to pretend that neither really exists.

But the fact is that we use power and exercise our ambitions just the
same—troubled though we may be by the proverbial New England conscience which "doesn't prevent you from doing anything—it just keeps
you from enjoying it!"

Reprinted from the *Harvard Business Review*, November-December 1956, pp. 25–29, by
permission of the authors and the publisher, © 1956 by the President and Fellows of Harvard
College. All rights reserved.
  1. V. O. Key Jr., *Politics, Parties and Pressure Groups*, 2d ed. (New York: Thomas Y.
Crowell Co., 1948), p. 3.
  2. R. H. Tawney, *Equality*, 4th ed. (London: George Allen & Unwin, Ltd., 1952),
p. 175.

The complexity of the problem is increased when we recall that the real source of power is not the superior but the subordinate. Men can only exercise that power which they are allowed by other men—albeit their positions are buttressed by economic, legal, and other props. The ultimate source of power is the group; and a group, in turn, is made up of people with consciousness and will, with emotion and irrationality, with intense personal interests and tenaciously held values.

The human being resists being treated as a constant. Knowledge, reason, and technical know-how will not suffice as means of control but give way to the arts of persuasion and inducement, of tactics and maneuver, of all that is involved in interpersonal relationships. Power cannot be given; it must be won. And the techniques and skills of winning it are at the same time the methods of employing it as a medium of control. This represents the political function of the power-holder.

In such a light, we see why the successful functioning and advancement of the executive is dependent, not only on those aspects of an enterprise which are physical and logical, but on morale, teamwork, authority, and obedience—in a word, on the vast intricacy of human relationships which make up the political universe of the executive.

The real question then becomes: How can power be used most effectively? What are some of the political strategems which the administrator must employ if he is to carry out his responsibilities and further his career? This is an area that has carefully been avoided by both students and practitioners of business—as if there were something shady about it. But facts are facts, and closing our eyes to them will not change them. Besides, if they are important facts, they should be brought into the open for examination.

Accordingly, we present here preliminary findings of the first stage of a fairly extensive investigation of just how the executive functions in his political-power environment. We have searched the biographies of well-known leaders of history, from Alexander to Roosevelt; we have explored the lives of successful industrialists like Rockefeller and Ford; and we have interviewed a number of contemporary executives.

There follows an account of certain tactics which we have found to be practiced by most men whose success rests on ability to control and direct the actions of others—no doubt, raw and oversimplified when reduced to a few black-and-white words, but for this very reason more likely to be provocative. With further refinement, these generalizations will serve as hypotheses in the succeeding stages of our research, but in the meantime we present them to businessmen to look at openly and objectively—to ask, "Do we not use just such techniques frequently?" and, if so, to ponder, "How can we best operate in this particular area, for our own interest as managers and for the good of people under us?"

Taking counsel

The able executive is cautious about how he seeks and receives advice. He takes counsel only when he himself desires it. His decisions must be made in terms of his own grasp of the situation, taking into account the views of others when he thinks it necessary. To act otherwise is to be subject, not to advice, but to pressure; to act otherwise too often produces vacillation and inconsistency.

Throwing a question to a group of subordinates is all too often interpreted as a delegation of power, and the executive may find himself answered with a decision instead of counsel. He must remember that he, not the group under him, is the responsible party. If an executive allows his subordinates to provide advice when he does not specifically call for it, he may find himself subject, not only to pressure, but to conflicting alignments of forces within his own ranks. A vague sort of policy which states, "I am always ready to hear your advice and ideas on anything," will waste time, confuse issues, dilute leadership, and erode power.

Alliances

In many respects, the executive system in a firm is composed of complexes of sponsor-protégé relationships.[3] For the protégé, these relationships provide channels for advancement; for the sponsor, they build a loyal group of followers. A wise administrator will make it a point to establish such associations with those above and below him. In the struggles for power and influence that go on in many organizations, every executive needs a devoted following and close alliances with other executives, both on his own level and above him, if he is to protect and to enhance his status and sphere of influence.

Alliances should not be looked upon, however, merely as a protective device. In addition, they provide ready-made systems of communication, through which the executive can learn firsthand how his decisions are being carried out, what unforeseen obstacles are being encountered, and what the level of morale in the organization is at any moment.

Maneuverability

The wise executive maintains his flexibility, and he never completely commits himself to any one position or program. If forces beyond his control compel a major change in company policy, he can gracefully bend with the wind and cooperate with the inevitable, thus maintaining his status.

An executive should preserve maneuverability in career planning as

3. See Norman H. Martin and Anselm S. Strauss, "Patterns of Mobility within Industrial Organizations," *Journal of Business,* April 1956, p. 101.

well. He ought never to get in a situation that does not have plenty of escape hatches. He must be careful, for instance, that his career is not directly dependent on the superior position of a sponsor. He should provide himself with transferable talents, and interfirm alliances, so that he will be able to move elsewhere if the conditions in his current organization become untenable.

Communication

During recent years emphasis has been placed on the necessity for well-dredged channels of communication which run upward, downward, and sideways. Top management should supply its subordinates with maximum information, according to this theory; subordinates, in turn, must report fully to their chiefs.

It is possible, however, that executives have been oversold on maximizing the flow of information. It simply is not good strategy to communicate everything one knows. Instead, it may often be advantageous to withhold information or to time its release. This is especially true with reference to future plans—plans which may or may not materialize; it is also valid in the case of information that may create schism or conflict within the organization; and it is prudent when another executive is a threat to one's own position. Furthermore, information is an important tactical weapon, and should be considered as such.

It would appear, then, that executives should be concerned with determining "who gets to know what and when" rather than with simply increasing the flow. Completely open communication deprives the executive of the exclusive power of directing information which should be his.

Compromising

The executive should accept compromise as a means of settling differences with his tongue in his cheek. While appearing to alter his view, he should continue to press forward toward a clear-cut set of goals. It is frequently necessary to give ground on small matters, to delay, to move off tangents, even to suffer reverses in order to retain power for future forward movement. Concessions, then, should be more apparent than real.

Negative timing

The executive is often urged to take action with which he is not in agreement. Sometimes pressure for such action arises from the expectations of subordinates, the influence of his associates with his superiors, the demands of custom and tradition, or other sources he would be unwise to ignore.

To give in to such demands would be to deny the executive's prerogative; to refuse might precipitate a dangerous crisis, and threaten his power. In such situations the executive may find it wise to use what might be called the technique of "negative timing." He initiates action, but the process of expedition is retarded. He is considering, studying, and planning for the problem; there are difficulties to be overcome and possible ramifications which must be considered. He is always *in the process* of doing something but never quite does it, or finally he takes action when it is actually too late. In this way the executive escapes the charge of dereliction, and at the same time the inadvisable program "dies on the vine."

Self-dramatization

Most vocal communication in which an executive engages—whether with his superiors, his colleagues, or his subordinates—is unpremeditated, sincere, spontaneous. His nonvocal communication—the impression projected by his posture, gestures, dress, or facial expressions—is commonly just as natural.

But executives would do well to reexamine this instinctive behavior, for many of them are overlooking an important political strategem. The skill of the actor—whose communication is "artistic" as opposed to "natural"—represents a potential asset to an administrator. Dramatic art is a process by which selections from reality are chosen and arranged by the artists for the particular purpose of arousing the emotions, of convincing, of persuading, of altering the behavior of the audience in a *planned direction*.

The actor's purpose is no different from that of the manager who wants to activate his subordinates in certain specific directions—to secure a certain response from those with whom he communicates. The actor's peculiar gift is in deliberately shaping his own speech and behavior to accomplish his purpose. The element of chance, the variable of the unknown, is diminished, if not removed; and rehearsal with some foreknowledge of what is to occur takes place. The *how* of communicating is considered as well as the *what*.

Of course, this is no easy task. The effectiveness of the actor's performance depends on his ability to estimate what will stimulate the audience to respond. And once he makes his choices, he must be able to use them skillfully. His voice and body must be so well disciplined, so well trained, that the images he chooses may be given life. The question is, How can an executive acquire the skill of artistic communication? How can he learn to dramatize himself?

The development of sharper powers of observation is the first step. Having witnessed effective communication—whether a TV drama or an actual meeting of the board of directors—the executive should try to determine what made it effective. He should pay attention to *how* a successful man handled himself, not what he said or did. Formal classes can provide the executive with control over his voice—its pitch, tone, color, speed, diction; training can do the same for his body—gesture, posture, and mime. Most important, the executive should seize any opportunity to gain actual experience in putting such skills to work, in amateur theatricals or "role-playing" sessions.

It would be foolish to deny that such skills cannot be entirely learned; to some extent they depend on the unknowns of flair, talent, and genius. But such an acknowledgement does not excuse the executive from making an effort, for the range of possible improvement is very great.

Confidence

Related to, but not identical with, self-dramatization is the outward appearance of confidence. Once an executive has made a decision, he must look and act decided. In some instances genuine inner conviction may be lacking, or the manager may find it difficult to generate the needed dynamics. The skillful executive who finds himself in such a situation will either produce the effect of certainty or postpone any contact with his associates in order to avoid appearing in an unfavorable light.

Thus, the man who constantly gives the impression of knowing what he is doing—even if he does not—is using his power and increasing it at the same time.

Always the boss

Warm personal relations with subordinates have sometimes been considered the mark of a good executive. But in practice an atmosphere of social friendship interferes with the efficiency of an operation and acts to limit the power of the manager. Personal feelings should not be a basis for action—either negative or positive. The executive should never permit himself to be so committed to a subordinate as a friend that he is unable to withdraw from this personal involvement and regard the man objectively as an element in a given situation.

Thus, a thin line of separation between executive and subordinate must always be maintained. The situation should be one of isolation and contact—of the near and far—of marginality. No matter how cordial he may be, the executive must sustain a line of privacy which cannot be transgressed; in the final analysis, he must always be the boss. If we assume, then, that the traditional "open-door" policy of the modern executive is good strategy, we must always ask the question: "How far open?"

The foregoing discussion will undoubtedly raise questions, and even indignation, in the minds of some readers. In the last two decades, the finger of censure has often been pointed at the interpersonal relations in the management of industrial organizations, questioning whether they are harmonious with a democratic society and ideology.[4] Executives have been urged to adopt practices and programs aimed at "democratizing" their businesses.

---

4. See Thomas C. Cochran, "Business and the Democratic Tradition," *Harvard Business Review*, March-April 1956, p. 39.

Perhaps they have even developed a sense of guilt from the realization of their own position of authority and that they cannot be completely frank, sincere, honest, and aboveboard in their interpersonal relations. We live in an era of "groupiness"; we are bombarded with admonitions which insist that everyone who is participating in an enterprise should have a part in the management of it.

In the light of such a trend even the terminology used in this article—"power," "maneuver," "tactics," "techniques"—appears disturbing when set down in black and white. But in fact it is neither immoral nor cynical to recognize and describe the actual daily practices of power. After all, sweeping them under the rug—making believe that they are not actually part of the executive's activity—does not cause them to vanish. Open and honest discussion of the political aspects in the administrator's job exposes these stratagems to the constructive spotlight of knowledge. They exist; therefore, we had better take a look at them and see what they are really like.

As we delve deeper into the study of political tactics in business management, the contrast with modern human relations theory and practice will stand out in ever-sharper relief. Mutual confidence, open communication, continuing consultation and participation by subordinates, friendship, and an atmosphere of democracy seem hard to reconcile with much of the maneuvering and power plays that go on in the nation's offices and factories every day.

Yet businessmen must develop some rationale of executive behavior which can encompass the idealism of democracy and the practicality of politics—and, at the same time, be justified in terms of ultimate values. If they do not, they will feel like hypocrites as the day-to-day operation of their offices clashes with their speeches before womens' clubs. The old cliché that "business is business" is no longer satisfying to the general public nor to the executive himself.

One way to try to fit human relations theory and political tactics together is to state that the means or ways of exercising power are neutral. In and of themselves, they have no moral value. They take on moral qualities only in connection with the ends for which they are used. Power can be used for good or ill according to this theory, and we should have the courage and knowledge to use it wisely. Conscious, deliberate, and skilled use of executive power means responsible use of power. If men in the past have employed power for evil ends, that is unfortunate; it is just as true that other men, if they had made use of business politics in an effective fashion, might have been a greater force for good.

The difficulty with this line of thought lies in the well-known pitfalls inherent in the timeless means-ends controversy. In real life, what are means and what are ends? Can you achieve good ends by bad means? If the way one man conducts his relationship with another has no moral implications, what human activity does have moral significance?

Others may take the position that "so long as my general philosophy is sound and moral, the specific actions I have to take in the course of my job don't matter." But one may question the validity of a philosophy of life that breaks down every time it comes into contact with reality.

Still another formula could be found in the statement, "The good of the company comes before that of an individual. If I have to violate moral codes and democratic principles in dealing with one man, that is too bad for him. But I cannot allow any single person to overshadow the interests of all our other employees, stockholders, and customers." The skeptical listener might then raise the issue of collectivism versus individualism, and ask whether the general welfare really overrides the worth and dignity of the individual. Can we build a society on the idea of the individual's importance if we violate the principle whenever it interferes with what we consider to be the good of the group?

There are, of course, other approaches, but they too are fraught with internal contradictions. The riddle, then, remains unsolved; the conflict between the use of power and the principles of democracy and enlightened management is unrelieved. Businessmen, who face this paradox every day in countless situations, cannot avoid the responsibility of explaining or resolving it. If a viable philosophy of management is to be developed, they must contribute their ideas—for the sake of their own peace of mind, if nothing else.

If this article succeeds in getting more businessmen to do some thinking along this line, then it will have served its purpose.

Why the Powerless
Do Not Revolt

Jean Lipman-Blumen

Given that men control greater institutional resources than women, why
don't they simply crush women into total submission and end the gender
power struggle once and for all? Earlier we suggested two reasons why
men use force infrequently against women. First, force is hardly an encouragement to love and affection. Second, if men want not only love but productivity, service, and work from women, those who are beaten down are
incapable of such efforts. Additional important reasons exist for men's reluctance to coerce women's compliance. And still other factors—structural, attitudinal, and existential—lead women and men to join forces to
protect the gender power balance.

Men's power position and their need for women

What are these other key aspects of the power relationship itself that not
only prevent men from using force, but predispose them to seek the apparent acquiescence, if not the enthusiastic endorsement, of women? One factor is the isolation that stems from the structural differentiation of gender
roles. If sex and gender roles define men and women as unalterably different, with men alone perceived as the appropriate wielders of power, then
men too are set apart, isolated in their lonely governing roles.

The existential condition—each individual's deep-seated awareness of
his or her own human frailty and uncertainty—makes even the most renowned king seek approval of his decisions and beliefs, validation of his
own existence. The common practice of princes surrounding themselves
with fawning courtiers, or of presidents, both national and corporate, of
encouraging an entourage of "yes-men," is not simply the result of power's
sweet nectar attracting obsequious bees. Of course, insincere and unrelent-
ing rubberstamping eventually frustrates the powerful, who occasionally
seek objective opinions, usually in vain. But the powerful conspire with the
less powerful to validate their own decisions, their own view of life.

Reprinted from Jean Lipman-Blumen, *Gender Roles and Power,* © 1984 by Prentice-
Hall, Englewood Cliffs, N.J., by permission of Prentice-Hall.

It is hardly surprising that men turn to women, both at home and at work, for emotional and moral validation. Thanks to gender roles defining women as society's emotional and moral arbiters, men's decisions in the public domain require recurrent validation and approval from women. Deprived of this legitimation of their experience and choices, men, as well as women, lose touch with reality and risk slipping through the looking-glass into the mad world of schizophrenia or megalomania. So men need women, defined by gender roles as more moral, emotional, and nurturant than men, to assure them that the choices they make as agents of power are good, even lovable. In those rare instances when women find themselves in seats of great institutional power, they too seek such reassurances.

The structural bases of male-female interdependence

Another reason why men, as the socially dominant group, ordinarily do not choose to use visible force to gain women's agreement with their decisions is that they live together in families, domestically unsegregated. Women and men are both separated from their own gender groups, particularly those of different social, economic, racial, and ethnic backgrounds. And women who do not participate in the occupational world are even more segregated from other non-kin women.

The definition of separate but complementary roles (or "two spheres") created by the sex-gender system leads to a sexual division of labor within the home and the marketplace that spawns a structured interdependence between men and women. The rise of the nuclear family, with all its sociological, psychological, economic, and political correlates, increases men's and women's emotional intimacy and interdependence. This socially induced interdependence fosters cooperation between men and women. The physical and emotional enclosure we call the family provides the psychological and structural humidity and nutrients for the tendrils of emotional intimacy and vulnerability—be they affection, love, hatred, or simply familiarity—to take root.

That men and women live together in social and sexual intimacy within households, if not always families, increases the likelihood that they will look to one another for help and reassurance, as well as for emotional and economic support. These circumstances provide the soil in which emotional interdependence can grow. Feminists argue that women's economic dependence on men has more seriously devastating outcomes than men's emotional reliance on women. Researchers who cite the higher mortality and morbidity figures of divorced, widowed, and single men might dispute this view.

The fact that women and men live in mutual dependence within families or households patterned on a division of labor dictated by sex and gender roles also provides a structural basis for the maintenance of this arrangement. Their own structured social and sexual intimacy, coupled with their separation from other non-kin members of their own gender, keeps both women and less powerful men from joining forces with similarly situated members of their own gender group. Negative social class, racial, and ethnic stereotypes help to maintain these divisions within gender groups. The long-term nature of these living arrangements also reduces the likelihood that men will impose their decisions on women by brute force. It simply would not work in the long run. Men, as well as women, understand the folk wisdom of that old adage, "Softly, softly, catch a monkey." Thus, structural arrangements of intimate family living promote the growth of social, sexual, and affectional bonds that ease the power struggle between individual women and men.

Attitudinal supports: How stereotypes divide the powerless

Although family living arrangements encourage interdependence and intimacy between the sexes, they tend to separate homebound women from other non-kin women; women in the labor force are less segregated from one another and more likely to join forces in their struggle for equality. Men's greater labor-force participation puts them in daily contact with other non-kin males. Moreover, men's—particularly powerful men's—membership in the ruling social group reduces their need for same-sex alliances, especially with men in less powerful positions. Even in terms of their dependence within the heterosexual union, men from the higher socioeconomic strata are less vulnerable than their mates; they almost always can attract other women with fewer resources to share their power and life style.

Thus, family living arrangements heighten the physical segregation of women who do not work outside the home. This physical separation of women from non-kin females of different socioeconomic, racial, and ethnic groups also provides the structural basis for inhibiting women from uniting to improve their power position relative to men. This structural basis for female segregation is strengthened by an attitudinal basis—negative stereotypes of other groups, including the women in those groups. Taken together, these factors limit the possibilities for women to create alliances with other women from different socioeconomic, racial, age and ethnic groups.

On one level, negative stereotypes of less powerful groups are fashioned by the powerful to maintain their own preeminence. Negative stereotypes depicting other groups as untouchables diminish the likelihood that women, the subordinate partners in heterosexual unions, will forsake this imperfect shelter for a potentially contaminating political or economic alliance with members of other stigmatized groups—particularly since whatever negative stereotypes describe a group as a whole are even more negatively applied to its women. Middle- and upper-class women (and less powerful men) are kept from alliances with their gender-mates from other socioeconomic, racial, age, and ethnic groups by the fear of contamination and loss of whatever limited advantages they currently have. Their working-class sisters, alternately disdainful and desirous of the life style of middle- and upper-class women, worry about the motivations of women above them in the social hierarchy. Rather than join those middle-class and occasional upper-class women who seek their help in reordering the power balance between male and female, working-class women suspect their motives as genocidal, elitist, and racist. The historical record often fuels their fears.

Add to this what women of all social classes, through the ages, have learned explicitly from their mothers and implicitly from their fathers: Given the barriers to women's own personal occupational and economic success, sexual competition among women for that scarce and valuable commodity—powerful men—is women's one dependable route to economic and social security. Until recently, when increasing occupational opportunities and greater acceptance of divorce and remarriage began to offer alternatives, the stage was elaborately set for fierce female sexual competition.

Working-class women, whose power chips have been the least valued by the dominant group, see access to resource-generating institutions as a cruel joke in which they repeatedly have been the victims of exploitative wages and health-jeopardizing work environments. Not surprisingly, they believe their best hope is entering the ranks of middle-class housewives, with whatever additional advantages their social telescope seems to magnify.

More affluent women have their own reasons for reluctance. They fear losing the vicarious status and power they now derive through their husbands' positions in the social hierarchy. Socialized from early childhood to achieve vicariously, first through their fathers and later through their husbands and sons, these affluent women are kept in line by control myths—another form of stereotype. Many of these women have been guided away from crucial enabling experiences—learning mathematics, science, finance, law—that would have broadened their personal options in the world beyond the family. Higher education may have radicalized some women, but it rarely gave them the critical tools to end their economic dependence on men.

More affluent women also have their own negative stereotypes of their less well-to-do sisters. They have been schooled to perceive their less affluent gender-mates as vulgar, ill-bred, ignorant, sexually promiscuous, lesbians, or welfare parasites. Belief in these stereotypes keeps all but a few of these vicariously successful women from joining women of less privileged socioeconomic, racial, and ethnic groups to reset the gender power balance. (We might note that less powerful men are prevented from uniting with other equally disenfranchised males across class, race, and ethnic lines by similar strategies.)

Other rationales

Negative stereotypes about outsiders are not the only attitudinal basis for maintaining the strength of the heterosexual power relationship. For the powerless to go on living intimately with those who most directly limit their power, other strong rationales must exist. The weight of tradition predisposes both women and men to take the social structure for granted, including the entire panoply of institutional arrangements based on laws, customs, and practices, rather than on individual talent.

Most women and men accept the structural arrangements as natural, each group believing the stereotypes that keep the complementary gender-role dance in harmony. Males attribute their own success to competence, women's more limited success to innate female incapacities. Women, socialized from childhood to concur in this belief, usually do. Females, raised to be spectators at both the childhood playground and the adult institutional games in which men star, receive only rare opportunities to test their own skills. Many women, forced by the crises of widowhood, family illness, or divorce to test their abilities at traditional male activites, find they easily learn the requisite skills. Many discover their own unsuspected talent for these games.

Some women, valuing their deep-seated appreciation of the less competitive, more cooperative life styles and strategies learned within traditional female gender roles, would prefer to infuse institutional structures and practices with their own special perspective. Other women, radicalized by higher education and labor-force participation, express growing doubts about the "natural," much less the "inevitable," quality of the existing social structure. They have begun to reject the traditional institutional structures, on the grounds that "the only game in town" is rigged. No matter. The dominant group and the remaining powerless whom they "support" and "protect" continue to accept the institutional arrangements as givens.

Males controlling institutional arrangements see their position as deserved, and they resist, as sociologist William J. Goode tells us, all efforts to chip away at their power.[1] Powerful men's sincere belief that they are more intelligent and competent than women promotes their indignant resistance to efforts to redress women's unequal status. They continue to misinterpret such efforts, including affirmative action, as strategies to offer incompetent women and other minority group members an unfair advantage in gender-segregated economic and political institutions. Men's own structural advantage, embedded like the rabbit in the landscapes of children's picture books, is just as hard for them to detect. Over time, foreground blends into background. The less powerful who have identified the

1. William J. Goode, Why men resist, in *Rethinking the Family: Some Feminist Questions,* ed., Barrie Thorne with Marilyn Yalom (New York: Longman Inc., 1982).

embedded rabbit as the structural arrangement known as "sex discrimination" find it nearly impossible to make the rabbit fade away into the background.

The blueprint problem: A strong existential force

Still another factor helps to maintain the gender power balance. It offers one more clue to why men particularly, but not without women's witting or unwitting collusion, seek to keep the sex-gender system in "proper" balance—that is, with a clear power discrepancy between women and men. For simplicity, we shall call this the *blueprint problem*.

Earlier, we alluded to the importance of the interconnections among institutions. Everywhere in society, social institutions are composed of roles rank-ordered into a value and dominance hierarchy. The general pattern is repeated in all institutions: the family, the occupational system, the political and legal system, the religious system, the economic system. Men are situated in the highest stratum in every social institution, with women consistently located in strata below men of their own social group. As long as this key power relationship between men and women remains in the traditional balance, *all* institutions are protected from change.

This brings us to a major thesis of this book: The power relationship between men and women is at the very heart of the social fabric. Once it begins to unravel, so do all other power relationships. Hence, despite the fact that women may be the numerical majority in the world population, they are subordinate everywhere to men of their own social group. Social science principles insist that variation in the political and economic systems of society will lead to variation in the relative importance and bargaining power of different groups. Nonetheless, in all known societies, despite differences in stage of development and political and economic structures, women's relative status and bargaining power are consistently less than that of men in their own cultures. Somehow, through structural arrangements and practices, legal mandates, customs, control myths, and a host of other social, psychological, political, legal, and economic phenomena, women are kept subordinate to men.

The need to maintain women's subordination at home and in the world at large is deep seated, since in some inchoate way both women and men understand that the power relationship between the genders is the blueprint for *all* other power relationships. Small changes in the gender power balance can be tolerated. Many unconsciously fear, however, that a major change, one in which women could negotiate the dominant role, would prove the undoing of all other power relationships modeled so carefully after this seemingly most stable and inevitable one.

This blueprint, itself presumably patterned after the divine relationship between God and humans portrayed in traditional Western religious systems, is then used to fashion all other power relationships. The blueprint itself becomes sacred. Its meaning becomes dangerous knowledge: that the

Divine Echo, the gender power relationship, is the model of all power relationships in all societal institutions, the model that keeps all others in place. The awareness of this dangerous truth threatens every political power relationship.

The parallel between sexual and political dominance is seen in relationships among ethnic, racial, economic, and national groups. Western colonialism in Africa, Asia, and Latin America, not to mention the American slavery experience, was based upon the relationship between sexual and political power relationships. Numerous students of colonialism, including Ashis Nandy, suggest that the basic condition of colonialism is a psychological acceptance of the states of dominance/masculinity and subordinance/femininity by the rulers and ruled, respectively. In a trenchant politico-psychoanalytic analysis of British colonialism in India, Nandy argues that

> Colonial ideology in British India was built of the cultural meanings of two fundamental categories of institutional discrimination in Britain— sex and age. . . . Colonialism . . . was congruent with the existing Western sexual stereotypes and the philosophy of life which they represented. It produced a cultural consensus in which political and socioeconomic dominance symbolized the dominance of men and masculinity over women and femininity.[2]

Eventually, both rulers and subjects accepted the notion of colonial rule as a "husbandly," "manly," or "lordly" prerogative. Nandy offers this as a description not of the micropolitics, but the macropolitics of colonialism. The notion of "protectorates" as unable to fend for themselves—less able, less educable, and more primitive than the colonial ruler—contains a metaphor too reminiscent of the female/male power balance to warrant dismissal as mere coincidence. The very language of colonialism evokes the domestic paradigm.

The inchoate awareness of the blueprint problem lies at the heart of seemingly disparate efforts to maintain the sex-gender system in its current balance. It is this barely conscious understanding that may be the connective tissue linking such apparently unrelated occurrences as opposition to the Equal Rights Amendment in the United States (where such legal equality would not be nonchalantly taken for granted); the unwillingness of Soviet husbands (whose wives have unusual equality in the work force) to share domestic chores within the family; and female clitoridectomies in Third World countries (where unbridled female sexual prowess allegedly would lead to a host of ills). Perhaps these are all last-ditch measures to ensure that the gender power balance stays at least symbolically tipped in men's favor.

---

2. Ashis Nandy, *The Intimate Enemy: Loss and Recovery of Self under Colonialism* (New Delhi: Oxford University Press, 1983), p. 4.

Men and women share the dangerous knowledge that the gender power relationship, echoing the divine power structure of traditional religions, is the model for all other power relationships in every societal institution. It reinforces and is reinforced by the interconnectedness of social institutions. Men and women also share the fear of the unknown, the fear of what would happen if women, mobilizing and valuing their own resources, negotiated for the dominant position. What, indeed, would happen to the fabric of society if the key pattern were to change? Would every institutional power arrangement eventually shift? Probably.

Why the powerless do not revolt

It is not difficult to understand why the powerful want to stay in charge: a deep-seated, often unidentified fear that all institutional power relationships might unravel, structurally induced myopia, tradition, belief in their own superior talents, the negotiated power to define, label, and rank-order. These are seductive incentives for wanting to remain in charge, even though control brings serious burdens. But what do the powerless derive from this structured inequality? Why do they remain? Why do the less powerful, in this case women, continue to validate male decision-making and negotiate in ways that maintain their subordinate position?

First, and most significant to women as well as men, is the blueprint problem we have just discussed. Second, women and men alike are socialized from infancy to accept the traditional definition of gender roles. Both sexes believe in the gender definitions created by their forebears and inculcated by their parents and other adults through word and deed. They are repeatedly taught through *control myths* about the supposedly innate nature—that is, differentiation—of males and females.

Two control myths in particular keep women from renegotiating the power relationship to allow them greater access to institutional resources. First is the control myth that assures women that men are more knowledgeable and capable; second is the myth that men have women's best interests at heart (colonialism revisited).

That men are more knowledgeable and capable is a control myth of enormous influence. For example, despite females' early verbal and mathematical advantages over males, they are set on the "proper" track by control myths that guide them into nonquantitative, nonscientific, non-financial, nonlegal courses of study to enter service, helping, people-oriented occupations. Institutional arrangements and practices, also shaped by control myths, keep any curious or rebellious individuals from straying into the other gender's territory. Eventually the control myth about men's greater knowledge and capability becomes a self-fulfilling prophecy.[3] First

3. Robert K. Merton, *Social Theory and Social Structure*, rev. ed. (Glencoe, Illinois: The Free Press, 1957).

we believe the definitions; then we act in accordance with them and, by so doing, we make them come true.

The second control myth—that men have women's best interests at heart, that men will protect these less knowledgeable, and therefore more dependent women—is also taught to men and women alike. For men, this means they believe they know better and more, and thus must take care of women and protect them from danger. Often, men see danger to women coming from other men, not themselves. And so they devise laws to protect women from those other men who would exploit and harm them. Protective legislation, notorious for protecting women and children not only from exploitation but from mobility-offering and high-salary jobs as well, was the joint accomplishment of women seeking protection and men who had their best interests at heart.

For women, the belief that men have their welfare at heart has several consequences. For one, they relax, let down their guard in the power struggle, and do not negotiate too hard. It seems pointless to antagonize a strong, wise, and especially a benevolent despot. Sexual and affectional ties to the benevolent ruler compound the issue. But believing in benevolent despots, even kindly rulers, means we believe that power is an *attribute* of a leader or ruler, a *commodity* that one has more or less of, rather than a *process* of decision-making and negotiation. But accepting the notion that men have women's and less powerful men's best interests at heart is to pin one's hopes on moral and ethnical rulers.

However, Lord Acton warned us that "Power tends to corrupt, and absolute power corrupts absolutely." The lesson Lord Acton would have us learn is that those we grant unchecked power—power that need not be constantly renegotiated—cannot remain moral and ethical. Women and powerless men cannot relax and hand over the reins and burdens of decision-making about critical world events, even to those who might indeed have their best interests at heart.

Sometimes, of course, even those who sincerely want the best for women do not actually know what that "best" is. For example, those loving fathers and husbands who protected their daughters and wives from financial burdens often left their shielded widow and children in the hands of those other men—notoriously bankers and lawyers—who did, indeed, exploit their financial ignorance. Women know better than anyone else what constitutes their best interests, just as men are the most competent judges of their own welfare. To rephrase an old truism: "Until men walk in women's moccasins," their claims to know women's best interests are suspect—and vice versa.

The overwhelming odds

Still another reason why women, like other less powerful groups, tend to remain in the subordinate position in a power relationship is that they perceive the institutional resources that men have as unattainable for women, except through their relationships with men. The disparity is too great; it is too wide to be bridged. The odds are overwhelming.

In large part this perception is based on fact, since the majority of independently wealthy women have become so through inheritance or marriage. And even those relatively few women who have entered entrepreneurial and professional roles rarely receive the same rewards—money, prestige, position, or access to still more sacrosanct institutions—as men. The small number who do are usually featured on the women's page, rather than on the financial or front page of the newspaper. The woman physician who works full time at her profession rarely has even the economic advantages, much less the leisure time (another important resource), of the male physician's full-time housewife.

A keen awareness of this substantial disparity between men's and women's resources and the genuine inaccessibility of institutional resources to women has kept many gender power relationships intact. This is what keeps many discontented wives locked into the bonds of acrimony with spouses they would rather divorce. This trap traps the trappers, as well. Men too are caught by this arrangement. Wives who will never be able to earn enough in the labor force to support themselves, much less their children, may require lifelong, debilitating alimony payments. The awareness of this huge and seemingly irreducible disparity in resources has ignited the flame of fear among many women whose lives have been based on vicarious or derivative access to resources. Many of these women understandably oppose any movement for change, which they sense threatens to reduce their current, if tenuous, access to resources.

Women's belief in debilitating control myths often teaches them that their strengths are their weaknesses. Strong verbal skills (called "talking too much" in women, and "articulateness" in men) are keys to leadership roles in organizations. Women are taught to restrain their talking—that is, their displays of intelligence—in such settings, lest they make negative female stereotypes self-fulfilling prophecies.

Men too, from early childhood and throughout life, are indoctrinated with beliefs, expectations, attitudes, and values that limit their total role repertoire, including their sex and gender roles. Males, no less than females, are subjected to this pervasive socialization, through parents, teachers, peers, media, art, and religion—through a host of societal forces that create near mutually exclusive, but complementary, roles. In the next chapter, we begin to consider how socialization occurs, and how it leaves both women and men poised for the gender power struggle.

Summary

Structural, attitudinal, and existential supports keep the gender power balance intact. Men, locked into their lonely decision-making roles, seek affirmation of their choices from women, defined as society's moral arbiters. Living together in households or families, men and women develop an intimate interdependence that encourages conscious and unconscious collusion between the genders to protect the power balance. Negative female stereotypes keep women from reaching across socioeconomic, racial, and ethnic boundaries to form power alliances with other women.

The gender power balance receives additional support from those who perceive it as the blueprint or model for all other power relationships. Its maintenance protects the stability of all other power relationships. Control myths that insist that men are more able than women but have women's best interests at heart contribute to the stability of male domination. Moreover, the disproportionate institutional resources that men control create overwhelming odds against which women feel it is futile to revolt.

This combination of structural, attitudinal, and existential forces operates to keep the gender power struggle on course. As we shall now see, male and female socialization to gender roles serves to reinforce this sexgender helix.

7

Groups: Group Pressures, Group Decisions, Group Conflicts

A paradox: Many managers hate groups. They complain about them. They recall Fred Allen's definition of a committee as a "group of people who individually do nothing, but as a group decide that nothing can be done." They think of Milton Berle's comment that a committee "keeps minutes and wastes hours." But managers spend huge amounts of their time in groups. They sit on committees and task forces, and they also create them. They go to meetings, and they call meetings for other people to come to.

Either managers are really stupid or else they find groups necessary. We'll bet on the latter. Groups, indeed, have become more and more important mechanisms for making decisions and for getting things done in organizations.

Managers need groups for many different reasons. In a complex world of large organizations, people have to put their heads together to coordinate their efforts. Knowledge and information, widely dispersed in many heads, need to be brought together. And group decisions are often better, by any standards, than those of a single person. Moreover, groups generate commitment by their members to their group decisions. And groups are great training devices for teaching the ropes to newcomers.

For all those reasons and more, groups are here to stay on the managerial scene.

The first paper in this section, Harold Leavitt's, plays a speculative game. If groups are so important for so many reasons, how might managers take much better advantage of them? Suppose, Leavitt proposes, we were to treat the small group rather than the individual as our basic unit of analysis. What might be some of the major positive and negative consequences?

The second paper, Edgar Schein's, looks more closely at the group's role as shaper and influencer of the behavior of its members. Driven in part from his studies of "brainwashing" of American prisoners in Korea, Schein shows how groups can pressure and persuade their members to change, sharply, prior attitudes and values. Groups are powerful agents of change!

And their power does not always result in positive outcomes, as Irving

Janis's paper shows. Janis looks at the phenomenon of "groupthink," the propensity of groups to become more concerned with their own process than with critical analyses of their tasks. He uses some major crises in U.S. history, such as Pearl Harbor, to make his telling points.

Then, in the last paper of this section, Kenwyn Smith's, we look at a pervasive and critical problem in human affairs—the problem of developing positive collaboration among groups. As groups become internally loyal and cohesive, they tend to treat other groups as troublemakers, if not outright enemies. The problem of intergroup conflict is not limited to the engineering group and the marketing group inside one company. It also underlies the difficulties encountered by the not-so-United Nations, or the Army versus the Air Force versus the Navy, or the Walloons versus the Flemish in Belgium, or blacks versus whites in the United States.

So groups are important, they're powerful, and they're dangerous. Let's try to understand them better.

Suppose We Took Groups Seriously

Harold J. Leavitt

Introduction

This chapter is mostly a fantasy, but not a utopian fantasy. As the title suggests, it tries to spin out some of the things that might happen if we really took small groups seriously; if, that is, we really used groups, rather than individuals, as the basic building blocks for an organization.

This seems an appropriate forum for such a fantasy. It was fifty years ago, at Hawthorne, that the informal face-to-face work group was discovered. Since then groups have been studied inside and out; they have been experimented with, observed, built, and taken apart. Small groups have become the major tool of the applied behavioral scientist. Organizational Development methods are group methods. Almost all of what is called participative management is essentially based on group techniques.

So the idea of using groups as organizational mechanisms is by no means new or fantastic. The fantasy comes in proposing to start with groups, not add them in; to design organizations from scratch around small groups, rather than around individuals.

But right from the start, talk like that appears to violate a deep and important value, individualism. But this fantasy will not really turn out to be anti-individualistic in the end.

The rest of this chapter will briefly address the following questions: (1) Is it fair to say that groups have not been taken very seriously in organizational design? (2) Why are groups even worth thinking about as organizational building materials? What are the characteristics of groups that might make them interesting enough to be worth serious attention? (3) What would it mean "to take groups seriously?" Just what kinds of things would have to be done differently? (4) What compensatory changes would probably be needed in other aspects of the organization, to have groups as the basic unit? And finally, (5), is the idea of designing the organization around

Reprinted from *Man and Work in Society,* edited by Eugene L. Cass and Frederick G. Zimmer, © 1975 by Western Electric Company, Inc., by permission of Van Nostrand Reinhold Company.

small face-to-face groups a very radical idea, or is it just an extension of a direction in which we are already going?

Haven't groups been taken seriously enough already?

The argument that groups have not been taken "seriously" doesn't seem a hard one to make. The contemporary ideas about groups didn't really come along until the '30s and '40s. By that time a logical, rationalistic tradition for the construction of organizations already existed. That tradition was very heavily based on the notion that the individual was the construction unit. The logic moved from the projected task backward. Determine the task, the goal, then find an appropriate structure and technology, and last of all fit individual human beings into predefined mansized pieces of the action. That was, for instance, what industrial psychology was all about during its development between the two world wars. It was concerned almost entirely with individual differences and worked in the service of structuralists, fitting square human pegs to predesigned square holes. The role of the psychologist was thus ancillary to the role of the designers of the whole organization. It was a back up, supportive role that followed more than it led design.

It was not just the logic of classical organizational theory that concentrated on the individual. The whole entrepreneurial tradition of American society supported it. Individuals, at least male individuals, were taught achievement motivation. They were taught to seek individual evaluation, to compete, to see the world, organizational or otherwise, as a place in which to strive for individual accomplishment and satisfaction.

In those respects the classical design of organizations was consonant with the then existent cultural landscape. Individualized organizational structures blended with the environment of individualism. All the accessories fell into place: individual incentive schemes for hourly workers, individual merit rating and assessment schemes, tests for selection of individuals.

The unique characteristic of the organization was that it was not simply a race track within which individuals could compete, but a system in which somehow the competitive behavior of individuals could be coordinated, harnessed and controlled in the interest of the common tasks. Of course one residual of all that was a continuing tension between individual and organization, with the organization seeking to control and coordinate the individual's activities at the same time that it tried to motivate him; while the competitive individual insisted on reaching well beyond the constraints imposed upon him by the organization. One product of this tension became the informal organization discovered here at Western; typically an informal coalition designed to fight the system.

Then it was discovered that groups could be exploited for what management saw as positive purposes, *toward* productivity instead of away from it. There followed the era of experimentation with small face-to-face groups. We learned to patch them on to existing organizations as bandaids to relieve tensions between individual and organization. We promoted co-ordination through group methods. We learned that groups were useful to discipline and control recalcitrant individuals.

Groups were fitted onto organizations. The group skills of individual members improved so that they could coordinate their efforts more effec-tively, control deviants more effectively and gain more commitment from subordinate individuals. But groups were seen primarily as tools to be tacked on and utilized in the pre-existing individualized organizational sys-tem. With a few notable exceptions, like Rensis Likert (1961), most did not design organizations around groups. On the contrary, as some of the ideas about small groups began to be tacked onto existing organizational methods, they generated new tensions and conflicts of their own. Managers complained not only that groups were slow, but that they diffused responsi-bility, vitiated the power of the hierarchy because they were too "demo-cratic and created small in-group empires which were very hard for others to penetrate." There was the period, for example, of the great gap between T-group training (which had to be conducted on "cultural islands") and the organization back home. The T-groupers therefore talked a lot about the "reentry problem," which meant in part the problem of movement from a new culture (the T-group culture) designed around groups back into the organizational culture designed around individuals.

But of course groups didn't die despite their difficulties. How could they die? They had always been there, though not always in the service of the organization. They turned out to be useful, indeed necessary, though often unrecognized tools. For organizations were growing, and professional-izing, and the need for better coordination grew even as the humanistic expectations of individuals also grew. So "acknowledged" groups (as dis-tinct from "natural," informal groups) became fairly firmly attached even to conservative organizations, but largely as compensating addenda very often reluctantly backed into by organizational managers.

Groups have never been given a chance. It is as though someone had insisted that automobiles be designed to fit the existing terrain rather than build roads to adapt to automobiles.

Are groups worth considering as fundamental building blocks?

Why would groups be more interesting than individuals as basic design units around which to build organizations? What are the prominent char-acteristics of small groups? Why are they interesting? Here are several answers:

First, small groups seem to be good for people. They can satisfy impor-tant membership needs. They can provide a moderately wide range of ac-tivities for individual members. They can provide support in times of stress and crisis. They are settings in which people can learn not only cognitively but empirically to be reasonably trusting and helpful to one another. Second, groups seem to be good problem finding tools. They seem to be useful in promoting innovation and creativity. Third, in a wide variety of decision situations, they make better decisions than individuals do. Fourth, they are great tools for implementation. They gain commitment from their members so that group decisions are likely to be willingly carried out. Fifth, they can control and discipline individual members in ways that are often extremely difficult through more impersonal quasi-legal disciplinary systems. Sixth, as organizations grow large, small groups appear to be useful mechanisms for fending off many of the negative effects of large size. They help to prevent communication lines from growing too long, the hierarchy from growing too steep, and the individual from getting lost in the crowd.

There is a seventh, but altogether different kind of argument for taking groups seriously. Thus far the designer of organizations seemed to have a choice. He could build an individualized *or* a groupy organization. A groupy organization will, de facto, have to deal with individuals; but what was learned here so long ago is that individualized organizations, must de facto, deal with groups. Groups are natural phenomena, and facts of organizational life. They can be created but their spontaneous development cannot be prevented. The problem is not shall groups exist or not, but shall groups be planned or not? If not, the individualized organizational garden will sprout groupy weeds all over the place. By defining them as weeds instead of flowers, they shall continue, as in earlier days, to be treated as pests, forever fouling up the beauty of rationally designed individualized organizations, forever forming informally (and irrationally) to harass and outgame the planners.

It is likely that the reverse could also be true, that if groups are defined as the flowers and individuals as the weeds, new problems will crop up. Surely they will, but that discussion can be delayed for at least a little while.

Who uses groups best?

So groups look like interesting organizational building blocks. But before going on to consider the implications of designing organizations around groups, one useful heuristic might be to look around the existing world at those places in which groups seem to have been treated somewhat more seriously.

One place groups have become big is in Japanese organizations (Johnson and Ouchi 1974). The Japanese seem to be very groupy, and much less concerned than Americans about issues like individual accountability. Japanese organizations, of course, are thus consonant with Japanese culture, where notions of individual aggressiveness and competitiveness are de-emphasized in favor of self-effacement and group loyalty. But Japanese organizations seem to get a lot done, despite the relative suppression of the individual in favor of the group. It also appears that the advantages of the groupy Japanese style have really come to the fore in large technologically complex organizations.

Another place to look is at American conglomerates. They go to the opposite extreme, dealing with very large units. They buy large organizational units and sell units. They evaluate units. In effect they promote units by offering them extra resources as rewards for good performance. In that sense conglomerates, one might argue, are designed around groups, but the groups in question are often themselves large organizational chunks.

Groups in an individualistic culture

An architect can design a beautiful building which either blends smoothly with its environment or contrasts starkly with it. But organization designers may not have the same choice. If we design an organization which is structurally dissonant with its environment, it is conceivable that the environment will change to adjust to the organization. It seems much more likely, however, that the environment will reject the organization. If designing organizations around groups represents a sharp counterpoint to environmental trends maybe we should abort the idea.

Our environment, one can argue, is certainly highly individualized. But one can also make a less solid argument in the other direction; an argument that American society is going groupy rather than individual this year. Or at least that it is going groupy as well as individual. The evidence is sloppy at best. One can reinterpret the student revolution and the growth of anti-establishment feelings at least in part as a reaction to the decline of those institutions that most satisfied social membership needs. One can argue that the decline of the Church, of the village and of the extended family is leaving behind a vacuum of unsatisfied membership and belongingness motives. Certainly popular critics of American society have laid a great deal of emphasis on the loneliness and anomie that seem to have resulted not only from materialism but from the emphasis on individualism. It seems possible to argue that, insofar as there has been any significant change in the work ethic in America, the change has been toward a desire for work which is socially as well as egoistically fulfilling, and which satisfies human needs for belongingness and affiliation as well as needs for achievement.

In effect, the usual interpretation of Abraham Maslow's need hierarchy may be wrong. Usually the esteem and self-actualization levels of motivation are emphasized. Perhaps the level that is becoming operant most rapidly is neither of those, but the social-love-membership level.

The rising role of women in American society also has implications for the groupiness of organizations. There is a moderate amount of evidence that American women have been socialized more strongly into affiliative and relational sorts of attitudes than men. They probably can, in general, more comfortably work in direct achievement roles in group settings, where there are strong relational bonds among members, than in competitive, individualistic settings. Moreover it is reasonable to assume that as women take a more important place in American society, some of their values and attitudes will spill over to the male side.

Although the notion of designing organizations around groups in America in 1974 may be a little premature, it is consonant with cultural trends that may make the idea much more appropriate ten years from now.

But groups are becoming more relevant for organizational as well as cultural reasons. Groups seem to be particularly useful as coordinating and integrating mechanisms for dealing with complex tasks that require the inputs of many kinds of specialized knowledge. In fact the development of matrix-type organizations in high technology industry is perhaps one effort to modify individually designed organizations toward a more groupy direction; not for humanistic reasons but as a consequence of tremendous increases in the informational complexity of the jobs that need to be done.

What might a seriously groupy organization look like?

Just what does it mean to design organizations around groups? Operationally how is that different from designing organizations around individuals? One approach to an answer is simply to take the things organizations do with individuals and try them out with groups. The idea is to raise the level from the atom to the molecule, and *select* groups rather than individuals, *train* groups rather than individuals, *pay* groups rather than individuals, *promote* groups rather than individuals, *design jobs* for groups rather than for individuals, *fire* groups rather than individuals, and so on down the list of activities which organizations have traditionally carried on in order to use human beings in their organizations.

Some of the items on that list seem easy to handle at the group level. For example, it doesn't seem terribly hard to design jobs for groups. In effect that is what top management already does for itself to a great extent. It gives specific jobs to committees, and often runs itself as a group. The problem seems to be a manageable one: designing job sets which are both big enough to require a small number of persons and also small enough to require only a small number of persons. Big enough in this context means not only jobs that would occupy the hands of group members but that would provide opportunities for learning and expansion.

Ideas like evaluating, promoting, and paying groups raise many more difficult but interesting problems. Maybe the best that can be said for such ideas is that they provide opportunities for thinking creatively about pay and evaluation. Suppose, for example, that as a reward for good work the group gets a larger salary budget than it got last year. Suppose the allocation for increases within the group is left to the group members. Certainly one can think up all sorts of difficulties that might arise. But are the potential problems necessarily any more difficult than those now generated by individual merit raises? Is there any company in America that is satisfied with its existing individual performance appraisal and salary allocation schemes? At least the issues of distributive justice within small groups would presumably be open to internal discussion and debate. One might even permit the group to allocate payments to individuals differentially at different times, in accordance with some criteria of current contribution that they might establish.

As far as performance evaluation is concerned, it is probably easier for people up the hierarchy to assess the performance of total groups than it is to assess the performance of individual members well down the hierarchy. Top managers of decentralized organizations do it all the time, except that they usually reward the formal leader of the decentralized unit rather than the whole unit.

The notion of promoting groups raises another variety of difficulties. One thinks of physically transferring a whole group, for example, and of the costs associated with training a whole group to do a new job, especially if there are no bridging individuals. But there may be large advantages too. If a group moves, its members already know how to work with one another. Families may be less disrupted by movement if several move at the same time.

There is the problem of selection. Does it make sense to select groups? Initially, why not? Can't means be found for selecting not only for appropriate knowledge and skill but also for potential ability to work together? There is plenty of groundwork in the literature already.

After the initial phase, there will of course be problems of adding or subtracting individuals from existing groups. We already know a good deal about how to help new members get integrated into old groups. Incidentally, I was told recently by a plant manager in the midwest about an oddity he had encountered; the phenomenon of groups applying for work. Groups of three or four people have been coming to his plant seeking employment together. They wanted to work together and stay together.

Costs and danger points

To play this game of designing organizations around groups, what might be some important danger points? In general, a group-type organization is somewhat more like a free market than present organizations. More decisions would have to be worked out ad hoc, in a continually changing way. So one would need to schedule more negotiation time both within and between groups.

One would encounter more issues of justice, for the individual vis-à-vis the group and for groups vis-à-vis one another. More and better arbitration mechanisms would probably be needed along with highly flexible and rapidly adaptive record keeping. But modern record keeping technology is, potentially, both highly flexible and rapidly adaptive.

Another specific issue is the provision of escape hatches for individuals. Groups have been known to be cruel and unjust to their deviant members. One existing escape route for the individual would of course continue to exist: departure from the organization. Another might be easy means of transfer to another group.

Another related danger of a strong group emphasis might be a tendency to drive away highly individualistic, nongroup people. But the tight organizational constraints now imposed do the same thing. Indeed might not groups protect their individualists better than the impersonal rules of present day large organizations?

Another obvious problem: If groups are emphasized by rewarding them, paying them, promoting them, and so on, groups may begin to perceive themselves as power centers, in competitive conflict with other groups. Intergroup hostilities are likely to be exacerbated unless we can design some new coping mechanisms into the organization. Likert's proposal for solving that sort of problem (and others) is the linking pin concept. The notion is that individuals serve as members of more than one group, both up and down the hierarchy and horizontally. But Likert's scheme seems to me to assume fundamentally individualized organizations in the sense that it is still individuals who get paid, promoted and so on. In a more groupy organization, the linking pin concept has to be modified so that an individual might be a part-time member of more than one group, but still a real member. That is, for example, a portion of an individual's pay might come from each group in accordance with that group's perception of his contribution.

Certainly much more talk, both within and between groups, would be a necessary accompaniment of group emphasis; though we might argue about whether more talk should be classified as a cost or a benefit. In any case careful design of escape hatches for individuals and connections among groups would be as important in this kind of organization as would stairways between floors in the design of a private home.

There is also a danger of over-designing groups. All groups in the organization need not look alike. Quite to the contrary. Task and technology should have significant effects on the shapes and sizes of different subgroups within the large organization. Just as individuals end up adjusting the edges of their jobs to themselves and themselves to their jobs, we should expect flexibility within groups, allowing them to adapt and modify themselves to whatever the task and technology demand.

Another initially scary problem associated with groups is the potential loss of clear formal individual leadership. Without formal leaders how will we motivate people? Without leaders how will we control and discipline people? Without leaders how will we pinpoint responsibility? Even as I write those questions I cannot help but feel that they are archaic. They are questions which are themselves a product of the basic individual building block design of old organizations. The problem is not leaders so much as the performance of leadership functions. Surely groups will find leaders, but they will emerge from the bottom up. Given a fairly clear job description, some groups, in some settings, will set up more or less permanent leadership roles. Others may let leadership vary as the situation demands, or as a function of the power that individuals within any group may possess relative to the group's needs at that time. A reasonable amount of process time can be built in to enable groups to work on the leadership problem, but the problem will have to be resolved within each group. On the advantage side of the ledger, this may even get rid of a few hierarchical levels. There should be far less need for individuals who are chiefly supervisors of other individuals' work. Groups can serve as hierarchical leaders of other groups.

Two other potential costs: With an organization of groups, there may be a great deal of infighting, and power and conflict issues will come even more to the fore than they do now. Organizations of groups may become highly political, with coalitions lining up against one another on various issues. If so, the rest of the organizational system will have to take those political problems into account, both by setting up sensible systems of intercommunications among groups, and by allocating larger amounts of time and expertise to problems of conflict resolution.

But this is not a new problem unique to groupy organizations. Conflict among groups is prevalent in large organizations which are political systems now. But because these issues have not often been foreseen and planned for, the mechanisms for dealing with them are largely ad hoc. As a result, conflict is often dealt with in extremely irrational ways.

But there is another kind of intergroup power problem that may become extremely important and difficult in groupy organizations. There is a real danger that relatively autonomous and cohesive groups may be closed, not only to other groups but more importantly to staff advice or to new technological inputs.

These problems exist at present, of course, but they may be exacerbated by group structure. I cannot see any perfect way to handle those problems. One possibility may be to make individual members of staff groups part time members of line groups. Another is to work harder to educate line groups to potential staff contributions. Of course the reward system, the old market system, will probably be the strongest force for keeping groups from staying old-fashioned in a world of new technologies and ideas.

But the nature and degree of many of the second order spinoff effects are not fully knowable at the design stage. We need to build more complete working models and pilot plants. In any case it does not seem obvious that slowdowns, either at the work face or in decision-making processes, would necessarily accompany group based organizational designs.

Some possible advantages to the organization

Finally, from an organizational perspective, what are the potential advantages to be gained from a group based organization? The first might be a sharp reduction in the number of units that need to be controlled. Control would not have to be carried all the way down to the individual level. If the average group size is five, the number of blocks that management has to worry about is cut to 20 percent of what it was. Such a design would also probably cut the number of operational levels in the organization. In effect, levels which are now primarily supervisory would be incorporated into the groups that they supervise.

By this means many of the advantages of the small individualized organization could be brought back. These advantages would occur within groups simply because there would be a small number of blocks, albeit larger blocks, with which to build and rebuild the organization.

But most of all, and this is still uncertain, despite the extent to which we behavioral scientists have been enamoured of groups, there would be increased human advantages of cohesiveness, motivation, and commitment, and via that route, both increased productivity, stronger social glue within the organization, and a wider interaction between organization and environment.

Summary

Far and away the most powerful and beloved tool of applied behavioral scientists is the small face-to-face group. Since the Western Electric researches, behavioral scientists have been learning to understand, exploit and love groups. Groups attracted interest initially as devices for improving the implementation of decisions and to increase human commitment and motivation. They are now loved because they are also creative and innovative, they often make better quality decisions than individuals, and because they make organizational life more livable for people. One can't hire an applied behavioral scientist into an organization who within ten minutes will not want to call a group meeting and talk things over. The group meeting is his primary technology, his primary tool.

But groups in organizations are not an invention of behavioral types. They are a natural phenomenon of organizations. Organizations develop informal groups, like it or not. It is both possible and sensible to describe most large organizations as collections of groups in interaction with one another; bargaining with one another, forming coalitions with one another, cooperating and competing with one another. It is possible and sensible too to treat the decisions that emerge from large organizations as a resultant of the interplay of forces among groups within the organization, and not just the resultant of rational analysis.

On the down side, small face-to-face groups are great tools for disciplining and controlling their members. Contemporary China, for example, has just a fraction of the number of lawyers in the United States. Partially this is a result of the lesser complexity of Chinese society and lower levels of education. But a large part of it, surprisingly enough, seems to derive from the fact that modern China is designed around small groups. Since small groups take responsibility for the discipline and control of their members many deviant acts which would be considered illegal in the United States never enter the formal legal system in China. The law controls individual deviation less, the group controls it more (Li 1971).

Control of individual behavior is also a major problem of large complex western organizations. This problem has driven many organizations into elaborate bureaucratic quasi-legal sets of rules, ranging from job evaluation schemes to performance evaluations to incentive systems; all individually based, all terribly complex, all creating problems of distributive justice. Any organizational design that might eliminate much of that legalistic superstructure therefore begins to look highly desirable.

Management should consider building organizations using a material now understood very well and with properties that look very promising, the small group. Until recently, at least, the human group has primarily been used for patching and mending organizations that were originally built of other materials.

The major unanswered questions in my mind are not in the understanding of groups, nor in the potential unity of the group as a building block. The more difficult unanswered question is whether or not the approaching era is one in which Americans would willingly work in such apparently contra-individualistic units. I think we are.

References

Johnson, Richard T., and William G. Ouchi. Made in America (under Japanese management). *Harvard Business Review,* September-October 1974.

Li, Victor. The Development of the Chinese Legal System, in John Lindbeck (ed.), *China: The Management of a Revolutionary Society.* Seattle: University of Washington Press, 1971.

Likert, Rensis. *New Patterns of Management.* New York: McGraw-Hill, 1961.

Management Development
as a Process of Influence
Edgar H. Schein

The continuing rash of articles on the subject of developing better managers suggests, on the one hand, a continuing concern that existing methods are not providing the talent which is needed at the higher level of industry and, on the other hand, that we continue to lack clear cut formulations about the process by which such development occurs. We need more and better managers, and we need more and better theories of how to get them.

In the present paper I would like to cast management development as the problem of how an organization can influence the beliefs, attitudes, and values (hereafter simply called attitudes) of an individual for the purpose of "developing" him, i.e., changing him in a direction which the organization regards to be in his own and the organization's best interests. Most of the existing conceptions of the development of human resources are built upon assumptions of how people learn and grow, and some of the more strikingly contrasting theories of management development derive from disagreements about such assumptions.[1] I will attempt to build on a different base: instead of starting with assumptions about learning and growth, I will start with some assumptions from the social psychology of influence and attitude change.

Building on this base can be justified quite readily if we consider that adequate managerial performance at the higher levels is at least as much a matter of attitudes as it is a matter of knowledge and specific skills, and that the acquisition of such knowledge and skills is itself in part a function of attitudes. Yet we have given far more attention to the psychology which underlies change in the area of knowledge and abilities than we have to the psychology which underlies change in attitudes. We have surprisingly few studies of how a person develops loyalty to a company, commitment to a job, or a professional attitude toward the managerial role; how he comes to

Reprinted from *Sloan Management Review* 2, no. 2 (Spring 1961): 41–50, by permission of the publisher. © 1961 by the Sloan Management Review Association. All rights reserved.
1. An excellent discussion of two contrasting approaches—the engineering vs. the agricultural—deriving from contrasting assumptions about human behavior can be found in D. McGregor, *The Human Side of Enterprise* (New York: McGraw-Hill, 1960), chap. 14.

have the motives and attitudes which make possible the rendering of decisions concerning large quantities of money, materials, and human resources; how he develops attitudes toward himself, his co-workers, his employees, his customers, and society in general which give us confidence that he has a sense of responsibility and a set of ethics consistent with his responsible position or at least which permit us to understand his behavior.

It is clear that management is becoming increasingly professionalized, as evidenced by increasing emphasis on undergraduate and graduate education in the field of management. But professionalization is not only a matter of teaching candidates increasing amounts about a set of relevant subjects and disciplines; it is equally a problem of preparing the candidate for a role which requires a certain set of attitudes. Studies of the medical profession (Merton et al.[2] for example) have turned their attention increasingly to the unraveling of the difficult problem of how the medical student acquires those attitudes and values which enable him to make responsible decisions involving the lives of other people. Similar studies in other professions are sorely needed. When these are undertaken, it is likely to be discovered that much of the training of such attitudes is carried out implicitly and without a clearly formulated rationale. Law schools and medical schools provide various kinds of experiences which insure that the graduate is prepared to fulfill his professional role. Similarly, existing approaches to the development of managers probably provide ample opportunities for the manager to learn the attitudes he will need to fulfill high-level jobs. But in this field, particularly, one gets the impression that such opportunities are more the result of intuition or chance than of clearly formulated policies. This is partly because the essential or pivotal aspects of the managerial role have not as yet been clearly delineated, leaving ambiguous both the area of knowledge to be mastered and the attitude to be acquired.

Existing practice in the field of management development involves activities such as indoctrination and training programs conducted at various points in the manager's career; systematic job rotation involving changes both in the nature of the functions performed (e.g., moving from production into sales), in physical location, and in the individual's superiors; performance appraisal programs including various amounts of testing, general personality assessment, and counseling both within the organization and through the use of outside consultants: apprenticeships, systematic coaching, junior management boards, and special projects to facilitate practice by the young manager in functions he will have to perform later in his career; sponsorship and other comparable activities in which a select group of young managers is groomed systematically for high-level jobs (i.e., made

---

2. R. K. Merton, G. G. Reader, and Patricia L. Kendall, *The Student-Physician* (Cambridge, Mass.: Harvard University Press, 1957).

into "crown princes"); participation in special conferences and training programs, including professional association meetings, human relations workshops, advanced management programs conducted in business schools or by professional associations like the American Management Association, regular academic courses like the Sloan programs offered at Stanford and MIT, or liberal arts courses like those offered at the University of Pennsylvania, Dartmouth, Northwestern, and so on. These and many other specific educational devices, along with elaborate schemes of selection, appraisal, and placement, form the basic paraphernalia of management development.

Most of the methods mentioned above stem from the basic conception that it is the responsibility of the business enterprise, as an institution, to define what kind of behavior and attitude change is to take place and to construct mechanisms by which such change is to occur. Decisions about the kind of activity which might be appropriate for a given manager are usually made by others above him or by specialists hired to make such decisions. Where he is to be rotated, how long he is to remain on a given assignment, or what kind of new training he should undertake is masterminded by others whose concern is "career development." In a sense, the individual stands alone against the institution where his own career is concerned, because the basic assumption is that the institution knows better than the individual what kind of man it needs or wants in its higher levels of management. The kind of influence model which is relevant, then, is one which considers the whole range of resources available to an organization.

In the remainder of this paper I will attempt to spell out these general themes by first presenting a conceptual model for analyzing influence, then providing some illustrations from a variety of organizational influence situations, and then testing its applicability to the management development situation.

A model of influence and change

Most theories of influence or change accept the premise that change does not occur unless the individual is *motivated* and *ready* to change. This statement implies that the individual must perceive some need for change in himself, must be able to change, and must perceive the influencing agent as one who can facilitate such change in a direction acceptable to the individual. A model of the influence process, then, must account for the development of the motivation to change as well as the actual mechanisms by which the change occurs.

It is usually assumed that pointing out to a person some of his areas of deficiency or some failure on his part in these areas is sufficient to induce in him a readiness to change and to accept the influencing agent's guidance or recommendations. This assumption may be tenable if one is dealing with deficiencies in intellectual skills or technical knowledge. The young manager can see, with some help from his superiors, that he needs a greater knowledge of economics or marketing or production methods and can accept the suggestion that spending a year in another department or six weeks at an advanced management course will give him the missing knowledge and/or skills.

When we are dealing with attitudes, however, the suggestion of deficiency or the need for change is much more likely to be perceived as a basic threat to the individual's sense of identity and to his status position vis-à-vis others in the organization. Attitudes are generally organized and integrated around the person's image of himself, and they result in stabilized, characteristic ways of dealing with others. The suggestion of the need for change not only implies some criticism of the person's image of himself but also threatens the stability of his working relationships because change at this level implies that the expectations which others have about him will be upset, thus requiring the development of new relationships. It is not at all uncommon for training programs in human relations to arouse resistance or to produce, at best, temporary change because the expectations of co-workers operate to keep the individual in his "normal" mold. Management development programs which ignore these psychological resistances to change are likely to be self-defeating, no matter how much attention is given to the actual presentation of the new desired attitudes.

Given these general assumptions about the integration of attitudes in the person, it is appropriate to consider influence as a process which occurs over time and which includes three phases:

1. *Unfreezing:*[3] an alteration of the forces acting on the individual, such that his stable equilibrium is disturbed sufficiently to motivate him and to make him ready to change; this can be accomplished either by increasing the pressure to change or by reducing some of the threats of resistance to change.

2. *Changing:* the presentation of a direction of change and the actual process of learning new attitudes. This process occurs basically by one of two mechanisms: *(a) identification*[4]—the person learns new attitudes by identifying with and emulating some other person who holds those attitudes or *(b) internalization*—the person learns new attitudes by being placed in a situation in which new attitudes are demanded of him as a way of solving problems which confront him and which he cannot avoid; he discovers the new attitudes essentially for himself, though the situation may guide him or make it probable that he will discover only those attitudes which the influencing agent wishes him to discover.

---

3. These phases of influence are a derivation of the change model developed by K. Lewin, "Frontiers in Group Dynamics: Concept, Method, and Reality in Social Science," *Human Relations* 1 (1957):5–42.

4. These mechanisms of attitude change are taken from H. C. Kelman, "Compliance, Identification, and Internalization: Three Processes of Attitude Change," *Conflict Resolution* 2 (1958):51–60.

3. *Refreezing:* the integration of the changed attitudes into the rest of the personality and/or into ongoing significant emotional relationships.

In proposing this kind of model of influence we are leaving out two important cases—the individual who changes because he is *forced* to change by the agent's direct manipulation of rewards and punishments (what Kelman calls "compliance") and the individual whose strong motivation to rise in the organizational hierarchy makes him eager to accept the attitudes and acquire the skills which he perceives to be necessary for advancement. I will ignore both of these cases for the same reason—they usually do not involve genuine, stable change but merely involve the adoption of overt behaviors which imply to others that attitudes have changed, even if they have not. In the case of compliance, the individual drops the overt behavior as soon as surveillance by the influence agent is removed. Among the upwardly mobile individuals, there are those who are willing to be unfrozen and to undergo genuine attitude change (whose case fits the model to be presented below) and those whose overt behavior change is dictated by their changing perception of what the environment will reward but whose underlying attitudes are never really changed or refrozen.

I do not wish to imply that a general reward-punishment model is incorrect or inappropriate for the analysis of attitude change. My purpose, rather, is to provide a more refined model in terms of which it becomes possible to specify the differential effects of various kinds of rewards and punishments, some of which have far more significance and impact than others. For example, as I will try to show, the rewarding effect of approval from an admired person is very different in its ultimate consequence from the rewarding effect of developing a personal solution to a difficult situation.

The processes of unfreezing, changing, and refreezing can be identified in a variety of different institutions in which they are manifested in varying degrees of intensity. The content of what may be taught in the influence process may vary widely from the values of communism to the religious doctrines of a nun, and the process of influence may vary drastically in its intensity. Nevertheless, there is value in taking as our frame of reference a model like that proposed and testing its utility in a variety of different organizational contexts, ranging from Communist "thought reform" centers to business enterprises' management development programs. Because the value system of the business enterprise and its role conception of the manager are not as clear-cut as the values and role prescriptions in various other institutions, one may expect the processes of unfreezing, changing, and refreezing to occur with less intensity and to be less consciously rationalized in the business enterprise. But they are structurally the same as in other organizations. One of the main purposes of this paper, then, will be to try to make salient some features of the influence of the organization on the attitudes of the individual manager by attempting to compare institutions in which the influence process is more drastic and explicit with the more implicit and less drastic methods of the business enterprise.

Illustrations of organizational influence

Unfreezing

The concept of unfreezing and the variety of methods by which influence targets can be unfrozen can best be illustrated by considering examples drawn from a broad range of situations. The Chinese Communists in their attempt to inculcate Communist attitudes into their youth or into their prisoners serve as a good prototype of one extreme. First and most important was the removal of the target person from those situations and social relationships which tended to confirm and reinforce the validity of the old attitudes. Thus the targets, be they political prisoners, prisoners of war, university professors, or young students, were isolated from their friends, families, and accustomed work groups and cut off from all media of communication to which they were accustomed. In addition, they were subjected to continuous exhortations (backed by threats of severe punishment) to confess their crimes and adopt new attitudes and were constantly humiliated in order to discredit their old sense of identity.

The isolation of the target from his normal social and ideological supports reached its height in the case of Western civilians who were placed into group cells with a number of Chinese prisoners who had already confessed and were committed to reforming themselves and their lone Western cell mate. In the prisoner of war camps such extreme social isolation could not be produced, but its counterpart was created by the fomenting of mutual mistrust among the prisoners, by cutting off any supportive mail from home, and by systematically disorganizing the formal and informal social structure of the POW camp (by segregation of officers and noncommissioned officers from the remainder of the group, by the systematic removal of informal leaders or key personalities, and by the prohibition of any group activity not in line with the indoctrination program).[5]

The Chinese did not hesitate to use physical brutality and threats of death and/or permanent nonrepatriation to enforce the view that only by collaboration and attitude change could the prisoner hope to survive physically and psychologically. In the case of the civilians in group cells, an additional and greater stress was represented by the social pressure of the cell mates who would harangue, insult, revile, humiliate, and plead with the resistant Westerner twenty-four hours a day for weeks or months on end, exhorting him to admit his guilt, confess his crimes, reform, and adopt Communist values. This combination of physical and social pressures is perhaps a prototype of the use of coercion in the service of unfreezing a target individual in attitude areas to which he is strongly committed.

5. E. H. Schein, *Brainwashing* (Cambridge, Mass.: Center for International Studies, M.I.T., 1961); and E. H. Schein, "Interpersonal Communication, Group Solidarity, and Social Influence," *Sociometry* 23:148–61.

A somewhat milder, though structurally similar, process can be observed in the training of a nun.[6] The novice enters the convent voluntarily and is presumably ready to change, but the kind of change which must be accomplished encounters strong psychological resistances because, again, it involves deeply held attitudes and habits. Thus the novice must learn to be completely unselfish and, in fact, selfless; she must adapt to a completely communal life; she must give up any source of authority except the absolute authority of God and of those senior to her in the convent; and she must learn to curb her sexual and aggressive impulses. How does the routine of the convent facilitate unfreezing? Again a key element is the removal of the novice from her accustomed routines, sources of confirmation, social supports, and old relationships. She is physically isolated from the outside world, surrounded by others who are undergoing the same training as she, subjected to a highly demanding and fatiguing physical regimen, constantly exhorted toward her new role and punished for any evidence of old behaviors and attitudes, and subjected to a whole range of social pressures ranging from mild disapproval to total humiliation for any failure.

Not only is the novice cut off from her social identity, but her entry into the convent separates her from many aspects of her physical identity. She is deprived of all means of being beautiful or even feminine; her hair is cut off and she is given institutional garb which emphasizes formlessness and sameness; she loses her old name and chronological age in favor of a new name and age corresponding to length of time in the convent; her living quarters and daily routine emphasize an absolute minimum of physical comfort and signify a total devaluation of anything related to the body. At the same time the threat associated with change is minimized by the tremendous support which the convent offers for change and by the fact that everyone else either already exhibits the appropriate attitudes or is in the process of learning them.

If we look at the process by which a pledge comes to be a full-fledged member of a fraternity, we find in this situation also a set of pressures to give up old associations and habits, a devaluation of the old self by humiliations ranging from menial, senseless jobs to paddling and hazing, a removal of threat through sharing of training, and support for good performance in the pledge role. The evangelist seeking to convert those who come to hear him attempts to unfreeze his audience by stimulating guilt and by devaluating their former selves as sinful and unworthy. The teacher wishing to induce motivation to learn sometimes points out deficiencies in the student's knowledge and hopes at the same time to induce some guilt for having those deficiencies.

Some of the elements which all unfreezing situations have in common

6. K. Hulme, *The Nun's Story* (Boston: Little, Brown, 1957).

are the following: (1) the physical removal of the influence target from his accustomed routines, sources of information, and social relationships; (2) the undermining and destruction of all social supports; (3) demeaning and humiliating experience to help the target see his old self as unworthy and thus to become motivated to change; and (4) the consistent linking of reward with willingness to change and of punishment with unwillingness to change.

Changing

Once the target has become motivated to change, the actual influence is most likely to occur by one of two processes. The target finds one or more models in his social environment and learns new attitudes by identifying with them and trying to become like them; or the target confronts new situations with an experimental attitude and develops for himself attitudes which are appropriate to the situation and which remove whatever problem he faces. These two processes—*identification* and *internalization*—probably tend to occur together in most concrete situations, but it is worthwhile, for analytical purposes, to keep them separate.[7]

The student or prisoner of the Chinese Communists took his basic step toward acquiring Communist attitudes when he began to identify with his more advanced fellow student or prisoner. In the group cell it was the discovery by the Western prisoner that his Chinese cell mates were humans like himself, were rational, and yet completely believed in their own and his guilt, which forced him to reexamine his own premises and bases of judgment and led him the first step down the path of acquiring the Communist point of view. In other words, he began to identify with his cell mates and to acquire their point of view as the only solution to getting out of prison and reducing the pressure on him. The environment was, of course, saturated with the Communist point of view, but it is significant that such saturation by itself was not sufficient to induce genuine attitude change. The prisoner kept in isolation and bombarded with propaganda was less likely to acquire Communist attitudes than the one placed into a group cell with more reformed prisoners. Having a personal model was apparently crucial.

In the convent the situation is essentially comparable except that the novice is initially much more disposed toward identifying with older nuns and has a model of appropriate behavior around her all the time in the actions of the others. It is interesting to note also that some nuns are singled out as particularly qualified models and given the appropriate name of "the living rule." It is also a common institution in initiation or indoctrination procedures to attach to the target individual someone who is labeled a

---

7. Both are facilitated greatly if the influence agent saturates the environment with the new message or attitude to be learned.

"buddy" or "big brother," whose responsibility it is to teach the novice "the ropes" and to communicate the kinds of attitudes expected of him.

In most kinds of training and teaching situations, and even in the sales relationship, it is an acknowledged fact that the process is facilitated greatly if the target can identify with the influence agent. Such identification is facilitated if the social distance and rank difference between agent and target are not too great. The influence agent has to be close enough to the target to be seen as similar to the target, yet must be himself committed to the attitudes he is trying to inculcate. Thus, in the case of the Chinese Communist group cell, the cell mates could be perceived as sharing a common situation with the Western prisoner and this perception facilitated his identification with them. In most buddy systems, the buddy is someone who has himself gone through the training program in the recent past. If the target is likely to mistrust the influence attempts of the organization, as might be the case in a management-sponsored training program for labor or in a therapy program for delinquents in a reformatory, it is even more important that the influence agent be perceived as similar to the target. Otherwise he is dismissed as a "company man" or one who has already sold out, and hence is seen as someone whose message or example is not to be taken seriously.

Internalization, the discovery of attitudes which are the target's own solutions to his perceived dilemmas, can occur at the same time as identification. The individual can use the example of others to guide him in solving his own problems without necessarily identifying with them to the point of complete imitation. His choice of attitude remains ultimately his own in terms of what works for him, given the situation in which he finds himself. Internalization is only possible in an organizational context in which, from the organization's point of view, a number of different kinds of attitudes will be tolerated. If there is a "party line," a company philosophy, or a given way in which people have to feel about things in order to get along, it is hardly an efficient procedure to let trainees discover their own solutions. Manipulating the situation in such a way as to make the official solution the only one which is acceptable can, of course, be attempted, but the hazards of creating real resentment and alienation on the part of the individual when he discovers he really had no choice may outweigh the presumed advantages of letting him think he had a choice.

In the case of the Chinese Communists, the convent, the revival meeting, the fraternity, or the institutional training program, we are dealing with situations in which the attitudes to be learned are clearly specified. In this kind of situation, internalization will not occur unless the attitudes to be learned happen to fit uniquely the kind of personal problem the individual has in the situation. For example, a few prisoners of the Communists reacted to the tremendous unfreezing pressures with genuine guilt when they discovered they held certain prejudices and attitudes (e.g., when they realized that they had looked down on lower-class Chinese in spite of their manifest acceptance of them). These prisoners were then able to internalize certain portions of the total complex of Communist attitudes, particularly those dealing with unselfishness and working for the greater good of others. The attitudes which the institution demanded of them also solved a personal problem of long standing for them. In the case of the nun, one might hypothesize that internalization of the convent's attitudes will occur to the extent that asceticism offers a genuine solution to the incumbent's personal conflicts.

Internalization is a more common outcome in those influence settings where the direction of change is left more to the individual. The influence which occurs in programs like Alcoholics Anonymous, in psychotherapy or counseling for hospitalized or incarcerated populations, in religious retreats, in human relations training of the kind pursued by the National Training Laboratories,[8] and in certain kinds of progressive education programs is more likely to occur through internalization or, at least, to lead ultimately to more internalization.

Refreezing

Refreezing refers to the process by which the newly acquired attitude comes to be integrated into the target's personality and ongoing relationships. If the new attitude has been internalized while being learned, this has automatically facilitated refreezing because it has been fitted naturally into the individual's personality. If it has been learned through identification, it will persist only so long as the target's relationship with the original influence model persists unless new surrogate models are found or social support and reinforcement is obtained for expressions of the new attitude.[9]

In the case of the convent such support comes from a whole set of expectations which others have of how the nun should behave, from clearly specified role prescriptions, and from rituals. In the case of individuals influenced by the Chinese Communists, if they remained in Communist China they received constant support for their new attitudes from superiors and peers; if they returned to the West, the permanence of their attitude change depended on the degree of support they actually received from friends and relations back home or from groups which they sought out in an attempt to get support. If their friends and relatives did not support Communist attitudes, the repatriates were influenced once again toward their original attitudes or toward some new integration of both sets.

8. National Training Laboratory in Group Development, *Explorations in Human Relations Training: An Assessment of Experience, 1947–53* (Washington, D.C.: National Education Association, 1953).

9. In either case the change may be essentially permanent, in that a relationship to a model or surrogate can last indefinitely. It is important to distinguish the two processes, however, because if one were to try to change the attitude, different strategies would be used depending upon how the attitude had been learned.

The importance of social support for new attitudes was demonstrated dramatically in the recent Billy Graham crusade in New York City. An informal survey of individuals who came forward when Graham called for converts indicated that only those individuals who were subsequently integrated into local churches maintained their faith. Similar kinds of findings have been repeatedly noted with respect to human relations training in industry. Changes which may occur during the training program do not last unless there is some social support for the new attitudes in the "back-home" situation.

The kind of model which has been discussed above might best be described by the term "coercive persuasion." The influence of an organization on an individual is coercive in the sense that he is usually forced into situations which are likely to unfreeze him, in which there are many overt and covert pressures to recognize in himself a need for change, and in which the supports for his old attitudes are in varying degrees coercively removed. It is coercive also to the degree that the new attitudes to be learned are relatively rigidly prescribed. The individual either learns them or leaves the organization (if he can). At the same time, the actual process by which new attitudes are learned can best be described as persuasion. In effect, the individual is forced into a situation in which he is likely to be influenced. The organization can be highly coercive in unfreezing its potential influence targets, yet be quite open about the direction of attitude change it will tolerate. In those cases where the direction of change is itself coerced (as contrasted with letting it occur through identification or internalization), it is highly unlikely that anything is accomplished other than surface behavioral change in the target. And such surface change will be abandoned the moment the coercive force of the change agent is lessened. If behavioral changes are coerced at the same time as other unfreezing operations are undertaken, actual influence can be facilitated if the individual finds himself having to learn attitudes to justify the kinds of behavior he has been forced to exhibit. The salesman may not have an attitude of cynicism toward his customers initially. If, however, he is forced by his boss to behave as if he felt cynical, he might develop real cynicism as a way of justifying his actual behavior.

Management development: Is it coercive persuasion?

Do the notions of coercive persuasion developed above fit the management development situation? Does the extent to which they do or do not fit such a model illuminate for us some of the implications of specific management development practices?

Unfreezing

It is reasonable to assume that the majority of managers who are being "developed" are not ready or able to change in the manner in which their organization might desire and therefore must be unfrozen before they can be influenced. They may be eager to change at a conscious motivation level, yet still be psychologically unprepared to give up certain attitudes and values in favor of untried, threatening new ones. I cannot support this assumption empirically, but the likelihood of its being valid is high because of a related fact which is empirically supportable. Most managers do not participate heavily in decisions which affect their careers, nor do they have a large voice in the kind of self-development in which they wish to participate. It is the manager's superior or a staff specialist in career development who makes the key decisions concerning his career.[10] If the individual manager is not trained from the outset to take responsibility for his own career and given a heavy voice in diagnosing his own needs for a change, it is unlikely that he will readily be able to appreciate someone else's diagnosis. It may be unclear to him what basically is wanted of him or, worse, the ambiguity of the demands put upon him combined with his own inability to control his career development is likely to arouse anxiety and insecurity which would cause even greater resistance to genuine self-assessment and attitude change.[11] He becomes preoccupied with promotion in the abstract and attempts to acquire at a surface level the traits which he thinks are necessary for advancement.

If the decisions made by the organization do not seem valid to the manager or, if the unfreezing process turns out to be quite painful to him, to what extent can he leave the situation? His future career, his financial security, and his social status within the business community all stand to suffer if he resists the decisions made for him. Perhaps the most coercive feature is simply the psychological pressure that what he is being asked to do is "for his own ultimate welfare." Elementary loyalty to his organization and to his managerial role demands that he accept with good grace whatever happens to him in the name of his own career development. In this sense, then, I believe that the business organization has coercive forces at its disposal which are used by it in a manner comparable to the uses made by other organizations.

Given the assumption that the manager who is to be developed needs to be unfrozen, and given that the organization has available coercive power to accomplish such unfreezing, what mechanisms does it actually use to unfreeze potential influence targets?

The elements essential to unfreezing are the removal of supports for the old attitudes, the saturation of the environment with the new attitudes to be acquired, a minimizing of threat, and a maximizing of support for any change in the right direction. In terms of this model it becomes immediately

10. T. M. Alfred, personal communication, 1960.
11. An even greater hazard, of course, is that the organization communicates to the manager that he is not expected to take responsibility for his own career at the same time that it is trying to teach him how to be able to take responsibility for important decisions!

apparent that training programs or other activities which are conducted in the organization at the place of work for a certain number of hours per day or week are far less likely to unfreeze and subsequently influence the participant than those programs which remove him for varying lengths of time from his regular work situation and normal social relationships.

Are appraisal interviews, used periodically to communicate to the manager his strengths, weaknesses, and areas for improvement, likely to unfreeze him? Probably not, because as long as the individual is caught up in his regular routine and is responding, probably quite unconsciously, to a whole set of expectations which others have about his behavior and attitudes, it is virtually impossible for him to hear, at a psychological level, what his deficiencies or areas needing change are. Even if he can appreciate what is being communicated to him at an intellectual level, it is unlikely that he can emotionally accept the need for change, and even if he can accept it emotionally, it is unlikely that he can produce change in himself in an environment which supports all of his old ways of functioning. This statement does not mean that the man's co-workers necessarily approve of the way he is operating or like the attitudes which he is exhibiting. They may want to see him change, but their very expectations concerning how he normally behaves operate as a constraint on him which makes attitude change difficult in that setting.

On the other hand, there are a variety of training activities which are used in management development which approximate more closely the conditions necessary for effective unfreezing. These would include programs offered at special training centers such as those maintained by IBM on Long Island and General Electric at Crotonville, New York; university-sponsored courses in management, liberal arts, and/or the social sciences; and, especially, workshops or laboratories in human relations such as those conducted at Arden House, New York, by the National Training Laboratories. Programs such as these remove the participant for some length of time from his normal routine, his regular job, and his social relationships (including his family, in most cases), thus providing a kind of moratorium during which he can take stock of himself and determine where he is going and where he wants to go.

The almost total isolation from the pressures of daily life in the business world which a mountain chateau such as Arden House provides for a two-week period is supplemented by other unfreezing forces. The de-emphasis on the kind of job or title the participant holds in his company and the informal dress remove some of the symbolic or status supports upon which we all rely. Sharing a room and bath facilities with a roommate requires more than the accustomed exposure of private spheres of life to others. The total involvement of the participant in the laboratory program leaves little room for reflection about the back-home situation. The climate of the laboratory communicates tremendous support for any efforts at self-examination and attempts as much as possible to reduce the threats inherent in change by emphasizing the value of experimentation, the low cost and risk of trying a new response in the protected environment of the lab, and the high gains to be derived from finding new behavior patterns and attitudes which might improve back-home performance. The content of the material presented in lectures and the kind of learning model which is used in the workshop facilitate self-examination, self-diagnosis based on usable feedback from other participants, and rational planning for change.[12]

The practice of rotating a manager from one kind of assignment to another over a period of years can have some of the same unfreezing effects and thus facilitate attitude change. Certainly his physical move from one setting to another removes many of the supports to his old attitudes, and in his new job the manager will have an opportunity to try new behaviors and become exposed to new attitudes. The practice of providing a moratorium in the form of a training program prior to assuming a new job would appear to maximize the gains from each approach, in that unfreezing would be maximally facilitated and change would most probably be lasting if the person did not go back to a situation in which his co-workers, superiors, and subordinates had stable expectations of how he should behave.

Another example of how unfreezing can be facilitated in the organizational context is the practice of temporarily reducing the formal rank and responsibilities of the manager by making him a trainee in a special program, or an apprentice on a special project, or an assistant to a high-ranking member of the company. Such temporary lowering of formal rank can reduce the anxiety associated with changing and at the same time serves officially to destroy the old status and identity of the individual because he could not ordinarily return to his old position once he had accepted the path offered by the training program. He would have to move either up or out of the organization to maintain his sense of self-esteem. Of course, if such a training program is perceived by the trainee as an indication of his failing rather than a step toward a higher position, his anxiety about himself would be too high to facilitate effective change on his part. In all of the illustrations of organizational influence we have presented above, change was defined as being a means of gaining status—acceptance into Communist society, status as a nun or fraternity brother, salvation, and so on. If participants come to training programs believing they are being punished, they typically do not learn much.

The above discussion is intended to highlight the fact that some management development practices do facilitate the unfreezing of the influence target but that such unfreezing is by no means automatic. Where programs fail, therefore, one of the first questions we must ask is whether they failed because they did not provide adequate conditions for unfreezing.

---

12. Although, as I will point out later, such effective unfreezing may lead to change which is not supported or considered desirable by the "back-home" organization.

Changing

Turning now to the problem of the mechanisms by which changes actually occur, we must confront the question of whether the organization has relatively rigid prescribed goals concerning the direction of attitude change it expects of the young manager or whether it is concerned with growth in the sense of providing increasing opportunities for the young manager to learn the attitudes appropriate to ever more challenging situations. It is undoubtedly true that most programs would claim growth as their goal, but the degree to which they accomplish it can only be assessed from an examination of their actual practice.

Basically the question is whether the organization influences attitudes primarily through the mechanism of identification or the mechanism of internalization. If the development programs stimulate psychological relationships between the influence target and a member of the organization who has the desired attitudes, they are thereby facilitating influence by identification but, at the same time, are limiting the alternatives available to the target and possibly the permanence of the change achieved. If they emphasize that the target must develop his own solutions to ever more demanding problems, they are risking that the attitudes learned will be incompatible with other parts of the organization's value system but are producing more permanent change because the solutions found are internalized. From the organization's point of view, therefore, it is crucial to know what kind of influence it is exerting and to assess the results of such influence in terms of the basic goals which the organization may have. If new approaches and new attitudes toward management problems are desired, for example, it is crucial that the conditions for internalization be created. If rapid learning of a given set of attitudes is desired, it is equally crucial that the conditions for identification with the right kind of models be created.

One obvious implication of this distinction is that programs conducted within the organization's orbit by its own influence agents are much more likely to facilitate identification and thereby the transmission of the "party line" or organization philosophy. On the other hand, programs like those conducted at universities or by the National Training Laboratories place much more emphasis on the finding of solutions by participants which fit their own particular needs and problems. The emphasis in the human relations courses is on "learning how to learn" from the participant's own interpersonal experiences and how to harness his emotional life and intellectual capacities to the accomplishment of his goals rather than on specific principles of human relations. The nearest thing to an attitude which the laboratory staff, acting as influence agents, does care to communicate is an attitude of inquiry and experimentation, and to this end the learning of skills of observation, analysis, and diagnosis of interpersonal situations is given strong emphasis. The training group, which is the acknowledged core of the laboratory approach, provides its own unfreezing forces by being unstructured as to the content of discussion. But it is strongly committed to a method of learning by analysis of the member's own experiences in the group, which facilitates the discovery of the value of an attitude of inquiry and experimentation.

Mutual identification of the members of the group with each other and member identifications with the staff play some role in the acquisition of this attitude, but the basic power of the method is that the attitude of inquiry and experimentation *works* in the sense of providing for people valuable new insights about themselves, groups, and organizations. To the extent that it works and solves key problems for the participants, it is internalized and carried back into the home situation. To the extent that it is learned because participants wish to emulate a respected fellow member or staff member, it lasts only so long as the relationship with the model itself, or a surrogate of it, lasts (which may, of course, be a very long time).

The university program in management or liberal arts is more difficult to categorize in terms of an influence model, because within the program there are usually opportunities both for identification (e.g., with inspiring teachers) and internalization. It is a safe guess in either case, however, that the attitudes learned are likely to be in varying degrees out of phase with any given company's philosophy unless the company has learned from previous experience with a given course that the students are taught a point of view consistent with its own philosophy. Of course, universities, as much as laboratories, emphasize the value of a spirit of inquiry and, to the extent that they are successful in teaching this attitude, will be creating potential dissidents or innovators, depending on how the home company views the result.

Apprenticeships, special jobs in the role of "assistant to" somebody, job rotation, junior management boards, and so on stand in sharp contrast to the above methods in the degree to which they facilitate, indeed almost demand, that the young manager learn by watching those who are senior or more competent. It is probably not prescribed that in the process of acquiring knowledge and skills through the example of others he should also acquire their attitudes, but the probability that this will happen is very high, if the trainee develops any degree of respect and liking for his teacher and/or supervisor. It makes little difference whether the teacher, coach, or supervisor intends to influence the attitudes of his trainee or not. If a good emotional relationship develops between them, it will facilitate the learning of knowledge and skills, and will, at the same time, result in some degree of attitude change. Consequently, such methods do not maximize the probability of new approaches being invented to management problems, nor do they really by themselves facilitate the growth of the manager in the sense of providing opportunities for him to develop solutions which fit his own needs best.

Job rotation, on the other hand, can facilitate growth and innovation provided it is managed in such a way as to insure the exposure of the trainee to a broad range of points of view as he moved from assignment to assignment. The practice of shifting the developing manager geographically as well as functionally both facilitates unfreezing and increases the likelihood of his being exposed to new attitudes. This same practice can, of course, be merely a convenient way of indoctrinating the individual by sending him on an assignment, for example, "in order to acquire the sales point of view from Jim down in New York," where higher management knows perfectly well what sort of a view Jim will communicate to his subordinates.

Refreezing

Finally, a few words are in order about the problem of refreezing. Under what conditions will changed attitudes remain stable, and how do existing practices aid or hinder such stabilization? Our illustrations from the non-industrial setting highlighted the importance of social support for any attitudes which were learned through identification. Even the kind of training emphasized in the National Training Laboratories programs, which tends to be more internalized, does not produce stable attitude change unless others in the organization, especially superiors, peers, and subordinates, have undergone similar changes and give each other stimulation and support, because lack of support acts as a new unfreezing force producing new influence (possibly in the direction of the original attitudes).

If the young manager has been influenced primarily in the direction of what is already the company philosophy, he will, of course, obtain strong support and will have little difficulty maintaining his new attitudes. If, on the other hand, management development is supposed to lead to personal growth and organizational innovation, the organization must recognize the reality that new attitudes cannot be carried by isolated individuals. The lament that we no longer have strong individualists who are willing to try something new is a fallacy based on an incorrect diagnosis. Strong individuals have always gained a certain amount of their strength from the support of others, hence the organizational problem is how to create conditions which make possible the nurturing of new ideas, attitudes, and approaches. If organizations seem to lack innovators, it may be that the climate of the organization and its methods of management development do not foster innovation, not that its human resources are inadequate.

An organizational climate in which new attitudes which differ from company philosophy can nevertheless be maintained cannot be achieved merely by an intellectual or even emotional commitment on the part of higher-ranking managers to tolerance of new ideas and attitudes. Genuine support can come only from others who have themselves been influenced, which argues strongly that at least several members of a given department must be given the same training before such training can be expected to have effect. If the superior of the people involved can participate in it as well, this strengthens the group that much more, but it would not follow from my line of reasoning that this is a necessary condition. Only some support is needed, and this support can come as well from peers and subordinates.

From this point of view, the practice of sending more than one manager to any given program at a university or human relations workshop is very sound. The National Training Laboratories have emphasized from the beginning the desirability of having organizations send teams. Some organizations like Esso Standard have created their own laboratories for the training of the entire management complement of a given refinery, and all indications are that such a practice maximizes the possibility not only of the personal growth of the managers, but of the creative growth of the organization as a whole.

Conclusion

In the above discussion I have deliberately focused on a model influence which emphasizes procedure rather than content, interpersonal relations rather than mass media, and attitudes and values rather than knowledge and skills. By placing management development into a context of institutional influence procedures which also include Chinese Communist thought reform, the training of a nun, and other more drastic forms of coercive persuasion, I have tried to highlight aspects of management development which have remained implicit yet which need to be understood. I believe that some aspects of management development are a mild form of coercive persuasion, but I do not believe that coercive persuasion is either morally bad in any a priori sense or inefficient. If we are to develop a sound theory of career development which is capable of including not only many of the formal procedures discussed in this paper but the multitudes of informal practices, some of which are more and some of which are less coercive than those discussed, we need to suspend moral judgments for the time being and evaluate influence models solely in terms of their capacity to make sense of the data and to make meaningful predictions.

Groupthink
Irving L. Janis

"How could we have been so stupid?" President John F. Kennedy asked after he and a close group of advisers had blundered into the Bay of Pigs invasion. For the last two years I have been studying that question, as it applies not only to the Bay of Pigs decision-makers but also to those who led the United States into such other major fiascos as the failure to be prepared for the attack on Pearl Harbor, the Korean War stalemate, and the escalation of the Vietnam War.

Stupidity certainly is not the explanation. The men who participated in making the Bay of Pigs decision, for instance, comprised one of the greatest arrays of intellectual talent in the history of American government— Dean Rusk, Robert McNamara, Douglas Dillon, Robert Kennedy, McGeorge Bundy, Arthur Schlesinger, Jr., Allen Dulles, and others.

It also seemed to me that explanations were incomplete if they concentrated only on disturbances in the behavior of each individual within a decision-making body: temporary emotional states of elation, fear, or anger that reduce a man's mental efficiency, for example, or chronic blind spots arising from a man's social prejudices or idiosyncratic biases.

I preferred to broaden the picture by looking at the fiascos from the standpoint of group dynamics as it has been explored over the past three decades, first by the great social psychologist Kurt Lewin and later in many experimental situations by myself and other behavioral scientists. My conclusion after poring over hundreds of relevant documents—historical reports about formal group meetings and informal conversations among the members—is that the groups that committed the fiascos were victims of what I call "groupthink."

"Groupy"

In each case study, I was surprised to discover the extent to which each group displayed the typical phenomena of social conformity that are regu-

Reprinted with permission from *Psychology Today Magazine*, November 1971. © 1971 American Psychological Association.

larly encountered in studies of group dynamics among ordinary citizens. For example, some of the phenomena appear to be completely in line with findings from social-psychological experiments showing that powerful social pressures are brought to bear by the members of a cohesive group whenever a dissident begins to voice his objections to a group consensus. Other phenomena are reminiscent of the shared illusions observed in encounter groups and friendship cliques when the members simultaneously reach a peak of "groupy" feelings.

Above all, there are numerous indications pointing to the development of group norms that bolster morale at the expense of critical thinking. One of the most common norms appears to be that of remaining loyal to the group by sticking with the policies to which the group has already committed itself, even when those policies are obviously working out badly and have unintended consequences that disturb the conscience of each member. This is one of the key characteristics of groupthink.

1984

I use the term groupthink as a quick and easy way to refer to the mode of thinking that persons engage in when *concurrence-seeking* becomes so dominant in a cohesive ingroup that it tends to override realistic appraisal of alternative courses of action. Groupthink is a term of the same order as the words in the Newspeak vocabulary George Orwell used in his dismaying world of *1984*. In that context, groupthink takes on an invidious connotation. Exactly such a connotation is intended, since the term refers to a deterioration in mental efficiency, reality testing, and moral judgments as a result of group pressures.

The symptoms of groupthink arise when the members of decision-making groups become motivated to avoid being too harsh in their judgments of their leaders' or their colleagues' ideas. They adopt a soft line of criticism, even in their own thinking. At their meetings, all the members are amiable and seek complete concurrence on every important issue, with no bickering or conflict to spoil the cozy, "we-feeling" atmosphere.

Kill

Paradoxically, soft-headed groups are often hard-hearted when it comes to dealing with outgroups or enemies. They find it relatively easy to resort to dehumanizing solutions—they will readily authorize bombing attacks that kill large numbers of civilians in the name of the noble cause of persuading an unfriendly government to negotiate at the peace table. They are unlikely to pursue the more difficult and controversial issues that arise when alternatives to a harsh military solution come up for discussion. Nor are they inclined to raise ethical issues that carry the implication that *this fine group of ours, with its humanitarianism and its high-minded principles, might be capable of adopting a course of action that is inhumane and immoral.*

Norms

There is evidence from a number of social-psychological studies that as the members of a group feel more accepted by the others, which is a central feature of increased group cohesiveness, they display less overt conformity to group norms. Thus we would expect that the more cohesive a group becomes, the less the members will feel constrained to censor what they say out of fear of being socially punished for antagonizing the leader or any of their fellow members.

In contrast, the groupthink type of conformity tends to increase as group cohesiveness increases. Groupthink involves nondeliberate suppression of critical thoughts as a result of internalization of the group's norms, which is quite different from deliberate suppression on the basis of external threats of social punishment. The more cohesive the group, the greater the inner compulsion on the part of each member to avoid creating disunity, which inclines him to believe in the soundness of whatever proposals are promoted by the leader or by a majority of the group's members.

In a cohesive group, the danger is not so much that each individual will fail to receive his objections to what the others propose but that he will think the proposal is a good one, without attempting to carry out a careful, critical scrutiny of the pros and cons of the alternatives. When groupthink becomes dominant, there also is considerable suppression of deviant thoughts, but it takes the form of each person's deciding that his misgivings are not relevant and should be set aside, that the benefit of the doubt regarding any lingering uncertainties should be given to the group consensus.

Stress

I do not mean to imply that all cohesive groups necessarily suffer from groupthink. All ingroups may have a mild tendency toward groupthink, displaying one or another of the symptoms from time to time, but it need not be so dominant as to influence the quality of the group's final decision. Neither do I mean to imply that there is anything necessarily inefficient or harmful about group decisions in general. On the contrary, a group whose members have properly defined roles, with traditions concerning the procedures to follow in pursuing a critical inquiry, probably is capable of making better decisions than any individual group member working alone.

The problem is that the advantages of having decisions made by groups are often lost because of powerful psychological pressures that arise when the members work closely together, share the same set of values and, above all, face a crisis situation that puts everyone under intense stress.

The main principle of groupthink, which I offer in the spirit of Parkinson's Law, is this: *The more amiability and esprit de corps there is among the members of a policy-making ingroup, the greater the danger that independent critical thinking will be replaced by groupthink, which is likely to result in irrational and dehumanizing actions directed against outgroups.*

Symptoms

In my studies of high-level governmental decision-makers, both civilian and military, I have found eight main symptoms of groupthink.

Invulnerability

Most or all of the members of the ingroup share an *illusion* of invulnerability that provides for them some degree of reassurance about obvious dangers and leads them to become over-optimistic and willing to take extraordinary risks. It also causes them to fail to respond to clear warnings of danger.

The Kennedy ingroup, which uncritically accepted the Central Intelligence Agency's disastrous Bay of Pigs plan, operated on the false assumption that they could keep secret the fact that the United States was responsible for the invasion of Cuba. Even after news of the plan began to leak out, their belief remained unshaken. They failed even to consider the danger that awaited them: a worldwide revulsion against the United States.

A similar attitude appeared among the members of President Lyndon B. Johnson's ingroup, the "Tuesday Cabinet," which kept escalating the Vietnam War despite repeated setbacks and failures. "There was a belief," Bill Moyers commented after he resigned, "that if we indicated a willingness to use our power, they [the North Vietnamese] would get the message and back away from an all-out confrontation. . . . There was a confidence—it was never bragged about, it was just there—that when the chips were really down, the other people would fold."

A most poignant example of an illusion of invulnerability involves the ingroup around Admiral H. E. Kimmel, which failed to prepare for the possibility of a Japanese attack on Pearl Harbor despite repeated warnings. Informed by his intelligence chief that radio contact with Japanese aircraft carriers had been lost, Kimmel joked about it: "What, you don't know where the carriers are? Do you mean to say that they could be rounding Diamond Head (at Honolulu) and you wouldn't know it?" The carriers were in fact moving full-steam toward Kimmel's command post at the time. Laughing together about a danger signal, which labels it as a purely laughing matter, is a characteristic manifestation of groupthink.

Rationale

As we see, victims of groupthink ignore warnings; they also collectively construct rationalizations in order to discount warnings and other forms of negative feedback that, taken seriously, might lead the group members to reconsider their assumptions each time they recommit themselves to past decisions. Why did the Johnson ingroup avoid reconsidering its escalation policy when time and again the expectations on which they based their decisions turned out to be wrong? James C. Thompson, Jr., a Harvard historian who spent five years as an observing participant in both the State

Department and the White House, tells us that the policymakers avoided critical discussion of their prior decisions and continually invented new rationalizations so that they could sincerely recommit themselves to defeating the North Vietnamese.

In the fall of 1964, before the bombing of North Vietnam began, some of the policymakers predicted that six weeks of air strikes would induce the North Vietnamese to seek peace talks. When someone asked, "What if they don't?" the answer was that another four weeks certainly would do the trick.

Later, after each setback, the ingroup agreed that by investing just a bit more effort (by stepping up the bomb tonnage a bit, for instance), their course of action would prove to be right. *The Pentagon Papers* bears out these observations.

In *The Limits of Intervention,* Townsend Hoopes, who was acting Secretary of the Air Force under Johnson, says that Walt W. Rostow in particular showed a remarkable capacity for what has been called "instant rationalization." According to Hoopes, Rostow buttressed the group's optimism about being on the road to victory by culling selected scraps of evidence from news reports or, if necessary, by inventing "plausible" forecasts that had no basis in evidence at all.

Admiral Kimmel's group rationalized away their warnings, too. Right up to December 7, 1941, they convinced themselves that the Japanese would never dare attempt a full-scale surprise assault against Hawaii because Japan's leaders would realize that it would precipitate an all-out war which the United States would surely win. They made no attempt to look at the situation through the eyes of the Japanese leaders—another manifestation of groupthink.

Morality

Victims of groupthink believe unquestioningly in the inherent morality of their ingroup; this belief inclines the members to ignore the ethical or moral consequences of their decisions.

Evidence that this symptom is at work usually is of a negative kind—the things that are left unsaid in group meetings. At least two influential persons had doubts about the morality of the Bay of Pigs adventure. One of them, Arthur Schlesinger, Jr., presented his strong objections in a memorandum to President Kennedy and Secretary of State Rusk but suppressed them when he attended meetings of the Kennedy team. The other, Senator J. William Fulbright, was not a member of the group, but the president invited him to express his misgivings in a speech to the policymakers. However, when Fulbright finished speaking the president moved on to other agenda items without asking for reactions of the group.

David Kraslow and Stuart H. Loory, in *The Secret Search for Peace in Vietnam,* report that during 1966 President Johnson's ingroup was concerned primarily with selecting bomb targets in North Vietnam. They based their selections on four factors—the military advantage, the risk to American aircraft and pilots, the danger of forcing other countries into the fighting, and the danger of heavy civilian casualties. At their regular Tuesday luncheons, they weighed these factors the way schoolteachers grade examination papers, averaging them out. Though evidence on this point is scant, I suspect that the group's ritualistic adherence to a standardized procedure induced the members to feel morally justified in their destructive way of dealing with the Vietnamese people—after all, the danger of heavy civilian casualties from U.S. air strikes was taken into account on their checklists.

Stereotypes

Victims of groupthink hold stereotyped views of the leaders of enemy groups: they are so evil that genuine attempts at negotiating differences with them are unwarranted, or they are too weak or too stupid to deal effectively with whatever attempts the ingroup makes to defeat their purposes, no matter how risky the attempts are.

Kennedy's groupthinkers believed that Premier Fidel Castro's air force was so ineffectual that obsolete B-26s could knock it out completely in a surprise attack before the invasion began. They also believed that Castro's army was so weak that a small Cuban-exile brigade could establish a well-protected beachhead at the Bay of Pigs. In addition, they believed that Castro was not smart enough to put down any possible internal uprisings in support of the exiles. They were wrong on all three assumptions. Though much of the blame was attributable to faulty intelligence, the point is that none of Kennedy's advisers even questioned the CIA planners about these assumptions.

The Johnson advisers' sloganistic thinking about "the Communist apparatus" that was "working all around the world" (as Dean Rusk put it) led them to overlook the powerful nationalistic strivings of the North Vietnamese government and its efforts to ward off Chinese domination. The crudest of all stereotypes used by Johnson's inner circle to justify their policies was the domino theory ("If we don't stop the Reds in South Vietnam, tomorrow they will be in Hawaii and the next week they will be in San Francisco," Johnson once said). The group so firmly accepted this stereotype that it became almost impossible for any adviser to introduce a more sophisticated viewpoint.

In the documents of Pearl Harbor, it is clear to see that the navy commanders stationed in Hawaii had a naive image of Japan as a midget that would not dare to strike a blow against a powerful giant.

Pressure

Victims of groupthink apply direct pressure to any individual who momentarily expresses doubts about any of the group's shared illusions or who questions the validity of the arguments supporting a policy alternative favored by the majority. This gambit reinforces the concurrence-seeking norm that loyal members are expected to maintain.

President Kennedy probably was more active than anyone else in raising skeptical questions during the Bay of Pigs meetings, and yet he seems to have encouraged the group's docile, uncritical acceptance of defective arguments in favor of the CIA's plan. At every meeting, he allowed the CIA representatives to dominate the discussion. He permitted them to give their immediate refutations in response to each tentative doubt that one of the others expressed, instead of asking whether anyone shared the doubt or wanted to pursue the implications of the new worrisome issue that had just been raised. And at the most crucial meeting, when he was calling on each member to give his vote for or against the plan, he did not call on Arthur Schlesinger, the one man there who was known by the president to have serious misgivings.

Historian Thompson informs us that whenever a member of Johnson's ingroup began to express doubts, the group used subtle social pressures to "domesticate" him. To start with, the dissenter was made to feel at home, provided that he lived up to two restrictions: (1) that he did not voice his doubts to outsiders, which would play into the hands of the opposition; and (2) that he kept his criticisms within the bounds of acceptable deviation, which meant not challenging any of the fundamental assumptions that went into the group's prior commitments. One such "domesticated dissenter" was Bill Moyers. When Moyers arrived at a meeting, Thompson tells us, the president greeted him with, "Well, here comes Mr. Stop-the-Bombing."

Self-censorship

Victims of groupthink avoid deviating from what appears to be group consensus; they keep silent about their misgivings and even minimize to themselves the importance of their doubts.

As we have seen, Schlesinger was not all hesitant about presenting his strong objections to the Bay of Pigs plan in a memorandum to the president and the secretary of state. But he became keenly aware of his tendency to suppress objections at the White House meetings. "In the months after the Bay of Pigs I bitterly reproached myself for having kept so silent during those crucial discussions in the cabinet room," Schlesinger writes in *A Thousand Days*. "I can only explain my failure to do more than raise a few timid questions by reporting that one's impulse to blow the whistle on this nonsense was simply undone by the circumstances of the discussion."

Unanimity

Victims of groupthink share an *illusion* of unanimity within the group concerning almost all judgments expressed by members who speak in favor of the majority view. This symptom results partly from the preceding one, whose effects are augmented by the false assumption that any individual who remains silent during any part of the discussion is in full accord with what the others are saying.

When a group of persons who respect each other's opinions arrives at a unanimous view, each member is likely to feel that the belief must be true. This reliance on consensual validation within the group tends to replace individual critical thinking and reality testing, unless there are clear-cut disagreements among the members. In contemplating a course of action such as the invasion of Cuba, it is painful for the members to confront disagreements within their group, particularly if it becomes apparent that there are widely divergent views about whether the preferred course of action is too risky to undertake at all. Such disagreements are likely to arouse anxieties about making a serious error. Once the sense of unanimity is shattered, the members no longer can feel complacently confident about the decision they are inclined to make. Each man must then face the annoying realization that there are troublesome uncertainties and he must diligently seek out the best information he can get in order to decide for himself exactly how serious the risks might be. This is one of the unpleasant consequences of being in a group of hardhearted, critical thinkers.

To avoid such an unpleasant state, the members often become inclined, without quite realizing it, to prevent latent disagreements from surfacing when they are about to initiate a risky course of action. The group leader and the members support each other in playing up the areas of convergence in their thinking, at the expense of fully exploring divergencies that might reveal unsettled issues.

"Our meetings took place in a curious atmosphere of assumed consensus," Schlesinger writes. His additional comments clearly show that, curiously, the consensus was an illusion—an illusion that could be maintained only because the major participants did not reveal their own reasoning or discuss their idiosyncratic assumptions and vague reservations. Evidence from several sources makes it clear that even the three principals—President Kennedy, Rusk, and McNamara—had widely differing assumptions about the invasion plan.

Mindguards

Victims of groupthink sometimes appoint themselves as mindguards to protect the leader and fellow members from adverse information that might break the complacency they shared about the effectiveness and morality of past decisions. At a large birthday party for his wife, Attorney General Robert F. Kennedy, who had been constantly informed about the Cuban invasion plan, took Schlesinger aside and asked him why he was opposed. Kennedy listened coldly and said, "You may be right or you may be wrong, but the president has made his mind up. Don't push it any further. Now is the time for everyone to help him all they can."

Rusk also functioned as a highly effective mindguard by failing to transmit to the group the strong objections of three "outsiders" who had learned of the invasion plan—Undersecretary of State Chester Bowles, USIA Director Edward R. Murrow, and Rusk's intelligence chief, Roger Hilsman. Had Rusk done so, their warnings might have reinforced Schlesinger's memorandum and jolted some of Kennedy's ingroup, if not the president himself, into reconsidering the decision.

Products

When a group of executives frequently displays most or all of these interrelated symptoms, a detailed study of their deliberations is likely to reveal a number of immediate consequences. These consequences are, in effect, products of poor decision-making practices because they lead to inadequate solutions to the problems under discussion.

First, the group limits its discussions to a few alternative courses of action (often only two) without an initial survey of all the alternatives that might be worthy of consideration.

Second, the group fails to reexamine the course of action initially preferred by the majority after they learn of risks and drawbacks they had not considered originally.

Third, the members spend little or no time discussing whether there are nonobvious gains they may have overlooked or ways of reducing the seemingly prohibitive costs that made rejected alternatives appear undesirable to them.

Fourth, members make little or no attempt to obtain information from experts within their own organizations who might be able to supply more precise estimates of potential losses and gains.

Fifth, members show positive interest in facts and opinions that support their preferred policy; they tend to ignore facts and opinions that do not.

Sixth, members spend little time deliberating about how the chosen policy might be hindered by bureaucratic inertia, sabotaged by political opponents, or temporarily derailed by common accidents. Consequently, they fail to work out contingency plans to cope with foreseeable setbacks that could endanger the overall success of their chosen course.

Support

The search for an explanation of why groupthink occurs has led me through a quagmire of complicated theoretical issues in the murky area of human motivation. My belief, based on recent social psychological research, is that we can best understand the various symptoms of groupthink as a mutual effort among the group members to maintain self-esteem and emotional equanimity by providing social support to each other, especially at times when they share responsibility for making vital decisions.

Even when no important decision is pending, the typical administrator will begin to doubt the wisdom and morality of his past decisions each time he receives information about setbacks, particularly if the information is accompanied by negative feedback from prominent men who originally had been his supporters. It should not be surprising, therefore, to find that individual members strive to develop unanimity and esprit de corps that will help bolster each other's morale, to create an optimistic outlook about the success of pending decisions, and to reaffirm the positive value of past policies to which all of them are committed.

Pride

Shared illusions of invulnerability, for example, can reduce anxiety about taking risks. Rationalizations help members believe that the risks are really not so bad after all. The assumption of inherent morality helps the members to avoid feelings of shame or guilt. Negative stereotypes function as stress-reducing devices to enhance a sense of moral righteousness as well as pride in a lofty mission.

The mutual enhancement of self-esteem and morale may have functional value in enabling the members to maintain their capacity to take action, but it has maladaptive consequences insofar as concurrence-seeking tendencies interfere with critical, rational capacities and lead to serious errors of judgment.

While I have limited my study to decision-making bodies in government, groupthink symptoms appear in business, industry, and any other field where small, cohesive groups make the decisions. It is vital, then, for all sorts of people—and especially group leaders—to know what steps they can take to prevent groupthink.

Remedies

To counterpoint my case studies of the major fiascos, I have also investigated two highly successful group enterprises, the formulation of the Marshall Plan in the Truman administration and the handling of the Cuban missile crisis by President Kennedy and his advisers. I have found it instructive to examine the steps Kennedy took to change his group's decision-making processes. These changes ensured that the mistakes made by his Bay of Pigs ingroup were not repeated by the missile-crisis ingroup, even though the membership of both groups was essentially the same.

The following recommendations for preventing groupthink incorporate many of the good practices I discovered to be characteristic of the Marshall Plan and missile-crisis groups:

1. The leader of a policy-forming group should assign the role of critical evaluator to each member, encouraging the group to give high priority to open airing of objections and doubts. This practice needs to be reinforced by the leader's acceptance of criticism of his own judgments in order to

discourage members from soft-pedaling their disagreements and from allowing their striving for concurrence to inhibit critical thinking.

2. When the key members of a hierarchy assign a policy-planning mission to any group within their organization, they should adopt an impartial stance instead of stating preferences and expectations at the beginning. This will encourage open inquiry and impartial probing of a wide range of policy alternatives.

3. The organization routinely should set up several outside policy-planning and evaluation groups to work on the same policy question, each deliberating under a different leader. This can prevent the insulation of an ingroup.

4. At intervals before the group reaches a final consensus, the leader should require each member to discuss the group's deliberations with associates in his own unit of the organization—assuming that those associates can be trusted to adhere to the same security regulations that govern the policymakers—and then to report back their reactions to the group.

5. The group should invite one or more outside experts to each meeting on a staggered basis and encourage the experts to challenge the views of the core members.

6. At every general meeting of the group, whenever the agenda calls for an evaluation of policy alternatives, at least one member should play devil's advocate, functioning as a good lawyer in challenging the testimony of those who advocate the majority position.

7. Whenever the policy issue involves relations with a rival nation or organization, the group should devote a sizable block of time, perhaps an entire session, to a survey of all warning signals from the rivals and should write alternative scenarios on the rivals' intentions.

8. When the group is surveying policy alternatives for feasibility and effectiveness, it should from time to time divide into two or more subgroups to meet separately, under different chairmen, and then come back together to hammer out differences.

9. After reaching a preliminary consensus about what seems to be the best policy, the group should hold a "second-chance" meeting at which every member expresses as vividly as he can all his residual doubts, and rethinks the entire issue before making a definitive choice.

How

These recommendations have their disadvantages. To encourage the open airing of objections, for instance, might lead to prolonged and costly debates when a rapidly growing crisis requires immediate solution. It also could cause rejection, depression, and anger. A leader's failure to set a norm might create cleavage between leader and members that could develop into a disruptive power struggle if the leader looks on the emerging consensus as anathema. Setting up outside evaluation groups might increase the risk of security leakage. Still, inventive executives who know their way around the organizational maze probably can figure out how to apply one or another of the prescriptions successfully, without harmful side effects.

They also could benefit from the advice of outside experts in the administrative and behavioral sciences. Though these experts have much to offer, they have had few chances to work on policy-making machinery within large organizations. As matters now stand, executives innovate only when they need new procedures to avoid repeating serious errors that have deflated their self-images.

In this era of atomic warheads, urban disorganization, and ecocatastrophes, it seems to me that policymakers should collaborate with behavioral scientists and give top priority to preventing groupthink and its attendant fiascos.

An Intergroup Perspective on Individual Behavior
Kenwyn K. Smith

The history of psychology has been filled with attempts to understand the behavior of people either in terms of their personality, or as an interaction of individual and environmental characteristics (Lewin 1947). In the latter case, the environment has been conceptualized at many levels, ranging from global influences of the culture at large to specific properties of the groups of which individuals are members. Although a great deal of attention has been given to group influences on individuals' beliefs, values, perceptions, and behaviors (Hackman 1976), to date the impact on individuals of forces generated by relationships *between* groups has been largely unexplored.

Since there now exists an expanding body of knowledge about intergroup processes (Sherif 1962; Rice 1969; Levine and Campbell 1972; Lorsch and Lawrence 1972; Smith 1974; Alderfer 1977; Alderfer, Brown, Kaplan, and Smith, in press), our concept of individual behavior can be significantly augmented by including this aspect of the social environment as a determinant of how people behave.

In this paper I explore the proposition that, when intergroup situations exist, *behavior can be viewed primarily as an enactment of the forces those intergroup processes generate.* This is not to claim that individual or group interpretations of the same behaviors have no validity. Rather, it is simply an assertion that if an analysis is made at an intergroup level, a substantial proportion of the variation in individual behavior is explainable in terms of the intergroup dynamics. I propose that intergroup processes: (1) color profoundly our perceptions of the world, and may play a critical role in determining how we construct our personal sense of reality; (2) help define our individual identities; and (3) contribute significantly to the emergence of behavior patterns that we traditionally label as leadership.

I wish to gratefully acknowledge the critiques offered by J. L. Suttle, E. J. Woodhouse, and C. P. Alderfer on an earlier version of this paper. The ideas introduced here have been developed and elaborated in K. K. Smith, *Groups in Conflict* (Dubuque, Iowa: Kendall/Hunt, 1982) and K. K. Smith and D. N. Berg, *Paradoxes of Group Life* (San Francisco: Jossey-Bass, 1987). © 1977 by K. K. Smith. Used with permission.

Each of these assertions will be explored and illustrated by examining salient data from three very different social systems: (1) the experiences of a high school principal, and the way his personal sense of reality has been influenced by the various intergroup forces in his school system; (2) the development of the individual identity of a "village lunatic" in an experiential laboratory; and (3) the repeated changes of leadership behaviors in a group of survivors from an aircraft crash.

The intergroup as a determiner of an individual's perceptions of reality

It has long been recognized that people in different groups often perceive and understand the same event in radically different ways, particularly when there is an "ingroup" and an "outgroup." In such cases, one group usually will perceive an event in highly favorable terms, while the other sees the same event in an entirely derogatory manner. This phenomenon, referred to as "ethnocentrism" by Levine and Campbell (1972), is so powerful that group members may be unable to develop a view of reality that is independent of the group they belong to. The phenomenon becomes additionally potent when a person is caught in the context of multiple intergroups that involve interlocking sequences of events across time, and when the groups exist in a hierarchy of power relationships. Under these circumstances, the way one constructs his or her sense of reality may be almost completely determined by the interplay of intergroup processes.

Smith (1974) illustrates such a situation in his description of how Lewis Brook, principal of the high school in Ashgrove (New England), constructed his sense of what was taking place within the school system. Brook's perspectives changed dramatically from moment to moment, and these changes often were related directly to changes in his relative position in the power hierarchy of intergroup relationships.

For example, on one occasion Principal Brook was vociferously berating the superintendent, his superior, for something the superintendent had recently "done to" him. Lewis's recounting of the episode was cut short by a teacher who entered his office. Whereupon Lewis, without a moment's pause, responded to the teacher exactly as the superintendent had interacted with him. When confronted with this resounding obviousness, Lewis refused (or was unable) to see the similarity. When the two sets of events were dissected so that Lewis was caught by the brutal certitude of the similarities, he responded, "But it's different! I have reasons for treating the teacher that way." And when it was suggested that perhaps the superintendent had reasons for his treatment of the principal, Lewis, with more than a hint of impatience in his voice, retorted, "But mine were reasons; the superintendent's were merely rationalizations!"

This observation led me to formulate a theory of hierarchical intergroup relations in which the behavior of a person can be examined from the rela-

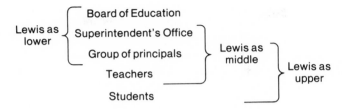

Figure 1. Constellation of intergroup relations with Lewis Brook in each of the three positions

tive positions of upper, middle, and lower in the organizational structures in which he or she is embedded. Lewis Brook, as principal of the Ashgrove high school, had three assistant principals and a staff of one hundred teachers who served the educational needs of some 1,400 children in the ninth to twelfth grades. Relative to these two groups, the teachers and the students, Lewis was in an *upper* position. Superimposed on the school was an administrative and political hierarchy of a superintendent and an elected Board of Education. In relation to these two groups, Lewis was in a *lower* position. Finally, Lewis was in a *middle* position in the constellation of relationships between his subordinates (the teachers and students) and his superiors (the superintendent's office). Brook's life as principal can be examined from each of these three relative positions in the hierarchical structure, as shown in figure 1. In particular, it is possible to see how his perceptions of events were influenced by the position he happened to occupy at the time they took place.

Lewis as a lower

When in a lower position, Brook regularly demonstrated a high degree of suspicion and excessive personal sensitivity. For example, on the day following each Board of Education meeting, Lewis would sit for long, anxious hours waiting for a call from the superintendent advising him of Board discussions that might be relevant to the life of his school. Usually no such call would come, and Lewis complained regularly and bitterly about how he was so faithfully ignored. But his protestation never triggered anything more than a retort from the superintendent that if anything relevant to his high school was discussed, he would be contacted within hours.

From the Board of Education's upper perspective, it was simple to conclude that if Lewis heard nothing it simply meant that the Board had not been debating anything relevant to his school's life. But from Lewis's lower perspective, hearing nothing did *not* mean that nothing was happening. Rather it meant "all hell is about to break loose," an inference that activated his "lower paranoia." Because Lewis assumed there was a conspiracy of silence, he would fantasize with meticulous dedication about all the possible things that could be "done to him," and would search for cues that might validate his worst suspicions. His failure to uncover a "plot" designed to undo him as principal was never interpreted by Lewis to mean that no such plot existed. Instead, he would conclude that his detection devices simply lacked the finesse required to detect what was happening in the "closed" ranks of the uppers.

Ironically, while Lewis was overcome with all this suspicion, reality for the Board of Education was that they were doing "nothing to anybody." In fact, they felt so paralyzed by their own stagnant inactivity that they would have been simultaneously dismayed and pleased to discover that someone, in his wildest imagination, was perceiving them as being in a state other than immobility. Ignorant of this alternative view, Lewis continued to construct a picture of the world about him that hung on trivial contingencies, but which for him was the pillar of his personal reality.

Brook's suspiciousness and oversensitivity when in a lower position can be seen as being a direct consequence of how people who feel powerless respond in intergroup exchanges with more powerful groups. Lower groups often develop strong protective devices and high cohesion to lessen their feelings of vulnerability. And one result of this response is that a lower group comes to define its essence in terms of this very cohesion and unity. In order to feed this sense of unity, members feel the need for the external threat to be continued. This creates a double bind: if the uppers cease to present a threat, that situation may be experienced by lowers as equally threatening, for it lessens the demand for their cohesion. This, in turn, recreates the sense of vulnerability of the lower group, because the *lack* of overt attack is a challenge to the very basis of unity on which group life is predicated. Either way it becomes imperative for members of the lower group to treat the uppers with suspicion. The bind reads as follows: "If they're getting at us, we've got to watch out. If they're not getting at us we've also got to watch out because they'll probably be getting at us in the long run by taking our unity away from us now by lessening the threat we feel." It is this process that ensures a lower group's paranoia and which, in my opinion, stirred Lewis Brook's intense feelings of sensitivity and suspiciousness when relating to his superiors.

Lewis as an upper

Despite the disdain Lewis felt about his superiors' failure to consult him on matters in which he believed he had a basic right to participate, he reacted toward his own subordinate teachers and students with an equally elitist air. When in his upper position, Lewis always had a myriad of reasons why it was impossible to let the teachers participate fully in decisions that influenced their lives. The teachers felt these reasons were without substance, and they were perpetually distressed by the lack of confidence shown toward them by their principal, who demanded that approval be obtained for even the most trivial and routine of tasks.

When Lewis was in an upper position, he acted out the tendency of superior groups to see the behavior of subordinates in pessimistic terms—the very behaviors that he reacted to so negatively when he was a lower. As a member of the upper group, Lewis, like other uppers, tended to delegate responsibilities very willingly, but not the authority required to carry through on those responsibilities. This behavior of superiors guarantees that the actions of subordinate groups will not fulfill satisfactorily the expectations implied when the responsibilities are delegated. Although such shortcomings are caused largely by the uppers' withholding of necessary authority, they also are used by the superiors as justification for their original unwillingness to delegate authority. This phenomenon ensures a self-reinforcing and self-repeating set of perceptions, in that it heightens the likelihood that the subordinate groups will be seen as less competent than is desirable.

An insidious dimension of this phenomenon is that it enables upper groups to avoid taking full responsibility for their own behavior. In taking for themselves the role of designing organizational policy—but then delegating the implementation of that policy to the middle group—the uppers are able to build for themselves the perfect defense against failure. They can always conclude that their own policy was good but that the middles simply failed to implement it satisfactorily. Negative feedback can then be viewed merely as an indicator that subordinate groups are not as competent as is necessary. And, at the same time, the superiors can continue to avoid confronting their own expertise (or lack thereof) as uppers. Such a process locks upper groups into a way of viewing the world that ensures they will see the behavior of subordinates in increasingly depreciating terms.

Lewis Brook, as a member of an upper group, was caught by this intergroup dynamic as strongly as he was by the double binds of suspiciousness when he was located in a lower position.

Lewis as a middle

When Brook was in a middle position, he was always espousing the need for "better communication" within the system. Despite this, he became caught in the trap of wanting to restrict information flow by making sure upper and lower groups communicated with each other only through him and his middle group. This situation is illustrated by the event described below.

Lewis was regularly embarrassed by learning about what was happening in his school for the first time from superiors who had been "leaked" information from below. Since he was an upper within the confines of the school itself, he often was unheeding to things teachers were trying to say to him. Therefore, they regularly felt the need to circumvent him in order to have their concerns attended to by the superintendent or the Board of Education. When teachers made attempts to contact the superintendent directly, Lewis became highly threatened and eventually decreed that no one could have access to the superintendent without first obtaining permission from one of the principals. By this action, Lewis clearly was working to preserve the centrality of his middle group's role as moderator of information flow.

Not to be daunted by this restriction on their liberties, the teachers found informal ways to gain access to the superintendent. The most frequently used device was to apply for study leave, even when not qualified for it. Such an application automatically led to an interview with the superintendent, which Lewis Brook allowed to occur without questioning his teachers. When ritualistically informed by the superintendent that they had not met the prerequisite conditions for study leave, the teachers willingly withdrew their applications and then confided the real reasons why they had sought an audience with him.

Lewis Brook never became aware of this practice, but he always felt distressed by the amount of information about his school of which the superintendent was aware. This distress only reinforced his dedication to make sure that teachers used his office alone as the means of communicating with the upper echelons of the system—an aspiration that he never realized.

To legitimize their own place in the system, middle groups need the uppers and lowers to be operating in a relatively polarized and noncommunicating fashion. Indeed, one of the ways for middle groups to be "confirmed" in the system is for them to become the central communication channel between the two extreme groups. This is possible primarily because both upper and lower groups use the withholding of information as a major strategy for dealing with each other. Upper groups limit information flow by using labels (such as "secret" or "in confidence") that designate who has legitimate access to what. For lowers, ground rules specifying what constitutes loyalty to the group determines what can be said to whom and under what circumstances, with the major concern being to minimize the vulnerability of the group.

If it were not for the rigid polarization of uppers and lowers, and their refusal to allow information to flow freely in the system, the middles might not be needed. But once the middle's role has become established as the communication link between upper and lower groups, the middles become very anxious to keep those polarized groups from talking frankly and openly. The middles become most threatened when the other two groups pass information to each other directly, or through any channel other than those the middles feel they have legitimized for the system. For this reason, the middles invest an inordinate amount of energy in defending the principle that all communication must pass through them. The net result of this dynamic is that middles will be constantly talking about the need to improve system-wide communication—while at the same time playing a vigorous role in restricting direct communication between other groups.

Summary

From the above account it is possible to recognize that intergroup processes cause groups at each of the three levels to become locked into a particular set of binds, and to create unique views of reality that are characteristic of those specific levels of the system. If these intergroup phenomena are conceded, it is predictable that an individual in a lower position will be supersensitive and suspicious of the activities of others. In an upper position, he or she will view the behavior of subordinates in a pessimistic light, and accordingly will delegate responsibility without the necessary authority. When in a middle position, the individual will espouse the need for greater communication, while acting to keep many communications restricted.

All these behaviors were exhibited by Lewis Brook in his role as Ashgrove's high school principal. It is easy to attribute these behaviors to Brook's unique personality. Yet, when viewed in the context of the intergroups operating in Brook's school system, it also becomes possible to understand how powerfully his own behavior and sense of reality were influenced by intergroup phenomena.

The intergroup as a determinant of individual identity

Smith (1976) describes how intergroup interactions in a five-day power laboratory led to the creation of an identity for one individual that other members of the social system came to symbolize as "the village lunatic."

A power laboratory is an experiential, social, and psychological simulation designed for people interested in experiencing and learning about the dynamics of power and powerlessness. The laboratory is structured to create three classes of people: (1) the powerful "elite," who have access to and control over all the basic resources of the society, such as food, housing, money, and so forth; (2) the "ins," who have minimal control over some resources, at the discretion of the elites; and (3) the powerless "outs" who are totally deprived and have no control over any community resources. All conditions of living, such as standards of housing, quality of food, and so on, are differentiated to heighten "class" differences. For example, the outs live in a ghetto-like life style, while the elites live in comparatively leisurely luxury. On arrival at the laboratory all members are "born into" one of these three classes, without individual choice.

In the power laboratory described by Smith, the elite group of seven arrived half a day before the middles, and produced a plan which would enable them to keep their eliteness hidden. They decided to act as if they were regular, nonelite participants, while they actually would be quietly and powerfully pulling the strings of the social system like backstage puppeteers.

The plan ran into trouble, however, within hours of the arrival of the nine middles. The "birth" trauma of the middles was quite extreme: at induction, they had all their belongings (save one change of underwear) taken from them, an event that stirred their anger and their determination to discern "who did this to us." Anthony, one of the middles, had brought with him a tape recorder that he wanted to use for his learning and post-laboratory reflections. He was not allowed to keep the recorder, however, and his resentment about this heightened his sensitivity as to who was powerful and who was powerless in the system. It took him very little time to differentiate the elites from the nonelites—simply by observing the interactions that took place among various participants. In response to his awareness, Anthony tried to initiate a public debate intended to flush out the elite group. He was generally unsuccessful in this, partly because others lacked his acumen in discerning what was taking place, and partly because of the skill of the elite group in keeping their identity hidden.

After half a day all but two members of the elite group had tired of the charade and had made public their real status. This made the middle group angry, and Anthony became even more determined to end the elites' game of phantomness. But this did not occur. The most influential member of the upper group—Richard, a tall, strong, bearded, black man—did not identify himself as an elite and remained with the middles, continuing to manipulate them to do exactly as the elites ordained.

The successful smoking out of most of the elite group fanned Anthony's fires. He became consumed with his fixation to force all the elites to become visible, Richard included. That was not to be, because Richard was blessed with a resolve equal to Anthony's and the two became bitterly pitted against each other. Anthony's energies were focused entirely on Richard's eviction from the middle group, while Richard, with a simple indifference to these pressures, worked at massaging the middles into accepting obediently their role as servants of the elites.

Whenever Richard attempted to make an initiative, Anthony immediately attempted to frustrate it by accurately, though boringly, accusing him of being an elite spy, and arguing that the middles should do nothing until such time as all the elites had been ousted. Eventually Richard became symbolized as a force for *activity* while Anthony came to be seen as someone reinforcing *stagnation*. Richard skillfully presented himself as the champion of the middles' cause, and successfully led negotiations with the elites for return of some of their personal belongings. This success elevated Richard to the sole leadership role in the bourgeoisie and he accordingly dealt with Anthony's accusations by simply dismissing them as part of a personal vendetta against him as the middles' leader.

The middle group did very little in the first day and a half other than debate the spy issue, and this inactivity produced such intense frustration that some reached the point of being willing to do anything, including being led down any path by Richard, simply to escape the paralysis of their inertia. Whether or not he was a spy ceased to matter much.

Anthony recognized that his group had adopted the spirit of going along with anything that produced activity, yet he could not reconcile himself to the fact that almost everything Richard proposed served to make the middles into the elite's lackeys. Soon Anthony's fight was being stifled by others in his group who would audibly groan their protest over his persistent regurgitation of a theme they all wanted to ignore. To buffer himself against this visible hostility, Anthony began to preface his remarks with a statement designed to lessen his vulnerability. He could have said, "I know I'm the only person who is concerned about this issue," but that's not the way he phrased his protective remarks. Instead he would say, "I know you think this is just my problem, but . . ."

By articulating this "buffer" statement in this way, Anthony provided other middles with the opportunity they had been looking for. By simply agreeing, "Yes, Anthony, that's just *your* problem," they could quickly close him down and avoid the agony of further monotonous reiteration of the spy theme.

The symbolization processes began to develop at a fast pace, and very soon the middle group had made "Anthony's problem" the receptacle for all of their frustrations. (Of course, the middles would have experienced frustration having to do with their need to keep their relationships with both elites and outs functional, independent of Anthony's role. As middles, they found that whenever they acted in the possible interest of the elites, the outs would abuse them for having been co-opted. And whenever they responded to pressures from the outs, the elites would treat them punitively and leave them feeling alienated and alone. The reality was that no matter what they did—even if they did nothing—the middles would end up feeling uncomfortable.)

Since the middles had begun to believe that the cause of their discomfort was "Anthony's problem," they came to view that "problem" in more extreme form as their sense of impotence heightened. Eventually they settled on the belief that "he really must be crazy." To make matters worse, Anthony had been successful enough to convince many of the middles that the spy issue was critical, but this only reverberated back on him: given the way the group's "problem" had become symbolized and projected into Anthony, it made more sense to many members of the middle group to suspect that Anthony was the real spy rather than Richard.

When this possibility was raised in the group, Anthony recognized that his battle was lost. By then he was so much on the periphery of the group that he knew there was little chance of his finding a comfortable place in the middle group. He therefore began to search for an alternative role in the system. The alternatives were, of course, very limited. The doors of the elites clearly were closed to him. That left only the outs—who in fact welcomed him with open arms. For them, the possibility of someone becoming *downwardly* mobile had real strategic value in this particular society, and they quickly grasped at the opportunity Anthony's plight presented. In addition, the outs had developed a strong emotional support system. They sensed Anthony's pain, and willingly reached out to provide him a haven.

Anthony became so overwhelmed by the level of acceptance and warmth accorded him by the outs that he quickly concluded that this was where he wanted to see out his days in the society. Here he ran into a new problem. It had been their common pain, their collective fears and uncertainties, and their desperate need for each other in psychological survival tasks that had forged the group of outs into its particular shape. Nothing in Anthony's middle experience paralleled those forces, and there was no way to revise the "out history" to allow Anthony to be made a full partner in the "real" life of the group. At best, he could become only an adopted son.

Anthony needed acceptance by the outs so badly that he was willing to comply uncritically to any of the group's wishes. And here, Anthony's "way of being" changed dramatically. The overly perceptive characteristics he displayed in his bourgeois period now became clouded by an obsessional overconforming to the norms of the out group—a response which attempted to compensate for his sense of historical exclusion from the outs' world, and to pay an adequate price for his acceptance by them.

Another event added appreciably to the complexity of everyone's perceptions of Anthony's behavior. At the time of Anthony's migration to the outs, Richard (keen to keep tranquility disjointed) returned to the relative comfort of the elite group. However, still wishing to maximize deception, the elites continued the charade by refusing to acknowledge that Richard had been one of them all along. Instead they described his move as "upward mobility," provided to Richard because of his good leadership behavior and his service to the society.

The impact of the dual departures of Richard and Anthony from the middles left a powerful vacuum. The remaining middles started to experiment with new behaviors. Collectively (though only temporarily) they gained a new sense of vitality. This caused them to lay, even more vehemently than previously, total responsibility for their earlier stagnation at Anthony's feet. They attributed none of it to Richard. For his departure they grieved. For Anthony's, they celebrated.

The remaining history of this laboratory was filled with examples of how tension in the system—the byproduct of unhandled intergroup conflict—became attributed to Anthony's "craziness." No matter what discomforting event occurred, it was symbolized as being Anthony's fault.

Why?

My basic thesis is that once the society had created for Anthony alone a totally unique experience within the society, and once a chance was provided for his behavior to be seen as "crazy," the system gave him an identity that powerfully served the needs of the intergroup exchanges. The "village lunatic" identity provided a receptacle for the craziness of the whole system—the deceit, the multiple and conflicting senses of reality, the myriad of covert, unarticulable processes, and so forth—which enabled the society at large to avoid having to confront its own pathology. In short, the social system had a vested interest in having Anthony become and remain crazy because it served admirably the continuation of the essential intergroup exchanges of the society at large.

And what became of Anthony himself?[1] Initially he was convinced his own perceptions were accurate. But across time, as others failed to see what was so obvious to him, he began to doubt his own sense of reality (even when he actually was perceiving correctly) and to wonder whether he was going mad. This eventually forced him to experience such discomfort that all of his energy became directed toward uncritically finding a place where he could feel support and acceptance. When the society transformed him into the "village lunatic," it created a form of madness aptly described by the poet Roethke, as mere "nobility of soul, at odds with circumstance."

One further question remains. What was it about Anthony as a person that caused him to become the lunatic? In my view, it was virtually accidental. The fact that he came originally with a tape recorder (and with a very high investment in being able to use it for his personal learning) meant that Anthony felt even more deprived than the others at induction time. This additional sense of deprivation heightened his activity to find out who the elites were much earlier than his fellow middles. Because he saw things differently than did the others, he started to become separated from the dominant sense of "reality" in the system. From there, the processes already described took off.

If Anthony had not come to this laboratory, would someone else have been made into a "lunatic" for the society's purposes? I suspect not. The forces which ended up focussing on him might well have been acted out in some other way—perhaps by creating another special identity for one individual, or by generating conditions of war between the groups, or even by the collapse of the society at large. The intergroup dynamics had to find *some* way to be acted out; the particular circumstances surrounding Anthony and his induction into the system were such that he became a convenient and useful vehicle for meeting that need.

The learning of overwhelming importance from this account is that often the personages or identities we take on may have very little to do with our own desires for ourselves, with our particular upbringings, or with our own values. Instead, they may, in fact, be mostly defined for us and forced

---

1. Anthony left the laboratory in good emotional health. During the critique phase of the experience, the staff of the laboratory spent a great deal of time with Anthony and others exploring how this "village lunatic" phenomenon had occurred.

upon us by external processes similar to those experienced by Anthony in the power laboratory.

The intergroup as a determinant of behaviors characterized as leadership

Perhaps one of the most gripping, passionate, and socially educative experiences ever recorded is the story of sixteen Uruguayan football players and their friends who not only survived an aircraft crash in the completely inaccessible heights of the Chilean Andes, but then existed for ten weeks in icy and desolate conditions with only the wrecked fuselage of the aircraft as their shelter and home (Read 1974).

Of the original forty-three people on board, sixteen were killed in the crash or died in the next few days from injuries. Seventeen days later the surviving twenty-seven were further reduced to a group of nineteen by an avalanche of snow that buried alive almost the whole group, eight of whom could not be dug out before they froze to death. After the avalanche, the group of survivors (reduced later by another three deaths) kept alive for fifty more days before two of their number, under unbelievable conditions, climbed a cliff-faced mountain of ice to a height of 13,500 feet, and eventually stumbled across civilization and help.

The story is a deeply touching account of human relationships under the most extreme survival conditions. In order to stay alive, it was necessary for group members, despite the repugnancy of the idea, to eat the raw flesh of the dead. Much of the early life and struggles of these survivors revolved around the agonies of acknowledging and accepting this imperative. As dreams of rescue faded, and as the struggle together under intense conditions heightened, the earlier revulsions became translated into a very mystical and religious experience—to the extent that several of the boys, when they realized that their own deaths were imminent, asked their comrades to feel free to eat their bodies.

In the discussion that follows, I will explore the social system composed of the survivors, and show how behaviors that traditionally would be described as personal "leadership" can be understood in terms of the relationships between various groups that emerged within that system. Specifically, I will propose that who becomes focal in leadership activities (and what leadership behaviors are seen as appropriate) changes radically from situation to situation—largely as a function of changing intergroup dynamics.

Immediately after the crash, many of the survivors were bleeding and in desperate need of medical care. In this initial phase, during which group life was defined by the visibility of wounded bodies, the key survival task was seen as caring for the bleeding. Accordingly, two of the group, who had been medical students in the earliest phases of their training, were automatically elevated to dominant status. An intergroup structure emerged which delineated all survivors into one of three classes—the wounded, the potential workers, and the doctors. The medical students were given tremendous power, despite the fact that their skills and competence in the setting were minimal, especially given that they had not facilities or medical supplies. Others willingly subjected themselves to directives the students issued around appropriate work or treatment programs. The need for medical help was so intense that the differential status of the survivors enabled limited skill to become symbolized as expert competence, which, in turn, gave the "doctors" inordinate power to influence everyone else's behavior.

Within a day or so, new demands appeared. The acquisition of food and water, and the preservation of hygiene in the fuselage—which constituted the only shelter from sub-zero temperatures, blizzards, and thoroughly treacherous conditions—became critical. These demands required a group structure that was radically different from the one that had developed in the period immediately after the crash. In particular, it became important for someone to play an overall "social maintenance" role to give coherence to the whole system. The captain of the football team, who had been overshadowed in the first day by the medical students, was reelevated to his former position. Beneath him were two groups of approximately equal status: (1) the medical team of two "doctors" and a couple of helpers, and (2) a group that searched battered luggage for tidbits of food, and who made water by melting snow on metal sheets and bottling it in old soda bottles. At a still lower level, was a group of the younger boys who served as a clean-up crew to maintain livable conditions in the cabin. The football captain himself became the general coordinator, and at noon each day he distributed the carefully rationed food to each person. In this role he clearly brought with him the ethos of his earlier influence as captain on the sports field.

The hierarchies of social influence changed during this period. The medical group now were granted authority related only to their specialist function, and they lost virtually all of their influence over nonmedical domains of the social system. For several days the football captain remained the key figure, mediating potential clashes over the food, and dealing with conflicts between the medical and work teams. Much of his power was predicated on his effusive optimism that they would all be rescued within a few days. He used this hope, which he constantly rekindled, as the major substance for social cohesion. But as time passed, and it became clear that rescue was not imminent, the hopes he had fostered began to sour and the captain's social maintenance skills slowly became devalued.

A new plight confronted the survivors several days after the crash. The food supplies were nearly exhausted. It was clear that if survival were to be sustained, the group maintenance orientation of the captain would no longer suffice. Parrado, who previously had played no significant role, moved to prominence. During the past few days he had been coping with the loss of both his mother and his sister, who had died from crash injuries. In the process, he had developed an unbelievable desire to survive. Parrado became the articulator of two new and key dimensions in the life of the group: (1) the suggestion that the only hope of rescue was for a group of expeditionaries to walk out of the mountains, and (2) the idea that life depended on consumption of the flesh of the dead, which was being preserved by the freezing cold. The force of these suggestions provided new energy for the group, and started the process of delineating new internal social structures within the mountain-top society.

At the same time, the role of the "doctors" was further diminished. With virtually no medical supplies, their "special expertise" had been exhausted. The worst cases had died, and it was now clear to everyone that there was very little more that could be offered in the medical domain. The collapse of the medical team's function added to the power vacuum and increased the uncertainty about social relationships among group members.

Eventually another new social structure did emerge. It was defined primarily by each person's willingness or reluctance to eat human flesh. Those who did so early, and with a reasonable degree of spontaneity, were the ones who maintained the physical energy to persevere—and thereby to provide vitality for the endurance of the social system itself. Those who could not bring themselves to overcome their natural abhorrence to the idea became weak, and eventually degenerated into a new "poorer class." A third group struggled with the tensions of survival on the one hand, and their natural revulsion to the consumption of human flesh on the other. In so doing, members of this group came to formulate a new way of symbolizing the activity. They developed a very mystical and spiritual interpretation of their group experience, reinterpreting the eating of the flesh of the dead as being parallel to a religious communion in which they would consume the body and blood of Christ. This resymbolization of experience facilitated survival by helping everyone respond to the imperative that they eat the flesh of the dead, no matter how strongly the idea initially had repelled them.

During this period, the football captain moved further from his earlier position of prominence. This was, in part, because of his unwillingness to take the lead in eating human flesh. But, in addition, the captain lost credibility because his repeated assurances that rescue was imminent came increasingly to sound hollow.

When the survivors eventually heard on a transistor radio that all rescue operations had been called off, the energy in the system changed dramatically. Despair and outrage hit members like clenched fists, and produced radically different responses in different people. Parrado was ready to leave on an expedition immediately, while others were ready to resign themselves to the inevitability of death. Despair was heightened further a couple of days later when an avalanche of snow caused the death of eight more persons, including the football captain. Reluctantly, it was concluded that

an expedition now offered the only hope for survival. And the internal social structure of the system went through yet another readjustment in response to this imperative.

Any social system can become subjected to crisis conditions which
produce extreme pressures from the outside, or from within. When this
happens, members of the system must respond to these pressures or else
risk long-term internal chaos. One common response is for clusters of
people to form which eventually evolve into critical groups for the system.
Moreover, the pressures that emerge from crisis experiences invariably demand that groups within the system relate to each other more intensely than
had previously been the case. Even the composition of these groups will
need to change. In the present case, the medical group was dominant initially, with others subservient to them. This structure was altered by the
emergence of the football captain as the major mediator between several
specialized work groups, and eventually by the emergence of an entirely
new social structure defined in terms of members' willingness to consume
human flesh.

When these changes are taking place in response to extreme pressures,
it often is most unclear what should happen to produce a new form of stability in which both directionality and internal coherence are present. What
an individual might do personally to provide leadership is unclear and
speculative. Instead, each new set of stresses causes changes in group
memberships or behaviors which, in turn, move the system toward some
new equilibrium. As this happens, power, authority, critical resources, and
ability to influence events become distributed differently than before. Only
when the directionality and coherence of the system achieve a reasonable
degree of stability is it possible to determine which behaviors actually
moved the system in productive directions, or served to keep the various
parts of the system integrated. Acts of leadership, then, are merely responses to the forces that emerge from the exchanges among groups within
the system, and it would *not* be valid to construe them as reflecting a conscious intent to lead. If, in hindsight, an act appears to have been one of
effective leadership, it may have been virtually accidental at the time it
happened—and identifiable as leadership only in retrospect. This phenomenon is especially visible in the next phase of the survivors' experiences.

As preparations for the expedition went forward, all energies were dedicated to that task. Medical duties had slipped from any prominence, and
the doctors simply took their place in the mainstream of the social structure. Four identifiable groups emerged as planning for the expedition proceeded. They were: (1) a collection of ten individuals who were designated
as too weak to undertake any significant walking; (2) three first choices for
the expedition, including one of the ex-doctors and Parrado, whose robust
constitution and steely resolve to escape had helped buoy the energy of the
fainthearted; (3) three cousins who were not fit for the expedition and who

previously had not played significant roles in the system—but who had co-alesced as a critical subgroup because of their strong support for each other in a common struggle (theirs, a blood relationship, was the only precrash grouping of friends that had not been fragmented by the ordeal); and (4) a trio of younger fellows who were potential expeditionaries—but who first had to be tested to prove their fitness.

Eventually a group of four was selected as the key expeditionaries. Once chosen, they became virtually a "warrior class" with extra rights and privileges. They were allowed to do anything that could be construed as bettering their physical condition. The whole group coddled them, both physically and psychologically, and everyone made sure that the only con-versations within their earshot were optimistic in tone.

Read (1974) reports that the expeditionaries were *not* the leaders of the society. They were basically a class apart, linked to the rest of the system by the group of cousins, whose cohesion was the only force available to balance the unbelievable power that had been given to the expeditionaries. Because the cousins were the only ones able to keep the "warriors" in check (and thereby keep the system in equilibrium) they became the major locus of power within the remainder of the system. They virtually ruled from then on. The cousins controlled food allocation, determined who should do what work, and mediated when the "workers" (those who cut meat, prepared water, attended to hygiene, and so forth) felt that some of the sick were merely "malingering" and therefore should not be fed unless they also worked.

Beneath the cousins, a second echelon of three emerged. These in-dividuals took roles equivalent to noncommissioned officers, receiving orders from above and giving them to those below. One of this trio, the second of the two doctors, became the "detective" in this phase of the so-ciety. He took upon himself the task of investigating misdemeanors and norm violations, and he flattered those more senior to him while bullying those more subservient.

It was several weeks before the expeditionaries departed. There were some valid reasons for the delay, but eventually everyone began to suspect that the ex-doctor was stalling and that he was using his expectant expedi-tionary status as a way of accruing privileges and minimizing work. At that point, his privileges were terminated. When one of the cousins volunteered to go in his place, the ex-doctor stirred himself and prepared for what proved to be a successful expedition: after a grueling ten-day trek, help was located and the remaining survivors were rescued.

One would have imagined that the ordeal was now over, but the system still had to face another extremely difficult event. Within a short time after the rescue, news leaked that the survivors had sustained themselves by consuming the flesh of the dead. This produced a strong reaction, especially among members of the press, who were poised to give world-wide publicity to this remarkable story. Religious figures, parents, and close friends were basically supportive during this period of new threat. But it soon became obvious that, if the survivors were ever to return to normal lives, it would be necessary for them to confront this issue together. So they called a press conference to tell their story.

The group debated at length as to who should explain the eating of human flesh. Several individuals felt they would be too emotional. It was eventually agreed that Delgado, who had been almost completely insignificant on the mountain top, should describe this aspect of their experience. His public presence and his eloquence—which of course had been of no value during the seventy-day ordeal—now came into its own, and he mediated brilliantly between the survivors, and the press, relatives, and other interested parties. His statement was a moving, passionate, religious, and emotional event, and through it he provided a way for everyone to resymbolize the meaning of the survival experience, thereby quelling criticism and laying to rest concerns over the consumption of the dead.

In this setting, Delgado's behavior, which to date had influenced nothing, was now seen by others as outstanding leadership. But did he lead? Or was it simply that his particular response to the tensions which intersected in his personhood in that situation touched the nerve fibers of the new sets of intergroup interactions, thereby triggering a new directionality and a wholesome coherence for the system?

Conclusion

The literature of organizational behavior is filled with concepts that help us understand the behavior of people in terms of their personal characteristics, or as a response to what takes place in the groups of which they are members. The material presented in this paper offers an alternative view: namely, that it is imperative to move beyond explanations that lie within people and within groups—and to include perspectives that derive from more global and systemic forces, including forces that derive from the dynamics of intergroups.

If, for example, the tools of personality theorists alone were applied to Lewis Brook in Ashgrove or to Anthony's identity struggle, we would obtain only a limited understanding of what affected their perceptions and their behaviors. Likewise, if we restricted our explorations of leadership among the aircraft survivors to traditional concepts that imply specific intentionality on the part of individuals (i.e., using notions such as participation, initiation of structure, socioemotional behavior, and so on), much of the essence of the leadership phenomena that developed on the mountain top would have been lost.

But how much relevance do the principles extracted from the materials presented in this paper have for understanding everyday experiences in everyday organizations? I submit, a great deal—and more than we usually realize or are comfortable acknowledging.

References

Alderfer, C. P. Group and intergroup relations. In J. R. Hackman and J. L. Suttle (Eds.). *Improving life at work: Behavioral science approaches to organizational change.* Pacific Palisades, Calif.: Goodyear, 1977.

Alderfer, C. P., Brown, L. D., Kaplan, R. E., & Smith K. K. *Group relations and organizational diagnosis.* London: Wiley, in press.

Hackman, J. R. Group influences on individuals in organizations. In M. D. Dunnette (Ed.). *Handbook of industrial and organizational psychology.* Chicago: Rand McNally, 1976.

Levine, R. A., & Campbell, D. T. *Ethnocentrism.* New York: Wiley, 1972.

Lewin, K. Frontiers in group dynamics. *Human Relations,* 1947, **1,** 5–41.

Likert, R. *New patterns of management.* New York: McGraw-Hill, 1964.

Lorsch, J. W., & Lawrence, P. R. *Managing group and intergroup relations.* Homewood, Ill.: Irwin, 1972.

Read, P. P. *Alive.* London: Pan Books, 1974.

Rice, A. K. Individual, group and intergroup processes. *Human Relations,* 1969, **22,** 565–585.

Sherif, M. (Ed.), *Intergroup relations and leadership.* New York: Wiley, 1962.

Smith, K. K. *Behavioral consequences of hierarchical structures.* Unpublished doctoral dissertation, Yale University, 1974.

Smith, K. K. The village lunatic. Unpublished manuscript, University of Melbourne, 1976.

8

Managing Conflict: Making Friends and Making Enemies

As organizations grow, subgroups take on special tasks. We set up a marketing department here, a manufacturing division there, a research division, an accounting department, and on and on. And we chop up our organization in other ways (and often they chop themselves up). Some people work at headquarters, some out in branch offices; some work on the twenty-fifth floor, others in the basement. Some wear white uniforms, others wear tweed jackets. Some eat in the executive dining room, others in the cafeteria, others out on the loading dock.

So what? Of course, the first consequence is that those departments, floors, uniforms, and eating places soon cause people to *feel* themselves to be members of those groups, to be "marketing people," or "basement people," or "field people." And when people identify themselves as group members, they also tend to see members of other groups as *different* from themselves. The next step is evaluative. They are not just different; they are not as good, or not to be trusted, or not our kind of people, and so on.

It's familiar stuff, this tendency for organizations (as well as nations, churches, and all other large institutions) to split and fragment into factions that begin to squabble and even in many cases to go to war with one another.

This section is about that huge and intransigent problem—about how conflicts happen, how organizations deal with them, and, to the extent that we know, how to prevent them.

Of course, if we really knew all the answers to these questions, we could put an end to war and make the United Nations work. But although we don't even know most of the answers, we know a little. And what we know can be important to the manager.

The three papers in this section attack the problem from related but different angles. Ruth Love's article on the "Absorption of Protest" takes a historical perspective, examining several cases in which large organizations, such as the Catholic Church and the U.S. Air Corps, have tried to deal with recalcitrant subgroups within their own ranks. What does a parent organization do when one of its offspring complains too loudly and begins to make too much trouble? What are the options, and what are their costs and benefits?

The article by Joanne Martin and Caren Siehl casts the issues in terms of conflicts between organizational cultures and the countercultures that develop within them. They use John DeLorean's relationship with General Motors as an example.

Finally, Louis Pondy's article tries to make order out of chaos, putting together several different ways of thinking about stages of organizational conflict and several types of conflict situations.

Life in organizations has never been a bed of roses. Conflict among units and between people is inevitable and often useful. Good managers expect it, understand it, and try to design organizations that minimize the costs of conflict and maximize the creative benefits they often provide.

The Absorption of Protest
Ruth Leeds Love

Introduction: The nonconformist and the enclave

The usual fate of the nonconformist who occupies a position of some responsibility in a complex organization has been established: the cleric who wavers from the true path goes on retreat; the maverick army officer is appointed to an innocuous position; the recalcitrant political party deputy is temporarily suspended.[1] If temporary suspension or relegation to an insignificant position does not suffice to curb the nonconformist, he is gradually eased out of the organization. But what happens when an organization is faced with not just a single nonconformist but with several who form a cohesive enclave in its midst? The organization—specifically incumbents of positions superordinate to the nonconformists—must now check not just one individual but many who could potentially divert organization resources from their current commitments, undermine organizational effectiveness, or form a front capable of capturing control of the organization.

To control a nonconforming enclave, the organization has to employ techniques other than those typically used to check a single nonconformist. An individual's nonconformity often as not stems primarily from personality factors, although structural determinants do contribute to it. The nonconformity of an enclave, which is shared by all its members, stems primarily from structural determinants rather than personality factors. Hence, different techniques are called for to check nonconforming enclaves.

There is one organizational technique—the subject of this chapter—that is particularly suited for controlling wayward groups. It consists of integrating the protest of the nonconforming enclave into the organization by converting it into a new legitimate subunit. Through conversion, the nonconforming enclave obtains a legitimate outlet for its nonconformity, and

Reprinted (except for postscript) from *New Perspectives in Organization Research*, ed. W. W. Cooper, H. J. Leavitt, and M. W. Shelly (New York: John Wiley & Sons, 1964), by permission of the publisher.

1. Amitai Etzioni, *A Comparative Analysis of Complex Organizations* (Glencoe, Ill.: The Free Press, 1961), pp. 241–44. This paper represents an expansion of an idea briefly discussed by Etzioni, pp. 245–48.

thereby contributes to the attainment of legitimate goals of the organization. The conversion from nonconforming enclave to legitimate subunit will be called the protest-absorbing process. Protest absorption might take as little as a year or as long as a generation. Regardless, by the end of the process, the nonconforming enclave and the top authorities of the organization reach an accommodation such that the enclave is given some autonomy to pursue a specific activity (usually the activity which was the focus of the nonconformity), but, at the same time, it is expected to abide by the regulations and restrictions to which all legitimate subunits adhere.

Protest absorption is a structural "weapon" available to the organization. It is a weapon insofar as it is used to control nonconforming groups. It is a structural weapon insofar as its effectiveness rests on formal changes in the organizational structure, that is, on the formal positions of subunits vis-à-vis each other. As will be seen, the weapon is unleashed through the exercise of *authority,* although *power* is a variable in the protest-absorption process. Protest absorption should not be confused with co-optation which comes about through power differentials between the co-opters and the co-opted regardless of the authority structure.[2] Although reductionist concepts like power and charisma are variables in the protest-absorption process, they are not the major explanatory concepts. Structure and authority are the key concepts to an understanding of protest absorption, although these terms will be used only rarely to avoid awkward phrasing.

Organizational analyses which generate theories about the organization as if all structures were cut from the same cloth must be qualified when applied to specific organizations, e.g., a prison, an army, or a factory. The development of a comparative approach permits the enrichment of organizational theories by adding statements of regularities within one type of organization to statements of universal uniformities. Given this consideration, the first step is to delineate the type of organization in which protest absorption is expected to be an effective weapon. Then we can characterize the nonconforming enclave and the process by which it is converted into a legitimate and quiescent unit. The appendix presents an outline of cases which *illustrate* the protest-absorption model. Since this paper represents both an exploratory study and a preliminary report, we are not concerned here with the frequency with which the model is approximated.

Normative organizations and the distribution of charisma[3]

Organizations can be characterized by the nature of the primary power that is used to control its lowest ranking participants. *Coercive* organizations, e.g., prisons, keep order through the use of physical force (or the threat of it); *utilitarian* organizations, e.g., factories, keep order primarily through

---

2. Philip Selznick, *TVA and the Grass Roots* (Berkeley: University of California Press, 1949).

3. Based on Etzioni, *A Comparative Analysis.*

monetary rewards; *normative* organizations, e.g., churches, elicit compliance through the allocation and manipulation of symbolic rewards. For reasons to be evident shortly, protest absorption is expected to occur most frequently in normative organizations.

Two other major characteristics distinguish the normative from the coercive and utilitarian organizations. First, a normative organization tends to demand a high degree of commitment and loyalty from its members, often to the point that members are expected to give their primary allegiance to the organization. The priest is symbolically wedded to the church; in those organizations where secular marriage is permitted, the wife is drawn into the structure and is known by its name, e.g., a navy wife.[4] Voluntary exiting from the organization is perceived as a sign of insufficient loyalty; for example, resignation from academic departments tends to precipitate feelings of resentment and rejection among the professors who remain.[5] Criticism of the organization's institutionalized norms and methods is also taken as a sign of insufficient loyalty.

Second, most offices in normative organizations have charisma ascribed to them. The performances associated with the position of priest or military officer are charismatic and are symbolized by such devices as special dress, badges of office, and ritual courtesies. The charismatic elements of a particular office enrich the organization's symbols and rituals with additional meaning, and increase their reward value for the loyalty and discipline which lowest-ranking members exhibit. Moreover, personal contact with an incumbent of a charismatic office is itself perceived as a reward by members. Thus charismatic power in its routinized form reinforces the normative power of the organization.

At the same time that charisma helps to generate loyalty and discipline among the personnel, it also is a potential disrupter of discipline and loyalty to the organization itself. The problem is present in latent form when the lower participants of the organization attribute the functionally specific charisma of office to a *particular* incumbent, and, in so doing, generalize the charisma so that it takes on diffuse characteristics. Where this occurs, the participants make personal commitments to the particular individual who occupies a charismatic office rather than to the office itself. If the charismatic officer uses these particularistic commitments for purposes that are functional to the organization as a whole (or for purposes that do not generate dysfunctions), then the problem remains latent. The case might be, however, that the charismatic employs these commitments to challenge organizational hegemony and integration, and to compete against regular subunits (sometimes laterally related) for resources, thereby undermining

---

4. Arthur K. Davis, "Bureaucratic Patterns in the Navy Officers Corps," in R. K. Merton et al., eds., *Reader in Bureaucracy* (Glencoe, Ill.: The Free Press, 1952).

5. Theodore Caplow and R. J. McGee, *The Academic Marketplace* (New York: Basic Books, 1958), p. 66.

the organization's allocation and reward system. (That such a situation might occur indicates both the desirability and the apparent impossibility of routinizing charisma.)

The potential strain between charisma and discipline is greatest in those organizations where the gift of grace parallels the formal organizational chart, being characteristic of many offices as well as the top ones, and yet where formal authority is centralized. The Catholic church and wartime military organizations are the major examples of organizations that have charisma distributed throughout their lines combined with a strong, centralized authority structure. Protest absorption is more likely to be used in these organizations to control nonconforming enclaves than in normative structures which have the potential for strain between charisma and discipline but lack a strong central authority (e.g., Protestant denominations and the early Catholic church).

The process of protest absorption

The potential strain between charisma and discipline erupts into a tempest in a tepid teapot with the formation of a nonconforming enclave. More often than not, the enclave is led by a charismatic who is concerned with devising new ways for carrying out his responsibilities more effectively. The leadership of the enclave is strengthened by able lieutenants. The enclave itself is endowed with a militant spirit; its members are eager to undertake large-scale tasks and to execute them with novel strategies. The organization, grown weak internally in one or several respects, either cannot or prefers not to initiate change (although from some objective perspective change might be functionally required if the organization is to continue being effective). Protest absorption has two major consequences for the organization; it checks the nonconforming enclave by turning it into a legitimate subunit which remains loyal to the organization and it permits the introduction of change. The descriptive model of protest absorption contains three parts: (1) the characteristics of the nonconforming enclave, (2) the state of the organization, and (3) the process of absorbing protest.

The nonconforming enclave

Two conditions are basic to the emergence of a nonconforming enclave. First, some members of a normative organization must attribute personal charisma to an official. This provides the official with an opportunity to lead a loyal following over which diffuse influence and control can be exercised. Second, the official must have tendencies toward nonconformity and unorthodoxy, and must disregard at least some traditional norms and strategies. Once the official has proved his capacity to acquire a personal following, he may be referred to as the enclave leader; once he leads in unorthodox directions, the enclave becomes a nonconforming group.

The leader's nonconformity stems in large measure from his position in

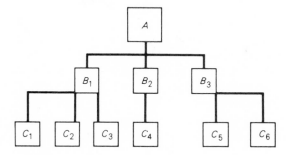

Figure 1. Boxes denote units in organization.

the organization. Assume that the leader is in unit C_4 (fig. 1). Assume further that C_4 is not functioning effectively with regard to its subunit goals. Lack of effectiveness could stem from one or several factors. For example, the unit is frequently peripheral and so does not receive the optimum quantity and quality of inputs; or the unit is a long-established one which has become more concerned with self-maintenance than with attainment of goals; or changes in the unit's environment have occurred which make present methods and procedures obsolete; or contingencies have emerged for which there is no formal provision. In short, the unit's responsibility for goals far exceeds its capacity for attainment of goals, thereby making it relatively ineffective.[6] One response to lack of effectiveness is to exercise trained incapacity, that is, to continue conforming to rules and procedures which have become inappropriate.[7] A second response is to search for new rules and procedures which would permit increased unit effectiveness. The first response is symptomatic of functional rationality and the second of substantive rationality.[8] The leader, either in his capacity as head of C_4 or as a member of it, exercises some degree of substantive rationality and assumes responsibility for devising methods which will make the unit more effective. Increased unit effectiveness would permit him to fulfill his own particular position more adequately.

In large measure, one's position determines whether one perceives the discrepancy between responsibility and control, and whether one chooses to respond functionally or substantively to it. The greater the responsibility for goal attainment or the greater the environmental contact associated with a given position, the more likely is the incumbent to respond substantively rather than functionally. In our simplified organization chart, the A level

6. See Etzioni, *A Comparative Analysis,* pp. 77–79, for a discussion of effectiveness.

7. R. K. Merton, *Social Theory and Social Structure,* rev. ed. (Glencoe, Ill.: The Free Press, 1957), p. 198.

8. Karl Mannheim, *Ideology and Utopia* (New York: Harcourt, Brace and Co., 1936), pp. 112–17.

has overall responsibility for organization goals; the *C* level is responsible for subunit goals. Moreover, both *A* and *C* levels have some contact with the environment. The *B* level serves internal coordination and communication functions. On a probability basis, then, the enclave leader is more likely to occupy a position in *A* or *C* than in *B*. To simplify presentation of our model, we assume that the enclave leader is located in *C*.

The leader's nonconformity is not to be confused with deviancy. Unlike a deviant, a nonconformist does not hide his dissent from the prevailing norms. He publicly challenges the efficacy of the existing norms and their applicability to specific situations in the hope of changing them without destroying the organization. The nonconformist justifies his challenge of the status quo by appealing to what the organization recognizes as its highest morality or its ultimate set of values.[9] The official who emerges as a leader of a nonconforming enclave is justified in saying, in the area of his specific responsibility, "It is written . . . but I say unto you . . ." on two counts. First, because he has charisma attributed to him, and second, because as a nonconformist he is oriented to existing rules only in a negative sense—to challenge them.[10]

Concomitant with his personal charisma and tendency toward nonconformity, the leader also has a flair for originality which permits him to create new strategies, ideologies, and symbols to counter those of the organization.[11] The development and implementation of new strategies come to represent the goal of the enclave. The new ideology and symbols serve as extensions to the leader's charisma in welding the enclave into a cohesive, dynamic group.

The charismatic rarely leads the enclave by himself.[12] He is usually assisted by lieutenants who support his unorthodox tactics and innovations,

9. If the leader appeals to a morality or values not recognized by the organization, the likelihood of protest absorption is reduced and the organization will resort to other means to check him. Orde Wingate was able to organize and arm Jews to quell Arab raids on the British pipelines in Palestine in the late 1930s, despite British policy not to give arms to Jews. Wingate also hoped that his Special Night Squad would form the basis for a Jewish army which would help to pave the way for Palestine's independence. Wingate's advocacy of a cause which extended beyond military purlieus led to his recall from Palestine, and probably helps to account for the rapid de-judification of the Special Night Squad. See Christopher Sykes, *Orde Wingate* (London: Collins, 1959).

10. R. K. Merton, "Social Problems and Sociological Theory," in R. K. Merton and R. A. Nisbet, eds., *Contemporary Social Problems* (New York: Harcourt, Brace and World, 1961), pp. 725–26; and Max Weber, *The Theory of Social and Economic Organization*, trans. A. M. Henderson and T. Parsons (New York: Oxford University Press; Glencoe, Ill.: The Free Press, 1947), p. 361.

11. Dorothy Emmet, *Function, Purpose and Powers* (London: Macmillan, 1958), p. 258. The problem of what an administrator should do with the single nonconformist, the "creative genius," the person with a flair who is "beyond good and evil," receives excellent treatment by Professor Emmet. She feels that a solution might develop if the administrator has the capacity to comprehend different roles; with such understanding the administrator might create a special role in the organization for the nonconformist. In the present context, protest absorption would require the administrator to have some understanding of structure. Emmet does not deal with the problems presented by a group of nonconformists.

12. See Weber, *The Theory of Social and Economic Organization*, p. 360.

and spearhead the enclave with their own missionary fire and ability to influence others. The leader, by granting his lieutenants some autonomy in a specialized area like procuring supplies, insures that they will remain subservient to him. Since the lieutenants are likely to promulgate their own ideas, a limited amount of autonomy may prevent rival ideas and methods from disrupting the unity of the enclave.

The energy and zeal of the nonconforming enclave are focused on innovations, which often assume the form of techniques intended to facilitate attainment of organizational goals. New techniques might be more effective in attaining existing goals by permitting higher output or they might revitalize goals which have grown fallow. (Later we shall have more to say about the enclave's objectives and their bearing on the protest-absorption process.) In essence, the enclave maintains a high commitment to the basic goals of the organization, and desires to display this commitment through recognition of its innovations. The commitment inspiring the nonconformists is frequently viewed as higher than that possessed by others in the organization. The perceived or alleged discrepancy between the extremely high degree of loyalty to basic organizational values exhibited by the nonconforming enclave and the moderate degree of loyalty exhibited by other organization participants is likely to provoke conflict. Other participants have little tolerance for the enthusiasm of the enclave, for, by comparison, they appear less diligent and less loyal to the organization.

The nonconforming enclave is further distinguished by an unorthodox atmosphere which permeates many aspects of its life. This atmosphere varies from extreme austerity and asceticism to romance, adventure, and heroic sacrifice. The unorthodox behavior of the enclave, whether reflected in the wearing of special clothing or in reckless courage, not only sets the enclave apart from the rest of the organization but also contributes to its cohesiveness and strength. A member can readily identify with a group symbolized by noticeable objects or mannerisms. If the group merits esteem from outsiders, it can be bestowed on easily recognized members. The symbols of unorthodoxy also facilitate recruitment in that they help publicize the group to potential members who share similar values and similar tendencies toward nonconformity.

In summary, the nonconforming enclave is characterized by a leader whose charisma of office has become personal. He pursues a course of action or cause which is perceived as unorthodox, and for which he creates symbols and an ideology. His immediate lieutenants are nonconformers in their own right, although less influential and original than the leader. The cause served is usually a means to revive allegedly neglected organizational goals or to achieve present organizational goals more effectively. Lastly, a peculiar aura, either of asceticism or of romance, envelops the enclave, contributing to its integration and highlighting its dedication to its cause.

The state of the organization

Although nonconformity can erupt at all times, a cohesive nonconforming enclave is likely to emerge in a context in which one or a combination of the following variations of organizational weakness is prevalent. If, over time, the legitimacy of the organization procedures decreases generally or within any subunit, charisma tends to shift from office to person among those dedicated to the ultimate purposes of the organization. If an organization is insensitive to potential nonconformity (due to such factors as inadequacies of communication networks), control mechanisms might not be activated in time to forestall a nonconforming official before he gains a personal following.[13] If an organization's internal authority is weak, owing to the corruption of officers responsible for enforcing conformity or owing to the lack of (or limited) control over enforcement facilities, then whatever control mechanisms the organization might employ are ineffectual. Finally, resources diverted outside the organization to meet an external challenge, or stoppage of inputs, limit the availability of the means needed to combat nonconformity.

Once the enclave emerges, mild checks to contain the nonconformity are no longer adequate. If the organizational elite ousts the leader, his immediate lieutenants could assume control of the enclave, or members of the enclave might follow their leader and form the beginnings of a competing structure. Such a possibility is particularly threatening when the organization enjoys a monopoly or duopoly position. If the organization is one of several of its kind, then one more similar structure in the environment makes little difference. Finally, if both the leader and the members of the enclave are dispersed throughout the organization, in an effort to disband the group, nonconformity might be spread rather than eliminated.

Given the inadequacy of control techniques which are typically applied to single nonconformists, the organizational elite must choose between several alternatives; condemnation, avoidance, expulsion, or protest absorption. The first three alternatives are not effective in containing the nonconformity unless the enclave itself is quite weak to begin with. Condemnation contains the danger of widening the rift between the enclave and the rest of the organization by forcing a polarization of issues.[14] Avoidance, which means consciously taking little account of the existence of the enclave,

13. In some instances the "following" emerges first and then casts about for a leader. According to Erle Wilson's less romantic account of the *Bounty* mutiny, the potential mutineers were ship's sailors, who, on becoming cognizant of each other's discontents, recruited Fletcher Christian to be their leader. Subsequent events indicated that the choice was not entirely fortunate, for Christian lacked the capacity to live up to the charisma which his followers attributed to him. See Erle Wilson, *Adams of the* Bounty (New York: Popular Library, 1959).

14. Z. Brzezinski, "Deviation Control: A Study in the Dynamics of Doctrinal Conflict," *American Political Science Review* 56 (1962): 9–10.

sidesteps the danger of polarization.[15] During the period that the organization elite obstensibly ignores the enclave, however, the enclave might grow in size and strength instead of drying out. Expulsion of the enclave represents a costly loss of resources which might yet be channeled to serve organizational goals.[16] Also, expulsion could lead to the emergence of a rival structure (albeit it does permit tightening of organizational ranks). The negative consequences which might result from attempting to control the enclave through condemnation, avoidance, or expulsion are particularly dysfunctional to the organization when it displays one or more signs of weakness. Although protest absorption also entails some dangers, it is a more promising way of checking nonconformity on several counts.

If protest absorption is successful, it not only eliminates the pocket of nonconformity but also strengthens the organization by providing it with the services of an energetic, devoted group. Moreover, the process permits the legitimation of innovation which better equips the organization to face external challenges or to attain its own goals more effectively. Protest absorption can also lead to the elimination of nonconformity without the emergence of a devoted group or the introduction of innovation. This form results when the organization provides the enclave with an "opportunity to fail." When the enclave protests about matters beyond its ken or original bailiwick, and it is accorded legitimacy in the area of protest, it is likely to fail because it lacks the skills and knowledge to carry out the now-legitimate activity. Any nonconformity which survives outright failure is expected to be sufficiently weakened so as to be eliminated easily. Should the enclave succeed despite its opportunity to fail, then the organization can reap the benefits. The risk accompanying protest absorption is that the nonconforming enclave may, during the time that the organization attempts to check it, gain access to the key power positions and, subsequently, assume control of the total structure.

The process of protest absorption

Once the nonconforming enclave has been converted into a new legitimate subunit, the organization is strengthened. During the protest-absorption process, however, the organization, especially that sector of it in which the enclave has erupted, faces a series of internal battles involving several levels of its hierarchy. The charismatic leader and his followers oppose those persons who formally are their immediate superiors. These shall be called the middle hierarchy and represent the enemy in the battles. Insofar as the

15. Ibid., pp. 11–12.
16. A recent report of the AFL-CIO council stated: "It is obvious that expulsion as such does not cure the offending practices. And, what is more important, once outside the federation the membership of such an organization is no longer accessible to corrective influences from the parent body through education and persuasion." (Quoted in the *Reporter,* 26 October 1961, p. 18.)

organization has a centralized top hierarchy which can exercise authority over the middle hierarchy, these battles tend not to be fought to the death of one or the other set of combatants. Instead, the top hierarchy intercedes and more or less arbitrarily terminates the conflict. Protest absorption essentially is a process whereby the top hierarchy attempts to balance the two opposing forces—members of the nonconforming enclave against members of the middle hierarchy who are the immediate superiors of the former.

In some instances, units which are laterally related to the nonconforming enclave will also be aligned with the middle hierarchy in opposing the enclave. In other cases, the opposition will be made up only of heads of laterally related units and an opposing middle hierarchy will be absent. The varying composition of the "enemy" depends upon the location of the enclave in the organizational structure. The general pattern, however, might be diagrammed as shown in fig. 2.

Assume that the enclave erupts in D_4. If the leader is the head of D_4, the enclave will encompass the entire unit. If the leader is only a member, the enclave will set itself up as D_4. In either case, the enclave will have to contend with C_2, who is responsible for D_1-D_4. Directly, or indirectly, the enclave will also have to contend with the other D units. The emergence of the nonconforming enclave creates increased competition for resources among the D units. In addition, they perceive themselves as being cast in an unfavorable light by the enthusiasm and heightened activity of the enclave. Hence, the D units will pressure C_2 to suppress the enclave. The D units do not always form part of the opposition to the enclave; another variation is that C_2 might also be directly in charge of one D unit as well as having general responsibility for the entire D section. Such structural variations in the formation of the opposition to the nonconforming enclave do

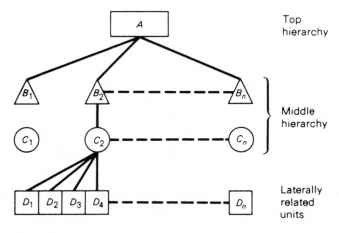

Figure 2.

not affect the general pattern of protest absorption, although they help to explain slight variations from case to case. Hence, for simplicity's sake, in describing the process we shall limit the opposition to the middle hierarchy, although the reader should bear in mind that the opposition can vary in its composition.

Incumbents of positions constituting the middle hierarchy are more likely to exhibit "trained incapacity" than incumbents of other levels. Hence, they are usually incapable of comprehending the significance of the enclave's protest. Furthermore, their positions are threatened by the enclave, both because it reveals that their loyalty to basic values of the organization is not as strong as it could be and because it indicates that they cannot make use of the authority vested in them to maintain order in their own bailiwicks. Their response to the enclave is to attempt to suppress it through such means as closing the communication links between the charismatic leader and the top hierarchy, restricting the enclave members' freedom of movement, and reducing the resources available to them. From the perspective of the middle hierarchy, the use of such techniques represents the full exercise of their rights of office.[17] From the perspective of the nonconforming enclave, such techniques are obstructions which indicate that the organization is against it, and hence, to carry out its cause, the enclave must try to be even more dynamic and more cohesive.

If the charismatic leader is to demonstrate his basic loyalty to organizational values and if he is to gain recognition and legitimation for his cause, he must have access to the top hierarchy. When such access via regular channels is barred, the leader develops his own routes to the top. Frequently this is done through an intermediary who is outside the organization but has legitimate access to the top echelon. Insofar as the charismatic leader is able to establish a particularistic relationship with such an intermediary which is beyond organizational control, he has relatively easy access to the top.

The particularistic communication line gives the nonconforming enclave some leverage in an attempt to have its cause recognized and legitimized. That the hierarchy is willing to use his power over the top hierarchy in behalf of the enclave is regarded by its members as a significant step forward and as a sign of incipient legitimation.

At the same time that a particularistic communication line gives the enclave hope that its cause will be successful it also produces potential instability and unreliability. First, the communication line is maintained at the will—or the whim—of the intermediary, which means that it can be opened and closed arbitrarily. Second, a particularistic request to the top

17. When legitimate techniques fail to quell the enclave, the middle hierarchy might resort to illegitimate or nonlegitimate ones. Paradoxically, it is at such times that the middle hierarchy overcomes its "trained incapacity."

hierarchy in behalf of the nonconforming enclave might elicit informal instructions to the middle hierarchy which it can easily overlook in its continued attempts to obstruct the enclave.

In some instances the charismatic leader need not resort to particularistic communication channels for he might be able to go to the top directly;[18] or the attention of the top hierarchy might be drawn to the nonconforming enclave as a result of the conflict between it and the middle hierarchy, especially if the conflict has affected task performance adversely.

Regardless of the means by which the attention of the top hierarchy is directed to the enclave, the leader who has gained this attention can demonstrate his basic loyalty to organizational values and communicate his ideas for their more effective realization in the hope of gaining official approval. Concerned with blocking such approval, the middle hierarchy urges the top to suppress the enclave. The top hierarchy is interested in enhancing general organizational effectiveness, and, by extension, is concerned with maintaining internal order. With its broader, more substantive, perspective, the top is more amenable to innovation than the middle hierarchy, especially when faced with internal weakness or external challenge. Hence, the top is more likely to accede some demands of the nonconforming enclave, especially if its leader is backed by a powerful intermediary, than to the insistence of the middle hierarchy that the enclave be thoroughly curbed or eliminated.

The first round in the protest-absorption process is completed when the top hierarchy recognizes the nonconforming enclave and gives it a modicum of autonomy to pursue its advocated innovation. This is followed by several more rounds of obstruction by the middle hierarchy, unorthodox communication to the top by the nonconforming enclave, and a gradually increasing grant of resources, autonomy, and legitimacy to the enclave by the top hierarchy. With each round the enclave comes closer to approximating a new legitimate subunit.

In exchange for autonomy and legitimacy from the top hierarchy, the enclave must agree to accept certain stabilizers. The stabilizers are mechanisms to insure the loyalty of the new unit to the organization and its conformity to organization regulations. First, the protest-absorbing unit is expected to develop rules, subject to approval by the top echelon, to guide its conduct; any changes in these rules are also subject to approval by the top. Second, the unit must accept a regular source of finance through which it will acquire all or most of its inputs. In this way, unauthorized appropriations of resources and competition with existing units for available resources are minimized, and the frustrations of an irregular source of income, typical of a group during its nonconformist period, are avoided. Third, and

---

18. The leader's ability to communicate with the top hierarchy directly is determined in large part by other capacities, roles, and statuses which he might have within or outside of the organization.

most important, the unit's activity is limited to a particular sphere of operation, usually that for which the leader and his followers advocated their
innovation.[19]

With the introduction of stabilizers, the leader's personal charisma becomes attenuated. The personal charisma is reconverted to charisma of
office as the leader (or his successor) assumes legitimate control of the protest-absorber unit. Furthermore, the most radical members of the former
enclave perceive the leader as bowing to the dictates of the top hierarchy,
thereby betraying the cause; they cease to accept the leader as a charismatic
figure, leave the unit, and, where possible, even the organization. The
more visible to his followers are the leader's negotiations with the top hierarchy, the more likely is this to be the case. In fact, the top hierarchy could
reduce the leader's personal charisma considerably by sending a representative directly to the members of the enclave to grant it legitimacy. By cir-
cumventing the leader, the top hierarchy gives the impression that it has
been wise enough to recognize the value of the enclave's cause of its own
accord and so no credit need be given to the leader who has spearheaded
the cause. Circumvention of the leader does present certain dangers, however. Such a procedure is most likely to be successful only if the representative has instructions to grant all or the most important of the enclave's
demands. Otherwise, enclave members are likely to perceive the visitation
of the representative as an attempt by the top hierarchy to sabotage the
cause. Since, in most cases, the top is unlikely to grant major concessions
in one fell swoop, this danger is almost always present and serves to
strengthen the enclave. A second danger is that the representative himself
might be affected by the leader's charisma and join the enclave rather than
fulfill his orders.

Occasionally other stabilizers are also introduced, e.g., limiting the size
of the protest-absorber unit, appointing a special supervisor to watch for
and check any excessive enthusiasm which the unit might display, and restricting the use it may make of its particularistic communication channel. Generally, these particular stabilizers are instituted if the newly
legitimized unit still remains somewhat recalcitrant in its adherence to organization rules.

The conformity of the unit if further enhanced through pressures arising
within it to replace the instability of its charismatic nature with the stabilizing characteristics which accompany routinization. The nonconforming
enclave, like the large-scale charismatic movement, faces "everyday"
problems of economic and administrative organization. For example, the

---

19. The nature of the task limitation imposed on the protest-absorber unit is in part determined by the form of the organization's division of labor, i.e., whether it is structured along
geographic lines such that each unit engages in the same task but in a different locality, or
around functionally specific lines where each unit engages in its own speciality, or is a combination of geography and functional specificity. See C. I. Barnard, *The Functions of the
Executive* (Cambridge, Mass.: Harvard University Press, 1938), p. 129ff.

unit at some point must provide for the selection of a successor to replace its charismatic leader. (The criteria for selection may be established either by the enclave or by the organization.)

The external pressures toward protest absorption and the internal pressures toward routinization eventually tame the nonconforming enclave and convert it into a quiescent unit concerned with maintaining order in its own bailiwick.[20] The unit may show signs of quiescence simultaneously with its legitimation through protest absorption, or after a period of dynamism during which it expands and gives devoted service to the organization. Its concern with expansion and innovation is replaced by one of self-maintenance. The zeal and energy of the unit are dissipated in legitimized action without being replenished. Once the original members of the unit are gone, or have become concerned with preserving their newly legitimized positions within the organization, the verve that sparked the unit when it was a nonconforming enclave cannot be sustained. Successors to key positions in the unit most likely have been socialized by the organization, and tend to resemble the middle hierarchy more than the original members of the enclave.

The unit's agreement to restrict itself to a specialized sphere of operation is itself another contributing factor to the emerging quiescent period. The agreement helps to preclude the possibility that the unit will attempt innovation beyond its allotted sphere; and whatever success the unit has in its speciality also drains it of further nonconformity. Success is its own detriment when the question of new risks arises: members of the unit prefer to maintain rather than gamble their resources and status on a new venture.

Another factor in the elimination of nonconformity from the unit is time itself. Norms which the enclave had revitalized once again become eroded through increasing lack of strict adherence to them. Members of the unit remain committed to their once-new methods even though they have become outmoded and ineffectual. The unit as a whole is no longer dedicated to the ultimate values of the organization but rests content with the sinecure provided it through protest absorption.

The factors that contribute to quiescence—cessation of innovation, dissipation of zeal and energy, emergent conservative tendencies, modification of norms, and the obsolescence of methods—also set the stage for new protest and new forms of nonconformity, which are likely to erupt because the unit legitimized through protest absorptions is more vulnerable to the strains between charisma and discipline than are other units. Its history of nonconformity remains unforgotten and lends it an aura of prestige, thereby distinguishing the former enclave from ordinary units. It is further distinguished by having institutionalized a more arduous socialization period for its recruits. Finally, its standards tend to be more strict and demanding than those of the organization as a whole, even with the corroding effects of

---

20. Robert Michels, *Political Parties* (New York: Dover Publications, 1959), pp. 174–75.

time. These factors not only militate against the complete integration of the unit into the organization but also make it extremely attractive to recruits, particularly to those who tend to be strongly or rigidly committed to its original values. In short, the unit, limited to its own sphere of action, tamed by stabilizers, concerned with its own well-being, and yet, endowed with the aura of its unorthodox past which facilitates recruitment of potential nonconformers, nurtures a fertile field for the regeneration of a nonconforming enclave and another cycle of protest absorption.

In summary, the process of protest absorption follows several steps. A nonconforming enclave is able to gain some power within the organization because the latter is internally weak or faced with an external crisis. To check the internal threat without further weakening itself, the organization forms a new administrative unit to absorb the enclave, based on the institutionalization of new norms. The emergence of the unit represents a *Sturm und Drang* period: the enclave demands more autonomy and resources so that it can pursue its course of action while the organization reluctantly grants some autonomy and resources, and permits some innovation, in order to maintain peace and overcome the crisis confronting it. The *Sturm und Drang* begins to subside when the enclave achieves the status of a more or less legitimate unit within the organization, and is virtually quelled as the unit loses its initial élan, no longer taking on new ventures and becoming concerned with its own maintenance. From the perspective of the top hierarchy of the organization, protest absorption is a process of encapsulation. The nonconforming enclave becomes encased in a network of stabilizers which limits its freedom of action.

Implications of protest absorption for the organization

In large measure, the significance of protest absorption for the organization as a whole depends upon the bearing which the enclave's cause has on the core policies and practices of the organization. From the standpoint of its proponents, the cause usually has a greater degree of significance for core policies than the top hierarchy is willing to acknowledge.

It is convenient to formalize what is generally involved here by means of a continuum in which the cause advocated by an enclave is scaled relative to the degree with which it is likely to affect core policies and practices. Then, as in fig. 3, the enclave can be characterized as to where it *aspires to be* on the continuum, and where it is *willing to be placed*. The organization can be characterized as to where it would *like* to locate the enclave, and where it is *willing to place it*. The shaded area indicates the range of acceptability for an enclave and its organization; in this instance there is an overlap, although this is not always the case. Moreover, the ranges of acceptability can shift in the course of the protest-absorption process.

Once these ranges are known, further statements can be made about

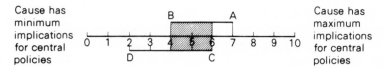

Figure 3. *A,* enclave desires cause to have value of 7. *B,* enclave willing to accept value of 4. *C,* organization willing to permit value of 6. *D,* organization prefers value of 2.

protest absorption. Where there is an overlap in ranges, protest absorption should prove more successful in controlling the enclave's nonconformity than where such an overlap does not exist. In the case where an overlap is absent (or in the case where the organization makes strong attempts to place the enclave below its minimum acceptable position—in fig. 3 this would be below 4), the enclave will retain its zeal and unorthodoxy in order to attempt to achieve its cause in the face of control measures. For as the enclave is forced toward the lower end of the continuum, its cause becomes more attenuated, and its chances are lessened for realizing the goals which sparked it in the first place.

Furthermore, by locating the ranges of acceptability, we can predict approximately the number of rounds the protest-absorption process is likely to undergo. More rounds can be anticipated as the overlap between the two ranges is lessened. For the organization will usually try to check the enclave by locating it as low on the continuum as it can, while the enclave will continue its nonconformist activity until it is located as high on the continuum as it can be.

The more that protest absorption takes place at the higher end of the continuum, the more likely it is that an organization's central policies and practices will undergo a change. This is likely, if only for the reason that the more central the protest-absorber unit is to the organization, the more probable it is that its members will be promoted upward in the hierarchy until they reach the top.[21] The variables which determine where, on the continuum, the enclave will ultimately be absorbed are those involved in the protest-absorption process itself: the degree of weakness of the organization, the strength of the nonconforming enclave, the power of the intermediary, the nature of the stabilizers, and so on. Thus the protest-absorption process can lead to a long-term chain reaction of major changes in the organization, as well as check nonconformity and introduce a particular innovation.

Finally, protest absorption can have implications for organizational pol-

---

21. The most cogent illustration of this process can probably be found in the history of the United States Air Force and of the submarine and aircraft carrier units in the United States Navy.

icy for dealing with nonconformity. An organization which has had long experience with nonconformity, e.g., the Catholic church, might institutionalize the rounds of protest absorption. This means that, as a nonconforming enclave emerges, it "automatically" will be converted into a new subunit over several stages, as it is able to meet criteria specified by the top hierarchy. If the adoption of protest absorption as a conscious organization policy is carried out effectively, an organization will strengthen its ability to cope with nonconformity and to implement changes flowing upward from the bottom.

Appendix

Some historical examples

Following a presentation of a middle-range theory model, ideally, one should develop indicators for the variables that make up the model, and then collect a sample of cases to test the model. Traditional limitations of time and space prevent the realization of the ideal. To facilitate comprehension of the protest-absorption model, however, the history of two nonconforming enclaves is presented in table 1. One enclave emerged within the Carmel Order in sixteenth-century Spain under the leadership of St. Teresa. The second enclave began when Claire Chennault was faced with the problem of developing a Chinese Air Force in the late 1930s.

Space does not permit even a skeleton consideration of other enclaves. Examples abound however. To name a few: Orde Wingate's Special Night Squad, his Gideon Force which fought in Ethiopia, and his long-range penetration unit known as the Chindits; the Cistercian Order which began as an enclave within the Benedictine Order, and the Trappist Order which emerged from the Cistercian Order, and so on. Our examples have been limited to military groups and to the cenobitic structures of the Catholic church, not only because these are normative organizations with strong centralized authorities but also because of availability of data. The reader should bear in mind, however, that nonconforming enclaves and their containment through protest absorption can occur in other normative organizations. An example is the Fund for the Republic which has been described as "Paul Hoffman's severance pay." In his unofficial biography of the Ford Foundation, Dwight MacDonald writes:

> The Foundation's trustees decided that (the program) should be implemented by a new agency, which finally emerged in December, 1952 as the Fund for the Republic. . . . Hoffman originally supported Hutchins in proposing it, and its establishment coincided with Hoffman's extrusion from the Foundation. . . . The Fund's elephantine gestation is perhaps explained by the dilemma of the Ford trustees . . . who found themselves being chivied by Hoffman and Hutchins into doing some-

Table 1. History of two nonconforming enclaves

	Discaled Carmelites, 1562–93	Flying Tigers, 1941–60
Organization	Catholic church	United States Army
Leader	St. Teresa	General C. L. Chennault
Lieutenants	St. John of the Cross	Colonel C. V. Haynes Colonel R. L. Scott
Cause	Greater concern with salvation. Revive asceticism of early Carmelites. Concern with action as well as contemplation, e.g., praying for the souls of others. This was to lead to emphasis on missionary work.	Develop and put into action fighter pilot tactics. Train American pilots in the use of fighter planes. Furnish air support for Chinese land forces and fight delaying action against Japanese.
Symbols	Alpargatas (hemp and rope sandals). Rough material for clothing.	Flying Tiger sharks painted on planes. Cowboy boots instead of regulation military boots.
State of organization	Carmel Order had its strict rule modified in 1432. By the sixteenth century, adherence to the modified rule had become lax. Nuns spent time in gossip rather than in prayer. Spanish church beginning to seethe with reform to meet challenge of Reformation.	Tactics for use of planes not developed at pace commensurate with technological progress. Tendency by military to view planes as auxiliary to infantry and artillery. Lack of preparation to deal with onset of World War II.
Middle hierarchy	Officials of Carmel Order in Spain and Italy	Generals Bissell and Stilwell
Top hierarchy	The pope	President Roosevelt
Intermediary	Philip II of Spain	Madame Chiang Kai-shek
Obstruction techniques	Teresa assigned for three-year period to head of a Carmel convent to halt her activities. Excommunication of nuns who voted for Teresa when her three-year term was concluded. Assigning Calced confessors to Discaled houses. Kidnapping and imprisoning friars loyal to Teresa.	Limiting allocation of supplies and personnel. Detaining Flying Tiger recruits in India, enroute to China, to indoctrinate them against Chennault. Attempting to select Chennault's chief of staff for him.
Stabilizers	Constitution for Discaled providing for a centralized government.	Induction of Flying Tigers into U.S. Army which meant that group would have to adhere to military regulations.

| Origin of enclave and rounds of protest absorption | Within convent at Avila, Teresa gained small following. Permission granted to start her own house.

1. Discalced established as separate province. 1579. Free to establish religious houses. Subject to General of Order of Spain.

2. Established as separate congregation, 1587. Subject to General of entire Carmel Order but elected its own Vicar-General.

3. Established by papal bull as separate order, 1593, subject only to pope.

4. In succeeding centuries Discalced Order engaged in missionary work and spread beyond the boundaries of Spain. | Chennault invited to China by Madame Chiang Kai-shek to develop Chinese Air Force. From 1936 to 1940, Chennault fought Japanese with whatever pilots and equipment drifted to China. From 1940 to 1941, American Volunteer Group organized; group commanded by Chennault and paid by Chinese government.

1. AVG transformed into China Air Task Force and inducted into USAAF, July 1942, subject to Bissell as head of parent 10th Air Force.

2. CATF converted into 14th Air Force, March 1943, subject to Stilwell's command as head of China-Burma-India theater.

3. No further rounds of protest absorption occurred, for General Marshall felt that Chennault should continue under Stilwell's command, but Stilwell was instructed to give Chennault all that he asked for.

4. 14th Air Force deactivated in 1960. |

Note: For references pertaining to table 1, see the following:

Discalced Carmelites:
Nigg, Walter, *Warriors of God*, New York: Alfred A. Knopf, 1959.
Peers, E. A., *Handbook to the Life and Times of St. Teresa and St. John of the Cross*, Westminster, Maryland: Newman Press, 1954.
———, *Spirit of Flame*, New York: Morehouse-Gorham, 1945.
St. Teresa, *Life of St. Teresa* (trans. by Rev. John Dalton), New York: P. J. Kennedy & Sons, N.D.
Zimmerman, B., *Carmel in England*, London: Burns & Oates, 1899.

Flying Tigers:
Romanus, C. F. and Sunderland, R., *Stilwell's Mission to China*, Washington, D.C.: Office of the Chief of Military History, Dept. of the Army, 1953.
Scott, R. L., *God is my Co-Pilot*, New York: Ballantine, 1959.
———, *Flying Tiger: Chennault of China*, New York: Doubleday, 1959.
Wedemyer, A. C., *Wedemyer Reports*, New York: Henry Holt, 1958.

thing that was as "controversial" as it was logical on the basis of the program they themselves had adopted.[22]

Postscript 1972

After this working paper was completed in 1962, no systematic effort was undertaken to test the hypothesis implicit in the description of the protest absorption process. But other research endeavors, and the militant, and at times violent, protest that has permeated many American institutions in recent years have stimulated some additional thoughts about protest absorption. I shall describe these briefly here.

Protest absorption in competitive organizations

Protest absorption is almost always shrouded with uncertainty, because it depends on the charismatic strength of the leader as he pursues his cause, among other reasons. His charisma might only be adequate through one round of absorption. But there is one structural characteristic that might compensate for the leader's deficiency and assure the establishment of a new legitimate subunit, and that is competition.

Among a set of organizations competing within the same market, either for resources or for clientele, the process of absorbing protest in one unit may have implications for structural change within a competing unit. Let us assume that organization A has, after much strife, converted a nonconforming enclave into a new legitimate subunit, with a delimited amount of autonomy to pursue its innovative ideas. Further, assume that the new subunit is visible to competing organizations. It may be the case that competing organization B is already faced with a similar nonconforming enclave. In this instance, B might convert the enclave into a legitimate subunit without as much conflict as occurred in A, to assure the maintenance of its competitive position. And this might occur regardless of the energies that the leader of the enclave brings to his cause, a particularistic link to the top leader of B, or the presence of other conditions that contribute to the protest-absorption process.[23]

Finally, organization C may not have a nonconforming enclave, but in response to protest absorption in A, it may introduce a new unit in order to maintain its competitive position. In this way protest absorption within one organization may have implications for structural change, if not protest absorption, for other organizations that compete in the same environment.

---

22. Dwight MacDonald, *The Ford Foundation* (New York: Reynal & Co., 1956), p. 71.
23. This hypothesis about the effects of competition on protest absorption emerged from a review of the histories of the news units within CBS and NBC. See Mitchell V. Charnley, *News by Radio* (New York: Macmillan, 1948); A. A. Schechter, *I Live on Air* (New York: Frederick A. Stokes, 1941); Francis Chase, Jr., *Sound and Fury* (New York: Harper & Bros., 1942); Eric Sevareid, *Not So Wild a Dream* (New York: Alfred Knopf, 1946), and other memoirs by broadcasters.

Protest and organizational learning

What has just been hypothesized about competing organizations implies that they learn from each other. The question that might be asked now is to what extent organizations which are functionally similar, such as universities, but are not competitive in the usual market sense, learn from each other in controlling nonconformity. Specifically, to what extent did the demand for and the institutionalization of such innovations as Black Studies programs or coed dormitories in one university affect the institutionalization process in other universities? The question is pertinent insofar as on some campuses such innovations emerged from the efforts of university officials to control nonconforming student enclaves. Probably a key explanatory variable for answering the question is the degree to which institutions of higher learning see themselves as similar to the university that is absorbing student protest by developing a new specialized curriculum.

The same types of questions about protest absorption could be raised vis-à-vis public school systems. Within the last five years some of the larger urban systems have been experimenting with innovative learning centers which replace the traditional public school for some students. Did these centers emerge from the efforts of school officials to control nonconforming enclaves or through other avenues?

Separation as an alternative to absorption

Certainly not all conforming enclaves are absorbed by their parent organizations. The history of Protestantism is, in large measure, the history of nonconforming sects that separated from their parent religions. The history of western political parties details the rise of splinter groups that either died out or established themselves as separate parties. Voluntary organizations also tend to produce splinter groups. A full account of the conditions leading to separation rather than absorption cannot be undertaken here, but a brief listing of them may serve to highlight the protest absorption process.

These conditions will be presented in the form of separate hypotheses. First, separation of the enclave, rather than its absorption, is more likely to occur when the parent organization lacks a long span of control. Where the middle hierarchy is short or absent the enclave is likely to pose a direct threat to the authority of the top leadership. Second, separation is more likely to occur when the enclave's cause directly challenges the premises underlying the organization's central policies. In both of these instances there is little room for arriving at solutions that would be acceptable both to the enclave and the top leadership. Third, separation is more likely when the organization feels it is sufficiently strong that it can afford to lose its protesting members, and face them as a part of its environment. (A small liberal arts college let the dissident members of its faculty go, to form a new type of college, at a time when Ph.Ds were beginning to be a glut on the market. The rift in the Sierra Club became complete as its membership was expanding rapidly.) Fourth, separation is more likely when an individual can easily obtain and shed member status in the organization. Fifth, separation rather than absorption is more likely to occur when the organization does not have a monopoly or partial monopoly on means and rewards. These last two conditions tend to be interrelated, and when they obtain, the enclave is more likely to believe that it can survive on its own.

Absorption and the content of protest

In view of the varieties of protest that institutions have sustained in recent years, the phrase of "protest absorption," which refers to the process by which a nonconforming enclave is checked through conversion into a new legitimate subunit, may be unfortunate. Even though the phrase is broader than the process it denotes, it shall be retained.

At least two types of protest within organizations have been evident in recent years, where protest absorption would not be feasible. The first type occurs when the protestors are advocating something for another party rather than for themselves. A case in point would be student objection to university actions such as research contracts with the Department of Defense. A university might create a new college that would have no defense contracts for protesting students to attend. But since these students are not likely to be involved in activities relating to such contracts in the first place, it is unclear how a new subcampus would dampen their protest.

The second type occurs when the protestors are advocating a change in the organization's central policies. Pertinent examples are the pressures within the Catholic church to change its position on the rule of clerical celibacy and on the use of contraceptives. Logically, protests on both matters could be handled through the creation of new subunits. For the former there could be a cenobitic order whose members would be permitted to marry. For the latter, subparishes could be established whose members would be permitted to use contraceptives. But the creation of such subunits would mean institutionalizing actions that contravene central beliefs (see figure 3 in the main text of the article).

All this suggests that the incidence of protest absorption within organizations broadly bears some kind of curvilinear relationship to societal change in general. When a society is extremely stable some of the conditions that produce a nonconforming enclave are probably absent, so the incidence of protest absorption would be very low. When a society has been accumulating extensive changes, nonconforming enclaves within organizations abound, but their protests are not always amenable to absorption through the creation of new subunits. Consequently, the incidence of protest absorption would be much smaller than the incidence of nonconforming enclaves. Between these extremes of stability and change, when conditions are present to produce nonconforming enclaves but the types of change that generate extreme pressures on an organization's central policies are absent, one might anticipate a much higher incidence of protest absorption.

Postscript 1979

Many observers of the American scene (e.g., Gary Trudeau in Doonesbury) see the 1970s as a formless decade, in contrast to earlier ones, not lending itself to easy symbolization. But from the perspective of protest absorption, the 1970s can be viewed as a decade in which many organizations were (and still are) faced with absorbing and institutionalizing changes stimulated by the 1960s social movements. These processes invite further reflection on the protest absorption theory. Here I shall elaborate on two points of the theory as they pertain to one outcome of the environmental movement. The two points are (1) that dispersal of the leader and members of the nonconforming enclave throughout the organization, in an effort to disband the group, might spread rather than eliminate the nonconformity; (2) that the protest of nonconforming enclaves is less amenable to absorption through the creation of new legitimate subunits the closer the subject of protest is to the organization's central beliefs and policies.

The environmental movement led to the passage of the National Environmental Policy Act of 1969 (NEPA), requiring federal agencies to address the latent as well as manifest consequences of their proposed construction projects, and resource extraction and utilization plans. Findings are to be published in environmental impact statements (EISs). The law requires that an agency publish a draft EIS which is to be viewed by other agencies, citizen groups, and individuals during a sixty to ninety-day public review period. The agency then prepares a final EIS which includes comments submitted during the review period, the agency's responses to the comments, and any revisions of the draft EIS stimulated by public review.

NEPA, in effect, is a mandate to have agencies improve their decision-making processes. Decisions about large construction projects and resource utilization are to be based on a more thorough understanding of the likely effects of a proposed undertaking on natural social environments. The EIS process is intended to broaden an agency's vision, to make it more sensitive to public concerns about its activities and their effects, to have it seriously contemplate alternative approaches for fulfilling its objectives, to make it more responsive to public concerns in choosing among alternative proposals, and to have an agency develop mitigation plans to dampen at least some of the anticipated unavoidable, adverse consequences of the alternative it has chosen to implement.

To comply with NEPA, federal agencies, in effect, had to permit the emergence of nonconforming enclaves within their organizations. Enclaves evolved through the hiring of relatively young, somewhat idealistic and very energetic persons with degrees in a variety of natural and social sciences, who were charged with preparing EISs, and with other responsibilities relating to the implementation of an "environmental sensitivity" in day-to-day affairs. For agencies whose professional positions were staffed almost exclusively by engineers, foresters, planners, or architects, the hiring of professionals in quite different disciplines marked a major new thrust. Typically, an agency would hire two or three "environmental specialists" at the outset, placing them in a subsection of the planning branch. Although the characteristics of the enclaves and the degree of cooperation they received from their organizations vary considerably from agency to agency, and from district office to district office within any one agency, in general they resemble the model of the nonconforming enclave. Enclave staffs had to be expanded rapidly to keep pace with court interpretations of what constituted legally acceptable impact statements. Some enclaves have as many as twenty to twenty-five members. Charismatic leaders have emerged in a number of them; in some enclaves, where the leader never emerged or where he was "exiled" to another unit of the organization, enclave members regarded themselves as committed to a charismatic idea, namely bringing about more "environmentally and socially sensitive" decisions.[24]

In the district offices of some agencies, middle management has used several bureaucratic tactics to check the enclaves and force them to produce EISs that discuss only the benign consequences of the proposed action and stress the adverse aspects of alternatives to it. By the same token, the enclaves have developed tactics to produce "full disclosure" EISs despite the censuring efforts of middle management. Also, some enclaves have sought to permeate a wide array of agency activities to stimulate "environmental sensitivity" in day-to-day actions. Such permeation is particularly important in agency planning branches where ideas for future construction and resource utilization projects are initiated. It is much easier to develop "environmentally sensitive" plans if such an orientation is considered throughout the planning process rather than tacked on after several years of planning,

---

24. For a discussion of charismatic ideas and their dependency on leaders for transmission see Peter Berger, "Charisma, Religious Innovation, and the Israelite Prophecy," *American Sociological Review* 28 (1963): 940–50; and Edward Shils, "Charisma, Order and Status," *American Sociological Review* 30 (1965): 199–212. In the context of a highly differentiated society with many voluntary organizations, the structure and networks are there for an idea without aid of a charismatic leader in the enclave itself. Enclave members can sustain commitment to the idea, and keep up with reinterpretations of it through memberships in professional and citizen organizations, through reading the literature published by these groups, and through nonwork activities allowing reaffirmation to the charismatic idea. In fact, such activities may bring enclave members in contact with charismatic leaders in nonwork settings like club activities and professional meetings.

during which time the project planning staff has developed a commitment to a particular course of action.

In some agency district offices, the enclaves experienced several rounds of protest absorption, often from subsections to sections within planning branches, and in a few instances to full-fledged branch status with their own sections. Several factors prompted these rounds: (1) increasing pressure from external sources like citizen groups to prepare comprehensive EISs, which required more labor; (2) increasing pressure from external sources to prepare EISs for a wide variety of agency undertakings, which also required more labor; (3) arguments presented by enclave leaders to higher management levels that work could be performed with greater quality and less delay if the environmental specialists had more autonomy, including developing their own budgets and schedules, and letting their own research contracts.

Meanwhile, the chiefs of nonplanning branches began to recognize the need for the permeation of "environmental sensitivity" in their areas of responsibility. They observed that failure to exercise such sensitivity led to delays in implementing actions and programs beyond the planning stage, or their cancellation or modification as citizen groups or other agencies used various legal tools (administrative appeals, court injunctions, etc.) to have environmentally insensitive actions halted.

This recognition had its own effect on the environmental enclaves. Generally, the enclaves worked most closely with planning branches, preparing EISs to accompany planning documents. But as other branches, in particular, those charged with construction and resource extraction supervision, and issuance of permits for activities to be engaged in by the private sector, developed the recognition, they turned to the environmental enclaves for assistance. (Prior informal contact with the environmental specialists helped encourage this recognition.) The enclaves responded to requests for help by working overtime, which was consistent with the youth and idealism of its members, and by hiring additional staff.

These responses, however, were usually not adequate for the increasing demands placed on the enclaves. As a result, work priorities shifted almost daily, and it became increasingly difficult to meet deadlines for the preparation of EISs. The need to cross department lines and go through time-consuming chains of command to obtain environmental assistance led to other solutions. Branch chiefs (other than planning) created new environmental positions within their units, often filling them by recruiting from the environmental enclaves. (In several instances, movement to these positions constituted promotions for the environmental specialists.)

Planning-branch heads also began to recognize the need for closer integration between various aspects of planning and environmental sensitivity, which led to further inroads on the environmental enclaves. Senior natural and social scientists were dispersed to different sections of planning branches. If the environmental enclave had achieved branch status, it was once again reduced to section or subsection status within the planning branch, with a smaller staff and lesser responsibility. Its main responsibility would be to coordinate all components of an EIS with other sections of the planning branch, and to rewrite a variety of study and planning documents into a relatively short and readable EIS. (The latter is consistent with new Council of Environmental Quality guidelines stipulating that EISs should summarize key research findings but should not present detailed studies.)

In summary, the passage of NEPA required federal construction and resource management agencies to bring an "environmental" orientation to their central policies which necessitated the utilization of training and skills the agencies had heretofore not found necessary. Initially, they responded to the law through establishing nonconforming enclaves of environmental specialists; some enclaves sustained several rounds of protest absorption. As pressures continued in the larger society to have "environmental" considerations influence decision and activities, agency managers created environmental positions within a variety of branches, often filling these with personnel from the enclaves, in an effort to institutionalize an environmental orientation throughout the agencies. (However, early in the history of some enclaves, some particularly zealous environmental specialists were ordered out of the enclaves into other sections in efforts to check them. Such transfers occurred after particularly abrasive incidents between enclave members and "old-time" agency members and were clearly regarded as "punishment.") Such dispersals, brought about partly because enclave members voluntarily applied for the new positions on a competitive basis, led to the devolution of the enclaves. Further devolution occurred when other members were transferred. With each type of dispersal, enclave members took with them many of the same responsibilities they had within the enclaves.

From the standpoint of the protest absorption theory, when external pressures are brought to bear on an organization's central policies which require the use of different skills and training, the organization may respond initially by developing a nonconforming enclave in its midst. Recruitment to the enclave is based on possession of the requisite skills to allow the organization to be responsive, to some degree, to pressures for change. For a while, the relationship between the enclave and the organization will follow the protest absorption model. But if external pressure for change in the organization's central policies continues, even an enclave that has undergone several rounds of protest absorption—becoming a new legitimate subunit—will not be able to handle all the demands placed on it. At this juncture, the organization will begin dispersing enclave specialists to new positions throughout the organization (or recruiting specialists from outside if necessary) in an effort to have its central policies change in a manner responsive to external pressure.

In conclusion, when the type of changes being demanded in an organization's central policies require skills and training that the organization has not used in the past, the formation of nonconforming enclaves and several rounds of protest absorption can be expected, followed by enclave devolution as positions based on the new skills are created throughout the organization.

Organizational Culture and Counterculture: An Uneasy Symbiosis

Joanne Martin
and Caren Siehl

Four sentences capture the essence of much of the recent organizational culture research. First, cultures offer an interpretation of an institution's history that members can use to decipher how they will be expected to behave in the future. Second, cultures can generate commitment to corporate values or management philosophy so that employees feel they are working for something they believe in. Third, cultures serve as organizational control mechanisms, informally approving or prohibiting some patterns of behavior. Finally, there is the possibility, as yet unsupported by conclusive evidence, that some types of organizational cultures are associated with greater productivity and profitability.

Most of this research shares a single set of simplifying assumptions. First, the perspective of the organization's top management is assumed because the functions studied serve to (1) transmit top management's interpretations of the meaning of events throughout the organization, (2) generate commitment to their practices and policies, and (3) help them control behavior in accordance with their objectives. Second, the functions of culture are portrayed as integrative, unifying the diverse elements of an organization. Third, organizational culture is treated as a monolithic phenomenon—one culture to a setting. Finally, many of these studies implicitly assume or explicitly assert that culture can be managed by using direct, intentional actions not unlike those used in other management tasks.

This particular set of simplifying assumptions may blind us to some important aspects of organizational culture. For example, studies of blue-collar workers' practices, such as "hassling" ratebusters, clearly indicate that cultural mechanisms can be used to undermine top-management objectives. Cultures can serve differentiating rather than integrating functions by, for example, expressing conflicts among parts of a society. Instead of being monolithic phenomena, organizational cultures are composed of various interlocking, nested, sometimes conflicting subcultures.

Finally, it is likely that cultural development, like other aspects of organizational functioning, is not as responsive to direct managerial attempts at control as many would like to believe. It may be that cultures cannot be straightforwardly created or managed by individuals. Instead, cultures may simply exist and managers may capitalize on cultural effects they perceive as positive or minimize those perceived as negative. Perhaps the most that can be expected is that a manager can slightly modify the trajectory of a culture, rather than exert major control over the direction of its development.

This article assumes that cultural mechanisms can undermine as well as support the objectives of the firm's top management. We argue that in addition to serving integrative functions, cultures can express conflicts and address needs for differentiation among organizational elements. Instead of treating culture as a monolithic phenomenon, we explore a counterculture's uneasy symbiotic relationship with the rest of an organization. Finally, we address the relationship between cultural development and managerial action by asking what a leader does, inadvertently or advertently, that seems to impact the development of a counterculture.

To examine a subculture in some depth, a few conceptual distinctions are needed. Edgar Schein has distinguished three levels of culture: basic assumptions, values or ideology, and artifacts (such as special jargon, stories, rituals, dress, and decor). We would add a fourth category, management practices. These are familiar management tasks, such as training, performance appraisal, allocation of rewards, hiring, and so forth. (Practices may or may not include artifacts. For example, a training program for new employees may be an occasion for telling organizational stories and may conclude with a ceremony.) Artifacts and practices express values, which may also be expressed as a corporate ideology or management philosophy. Underlying those values are even deeper assumptions, which rest at a preconscious level of awareness. Schein argues persuasively that because assumptions are taken for granted, they are difficult to study except through the use of long-term observation and in-depth, clinical interviewing techniques. (See the article by Alan L. Wilkins on page 24 of *Organizational Dynamics,* Autumn 1983, for a description of such a technique.) Because of the methodological difficulty of studying assumptions, we restrict our attention to artifacts, practices, and values, reserving some tentative speculations about assumptions for the concluding discussion.

Next, a distinction needs to be drawn between an organization's dominant culture and the various subcultures that might coexist with it. A dominant culture expresses, through artifacts, core values that are shared by a majority of the organization's members. At least three types of subcultures are conceivable: enhancing, orthogonal, and countercultural. An enhancing subculture would exist in an organizational enclave in which adherence to the core values of the dominant culture would be more fervent than in the rest of the organization. In an orthogonal subculture, the members would simultaneously accept the core values of the dominant culture and a separate, unconflicting set of values particular to themselves. For example, an accounting division and research and development (R&D) department may both endorse the values of their firm's dominant culture, while retaining separate sets of values related to their occupational identities, such as "going by the numbers" for the accounting department and "valuing innovation" in the R&D department.

The third type of subculture, a counterculture, is the focus of this article. We propose that some core values of a counterculture should present a direct challenge to the core values of a dominant culture. Thus a dominant culture and a counterculture should exist in an uneasy symbiosis, taking opposite positions on value issues that are critically important to each of them. This article explores the adequacy of this proposition by collecting artifacts from a dominant culture and a counterculture and determining what values those artifacts express. We expect that some artifacts from a counterculture will ridicule a subset of the dominant culture's values, while other countercultural artifacts will express support for an alternative set of values.

To find a setting in which we can study this issue, we need to know what types of organizational conditions are likely to give rise to a counterculture. Ruth Leeds Love's discussion of the absorption of protest offers a solution. She posits that organizations that are strongly centralized, but permit a decentralized diffusion of power, are likely to spawn what she terms a "nonconforming enclave." An organizational member challenges some aspect of the dominant culture. If the challenger is a charismatic leader, Love proposes that the organization will absorb the potential for protest by giving the charismatic person limited power, some formal structural autonomy, and a tacit mandate to gather followers and create a nonconforming enclave. This strategy has advantages from the dominant coalition's point of view. If the enclave functions innovatively, within the institution's latitude of tolerance, the institution benefits. If not, the institution has isolated the deviance. The structural autonomy serves as a boundary, defining the limits of acceptable behavior and possibly making the unwanted enclave easier to destroy.

To translate Love's proposition into the terminology introduced above, a counterculture should be most likely to arise in a strongly centralized institution that has permitted significant decentralization of authority to occur. The counterculture will be likely to emerge within a structural boundary and, interestingly, it may well have a charismatic leader.

The GM case

Organizational setting

General Motors (GM) is a well-documented case that fits the description outlined by Love. The firm is strongly centralized in that authority and responsibility for financial control and the long-range strategy of the firm rest in the hands of the corporate headquarters. Nevertheless the divisions, such as Pontiac and Chevrolet, have considerable autonomy on operating issues. The rationale for this structure was provided in former GM president and chairman of the board Alfred P. Sloan Jr.'s famous "Organizational Study" (released in 1920). The plan's description of an inevitable tension between centralization and decentralization accurately describes the firm today.

One division of GM was headed for some years by John DeLorean. This formal position of leadership gave him visibility, resources, and power; these were apparently augmented by such charismatic attributes as personal magnetism and dramatic flair. (Although DeLorean encountered business and personal difficulties after his departure from GM, this article focuses exclusively on his years with GM.)

Procedure

In the first stage of this research, the available published literature on GM was surveyed and several present and former GM employees interviewed by means of an open-ended format. The objective of this stage of the research effort was to gain a relatively broad base of knowledge about the corporation, with particular focus on the dominant culture.

In the second stage of the research effort, two views of the corporation were selected for an in-depth content analysis. The first is a "corporate history" of GM, Ed Cray's *Chrome Colossus: General Motors and Its Times* (McGraw-Hill, 1980). This book was selected for several reasons. It is recent. Unlike many others, it reports some information that is critical of the firm. It is comprehensive and provides a detailed picture, particularly of the firm's dominant culture. The second view selected was J. P. Wright's description of DeLorean's activities, *On A Clear Day You Can See General Motors* (Wright Enterprises, 1979). This book was selected because it is the most thorough published account of DeLorean's activities at GM.

Because culture is a socially constructed reality, it would be an exercise in futility to try to capture a single "objective" picture of a culture or subculture. Undoubtedly Cray and Wright have views of the issues and events discussed below that are somewhat different from others' views. It is impossible to avoid bias in the perception of a socially constructed reality; indeed, in some senses, that bias is the focus of this investigation.

One important limitation of these data sources merits mention. Cray and Wright focus primarily on the activities of relatively high-ranking executives. They do not attempt to explore how these leaders' activities were perceived by their subordinates. Thus the present article focuses on leader activities rather than subordinate reactions to such activities.

Core Values

Three related core values were repeatedly stressed (although terminology varied) in the various portrayals of the dominant culture at GM: respecting authority, fitting in, and being loyal. The description below begins with the dominant culture and describes the cultural artifacts that express these three core values. Next, the artifacts from DeLorean's division are examined to determine if they ridicule the dominant culture's values or express an alternative set of values, thus providing evidence of an uneasy symbiotic relationship between a dominant and a counterculture. In this latter part of the article, DeLorean's activities are studied to determine how they contribute, deliberately or inadvertently, to the development of a counterculture.

Respecting authority: Jargon and rituals of deference

One core value of GM's dominant culture involved the importance of paying deference to the top corporate management. The special language or jargon used to refer to these executives' domains and activities reflected this core value. The top team's offices were located in an I-shaped end of the fourteenth floor of the huge GM headquarters building. Company jargon referred to this domain as "the fourteenth floor" and to these offices as "executive row." Apparently even GM's critics spoke these words with some deference. The high status of these top executives was also evident in the derogatory terms used to refer to their subordinates. Each member of the top management team was assigned a junior executive, who acted as an assistant and secretary. These subordinates were called "dog robbers," a term that originally referred to the servants in large households who were assigned the undesirable task of cleaning up dog droppings.

Another type of cultural artifact is a ritual—that is, an activity composed of a formalized or patterned sequence of events that is repeated over and over again. GM had many rituals that supported the core value of deference owed authority. For example, subordinates were expected to meet their superiors from out of town at the airport, carry their bags, pay their hotel and meal bills, and chauffeur them around day and night. The higher the status of the superior, the more people would accompany him on the flight and the larger the retinue that would wait at the airport. A chief engineer would be met by at least one assistant engineer and perhaps a local plant official; a divisional general manager would travel with at least one executive from his office and would be met at the airport by the local plant manager, the heads of the regional and zone sales offices, and the local public relations director. If the chairman of the board decided to visit field offices, dozens of people would be involved in accompanying and meeting him.

Adherence to the airport ritual was not merely a social nicety, as DeLorean learned to his dismay on an occasion when he failed to meet his boss, Peter Estes, at the airport. Estes stormed into DeLorean's shower, nearly tearing the shower door off its hinges, shouting with atypical rage, "Why the hell wasn't someone out to meet me at the airport this morning? You knew I was coming, but nobody was there. Goddamnit, I served my time picking up my bosses at the airport. Now you guys are going to do this for me" (from J. P. Wright's *On A Clear Day You Can See General Motors* [Wright Enterprises, 1979]). The airport ritual communicated the message that no part of an executive's work was more important than helping superiors, even by meeting their most mundane needs. It is hardly surprising that Estes was somewhat perturbed, since DeLorean's refusal to adhere to the ritual clearly flouted a core value of GM's dominant culture and sent a crystal-clear message of disrespect for Estes' authority.

Fitting in: Communicating invisibility by visible cues

It is no accident that few people could have recognized GM's chairman of the board Thomas Murphy, although the faces of his peers, such as Henry Ford of Ford and William Paley of CBS, frequently graced the television screen, the front pages of newspapers, and the covers of news magazines. GM employees who found themselves the object of attention from the news media could expect a severe reprimand for disregarding another core value of GM's dominant culture: Ideal GM employees were invisible people who could fit in without drawing attention to themselves.

The core value of invisibility was expressed through such visible cultural artifacts as dress and decor. GM's dress norms in the 1960s required a dark suit, a light shirt, and a muted tie. This was a slightly more liberal version of the famous IBM dress code that required a dark suit, a sparkling white shirt, and a narrow blue or black tie. When all employees wear the same uniform, no single employee stands out.

Rules on office decor also expressed the value of invisibility. Even on the fourteenth floor, office decor was standardized. The carpeting was a nondescript blue-green and the oak paneling was a faded beige. When DeLorean was promoted to headquarters he requested brighter carpeting, sanding and restaining of the paneling, and some more modern, functional furniture. The man in charge of office decoration was apologetic, but firm: "We decorate the offices only every few years. And they are all done the same. It's the same way with the furniture. Maybe I can get you an extra table or a lamp . . ." (Wright, op. cit.).

The invisible GM employee was a "team player." Executives signalled their willingness to be team players by engaging in public, symbolic acts of conformity. Many of these activities centered on the act of eating. When executives were in town, for example, they were expected to eat in the executive dining room, where conversation usually consisted of bitching and office gossip, apparently irrelevant to serious business issues.

These meals were rituals. The executives were isolated in a separate room at predictable times. They said predictable sorts of things. Although at the manifest level these activities may have seemed irrelevant to the company's business, at a deeper level the eating ritual communicated several important aspects of the value of fitting in. Participation in the ritual required sacrifice of one's personal time that could have been spent having lunch with friends from outside GM or with one's family. When the conversation concerned gossip or complaints about GM, the talkers were taking personal risks by exposing themselves as "back-biters" or "tale-tellers," while listeners were initiated into an "in-group" of confidants sharing private knowledge. Precisely because topics of conversation were private and in a sense forbidden, the eating ritual was important. It signalled a willing sacrifice of time, an extension of the company into the more private and personal aspects of employees' lives, and a visible manifestation of willingness to fit in.

Failure to participate in the eating ritual was seen as a direct and unambiguous challenge: "Why doesn't he have dinner with the other executives? He's not acting like a team player" (Wright, op. cit.). Costs of such a challenge were clear. Standard management practices punished those who failed to fit in. For example, performance appraisals were not based solely on objective criteria—the work records of those who were promoted were often inferior to those of people who languished in lower-level positions. Performance appraisals relied heavily on subjective criteria, which included an assessment of an employee's private life. Top executives were expected to behave in a decorous fashion, avoid fads, and (at least publicly) maintain the appearance of a stable married life. "He's not a team player" was a frequent, and many times the only, obstacle to an executive's promotion (Wright, op. cit.).

Being loyal: Inferring the dominant view from what is absent

Another core value central to the GM philosophy was loyalty to one's boss, which was a special case of loyalty to GM's management, which in turn was sometimes portrayed as a special case of loyalty to the country. For example, a top GM executive testifying before Congress in the 1950s drew no distinction between what was good for GM and what was good for the entire country (from Ed Cray's *Chrome Colossus: General Motors and Its Times* [McGraw-Hill, 1980]).

One artifact of the dominant culture that expressed the value placed on loyalty was the retirement dinner. At these dinners, as at other rituals, the content of what was to be said and the sequence of events was prescribed. A prototypical retirement dinner began with a description of the retiree's early background, perhaps with evocations of his hard-working parents and the elm-lined streets of his hometown. His first job, perhaps as a newsboy, would be recalled, followed by a brief recap of the halcyon days of his undergraduate career when, inevitably, he was a uniformed member, if not a star, of some sport team. The retiree's history as a GM employee would then be recounted in detail, beginning with his first job, hopefully a humble one that preserved the purity of the Horatio Alger aspect of his story. Next, his steady (always steady) rise through the corporate hierarchy would be counterpointed with allusions to his charming wife and lovely children.

Usually retirement dinner programs ended with a few joking allusions to the retiree's idiosyncracies and a promise. The retiree and the company representatives pledged continuing mutual respect, admiration, and loyalty. This pledge included a kind of proto-immortality, as the organization promised not to forget the retiree's invaluable contributions and offered him a safe passage to life outside the corporation's doors.

If the content of what is said and the sequence of what is done is prescribed in a ritual, then departure from these routines should cause consternation, as in DeLorean's failure to perform the airport ritual for his boss. If the primary purpose of the retirement dinner at GM was to reward past and ensure future loyalty, then reactions to deviations from the expected behavior pattern should make this purpose clear.

A speaker at one GM retirement dinner committed two cardinal sins. He admitted that the company had once been in severe trouble and he blamed the debacle on the ill-considered decisions of a top GM executive. Even the usually critical DeLorean was shocked by the speaker's behavior, which he criticized as a "vicious verbal attack," "uncalled-for," and "vituperative." Others present were also dismayed, "shaking their heads and looking puzzled," and ". . . caught between modest surprise and downright embarrassment." Such a departure from the ritual protocol was exceedingly rare: "It was the first time I had ever heard a General Motors executive openly criticize another one, past or present, in front of corporate management" (Wright, op. cit.). The critical speech was so disruptive because it contradicted the ritual's basic purpose: to celebrate retiring and present GM employees for their loyalty to top GM executives and to the firm as a whole.

One cultural artifact, not yet discussed, is the organizational story. Such stories are anecdotes, ostensibly true, about a sequence of events drawn from the company's history. The stars of an organizational story are company employees, and the stories' morals concern the firm's core values and underlying assumptions.

Loyalty was so central to the GM philosophy that it is evident in what is absent from, as well as what is included in, the dominant culture's artifacts. Students of Japanese corporate cultures have noted the difficulty of interpreting cultural phenomena. To appreciate the shape and placement of a rock in a Japanese garden, the educated viewer focuses on the empty spaces around the rock. Similarly, the process of "reading" the content of a culture requires attention to disruptions and to what is absent or unsaid, because these are also clues to what is expected.

Thus reinforcement of the value of loyalty can also be seen in the type of organizational stories that were not found in this organizational setting. For example, Wright began his discussion of the loyalty issue with the telling observation that GM had no "prodigal son returns" story about an executive who left his "corporate home," because those who left were considered deserters and were not generally welcomed back.

The development of a counterculture; questioning
deference to authority

DeLorean expressed his opposition to deference to authority by telling this
organizational story:

> In preparing for the sales official's trip to this particular city, the
> Chevrolet zone sales people learned from Detroit that the boss liked to
> have a refrigerator full of cold beer, sandwiches, and fruit in his room
> to snack on at night before going to bed. They lined up a suite in one
> of the city's better hotels, rented a refrigerator, and ordered the food
> and beer. However, the door to the suite was too small to accommo-
> date the icebox. The hotel apparently nixed a plan to rip out the door
> and part of the adjoining wall. So the quick-thinking zone sales people
> hired a crane and operator, put them on the roof of the hotel, knocked
> out a set of windows in the suite, and lowered and shoved the refrig-
> erator into the room through this gaping hole.
>
> That night the Chevrolet executive wolfed down cold-cut sand-
> wiches, beer, and fresh fruit, no doubt thinking, "What a great bunch
> of people we have in this zone." The next day he was off to another
> city and most likely another refrigerator, while back in the city of his
> departure the zone people were once again dismantling hotel windows
> and removing the refrigerator by crane. [Wright, op. cit.]

The "refrigerator story" carries at least two messages. First, it is common practice at GM to engage in expensive and time-consuming efforts to
defer to even minor wishes of people in authority positions. Second, the
tone of the story implies that people who engage in these activities sometimes go to ridiculous extremes.

The "refrigerator story" is an example of a cultural artifact that has
"boomeranged" against the dominant culture. At first the story appears to
be another illustration of the importance of deference to authority, then it
becomes clear that the story portrays a situation in which this value has
been carried to a ridiculous extreme. When cultural artifacts boomerang,
they call into question those core values that at first they seem to reinforce.
Boomeranging cultural artifacts can breed a deep alienation from the dominant culture's core values, undermining rather than supporting top management's objectives.

We posited that a counterculture would undermine the dominant culture's values, as evident in the "refrigerator story," and that it would
produce cultural artifacts supporting an alternative set of core values. The
story-creation process is one means of expressing alternative values. The
process begins when a visible, often powerful and charismatic figure responds to a situation in a dramatic fashion, role modeling the behavior that
would be expected of employees who might someday face a similar situa-

tion. If the central character is sufficiently noteworthy, the event sufficiently dramatic, and the behavior clearly relevant to future activities, then
the role-modeled event may be recounted and eventually transformed into
an organizational story.

The story-creation process is one way in which an individual actor can
help create a counterculture, though it is important to note that the process
can occur without the central actor's intentional cooperation. Even if an
actor does intend to create a story, the transformation of an event into a
shared organizational story depends largely on whether organizational
members find it sufficiently interesting to repeat.

DeLorean, for example, repeatedly created such stories. For example,
wanting to replace deference to authority with task-oriented efficiency, he
decided to discourage the practice of meeting superiors at airports. Instead
of issuing an edict by memo, he role-modeled the behavior he wanted on
an occasion when he was scheduled to speak to a luncheon of McGraw-Hill
editors and executives in midtown Manhattan. DeLorean found his own
ride from the airport to the McGraw-Hill offices. The McGraw-Hill people
were used to GM executives who traveled with "retinues befitting only the
potentates of great nations"; when they questioned DeLorean about the
whereabouts of his subordinates, DeLorean complacently replied that he
hoped they were back in Detroit getting some work done. DeLorean noted
with some pride that he subsequently heard that the "McGraw-Hill incident" had been retold many times, both by his subordinates and by
McGraw-Hill employees (Wright, op. cit.).

This incident was transformed into an organizational story for several
reasons. The star was DeLorean, a controversial and powerful figure. The
events were sufficiently dramatic to be interesting and had clear implications for the types of behavior that would be considered appropriate for
DeLorean's subordinates. If a similar situation arose, subordinates sur-
mised that they should not meet DeLorean at the airport unless there was
specific business to conduct en route. Finally, the events were noteworthy
because they expressed a value that contradicted a core value of the dominant culture. In DeLorean's division, job performance was more important
than deference to authority.

An alternative to fitting in: The limits of acceptable deviance

DeLorean was opposed to the value placed by the dominant culture on
team play and fitting in. Instead, he valued dissent and independence. Sensibly, he backed his values with practices—changing, for example, the
performance appraisal system in his division. No longer were subjective
criteria, indicating willingness to fit in, considered relevant. Instead, performance was measured on the basis of criteria that were as objective as
possible.

DeLorean reinforced this value with cultural artifacts as well as practices. For example, he made a point of claiming that he would rely on objective performance appraisal criteria, even when the results ran counter to his own subjective opinions. He backed this claim with an anecdote, which he claimed became a shared organizational story. The central figure in the story, aside of course from DeLorean himself, was a disagreeable man whose performance record was superlative. Despite his personal dislike of the man, DeLorean promoted him four times, admitting that he tried to "stay the hell away from him" (Wright, op. cit.).

This anecdote has two intriguing central characters. DeLorean's strong dislike of his subordinate adds an element of personal interest. In addition, the anecdote clearly prescribes how DeLorean would have his subordinates behave when they assessed the behavior of a disliked subordinate. In this example, DeLorean articulated a core value that was counter to the core values of the dominant culture, he backed that new value by implementing consistent performance appraisal practices, and he dramatized and illustrated the value by role modeling the desired behavior. Although DeLorean's retrospective account may exaggerate the intentionality and impact of his behavior, it is plausible that these activities contributed to the development of a counterculture among DeLorean's subordinates.

DeLorean also used other techniques to facilitate the development of a counterculture. For example, when he was promoted to head the Chevrolet division, he used decor changes to symbolize his declaration of independence. The division's lobby and executive offices were refurbished with bright carpets, the paneling was sanded and restained, and modern furniture was brought in. In accord with the espoused values of independence and dissent, executives were allowed "within reasonable limits" to decorate their offices to fit their individual tastes.

In his own dress DeLorean role-modeled an apparently carefully calibrated willingness to deviate from the dominant culture's emphasis on fitting in. DeLorean's dark suits had a continental cut. His shirts were off-white with wide collars. His ties were suitably muted, but wider than the GM norm. His deviations were fashionable, for the late 1960s, but they represented only a slight variation on the executive dress norms of the dominant culture.

If a counterculture is to survive within the context of a dominant culture a delicate balancing act must be performed. DeLorean apparently did not hesitate to initiate stories and implement practices that directly challenged the dominant culture's core values. His use of visible cultural artifacts (not easily hidden from visiting outsiders) was more subtle, perhaps deliberately more circumspect. Although the extent of his intentionality is unclear, DeLorean's deviance appears carefully calibrated to remain within, but test the limits of, the dominant culture's latitude of acceptance.

Opposing demands for unquestioning loyalty

The Corvair disasters provided superb raw material for a "boomerang" challenge to the dominant culture's emphasis on loyalty. The story begins as a seemingly straightforward presentation epitomizing GM's finest characteristics. Initially the Corvair was seen as an innovative, appealing product—the best that GM minds could produce. The rear placement of the engine, the independent swing-axle suspension system, and the sporty styling gave the Corvair a racy image designed to appeal to the young.

At this point the Corvair story boomerangs: It takes a sudden turn and becomes a scathing indictment of the values it first appeared to endorse. Several GM employees raised objections to the car because of their concern about the lack of safety of the rear engine and the fact that the swing-axle design had a tendency to make the car directionally unstable and difficult to control, with a propensity to flip over at high speeds (Cray, op. cit.). Despite evidence supporting the validity of these objections, GM management told the dissenters to stop objecting and join the team or find some other place to work (Wright, op. cit.).

DeLorean concluded the Corvair story by enumerating the deaths caused by its faulty design and the negative effects its production had on the firm. These disastrous consequences included a "Watergate mentality" that led to attempts to buy and destroy evidence of owner complaints about the car, millions of dollars in legal expenses and out-of-court settlements, and extensive damage to GM's reputation. DeLorean explicitly stated the moral to the Corvair story in terms of the "group think" dangers of an overemphasis on loyalty:

> There wasn't a man in top GM management who had anything to do with the Corvair who would purposely build a car that he knew would hurt or kill people. But, as a part of a management team pushing for increased sales and profits, each gave his individual approval in a group to decisions which produced the car in the face of serious doubts that were raised about its safety, and then later sought to squelch information which might prove the car's deficiencies. [Wright, op. cit.]

It is noteworthy that this contribution to the creation of a counterculture within DeLorean's division includes no direct action. Instead, DeLorean merely offers, in this boomerang story, a reinterpretation of past events.

Conclusion

This analysis of the dominant culture at GM revealed three core values. Deference to authority was represented in the airport ritual and jargon, such as "dog robbers." The value of being invisible was expressed through management practices, such as subjective performance appraisal criteria, and through visible artifacts, such as conservative dress, standardized office decor, and public eating rituals. The value of loyalty was so central that it was evident in what was absent—a retirement dinner ritual that was disrupted and a prodigal son story that was missing.

Evidence of a counterculture was also found. In addition to ridiculing the values of the dominant culture, DeLorean articulated an alternative set of core values, preferring productivity to deference, objective measures of performance to subjective indicators of conformity, and independence to blind loyalty. Clearly the dominant and countercultures take opposite positions on value issues of central importance to both.

Several of DeLorean's activities apparently influenced the development of this uneasy symbiosis. First, he used "boomeranging" cultural artifacts, such as the "refrigerator" and "Corvair" stories, to ridicule the values of the dominant culture. Second, he articulated the countercultural values openly, through management practices such as objective performance appraisal criteria, and through the story creation process, as in the "McGraw-Hill" story. In addition, his use of such visible cultural artifacts as dress and decor communicated more subtly the limits of acceptable deviance.

While a manager alone may not be able to create or "manage" a culture, DeLorean's activities suggest that several managerial techniques may have a detectable impact on the trajectory of a culture's, or a subculture's, development. Those techniques include implementation of practices that are consistent with preferred values, articulation of "boomerangs," attempts to create organizational stories, and carefully calibrated uses of visible artifacts.

If DeLorean's activities are to serve as a source of cultural management ideas, it is important to discuss the limitations of his achievements at GM. It is true that for a time he maintained a delicate balance, fostering the development of a counterculture that rested within the dominant culture's latitude of tolerance. Eventually, however, DeLorean's dissent met with disfavor, and he left GM to found a company of his own.

DeLorean's history at GM raises some interesting questions that are addressed in Love's analysis of the absorption of protest. A counterculture can serve some useful functions for a dominant culture, articulating the boundaries between appropriate and inappropriate behavior and providing a safe haven for the development of innovative ideas. Did GM's top management want DeLorean's counterculture to succeed, and were they disappointed when his deviance went beyond their latitude of tolerance? Or, as implied in the analysis of the basic assumptions underlying the dominant culture's core values, had GM permitted DeLorean's counterculture to grow and die in order to provide an object lesson for other potential deviants? Or was the strength of the counterculture an unanticipated and unwelcome surprise to the dominant culture? No matter which of these alternatives comes closest to the truth, clearly it is a complex process, beyond the control of any one individual, to maintain the uneasy symbiotic relationship that exists between a dominant culture and a counterculture.

Selected bibliography

Organizational culture research has its roots in Philip Selznick's *Leadership and Administration* (Row, Peterson, 1957) and Burton Clark's *The Distinctive College: Antioch, Reed, and Swarthmore* (Aldine, 1970). Four books, oriented toward the professional manager, are largely responsible for the recent renaissance of interest in this topic. William Ouchi's *Theory Z: How American Business Can Meet the Japanese Challenge* (Addison-Wesley, 1981) and Richard Pascale and Anthony Athos's *The Art of Japanese Management* (Simon & Schuster, Inc., 1981) drew heavily on Japanese models of corporate culture. Thomas Peters and Robert Waterman studied the cultures of unusually profitable American companies in *In Search of Excellence* (Harper & Row, 1982), as did Terrence Deal and Allan Kennedy in *Corporate Cultures* (Addison-Wesley, 1982).

Some have taken a critical view of the work that aroused this interest in culture. Edgar Schein disputed the reliance on Japanese models in "Does Japanese Management Style Have a Message for American Managers?" (*Sloan Management Review,* Fall 1981). The claim that cultures express an institution's distinctive competence or unique accomplishment was questioned by Joanne Martin, Martha Feldman, Mary Jo Hatch, and Sim Sitkin in "The Uniqueness Paradox in Organizational Stories" (*Administrative Science Quarterly,* September 1983).

Others have taken a closer look at particular cultural phenomena. Organizational stories, legends, and myths have been studied by Alan Wilkins (see his article in this issue for references) and Joanne Martin—for example, see "Stories and Scripts in Organizational Settings" in Albert Hastorf's and Alice Isen's (editors) *Cognitive Social Psychology* (Elsevier-North Holland, 1982). For an excellent sampling of papers about a wide range of cultural phenomena, including organizational stories, rituals, humor, and jargon, see the collection edited by Louis Pondy, Peter Frost, Gareth Morgan, and Thomas Dandridge, *Organizational Symbolism* (JAI Press, 1983). Ruth Leeds Love's discussion of absorption of protest appears in Harold Leavitt and Louis Pondy's *Readings in Managerial Psychology,* 2nd Edition (University of Chicago Press, 1974).

Another approach has been to study the functions served by different types of cultures. For example, John Van Maanen and Stephen Barley have studied occupations in "Occupational Communities: Culture and Control in Organizations," in Barry Staw and Larry Cummings's (editors) *Research in Organizational Behavior,* Vol. 6 (JAI Press, in press). Caren Siehl and Joanne Martin have studied the enculturation process for new employees, producing a quantitative, easily administered measure of culture in "Symbolic Management: Can Culture Be Transmitted?", a chapter in the *Annual Leadership Series,* Vol. 7 (Southern Illinois University Press, in press). Although the recent academic research is scattered in a variety of scholarly journals, books integrating this literature are being written by a number of people, including Edgar Schein, Meryl Louis, and Joanne Martin.

This article draws evidence concerning the dominant and countercultures at General Motors primarily from two sources: Ed Cray's *Chrome Colossus: General Motors and Its Times* (McGraw-Hill, 1980) and J. P. Wright's *On A Clear Day You Can See General Motors* (Wright Enterprises, 1979). Because Wright writes of DeLorean's experiences in the first person, for the sake of clarity Wright's book is cited as representing DeLorean's point of view. Because DeLorean has disowned Wright's efforts, however, it is highly likely that their opinions differ on some issues. In such cases the book is probably more representative of Wright's opinions than DeLorean's, in spite of the former's use of the first person. The past tense is used throughout this article's descriptions of General Motors, because some information may no longer be accurate.

A number of other references on General Motors were useful, including particularly the works of A. D. Chandler, including *Giant Enterprise: Ford, General Motors, and the Automobile Industry* (Harcourt, Brace & World, 1964) and *Strategy and Structure: Chapters in the History of Industrial Enterprise* (MIT Press, 1969), Peter Drucker's *Concept of the Corporation* (John Day Co., 1972), Ralph Nadar's *Unsafe at Any Speed* (Grossman, 1972), and Alfred P. Sloan Jr.'s *My Years With General Motors* (McFadden-Bartell Corp., 1965).

Acknowledgments

The authors wish to thank the following people, who gave us particularly helpful comments on an earlier draft of this article: Susan Kreiger, Hal Leavitt, Meryl Louis, Gerald Salancik, and Edgar Schein. A preliminary version of this article was presented as part of the symposium "Can Culture Be Managed?" at the annual meeting of the Academy of Management in New York City in August 1982.

Organizational Conflict:
Concepts and Models
Louis R. Pondy

There is a large and growing body of literature on the subject of organizational conflict. The concept of conflict has been treated as a general social phenomenon, with implications for the understanding of conflict within and between organizations.[1] It has also assumed various roles of some importance in attempts at general theories of management and organizational behavior.[2] Finally, conflict has recently been the focus of numerous empirical studies of organization.[3]

Reprinted with permission from *Administrative Science Quarterly*, vol. 12, no. 2, 1967.

1. Jessie Bernard, T. H. Pear, Raymond Aron, and Robert C. Angell, *The Nature of Conflict* (Paris: UNESCO, 1957); Kenneth Boulding, *Conflict and Defense* (New York: Harper, 1962); Lewis Coser, *The Functions of Social Conflict* (Glencoe, Ill.: Free Press, 1956); Kurt Lewin, *Resolving Social Conflict* (New York: Harper, 1948); Anatol Rapaport, *Fights, Games, and Debates* (Ann Arbor: University of Michigan Press, 1960); Thomas C. Schelling, *The Strategy of Conflict* (Cambridge, Mass.: Harvard University Press, 1961); Muzafer Sherif and Carolyn Sherif, *Groups in Harmony and Tension* (Norman, Okla.: University of Oklahoma Press, 1953); Georg Simmel, *Conflict,* trans. Kurt H. Wolff (Glencoe, Ill.: Free Press, 1955).

2. Bernard M. Bass, *Organizational Psychology* (Boston, Mass.: Allyn and Bacon, 1965); Theodore Caplow, *Principles of Organization* (New York: Harcourt, Brace, and World, 1964); Eliot D. Chapple and Leonard F. Sayles, *The Measure of Management* (New York: Macmillan, 1961); Michel Crozier, *The Bureaucratic Phenomenon* (Glencoe, Ill.: Free Press, 1964); Richard M. Cyert and James G. March, *A Behavioral Theory of the Firm* (Englewood Cliffs, N.J.: Prentice-Hall, 1963); Alvin W. Gouldner, *Patterns of Industrial Bureaucracy* (Glencoe, Ill.: Free Press, 1954); Harold J. Leavitt, *Managerial Psychology* (Chicago: University of Chicago Press, 1964); James G. March and Herbert A. Simon, *Organizations* (New York: Wiley, 1958); Philip Selznick, *TVA and the Grass Roots* (Berkeley: University of California Press, 1949); Victor Thompson, *Modern Organization* (New York: Knopf, 1961).

3. Joseph L. Bower, The Role of Conflict in Economic Decision-making Groups, *Quarterly Journal of Economics* 79 (May 1965), 253–257; Melville Dalton, *Men Who Manage* (New York: Wiley, 1959); J. M. Dutton and R. E. Walton, "Interdepartmental Conflict and Cooperation: A Study of Two Contrasting Cases," dittoed, Purdue University, October 1964; William Evan, Superior-Subordinate Conflict in Research Organizations, *Administrative Science Quarterly* 10 (June 1965), 52–64; Robert L. Kahn, et al. *Studies in Organizational Stress* (New York: Wiley, 1964); L. R. Pondy, Budgeting and Inter-Group Conflict in Organizations, *Pittsburgh Business Review* 34 (April 1964), 1–3; R. E. Walton, J. M. Dutton, and H. G. Fitch, *A Study of Conflict in the Process, Structure, and Attitudes of Lateral Relationships* (Institute Paper No. 93; Lafayette, Ind.: Purdue University, November 1964); Harrison White, Management Conflict and Sociometric Structure, *American Journal of Soci-*

Slowly crystallizing out of this research are three conceptual models designed to deal with the major classes of conflict phenomena in organizations.[4]

1. *Bargaining model.* This is designed to deal with conflict among interest groups in competition for scarce resources. This model is particularly appropriate for the analysis of labor-management relations, budgeting processes, and staff-line conflicts.

2. *Bureaucratic model.* This is applicable to the analysis of superior-subordinate conflicts or, in general, conflicts along the vertical dimension of a hierarchy. This model is primarily concerned with the problems caused by institutional attempts to control behavior and the organization's reaction to such control.

3. *Systems model.* This is directed at lateral conflict, or conflict among the parties to a functional relationship. Analysis of the problems of coordination is the special province of this model.

Running as common threads through each of these models are several implicit orientations. The most important of these orientations follow:

1. Each conflict relationship is made up of a sequence of interlocking conflict episodes; each episode exhibits a sequence or pattern of development, and the conflict relationship can be characterized by stable patterns that appear across the sequence of episodes. This orientation forms the basis for a working definition of conflict.

2. Conflict may be functional as well as dysfunctional for the individual and the organization; it may have its roots either within the individual or in the organizational context; therefore, the desirability of conflict resolution needs to be approached with caution.

3. Conflict is intimately tied up with the stability of the organization, not merely in the usual sense that conflict is a threat to stability, but in a much more complex fashion; that is, conflict is a key variable in the feedback loops that characterize organizational behavior. These orientations are discussed before the conceptual models are elaborated.

A working definition of conflict

The term "conflict" has been used at one time or another in the literature to describe: *(1) antecedent conditions* (for example, scarcity of resources, policy differences) of conflictful behavior, *(2) affective states* (e.g., stress, tension, hostility, anxiety, etc.) of the individuals involved, *(3) cognitive states* of individuals, i.e., their perception or awareness of conflictful situations, and *(4) conflictful behavior,* ranging from passive resistance to overt

---

ology 67 (September 1961), 185–199; Mayer N. Zald, Power Balance and Staff Conflict in Correctional Institutions, *Administrative Science Quarterly* 7 (June 1962), 22–49.

4. The following conceptualization draws heavily on a paper by Lawrence R. Ephron, Group Conflict in Organizations: A Critical Appraisal of Recent Theories, *Berkeley Journal of Sociology* 6 (Spring 1961), 53–72.

aggression. Attempts to decide which of these classes—conditions, attitude, cognition, or behavior—is really conflict is likely to result in an empty controversy. The problem is not to choose among these alternative conceptual definitions, since each may be a relevant stage in the development of a conflict episode, but to try to clarify their relationships.

Conflict can be more readily understood if it is considered a dynamic process. A conflict relationship between two or more individuals in an organization can be analyzed as a sequence of conflict episodes. Each conflict episode begins with conditions characterized by certain conflict potentials. The parties to the relationship may not become aware of any basis of conflict, and they may not develop hostile affections for one another. Depending on a number of factors, their behavior may show a variety of conflictful traits. Each episode or encounter leaves an aftermath that affects the course of succeeding episodes. The entire relationship can then be characterized by certain stable aspects of conditions, affect, perception, and behavior. It can also be characterized by trends in any of these characteristics.

This is roughly analogous to defining a "decision" to include activities preliminary to and following choice, as well as the choice itself. In the same sense that a decision can be thought of as a process of gradual commitment to a course of action, a conflict episode can be thought of as a gradual escalation to a state of disorder. If choice is the climax of a decision, then by analogy, open war or aggression is the climax of a conflict episode.

This does not mean that every conflict episode necessarily passes through every stage to open aggression. A potential conflict may never be perceived by the parties to the conflict, or if perceived, the conflict may be resolved before hostilities break out. Several other alternative courses of development are possible. Both Coleman and Aubert make these points clearly in their treatments of the dynamics of conflict.[5]

Just as some decisions become programmed or routinized, conflict management in an organization also becomes programmed or institutionalized sometimes. In fact, the institutionalization of means for dealing with recurrent conflict is one of the important aspects in any treatment of the topic. An organization's success hinges to a great extent on its ability to set up and operate appropriate mechanisms for dealing with a variety of conflict phenomena.

Five stages of a conflict episode are identified: (*1*) latent conflict (conditions), (*2*) perceived conflict (cognition), (*3*) felt conflict (affect), (*4*) manifest conflict (behavior), and (*5*) conflict aftermath (conditions). The elaboration of each of these stages of a conflict episode will provide the substance for a working definition. Which specific reactions take place

5. James S. Coleman, *Community Conflict* (Glencoe, Ill.: Free Press, 1957); Vilhelm Aubert, Competition and Dissensus: Two Types of Conflict and Conflict Resolution, *Journal of Conflict Resolution* 7 (March 1963), 26–42.

at each stage of a conflict episode, and why, are the central questions to be answered in a theory of conflict. Only the framework within which those questions can be systematically investigated is developed here.

Latent conflict

A search of the literature has produced a long list of underlying sources of organizational conflict. These are condensed into three basic types of latent conflict: (*1*) competition for scarce resources, (*2*) drives for autonomy, and (*3*) divergence of subunit goals. Later in the paper each of these fundamental types of latent conflict is paired with one of the three conceptual models. Briefly, competition forms the basis for conflict when the aggregated demands of participants for resources exceed the resources available to the organization; autonomy needs form the basis of conflict when one party either seeks to exercise control over some activity that another party regards as his own province or seeks to insulate itself from such control; goal divergence is the source of conflict when two parties who must cooperate on some joint activity are unable to reach a consensus on concerted action. Two or more types of latent conflict may, of course, be present simultaneously.

An important form of latent conflict, which appears to be omitted from this list, is role conflict. The role conflict model treats the organization as a collection of role sets, each composed of the focal person and his role senders. Conflict is said to occur when the focal person receives incompatible role demands or expectations from the persons in his role set.[6] This model has the drawback that it treats the focal person as merely a passive receiver rather than as an active participant in the relationship. It is argued here, that the role conflict model does not postulate a distinct type of latent conflict. Instead, it defines a conceptual relationship, the role set, which may be useful for the analysis of all three forms of latent conflict described.

Perceived conflict

Conflict may sometimes be perceived when no conditions of latent conflict exist, and latent conflict conditions may be present in a relationship without any of the participants perceiving the conflict.

The case in which conflict is perceived when no latent conflict exists can be handled by the so-called semantic model of conflict.[7] According to this explanation, conflict is said to result from the parties' misunderstanding of each others' true position. It is argued that such conflict can be resolved by improving communications between the parties. This model has been the basis of a wide variety of management techniques aimed at improving interpersonal relations. Of course, if the parties' true positions *are* in opposition, then more open communication may only exacerbate the conflict.

The more important case, that some latent conflicts fail to reach the

6. Kahn, et al., *op. cit.*, pp. 11–35.
7. Bernard, Pear, Aron, and Angell, *op. cit.*

level of awareness also requires explanation. Two important mechanisms that limit perception of conflict are the suppression mechanism and the attention-focus mechanism.[8] Individuals tend to block conflicts that are only mildly threatening out of awareness.[9] Conflicts become strong threats, and therefore must be acknowledged, when the conflicts relate to values central to the individual's personality. The suppression mechanism is applicable more to conflicts related to personal than to organizational values. The attention-focus mechanism, however, is related more to organizational behavior than to personal values. Organizations are characteristically faced with more conflicts than can be dealt with, given available time and capacities. The normal reaction is to focus attention on only a few of these, and these tend to be the conflicts for which short-run, routine solutions are available. For organizations successfully to confront the less programmed conflicts, it is frequently necessary to set up separate subunits specifically to deal with such conflicts.

Felt conflict

There is an important distinction between perceiving conflict and feeling conflict. *A* may be aware that *B* and *A* are in serious disagreement over some policy, but it may not make *A* tense or anxious, and it may have no effect whatsoever on *A*'s affection towards *B*. The personalization of conflict is the mechanism which causes most students of organization to be concerned with the dysfunctions of conflict. There are two common explanations for the personalization of conflict.

One explanation is that the inconsistent demands of efficient organization and individual growth create anxieties within the individual.[10] Anxieties may also result from identity crises or from extra-organizational pressures. Individuals need to vent these anxieties in order to maintain internal equilibrium. Organizational conflicts of the three latent types described earlier provide defensible excuses for displacing these anxieties against suitable targets. This is essentially the so-called tension-model.[11]

A second explanation is that conflict becomes personalized when the whole personality of the individual is involved in the relationship. Hostile feelings are most common in the intimate relations that characterize total institutions, such as monasteries, residential colleges, and families.[12] In

8. These two mechanisms are instances of what Cyert and March, *op. cit.*, pp. 117–118, call the "quasi-resolution" of conflict.

9. Leavitt, *op. cit.*, pp. 53–72.

10. Chris Argyris, *Personality and Organization: The Conflict Between the System and the Individual* (New York: Harper, 1957).

11. Bernard, Pear, Aron, and Angell, *op. cit.*

12. It should be emphasized that members of total institutions characteristically experience both strong positive *and* negative feelings for one another and toward the institution. It may be argued that this ambivalence of feeling is a primary cause of anxiety. See Coser, *op. cit.*, pp. 61–65; and Amitai Etzioni and W. R. Taber, Scope, Pervasiveness, and Tension Management in Complex Organizations, *Social Research* 30 (Summer 1963), 220–238.

order to dissipate accumulated hostilities, total institutions require certain safety-valve institutions such as athletic activities or norms that legitimize solitude and withdrawal, such as the noncommunication norms prevalent in religious orders.

Thus, felt conflict may arise from sources independent of the three types of latent conflict, but latent conflicts may provide appropriate targets (perhaps symbolic ones) for undirected tensions.

Manifest conflict

By manifest conflict is meant any of several varieties of conflictful behavior. The most obvious of these is open aggression, but such physical and verbal violence is usually strongly proscribed by organizational norms. Except for prison riots, political revolutions, and extreme labor unrest, violence as a form of manifest conflict in organizations is rare. The motivations toward violence may remain, but they tend to be expressed in less violent form. Dalton has documented the covert attempts to sabotage or block an opponent's plans through aggressive and defensive coalitions.[13] Mechanic has described the tactics of conflict used by lower-level participants, such as apathy or rigid adherence to the rules, to resist mistreatment by the upper levels of the hierarchy.[14]

How can one decide when a certain behavior or pattern of behavior is conflictful? One important factor is that the behavior must be interpreted in the context in which it takes place. If A does not interact with B, it may be either because A and B are not related in any organizational sense, or because A has withdrawn from a too stressful relationship, or because A is deliberately frustrating B by withdrawing support, or simply because A is drawn away from the relationship by other competing demands upon his time. In other words, knowledge of the organizational requirements and of the expectations and motives of the participants appears to be necessary to characterize the behavior as conflictful. This suggests that behavior should be defined to be conflictful if, and only if, some or all of the participants perceive it to be conflictful.

Should the term *manifest conflict* be reserved for behavior which, in the eyes of the actor, is deliberately and consciously designed to frustrate another in the pursuit of his (the other's) overt or covert goals? But what of behavior which is not *intended* to frustrate, but does? Should not that behavior also be called conflictful? The most useful definition of manifest conflict seems to be that behavior which, in the mind of the actor, frustrates the goals of at least some of the other participants. In other words, a member of the organization is said to engage in conflictful behavior if he con-

---

13. Dalton, *op. cit.*
14. David Mechanic, "Sources of Power of Lower Participants in Complex Organizations," in W. W. Cooper, H. J. Leavitt, and M. W. Shelly (eds.), *New Perspectives in Organization Research* (New York: Wiley, 1964), pp. 136–149.

sciously, but not necessarily deliberately, blocks another member's goal achievement. He may engage in such behavior *deliberately* to frustrate another, or he may do so in spite of the fact that he frustrates another. To define manifest conflict in this way is to say that the following question is important: "Under what conditions will a party to a relationship *knowingly* frustrate another party to the relationship?" Suppose *A* unknowingly blocks *B*'s goals. This is not conflictful behavior. But suppose *B* informs *A* that he perceives *A*'s behavior to be conflictful; if then *A* acknowledges the message and *persists* in the behavior, it is an instance of manifest conflict.

The interface between perceived conflict and manifest conflict and the interface between felt conflict and manifest conflict are the pressure points where most conflict-resolution programs are applied. The object of such programs is to prevent conflicts which have reached the level of awareness or the level of affect from erupting into noncooperative behavior. The availability of appropriate and effective administrative devices is a major factor in determining whether conflict becomes manifest. The collective bargaining apparatus of labor-management disputes and budgeting systems for internal resource allocation are administrative devices for the resolution of interest-group conflicts. Evan and Scott have described due process or appeal systems for resolving superior-subordinate conflicts.[15] Mechanisms for resolving lateral conflicts among the parties to a functional relationship are relatively undeveloped. Transfer-pricing systems constitute one of the few exceptions. Much more common are organizational arrangements designed to *prevent* lateral conflicts, e.g., plans, schedules, and job descriptions, which define and delimit subunit responsibilities. Another alternative is to reduce the interdependence between conflicting subunits by introducing buffers, such as inventories, which reduce the need for sales and production departments in a business firm to act in perfect accord.

The mere availability of such administrative devices is not sufficient to prevent conflict from becoming manifest. If the parties to a relationship do not value the relationship, or if conflict is strategic in the pursuit of subunit goals, then conflictful behavior is likely. Furthermore, once conflict breaks out on some specific issue, then the conflict frequently widens and the initial specific conflict precipitates more general and more personal conflicts which had been suppressed in the interest of preserving the stability of the relationship.[16]

15. Evan, *op. cit.;* William G. Scott, *The Management of Conflict: Appeals System in Organizations* (Homewood, Ill.: Irwin, 1965). It is useful to interpret recent developments in leadership and supervision (e.g., participative management, Theory Y, linking-pin functions) as devices for preventing superior-subordinate conflicts from arising, thus, hopefully, avoiding the problem of developing appeals systems in the first place.

16. See Coleman, *op. cit.*, pp. 9–11, for an excellent analysis of this mechanism. A chemical analogue of this situation is the supersaturated solution, from which a large amount of chemical salts can be precipitated by the introduction of a single crystal.

Conflict aftermath

Each conflict episode is but one of the sequence of such episodes that constitute the relationships among organization participants.[17] If the conflict is genuinely resolved to the satisfaction of all participants, the basis for a more cooperative relationship may be laid; or the participants, in their drive for a more ordered relationship, may focus on latent conflicts not previously perceived and dealt with. On the other hand, if the conflict is merely suppressed but not resolved, the latent conditions of conflict may be aggravated and explode in more serious form until they are rectified or until the relationship dissolves. This legacy of a conflict episode is here called "conflict aftermath."[18]

However, the organization is not a closed system. The environment in which it is embedded may become more benevolent and alleviate the conditions of latent conflict, for example, by making more resources available to the organization. But a more malevolent environment may precipitate new crisis. The development of each conflict episode is determined by a complex combination of the effects of preceding episodes and the environmental milieu. The main ideas of this view of the dynamics of conflict are summarized in figure 1.

Functions and dysfunctions of conflict

Few students of social and organizational behavior have treated conflict as a neutral phenomenon to be studied primarily because of scientific curiosity about its nature and form, its causes, and its effects. Most frequently the study of conflict has been motivated by a desire to resolve it and to minimize its deleterious effects on the psychological health of organizational participants and the efficiency of organization performance. Although Kahn and others pay lip service to the opinion that, "one might well make a case for interpreting some conflict as essential for the continued development of mature and competent human beings," the overriding bias of their report is with the "personal costs of excessive emotional strain," and, they state, "the fact that common reactions to conflict and its associated tensions are often dysfunctional for the organization as an ongoing social system and self-defeating for the person in the long run."[19] Boulding recognizes that some optimum level of conflict and associated personal stress and tension are necessary for progress and productivity, but he portrays conflict primarily as a personal and social cost.[20] Baritz argues that

17. The sequential dependence of conflict episodes also plays a major role in the analysis of role conflicts by Kahn, et al., *op. cit.*, pp. 11–35. Pondy, *op. cit.*, has used the concept of "budget residues" to explain how precedents set in budgetary bargains guide and constrain succeeding budget proceedings.

18. Aubert, *op. cit.*

19. Kahn, et al., *op. cit.*, p. 65.

20. Boulding, *op. cit.*, pp. 305–307.

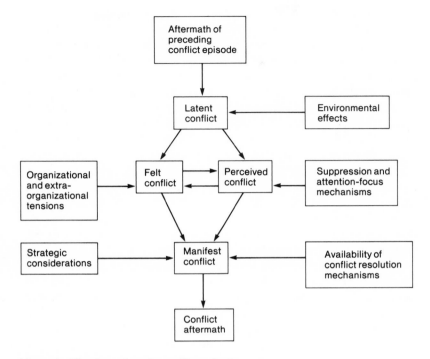

Figure 1. The dynamics of a conflict episode

Elton Mayo has treated conflict as "an evil, a symptom of the lack of social skills," and its alleged opposite, cooperation, as "symptomatic of health." [21] Even as dispassionate a theory of organization as that of March and Simon defines conflict conceptually as a "*breakdown* in the standard mechanisms of decision making"; i.e., as a malfunction of the system.[22]

It has become fashionable to say that conflict may be either functional or dysfunctional and is not necessarily either one. What this palliative leaves out is that the effects of conflict must be evaluated relative to some set of values. The argument with those who seek uniformly to abolish conflict is not so much with their a priori assertion that conflict is undesirable, as it is with their failure to make explicit the value system on which their assertion rests.

For the purposes of this research, the effects of organizational conflict

21. Loren Bartiz, *The Servants of Power* (Middletown, Conn.: Wesleyan University Press, 1960), p. 203.

22. March and Simon, *op. cit.*, p. 112, italics mine. At least one author, however, argues that a "harmony bias" permeates the entire March-Simon volume. It is argued that what March and Simon call conflicts are mere "frictions" and "differences that are not within a community of interests are ignored." See Sherman Krupp, *Pattern in Organization Analysis* (New York: Holt, Rinehart and Winston, 1961), pp. 140–167.

on individual welfare are not of concern. Conflict may threaten the emotional well-being of individual persons; it may also be a positive factor in personal character development; but this research is not addressed to these questions. Intraindividual conflict is of concern only insofar as it has implications for organizational performance. With respect to organizational values, *productivity,* measured in both quantitative and qualitative terms, is valued; other things being equal, an organization is "better" if it produces more, if it is more innovative, and if its output meets higher standards of quality than other organizations. *Stability* is also valued. An organization improves if it can increase its cohesiveness and solvency, other things being equal. Finally *adaptability* is valued. Other things being equal, organizations that can learn and improve performance and that can adapt to changing internal and environmental pressures are preferred to those that cannot. In this view, therefore, to say that conflict is functional or dysfunctional is to say that it facilitates or inhibits the organization's productivity, stability, or adaptability.

Clearly, these values are not entirely compatible. An organization may have to sacrifice quality of output for quantity of output; if it pursues policies and actions that guarantee stability, it may inhibit its adaptive abilities. It is argued here that a given conflict episode or relationship may have beneficial or deleterious effects on productivity, stability, and adaptability. Since these values are incompatible, conflict may be simultaneously functional and dysfunctional for the organization.

A detailed examination of the functional and dysfunctional effects of conflict is more effectively made in the context of the three conceptual models. Underlying that analysis is the notion that conflict disturbs the "equilibrium" of the organization, and that the reaction of the organization to disequilibrium is the mechanism by which conflict affects productivity, stability, and adaptability.

Conflict and equilibrium

One way of viewing an organization is to think of each participant as making contributions, such as work, capital, and raw materials, in return for certain inducements, such as salary, interest, and finished goods. The organization is said to be in "equilibrium," if inducements exceed contributions (subjectivity valued) for every participant, and in "disequilibrium" if contributions exceed inducements for some or all of the participants. Participants will be motivated to restore equilibrium either by leaving the organization for greener pastures, when the disequilibrium is said to be "unstable," or by attempting to achieve a favorable balance between inducements and contributions within the organization, when it is considered "stable." Since changing organizational affiliation frequently involves sizable costs, disequilibria tend to be stable.

If we assume conflict to be a cost of participation, this inducements-contributions balance theory may help in understanding organizational reactions to conflict. It suggests that the perception of conflict by the participants will motivate them to reduce conflict either by withdrawing from the relationship, or by resolving the conflict within the context of the relationship, or by securing increased inducements to compensate for the conflict.

The assumption that conflict creates a disequilibrium is implicit in nearly all studies of organizational conflict. For example, March and Simon assume that "where conflict is perceived, motivation to reduce conflict is generated," and conscious efforts to resolve conflict are made.[23] Not all treatments of the subject make this assumption, however. Harrison White attacks the March-Simon assumption of the disequilibrium of conflict as "naive."[24] He bases his assertion on his observation of chronic, continuous, high-level conflict in administrative settings. This, of course, raises the question, "Under what conditions *does* conflict represent a disequilibrium?"

To say that (perceived) conflict represents a state of disequilibrium and generates pressures for conflict resolution is to say three things: (*1*) that perceived conflict is a cost of participation; (*2*) that the conflict disturbs the inducements-contributions balance; and (*3*) that organizational members react to perceptions of conflict by attempting to resolve the conflict, *in preference to* (although this is not made explicit in the March-Simon treatment) other reactions such as withdrawing from the relationship or attempting to gain added inducements to compensate for the conflict.

1. *Conflict as a cost.* Conflict is not necessarily a cost for the individual. Some participants may actually enjoy the "heat of battle." As Hans Hoffman argues, "The unique function of man is to live in close creative touch with chaos and thereby experience the birth of order."[25]

Conflict may also be instrumental in the achievement of other goals. One of the tactics of successful executives in the modern business enterprise is to create confusion as a cover for the expansion of their particular empire,[26] or, as Sorensen observes, deliberately to create dissent and competition among one's subordinates in order to ensure that he will be brought into the relationship as an arbiter at critical times, as Franklin D. Roosevelt did.[27] Or, conflict with an out-group may be desirable to maintain stability within the in-group.

In general, however, conflict can be expected to be negatively valued;

23. March and Simon, *op. cit.*, pp. 115, 129.

24. Harrison White, *op. cit.*

25. Quoted in H. J. Leavitt and L. R. Pondy, *Readings in Managerial Psychology* (Chicago: University of Chicago Press, 1964), p. 58.

26. Dalton, *op. cit.*

27. Theodore Sorensen, *Decision Making in the White House* (New York: Columbia University Press, 1963), p. 15. This latter tactic, of course, is predicated on the fact that, *for the subordinates,* conflict is indeed a cost!

particularly if conflict becomes manifest, and subunit goals and actions are blocked and frustrated. Latency or perception of conflict should be treated as a cost, only if harmony and uniformity are highly valued. Tolerance of divergence is not generally a value widely shared in contemporary organizations, and under these conditions latent and perceived conflict are also likely to be treated as costly.

2. *Conflict as a source of disequilibrium.* White's observation of *chronic* conflict creates doubt as to whether conflict represents a disequilibrium.[28] He argued that if conflict *were* an unstable state for the system, then only transient conflict or conflict over shifting foci would be observable. Even if organizational participants treat conflict as a cost, they may still endure intense, chronic conflict, if there are compensating inducements from the organization in the form of high salary, opportunities for advancement, and others. To say that a participant will endure chronic conflict is not to deny that he will be motivated to reduce it; it is merely to say that if the organizational member is unsuccessful in reducing conflict, he may still continue to participate if the inducements offered to him exceed the contributions he makes in return. Although conflict may be one of several sources of disequilibrium, it is neither a necessary nor a sufficient condition of disequilibrium. But, as will be shown, equilibrium nevertheless plays an important role in organizational reactions to conflict.[29]

3. *Resolution pressures a necessary consequence of conflict.* If conflicts are relatively small, and the inducements and contributions remain in equilibrium, then the participants are likely to try to resolve the conflict within the context of the existing relationship.[30] On the other hand, when contributions exceed inducements, or when conflict is intense enough to destroy the inducements-contributions balance and there is no prospect for the reestablishment of equilibrium, then conflict is likely to be reduced by dissolving the relationship. Temporary imbalances, of course, may be tolerated; i.e., the relationship will not dissolve if the participants perceive the conflicts to be resolvable in the near future.

What is the effect of conflict on the interaction rate among participants?

28. Harrison White, *op. cit.*

29. Conflict may actually be a source of equilibrium and stability, as Coser, *op. cit.*, p. 159, points out. A multiplicity of conflicts internal to a group, Coser argues, may breed solidarity, provided that the conflicts do not divide the group along the same axis, because the multiplicity of coalitions and associations provide a web of affiliation for the exchange of dissenting viewpoints. The essence of his argument is that some conflict is inevitable, and that it is better to foster frequent minor conflicts of interest, and thereby gradually adjust the system, and so forestall the accumulation of latent antagonisms which might eventually disrupt the organization. Frequent minor conflicts also serve to keep the antagonists accurately informed of each other's relative strength, thereby preventing a serious miscalculation of the changes of a successful major conflagration and promoting the continual and gradual readjustment of structure to coincide with true relative power.

30. For example, labor unions, while they wish to win the economic conflict with management, have no interest in seeing the relationship destroyed altogether. They may, however, choose to threaten such disruptive conflict as a matter of strategy.

It depends on the stability of the relationship. If the participants receive inducements in sufficient amounts to balance contributions, then perception of conflict is likely to generate pressures for *increased* interaction, and the content of the interaction is likely to deal with resolution procedures. On the other hand, if conflict represents a cost to the participant and this cost is not compensated by added inducements, then conflict is likely to lead to *decreased* interaction or withdrawal from the relationship.

To summarize, conflict is frequently, but not always, negatively valued by organization members. To the extent that conflict *is* valued negatively, minor conflicts generate pressures towards resolution without altering the relationship; and major conflicts generate pressures to alter the form of the relationship or to dissolve it altogether. If inducements for participation are sufficiently high, there is the possibility of chronic conflict in the context of a stable relationship.

Three conceptual models of organizational conflict

As Ephron points out, only a very abstract model is likely to be applicable to the study of all organizational conflict phenomena.[31] To be useful in the analysis of real situations, a general theoretical framework must at least fit several broad classes of conflict, some or all of which may occur within the same organization. This suggests that different ways of abstracting or conceptualizing a given organization are required, depending on what phenomena are to be studied. The three models of organization described at the beginning of this paper are the basis of the general theory of conflict presented here.

Bargaining model

A reasonable measure of the potential conflict among a set of interest groups is the discrepancy between aggregated demands of the competing parties and the available resources. Attempts at conflict resolution usually center around attempting either to increase the pool of available resources or to decrease the demands of the parties to the conflict. Because market mechanisms or elaborate administrative mechanisms have usually evolved to guarantee orderly allocation of scarce resources, bargaining conflicts rarely escalate to the manifest level, except as strategic maneuvers.[32] Walton and McKersie describe such conflicts as complex relationships which involve both integrative (cooperative) and distributive (competitive) subprocesses.[33] Each party to the conflict has an interest in making the total resources as large as possible, but also in securing as large a share of them

---

31. Ephron, *op. cit.*, p. 55.

32. However, the Negro demonstrations of the 1960s and the labor riots of the early twentieth century testify to the futility of managing interest-group conflicts when mechanisms for resolution are not available or when the parties in power refuse to create such mechanisms.

33. R. E. Walton and R. B. McKersie, *A Behavioral Theory of Labor Negotiations* (New York: McGraw-Hill, 1965).

as possible for itself. The integrative subprocess is largely concerned with joint problem solving, and the distributive subprocess with strategic bargaining. A major element of strategy in strategic bargaining is that of attitudinal structuring, whereby each party attempts to secure the moral backing of relevant third parties (for example, the public or the government).

An important characteristic of interest-group conflicts is that negotiation is frequently done by representatives who face the dual problems of (*1*) securing consensus for the negotiated solution among respective group members, and (*2*) compromising between the demands for flexibility by his opposite number and the demands for rigidity by his own group.[34] The level of perceived conflict will increase as the deadline for a solution approaches; and interest-group conflicts are invariably characterized by deadline pressures.

Most of Walton and McKersie's framework has been developed and applied within the context of labor-management relations. But the interest-group model is not limited to this sphere of activity. Pondy has described the process of capital budgeting as a process of conflict resolution among departments competing for investment funds.[35] Wildavsky has described government budgeting as a political process involving paraphernalia of bargaining among legislative and executive interest groups.[36] Just as past labor agreements set precedents for current labor agreements, budgeting is an incremental process that builds on the residues of previous budgetary conflicts. But, whereas the visible procedures of bargaining are an accepted part of labor-management relations, there are strong pressures in budgeting (particularly *business* budgeting) to conceal the bargaining that goes on and to attempt to cloak all decisions in the guise of rationality.[37]

Bureaucratic model

The bureaucratic model (roughly equivalent to Ephron's "political" model) is appropriate for the analysis of conflicts along the *vertical* dimension of a hierarchy, that is, conflicts among the parties to an authority relation. Vertical conflicts in an organization usually arise because superiors attempt to control the behavior of subordinates, and subordinates resist such control. The authority relation is defined by the set of subordinate activities over which the subordinate has surrendered to a superior the legitimacy to exercise discretion.[38] The potential for conflict is thus present when the superior

34. These two negotiator problems are termed "factional conflict" and "boundary conflict" by Walton and McKersie, *op. cit.*, p. 283 ff.

35. Pondy, *op. cit.*

36. Aaron Wildavsky, *The Politics of the Budgetary Process* (Boston: Little, Brown, 1964).

37. March and Simon, *op. cit.*, p. 131.

38. This set of activities is usually called the "zone of indifference" or "zone of acceptance." See Chester Barnard, *The Functions of the Executive* (Cambridge, Mass.: Harvard University Press, 1960), pp. 168–170; and Herbert A. Simon, *Administrative Behavior* (New York: Macmillan, 1960), pp. 11–13.

and subordinate have different expectations about the zone of indifference. The subordinate is likely to perceive conflict when the superior attempts to exercise control over activities outside the zone of indifference; and the superior perceives conflict when his attempts at control are thwarted. Superiors are likely to interpret subordinate resistance as due to resentment of the exercise of *personal* power. A typical bureaucratic reaction to subordinate resistance is therefore the substitution of impersonal rules for personal control. As numerous students of bureaucracy are quick to point out, however, the unanticipated reaction to rules is more conflict, not less. The usual reasoning goes as follows: The imposition of rules defines the authority relation more clearly and robs the subordinate of the autonomy provided by ambiguity. Replacing supervision with control by rules invariably narrows the subordinate's freedom of action, makes his behavior more predictable to others, and thus weakens his power position in the organization. Control over the conditions of one's own existence, if not over others', is highly valued in organizations, particularly in large organizations. The subordinate therefore perceives himself to be threatened by and in conflict with his superiors, who are attempting to decrease his autonomy.

But why should autonomy be so important? What is the drawback to being subject to a benevolent autocrat? The answer, of course, is that autocrats seldom are or seldom remain benevolent. There is no assurance that the superior's (the organization's) goals, interests, or needs will be compatible with those of the subordinate, especially when: (*1*) organizations are so large that the leaders cannot identify personally with the rank and file; (*2*) responsibilities are delegated to organizational subunits, and subunit goals, values, etc. become differentiated from those of the hierarchy; and (*3*) procedures are formalized, and the organization leaders tend to treat rank and file members as mere instrumentalities or executors of the procedures.

In short, numerous factors influence goals and values along the vertical dimension of an organization; therefore, because subordinates to an authority relation can not rely on superiors to identify with their goals, autonomy becomes important. This leads to resistance by subordinates to attempts by superiors to control them, which in turn generates pressures toward routinization of activities and the institution of impersonal rules. This may lead to relatively predictable, conflict-free behavior, but behavior which is rigid and largely immune to personal persuasion. It is ironic that these very factors provide the potential for conflict when the organization must adapt to a changing environment. Rigidity of behavior, which minimizes conflict in a stable environment, is a major source of conflict when adaptability is required.

Research on leadership and on role conflict also provides important insights into vertical conflict. Whereas bureaucratic developments have sought to minimize conflict by altering the *fact* of supervision (for example, the use of impersonal rules and emphasis on procedure), leadership developments have sought to alter the *style* of supervision (for example, Likert's "linking pin" proposal and the various techniques of participative management).[39] Instead of minimizing dependence and increasing autonomy, leadership theorists have proposed minimizing conflict by using personal persuasion and group pressures to bring subordinate goals more closely into line with the legitimate goals of the organization. They have prescribed solutions which decrease autonomy and increase dependence. By heightening the individual's involvement in the organization's activities, they have actually provided the basis for the intense personal conflict that characterizes intimate relations.[40]

Both the bureaucratic and the leadership approaches to vertical conflict, as discussed here, take the superior-subordinate dyad as the unit of analysis. The role-conflict approach opens up the possibility of examining the conflicts faced by a man-in-the-middle between the demands of his subordinates and the demands of his superiors. Blau and Scott have suggested that effective leadership can occur only on alternative levels of a hierarchy.[41] The "man-in-the-middle" must align himself with the interests of either his superior or his subordinate, and in so doing he alienates the other. Of the three conceptual models of conflict, the bureaucratic model has probably received the most attention from researchers from a wide variety of disciplines. Partly because of this diversity, and partly because of the ease with which researchers identify with values of efficiency or democracy, this model is the least straightforward of the three.

Systems model

The systems model, like Ephron's "administrative" model, derives largely from the March-Simon treatment of organizational conflict.[42] It is appropriate for the analysis of conflicts among the parties to a functional relationship. Or to use Walton's terminology, the systems model is concerned with "lateral" conflicts or conflicts among persons at the same hierarchical level.[43] Whereas the authority-structure model is about problems of control, and the interest-group model is about problems of competition, the systems model is about problems of coordination.

The dyad is taken as the basic building block of the conceptual system. Consider two individuals, each occupying some formal position in an organization and playing some formal role with respect to the other. For ex-

39. Rensis Likert, *New Patterns of Management* (New York: McGraw-Hill, 1961). See, for example, Chris Argyris, *Interpersonal Competence and Organizational Effectiveness* (Homewood, Ill.: Dorsey, 1962), or Douglas McGregor, *The Human Side of Enterprise* (New York: McGraw-Hill, 1960).

40. Coser, *op. cit.*, pp. 67–72.

41. Peter Blau and Richard Scott, *Formal Organizations* (San Francisco: Chandler, 1962), pp. 162–163.

42. March and Simon, *op. cit.*, pp. 112–135.

43. R. E. Walton, *Theory of Conflict in Lateral Organizational Relationships* (Institute Paper No. 85; Lafayette, Ind.: Purdue University, November 1964).

ample, *A* is the production manager and *B* the marketing manager of the *XYZ* company. The production manager's position is defined by the responsibility to use resources at his disposal (for example, raw materials, workers, machines) to manufacture specified products with certain constraints of quantity, quality, cost, time, and perhaps procedure. The marketing manager's position is defined by the responsibility to use resources at his disposal (for example, promotional media, salesmen, salable goods) to market and sell the company's products within certain constraints, and so on. The constraints under which each manager operates and the resources at his disposal may be set for him by himself, by the other manager, or by someone else either in or outside of the company. The role of each with respect to the other is specified by the set of directions, requests, information, and goods which he minimally must or maximally may give to or receive from the other manager. The roles may also specify instances of and procedures for joint selection of product mix, schedules, and so on. These *formal* specifications of position and role are frequently described in written job descriptions, but may also form a part of a set of unwritten, stable, widely shared expectations legitimized by the appropriate hierarchical authorities. If certain responsibilities and activities are exercised without legitimization, that is, without the conscious, deliberate recognition and approval of the appropriate authorities, then they constitute *informal* positions and roles. Such expectations may still be widely shared, and are not necessarily illegitimate, i.e., specifically proscribed by the hierarchical authorities.

The fundamental source of conflict in such a system arises out of the pressures toward suboptimization. Assume first that the organization is goal-oriented rather than procedure-oriented. The subunits in a goal-oriented system will, for various reasons, have different sets of active goals,[44] or different preference orderings for the same set of goals. If in turn, two subunits having differentiated goals are functionally interdependent, then conditions exist for conflict. Important types of interdependence matter are: (*1*) common usage of some service or facility, (*2*) sequences of work or information flow prescribed by task or hierarchy, and (*3*) rules of unanimity or consensus about joint activity.

Two ways of reducing conflict in lateral relationships, if it be desirable to do so, therefore, are to reduce goal differentiation by modified incentive systems, or by proper selection, training, or assignment procedures; and to reduce functional interdependence. Functional interdependence is reduced by (*1*) reducing dependence on common resources; (*2*) loosening up schedules or introducing buffers, such as inventories or contingency funds; and (*3*) reducing pressures for consensus. These techniques of preventing con-

---

44. Following Simon, we treat a goal as any criterion of decision. Thus, both purposes and constraints are taken to be goals. See Herbert A. Simon, On the Concept of Organizational Goal, *Administrative Science Quarterly* 9 (June 1964), 1–22.

flict may be costly in both direct and indirect costs. Interpersonal friction is one of the costs of "running a tight ship."

If the parties to the conflict are flexible in their demands and desires,[45] the conflict is likely to be perceived only as a transient disturbance. Furthermore, the conflict may not be perceived, if alternative relationships for satisfying needs are available. This is one of the persuasive arguments for building in redundant channels of work and information flow.

Some relationships may be traditionally conflictful (e.g., administration-faculty, sales-production, and others). The parties to such a relationship have a set to expect conflict, and therefore may perceive conflict when none exists.

As to the forms of manifested conflict, it is extremely unlikely that any violent or aggressive actions will occur. First, strongly held norms proscribe such behavior. Secondly, the reaction of other parties to the relationship is likely to be that of withdrawing all cooperation. A much more common reaction to perceived conflict is the adoption of a joint decision process characterized by bargaining rather than problem solving. Walton, Dutton, and Fitch have described some of the characteristics of a bargaining style: careful rationing of information and its deliberate distortion; rigid, formal, and circumscribed relations; suspicion, hostility, and disassociation among the subunits.[46] These rigidities and negative attitudes, of course, provide the potential for conflict over other issues in future episodes of the relationship.

Summary

It has been argued that conflict within an organization can be best understood as a dynamic process underlying a wide variety of organizational behaviors. The term conflict refers neither to its antecedent conditions, nor individual awareness of it, nor certain affective states, nor its overt manifestations, nor its residues of feeling, precedent, or structure, but to all of these taken together as the history of a conflict episode.

Conflict is not necessarily bad or good, but must be evaluated in terms of its individual and organizational functions and dysfunctions. In general, conflict generates pressures to reduce conflict, but chronic conflict persists and is endured under certain conditions, and consciously created and managed by the politically astute administrator.

Conflict resolution techniques may be applied at any of several pressure points. Their effectiveness and appropriateness depends on the nature of the conflict and on the administrator's philosophy of management. The tension model leads to creation of safety-valve institutions and the semantic

---

45. Such flexibility is one of the characteristics of a problem-solving relationship. Conversely, a bargaining relationship is characterized by rigidity of demands and desires.
46. Walton, Dutton, and Fitch, *op. cit.*

model to the promotion of open communication. Although these may be perfectly appropriate for certain forms of imagined conflict, their application to real conflict may only exacerbate the conflict.

A general theory of conflict has been elaborated in the context of each of three conceptual models: (*1*) a bargaining model, which deals with interest groups in competition for resources; (*2*) a bureaucratic model, which deals with authority relations and the need to control; and (*3*) a systems model, which deals with functional relations and the need to coordinate.

9 The Manager's Job

In this section we look at what managers *do,* what they don't do, and what they ought to do. The focus is on managing, with emphasis on the *-ing,* on doing it, making it happen, inside the organizational maze.

Over the years, many people have tried, from many perspectives, to describe and define the managing process. Working managers have tried it, and sometimes saliently and effectively, as, for example, Chester Barnard, many years ago in his classic work, *The Functions of the Executive.* Many academics have tried it, too. A few decades ago, academics tried to do it using a logical, deductive, normative process. First, they specified an ideal organizational structure, then defined managerial jobs within them, and then listed the "proper" duties and responsibilities of each job. Following that rather formalistic period, we turned to more empirical methods. By the 1950s, organizational anthropologists were trying to understand the managing process by living inside organizations, just as they had lived inside tribal communities in faraway places. They tried from that vantage point to observe and document the customs and activities of that strange race called managers. More recently still, we moved over a bit to the straightforward method of following real managers around, notepad in hand, writing down everything those managers did; then we tried to categorize and make sense out of our observations.

The first three papers in this section are from that last tradition, the tradition of following managers around. John Kotter, as the title of his paper suggests, looks at what effective managers do all day, minute by minute. He then draws some interesting and useful conclusions about what makes good managers good. Robert Kaplan focuses on the manager's networks of relationships. With whom do managers talk? When? How often? Why? From whom do they seek counsel? And with whom don't they communicate?

Henry Mintzberg, like Kotter, has carefully observed managers in situ for many years. He tries, through analysis, to draw conclusions about how managers decide what to do and how to do it.

The Harold Leavitt paper is a little different. It is not based on direct empirical research. Rather, it is an argument derived from some general observations about the managing process. Leavitt argues that managing is not just about action, nor just about analysis, but also about some soft stuff, such as imagination and a sense of mission; good managers don't just solve problems, they also create them. So this last paper proposes a three-phase model of what managing is all about: an active, implementing phase; an analytic problem-solving phase; and a mission-oriented, pathfinding phase.

After you, the reader, have looked over this section, you might take a shot at thinking about what kind of general model of the managing process you yourself are carrying around, way back in the deeper recesses of your mind.

What Effective General Managers Really Do
John P. Kotter

Here is a description of a reasonably typical day in the life of a successful executive. The individual in this case is Michael Richardson, the president of an investment management firm.

7:35 A.M.—He arrives at work after a short commute, unpacks his briefcase, gets some coffee, and begins a "to do" list for the day.

7:40—Jerry Bradshaw, a subordinate, arrives at his office, which is right next to Richardson's. One of Bradshaw's duties is to act as an assistant to Richardson.

7:45—Bradshaw and Richardson converse about a number of topics. Richardson shows Bradshaw some pictures he recently took at his summer home.

8:00—Bradshaw and Richardson talk about a schedule and priorities for the day. In the process, they touch on a dozen different subjects and issues relating to customers, and other subordinates.

8:20—Frank Wilson, another subordinate, drops in. He asks a few questions about a personnel problem and then joins in the ongoing discussion. The discussion is straightforward, rapid, and occasionally punctuated with humor.

8:30—Fred Holly, the chairman of the firm and Richardson's "boss," stops in and joins in the conversation. He asks about an appointment scheduled for 11 o'clock and brings up a few other topics as well.

8:40—Richardson leaves to get more coffee. Bradshaw, Holly, and Wilson continue their conversation.

8:42—Richardson comes back. A subordinate of a subordinate stops in and says hello. The others leave.

8:43—Bradshaw drops off a report, hands Richardson instructions that go with it, and leaves.

8:45—Joan Swanson, Richardson's secretary, arrives. They discuss her new apartment and arrangements for a meeting later in the morning.

Reprinted by permission from the *Harvard Business Review,* November-December 1982.
©1982 by the President and Fellows of Harvard College. All rights reserved.

8:49—Richardson gets a phone call from a subordinate who is returning a call from the day before. They talk primarily about the subject of the report Richardson just received.

8:55—He leaves his office and goes to a regular morning meeting that one of his subordinates runs. There are about 30 people there. Richardson reads during the meeting.

9:09—The meeting is over. Richardson stops one of the people there and talks to him briefly.

9:15—He walks over to the office of one of his subordinates, who is corporate counsel. His boss, Holly, is there too. They discuss a phone call the lawyer just received. While standing, the three talk about possible responses to a problem. As before, the exchange is quick and includes some humor.

9:30—Richardson goes back to his office for a meeting with the vice chairman of another firm (a potential customer and supplier). One other person, a liaison with that firm and a subordinate's subordinate, also attends the meeting. The discussion is cordial. It covers many topics, from their products to U.S. foreign relations.

9:50—The visitor and the subordinate's subordinate leave. Richardson opens the adjoining door to Bradshaw's office and asks a question.

9:52—Richardson's secretary comes in with five items of business.

9:55—Bradshaw drops in, asks a question about a customer, and then leaves.

9:58—Frank Wilson and one of his people arrive. He gives Richardson a memo and then the three talk about the important legal problem. Wilson does not like a decision that Richardson has tentatively made and urges him to reconsider. The discussion goes back and forth for 20 minutes until they agree on the next action and schedule it for 9 o'clock the next day.

10:35—They leave. Richardson looks over papers on his desk, then picks one up and calls Holly's secretary regarding the minutes of the last board meeting. He asks her to make a few corrections.

10:41—His secretary comes in with a card for a friend who is sick. He writes a note to go with the card.

10:50—He gets a brief phone call, then goes back to the papers on his desk.

11:03—His boss stops in. Before Richardson and Holly can begin to talk, Richardson gets another call. After the call, he tells his secretary that someone didn't get a letter he sent and asks her to send another.

11:05—Holly brings up a couple of issues, and then Bradshaw comes in. The three start talking about Jerry Phillips, who has become a difficult problem. Bradshaw leads the conversation, telling the others what he has done during the last few days regarding this issue. Richardson and Holly ask questions. After a while, Richardson begins to take notes. The exchange, as before, is rapid and straightforward. They try to define the problem and outline possible alternative next steps. Richardson lets the discussion roam away from and back to the topic again and again. Finally, they agree on a next step.

12:00 Noon—Richardson orders lunch for himself and Bradshaw. Bradshaw comes in and goes over a dozen items. Wilson stops by to say that he has already followed up on their earlier conversation.

12:10 P.M.—A staff person stops by with some calculations Richardson had requested. He thanks her and has a brief, amicable conversation.

12:20—Lunch arrives. Richardson and Bradshaw go into the conference room to eat. Over lunch they pursue business and nonbusiness subjects. They laugh often at each other's humor. They end the lunch talking about a potential major customer.

1:15—Back in Richardson's office, they continue the discussion about the customer. Bradshaw gets a pad, and they go over in detail a presentation to the customer. Then Bradshaw leaves.

1:40—Working at his desk, Richardson looks over a new marketing brochure.

1:50—Bradshaw comes in again; he and Richardson go over another dozen details regarding the presentation to the potential customer. Bradshaw leaves.

1:55—Jerry Thomas comes in. He is a subordinate of Richardson, and he has scheduled for the afternoon some key performance appraisals, which he and Richardson will hold in Richardson's office. They talk briefly about how they will handle each appraisal.

2:00—Fred Jacobs (a subordinate of Thomas) joins Richardson and Thomas. Thomas runs the meeting. He goes over Jacobs's bonus for the year and the reason for it. Then the three of them talk about Jacob's role in the upcoming year. They generally agree and Jacobs leaves.

2:30—Jane Kimble comes in. The appraisal follows the same format as for Fred Jacobs. Richardson asks a lot of questions and praises Kimble at times. The meeting ends on a friendly note of agreement.

3:00—George Houston comes in; the appraisal format is repeated again.

3:30—When Houston leaves, Richardson and Thomas talk briefly about how well they have accomplished their objectives in the meetings. Then they talk briefly about some of Thomas's other subordinates. Thomas leaves.

3:45—Richardson gets a short phone call. His secretary and Bradshaw come in with a list of requests.

3:50—Richardson receives a call from Jerry Phillips. He gets his notes from the 11 o'clock meeting about Phillips. They go back and forth on the phone talking about lost business, unhappy subordinates, who did what to whom, and what should be done now. It is a long, circular, and sometimes emotional conversation. Near the end, Phillips is agreeing with Richardson on the next step and thanking him.

4:55—Bradshaw, Wilson, and Holly all step in. Each is following up on different issues that were discussed earlier in the day. Richardson briefly tells them of his conversation with Phillips. Bradshaw and Holly leave.

5:10—Richardson and Wilson have a light conversation about three or four items.

5:20—Jerry Thomas stops in. He describes a new personnel problem and the three of them discuss it. More and more humor starts coming into the conversation. They agree on an action to take.

5:30—Richardson begins to pack his briefcase. Five people briefly stop by, one or two at a time.

5:45—He leaves the office.

In at least a dozen ways, Richardson's day is typical for a general manager. The daily behavior of the successful GMs I have studied generally conforms to these patterns (see the appendix for a description of the study):

1. They spend most of their time with others. The average GM spends only 25% of his working time alone, and this is spent largely at home, on airplanes, or while commuting. Few spend less than 70% of their time with others, and some spend up to 90% of their work time this way.

2. The people they spend time with include many in addition to their direct subordinates and boss. GMs regularly go around the formal chain of command. They also regularly see people who often appear to be unimportant outsiders.

3. The breadth of topics in these discussions is extremely wide. The GMs do not limit their focus to planning, business strategy, staffing, and other "top management concerns." They discuss virtually anything and everything even remotely associated with their businesses and organizations.

4. In these conversations, GMs typically ask a lot of questions. In a half-hour conversation, some will ask literally hundreds.

5. During these conversations, the GMs rarely seem to make "big" decisions.

6. These discussions usually contain a considerable amount of joking and kidding and concern non-work-related issues. The humor is often about others in the organization or industry. Nonwork discussions are usually about people's families, hobbies, or recent outside activities (e.g., golf scores).

7. In not a small number of these encounters, the substantive issue discussed is relatively unimportant to the business or organization. That is, GMs regularly engage in activities that even they regard as a waste of time.

8. In these encounters, the executives rarely give orders in a traditional sense. That is, they seldom "tell" people what to do.

9. Nevertheless, GMs frequently engage in attempts to influence others. However, instead of telling people what to do, they ask, request, cajole, persuade, and intimidate.

10. In allocating their time with others, GMs often react to others' initiatives. Much of the typical GM's day is unplanned. Even GMs who have a heavy schedule of planned meetings often end up spending a lot of time on topics that are not on the official agenda.

11. Most of their time with others is spent in short, disjointed conversations. Discussions of a single question or issue rarely last more than ten minutes. And it is not at all unusual for a GM to cover ten unrelated topics in a five-minute interaction.

12. They work long hours. The average person I have studied works just under 60 hours per week. Not many work fewer than 55 hours per week. Although some of their work is done at home, while commuting to work, or while traveling, they spend most of their time at their places of work.

These patterns in daily behavior, which Richardson's day illustrates, are basically consistent with other studies of managerial behavior,[1] especially those of high-level managers.[2] Nevertheless, as Henry Mintzberg has pointed out,[3] this behavior seems hard to reconcile, on the surface at least, with traditional notions of what top managers do (or should do). It is hard to fit the behavior into categories like "planning," "organizing," "controlling," "directing," "staffing," and so on.

And even if one tries, two conclusions surface: (1) The "planning" and "organizing" that these people do does not seem very systematically done; it seems rather hit or miss, rather sloppy. (2) A lot of behavior ends up being classified as "none of the above." The implication is that these are things that top managers should not be doing. Nevertheless, hit or miss is precisely how planning and organizing manifest themselves in the daily behavior of effective executives, and for perfectly understandable reasons.

How effective executives approach their jobs

To understand why effective GMs behave as they do, it is essential first to recognize the types of challenges and dilemmas found in most of their jobs, the two most fundamental of which are:

> Figuring out what to do despite uncertainty, great diversity, and an enormous amount of potentially relevant information.
>
> Getting things done through a large and diverse set of people despite having little direct control over most of them.

The severity of these challenges in complex organizations is much greater than most nonexecutives would suspect. And the implications of these job demands for the traditional management functions of planning, staffing, organizing, directing, and controlling are very powerful.

Implications for traditional management functions	Dilemmas inherent in the job	
	Figuring out what to do despite great uncertainty, great diversity, and an enormous quantity of potentially relevant information.	Getting things done through a large and diverse group of people despite having little direct control over most of them.
Planning	Planning is very difficult to do well in such a context. It requires a lot of time and attention, not just a series of meetings once a year. It requires some good information systems to sort out the noise and focus on essential data.	Planning must be done in a way that does not exacerbate the already very difficult human environment. One must therefore be very careful regarding what is put on paper or said to others.
Staffing and organizing	Some type of sound plan or map is essential, because without it there is no rational basis for "staffing" and "organizing."	The resources one needs to get the job done include many people besides direct subordinates. Hence, some form of "staffing" and "organizing" activity must be aimed at many others and this activity will have to rely mainly on methods other than formal staffing and organizing procedures.
Directing and controlling	Some type of sound plan or map is essential, because without it, it is impossible to know where to direct one's attention among the infinite possibilities. Without it, one cannot know what to direct or control.	A fairly strong set of cooperative relationships to those resources on which one is dependent is essential, or one simply will not be able to "direct" and "control."

Exhibit 1. Behavioral implications, given the nature of GM jobs, for the traditional management functions

Exhibit 1 suggests that the very nature of executive jobs requires a complex and subtle approach to planning, organizing, staffing, and so forth. The approach needs to take into account the uncertainty involved, as well as the diversity and volume of potentially relevant information. It must also come to grips with the difficult human environment; it must somehow help executives get things done despite their dependency on a large number of people, many of whom are not their subordinates.

An examination of effective general managers suggests that they have found just such an approach, a central part of which might be usefully thought of as "agenda setting" and "network building."

Agenda setting

During their first six months to a year in a new job, GMs usually spend considerable time establishing their agendas. Later, they continue to update them but in a less time-consuming process.

Effective executives develop agendas that are made up of loosely connected goals and plans that address their long-, medium-, and short-term responsibilities. The agendas usually address a broad range of financial, product/market, and organizational issues. They include both vague and specific items. Exhibit 2 summarizes the contents of a typical GM's agenda.

Time frame	Key issues		
	Financial	**Business product/ market**	**Organizational people**
Long run 5 to 20 years	A vague notion of revenues or ROI desired in 10 to 20 years.	Only a vague notion of what kind of business (products and markets) the GM wants to develop.	Vague; sometimes includes a notion about the type of company the GM wants and the caliber of management that will be needed.
Medium run 1 to 5 years	A fairly specific set of goals for sales and income and ROI for the next five years.	Some goals and plans for growing the business, such as: (a) introduce three new products before 1985, and (b) explore acquisition possibilities in the communications industry.	A short list of items, such as: (a) by 1983 we will need a major reorganization, and (b) find a replacement for Corey by 1984.
Short run zero to 12 months	A very detailed list of financial objectives for the quarter and the year in all financial areas: sales, expenses, income, ROI, and so on.	A set of general objectives and plans aimed at such things as: (a) the market share for various products, and (b) the inventory levels of various lines.	A list of items, such as: (a) find a replacement for Smith soon, and (b) get Jones to commit himself to a more aggressive set of five-year objectives.

Exhibit 2. A GM's typical agenda

Although most corporations today have formal planning processes that produce written plans, GMs' agendas always include goals, priorities, strategies, and plans that are not in these documents. This is not to say that formal plans and the GMs' agendas are incompatible. Generally they are very consistent, but they differ in at least three important ways:

First, the formal plans tend to be written mostly in terms of detailed financial numbers. GMs' agendas tend to be less detailed in financial objectives and more detailed in strategies and plans for the business or the organization.

Second, formal plans usually focus entirely on the short and moderate run (3 months to 5 years), while GMs' agendas tend to focus on a broader time frame, which includes the immediate future (1 to 30 days) and the longer run (5 to 20 years).

Finally, the formal plans tend to be more explicit, rigorous, and logical, especially regarding how various financial items fit together. GMs' agendas often contain lists of goals or plans that are not as explicitly connected.

Executives begin the process of developing these agendas immediately after starting their jobs, if not before. They use their knowledge of the businesses and organizations involved along with new information received each day to quickly develop a rough agenda—typically, this contains a very loosely connected and incomplete set of objectives, along with a few specific strategies and plans. Then over time, as more and more information is gathered, they incrementally (one step at a time) make the agendas more complete and more tightly connected.

In gathering information to set their agendas, effective GMs rely more on discussions with others than on books, magazines, or reports. These people tend to be individuals with whom they have relationships, not necessarily people in the "appropriate" job or function (e.g., such as a person in the planning function). In this way, they obtain information continuously, day after day, not just at planning meetings. And they do so by using their current knowledge of the business and organization and of management in general to help them direct their questioning, not by asking broad or general questions. In other words, they find ways within the flow of their workdays to ask a few critical questions and to receive in return some information that would be useful for agenda-setting purposes.

With this information, GMs make agenda-setting decisions both consciously (or analytically) and unconsciously (or intuitively) in a process that is largely internal to their minds. Indeed, important agenda-setting decisions are often not observable. In selecting specific activities to include in their agendas, GMs look for those that accomplish multiple goals, that are consistent with all other goals and plans, and that are within their power to implement. Projects and programs that seem important and logical but do not meet these criteria tend to be discarded or are at least resisted.

Almost all effective GMs seem to use this type of agenda-setting process, but the best performers do so to a greater degree and with more skill.

For example, the "excellent" performers I have studied develop agendas based on more explicit business strategies that address longer time frames and that include a wider range of business issues. They do so by more aggressively seeking information from others (including "bad news"), by more skillfully asking questions, and by more successfully seeking out programs and projects that can help accomplish multiple objectives at once.[4]

Network building

In addition to setting agendas, effective GMs allocate significant time and effort when they first take their jobs to developing a network of cooperative relationships among those people they feel are needed to satisfy their emerging agendas. Even after the first six months, this activity still takes up considerable time; but generally, it is most intense during the first months in a job. After that, their attention shifts toward using the networks to both implement and help in updating the agendas.

This network-building activity, as I have observed it and had it described to me, is aimed at much more than just direct subordinates. GMs develop cooperative relationships with and among peers, outsiders, their bosses' boss, and their subordinates' subordinates. Indeed, they develop relationships with (and sometimes among) any and all of the hundreds or even thousands of people on whom they feel dependent because of their jobs. That is, just as they create an agenda that is different from, although generally consistent with, formal plans, they also create a network that is different from, but generally consistent with, the formal organization structure (see exhibit 3 for a typical GM's network).

In these large networks, the nature of the relationships varies significantly in intensity and in type; some relationships are much stronger than others, some much more personal than others, and so on. Indeed, to some degree, every relationship in a network is different because it has a unique history, it is between unique people, and so forth.

GMs develop these networks of cooperative relationships using a wide variety of face-to-face methods. They try to make others feel legitimately obliged to them by doing favors or by stressing their formal relationships. They act in ways to encourage others to identify with them. They carefully nurture their professional reputations in the eyes of others. They even maneuver to make others feel that they are particularly dependent on the GMs for resources, or career advancement, or other support.

In addition to developing relationships with existing personnel, effective GMs also often develop their networks by moving, hiring, and firing subordinates. Generally, they do so to strengthen their ability to get things done. In a similar way, they also change suppliers or bankers, lobby to get different people into peer positions, and even restructure their boards to improve their relationships with a needed resource.

Furthermore, they also sometimes shape their networks by trying to

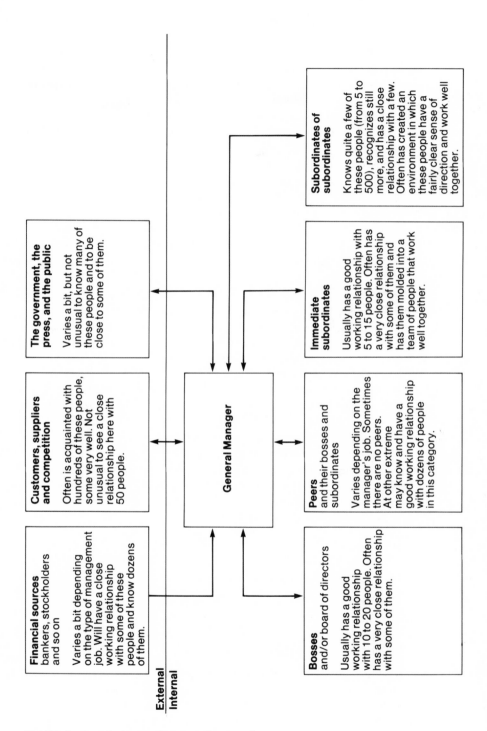

External
Internal

Financial sources
bankers, stockholders and so on

Varies a bit depending on the type of management job. Will have a close working relationship with some of these people and know dozens of them.

Customers, suppliers and competition

Often is acquainted with hundreds of these people, some very well. Not unusual to see a close relationship here with 50 people.

The government, the press, and the public

Varies a bit, but not unusual to know many of these people and to be close to some of them.

Subordinates of subordinates

Knows quite a few of these people (from 5 to 500), recognizes still more, and has a close relationship with a few. Often has created an environment in which these people have a fairly clear sense of direction and work well together.

General Manager

Bosses
and/or board of directors

Usually has a good working relationship with 10 to 20 people. Often has a very close relationship with some of them.

Peers
and their bosses and subordinates

Varies depending on the manager's job. Sometimes there are no peers. At other extreme may know and have a good working relationship with dozens of people in this category.

Immediate subordinates

Usually has a good working relationship with 5 to 15 people. Often has a very close relationship with some of them and has them molded into a team of people that work well together.

Exhibit 3. A typical general manager's network

create certain types of relationships *among* the people in various parts of the network. That is, they try to create the appropriate "environment" (norms and values) they feel is necessary to implement their agendas. Typically this is an environment in which people are willing to work hard on the GM's agenda and cooperate for the greater good. Although executives sometimes try to create such an environment among peers, bosses, or outsiders, they do so most often among their subordinates.

Almost all effective GMs use this network-building process, but the best performers do so more aggressively and more skillfully. "Excellent" performers, for example, create networks with many talented people in them and with strong ties to and among their subordinates. They do so by using a wide variety of methods with great skill. The "good/fair" performers tend to use fewer network-building methods, employ them less aggressively, and in the process, create weaker networks.[5]

Execution: Getting networks to implement agendas

After they have largely developed their networks and agendas, effective GMs tend to shift their attention toward using the networks to implement their agendas. In doing so, they marshal their interpersonal skills, budgetary resources, and information to influence people and events in a variety of direct and indirect ways.

In implementing their agendas, GMs often call on virtually their entire network of relationships to help them. They do not limit their assistance to direct subordinates and a boss; when necessary, they use any and all of their relationships. During my time with GMs, I have seen some of them call on peers, corporate staff people, subordinates reporting three or four levels below them, bosses reporting two or three levels above them, suppliers or customers, even competitors, to help them get something done. There is no category of people that was never used. And in each case, the basic pattern was the same:

> The GM was trying to get some action on items in his agenda that he felt would not be accomplished without intervention on his part.
>
> The people he approached could be of help, often uniquely so.
>
> The people he approached were part of his network.
>
> The GM chose people and an approach with an eye toward achieving multiple objectives at once and doing so without inadvertently disturbing important relationships in the network.

Having approached people, GMs often influence them by simply asking or suggesting that they do something, knowing that because of their relationship with the person, he or she will comply. In some cases, depending on the issue involved and the nature of the relationship they also use their knowledge and information to help persuade these people. Under other circumstances, they will use resources available to them to negotiate a trade. And occasionally, they even resort to intimidation and coercion.

Effective GMs also often use their networks to exert indirect influence on people, including people who are not a part of that network. In some cases, GMs will convince one person who is in their network to get a second, who is not, to take some needed action. More indirectly still, GMs will sometimes approach a number of different people, requesting them to take actions that would then shape events that influence other individuals. Perhaps the most common example of indirect influence involves staging an event of some sort. In a typical case, the GM would set up a meeting or meetings and influence others through the selection of participants, the choice of an agenda, and often by his own participation.

Unlike the case of direct influence, GMs achieve much of their more indirect influence through symbolic methods. That is, they use meetings, architecture, language, stories about the organization, time, and space as symbols in order to get some message across indirectly.

All effective GMs seem to get things done this way, but the best performers do so more than others and with greater skill. That is, the better performers tend to mobilize more people to get more things done, and do so using a wider range of influence tactics. "Excellent" performers ask, encourage, cajole, praise, reward, demand, manipulate, and generally motivate others with great skill in face-to-face situations. They also rely more heavily on indirect influence than the "good" managers, who tend to rely on a more narrow range of influence techniques and apply them with less finesse.[6]

How the job determines behavior

Most of the visible patterns in daily behavior seem to be direct consequences of the way GMs approach their job, and thus consequences of the nature of the job itself and the type of people involved. More specifically, some of these patterns seem to derive from the approach taken to agenda setting, others from network building, others from how they tend to use networks to implement agendas, and still others from the approach in general.

Spending most of the time with others (pattern 1) seems to be a natural consequence of the GM's overall approach to the job and the central role the network of relationships plays. As we saw earlier, GMs develop a network of relationships with those the job makes them dependent on and then use that network to help create, implement, and update an organizational agenda. As such, the whole approach to the job involves interacting with people. Hence it should not be surprising to find that on a daily basis, GMs spend most of their time with others.

Likewise, because the network tends to include all those the GM is dependent on, it is hardly surprising to find the GM spending time with many besides a boss and direct subordinates (pattern 2). And because the agenda tends to include items related to all the long-, medium-, and short-run responsibilities associated with the job, it is to be expected that the breadth of topics covered in daily conversations might be very wide (pattern 3).

A few of the other patterns seem to be a direct consequence of the agenda-setting approach employed by GMs. As we saw earlier, agenda setting involves gathering information on a continuous basis from network members, usually by asking questions. That GMs ask a lot of questions (pattern 4) follows directly. With the information in hand, we saw that GMs create largely unwritten agendas. Hence, major agenda-setting decisions are often invisible; they occur in the GM's mind (pattern 5).

We also saw that network building involves the use of a wide range of interpersonal tactics. Since humor and nonwork discussions can be used as effective tools for building relationships and maintaining them under stressful conditions, we should not be surprised to find these tools used often (as we do—pattern 6). Since maintaining relationships requires that one deal with issues that other people feel are important (regardless of their centrality to the business), it is also not surprising to find the GMs spending time on substantive issues that seem unimportant to us and them (pattern 7).

As I indicated earlier, after the initial period on the job the thrust of the GMs' approach is to use their networks to implement their agendas. They do so using a wide variety of direct and indirect influence methods. Ordering is only one of many methods. Under these circumstances, one would expect to find them rarely ordering others (pattern 8) but spending a lot of time trying to influence others (pattern 9).

The efficiency of seemingly inefficient behavior

Of all the patterns visible in daily behavior, perhaps the most difficult to understand, or at least appreciate, are that the executives do not plan their days in advance in much detail but instead react (pattern 10) and that conversations are short and disjointed (pattern 11). On the surface at least, behaving this way seems particularly unmanagerial. Yet these patterns are possibly the most important and efficient of all.

The following is a typical example of the effectiveness and efficiency of "reactive" behavior. On his way to a meeting, a GM bumped into a staff member who did not report to him. Using this opportunity, in a two-minute conversation he: (a) asked two questions and received the information he needed; (b) reinforced their good relationship by sincerely complimenting the staff member on something he had recently done; and (c) got the staff member to agree to do something that the GM needed done.

The agenda in his mind guided the executive through this encounter, prompting him to ask important questions and to request an important action. And his relationship with this member of his network allowed him to get the cooperation he needed to do all this very quickly. Had he tried to plan this encounter in advance, he would have had to set up and attend a meeting, which would have taken at least 15 to 30 minutes, or 750% to 1,500% more time than the chance encounter. And if he had not already had a good relationship with the person, the meeting may have taken even longer or been ineffective.

In a similar way, agendas and networks allow GMs to engage in short and disjointed conversations, which can be extremely efficient. The following set of very short discussions, taken from a day in the life of John Thompson, a division manager in a financial services corporation, is typical in this regard. The conversation occurred one morning in Thompson's office. With him were two of his subordinates, Phil Dodge and Jud Smith:

THOMPSON: "What about Potter?"

DODGE: "He's OK."

SMITH: "Don't forget about Chicago."

DODGE: "Oh yeah." [Makes a note to himself.]

THOMPSON: "OK. Then what about next week?"

DODGE: "We're set."

THOMPSON: "Good. By the way, how is Ted doing?"

SMITH: "Better. He got back from the hospital on Tuesday. Phyllis says he looks good."

THOMPSON: "That's good to hear. I hope he doesn't have a relapse."

DODGE: "I'll see you this afternoon." [Leaves the room.]

THOMPSON: "OK. [To Smith.] Are we all set for now?"

SMITH: "Yeah." [He gets up and starts to leave.]

LAWRENCE: [Steps into the doorway from the hall and speaks to Thompson.] "Have you seen the April numbers yet?"

THOMPSON: "No, have you?"

LAWRENCE: "Yes, five minutes ago. They're good except for CD, which is off by 5%."

THOMPSON: "That's better than I expected."

SMITH: "I bet George is happy."

THOMPSON: [Laughing.] "If he is, he won't be after I talk to him." [Turner, Thompson's secretary, sticks her head through the doorway and tells him Bill Larson is on the phone.]

THOMPSON: "I'll take it. Will you ask George to stop by later? [Others leave and Thompson picks up the phone.] Bill, good morning, how are you? . . . Yeah. . . . Is that right? . . . No, don't worry about it. . . . I think about a million and a half. . . . Yeah. . . . OK. . . . Yeah, Sally enjoyed the other night too. Thanks again. . . . OK. . . . Bye."

LAWRENCE: [Steps back into the office.] "What do you think about the Gerald proposal?"

THOMPSON: "I don't like it. It doesn't fit with what we've promised Corporate or Hines."

LAWRENCE: "Yeah, that's what I thought too. What is Jerry going to do about it?"

THOMPSON: "I haven't talked to him yet. [He turns to the phone and dials.] Let's see if he's in."

This dialogue may seem chaotic to an outsider, but that's only because an outsider does not share the business or organizational knowledge these managers have and does not know Thompson's agenda. That is, an outsider would not know who Potter, Ted, Phyllis, Bill Larson, Sally, Hines, or Jerry are, or what exactly "Chicago," "April numbers," "CD," or the "Gerald proposal" refer to. Nor would an outsider know what role Potter or Hines plays in Thompson's agenda. But to someone with that knowledge, the conversations make sense.

But more important, beyond being "not chaotic," these conversations are in fact amazingly efficient. In less than two minutes Thompson accomplished all of the following:

1. He learned that Mike Potter agreed to help on a particular problem loan. That problem, if not resolved successfully, could have seriously hurt Thompson's plan to increase the division's business in a certain area.

2. He reminded one of his managers to call someone in Chicago in reference to that loan.

3. He found out that the plans for the next week, about that loan, were all set. These included two internal meetings and a talk with the client.

4. He learned that Ted Jenkins was feeling better after an operation. Ted worked for Thompson and was an important part of Thompson's plans for the direction of the division over the next two years.

5. He found out that division income for April was on budget except in one area, which reduced pressures on him to focus on monthly income and to divert attention away from an effort to build revenues in one area.

6. He initiated a meeting with George Masolia to talk about the April figures. Thompson had been considering various future alternatives for the CD product line, which he felt must get on budget to support his overall thrust for the division.

7. He provided some information (as a favor) to Bill Larson, a peer in another part of the bank. Larson had been very helpful to Thompson in the past and was in a position to be very helpful in the future.

8. He initiated a call to Jerry Wilkins, one of his subordinates, to find out his reaction to a proposal from another divison that would affect Thompson's division. He was concerned that the proposal could interfere with the division's five-year revenue goals.

In a general sense, John Thompson and most of the other effective GMs I have known are, as one HBR author recently put it, "adept at grasping and taking advantage of each item in the random succession of time and issue fragments that crowd [their] day[s]." [7] This seems to be particularly true for the best performers. And central to their ability to do so are their networks and agendas. The agendas allow the GMs to react in an opportunistic (and highly efficient) way to the flow of events around them, yet knowing that they are doing so within some broader and more rational framework. The networks allow terse (and very efficient) conversations to happen; without them, such short yet meaningful conversations would be impossible. Together, the agenda and networks allow the GMs to achieve the efficiency they need to cope with very demanding jobs in fewer than 60 hours per week (pattern 12), through daily behavior patterns that on the surface can look "unmanagerial."

What should top managers do?

Some of the most important implications of all this include the following:

1. At the start, putting someone in a GM job who does not know the business or the people involved, because he is a successful "professional manager," is probably very risky. Unless the business is easy to learn, it would be very difficult for an individual to learn enough, fast enough, to develop a good agenda. And unless it is a small situation with few people involved, it would be difficult to build a strong network fast enough to implement the agenda.

Especially for large and complex businesses, this condition suggests that "growing" one's own executives should have a high priority. Many companies today say that developing their own executives is important, but in light of the booming executive search business, one has to conclude that either they are not trying very hard or that their efforts simply are not succeeding.

2. Management training courses, both in universities and in corporations, probably overemphasize formal tools, unambiguous problems, and situations that deal simplistically with human relationships.

Some of the time-management programs, currently in vogue, are a good example of the problem here. Based on simplistic conceptions about the nature of managerial work, these programs instruct managers to stop letting people and problems "interrupt" their daily work. They often tell potential executives that short and disjointed conversations are ineffective. They advise that one should discipline oneself not to let "irrelevant" people and topics get on one's schedule. In other words, they advise people to behave differently from the effective executives in this study. Seminars on "How to Run Meetings" are probably just as bad.

Another example of inappropriate courses is university-based executive training programs that emphasize formal quantitative tools. These programs are based, at least implicitly, on the assumption that such tools are central to effective performance. All evidence suggests that while they are sometimes relevant, they are hardly central.

3. People who are new in general management jobs can probably be gotten up to speed more effectively than is the norm today. Initially, a new GM usually needs to spend considerable time collecting information, establishing relationships, selecting a basic direction for his or her area of responsibilities, and developing a supporting organization. During the first three to six months, demands from superiors to accomplish specific tasks, or to work on pet projects, can often be counterproductive. Indeed, anything that significantly diverts attention away from agenda setting and network building can prove to be counterproductive.

In a more positive sense, those who oversee GMs can probably be most helpful initially if they are sensitive to where the new executive is likely to have problems and help him or her in those areas. Such areas are often quite predictable. For example, if people have spent their careers going up the ladder in one function and have been promoted into the general manager's job in an autonomous division (a common occurrence, especially in manufacturing organizations), they will probably have problems with agenda setting because of a lack of detailed knowledge about the other functions in the division.

On the other hand, if people have spent most of their early careers in professional, staff, or assistant-to jobs and are promoted into a GM's job where they suddenly have responsibility for hundreds or thousands of people (not an unusual occurrence in professional organizations), they will probably have great difficulty at first building a network. They don't have many relationships to begin with and they are not used to spending time developing a large network.

In either case, a GM's boss can be a helpful coach and can arrange activities that foster instead of retard the types of actions the new executive should be taking.

4. Finally, the formal planning systems within which many GMs must operate probably hinder effective performance.

A good planning system should help a GM create an intelligent agenda and a strong network that can implement it. That is, it should encourage the GM to think strategically, to consider both the long and short term, and regardless of the time frame, to take into account financial, product/market, and organizational issues. Furthermore, it should be a flexible tool that the executive can use to help build a network. It should give the GM leeway and options, so that, depending on what kind of environment among subordinates is desired, he or she can use the planning system to help achieve the goals.

Unfortunately, many of the planning systems used by corporations do nothing of the sort. Instead, they impose a rigid "number crunching" requirement on GMs that often does not require much strategic or long-range thinking in agenda setting and which can make network building and maintenance needlessly difficult by creating unnecessary stress among people.

Indeed, some systems seem to do nothing but generate paper, often a lot of it, and distract executives from doing those things that are really important.

Appendix

Conducted between 1976 and 1981, this study focused on a group of successful general managers in nine corporations. I examined what their jobs entailed, who they were, where they had come from, how they behaved, and how this all varied in different corporate and industry settings.

The participants all had some profit center and multifunctional responsibility. They were located in cities across the United States. They were involved in a broad range of industries, including banking, consulting, tire and rubber manufacture, TV, mechanical equipment manufacture, newspapers, copiers, investment management, consumer products, and still others. The businesses they were responsible for included some doing only $1 million to $10 million in sales, others in the $10 million to $50 million range, the $50 million to $100 million range, the $100 million to $1 billion range, and some doing $1 billion or more. On average, these executives were 47 years old. In 1978, they were paid (on average) about $150,000 (that is, well over $200,000 in 1982 dollars). And all, when selected, were believed to be performing well in their jobs.

Data collection involved three visits to each GM over 6 to 12 months. Each time I interviewed them for at least five hours, often more. I observed their daily routine for about 35 hours, and I interviewed for an hour each the dozen or so key people with whom each worked. The GMs filled out two questionnaires and gave me relevant documents, such as business plans, appointment diaries, and annual reports. From these various sources, I obtained information on the GMs' backgrounds, personalities, jobs, job contexts, behavior, and performance. Because data collection involved considerable effort for each individual, I had to limit the number of GMs selected for study to 15.

I measured the performance of the GMs by combining "hard" and "soft" indexes. The former included measures of revenue and profit growth, both in an absolute sense and compared with plans. The latter included opinions of people who worked with the GMs (including bosses, subordinates, and peers), as well as, when possible, industry analysts. Using this method, I judged most of the GMs to be doing a "very good" job. A few were rated "excellent" and a few "good/fair."

Notes

1. Such as Sune Carlson, *Executive Behavior: A Study of the Work Load and the Working Methods of Managing Directors* (Stockholm, Sweden: Strombergs, 1951); Thomas Burns, "Management in action," *Operational Research Quarterly* 8 (1957); Rosemary Stewart, "To understand the manager's job: Consider demands, constraints, choices," *Organiza-*

tional Dynamics, Spring 1976, p. 22; Michael Cohen and James March, *Leadership and Ambiguity* (New York: McGraw-Hill, 1974); R. Dubin and S. L. Spray, "Executive behavior and interaction," *Industrial Relations* 3 (1964): 99; and E. Brewer and J. W. C. Tomlinson, "The manager's working day," *Journal of Industrial Economics* 12 (1964): 191.

2. See Morgan McCall, Ann Morrison, and Robert Hannan, "Studies of managerial work: Results and methods," Technical Report No. 9 (Greensboro, N.C.: Center for Creative Leadership, 1978). This excellent report summarizes dozens of different studies ranging from Sune Carlson's groundbreaking work in 1951 to recent work by Mintzberg, Stewart, and others.

3. See "The manager's job: Folklore or fact," *Harvard Business Review,* July–August 1975, p. 49.

4. Although these patterns are not widely recognized in today's conventional wisdom on management, there is evidence from other studies that GMs and other top managers do use such a process. See, for example, James Brian Quinn, *Strategies for Change: Logical Incrementalism* (Homewood, Ill.: Richard D. Irwin, 1980); Henry Mintzberg, *The Nature of Managerial Work* (New York: Harper & Row, 1973); H. Edward Wrapp, "Good managers don't make policy decisions," *Harvard Business Review,* September–October 1967, p. 91; Charles Lindblom, "The science of 'muddling through'," *Public Administration Review* 19 (1959): 79; James March and Herbert Simon, *Organizations* (New York: John Wiley, 1958); Chester Barnard, *The Functions of the Executive* (Cambridge, Mass.: Harvard University Press, 1939); Rosemary Stewart, "Managerial agendas— Reactive or proactive," *Organizational Dynamics,* Autumn 1979, p. 34; Frank Aguilar, *Scanning the Business Environment* (New York: Macmillan, 1967); and Michael McCaskey, "A contingency approach to planning: Planning with goals and planning without goals," *Academy of Management Journal,* June 1974, p. 91.

5. Although there is not a great deal of supporting evidence elsewhere, some does exist that is consistent with these findings. See, for example, John F. Gabarro, "Socialization at the top—How CEOs and their subordinates evolve interpersonal contacts," *Organizational Dynamics,* Winter 1979, p. 2; Jeffrey Pfeffer and Jerry Salancik, "Who gets power and how they hold on to it," *Organizational Dynamics,* Winter 1977, p. 2; John P. Kotter, "Power, dependence, and effective management," *Harvard Business Review,* July–August 1977, p. 125; Melville Dalton, *Men Who Manage* (New York: John Wiley, 1959); and Richard Tanner Pascale and Anthony G. Athos, *The Art of Japanese Management* (New York: Simon & Schuster, 1981).

6. Once again, this type of behavior has been recognized and discussed in some management literature, but not in a great deal of it. See recent work by Thomas J. Peters and Jeffrey Pfeffer, in particular. For example, see Thomas J. Peters, "Symbols, patterns, and settings: An optimistic case

for getting things done," *Organizational Dynamics,* Autumn 1978; and Jeffrey Pfeffer, "Management as symbolic action," in *Research in Organizational Behavior,* vol. 3, ed. L. L. Cummings and Barry M. Staw (Greenwich, Conn.: JAI Press, 1980). Also, see M. Andrew Pettigrew, *The Politics of Organizational Decision Making* (London: Tavistock Publications, 1973); and John P. Kotter, "Power, dependence, and effective management," *Harvard Business Review,* July–August 1977, p. 125.

7. Thomas J. Peters, "Leadership: Sad facts and silver linings," *Harvard Business Review,* November–December 1979, p. 164.

Trade Routes: The
Manager's Network
of Relationships
Robert E. Kaplan

[B. J. Sparksman] had a good working relationship with his four
bosses and a close mentor-protégé relationship with one of them. He
had cordial-to-good relations with his peers, some of whom were
friends and all of whom were aware of his track record. . . . He also
had a good working relationship with many of the subordinates of his
peers (hundreds of people) based mostly on his reputation. B. J. had a
close and strong working relationship with all but one of his main
direct reports because they respected him, because he was the boss,
and because he had promoted some of them into their current positions. . . . B. J. also knew the vast majority of his subordinates'
subordinates, if only by reputation, the fact that he was the boss, and
the fact that he tried to treat them fairly and with respect. Outside
the firm, B. J. maintained fairly strong relationships with dozens of
top people in firms that were important clients for his organization. . . . He also had relationships with dozens of other important
people in his local community (from *The General Managers* [Free
Press, 1982] by John P. Kotter).

Not all managers have a network that explodes in all directions like this
one. But it is increasingly the fate of modern managers at all levels of today's institutions to work with a large and varied set of people in- and outside their organizations. A network is a reciprocating set of relationships
that stabilizes the manager's world and gives it predictability.

Networks can stretch horizontally as well as vertically, as exhibit 1
shows. The vertical sector of a network often includes not only boss and
immediate subordinates, but also one's boss's superiors as well as one's
subordinates' subordinates. The lateral sector encompasses people at the
same level (peers) and at lower and higher levels (lateral subordinates and

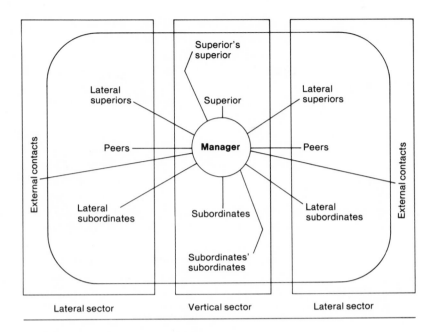

Exhibit 1. The sectors of a manager's network

lateral superiors). The lateral relationship also includes people who are outside the organization (external contacts).

The literature on leadership and management has been preoccupied with superior-subordinate relationships and has paid much less attention to lateral relationships. Because of this and because most managers spend most of their time not with superiors and subordinates but with people outside of the vertical channel, this article will highlight managers' lateral relationships.

Lateral relationships are important to the manager, whatever the manager's line of work and station in organizational life. Take the case of a lower-level manager in an inner-city manpower agency who directed a program that taught job-search skills to unemployed adults. In addition to his superior and his program staff, several peers were also indispensable to him and his program. To send participants to his program along with the appropriate paperwork, he depended on two managers who ran skill-training programs and another who was in charge of the agency's intake function. He also sorely needed the cooperation of the payroll clerks (lateral subordinates) to put the new participants who trickled into the program on the payroll, to pay both participants and staff, and to clear up any payroll snafus promptly. Furthermore, he depended on the purchasing manager to authorize him to buy equipment and supplies—made difficult by the fact that it always took several calls to get through to the purchasing manager. The program manager could not function without recourse to his lateral relationships. (*Note:* This example, and all other examples in the text not attributed to other authors, come from 55 interviews we conducted with managers and from informal observations made during ten management-development programs.)

From an entirely different walk of organizational life, the chief executive officer of Lockheed, Daniel Haughton, relied no less on lateral relationships. According to John Newhouse ("The Sporting Game," *The New Yorker,* July 5, 1982), in the late 1960s Lockheed Corporation began its program to build a wide-bodied plane, the L-1011, and in 1969 contracted with Rolls-Royce for the British aircraft engine company to design and manufacture the huge jet engine, the RB211, for the aircraft. By early 1971 Rolls-Royce, with the job half completed and costs running far ahead of projections, nearly went under. To save the contract, Lockheed, itself in financial crisis, had to help Rolls-Royce secure renewed financial backing from the British government. This quest plunged Haughton into months of negotiations with lateral contacts, all of them external to Lockheed. These included Lord Carrington, the British Secretary of State for Defence; Edward Heath, the British Prime Minister; a syndicate of Lockheed's 24 bankers, who had to decide whether to save the L-1011 or put Lockheed into receivership; and the six U.S. airlines that had ordered L-1011s and were alarmed at the prospect of either not receiving their planes or being asked to agree to a higher price. The U.S. government, interested in supporting the aerospace industry during the 1971 recession, also got involved through President Richard Nixon and Assistant Secretary of Defense David Packard.

After six months of feverish travelling and innumerable meetings, Haughton put together an agreement acceptable to his corporation and all the lateral parties involved. The British government pledged to pay for all further costs of supplying the engine; Lockheed agreed to pay $180,000 more for each engine; the six customer airlines agreed to pay $140,000 more for each airplane; Lockheed's creditor banks agreed to extend the corporation's line of credit, provided the U.S. government guaranteed repayment; and Congress narrowly approved a bill that guaranteed Lockheed's loans. As Newhouse wrote, Haughton is credited with accomplishing this feat "by tireless efforts, diplomatic skill, and the fact that he was trusted by all sides."

Both of these examples point up how important lateral relationships are in a manager's network, and they also show how important reciprocity is to lateral relationships. These relationships are the manager's trade routes.

Why trade?

Managers enter trade relationships with lateral network members for one compelling reason: They depend on these people and literally can't get their jobs done without them. Like nations, managers are not self-sufficient and must engage in "foreign trade" to get what they need. Referring to large corporations, Rosabeth Moss Kanter, in *Men and Women of the Corporation,* observed that "Beyond the people in the most routine functions, no one has within a small domain all of the things he or she needs to carry out his or her job." Managers may be influential, but they cannot escape being dependent. An executive interviewed by John P. Kotter for *Power and Management* described the plight of the manager:

> My son, my wife, and many of my professional friends have very in-accurate conceptions of what I really do for a living. . . . Most of these misperceptions are based on the implicit assumption that I some-how have control over all or most of the resources I need to do my job. . . . In reality, of course, in addition to my direct subordinates, there are hundreds of people whom I have no direct control over but who can affect the performance of my job. At least two dozen of these people are crucial. . . . All of this adds up, and leaves me in a much more vulnerable position than most people realize.

Managers open trade routes with their peers because without these informal arrangements managers are rendered powerless and ineffective. In an anthropological study of informal relationships—which he called cliques—many of which were horizontal, Melville Dalton (*Men Who Manage,* Wiley, 1959) found effective managers were "adroit at moving in and out of clique activities, [but less effective managers] . . . were unable to form cliques or to participate in clique behavior to win the informal strength eventually necessary for larger official action."

That managers have little or no formal authority over their counterparts in other spheres accentuates the need for managers to create some basis for cooperation. Because they are in no position to command cooperation or the resources they need, managers resort, in most cases, to trade: They obtain what they need by providing others with what they, in turn, require.

Reciprocity: The first principle of trade

Unlike nations, managers usually do not trade goods; they trade services. Put another way: Managers trade power, or the ability to get things done. They provide services to others in exchange for the services that they themselves require.

What kinds of services do managers need from their lateral sector? They need people to provide accurate information, make technical expertise available, give advice, provide political backing, authorize changes, and lend moral support. Because managers are often pressed for time, they usually need these things quickly. As one manager told us: "I've worked at building my contacts in other departments so that when I need something done that involves another department, I have someone who will give me a fast, cooperative answer."

Managers obtain these services by setting up reciprocal relationships. They come to the lateral sector with "salable commodities." Dalton found that purchasing agents, for example, go to great lengths to learn about the products so that they can deal with company engineers on equal terms. As one manager in the health care field put it: "You persist and, hell, you make a lot of friends in this business. I do things for them and they do things for me." In her study of one corporation, Kanter found that:

> Peer alliances often worked through direct exchange of favors. On lower levels information was traded; on higher levels bargaining and trade often took place around good performers and job openings. In a senior executive's view, it worked like this: A good job becomes available. A list of candidates is generated. That's refined down to three or four. That is circulated to a select group that has an opportunity to look it over. Then they can make bargains among themselves. A manager commented, "There's lots of 'I owe you one.'" If you can accumulate enough chits, that helps you get what you need; but then, of course, people have to be in a position to cash them in.

Managers get what they want, provided they have what their fellow managers need. Commodities have value only if they are relevant to another person's needs. If manager A, for example, is responsible for succession planning and influences people's careers, but manager B, in his mid-forties, no longer yearns for rapid promotion, then A's power in this respect is lost on B.

Because managers can only get in proportion to what they can give, they work hard to accumulate valued resources. One executive told us how he built a knowledge base when he took over corporate employee relations:

> I wanted a base that was different from what the groups reporting to me had and also from what my superiors had so I established a series of contacts in other American industries until I knew on a first-name basis my counterpart at IBM, TRW, Procter & Gamble, DuPont, and General Electric, and I could get their input—input which the people in my organization didn't have.

By developing exclusive sources of information, this executive operated on the principle that power accrues to the person with resources that are not readily available elsewhere.

When managers trade, they may sometimes give and get at the same time. Dalton described how a horizontal clique of managers coalesces to fend off a common danger—for example, a threatened reorganization or the introduction of an unwanted control system. These managers simultaneously lend each other support for the common cause.

But managers often do not reciprocate a service at the time that it is given. Because it is only over time that a balance has to be struck, managers can take turns being of service to each other. The giver obligates the receiver, who later discharges the obligation. A university administrator, lobbying for a state appropriation to support a construction project on campus, cashed in on a series of favors he had done for a former state official: "When he left state government, I had helped him get a job first as the head of a community agency and then as a staff member for a Congressional committee. During the fight for the appropriation, he became a key guy for me. He was instrumental in getting the Catholic church to apply pressure to the Governor." Managers will allow network members to open charge accounts so long as the debt is later repaid in needed services. They exchange help for the promise of future help.

In addition to promises, managers will also accept another kind of intangible return for services rendered: recognition. One party does another a favor, and the other party completes the exchange by expressing appreciation. Peter M. Blau (*Bureaucracy in Modern Society,* Wiley, 1964) found that law enforcement agents regularly exchanged intangible for tangible commodities by consulting on difficult cases:

> By asking for advice [an agent] implicitly pays his respect to the superior proficiency of his colleague. . . . The consultant gains prestige, in return for which he is willing to devote some time to the consultation and permit it to disrupt his work. . . . The expert whose advice was often sought by colleagues [also] obtained social evidence of his superior abilities.

Similarly, experienced managers who give advice and counsel to a junior manager get confirmation of their status as well as the satisfaction of bringing a promising individual along.

Managers also place a value on another sort of recognition—the kind that affects their reputation, job security, and careers. One manager stated flatly: "My performance rating depends on the feedback my superiors receive from my lateral contacts." It is well known that careers rise and fall with the impressions formed by higher-level managers. So if recognition seems an insubstantial form of payment now, it can translate into quite tangible returns later on.

The principle of reciprocity may seem obvious, but some managers don't have an instinctive appreciation of it. A manager from a Big Eight accounting firm, for example, attended a management training program because he had been told that he was, inexplicably to him, "threatening" to other people. Because of this threatening quality, his relationships within the firm had suffered. He discovered in the training program that, being extremely ambitious, he singlemindedly pursued his own agendas to the exclusion of what anyone else might want or need. He didn't create reciprocal relationships: His relationships were long on take and short on give. He learned that to reduce the threat to others and to build connections, he needed to invest in other people's agendas.

A cautionary note: Giving is always, at some level, self-interested, done to tuck away an expectation of later return or to reap a psychic reward. None of this is objectionable or counterproductive, although it can slip into manipulation. A wry example is the cartoon showing a manager on the phone saying to a colleague (his hand over the mouthpiece): "It's the copier rep asking how my children are—must be contract time." When the psychic or social satisfactions one offers are self-serving and insincere, the attempt at giving backfires.

Trade advantages

When managers go after services from people in the lateral sector of their networks, they may bring power beyond their willingness to respond in kind. Four factors further empower managers vis-à-vis their trading partners: their reputation, their alliances, the importance of their position to the organization, and their favored standing with the network member.

Reputation

Power goes to those managers with a reputation for using power well—that is, for making things happen with the resources available to them. People are quicker to support individuals who consistently get results. The better a person's reputation, the more likely one's investment in that person will pay off.

Managers earn a good reputation to the extent that they have succeeded at extraordinary and visible assignments. Those managers who take on extraordinary projects—pulling an organization out of a tail spin, presiding over the development of a new product, redefining the organization's mission—win recognition that, in turn, makes it easier for them to mobilize support for their next undertaking.

Managers also earn and preserve their reputations by linking themselves, as much as possible, to winning causes. As one executive counselled:

> You have to know enough about your plans in the organization that
> you don't take on the impossible task. Even if the idea is a good one,
> it may be an idea ahead of its time, or it may be beyond your scope in
> the organization.

By taking a realistic view of how much power they have and by gauging accurately a project's prospects for success, managers build a track record that enhances their attractiveness as trading partners, thus increasing their power.

A manager's opportunity for advancement, perceived or real, can also enhance his or her reputation. Other managers, on the lookout for powerful people to ally themselves with, are more than ready to hitch themselves to a rising star. In this case, managers moving up gain power because of the promise of future power accruing to themselves and to those who join forces with them.

Alliances

As managers enter a transaction with any one person, their power to get what they want derives, in part, from their connections to others. A glamorous example was Philip Graham, later the publisher of the *Washington Post,* who worked in a small group that President Franklin Roosevelt put together on the eve of World War II to mobilize American industry for the war effort. As David Halberstam described the activities of Philip Graham in his book, *The Powers That Be* (Dell, 1979):

> He was brilliant at his job, cutting through red tape, getting things done, slipping past the bureaucracy which was in no way as passionate as he was about preparing America for war. He was smart and clever and fearless and dazzlingly well connected. . . . He was also Frankfurter's protégé and Eugene Meyer's son-in-law and important people tended to take his phone calls as they did not take the phone calls of most twenty-five-year-olds. [Felix Frankfurter was at that time Chief Justice of the Supreme Court, and Eugene Meyer was a wealthy industrial magnate who later bought the *Washington Post* and made Graham publisher.]

Managers can operate laterally to the extent that they are well-connected elsewhere. In his study of gangs, William Whyte found that a gang leader's reputation in the community depended on his standing in the gang (the converse was also true). Managers launching innovative projects enjoy more success in recruiting peers as collaborators if they have won the support of top management for the project—and again the converse is also true.

Alliances help managers because they give potential trade partners an added incentive to help. If other powerful people support a project, then it looks like a better bet to someone being approached for help. In general, allies are a reason to go along with a request lest one lose favor with these people and hurt one's trading relationships with them.

Position

Managers are only as important as the positions they occupy. If the position is critical to the organization, then the manager acquires a kind of legitimate power to make demands on others for cooperation. As one manager said to us: "My peers are responsive to me because the functions that I manage are the lifeblood of the organization. I manage the people who provide readings on their vital signs, and consequently my presence in their office implies that there's a vital-sign concern . . . that needs to be dealt with."

Many times a critical position accrues power because the position is located in a function indispensable to the organization. This puts the manager in charge of a "critical contingency," as Gerald R. Salancik and Jeffrey Pfeffer put it (*Organizational Dynamics,* Winter, 1977). Kanter has noted that "For the system, the most power goes to those people in those functions that provide greater control over what the organization currently finds problematic: sales and marketing people when markets are competitive [and so on]." In a computer company like IBM, for example, the engineers who design new products and the production managers who get the products out are one-down to the marketing managers who, in the highly volatile computer industry, find and create the demand for new products. Managers in a function of strategic importance to the organization can make claims on the cooperation of their peers in the name of service to the organization.

Favored standing

With some trading partners, managers achieve a sort of "favored nation status." Managers have an edge if they are on friendly terms with lateral contacts, share a common work history, or share similar demographic characteristics.

Several mayors in the study done by John P. Kotter and Paul Lawrence created cooperative relationships on the basis of friendship. Acquaintances also give the manager leverage, although mayors who cultivated numerous acquaintances spent many an evening at social and political functions. For the satisfaction and utility gained, managers develop personal as well as work connections with colleagues, Kotter has argued. A high-level manager in a hospital commented: "I spend a fair amount of time knowing the personal and professional side of the people I work with. I'll know that they play golf or that they are working on such and such system. It's never all business." In a study of the lateral relations of purchasing agents, George Strauss (*Administrative Science Quarterly,* June 1962) found that most agents prefer to deal with friends, that friendship gets proposals accepted more quickly, but that it is a mistake to rely on friendship alone.

Managers have a leg up if they share a common work history with the people on whom they must depend. A manager's track record is enhanced in the eyes of others when those others worked to achieve the same successes. This is power gained from "past cooperative victories," as Dalton put it. A financial manager explained the good response he gets from accountants in City Hall as follows: "For two years I worked closely with the current deputy controller and we had a good relationship. We still have. That's one reason he stayed here with me till midnight last week working on those audits." There is something almost romantically binding about accomplishing a difficult task together. A history of successfully working together creates a responsiveness that makes life easy for the manager. The program manager mentioned in the beginning of this article explained the good response he got from the payroll department in these terms: "The payroll manager and I have worked closely together for some time and know each other's styles. Usually she'll lean over backwards, and I'll do the same. She'll even respond to my secretary's requests."

A shared history one step removed—holding the same job at different times—can also pay dividends. A manager reported being on the same wave-length with a peer who succeeded him in a planning and development job: "Because I had his job before I got this one, I understand his problems in a way that I don't understand some of the other problems." This peer obviously gained an advantage with the manager, who identified so closely with the peer's situation. Herein lies the logic of job rotation, a common practice in some Japanese firms.

When a manager enters an exchange, it is more likely to go well if, other things being equal, the demographic characteristics of the other party match up with those of the manager. Similarities in skin color, gender, age, country of origin, and socio-economic status smooth the way for each party to identify with and reach the other.

This is not to say that demographic differences inevitably raise barriers. In one case, a black manager formed a strong relationship with a white manager at his level because they both came of age during the same period. "We both went to college in the '60s and share enthusiasms from that time. We make references that go over most other people's heads." Their generational commonality overrode the racial difference.

Some factors that empower managers lie outside the relationship to the other individual—the manager's reputation, alliances, and position. Other factors lie within the relationship itself—favored standing with the other party stemming from friendship, shared work history, and similar demographic characteristics. Yet another asset, discussed next, is the skill that managers bring to interpersonal transactions.

Diplomatic skill

As in foreign trade, trade among managers depends on the diplomatic ability of those involved. Managers strike deals and deliver services by making contact with one another, and they trade no more successfully than they handle the interpersonal medium. The requisite diplomatic skills all boil down to a talent for give-and-take accompanied by a sense of when to use which skill. One manager, adept at having brief, productive conversations, was described as having an "excellent quick-contact style." But invariably using the same mode of contact, no matter how adeptly, leads to ruin, or at least to impaired effectiveness. One high-level manager advised: "You have to have good communication skills, but you also have to know when to key in on some skills and when not to."

To trade successfully, managers need to call upon several skills, each of which entails versatility.

Varying one's participation in conversations

To achieve give-and-take in conversations, managers must be able to talk and to listen, as the occasion requires. Human beings seem to be divided into two categories—"producers," who in conversations specialize in producing words, ideas, information; and "elicitors" who specialize in bringing out other people. Managers who overspecialize in either of these roles hurt their effectiveness. They must be able both to hold up their end of conversation and to take in the contributions of others.

One manager we know, for example, prided himself in being a good communicator. "KISS" was the way he put it: Keep It Short and Sweet. He had even developed his own ABC's of effective communication—A (for Accurate), B (for Brief), C (for Clear), D (for Direct), and so on. He was a skilled and, in spite of his credo, a long-winded producer but not nearly as good an elicitor and listener. He had a habit of remaining impassive, giving no facial reinforcement, when other people spoke. And when someone disagreed with him, he either ignored the comment or bristled visibly. This deficiency hurt him as a conversational partner; he dealt out a good deal better than he took in.

Another dimension of conversational flexibility is the ability to vary the length of a conversation. Some managers favor a hit-and-run approach: Sit people down, hit them with your issue, and run off before they can respond. Others are notorious for lengthy conversations, no matter the issue. The trick is to be equally at ease in either mode. Frederick Richardson (cited by Leonard Sayles) offers the following words of wisdom: Beware of overly regular contact rhythms.

Apportioning contact time

How do managers distribute the time they can spend with other people? While, as we have seen, managers must invest in relationships, job demands should determine how the manager apportions contact time. Form should follow function. The 15 general managers that Kotter studied did invest most heavily in the relationships they needed most.

But, like conversational handicaps, distortions in contact patterns can hamper managers. Responding to their emotional needs instead of to job demands, managers may avoid relationships that make them uncomfortable. Managers who are phobic about people with greater power may neglect upward relationships. Managers of staff functions have jobs that dictate heavy contact with people at the same level, but they may choose instead to associate with their subordinates out of distaste for the conflict and tension touched off by lateral relationships. The rub is that neglected relationships won't produce any of the things that managers need.

Repertoire of influence tactics

As they go in quest of help, managers encounter a wide range of interpersonal situations that require a wide repertoire of behaviors for reaching people. In lateral relationships managers are not in a position to give orders, so they resort to persuasion, camaraderie, negotiation, bargaining. Lateral relationships put a premium on knowing when to act tough (for example, when conflict is built into the situation) and when to use softer methods (for example, when there is basic agreement). The program manager mentioned previously varied his approach according to how much resistance he ran into: "Depending on how other people respond, I can go from being pleasant to very dominating."

In Kotter's study of general managers, the better performers used a larger set of influence tactics and did so with greater skill. "The 'excellent' performers asked, encouraged, cajoled, praised, rewarded, demanded, manipulated, and generally motivated others with great skill in face-to-face situations." The managers' arsenal also typically included references to sports and family as well as liberal doses of joking and humor.

Mixing the mode of contact

In doing business, managers have a number of options available to them— the telephone, written communication (including, in some companies, electronic mail), and face-to-face contact, which can take the form of scheduled or unscheduled meetings held in groups or on a one-to-one basis.

Face-to-face contact is an immediate and powerful medium. Of the various forms of such contact, group meetings serve some important purposes, but there is evidence to suggest that one-to-one contact is the *sine qua non* of managerial life: Richardson found that the more effective research and development managers in his sample spent 45-to-65 percent of their time in one-to-one contact. On the other side of the coin, Peter Drucker has cautioned managers against spending more than 40 percent of their time in group meetings.

The smart money is on using the different mediums not singly but in happy combinations. Group meetings should be accompanied by premeeting huddles with key individuals to line up support and by post-meeting check-ins to clarify action taken and to smooth any ruffled feathers. Memos, when necessary, are more likely to get results when accompanied by a conversation to warn, clarify, explain, prod, sell, or soothe.

Fluency in a number of languages

On the international scene, it pays to know the languages of other countries. In organizational life, it helps to speak the specialized languages of the organization, however haltingly. A highly placed manager in a medical setting said: "With a systems person I talk a little differently than when I talk with a professor in obstetrics and gynecology or to a dean, or a clerk, or what have you. This is particularly important in this organization where we have an array of services all the way from housekeeping to neurosurgery." Among the 20 mayors whom Kotter and Lawrence studied, for example, the capacity to speak the different interpersonal languages of the community varied greatly. At one extreme was a mayor who always acted like a corporate executive, no matter what the setting. At the other was Richard C. Lee of New Haven, Connecticut, whose repertoire was extensive. Lee was described by Kotter and Lawrence as follows:

> When he is with the Irish, his ethnic background comes out and he looks like he grew up in Dublin. When he is at the university, he is a wise old man. Over at the Chamber he is a shrewd capitalist. With the unions he is a cigar-chomping tough guy. He's not just "acting" either. He really knows how to talk the language of each of those groups.

Lee didn't acquire this fluency out of thin air: It was born of a broad range of developmental experiences, including jobs in several different major institutions in the city and intensive contact with the city's major ethnic and racial groups.

Managers are only as interpersonally skilled as their organizations allow them to be. One organization we know of cramped the style of its managers by dealing heavily in one medium—the memo. Because of too much written contact and too little face-to-face contact, the pace of managerial work slowed to a crawl. Whatever the predispositions of the individual managers, they became captive to the overall pattern. In the next section, we look at other restraints of trade.

Trade barriers

In trying to establish lateral trade relationships, managers sometimes come up against formidable barriers. People don't get along; they are rivals; they work for different organizations; they are separated by potent demographic differences. Of the many possible barriers, we look at just three: functional differences, functional and level differences combined, and disparities in degrees of dependence.

Functional differences

It is no mean task to transact business in "the no man's land of interdepartmental relations," in Sayles's phrase. The parties to a cross-functional relationship belong to units with different goals, different interests, different cultures, and different languages. They often report to different people, further widening the gap. Finally, they may have little occasion to interact and therefore little opportunity to accommodate to each other's styles of working and relating. In an interview with the author, one executive described how key players at high levels assumed different organizational postures in the following way:

> Here you have a vice-president of manufacturing whose performance is measured by the "numbers"—how many good pieces the factory gets into the tote box, rework and scrap figures, whether the production schedules are met at the end of the month. And then you have a human resources executive who is responding to a different set of measurements and whose accomplishments may or may not support the manufacturing executive. And then there is the sales executive pushing, as he should, for finished, high-quality units he can sell to the customers. So executives are people coming from different places, responding to different pressures. Whoever you are—the chief executive officer, the president, or a vice-president—you have to build networks with all those people.

As we have already seen, the key to building networks across jurisdictions is to swap services—that is, to find a basis for reciprocal action.

Functional plus level differences

Trade barriers climb higher when the functional difference inherent in lateral relationships is augmented by a hierarchical difference. The added difference is sure to make life difficult for the manager when it is charged with organizational significance. In a chemical plant, for example, second- and third-level supervisors were separated by an unwritten corporate rule that kept people from ascending beyond second-level management without an engineering degree, symbolized by a ring made of iron and worn on the right pinkie finger—thus the "iron ring syndrome." As a result, most second-level managers had worked their way up from the ranks of the workers and were going no further, and all third-level managers had college educations and varying degrees of opportunities to advance further. Thus lateral relationships between second- and third-level managers posed a particular challenge, and diagonal pairs of managers on the two levels had widely varying degrees of success in meeting this challenge.

Relationships with lateral superiors often give managers fits. The upward diagonal relationships can be troublesome for a number of reasons, itemized by Rosemary Stewart:

> [Lateral superiors] can be important to one's career, so making an unfavorable impression can matter more than with peers: They may be in a position to trim down a project that one is putting forward; they may

be more demanding than peers in their service requirements; and they will probably be less familiar than one's own boss so that it will be harder to judge how they will react.

Lacking the immediate superior's responsibility to the individual, the lateral superior may be inaccessible and unresponsive. A woman manager in charge of her organization's affirmative action program desperately needed support and information from a lateral superior and his subordinate managers. She attributed his resistance to the notion that "He is one of the worst for resenting somebody who's not on his level communicating with him or feeling like they have a right to." Powerless because of a combination of gender, function, and level, she had no recourse with him. "I get practically nothing from his subordinates, either; any information I get from them has to be okayed by him."

In their attempts to build lateral upward relationships, managers are often hampered by scanty opportunities to interact. A manager in a food-service firm worried that his underdeveloped relationships with lateral superiors would hurt his chances for promotion: "I don't promote myself well. I don't mention casually that I've done something great. I don't joke or tell stories or give presentations to get visibility because those things are much less natural to me than personal relationships. But around what can I develop a personal relationship with them?"

The key to building relationships with lateral superiors is finding legitimate reasons for contact. If managers appear to be currying favor, they may only set the relationship back. It is best to cultivate such a relationship in the normal course of one's work by, for example, serving on the same task force or executing an assignment in the other manager's area. Special projects put the manager in touch with lateral superiors and give the manager a chance to shine. Kanter gives an example of how a relationship with a lateral superior might unfold:

> One salesman with a problem he wanted to solve for a customer described Indsco as "like the Army, Air Force, and Navy—we have a formal chain of command." The person who could make the decision on his problem was four steps removed from him, not in hierarchical rank but according to operating procedure. Ordinarily, he would not be able to go directly to him, but they had developed a relationship over a series of sales meetings, during which the more powerful person had said, "Please drop by anytime you're at headquarters." So the salesman found an occasion to "drop by," and in the course of the casual conversation mentioned his situation. It was solved immediately.

Unequal dependence

Relationships with lateral superiors are a special case of relating to people who depend on the manager less than the manager depends on them. Managers can't readily set up a reciprocal relationship unless they are in a position to reciprocate. The manager's influence with someone is tied to how much the other person depends on the manager. Managers of staff functions that line managers regard as inessential run into this roadblock. As a result, they have to work harder at being acceptable personally. They also must find a way to sell their service to their unreceptive peers and thereby offset their own heavy dependence.

Consider the plight of a manager who, as a result of a reorganization, was assigned a new position designed to give the U.S. domestic organization greater control over operations in other countries. His job was to bridge a gap between headquarters and operations in South America. Because of the matrix arrangement, he had no direct control over the South American managers he had to work with. He recounted: "I made some friends, but basically I was as welcome as a skunk in church. They couldn't tell me not to come to Peru or Chile—but once I got there, they said: 'So what?' I fought the battle for two years, flying everywhere. But overall it was a very unhappy experience." In fact, he tried to overcome his peers' resistance by finding a way to be useful to them. "I had to get inside people's knickers by understanding their problems and bringing help. I was more welcome if I could bring something to the party." Unfortunately, this manager's sound strategy of trying to induce a need met with only limited success.

Building networks is tantamount to bridging gaps. The more differences that coincide in a relationship, the greater the gap and the harder a manager must work to form a relationship. Managers cross divides by doing the things described in the last three sections—setting up reciprocity, putting themselves in advantageous positions, and making good contact. No matter what the gap, the only alternative is to set about creating a successful history by getting down to work so that the bits of productive exchanges eventually add up to something worthwhile for the manager.

Growing networks

Organizations cannot grant networks to managers. Managers must cultivate networks. This is something that managers do deliberately and also something that happens naturally. Asked how he goes about cultivating relationships, one manager said:

> It depends on what you consider cultivating. I could argue that every time I answer the phone or every time someone drops in my office, I'm cultivating a contact.

As managers field requests, relationships develop almost on their own.

How long does it take to develop a network? If there are no big obstacles, relationships for getting routine things done can sprout almost like weeds. But relationships strong enough to stand up under heavy pressure are another story. Sturdy relationships take time to develop. Executives with many years in the same organization especially value their long-time contacts. An executive who has so far spent his entire 25-year career in one textile firm asserted: "I can't overestimate the importance of good interpersonal relationships. Growing up in the company, I have worked with all these guys. I know them; they know me. These relationships help tremendously in a crisis situation or when you need something quickly." History matters. Relationships gain strength as both parties show that they can and will come through for each other.

Managers have no choice but to keep growing their networks. They never have the luxury of sitting back and saying: "Now I can relax: I've got all the connections I need." Networks are dynamic, like the mobile society we live in.

Every time managers change jobs, as the upwardly mobile ones do every two years or so, they must rebuild their networks. Kotter found that general managers spend the first six months in a new job investing heavily in forming new bonds. The more different the new job is from the manager's previous experience, the more overhauling the network will need. When managers parachute into a different organization in a totally different field, they may need to rebuild their networks from scratch. On the other hand, when a manager moves to the next level or a neighboring function, he or she can get away with less network-building because large portions of the existing network then become portable.

If managers stay put, the world nevertheless changes around them. Faces change, with the rate of change linked to rates of turnover and mobility in that organization. The job of growing networks is never done.

Harvesting networks

Networks aren't built to serve some vague global purpose, but to get help on the manager's specific tasks. To reap the full benefit of their networks, managers must excel not only at growing but also at harvesting. Managers get work done by activating their relationships selectively. Leaders call upon what Warren Bennis calls their "executive constellations," by forming task forces for a particular assignment and reassembling others for a different assignment. John Friend, John Power, and C. J. L. Yewlett (*Public Planning: The Intercorporate Dimension,* Tavistock, 1964) stated that to make effective use of a network, managers mobilize their networks "in an intelligently selective way," which depends on knowing both the structure of the problem and the structure of the human relationships around the problem. A hospital administrator displayed this sense in talking about how he conceptualized the startup of a new project.

> I knew everybody that this project was going to impact in one way or another—systems, fiscal, the medical school, medical records, on

down the line. I had to use my technical knowledge and the personal rapport that I had or didn't have with the individuals. I was kind of making a web of people and trying to bring them together to get something done.

To launch the project, he involved the people affected, calling upon relationships he already had and developing the ones he didn't have. Innovative projects in particular put a premium on the manager's ability to activate relationships—to define the project and to build a coalition of sponsors and collaborators to implement the project.

The notion of a network is simply another lens through which to view the work of a manager. Although fast becoming a cliché, the concept is nevertheless useful because it portrays the manager's relationships in context. It affords us a view that is faithful to the complex and richly textured setting in which most managers work.

Conclusion

A manager's connections often reach, like tentacles, throughout the organization (and outside it). The *number* of people is striking, but no less so than the diversity. Network members differ on organizational factors such as job, level, history, and future in the organization; on sociological factors such as age, sex, race, religion, ethnic background, education, and socio-economic status; and on personal factors such as openness to influence, ability to communicate, and commitment to work. It is no small task to establish reliable relationships with so many different people. As a manager of packaging engineering put it, "The manager's role is to keep a friendly relationship with strange bedfellows."

Networks, with their emphasis on peer relationships, seem to have special relevance for middle managers, embedded as they are in a vertical channel and lateral work flow. Walter Tornow and Patrick Pinto (*Journal of Applied Psychology*, 1976), in a job analysis of 433 low-, middle-, and high-level managers, found that middle managers scored higher than the other two groups on "coordinating the efforts of those over whom one has no direct control" and "working across existing organizational boundaries." Middle managers develop a classic Hub-type network, in Stewart's terms; general managers exemplify this type (see the quotation at the beginning of this paper).

But networks are by no means the exclusive preserve of middle managers. According to Stewart, upper-level managers typically use Apex-type networks, which extend primarily downward in the organization and laterally into the outside world. The example of the Lockheed CEO given earlier played up his external relationships, leaving, however, his indispensable downward internal relationships in the background. Kotter found that over the course of their careers, high-level managers may accumulate hundreds, if not thousands, of contacts of varying degrees of importance. One management expert cited by Packard commented that the managers "who have really arrived will be spider-webbed off in several directions by a mysterious cross-hatching."

Lower-level managers may operate in a smaller sphere, both vertically and horizontally, but networks still figure prominently in their work lives. The program manager described in the introduction needed equally his staff to run the program and his peers to support the program, not to mention his boss to run interference. ("If my Mastercharge card doesn't work, I borrow his American Express card.")

Few managers function autonomously, having what Stewart called a solo network, and even these managers spend a sizeable chunk of their time interacting. Nowhere does John Donne's poetic dictum, "No man is an island," apply with greater force than to the world of managers.

Selected bibliography

The work of four students of managerial relationships provided information for this article. Rosabeth Moss Kanter wrote about power and relationships in *Men and Women of the Corporation* (Basic Books, 1977) and about peer relationships in a *Harvard Business Review* article called "The Middle Manager as Innovator" (July–August 1982). John P. Kotter examined power and dependency in *Power in Management* (AMACOM, 1979), and he treated networks explicitly in the research reported in *Managers in Action* (Wiley, 1976) written with Paul Lawrence, and in *The General Managers* (Free Press, 1982). Leonard Sayles shed light on work-flow relationships and social contact in the manager's job in *Managerial Behavior* (McGraw-Hill, 1966). Finally, Rosemary Stewart in *Contrasts in Management* (McGraw-Hill, 1976) investigated types of networks as they vary with types of managers' jobs.

Acknowledgments

I would like to thank Mignon Mazique for help as a collaborator at an early stage of the research, David DeVries and Michael Lombardo for their comments on an earlier draft, Bill Drath for his help in imposing conceptual order on a recalcitrant subject, and Alice Warren for indefatigably typing and retyping this paper.

Managerial Work: Analysis from Observation

Henry Mintzberg

What do managers do? Ask this question and you will likely be told that managers plan, organize, coordinate, and control. Since Henri Fayol (1) first proposed these words in 1916, they have dominated the vocabulary of management. (See, for example, Drucker [2], Gulick [3] and Kelly [4]). How valuable are they in describing managerial work? Consider one morning's work of the president of a large organization:

As he enters his office at 8:23, the manager's secretary motions for him to pick up the telephone. "Jerry, there was a bad fire in the plant last night, about $30,000 damage. We should be back in operation by Wednesday. Thought you should know."

At 8:45, a Mr. Jamison is ushered into the manager's office. They discuss Mr. Jamison's retirement plans and his cottage in New Hampshire. Then the manager presents a plaque to him commemorating his thirty-two years with the organization.

Mail processing follows: An innocent-looking letter, signed by a Detroit lawyer, reads: "A group of us in Detroit has decided not to buy any of your products because you used that antiflag, antiAmerican pinko, Bill Lindell, on your Thursday night TV show." The manager dictates a restrained reply.

The 10:00 meeting is scheduled by a professional staffer. He claims that his superior, a high-ranking vice-president of the organization, mistreats his staff, and that if the man is not fired, they will all walk out. As soon as the meeting ends, the manager rearranges his schedule to investigate the claim and to react to this crisis.

Which of these activities may be called planning, and which may be called organizing, coordinating, and controlling? Indeed, what do words such as "coordinating" and "planning" mean in the context of real activity? In fact, these four words do not describe the actual work of managers at all;

Reprinted by permission from Henry Mintzberg, "Managerial Work: Analysis from Observation," *Management Science*, October 1971, B97–B110.

they describe certain vague objectives of managerial work. "They are just ways of indicating what we need to explain" (5, p. 537).

Other approaches to the study of managerial work have developed, one dealing with managerial decision-making and policy-making processes, another with the manager's interpersonal activities. (See, for example, Braybrooke and Lindblom [6] and Gibb [7]). And some empirical researchers, using the "diary" method, have studied what might be called managerial "media"—by what means, with whom, how long, and where managers spend their time.[1] But in no part of this literature is the actual content of managerial work systematically and meaningfully described.[2] Thus, the question posed at the start—what do managers do?—remains essentially unanswered in the literature of management.

This is indeed an odd situation. We claim to teach management in schools of both business and public administration; we undertake major research programs in management; we find a growing segment of the management science community concerned with the problems of senior management. Most of these people—the planners, information and control theorists, systems analysts, etc.—are attempting to analyze and change working habits that they themselves do not understand. Thus, at a conference called at M.I.T. to assess the impact of the computer on the manager; and attended by a number of America's foremost management scientists, a participant found it necessary to comment after lengthy discussion (14, p. 198):

> I'd like to return to an earlier point. It seems to me that until we get into the question of what the top manager does or what the functions are that define the top management job, we're not going to get out of the kind of difficulty that keeps cropping up. What I'm really doing is leading up to my earlier question which no one really answered. And that is: Is it possible to arrive at a specification of what constitutes the job of a top manager?

His question was not answered.

Research study on managerial work

In late 1966, I began research on this question, seeking to replace Fayol's words by a set that would more accurately describe what managers do. In essence, I sought to develop by the process of induction a statement of managerial work that would have empirical validity. Using a method called

---

1. Carlson (8) carried out the classic study just after World War II. He asked nine Swedish managing directors to record on diary pads details of each activity in which they engaged. His method was used by a group of other researchers, many of them working in the United Kingdom. (See Burns [9, 10]; Horne and Lupton [11]; and Stewart [12].

2. One major project, involving numerous publications, took place at Ohio State University and spanned three decades. Some of the vocabulary used followed Fayol. The results have generated little interest in this area. (See, for example, Hemphill [13]).

"structured observation," I observed for one-week periods the chief executives of five medium to large organizations (a consulting firm, a school system, a technology firm, a consumer goods manufacturer, and a hospital).

Structured as well as unstructured (i.e., anecdotal) data were collected in three "records." In the *chronology record,* activity patterns throughout the working day were recorded. In the *mail record,* for each of 890 pieces of mail processed during the five weeks, the purpose, format, and sender, the attention it received, and the action it elicited were recorded. And, recorded in the *contact record,* for each of 368 verbal interactions, were the purpose, the medium (telephone call, scheduled or unscheduled meeting, tour), the participants, the form of initiation, and the location. It should be noted that all categorizing was done during and after observation so as to ensure that the categories reflected only the work under observation. Mintzberg's study (15) contains a fuller description of this methodology and a tabulation of the results of the study.

Two sets of conclusions are presented below. The first deals with certain characteristics of managerial work, as they appeared from analysis of the numerical data (e.g., How much time is spent with peers? What is the average duration of meetings? What proportion of contacts are initiated by the manager himself?). The second describes the basic content of managerial work in terms of ten roles. This description derives from an analysis of the data on the recorded *purpose* of each contact and piece of mail.

The liberty is taken of referring to these findings as descriptive of managerial, as opposed to chief executive, work. This is done because many of the findings are supported by studies of other types of managers. Specifically, most of the conclusions on work characteristics are to be found in the combined results of a group of studies of foremen (16, 17), middle managers (9– 12), and chief executives (8). And although there is little useful material on managerial roles, three studies do provide some evidence of the applicability of the role set. Most important, Sayles' empirical study of production managers (18) suggests that at least five of the ten roles are performed at the lower end of the managerial hierarchy. And some further evidence is provided by comments in Whyte's study of leadership in a street gang (19) and Neustadt's study of three U.S. presidents (20). (Reference is made to these findings where appropriate.) Thus, although most of the illustrations are drawn from my study of chief executives, there is some justification in asking the reader to consider when he sees the terms "manager" and his "organization" not only "presidents" and their "companies," but also "foremen" and their "shops," "directors" and their "branches," "vice-presidents" and their "divisions." The term *manager* shall be used with reference to all those people in charge of formal organizations or their subunits.

Some characteristics of managerial work

Six sets of characteristics of managerial work derive from analysis of the data of this study. Each has a significant bearing on the manager's ability to administer a complex organization.

Characteristic 1. The manager performs a great quantity of work at an unrelenting pace

Despite a semblance of normal working hours, in truth managerial work appears to be very taxing. The five men in this study processed an average of thirty-six pieces of mail each day, participated in eight meetings (half of which were scheduled), engaged in five telephone calls, and took one tour. In his study of foremen, Guest (16) found that the number of activities per day averaged 583, with no real break in the pace.

Free time appears to be very rare. If by chance a manager has caught up with the mail, satisfied the callers, dealt with all the disturbances, and avoided scheduled meetings, a subordinate will likely show up to usurp the available time. It seems that the manager cannot expect to have much time for leisurely reflection during office hours. During "off" hours, our chief executives spent much time on work-related reading. High-level managers appear to be able to escape neither from an environment which recognizes the power and status of their positions nor from their own minds which have been trained to search continually for new information.

Characteristic 2. Managerial activity is characterized by variety, fragmentation, and brevity

There seems to be no pattern to managerial activity. Rather, variety and fragmentation appear to be characteristic, as successive activities deal with issues that differ greatly both in type and in content. In effect the manager must be prepared to shift moods quickly and frequently.

A typical chief executive day may begin with a telephone call from a director who asks a favor (a "status request"); then a subordinate calls to tell of a strike at one of the facilities (fast movement of information, termed "instant communication"); this is followed by a relaxed scheduled event at which the manager speaks to a group of visiting dignitaries (ceremony); the manager returns to find a message from a major customer who is demanding the renegotiation of a contract (pressure); and so on. Throughout the day, the managers of our study encountered this great variety of activity. Most surprisingly, the significant activities were interspersed with the trivial in no particular pattern.

Furthermore, these managerial activities were characterized by their brevity. Half of all the activities studied lasted less than nine minutes and only ten percent exceeded one hour. Guest's foremen averaged 48 seconds per activity, and Carlson (8) stressed that his chief executives were unable to work without frequent interruption.

In my own study of chief executives, I felt that the managers demonstrated a preference for tasks of short duration and encouraged interruption. Perhaps the manager becomes accustomed to variety, or perhaps the flow of "instant communication" cannot be delayed. A more plausible explanation might be that the manager becomes conditioned by his workload. He develops a sensitive appreciation for the opportunity cost of his own time. Also, he is aware of the ever-present assortment of obligations associated with his job—accumulations of mail that cannot be delayed, the callers that must be attended to, the meetings that require his participation. In other words, no matter what he is doing, the manager is plagued by what he must do and what he might do. Thus, the manager is forced to treat issues in an abrupt and superficial way.

Characteristic 3. Managers prefer issues that are current, specific and ad hoc

Ad hoc operating reports received more attention than did routine ones; current, uncertain information—gossip, speculation, hearsay—which flows quickly was preferred to historical, certain information; "instant communication" received first consideration; few contacts were held on a routine or "clocked" basis; almost all contacts concerned well-defined issues. The managerial environment is clearly one of stimulus-response. It breeds not reflective planners, but adaptable information manipulators who prefer the live, concrete situation, men who demonstrate a marked action orientation.

Characteristic 4. The manager sits between his organization and a network of contacts

In virtually every empirical study of managerial time allocation, it was reported that managers spent a surprisingly large amount of time in horizontal or lateral (nonline) communication. It is clear from this study and from that of Sayles (18) that the manager is surrounded by a diverse and complex web of contacts which serves as his self-designed external information system. Included in this web can be clients, associates, and suppliers, outside staff experts, peers (managers of related or similar organizations), trade organizations, government officials, independents (those with no relevant organizational affiliation), and directors or superiors. (Among these, directors in this study and superiors in other studies did *not* stand out as particularly active individuals.)

The managers in this study received far more information than they emitted, much of it coming from contacts, and more from subordinates who acted as filters. Figuratively, the manager appears as the neck of an hourglass, sifting information into his own organization from its environment.

Characteristic 5. The manager demonstrates a strong preference
for the verbal media

The manager has five media at his command—mail (documented), telephone (purely verbal), unscheduled meeting (informal face-to-face), scheduled meeting (formal face-to-face), and tour (observational). Along with
all the other empirical studies of work characteristics, I found a strong pre-
dominance of verbal forms of communication.

Mail

By all indications, managers dislike the documented form of communication. In this study, they gave cursory attention to such items as operating
reports and periodicals. It was estimated that only thirteen percent of the
input mail was of specific and immediate use to the managers. Much of
the rest dealt with formalities and provided general reference data. The
managers studied initiated very little mail, only twenty-five pieces in the
five weeks. The rest of the outgoing mail was sent in reaction to mail received—a reply to a request, an acknowledgment, some information forwarded to a part of the organization. The managers appeared to dislike this
form of communication, perhaps because the mail is a relatively slow and
tedious medium to use.

Telephone and unscheduled meetings

The less formal means of verbal communication—the telephone, a purely
verbal form, and the unscheduled meeting, a face-to-face form—were
used frequently (two-thirds of the contacts in the study) but for brief encounters (average duration of six and twelve minutes, respectively). They
were used primarily to deliver requests and to transmit pressing information to those outsiders and subordinates who had informal relationships
with the manager.

Scheduled meetings

These tended to be of long duration, averaging sixty-eight minutes in this
study, and absorbing over half the managers' time. Such meetings provided
the managers with their main opportunities to interact with large groups
and to leave the confines of their own offices. Scheduled meetings were
used when the participants were unfamiliar to the manager (e.g., students
who request that he speak at a university), when a large quantity of information had to be transmitted (e.g., presentation of a report), when ceremony had to take place, and when complex strategy-making or negotiation
had to be undertaken. An important feature of the scheduled meeting was
the incidental, but by no means irrelevant, information that flowed at the
start and end of such meetings.

Tours

Although the walking tour would appear to be a powerful tool for gaining information in an informal way, in this study tours accounted for only three percent of the manager's time.

In general, it can be concluded that the manager uses each medium for particular purposes. Nevertheless, where possible, he appears to gravitate to verbal media since these provide greater flexibility, require less effort, and bring faster response. It should be noted here that the manager does not leave the telephone or the meeting to get back to work. Rather, communication is his work, and these media are his tools. The operating work of the organization—producing a product, doing research, purchasing a part—appears to be undertaken infrequently by the senior manager. The manager's productive output must be measured in terms of information, a great part of which is transmitted verbally.

Characteristic 6. Despite the preponderance of obligations, the manager appears to be able to control his own affairs

Carlson suggested in his study of Swedish chief executives that these men were puppets, with little control over their own affairs. A cursory examination of our data indicates that this is true. Our managers were responsible for the initiation of only thirty-two percent of their verbal contacts and a smaller proportion of their mail. Activities were also classified as to the nature of the managers' participation, and the active ones were outnumbered by the passive ones (e.g., making requests vs. receiving requests). On the surface, the manager is indeed a puppet, answering requests in the mail, returning telephone calls, attending meetings initiated by others, yielding to subordinates' requests for time, reacting to crises.

However, such a view is misleading. There is evidence that the senior manager can exert control over his own affairs in two significant ways: (1) It is he who defines many of his own long-term commitments, by developing appropriate information channels which later feed him information, by initiating projects which later demand his time, by joining committees or outside boards which provide contacts in return for his services, and so on. (2) The manager can exploit situations that appear as obligations. He can lobby at ceremonial speeches; he can impose his values on his organization when his authorization is requested; he can motivate his subordinates whenever he interacts with them; he can use the crisis situation as an opportunity to innovate.

Perhaps these are two points that help distinguish successful and unsuccessful managers. All managers appear to be puppets. Some decide who will pull the strings and how, and they then take advantage of each move that they are forced to make. Others, unable to exploit this high-tension environment, are swallowed up by this most demanding of jobs.

The manager's work roles

In describing the essential content of managerial work, one should aim to model managerial activity, that is, to describe it as a set of programs. But an undertaking as complex as this must be preceded by the development of a useful typological description of managerial work. In other words, we must first understand the distinct components of managerial work. At the present time we do not.

In this study, 890 pieces of mail and 368 verbal contacts were categorized as to purpose. The incoming mail was found to carry acknowledgments, requests and solicitations of various kinds, reference data, news, analytical reports, reports on events and on operations, advice on various situations, and statements of problems, pressures, and ideas. In reacting to mail, the managers acknowledged some, replied to the requests (e.g., by sending information), and forwarded much to subordinates (usually for their information). Verbal contacts involved a variety of purposes. In 15% of them activities were scheduled, in 6% ceremonial events took place, and a few involved external board work. About 34% involved requests of various kinds, some insignificant, some for information, some for authorization of proposed actions. Another 36% essentially involved the flow of information to and from the manager, while the remainder dealt specifically with issues of strategy and with negotiations. (For details, see Mintzberg [15]).

In this study, each piece of mail and verbal contact categorized in this way was subjected to one question: Why did the manager do this? The answers were collected and grouped and regrouped in various ways (over the course of three years) until a typology emerged that was felt to be satisfactory. While an example, presented below, will partially explain this process to the reader, it must be remembered that (in the words of Bronowski [21, p. 62]): "Every induction is a speculation and it guesses at a unity which the facts present but do not strictly imply."

Consider the following sequence of two episodes: A chief executive attends a meeting of an external board on which he sits. Upon his return to his organization, he immediately goes to the office of a subordinate, tells of a conversation he had with a fellow board member, and concludes with the statement: "It looks like we shall get the contract."

The purposes of these two contacts are clear—to attend an external board meeting, and to give current information (instant communication) to a subordinate. But why did the manager attend the meeting? Indeed, why does he belong to the board? And why did he give this particular information to his subordinate?

Basing analysis on this incident, one can argue as follows: The manager belongs to the board in part so that he can be exposed to special information which is of use to his organization. The subordinate needs the information but has not the status which would give him access to it. The chief executive does. Board memberships bring chief executives in contact with one another for the purpose of trading information.

Two aspects of managerial work emerge from this brief analysis. The manager serves in a "liaison" capacity because of the status of his office, and what he learns here enables him to act as "disseminator" of information into his organization. We refer to these as *roles*—organized sets of behaviors belonging to identifiable offices or positions (22). Ten roles were chosen to capture all the activities observed during this study.

All activities were found to involve one or more of three basic behaviors—interpersonal contact, the processing of information, and the making of decisions. As a result, our ten roles are divided into three corresponding groups. Three roles—labelled *figurehead, liaison,* and *leader*—deal with behavior that is essentially interpersonal in nature. Three others—*nerve center, disseminator,* and *spokesman*—deal with information-processing activities performed by the manager. And the remaining four—*entrepreneur, disturbance handler, resource allocator,* and *negotiator*—cover the decision-making activities of the manager. We describe each of these roles in turn, asking the reader to note that they form a *gestalt,* a unified whole whose parts cannot be considered in isolation.

The interpersonal roles

Three roles relate to the manager's behavior that focuses on interpersonal contact. These roles derive directly from the authority and status associated with holding managerial office.

Figurehead

As legal authority in his organization, the manager is a symbol, obliged to perform a number of duties. He must preside at ceremonial events, sign legal documents, receive visitors, make himself available to many of those who feel, in the words of one of the men studied, "that the only way to get something done is to get to the top." There is evidence that this role applies at other levels as well. Davis cites the case of the field sales manager who must deal with those customers who believe that their accounts deserve his attention.

Leader

Leadership is the most widely recognized of managerial roles. It describes the manager's relationship with his subordinates—his attempts to motivate them and his development of the milieu in which they work. Leadership actions pervade all activity—in contrast to most roles, it is possible to designate only a few activities as dealing exclusively with leadership (these mostly related to staffing duties). Each time a manager encourages a subordinate, or meddles in his affairs, or replies to one of his requests, he is playing the *leader* role. Subordinates seek out and react to these leadership clues, and, as a result, they impart significant power to the manager.

Liaison

As noted earlier, the empirical studies have emphasized the importance of lateral or horizontal communication in the work of managers at all levels. It is clear from our study that this is explained largely in terms of the *liaison* role. The manager establishes his network of contacts essentially to bring information and favors to his organization. As Sayles notes in his study of production supervisors (18, p. 258), "The one enduring objective [of the manager] is the effort to build and maintain a predictable, reciprocating system of relationships. . . ."

Making use of his status, the manager interacts with a variety of peers and other people outside his organization. He provides time, information, and favors in return for the same from others. Foremen deal with staff groups and other foremen; chief executives join boards of directors, and maintain extensive networks of individual relationships. Neustadt notes this behavior in analyzing the work of President Roosevelt (20, p. 150):

> His personal sources were the product of a sociability and curiosity that reached back to the other Roosevelt's time. He had an enormous acquaintance in various phases of national life and at various levels of government; he also had his wife and her variety of contacts. He extended his acquaintanceships abroad; in the war years Winston Churchill, among others, became a "personal source." Roosevelt quite deliberately exploited these relationships and mixed them up to widen his own range of information. He changed his sources as his interests changed, but no one who had ever interested him was quite forgotten or immune to sudden use.

The informational roles

A second set of managerial activities relates primarily to the processing of information. Together they suggest three significant managerial roles, one describing the manager as a focal point for a certain kind of organizational information, the other two describing relatively simple transmission of this information.

Nerve Center

There is indication, both from this study and from those by Neustadt and Whyte, that the manager serves as the focal point in his organization for the movement of nonroutine information. Homans, who analyzed Whyte's study, draws the following conclusions (19, p. 187):

> Since interaction flowed toward [the leaders], they were better in-
> formed about the problems and desires of group members than were

any of the followers and therefore better able to decide on an appropriate course of action. Since they were in close touch with other gang leaders, they were also better informed than their followers about conditions in Cornerville at large. Moreover, in their positions at the focus of the chains of interaction, they were better able than any follower to pass on to the group decisions that had been reached.

The term *nerve center* is chosen to encompass those many activities in which the manager receives information.

Within his own organization, the manager has legal authority that formally connects him—and only him—to *every* member. Hence, the manager emerges as *nerve center* of internal information. He may not know as much about any one function as the subordinate who specializes in it, but he comes to know more about his total organization than any other member. He is the information generalist. Furthermore, because of the manager's status and its manifestation in the *liaison* role, the manager gains unique access to a variety of knowledgeable outsiders including peers who are themselves *nerve centers* of their own organizations. Hence, the manager emerges as his organization's *nerve center* of external information as well.

As noted earlier, the manager's nerve center information is of a special kind. He appears to find it most important to get his information quickly and informally. As a result, he will not hesitate to bypass formal information channels to get it, and he is prepared to deal with a large amount of gossip, hearsay, and opinion which has not yet become substantiated fact.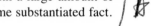

Disseminator

Much of the manager's information must be transmitted to subordinates. Some of this is of a *factual* nature, received from outside the organization or from other subordinates. And some is of a *value* nature. Here, the manager acts as the mechanism by which organizational influencers (owners, governments, employee groups, the general public, etc., or simply the "boss") make their preferences known to the organization. It is the manager's duty to integrate these value positions, and to express general organizational preferences as a guide to decision made by subordinates. One of the men studied commented: "One of the principal functions of this position is to integrate the hospital interests with the public interests." Papandreou describes his duty in a paper published in 1952, referring to management as the "peak coordinator" (24).

Spokesman

In his *spokesman* role, the manager is obliged to transmit his information to outsiders. He informs influencers and other interested parties about his organization's performance, its policies, and its plans. Furthermore, he is expected to serve outside his organization as an expert in its industry. Hospital administrators are expected to spend some time serving outside as public experts on health, and corporation presidents, perhaps as chamber of commerce executives.

The decisional roles

The manager's legal authority requires that he assume responsibility for all of his organization's important actions. The *nerve center* role suggests that only he can fully understand complex decisions, particularly those involving difficult value trade-offs. As a result, the manager emerges as the key figure in the making and interrelating of all significant decisions in his organization, a process that can be referred to as *strategy-making*. Four roles describe the manager's control over the strategy-making system in his organization.

Entrepreneur

The *entrepreneur* role describes the manager as initiator and designer of much of the controlled change in his organization. The manager looks for opportunities and potential problems which may cause him to initiate action. Action takes the form of *improvement projects*—the marketing of a new product, the strengthening of a weak department, the purchasing of new equipment, the reorganization of formal structure, and so on.

The manager can involve himself in each improvement project in one of three ways: (1) He may *delegate* all responsibility for its design and approval, implicitly retaining the right to replace that subordinate who takes charge of it. (2) He may delegate the design work to a subordinate, but retain the right to *approve* it before implementation. (3) He may actively *supervise* the design work himself.

Improvement projects exhibit a number of interesting characteristics. They appear to involve a number of subdecisions, consciously sequenced over long periods of time and separated by delays of various kinds. Furthermore, the manager appears to supervise a great many of these at any one time—perhaps fifty to one hundred in the case of chief executives. In fact, in his handling of improvement projects, the manager may be likened to a juggler. At any one point, he maintains a number of balls in the air. Periodically, one comes down, receives a short burst of energy, and goes up again. Meanwhile, an inventory of new balls waits on the sidelines and, at random intervals, old balls are discarded and new ones added. Braybrooke and Lindblom (6) and Marples (25) touch on these aspects of strategy-making, the former stressing the disjointed and incremental nature of the decisions, and the latter depicting the sequential episodes in terms of a stranded rope made up of fibers of different lengths, each of which surfaces periodically.

Disturbance Handler

While the *entrepreneur* role focuses on voluntary change, the *disturbance handler* role deals with corrections which the manager is forced to make. We may describe this role as follows: The organization consists basically of specialist operating programs. From time to time, it experiences a stimulus that cannot be handled routinely, either because an operating program has broken down or because the stimulus is new and it is not clear which operating program should handle it. These situations constitute disturbances. As generalist, the manager is obliged to assume responsibility for dealing with the stimulus. Thus, the handling of disturbances is an essential duty of the manager.

There is clear evidence for this role both in our study of chief executives and in Sayles' study of production supervisors (18, p. 162):

> The achievement of this stability, which is the manager's objective, is a never-to-be-attained ideal. He is like a symphony orchestra conductor, endeavoring to maintain a melodious performance in which contributions of the various instruments are coordinated and sequenced, patterned and paced, while the orchestra members are having various personal difficulties, stagehands are moving music stands, alternating excessive heat and cold are creating audience and instrument problems, and the sponsor of the concert is insisting on irrational changes in the program.

Sayles goes further to point out the very important balance that the manager must maintain between change and stability. To Sayles, the manager seeks "a dynamic type of stability" (p. 162). Most disturbances elicit short-term adjustments which bring back equilibrium; persistent ones require the introduction of long-term structural change.

Resource Allocator

The manager maintains ultimate authority over his organization's strategy-making system by controlling the allocation of its resources. By deciding who will get what (and who will do what), the manager directs the course of his organization. He does this in three ways:

(1) *In scheduling his own time,* the manager allocates his most precious resource and thereby determines organizational priorities. Issues that receive low priority do not reach the *nerve center* of the organization and are blocked for want of resources.

(2) In designing the organizational structure and in carrying out many improvement projects, the manager *programs the work of his subordinates*. In other words, he allocates their time by deciding what will be done and who will do it.

(3) Most significantly, the manager maintains control over resource allocation by the requirement that he *authorize all significant decisions* before they are implemented. By retaining this power, the manager ensures that different decisions are interrelated—that conflicts are avoided, that resource constraints are respected, and that decisions complement one another.

Decisions appear to be authorized in one of two ways. Where the costs and benefits of a proposal can be quantified, where it is competing for specified resources with other known proposals, and where it can wait for a certain time of year, approval for a proposal is sought in the context of a formal *budgeting* procedure. But these conditions are most often not met—timing may be crucial, nonmonetary costs may predominate, and so on. In these cases, approval is sought in terms of an *ad hoc request for authorization*. Subordinate and manager meet (perhaps informally) to discuss one proposal alone.

Authorization choices are enormously complex ones for the manager. A myriad of factors must be considered (resource constraints, influencer preferences, consistency with other decisions, feasibility, payoff, timing, subordinate feeling, etc.). But the fact that the manager is authorizing the decision rather than supervising its design suggests that he has little time to give to it. To alleviate this difficulty, it appears that managers use special kinds of *models* and *plans* in their decision-making. These exist only in their minds and are loose, but they serve to guide behaviors. Models may answer questions such as, "Does this proposal make sense in terms of the trends that I see in tariff legislation?" or "Will the EDP department be able to get along with marketing on this?" Plans exist in the sense that, on questioning, managers reveal images (in terms of proposed improvement projects) of where they would like their organizations to go: "Well, once I get these foreign operations fully developed, I would like to begin to look into a reorganization," said one subject of this study.

Negotiator

The final role describes the manager as participant in negotiation activity. To some students of the management process (2, p. 343), this is not truly part of the job of managing. But such distinctions are arbitrary. Negotiation is an integral part of managerial work, as this study notes for chief executives and, as that of Sayles made very clear for production supervisors (18, p. 131): "Sophisticated managers place great stress on negotiations as a way of life. They negotiate with groups who are setting standards for their work, who are performing support activity for them, and to whom they wish to 'sell' their services."

The manager must participate in important negotiation sessions because he is his organization's legal authority, its *spokesman,* and its *resource al-*

locator. Negotiation is resource trading in real time. If the resource commitments are to be large, the legal authority must be present.

These ten roles suggest that the manager of an organization bears a great burden of responsibility. He must oversee his organization's status system; he must serve as a crucial informational link between it and its environment; he must interpret and reflect its basic values; he must maintain the stability of its operations, and he must adapt it in a controlled and balanced way to a changing environment.

Management as a profession and as a science

Is management a profession? To the extent that different managers perform one set of basic roles, management satisfies one criterion for becoming a profession. But a profession must require, in the words of the *Random House Dictionary,* "knowledge of some department of learning or science." Which of the ten roles now requires specialized learning? Indeed, what school of business or public administration teaches its students how to disseminate information, allocate resources, perform as figurehead, make contacts, or handle disturbances? We simply know very little about teaching these things. The reason is that we have never tried to document and describe in a meaningful way the procedures (or programs) that managers use.

The evidence of this research suggests that there is as yet no science in managerial work—that managers do not work according to procedures that have been prescribed by scientific analysis. Indeed, except for his use of the telephone, the airplane, and the dictating machine, it would appear that the manager of today is indistinguishable from his predecessors. He may seek different information, but he gets much of it in the same way—from word-of-mouth. He may make decisions dealing with modern technology but he uses the same intuitive (that is, nonexplicit) procedures in making them. Even the computer, which has had such a great impact on other kinds of organizational work, has apparently done little to alter the working methods of the general manager.

How do we develop a scientific base to understand the work of the manager? The description of roles is a first and necessary step. But tighter forms of research are necessary. Specifically, we must attempt to model managerial work—to describe it as a system of programs. First, it will be necessary to decide what programs managers actually use. Among a great number of programs in the manager's repertoire, we might expect to find a time-scheduling program, an information-disseminating program, and a disturbance-handling program. Then, researchers will have to devote a considerable amount of effort to studying and accurately describing the content of each of these programs—the information and heuristics used. Finally, it will be necessary to describe the interrelationships among all of these programs so that they may be combined into an integrated descriptive model of managerial work.

When the management scientist begins to understand the programs that managers use, he can begin to design meaningful systems and provide help for the manager. He may ask: Which managerial activities can be fully re-programmed (i.e., automated)? Which cannot be reprogrammed because they require human responses? Which can be partially reprogrammed to operate in a man-machine system? Perhaps scheduling, information-collecting, and resource-allocating activities lend themselves to varying degrees of reprogramming. Management will emerge as a science to the extent that such efforts are successful.

Improving the manager's effectiveness

Fayol's fifty-year-old description of managerial work is no longer of use to us. And we shall not disentangle the complexity of managerial work if we insist on viewing the manager simply as a decision-maker or simply as a motivator of subordinates. In fact, we are unlikely to overestimate the complexity of the manager's work, and we shall make little headway if we take overly simple or narrow points of view in our research.

A major problem faces today's manager. Despite the growing size of modern organizations and the growing complexity of their problems (par-ticularly those in the public sector), the manager can expect little help. He must design his own information system, and he must take full charge of his organization's strategy-making system. Furthermore, the manager faces what might be called the *dilemma of delegation*. He has unique access to much important information but he lacks a formal means of disseminating it. As much of it is verbal, he cannot spread it around in an efficient man-ner. How can he delegate a task with confidence when he has neither the time nor the means to send the necessary information along with it?

Thus, the manager is usually forced to carry a great burden of responsi-bility in his organization. As organizations become increasingly large and complex, this burden increases. Unfortunately, the man cannot signifi-cantly increase his available time or significantly improve his abilities to manage. Hence, in the large, complex bureaucracy, the top manager's time assumes an enormous opportunity cost and he faces the real danger of be-coming a major obstruction in the flow of decisions and information.

Because of this, as we have seen, managerial work assumes a number of distinctive characteristics. The quantity of work is great; the pace is un-relenting; there is great variety, fragmentation, and brevity in the work ac-tivities; the manager must concentrate on issues that are current, specific, and ad hoc, and to do so, he finds that he must rely on verbal forms of communications. Yet it is on this man that the burden lies for designing and operating strategy-making and information-processing systems that are to solve his organization's (and society's) problems.

The manager can do something to alleviate these problems. He can learn more about his own roles in his organization, and he can use this information to schedule his time in a more efficient manner. He can recognize that only he has much of the information needed by his organization. Then, he can seek to find better means of disseminating it into the organization. Finally, he can turn to the skills of his management scientists to help reduce his workload and to improve his ability to make decisions.

The management scientist can learn to help the manager to the extent he can develop an understanding of the manager's work and the manager's information. To date, strategic planners, operations researchers, and information system designers have provided little help for the senior manager. They simply have had no framework available by which to understand the work of the men who employed them, and they have had poor access to the information which has never been documented. It is folly to believe that a man with poor access to the organization's true *nerve center* can design a formal management information system. Similarly, how can the long-range planner, a man usually uninformed about many of the *current* events that take place in and around his organization, design meaningful strategic plans? For good reason, the literature documents many manager complaints of naïve planning and many planner complaints of disinterested managers. In my view, our lack of understanding of managerial work has been the greatest block to the progress of management science.

The ultimate .solution to the problem—to the overburdened manager seeking meaningful help—must derive from research. We must observe, describe, and understand the real work of managing; then and only then shall we significantly improve it.

References

1. Fayol, Henri. *Administration industrielle et générale,* Dunods, Paris, 1950 (first published 1916).

2. Drucker, Peter F. *The Practice of Management,* Harper and Row, New York, 1954.

3. Gulick, Luther H. "Notes on the Theory of Organization," in Luther Gulick and Lyndall Urwick (eds.), *Paper on the Science of Administration,* Columbia University Press, New York, 1937.

4. Mackenzie, R. Alex. "The Management Process in 3D," *Harvard Business Review* (November–December 1969), pp. 80–87.

5. Braybrooke, David. "The Mystery of Executive Success Reexamined," *Administrative Science Quarterly* 8 (1964), 533–60.

6. Braybrooke, David, and Lindblom, Charles E. *A Strategy of Decision,* Free Press, New York, 1963.

7. Gibb, Cecil A. "Leadership," chapter 31 in Gardner Lindzey and Elliot A. Aronson (eds.), *The Handbook of Social Psychology,* Vol. 4, second edition, Addison-Wesley, Reading, Mass., 1969.

8. Carlson, Sune. *Executive Behavior,* Strömbergs, Stockholm, 1951.

9. Burns, Tom. "The Directions of Activity and Communications in a Departmental Executive Group," *Human Relations* 7 (1954), 73–97.

10. Burns, Tom. "Management in Action," *Operational Research Quarterly* 8 (1957), 45–60.

11. Horne, J. H., and Lupton, Tom. "The Work Activities of Middle Managers: An Exploratory Study," *The Journal of Management Studies* 2 (1965), 14–33.

12. Stewart, Rosemary. *Managers and Their Jobs,* Macmillan, London, 1967.

13. Hemphill, John K. *Dimensions of Executive Positions,* Bureau of Business Research Monograph Number 98, Ohio State University, Columbus, 1960.

14. Myers, Charles A. (Ed.). *The Impact of Computers on Management,* MIT Press, Cambridge, Mass., 1967.

15. Mintzberg, Henry. "Structured Observation as a Method to Study Managerial Work," *The Journal of Management Studies* 7 (1970), 87–104.

16. Guest, Robert H. "Of Time and the Foreman," *Personnel* 32 (1955–56), 478–86.

17. Kelly, Joe. "The Study of Executive Behavior by Activity Sampling," *Human Relations* 17 (1964), 277–87.

18. Sayles, Leonard R. *Managerial Behavior: Administration in Complex Enterprises,* McGraw-Hill, New York, 1964.

19. Whyte, William F. *Street Corner Society,* second edition, University of Chicago Press, 1955.

20. Neustadt, Richard E. *Presidential Power: The Politics of Leadership,* The New American Library, New York, 1964.

21. Bronowski, J. "The Creative Process," *Scientific American* 199 (1958), 59–65.

22. Sarbin, T. R., and Allen, V. L. "Role Theory," in Gardner Lindzey and Elliot A. Aronson (eds.), *The Handbook of Social Psychology,* Vol. I, second edition, Addison-Wesley, Reading, Mass., 1968, pp. 488–567.

23. David, Robert T. *Performance and Development of Field Sales Managers,* Division of Research, Graduate School of Business Administration, Harvard University, Boston, 1957.

24. Papandreou, Andreas G. "Some Basic Problems in the Theory of the Firm," in Bernard F. Haley (ed.), *A Survey of Contemporary Economics,* Vol. II, Irwin, Homewood, Illinois, 1952, pp. 183–219.

25. Marples, D. L. "Studies of Managers: A Fresh Start?" *The Journal of Management Studies* 4 (1967), 282–99.

Pathfinding, Problem Solving, and Implementing: The Management Mix

Harold J. Leavitt

Every couple of decades managers and academics scratch their heads and once again ponder some tough old questions like these: What is managing *really* all about? What are managers doing right? What are they doing wrong? What should they *really* be trying to do?

Even though such questions will never be finally answered, they are healthy, indicative of a recurrent readiness to change and to experiment. This time around, they seem especially important, driven partly by anxiety and uncertainty about what it will take to cope with the volatile, complex, and fast-changing world that lies ahead.

This small book tries to focus more clearly on questions of this kind, and to suggest partial and temporary answers to some of them. It begins with a simple three-part description of what the managing process looks like in the late 1980s. Those three parts then serve as handles for examining where American management has gone right and gone wrong in recent years, and what kinds of corrections and changes seem to be in order.

The book's general argument is that we have unintentionally neglected the visionary, pathfinding part of the managing process over the last 20 years. We have, at our peril, put most of our energies into two other areas—into planful, analytic, systematic methods of problem solving and into the action and people-oriented implementing parts of managing. Only since the early 1980s have the bills from that neglect of pathfinding become obvious. We are right now in a healthy but hectic period of repayment, regrouping, and renewal.

This first chapter outlines the three-part model of the managing process and briefly describes each of the three parts. The main purpose of the chapter is to lay the groundwork for understanding why the neglect of pathfinding by managers and educators alike has come close to costing us our managerial shirts.

Reprinted from Harold Leavitt, *Corporate Pathfinders* (Homewood, Ill.: Dow Jones–Irwin, 1986), pp. 1–24.

The three parts into which this model divides managing are these: #1 pathfinding, #2 problem solving, and #3 implementing.

Consider them in reverse order, starting with #3 *implementing,* because that one is such a pervasive element of our image of the modern manager. For here lies the macho mover-and-shaker part of the managing process, as well as the office politics and manipulative parts, and even the participative, human relations parts. It is this implementing side of managing that shows up most often in soap opera managers and in movie versions of the manager. Implementing is about *action,* about getting things done through people, making things happen. Implementing is getting the bricks laid, the services rendered, and the product delivered. Implementing is *doing* things *through others.* Managers are people who get things done. They persuade, cajole, influence, command.

But managing is not just about implementing. It is also about *problem solving.* Managers have to organize, plan, and make decisions. Good managing takes some IQ points as well as some capacity to get things done. Managing means taking hold of complex, messy, ill-defined problems and converting them into organized, systematized forms. Managers have to make rational decisions about products, people, and markets; they have to allocate scarce resources sensibly. Managers must be thinkers as well as doers. They have to make order out of chaos.

Behind both the problem solving and implementing parts of managing, there lurks still another part of the process, the much fuzzier, less observable #1 part, here called *pathfinding.* Pathfinding is the major focus of this book, and while ephemeral and hard to measure, it is an incontrovertibly real and critical part of the managing process.

#1 pathfinding is about getting the right questions rather than the right answers. It is about making problems rather than solving them. It is *not* about figuring out the best way to get there from here, nor even about making sure that we get there. It is rather about pointing to where we ought to try to go.

#1 pathfinding, that is, is about mission, purpose, and vision; #2 problem solving is about analysis, planning, and reasoning; and #3 implementing is about doing, changing, and influencing. Our model of managing is about those three critical sets of activities and about the back-and-forth interactions among the three.

The model can be pictured this way:

A Model of the Managing Process		
#1	#2	#3
Pathfinding	Problem Solving	Implementing

The wavy vertical lines are there to show that the boundaries between the pieces are often foggy, and to suggest that movement from any one to any other can be both difficult and critical. It is not enough, that is, for the manager to be competent in one of these three, or even in all three at once. The manager had also better be skillful at moving across the harsh terrain that often separates them.

That three-part view of managing can (and will) be applied at several levels. For the individual manager, the three parts can be treated as three styles of managing. Some managers, that is, use predominantly pathfinding styles; others are problem solvers; still others are implementers. Most of us mix the three styles, presumably to fit appropriate situations. But are we really that flexible? Can we learn new styles late in life? How? Aren't the three parts of managing mutually contradictory?

At that same individual level, educational questions arise. In the education of managers, should we try to teach a blend of all three and shoot for "balanced excellence"? Have business schools taught any pathfinding at all? Could they? Or should they try? Later chapters examine such questions from an individual perspective.

The three parts—pathfinding, problem solving, and implementing—can also be looked at from an organizational perspective. Do organizations need pathfinding individuals? In what proportions? At the top? Throughout the organization? Should the three parts of the process be specialized, with each the responsibility of a particular group or level? Should we let R&D, for example, do the pathfinding, while engineering does the problem solving and sales does the implementing? Or should the CEO be the pathfinder, with the staff people the problem solvers and all the rest the implementers?

Do large ongoing organizations need more pathfinding types? Won't that erode discipline and lead to anarchy? How can the individualistic, high-risk pathfinding style be integrated into the participative kind of implementation that has grown so prevalent in recent years?

This three-part model can be considered at a societal level as well. To what extent is pathfinding part of the heritage of most Western nations? Has some of that heritage been lost? Have recent educational policies and practices encouraged or suppressed pathfinding tendencies? Has the growth of very large organizations discouraged individualistic pathfinding? Do the cultures of most organizations, especially large and old ones, need a good shot of pathfinding style—a mood of urgency, a push toward innovation, a salient sense of mission?

Implementing

Let's add a little meat to these bones by looking at each part of that three-part model in more depth. Again we start at the #3 end.

Implementing is not done by managers alone. Each of us implements all the time, whether or not we wear managerial hats. We mow the lawn, drive the car, fix the lamp, cook the dinner. But when implementing is part of the managing process, it has a couple of attributes that distinguish it from implementing in nonmanagerial settings.

First, managerial implementing is always done through other people. That's of course not at all a new idea. My old mentor Douglas McGregor used to define all of managing that way: "Managing is getting things done through people." While in other parts of life we can often implement our own decisions, managing human organizations invariably requires convincing other people to mow our lawns and cook our dinners. Implementing in organizations almost always requires the manager to persuade or command or manipulate or force other people to change their present behavior, to do what the manager wants done instead of what those people are now doing. *Managerial implementing is therefore a highly social activity.*

Second, managerial implementing involves changing other people's behavior, and therefore *it is a highly emotional activity.* Everything the social sciences know about changing behavior says that people change for emotional reasons far more than for rational reasons. It's love, hate, greed, loyalty, jealousy, and passion, much more than cool, pure reason, that drive us to change our ways. So the implementing part of managing has more to do with people's hearts than with their brains. It is not through logic and rationality that we persuade our employees to improve quality or increase productivity. It is through pride or ambition or loyalty. Getting people to do what you want them to do is much more a gutsy than an intellectual process.

But what's new? Hasn't that always been the case? Yes, but in our new world of knowledge and information, the role of emotionality has, paradoxically, gotten bigger, not smaller. In the old world of mostly physical arm-and-leg work, and in the social environment of those days, implementing was mostly focused on the fear-provoking emotionality of command and control or on the emotionality of paternalistic protectionism. In today's more professional, more educated, and more egalitarian organizational world, implementing becomes an issue of persuasion, negotiation, and inspiration rather than of command or protection.

Skill in working with human emotionality is not only rare in managers; it is often seen as "unmanagerial." Recent generations of young managers have, in general, been taught to use their heads much more than their hearts. They are supposed to learn to be rational, objective, hardheaded, professional. But when managers try to influence emotional human beings with exclusively rational tools, trouble starts.

Where and how, then, does one learn implementing skills? Imagine a teenager asking you something like that. "I really like that implementing stuff. I'd love to learn how to win friends and influence people. But how do I learn to become a great implementer? What should I study? What occupation should I try?"

It is not very difficult to identify some occupations in which implementing skills are critical to effective performance. How about direct selling? Or line supervision in a manufacturing plant? Surely platoon leaders in the Marine Corps had also better learn to be pretty good at implementing. They are helped along, of course, by rank, military structure, and all the rest, but in the last analysis it's the platoon leader who has to get those 50 marines to take that hill.

Litigating lawyers had better understand emotional implementing too. They have to persuade judges and jurors, to cajole and browbeat and sweet-talk witnesses. The litigators I have encountered in American law firms are killers, competitors. They are often singled out by other lawyers as a special subgenus of the legal species. Litigators worry about whether to select younger women for this jury or whether they would be better off with older men. They focus on the idiosyncrasies and characteristics of the opposing lawyers and on those of the judge. They work on people's prejudices and impulses, just as a very good salesperson does.

The band of occupations that can offer a young person practice in implementing is very broad indeed. It includes not only second lieutenants, lobbyists, and salespeople but also psychiatrists, counselors, organizational development people, and others in the "helping professions." Whether they acknowledge it or not, the members of these professions too try to change people's behavior by largely emotional means.

So what may seem like a collection of very strange bedfellows fits into this implementing part of the world of managing. Two bonds tie them all together. First, in all the varied kinds of managerial implementing, *human emotionality is the essence* from which change is made.

Second, most members of these implementing occupations think *small*. They think about people singly or in small numbers. For most skilled managerial implementers, human beings are *real*. They have names, faces, personalities, individual idiosyncrasies. They are not masses or statistics or hired hands, as they often are for extreme #2 problem solvers. So it should come as no surprise that when #3 implementers try to design large organizations, they usually want to use small groups as their building blocks, piling up pyramids composed of many small human units.

Problem solving

Let's turn now for a closer look at the #2 problem solving piece of the managing process. If the key word for #3 implementing is *action,* then the key word for #2 problem solving is *analysis.* Problem solving (at least as we in the Western world see it) is about reason and logic. It is about orderly, systematic approaches to problems. It is about planning and coordinating.

We know a good deal about how to teach problem solving skills, much more than we know about how to teach implementing skills. Indeed, that's what most education is all about. Reading, writing, and arithmetic are all analytic problem solving skills. A caricature of the complete #2 problem solver does not look at all like the fast-moving, fast-talking caricature of the implementer. The problem solver casts an intellectually reserved shadow. The image is of the steel-trap mind poring over the printout by lamplight, figuring out the right answer, the logical solution, the defensible decision, the optimal strategy.

If that inquiring teenager likes the #2 problem solving image and asks you where a young person ought to go for training to become a great problem solver, the answer should be quite easy. One good place to go is the Modern American Business School. Something like 80 percent of the contemporary MBA curriculum has been focused on the #2 analytic problem solving part of managing. That's the place to learn about linear programming, systems analysis, operations research, and econometric methods, about how to build marketing models and how to do financial analyses. Look at the catalog of any MBA school. The course titles use the word *analysis* again and again: Financial Analysis, Market Analysis, Decision Analysis, Economic Analysis. Go to business school to learn to program what has previously been unprogrammable.

But business school is only one of the places where the young person can learn how to do analytic problem solving. He or she might also try engineering or accounting or management consulting or tax law. All of those professions require high levels of analytic skills. They require logic, consistency, and orderliness. While it's likely that members of those professions are sometimes talented in other ways too, analytic skill remains a sine qua non for competence in all of them.

Given all of that emphasis on analysis and logic, it is no surprise that all-out #2 types take a dim view of emotionality. While for #3 implementers emotionality is the raw material of change, for orthodox #2s that same emotionality is likely to be seen as noise in the system, as a sign of human imperfection. In a few million years the full rationality that God so clearly intended will evolve. Real men aren't emotional. So one of the trouble spots in the managing process is located at the junction of #2 and #3, where rational problem solvers meet emotional implementers.

Notice too that analytic occupations carry very high status in Western society, in contrast to the somewhat lower status usually ascribed to many of the implementing occupations, such as selling or manufacturing management. It's OK for your son or daughter to enter any one of them. And they pay well too. Among MBA students, for example, it has been the jobs in consulting and financial analysis that have been viewed as the most desirable ones, at least until recently. Selling has been viewed as low class, and manufacturing as too dirty.

A caveat: While much of the problem solving part of managing can be learned through quantitative, analytic training, not *all* of it can be picked up that easily. There is, as every manager knows, more to real-world problem solving than can be found in the problem sets at the end of the chapters in the accounting text. There is more uncertainty in the real world, more unforeseeable variability. So such words as *judgment, experience, wisdom,* and *good sense* have stayed on our recruiting checklists, even as #2-type academics seek ways of making them unnecessary.

Pathfinding

If implementing includes large emotional components and if problem solving includes large rational and analytic components, how can one characterize the #1 pathfinding part of the managing process? The central issue of pathfinding is not influence or persuasion, nor is it reasoning or systematic analysis. The key word here is *mission*. The pathfinding part of managing is the homeland of the visionary, the dreamer, the innovator, the creator, the entrepreneur, and the charismatic leader. The central questions are very difficult and often unaddressed: How do I decide what I want to be when I grow up? What should this organization try to become if it could become anything imaginable? What do we really want to do with this company?

The #1 pathfinding world is highly personal and subjective, with answers, where there are any, emerging more from within the self than from a diagnosis of what's out there. Pathfinding is the ephemeral part of managing that deals with values, aesthetics, and beliefs. Putting faith before evidence, pathfinders often violate #2 problem solving precepts. But they also build new worlds.

Do we even need such soft, subjective stuff to manage the modern organization? The answer is unequivocally yes, whether we derive it from social or political or organizational observation. The pathfinding role has always been a critical driving force in the rise of human institutions. From the founding of the United States to the development of IBM to the birth pangs of that new little start-up company, the beliefs and visions of a few stubborn souls have always driven innovation and development.

By far the best illustration of a pathfinding statement that I can offer is familiar to all Americans. It is the second sentence of the American Declaration of Independence: "We hold these truths to be self-evident, that all men are created equal, that they are endowed by their Creator with certain unalienable Rights, that among these are Life, Liberty and the pursuit of Happiness."

What an assertive, pathfinding declaration that is! It must have driven the #2 problem solvers of the day absolutely wild. All men are created equal? How do you know? What's the genetic evidence? "Rights" like "Liberty" or "the pursuit of Happiness"? How do you measure such stuff? "Self-evident" truths? No evidence required? No data to support them? And could anyone, even armed with the most clear and potent evidence, have changed those Founding Fathers' minds? They weren't to be distracted by mere facts!

The pathfinders whom most of us would cite as memorable are also necessarily skillful as implementers. We only remember them if other people have joined up with their visions. Visionaries who do *not* influence others to follow them are simply forgotten. Or if they are remembered at all, they are remembered as impractical dreamers, not as men and women of vision. Indeed, that almost defines a *charismatic leader:* A charismatic leader is a #1 pathfinder who is also successful at #3 implementing—someone with a sense of mission who can also get others to join in.

Pathfinders need not be heroes. They are not always lovable or even smart. People with unusual ideas, strong commitments, and deep beliefs may also be intransigent, single-minded, unforgiving, or simply stupid. It's not just the good guys, the Jesus Christs and Martin Luther Kings, who qualify as pathfinders. Some great pathfinders were more than a bit unpleasant; some were very bad fellows. Adolf Hitler belongs in that set, as does Jim Jones of Jonestown in Guyana, and probably so too do many of the robber barons of European and American industrial history.

In business, the pathfinders are easiest to spot among entrepreneurs and founders of companies. Watson of IBM, Hewlett and Packard, Land of Polaroid, and Freddie Laker were all people dedicated to building their dreams into realities. Such pathfinders are not always pleasant or friendly, and they may not be successful in the long run, but they are all stubborn, committed believers with strong, clear notions of good and bad.

Pathfinders also turn up in old established companies, but less frequently. When they do, they inject new mission and purpose into old organizations. In the early 1980s Lee Iacocca, for example, may have done just that at Chrysler, and Carlson at SAS. In both cases they have turned around their companies' spirits as well as their P&Ls.

To what education and which professions, then, should we direct young people who decide that pathfinding is what excites them?

It's much harder to answer that question for #1 pathfinding than it was for #2 problem solving or #3 implementing. Pathfinders seem far easier to identify than to develop. Perhaps we should point young people in directions quite unrelated to the contemporary management scene. We could suggest that they seek their fortunes among artists and architects, or among philosophers and religionists, or among theoretical physicists; or perhaps we should recommend a broad liberal education, if such a thing still exists.

Indeed, one can argue that management education as we now practice it would do very little to enhance pathfinding abilities. Our methods of educating and developing new managers have not only neglected pathfinding; they have often downright clobbered it. While problem solvers and implementers, whether in companies or in universities, fight like the devil with one another, they also share a common interest (sometimes unconscious) in keeping the pathfinders out.

For obvious reasons, #2 problem solvers don't want stubborn, intractable, impractical visionaries around. Pathfinders can seldom offer (and seldom care to offer) hard evidence for their choices; and hard evidence is the essence of modern problem solving. Pathfinders often ignore the rules, or act impulsively, or wave off what they see as trivial details.

Here in northern California's Silicon Valley one version of the clash between #1 and #2 styles has occurred several times in recent years. It happens as small companies succeed and grow larger. At some point, the venture capitalists or other investors convince the #1-type founders that their now chaotic organization needs discipline and control. So a #2-type COO is brought aboard. Occasionally the marriage works, but frequently the freewheeling #1 style of the founder is just too disruptive for the control-oriented #2 manager (or vice versa), so sparks fly, heads roll, and energy is diverted from the main target just when it is needed most.

#3 implementers are also likely to feel cool toward those unmalleable, individualistic pathfinders. Contemporary #3 types are particularly oriented toward teamwork, consensus, and cooperation among an organization's members. No matter how positively we may value such styles, they do not fit neatly with the stubborn, determined individualism of pathfinders. #1 pathfinders often become team leaders, but they are seldom good team players.

Outstanding pathfinders, problem solvers, and implementers: Some examples

Occasionally rare and unique personalities turn up who leave their mark in history almost entirely as implementers, or problem solvers, or pathfinders. They are so good at that one part of managing that it completely overshadows the other two. It's worth identifying a few such extraordinary people, people known to almost all of us, to help draw a clearer picture of the differences among the three parts.

Who, for example, among great public figures familiar to all of us, is the implementer par excellence? Who is preeminent among the problem solvers? Who are the outstanding pathfinders?

Certainly one ideal nominee for an Oscar among implementers would be Lyndon Baines Johnson, at least that part of him that keeps coming through in his biographies. Implementing can be done in many ways, and Johnson's was only one way. He was so good at it, however, and it was so central to his managing style that he serves as an excellent example.

As president, Johnson was certainly not considered by most observers to have been a particularly great #2 intellect, nor a great planner or organizer. Neither was he regarded as a great #1 visionary pathfinder. He did, the reader will remember, try to establish a mission for America, his Great Society, but that notion somehow never took hold, perhaps because many Americans weren't sure he really believed in it himself.

But Johnson will always be remembered as a top-notch implementer. His skill at twisting the arms and stroking the egos of congressmen was legendary. He could shuffle greed, love, fear, and sentimentality to get what he wanted. He could make compromises, negotiate workable solutions. He could get it done. In one sense, he was a very good planner too. He did his homework before taking on the people he wanted to influence. He learned all about their children and their lovers and their hobbies and their hangups. And he used whatever tactics were needed to do the job. He got things implemented through people.

The stories left behind from the Johnson presidency reflect those characteristics. Johnson's memorable quotations were invariably pragmatic and earthy. One of his favorites: "Don't spit in the soup; we all have to eat."

On one occasion, the story goes, an aide came to him to ask, "Mr. President, why are you climbing into bed with Joe Smith, who has always been your enemy? For years that guy has been trying to destroy you, and now you seem to be forming an alliance with him." Johnson is said to have replied, "I'd rather have him inside the tent pissing out than outside pissing in."

No statesmanlike rhetoric here. Those Johnsonisms are not likely to make *The World's Great Quotations,* but they catch Johnson's pragmatic emphasis on doing what one has to do to get the damn job done. And they surely also illustrate his awareness of the relevance of human emotionality in the implementing process. Typical of the approach of excellent implementers, these quotations illustrate two key characteristics of #3 skill— attention to emotionality and attention to the individual.

After some hesitation, I have decided to include one more remark that has been ascribed, truly or falsely, to President Johnson. The remark is worth reporting, not because it is off-color, but because it so clearly demonstrates Johnson's faith that implementing is what *really* counts. "When you grab 'em by the balls," the remark goes, "their hearts and minds will soon follow." Translated, that would read, "If you catch people where their #3 emotions are, then the #2 rationality and their #1 values will adapt themselves to fit." In this rather cynical ideology, emotionality dominates both logic and morality. While Johnson's application of that ideology looks especially manipulative, the ideology itself underlies the practice of many other types of implementers.

It's not too difficult to find other examples of excellent implementers. During World War II General George Patton was a flamboyant example, out there at the head of his troops, his twin pearl-handled revolvers at his side. And Ronald Reagan has shown extraordinary skill at social influence, both through his mastery of the media and in face-to-face dealings with congressmen. Remember, for example, how, early in his first term, he got those AWAC planes for the Saudis? While commentators were insisting that he couldn't possibly push the deal through, he did. And the newspapers talked about how his personal charm had swung the votes his way.

Incidentally, was any #1 mission involved in that deal? Or was any of the deal part of a grand #2 plan? Most observers seemed to feel that in that case #3 was all there was.

Doesn't Lee Iacocca belong on any list of great recent managerial implementers? He may be good at #1 and #2 as well, but his affable personal implementing style and his effective exploitation of the emotional aspects of managing have been extraordinary.

Each of us could probably make a private list of "implementers I have known"—from a particular teacher who counseled and guided us, to the company tactician who always seemed to know just when to push hard and when to back off, to that extraordinary sales rep who somehow made those impossible sales, to the negotiator who always seemed to get a better deal than anyone else.

If Johnson serves as a caricature of the extreme and skillful implementer, who can similarly exemplify the far-out problem solver? The epitome of rational, analytic intelligence? The person who could decompose very complex problems and then reassemble them into a clear controllable form? Does your vice president for finance fit the mold? Or your chief industrial engineer? How about David Stockman, recently the director of the U.S. Budget Bureau?

One public figure of a couple of decades ago who fitted that image perfectly, at least by media stereotype, was Robert McNamara during his tenure as U.S. secretary of defense. The later McNamara of the World Bank appears much more mellow than did the earlier Department of Defense version. McNamara in those early years was much admired by many of his contemporaries chiefly because of his brilliantly orderly, systematic, and rational mind. In contrast to the stories about LBJ (under whom McNamara served), the stories about McNamara reflect just those #2 qualities. Here's one:

McNamara is attending a presentation at which the presenter shows slide after slide full of graphs and charts and numbers. At the 105th slide, McNamara says, "Stop! Slide number 105 contradicts slide number 6." And sure enough, he is right! Everyone in attendance is awed by his capacity to order and process such massive quantities of information. Some Washington veterans still count McNamara as the greatest civil servant of his time. They usually cite his incisive, analytic, logical qualities as the main reason.

However, at least as the stories go, the McNamara of those DOD days was not nearly as effective in implementing his decisions as he was in making them, and history books are not likely to picture him as a great visionary (though that is probably quite unjust). There are Washington old-timers who still turn beet red with anger at the mention of his name. When they calm down enough to say why, it is almost always to complain that he tried to "take over," to reduce other people's autonomy. Some generals in Vietnam and some legislators in Washington, themselves pretty good #3 implementers, viewed him as an intruder into their autonomous territories and resisted those carefully worked-out controls imposed from the Pentagon.

While it is difficult to identify senior managers who manifest extreme #2 posture in these late 1980s, such managers were less rare in the 60s and 70s. In those years, executives like Roy Ash at Litton Industries and Harold Geneen at ITT were seen as the very model of modern managers— brilliant, tough, systematic, coldly rational.

Analytic think tanks like the Rand Corporation flourished in those decades too. And small analytic-planning groups played a powerful role in France. The stereotype of the cool analytic MBA also came into its own in that period too, and it became so popular with managers that the number of such MBAs multiplied, as did the number of business schools that produced them. The 1960s and 70s were the decades when corporate staffs grew fat and great conglomerates roamed the earth.

Examples of #1 pathfinders, however, seem to turn up throughout human history. They include great religious figures like Jesus and Mohammed; leaders of nations like Mahatma Gandhi, Vladimir Ilyich Lenin, Charles de Gaulle, Lee Kuan Yew, and Golda Meir; and pioneers in the professions like Florence Nightingale and Sigmund Freud.

Other less attractive personages also belong on the pathfinder list: Adolf Hitler, Muammar al-Qaddafi, Napoleon Bonaparte, and Attila the Hun. My favorite candidate for recent top-of-the-line pathfinder is Dr. Martin Luther King, Jr. His most remembered phrase is "I have a dream." That's as pathfinding a phrase as one can imagine. Of course, Dr. King must be counted as a great implementer as well. Followers flocked to act upon his dream. He too changed behavior by emotional means, though he used a style quite different from President Johnson's.

Just for practice, imagine how differently either Robert McNamara or Lyndon Johnson, given the same intent as King's, might have approached the same problem of changing race relations in America.

McNamara would have worked out a grand strategy, wouldn't he? He would have been sure that all of the staff work had been done, the information gathered and analyzed, the contingencies planned for. He would have done an admirably professional job.

President Johnson's approach? Perhaps he would have identified the key players, figured out which people really had the power. Then perhaps he would have worked on those people, one at a time, using every weapon that he could muster to line them up—from the prestige of his office, to promises of support for their pet projects, to personal persuasion.

Would either of them have shown the passionate, resolute, self-sacrificing style used by Dr. King? I think not.

In the corporate world, pathfinders are, thank heaven, not yet an entirely endangered species. They can most often (but not always) be found among founders of companies, in part because successful founders are apt to get more public attention than second- or third-generation managers.

Some recent examples: Messrs. Hewlett and Packard seem to have truly committed themselves to a clear set of organizational values. They have captured and transmitted much of their intent with the phrase "the H-P way." That phrase really means something to H-P people everywhere. It describes a style of openness, honesty, and mutual support and respect reminiscent of the best of small-town America. At Apple Computer, in contrast, Steve Jobs and Company tried to pursue a very different vision— a brash, innovative, almost arrogant organizational culture. Some observers saw that pursuit as a somewhat flaky new children's crusade; for others, it was a youthful cultural revolution, ideally appropriate to its time, its place, and its product.

But in older companies too, pathfinders arise. Pehr Gyllenhammer at Volvo has pushed long, hard, and effectively for a more humane and productive alternative to the old assembly line. He has argued saliently for keeping most of Volvo's operations in its native Sweden despite high labor costs, because he believes in fighting the productivity battle in more positive ways than by escaping to cheap labor overseas.

So Volvo has tried to stay competitive (and so far it has worked) by innovating in both the technology and the sociology of production—building quality cars and trucks with small teams, using appropriate tools, and even modifying the design of its products to fit coherently into the total system. So far, it's doing pretty well.

Ren McPherson, at Dana Corporation, has also successfully pushed his vision of people-based productivity into an otherwise unglamorous old auto parts company. He too did it by using personal passion and determination, injecting pride and enthusiasm into the organization.

In all of these cases the pathfinding leaders have backed up their own pathfinding leadership with effective #3 participative-type implementation, providing us with living examples of successful marriages between #1 and #3. In later chapters that #1 – #3 relationship gets a closer look, and so do some of the obstacles that frequently beset such marriages.

Surely the reader can (and should) add to this list from personal experience. Pathfinders—dedicated, purposive people—are not to be found only among the famous and infamous, or only at the tops of large organizations. Small entrepreneurial companies are very often led by people with such dedication to particular visions and values, and deep within large organizations, often in the face of enormous bureaucratic roadblocks, the dedicated champions of new ideas and important causes still make their voices heard.

Does the managerial world need more pathfinding?

There are some persuasive arguments on both sides of the question of the importance of pathfinding, especially in large organizations. On the pro side:

— Innovations are almost always the products of pathfinding individuals and small groups, almost never the products of large, highly structured bureaucracies.

— Breakthroughs in any field typically emerge from a combination of thorough understanding of the existing rules *and* a risk-taking readiness to break out of them, to march to different drummers.

— One can also cite the usual broader arguments: the knowledge explosion, ever faster technological change, a crowded and small organizational world. For those reasons and more, organizations need both innovation and direction. They need a constant flow of innovations in products and services because competitors will kill them if they stand still. Intercontinental airplanes knock off passenger liners. Slide rules give way to calculators. Transistors not only destroy vacuum-tube makers but also displace old ways of building watches, radios, and computers. Organizations need direction and purpose lest they be lost in the buffeting storms of competition, regulation, and social change. And individuals need purpose lest *they* be lost in meaningless ennui. The pathfinding part of managing is about both innovation and purpose.

— But let's not try to justify #1 by using only #2-type arguments. There are powerful #1-type reasons for building more pathfinding into Western management. Pathfinding is our heritage, in the United States and almost all other Western countries. Our traditions and our self-esteem commit us to changing the world, to developing the new and the better. Independence, achievement, and daring are integral to our value systems. Pathfinding is what we claim to believe in. We should build it into ourselves and our organizations just because it is our heritage, and just because we believe it is good.

— Just in case the hardheaded reader wants a more practical reason to supplement all of that sentimental junk, here's one: Our traditions of individualism, of independent effort, of starting new fires may just constitute one of our few comparative advantages over the Japanese, with their traditions of conformity, obedience, and self-subordination.

Perhaps it's appropriate here to cite just a few arguments against pushing the pathfinding idea too far:

— How can you run a company full of independent, rule-breaking, intractable pathfinders? That's an invitation to anarchy.

— It's always (well, almost always) been the well-organized, disciplined army that wins the war. Precision and planfulness, not vision and stubbornness, make the difference between success and failure.

— Those imaginative dreamers are a dime a dozen. They're almost always unrealistic and impractical. They bite off more than they can chew, and they won't spit it out no matter how obvious it is that they're wrong. They can kill a company by stubbornly refusing to abandon their dogmatic beliefs.

— The job of managers is to understand the world as it exists and to deal with it, not to take on the impossible job of making it over.

10

Designing Organizational Cultures: Myth, Ritual, and Symbol

Over the last decade, the concept of *organizational culture* has come into wide use in managerial circles. Culture is an umbrella concept, difficult to define. We can sense it when we enter a society or organization that is new (to us), but we often can't see it or measure it. Culture is what its members share—beliefs, values, assumptions—often unconsciously. Culture provides the community, the sameness, the consensus that makes those people unique and special. Often our cultural beliefs are so much a part of the atmosphere (like fresh air) that we don't become aware of them until we discover they are no longer there. We realize how American or Chinese or French we really are when we get out of that airplane and find ourselves suddenly in the middle of someone else's strange culture.

But why has the concept of organizational culture now become so important? After all, cultures have always existed, everywhere. The answers from the manager's point of view include these:

If culture means common beliefs and values, shared by (almost) everyone in my organization, then culture is very important indeed! If our people all believe, for example, in hard work, high quality, and cooperation, and if they feel loyal and committed to our company, what a great and productive company we'll have! But if they believe only in getting more money for less work, if quality is of no importance, if the norm is competition rather than cooperation, then I have some managerial problems on my hands.

So a "strong" culture is a control system—a *self*-control system. And if that strong culture is one that values what is in the organization's interests, then that manager is a lucky manager. Managing such a shop is easy. Everybody is already motivated in the right direction and loyal and cooperative.

Next obvious question: Do cultures just happen? Or can managers manage them? Can I shape and develop my company's culture? Yes, and also no. It isn't easy, and it usually isn't fast.

This section examines the whole idea of culture and its management, including the use of devices to help with culture management, such as developing organizational myths and stories (David Boje et al.) and ceremonies and rituals (Harrison Trice et al.). The general issue is covered in Thomas Peters's "Symbols, Patterns, and Settings." And the final paper, by Richard Pascale, looks at ways of socializing new employees into old cultures.

A request to the reader: As you consider these writings, please keep a few caveats in mind. What about the ethics of all this, of trying to shape and direct the beliefs and values of your employees into a single pattern? Is that right? And if you succeed, mightn't you find that you have created a monster of unchangeable rigidity? But if you don't do anything, won't a culture grow anyway? And is that "natural" culture necessarily better than the one you might cultivate?

Myth Making: A Qualitative Step in OD Interventions
David M. Boje,
Donald B. Fedor, and
Kendrith M. Rowland

Organizational participants, consultants, and researchers will attest that organizations are not perfectly rational or logical systems (e.g., March & Olsen 1976). Organizations are replete with competing ideologies and goals that result from the uncertainty pervading them. Organizations must function within turbulent environments (Perrow 1972; Emery & Trist 1965), with complex technologies (Thompson 1967), and threatening political climates (Tushman 1977). Instead of clear-cut paths to achieving goals and objectives, people in organizations, as well as consultants working with them, are forced to sift through incomplete or conflicting stories, observations, and opinions to make sense out of the dynamics in them and their relationships to the environment.

This milieu of uncertainty is the foundation upon which organizational cultures arise to provide a framework within which shared meanings are developed. Organizational culture, as used here, includes the unique language, symbols, metaphors, and myths that arise from the organization's situation and the interactions of its participants. These particular components of culture facilitate the feelings of rational action in the midst of otherwise overpowering uncertainty and political maneuvering. Myths in this context represent one way in which other elements of organizational culture are conceptually organized into a system of organizationally relevant logic.

The myth-making system in organizations

Myth making is an adaptive mechanism whereby groups in an organization maintain logic frameworks within which to attribute meaning to activities and events. The meanings that organize past activities and events into a system of logic then become the basis for legitimizing present and future behaviors. A myth-making system is evident to some degree in every organization. Without such an adaptive system, the technological and adminis-

Reprinted with the permission of NTL Institute from *The Journal of Applied Behavioral Science* 18, no. 1:17–28, © 1982.

trative structure would lack sufficient shared meaning to serve as a basis for coordinated behavior in the face of excessive uncertainty.

For those who become socialized into an organization, myths constitute a factual and highly objective reality. They are a major part of the taken-for-granted assumptions and common-sense theories of organizational experience. In general, we hold myths to be social attempts to "manage" certain problematic aspects of modern organizations through definitions of truth and rational purpose. This process of "management" results in a composite of standard operating procedures and organizational characteristics, such as acceptable practices concerning the treatment of subordinates and procedures for their placement, transfer, and promotion. A myth is constructed to exemplify why the given practices and procedures are the "only way" the organization can function effectively. March and Simon (1958) point out how unlike the "economic man" we are in the way we "bound" our world to make it *seem* rational. Myths are a form of "bounding," permitting meaningful organizational behavior to occur, while glossing over excessive complexity, turbulence, or ambiguity. Myths narrow the horizon in which organizational life is allowed to make sense.

Because friendship and/or work groups within an organization face different environments and are made up of individuals with different backgrounds and skills, the dominant myths for each group can vary significantly. Myths collide and compete in the ongoing negotiation of power and privilege among groups attempting to determine the dominant myth-making system. Once a myth is accepted as a basis for a group's belief structure, however, it will be strongly resistant to change.

Myth making and organization development

Interventions by OD consultants not only affect the structure and process of human interaction, but also the delicate fabrics of socially constructed realities (Berger & Luckman 1967). In their attempts to examine the organization's myth system, OD consultants often substitute their own myths for those of the client organization. In theory, many OD techniques (e.g., survey feedback, process analysis, confrontation meeting) focus on the discrepancy between story and action to promote organizational change. An assumption among some consultants is that all myths are dysfunctional to the accomplishment of organizational goals. The revelation of these inconsistencies will presumably facilitate more effective modes of behavior.

There is, however, some disagreement as to the need to demythify the practice of OD. Margulies (1972), for example, describes the OD consultant as somewhere between an applier of behavioral science principles and a "magician" employing such tactics as placebos and myth making to effect change. Almost to the other extreme, French and Bell (1973) define OD as the application of behavioral science principles that completely demythify poorly understood organizational phenomena. Unfortunately, the consultant attempting to alter components of a dominant myth often confronts great resistance when a change strategy threatens to unlock inconsistencies or ambiguities that are being explained and even controlled through the current myth structure. Since, in our opinion, the client organization and the OD consultant both use myths, an intervention becomes an occasion for potential myth conflict between client and practitioner.

A typology of organizational myths

There are numerous functions of myth making that benefit both client and consultant. Our typology of myth functions draws upon the work of Thompson (1967) and categorizes myths in accordance with whether they deal with *standards of desirability* (1 and 2) or with *cause and effect* relationships (3 and 4).

> *Myths concerning standards of desirability*
> 1. Myths that create, maintain, and legitimize past, present, or future actions and consequences
> 2. Myths that maintain and conceal political interests and value systems
>
> *Myths concerning cause and effect relationships*
> 3. Myths that help explain and create cause and effect relationships under conditions of incomplete knowledge
> 4. Myths that rationalize the complexity and turbulence of activities and events to allow for predictable action taking

We believe myth making will be most obvious in organizations where standards of desirability and cause and effect relationships are unknown or in dispute. These four categories are designed as a heuristic framework within which to further consider and analyze the functions of myths in organizations.

Myths that create, maintain, and legitimize past, present, and future actions and consequences

Margulies (1972) has pointed out how the myths of "newness" and "rational scientific principles" can give added legitimacy to the consultant in gaining entrance into the client organization and generating the support of influential people once inside. War stories (Mitroff & Kilmann 1976) can also be used by both client and consultant to legitimize the continuance of techniques that worked well in the past and to target the scope and direction of interventions.

Besides anchoring the present in the past and providing legitimacy, myths can be important creators of organizational futures. Clark (1972) and Pettigrew (1976) have reported how entrepreneurs and reformers at times have pushed aside old structures in favor of the image of the future they intend to create. Sproull and Weiner (1976) have documented how this type of process was of prime importance to the creation of the National Institute of Education. Images of the future were molded and shaped in ways that allowed the mobilization of support and legitimization of policy statements. Influential persons involved in the myth creation also aided this process by giving their prestige and reputation to this myth, thus helping it attain greater concrete reality.

King (1974) has described how "expectation effects" explain the results of many OD efforts. One group of clients, for example, was told their intervention would lead to greater productivity, while the other group was told that improvements in interpersonal relationships would result. King found that the expectations conveyed before the intervention predicted its outcome. Myths about the past can also mobilize support and provide protection against threatening groups. In other words, myths create a momentum of their own.

Myths that maintain and conceal political interests

Pfeffer (1977) has described how myths can be used by the dominant coalition in an organization to camouflage its power, make decisions in secret, and hide the results of those decisions. Myths are inexorably intertwined in an organization's power structure. This is often not the power hierarchy defined by the organizational chart. Instead, actual power groups often use the rationalizing function of a myth to justify actions that might appear selfish or unethical. For example, when the federal government decided to create the Tennessee Valley Authority (TVA), it was done under the guise of providing cheap and efficient electrical power to that region (Selznick 1966). The political motive, to prohibit the growth of powerful private interests, was shielded by the myth of benevolence.

There is a further interaction between power and its supporting myth. While power groups have the ability to maintain and impose their own myth structure on others, the myth provides the framework for the full and unquestioned use of such power. The U.S. auto industry serves as a recent example. For many years, executives of the major auto companies were convinced that the domestic car buyer would never settle for a small, compact car. The lack of success with a few of them (e.g., the Vega and the Pinto) served only to support this idea. Internal planners and external critics argued in vain for resource allocations (and a better quality product) in the face of this overriding belief. Only when the evidence became overwhelming (i.e., a drastic drop in sales and profits) did the auto makers reexamine the "big car" myth.

Myths that help explain and create cause and effect relationships

Under conditions of incomplete knowledge, myths function to support decision making and rationality by creating cause and effect relationships. This allows organizational actors to assign causes to the present, once meaning is determined for the past. Problems can arise when knowledge gained from the past is built in as an assumption regarding the future. Since the assigned cause and effect relationship is usually consistent with the current dominant myth, "data" derived from prior activities and events will tend to support that myth and the existing power structure.

Women's groups, for example, have charged that men have perpetuated a myth about female unreliability in order to exclude them from better and higher paying jobs. The belief was that most women were only working until they could get married, get their husband through school, and the like. In other words, a woman's career was naturally (or instinctively) secondary to her family. By providing a rationale for not promoting women, a self-fulfilling prophecy developed. Not surprisingly, most women chose to leave the labor force when other opportunities were available. That is, the data supported the dominant myth.

Myths that rationalize complexity and turbulence to allow for taking predictable action

Myths of this type play an important role in providing the illusion of rational intention and action and in creating predictability in the face of random and evolutionary forces. Many actors are predisposed to see every action as the result of an *a priori* goal. Every effect must have causal intent. Even if an action is unintended, many search out "latent" goals that explain its origin. Consultants may be making a mythical assumption in treating organizations as identifiable, measurable, analyzable, and changeable (Greenfield 1973). Here, the socially constructed reality of the consultant affects the actions and consequences of system actors.

Myths may be used to simplify the complexity of the flow of events by resorting to ethical codes (Emery & Trist 1965) or standards of acceptability. Rather than respond to the turbulence of the environment directly, organizations often enact a simpler environment of rules and rituals for reaching their decisions.

Mintzberg (1973) has noted that many executives mythically adopt the planning, organizing, directing, and controlling model of management, when in fact they make decisions in haste and work in fast-paced environments with frequent interruptions. Managers are also bombarded by competing demands from their superiors, subordinates, and peers. When subordinates make requests or demands to alter certain procedures, the manager will frequently invoke the myth of "tradition" or "past success." Procedures become embedded in the fabric of organizational life and become "the way things are done here." Essentially, the myth in this case provides the manager with a ready-made rationale to avoid re-examining certain aspects of the system. The result is to gloss over much of the potential complexity in the organization's internal processes.

In summary, organizational myths are neither inherently positive nor negative. They are facts of organizational existence that serve as another factor to be considered, analyzed, and potentially altered or incorporated in change efforts. Unlike French and Bell (1973), we do not advocate simply sweeping aside "dysfunctional" myths. Instead, the myth system of certain groups may have to be taken as a given, modified, or enriched depending upon the anticipated scope and objectives of the organizational development effort. The first step must be to determine what myth system(s) are functioning in the organization.

Structural analysis of myths and myth making

One problem with analyzing myths is that the consultant must translate the client organization's *reconstructions* (i.e., stories, sagas, retrospections, linguistic categories) into common and opposing themes before he or she can derive the logic of the myth-making system. This requires a more qualitative process akin to psychoanalysis to investigate the client's reconstruction of "why" a certain event or activity occurred. A recommendation of structural anthropologists, particularly Levi-Strauss (1955, 1963), is to identify the episodes of the mythical account throughout the client organization and then to analytically infer the underlying structure of the myth-making system.

For example, suppose we ask people how or why a certain tradition or rule came into being. Techniques, like phenomenological interviewing, that allow individuals to freely recount episodes seem appropriate here (Massarik, 1979). People may reconstruct differing historical accounts of that event, depending upon their tenure, level, specialization, industry environment, and a host of other contextual variables. This contextual variance ought to be studied rather than controlled since it may reveal the logical themes that bind the accounts together.

We will not discover the meaning of organizational myths in a single convention, rule, procedure, or philosophic tidbit. Nor will we discover it in averages or tests of co-variation. A myth-making system is revealed in the logic that connects a wide variety of seemingly disjointed elements. The elements of the underlying theme occur in sets, the meaning of which is discovered by contrasting one element with other elements in context rather than a single element with itself.

Unobtrusive elements, such as codes of ethics, procedures for hiring, rules for budgeting, and symbols of office, are assumed here to be fundamental elements, which under systematic analysis may reveal the underlying socially constructed logic that interrelates them. An observed action, practice, or ritualistic behavior has no meaning except in the context of other historical elements. By analyzing these relationships across time and context, the myths should become more obvious—i.e., more obvious in the same sense that words have more meaning in the context of a sentence. Organizations, for example, in which family imagery and metaphors (e.g., "the old man," "the parent office") are employed, suggest behavioral patterns and appraisal systems quite contrary to a setting where we hear stories of "empire builders," "domains," and "young princes."

The consultant may wonder what to focus on in the client organization's reconstructions. Some suggestions are, (1) Recurring metaphors and themes that appear across rationalizing accounts (e.g., racial imagery, historical labels); (2) Categorizing dimensions employed in the accounts, such as status differentiations: us *vs.* them, good *vs.* bad, appropriate *vs.* inappropriate, formal *vs.* informal; (3) Underlying oppositions and contradictions; the coexistence of mutually exclusive or competing beliefs (e.g., "the common good" in the face of piece-rate incentives).

While we know of no current efforts to apply such an analytical framework to the study of organizational myth making, we believe the above guidelines coupled with research into the implications of different organization structures could reveal unseen aspects of formal organizations and human behavior in them.

The use of myth data in OD

For the OD consultant, the critical issue is the diagnosis of myth making and the associated implications for organizational health. Consultants, as unsocialized intruders, are told many stories about the organization. These should be carefully recorded to capture the subtle variations among the versions told in different units and at various levels. These reconstructions may give clues to the state of the system and where there is impetus for change.

As the "intruder" gains entrance, he or she quickly learns a new language. To the extent that language not only determines what we see, but how we interpret what we see, careful documentation of organizational and group language is in order.

The consultant will know if he or she has isolated the important aspects of myth making when he or she begins to be able to predict and interpret behavior the same way as the client. The consultant who employs the same categories and "actions in use" soon ceases to be viewed as the intruder. If the practitioner is able to identify the relevant organizational myths that support the decision-making process, the following is a partial list of the potential uses of such data.

The myth-making life cycle

A problem often encountered is the timing of change. For the purpose of selecting an appropriate intervention point, a life-cycle concept can be applied to the myth-making process. Organizational development theorists (e.g., Cohen, Fink, Gadon & Willits 1976) have stated that the best time to

Table 1. The myth-making life cycle

Myth Stage	Company Situation	Myth Development
I. Development	Rapid growth, high profitability, bright future outlook: no real competition.	Myth is successfully guiding decision making and organizational strategy. "Developing myth"
II. Maturation	Company's growth slowing, but still recognized as solid leader. Some competition which is inconsequential.	Myth and company identity completely intertwined. Myth strength still high. "Solid myth"
III. Decline	Competition has become substantial. Profitability slipping. Mission is a hindrance to action.	Most organizational units looking for ways to bolster myth, but some groups beginning to develop competing myths for renewal. "Myth Split"
IV. Reformulation	Company's situation has deteriorated to the point that precipitates a change in leadership.	Myth redefined to include new quality range for products. "Myth shift"

intervene is when sufficient tension exists in the system to motivate organizational actors to seek alternate methods for action. This occurs when the environment begins to withdraw expected reinforcements. As a heuristic device, four stages of a myth cycle are developed below. The example is a small company that finds its environment changing from one of non-competition to strong competition. Table 1 shows the four potential stages this company's myth-making system might experience. In this case, the company's defined mission—to produce only the finest quality products regardless of cost—will be used as the dominant organizational myth.

The ability to maintain a myth will be dependent upon a group's relative power within the organization. How each group then perceives its goal as being convergent with, or divergent from the organization's will help determine that group's acceptance of the overall organizational myth. The point is that myth evolution does not have to be a smooth process, but can be erratic, depending upon the support the organizational myth receives from divergent groups and the environment.

It is hypothesized that each myth stage will afford different opportunities for change efforts. Stage III, "Decline," in Table 1 corresponds to the period of developing tension. In the decline stage, the dominant myth is becoming detrimental to the organization's ability to react to its changing environment. At this stage, an intervention in the myth structure would be possible because of the internal strife, while at the same time averting further economic loss and subsequent disruption. Stage IV, "Reformulation," represents a final breakdown of the dominant myth structure. At this stage, there can be great tension and open conflict between myths that are vying for dominance.

The previous example of the U.S. auto industry will provide a case in point. The dominant myth that the average consumer would not purchase a compact car held sway until it nearly destroyed a major producer. In this case, the decline phase for this myth might have occurred when the environment began to withdraw its support, as evidenced by higher gasoline prices and the growing market share captured by foreign competitors. Presumably, re-examination of the myth would have been appropriate at this stage, averting the dramatic reformulation that was necessary to prevent disaster for the industry. It must be noted, however, that prior to the decline stage, intervention attempts would most likely have failed because of the dominant myth's past record of success.

Consultants may feel that the level of organizational diagnosis must correspond only to the anticipated "depth" of the intervention. Therefore, if the change is focused at the individual level, the relevant information would be background, attitude, and skill data.

Fleishman (1953), however, has noted the futility of training individuals and then returning them to groups that hold beliefs in opposition to those supporting the training. Since the dominant myth provides the basis for the group's definition of meaning and acceptable behavior, attempts to change individual behavior must still take into account the myth structure. Even for interventions that are not intended to change the myth, new behavioral or attitudinal components introduced into the system must be complementary.

For major interventions focused at altering a given myth or set of myths, the degree of change desired and the system's propensity to accept such change will be important factors. The greater the change required, presumably the further advanced the myth life cycle would be. This assumes that the system's resistance to change corresponds to a life-cycle progression. In either case, myth analysis becomes an important aspect of any diagnostic effort.

Seats of power

For an intervention to be successful, organizational groups with the power to institute or impede change must be involved in, if not take ownership of, the intervention. Diagnosing the seats of power within the organization can be facilitated by the analysis of the myth structure. The ability of a given group to impose its myth on other organizational members, as evidenced by how decisions are made, is an indicator of real organizational power.

Changing the alignment of power groups will necessitate accounting for such a shift in the organization's myth-making system.

The soft side of diagnosis

French, Bell, and Zawacki (1979), when discussing survey feedback as a diagnostic tool, state that "a successful change effort begins with rigorous measurement of the way in which the organization is presently functioning" (p. 185). From the preceding discussion, it becomes apparent that this diagnosis cannot and should not be restricted to "hard" data. Indirect data-gathering techniques must be defined and eventually refined for OD practitioners. This traditionally "soft" area of diagnosis has been left up to the individual consultant's intuition or style.

Since individuals within the organization rely upon the myth as an un-questioned basis for interpretation and decision making, it may not be appropriate to question them directly about these assumptions. Interventions, built on such models as Walton's (1969) third-party, peace making model, which rely upon organizational actors to reveal their assumptions, may not provide an accurate assessment of the myth-making system. The myth that underlies the perceptions of reality will be too deeply imbedded in the cognitive framework to be discerned by introspection concerning "hard" data. Diagnosis must include the collection of multilevel information through participant observation and ethnographic analysis (Pettigrew 1979) to completely determine the client system's need for, and the receptivity to, an intervention.

Myth-making interventions

In this section, we would like to propose possible interventions into the myth-making process of organizations. Our discussion here is tentative and meant to be more exploratory than prescriptive.

Demythifying

French and Bell (1973), as noted earlier, have suggested that OD consultants should concern themselves more with applying behavioral science principles in their intervention strategies. The suggested intervention, in this case, is the substitution of the lawful patterns of the behavioral sciences for the often subconscious myth patterns of clients. Practitioners, therefore, should spend more time training system actors in the principles of the behavioral sciences and developing skills for diagnosing and counter-acting common organizational myths. We wonder whether the behavioral sciences have advanced to the point of being able to advocate confidently their "truths" over the "realities" of the people who work and live in complex organizations.

Myth exchange

The basic assumption of this intervention is that if we dig deep enough into the relationships between actors in complex organizations, a significant part of those relationships will be based upon myths. Interventions focused upon allowing one actor to be able to see through the filters employed by other actors may help to improve communication and understanding. The first step for the practitioner is to demonstrate the existence of different logic systems and filters for viewing reality. System actors must learn to identify different organizational myths as alternative views of reality. The second step in this intervention is Maruyama's (1974) technique of "transpection," through which the actor attempts to "bracket" her or his own mythical thinking and reason in terms of the logics held by other actors, so that she or he can see the same reality others are seeing. Learning the other's language is a necessary prerequisite to entertaining the other's logic.

The next important step in the exchange is being able to have Actor A (having understood and being able to see with the frames used by Actor B) explain to Actor B just how she or he sees B's world. Practitioners employ similar interventions when they ask participants to engage in "imaging." In imaging, actors are asked to describe how other actors see them. This requires that a three-step process be followed: (1) recognizing differing myths, (2) being able to see the world the way others see it, and (3) being able to communicate what is seen in the logic categories of the original myth before exchange.

Myth balancing

The OD consultant can often note the existence of apparently mutually exclusive activities and events in organizations. Demythifying and exchange interventions may not be enough to cause adjustments in firmly held patterns of belief. Perhaps the intervention to employ here is to balance existing myths with a more multi-faceted or dialectical view of reality.

If the relevant myth suggests a rational goal perspective for all action, the practitioner might temper this perspective with a greater emphasis on the use of problem and goal discovery. On the other hand, suppose actors presume that there is little they can do to counteract the uncertainty of their environments. In this case, a greater understanding of planning and goal-setting models for action might help participants gain greater control over their environment.

In myth balancing, the focus is not on shattering people's deeply held myths, but in providing them with a fruitful way of thinking about their experiences. Rather than picking up on one or the other side of opposing views, the intervention should give participants a balanced view of reality:

to allow for the incorporation of existing beliefs by way of modification and balance, rather than rejection.

Myth enrichment

People like to reconstruct their experiences in a way that puts them in a better light. Their enhanced image of themselves and their organization can promote a higher quality of working life. Here the intervention should cultivate an enriched meaning of the organization and the roles and relationships of those working in it.

There are periods in an organization's life cycle when a crisis of meaning pervades: that is, when cohesion and logic have withered away or been shattered by rapidly changing or turbulent environments. In such cases, the myth-making system exists in a state of future shock. Interventions, which can aid the organization in finding meaningful interpretations and enrich feelings of purpose, direction, and importance, are appropriate.

If, on the other hand, the investigation involves the uncovering of dysfunctional or negative thought structures, then a useful intervention might be to substitute alternative imagery. Giving the client an enriched language may improve the perceptions of human relationships. Inventing and socializing participants into new myths may give social structure and process new meaning.

Summary

We envision this line of inquiry as having implications for the kinds of organizational interventions we would expect to see in the future. If we want to intervene in the cultural side of organizations, we must try to understand why and for what purposes myth making occurs. We have suggested that myths emerge to mediate and otherwise "manage" basic organizational dilemmas, such as unchartered ambiguities, basic uncertainties, turbulent environments, poorly understood technologies, and demands for depersonalization and rationalization of human action and purpose.

We have suggested that myths perform a variety of functions, such as: (1) legitimizing and rationalizing actions and consequences that are intended or completed; (2) moderating political interests and value systems; (3) explaining and creating cause and effect relationships; and (4) creating an environment where turbulence and complexity are buffered through rationalization and social reconstruction. To this list, we have added a final opinion: that myth making may fulfill a useful and healthy function in enriching human interaction.

Finally, we have offered a number of suggestions concerning the uses of myths for organizational diagnosis, and the types of interventions that might take advantage of myths and myth making in organizations. We believe the orientation and framework we have presented represents an alternative, useful way of studying organizations as cultural phenomena and enriching the meaning of organizational life.

References

Berger, P. L., & Luckman, T. *The social construction of reality.* Garden City, N.Y.: Anchor Books, 1967.

Clark, B. R. The organizational saga in higher education. *Administrative Science Quarterly* 1972, *17*, 178–184.

Cohen, A. R., Fink, S. L., Gadon, H., & Willits, R. D. *Effective behavior in organizations.* Homewood, Ill.: Irwin, 1976.

Emery, F. E., & Trist, E. L. The casual texture of organizational environment. *Human Relations,* 1965, *18*, 21–32.

Fleishman, E. A. Leadership climate, human relations training, and supervisory behavior. *Personnel Psychology,* 1953, *6*, 205–222.

French, W. L., & Bell, C. H. *Organization development: Behavioral science interventions for organization improvement.* Englewood Cliffs, N.J.: Prentice-Hall, 1973.

French, W. L., Bell, C. H., & Zawacki, R. A. *Organizational development: Theory, practice and research.* Dallas: Business Publications, 1979.

Greenfield, T. B. Organizations as social inventions: Rethinking assumptions about change. *Journal of Applied Behavioral Science,* 1973, *9*, 551–574.

King, A. S. Expectation effects in organizational change. *Administrative Science Quarterly,* 1974, *19*, 221–230.

Levi-Strauss, C. The structural study of myths. *Journal of American Folklore,* 1955, *68*, 428–444.

Levi-Strauss, C. *Structural anthropology.* New York: Basic Books, 1963.

March, J. G., & Olsen, J. P. *Ambiguity and choice in organizations.* Bergen, Norway: Universitetsforlaget, 1976.

March, J. G., & Simon, H. A. *Organizations.* New York: John Wiley, 1958.

Margulies, N. The myth and magic in OD: Powerful and neglected forces. *Business Horizons,* 1972, *15*, 77–82.

Maruyama, M. Paradigms and communication. *Technological Forecasting and Social Change,* 1974, *6*, 3–32.

Massarik, F. *Phenomenological interviewing.* Working paper, Behavioral and Organizational Science Study Center, University of California, Los Angeles, 1979.

Mintzberg, H. *The nature of managerial work.* New York: Harper & Row, 1973.

Mitroff, I. I., & Kilmann, R. H. On organization stories: An approach to the design and analysis of organizations through myths and stories. In R. H. Kilmann, D. P. Slevin, & L. R. Pondy (Eds.), *The manage-*

ment of organization design, Vol. I. New York: North Holland, 1976, pp. 189–208.

Perrow, C. *Complex organizations.* Glenview, Ill.: Scott, Foresman, 1972.

Pettigrew, A. M. *The creation of organizational structure.* Paper presented at Joint EIASM-Dansk Management Seminar on Entrepreneurs and the Process of Institution Building, Copenhagen, Denmark, May 1976.

Pettigrew, A. M. On studying organizational cultures. *Administrative Science Quarterly,* 1979, *24,* 570–581.

Pfeffer, J. Power and resource allocation in organizations. In B. M. Staw & G. R. Salancik (Eds.), *New directions in organizational behavior.* Chicago: St. Clair Press, 1977.

Selznick, P. *TVA and the grass roots.* New York: Harper & Row, 1966.

Sproull, L., & Weiner, S. *Easier "seen" than done: The function of cognitive images in establishing a new bureaucracy.* Unpublished manuscript, Stanford University, 1976.

Thompson, J. P. *Organizations in action.* New York: McGraw-Hill, 1967.

Tushman, M. L. A political approach to organizations: A review and rationale, *Academy of Management Review,* 1977, *2,* 206–216.

Walton, R. E. *Interpersonal peacemaking: Confrontations and third-party consultation.* Reading, Mass.: Addison-Wesley, 1969.

The Role of Ceremonials in Organizational Behavior
Harrison M. Trice,
James Belasco, and
Joseph A. Alutto

The analysis of organizational phenomena may be predicated upon numerous theoretical or empirical bases. For example, it is possible to adopt a strictly structural Weberian analysis of authority and power, a Parsonian functional analysis of interdependencies between organizational sub-units, or a "human relations" approach to the investigation of individual sentiments and internal or external group interactions.[1] Each of these perspectives, however, incorporates the implicit assumption that directly discernible links exist between the observable substance of organizational activities and the eventual achievement of specific system goals.

Although some researchers continue to assume that formal industrial systems have unidimensional goals centering around publicly stated organizational missions, it has been recognized increasingly that organizations allocate considerable human and physical resources to the simultaneous achievement of multiple goals, many of which appear to possess relevance for the fulfillment of objectives other than production or profit. Activities directed toward nonproduction goals have been identified as serving either system maintenance or adaptation functions and have been discussed most often under the rubric of goal displacement. Merton,[2] Selznick,[3] Messinger,[4] and Gusfield,[5] for instance, have identified and analyzed situa-

Reprinted with permission from *Industrial and Labor Relations Review* 23, no. 1 (October 1969): 40–51. © 1969 by New York State School of Industrial and Labor Relations, Cornell University.

1. For discussion and examples of such approaches see A. Etzioni, ed., *Complex Organizations* (New York: Holt, Rinehart and Winston, 1966); J. March, ed., *Handbook of Organizations* (Chicago: Rand-McNally, 1965); Robert K. Merton, *Social Theory and Social Structure* (Glencoe, Ill.: The Free Press, 1957); and N. Smelser, *Social Change In The Industrial Revolution* (Chicago: University of Chicago Press, 1959).

2. Merton, *op. cit.*, pp. 199–202.

3. Philip Selznick, *Leadership in Administration: A Sociological Interpretation* (Evanston, Ill.: Row, Peterson, 1957).

4. Sheldon L. Messinger, "Organizational transformation: A case study of a declining social movement," *American Sociological Review* 20, no. 1 (February 1955): 3–10.

5. Joseph R. Gusfield, "Social structure and moral reform: A study of the Woman's Christian Temperance Union," *American Journal of Sociology* 61, no. 3 (November 1955): 221–32.

tions in which the initial profit-production system goals were replaced by objectives related to simply the continuance of current procedures and structures.

Despite the recognition and acceptance of goal-displacement phenomena and the prevalence of organizational activities devoted to systems maintenance, most perspectives for the analysis of organizations include (either implicitly or explicitly) a postulate concerning the existence of overt, easily directed relationships between the allocation of system resources and the attainment of system goals. For example, although the role performances of "personnel administrators" have been categorized as organizational activities primarily directed toward the fulfillment of system maintenance requirements,[6] the assumption continues that there are connections between the actual substance of personnel administrator role behaviors and the attainment of system maintenance goals. Consequently, when investigating the achievement of maintenance functions, researchers often observe the actions of personnel administrators (for example, as they search out and listen to employee complaints) and attempt to determine the relative effectiveness of their behavior. This approach is predicated on the supposition that the more effectively such activities are carried out, the greater will be the probability of achieving desired organizational maintenance goals. Omitted from consideration is the question of whether or not the mere exhibition of these activities (seeking and recognizing employee complaints) has as great an organizational significance as an empirical estimate of performance efficiency and effectiveness. Stated somewhat differently, it might be profitable to determine the degree to which the simple occurrence or existence of personnel role behaviors (rather than the relative capabilities of any particular personnel administrator) contributes to the achievement of system maintenance.

This article suggests that determination of the actual substantive (i.e., manifest) efficiency or effectiveness with which personnel activities are conducted may have less relevance for an understanding of how institutional maintenance is achieved than would an analysis of the latent or symbolic value of such activities. Furthermore, it is contended that the investigation of organizational ceremonials is of particular utility for understanding how personnel administrators contribute to the achievement of general system goals. In essence, the purpose of this study is to systematically explore ceremonial aspects of personnel roles, with particular emphasis on the organizational significance of such activities.

Ceremonials in organizations

The discussion of ceremonials is usually associated with anthropological descriptions of primitive peoples. In reality, of course, ceremonials consti-

6. D. Katz and R. Kahn, *The Social Psychology of Organizations* (New York: John Wiley and Sons, 1966).

tute an essential element of all social systems, partially because they serve to stabilize and perpetuate the structure and functioning of system sub-units.[7] For present purposes, ceremonials are considered to be distinct sets of system practices, procedures, and techniques—which are accepted and desired by system members, which are associated with both "assumed" and "actual" contributions to organizational existence and which may or may not be known to system members. The survival of a ceremonial is not dependent on logically or empirically derived measures of effectiveness, value, or utility; its existence often is based on random learning or superstition.[8] Consequently, it is possible for organizational members to neither agree on nor know with any certainty the value or purpose of a ceremonial, while they continue to participate in and support such activities.

Generally (within organizational systems) ceremonials serve to structure, validate, and stabilize collective action, in part due to their being "passed along" to newcomers during periods of socialization. In this manner ceremonials provide perceptual and cognitive structuring for individuals confronted with new or ambiguous organizational stimuli. In so doing, ceremonials invest associated organizational behaviors with reality and legitimacy which enable the system and its members to undertake actions required for continued existence or growth.

Organizations tend to use ceremonials in at least three ways. First, they are employed during the socialization process to which all members are exposed in order to modify the initial perceptions of the newcomers. Socialization practices are designed to produce a set of values, norms, attitudes, and expectations in individuals which will be supportive of overall system operations. During such processes, emphasis is also placed on extinguishing potentially disruptive or dysfunctional behavioral tendencies.[9] As discussed below, selection and training phenomena encompass ceremonials of significant relevance for the socialization of system members.

Second, by generating consistency between the expectations of related role performers within a system, ceremonials perform valuable stabilizing functions. Such ceremonial activities act to support and sustain the authority of individual decision makers and, in a wholistic sense, the organization as an operational unit. Ceremonials serve this valuable function

7. For example see R. Linton, "A neglected aspect of social organizations," *American Journal of Sociology* 45, no. 6 (May 1940): 870–86; R. Linton, "Age and sex categories," *American Sociological Review* 7, no. 5 (October 1942): 589–603; and F. Young, "The function of male initiation ceremonies: A cross cultural text of an alternative hypothesis," *American Journal of Sociology* 67, no. 4 (January 1962): 370–96.

8. However, see the discussion of "survivals" in A. Gouldner, "The norm of reciprocity: A preliminary statement," *American Sociological Review* 25, no. 2 (April 1960): 161–78.

9. For example, see E. Gross, "Some functional consequences of primary controls in formal work organizations," *American Sociological Review* 18, no. 4 (August 1953): 368–73; and J. Alutto, "Identification: State and process considerations," *Cornell Journal of Social Relations* 2 (Spring 1967): 45–60.

especially during periods of role transition; they stabilize aspects of organizational structure and operation prior to, during, and following role change. In this respect ceremonials are employed to ease and quicken the transformation of organizational identities for system members.

Additionally, in an objective sense ceremonials facilitate the reduction of anxieties and ambiguities often experienced by members. This is particularly true when the problem or crisis requires the employment of nonsalient or nonexistent knowledge. System ceremonials may serve, at least in the short run, as acceptable substitutes for "real solutions" through generating affective feelings of familiarity, tension reduction, and certainty (whether real or imagined).

It should be borne in mind that ceremonials serve to structure the perceptions and expectations of both the participating role performers and others in the organization. Frequently, the ability to distinguish between the mythical and actual outcomes of ceremonials is retained only by individuals who may be characterized as interested nonsystem members or observers.[10] The perspectives of such individuals are not restricted by the system-wide acceptance of assumed relationships between specific activities and the fulfillment of particular organizational goals. Therefore, in order to determine the actual contributions of ceremonial activities to organizational structure and functioning, one should consider adopting at least three perspectives—that of the individual directly participating in ceremonial activities, that of related role performers within the organizational milieu, and that of outside observers.

Relevance of ceremonials for personnel administrators

One method of demonstrating the use of ceremonials in formal work organizations is to focus on the ceremonial aspects of one organizational position, the traditional system justification for such activities expressed in terms of associated goal achievements, and the actual impacts of such exhibited behaviors regardless of system assumptions. The particular focus of this article is on the role of the personnel administrator. The selection of this position was determined, in part, by literature suggesting that personnel activities contribute primarily to the achievement of maintenance goals rather than profit-production goals. This is relevant, since given the previously stated definition of a "ceremonial," we believe analysis of organizational ceremonials may be most appropriate to an understanding of activities contributing to the attainment of maintenance goals.

Unfortunately, of the many role behaviors exhibited by personnel administrators, those of basically a ceremonial nature probably are least

10. These individuals may be said to be nonsocialized, concerned, and relatively independent of system rewards.

understood by organizational analysts. A review of relevant literature reveals the identification and discussion of almost every conceivable personnel activity and related system consequence with little reference to their possible mythical or symbolic natures.[11] Conversely, it is curious that ceremonial aspects of personnel roles were among the first issues mentioned and described during our recent interviews with practicing personnel administrators. Furthermore, these role performers consistently indicated that ceremonial activities constitute an extensive and essential subset of their behaviors.[12]

As will become apparent, the observations reported here are basically impressionistic and qualitative in character. They have, however, been generated by in-depth interviews and observational data collected from over three hundred subjects. The subject pool consisted of one hundred ten personnel administrators from all levels and approximately two hundred twenty officials defined by personnel administrators as significant. The collection of research data and the generation, modification, and clarification of ideas presented in this study occurred during the period from 1966 to 1969.[13] Thus it should be noted that the identification of relevant ceremonial activities, as well as the exploration of their supposed and actual effects,[14] is predicated on the observations of personnel administrators, other management officials, and the authors.

11. See, for instance, Dale Hemming and Wendell French, "The Mythical Personnel Manager," *California Management Review* 3, no. 4 (Summer 1961): 24–38; Dalton E. McFarland, "The scope of the industrial relations function," *Personnel* 36, no. 1 (January–February 1959): 42–51; and Charles Myers and John Turnbull, "Line and staff in industrial relations," *Harvard Business Review* 34, no. 4 (July–August 1956): 113–21.

12. One *caveat* is important at this juncture. While this article places emphasis on ceremonial dimensions of the personnel role, the reader should not forget substantive aspects of that role. Similarly, our purpose is not to suggest that organizational life is composed solely or even mainly of ceremony and ritual. We intend merely to highlight determinants and consequences of ceremonials in organizations, specifically those associated with activities of personnel administrators.

13. This information was gathered in a series of structured interviews with and observations of personnel administrators and relevant role definers. The average length of an interview/observation series extended over 12 hours, with many exceeding 40 hours.

The data were gathered as part of a national study of personnel managers (who are members of the American Society of Personnel Administrators) and from an intensive study of personnel administrators located on the Niagara Frontier in western New York.

The first study was sponsored in part by the Society and by the New York State School of Industrial and Labor Relations, Cornell University; the second was sponsored in part by the Department of Organization, School of Management, State University of New York at Buffalo.

14. It should be apparent that such assumptions may be completely correct, partially fulfilled, or completely invalid (i.e., entirely mythical). Not surprisingly, it was discovered that most traditionally accepted assumptions were partially correct or justified on the basis of the "actual" consequences of ceremonial activities. In such instances, however, the anticipated outcomes, while present and easily identified, were often of secondary importance when compared with other unanticipated consequences.

Legitimation process

As has been stated, ceremonials are utilized to affect the perceptions and expectations of individuals prior to their initial participation in organizational activities, throughout the various stages of their membership in the system, and prior to their departure. Organizationally relevant modifications in attitudes and expectations often occur as a result of the officiation of personnel administrators at times of difficult role changes. Such participation clearly constitutes a set of ceremonial activities directed toward securing legitimacy for the proposed change. In this context, legitimation is defined in the Gross, Mason, and McEachern sense of the proclamation of the institutional legality of the change, which justifies its acceptance by both the role performer and his significant others.[15] The office of personnel administrator can legitimate system changes because it tends to be the single organizational repository of systematically derived "scientific" information concerning members and their motivations. As a consequence, the acceptance and support by personnel administrators lends an air of scientific validity to changes in status or position. Organizational members appear to reason, "If the specialist approves an action, the approval is justified on scientific grounds; and if a change is scientifically correct, it should be accepted by all concerned." This perceived stamp of scientific validity and legitimacy conferred by personnel administrators tends to facilitate the resolution of system member uncertainties about the suitability of individuals in instances of promotion as well as about lack of justice in cases of termination.

Furthermore, the visible participation of personnel administrators provides legitimacy by symbolizing a corporatewide approval of organizational changes. Any given line official, such as a plant manager, usually can speak only for a particular functional organizational group, since the authority inherent in his position is limited to that group. Personnel administrators, however, represent authority which appears to cross functional and organizational lines. Thus, not only is an individual's status change approved by line officials in a given department, but also through participation of the personnel administrator this change is stamped "approved" by the broader corporate organization. In this manner also, the participation in change activities by personnel administrators serves to structure the perceptions or expectations of organizational members and, simultaneously, to resolve associated tensions concerning the appropriateness of particular changes.

Personnel administrators appear to symbolize not only broad corporate

---

15. N. Gross, W. Mason, and A. McEachern, *Explorations in Role Analysis* (New York: John Wiley and Sons, 1958).

interests but also more general, societal concerns for social and individual justice. As the officially designated and informally recognized "keeper of the corporate conscience" concerning the fair and just treatment of human beings in the organization, the presence of a personnel administrator at times of status and role change apparently serves to indicate the change is just and fair for all concerned, especially for those who may *not* have been chosen. It is through the ceremonial intervention of this designated official that the perceptions and expectations of both the individual involved and related role partners are modified, while tensions associated with doubts about the wisdom of a change are resolved.

In some respects the legitimating function performed by personnel administrators closely parallels that of priests who officiate at the various stages of a person's life and death. Both the priest and the personnel administrator are assumed to represent a source of authority greater than that of the individuals involved. This authority is used, additionally, to sanction various occurrences which, without legitimation, are cause for great concern.

Interestingly, however, such ceremonials result in the legitimation of *both* individuals experiencing change (as discussed above) and participating personnel administrators. In the manner of a self-fulfilling prophecy, the physical presence of personnel administrators during critical periods (hiring, evaluation, training, promotion, dismissal) suggests to organizational members that personnel administrators are essential to these activities. Thus, while it is true that the participation of personnel managers in hiring or promotion ceremonials facilitates the legitimation of associated changes, these ceremonial activities also result in the legitimation of personnel administrators themselves.

It should be noted that this legitimation by association has beneficial outcomes for personnel administrators. Regardless of intention, increased participation by personnel officials in ceremonial activities may result in greater resource allocations to personnel functions than would occur otherwise. Furthermore, the power of personnel administrators may be increased by the type of symbolic rewards which organizational members often presume to be within the legitimate control of such officials: promotions, transfers, job evaluations, pay schedules, training opportunities, etc. The assumption that they control such highly valued and visible rewards may increase the ability of personnel officials to influence the behavior of others.

Ceremonials of relevance for individual role performers

Selection and placement activities provide excellent examples of legitimation practices with the main goal of structuring the expectations of individuals. Most selection and placement procedures involve elaborate testing and interviewing. Despite the fact that when judged solely on the basis of empirical evidence most of these procedures prove not to be particularly accurate in identifying the right person for the right job, they persist and proliferate.[16] The continuous employment of these procedures may depend on their symbolic value as ceremonials rather than any demonstrable utility as selection devices.

Elaborate selection procedures (aptitude tests, psychological tests, stress interviews, etc.) confront the applicant with a series of difficult and ambiguous situations which he assumes have a direct relationship to success in the job to which he aspires. In addition, the applicant knows these tests will be scored and his score compared with others. This provides the applicant with further incentive to perform well on the trials. Test difficulty, combined with heightened motivation to succeed, increases the value of the reward for performing well, i.e., acceptance into the organization; after all, "that which is difficult is more rewarding than that which is obtained easily." In essence, individuals appear to believe that if entry into an organization is a result of success in a series of difficult trials, then membership in that system must be valuable. Sophisticated selection procedures, then, increase the value of organizational membership, not only for the new initiate but also for the currently employed organizational member. For him the entry procedures provide evidence of the selectivity exercised by the organization: a process through which only those of greatest ability and value, himself included, are accepted.

In short, although selection procedures may not possess power to consistently select the "right" man for a job, they may facilitate the continuous and crucial organizational task of socializing both new and old system members. As a result of their apparent scientific rigor and of the legitimacy they effect, selection procedures (1) increase the commitment of a new initiate to the organization and thereby render him more susceptible to influence from the organization; (2) reinforce the perceptions and commitments of current members by reaffirming the value of system membership; (3) resolve questions for other system members concerning the competence and dependability of the individual; and (4) may establish a self-fulfilling prophecy by structuring the expectations of system colleagues in such a manner that those who perform exceptionally well during the trials tend to be organizationally successful since others *expect* them to succeed. Therefore, as the chief managers, interpreters, and general manipulators of selection and placement procedures, personnel administrators perform a vital ceremonial function.

16. H. G. Heneman, Jr., *Manpower Management: New Wrapping on Old Merchandise* (Minneapolis, Minn.: Industrial Relations Center, University of Minnesota, 1960); G. W. England and D. G. Peterson, "Selection and placement—The past ten years," in H. G. Heneman, ed., *Employment Relations Research* (New York: Harper and Brothers, 1960), pp. 43–72; and M. D. Dunwitte, "Personnel Management," *Seminal Review of Psychology* 13 (1962): 285–314.

Rites of passage

Organizational ceremonies concerned primarily with legitimation include a subset of activities which may be called "rites of passage."[17] These are employed in the socialization of individual actors and their role partners in new organizational positions. In effect, these ceremonial activities are designed to speed the acquisition of particular skills and expectations required to effectively consummate role changes.

In general, rites of passage have three distinct stages. First, the member in transition is removed from interaction with those performing organizational roles he will abandon. Along with others in transition between roles, the individual progresses, during a second stage, through a series of activities which bring him into close and frequent contact with persons occupying positions related to, and perhaps identical with, those he will enter. These interactions provide information about the technical and emotional demands to which he is expected to respond in his new position. In the final phase, ceremonial activities conclude with the introduction of the "changed" person into a new system of associations and expectations. Although little of a concrete, tangible nature actually may change, the individual progresses through a series of experiences which facilitate the acquisition of appropriate new role behaviors. Regardless of whether or not the intitiate has been exposed to training procedure which actually produced new skills or knowledge, the rite of passage forces him into a pattern of behavior relevant to his new role.[18]

Many managerial and supervisory training programs actually constitute effective rites of passage. For example, in one company included in our interview sample, all candidates for supervisory positions were given a two-day battery of screening tests, including supervisory aptitude scales and intelligence measures. As the first step in the rite, those who "passed" (and there were many who did not) were removed from their current jobs and placed in isolated training units where line supervisors instructed them in technical procedures and problems of supervision. At this point, once again, some did not "pass." At the third (or reincorporation) phase, occurring at the conclusion of training, the company put on an induction ceremony which included a speech by the production superintendent outlining the program the new initiates had been through and a cocktail party with the new supervisors as guests of honor. When the newly appointed foreman actually assumed his role, a brief shutdown of work occurred, and those employees he was to supervise heard about his "ordeal." Interestingly, ob-

17. Arnold van Gennep, *The Rites of Passage* (Chicago: University of Chicago Press, 1960). This book was translated by Monika B. Vizedom and Gabrielle L. Caffee.

18. For a discussion of the dynamics underlying the acquisition of roles see J. Alutto, "Role theory in propositional form" (Ph.D. dissertation, New York State School of Industrial and Labor Relations, Cornell University, 1968), pp. 61–81.

jective measurements undertaken by a system outsider indicate that neither the testing nor the training achieved any of their explicit goals. There appeared to be considerable belief on the part of many organizational members, however, that supervisors chosen and trained through these procedures performed their jobs well and acted like members of management. As a result, the procedures and practices have persisted.

The above provides examples of the various levels at which the impacts of ceremonials may be assessed. For the individual, the testing and training procedures serve to structure his expectations and perceptions of, and commitments to a new organizational role. The "trainee" experiences obvious organizational approval of his altered status and also gains some insight into the demands and expectations of others relevant to his new position. For other organizational members, the training procedures serve to reduce their anxieties concerning the desirability of the proposed change and, by transmitting cues to the effect that the new member is competent, also serve to establish the requisite conditions for meaningful role relationships. While it may be "objectively" true that overall initial selection decisions could have been generated as effectively by random identifications of trainees, organizational members believed the decisional criteria were appropriate and useful. Thus, the impact of training ceremonials rests with the belief in and acceptance by system members and not with empirical determinations of effectiveness.

Stability or equilibrium functions

An additional function of ceremonials is their contribution to the maintenance or achievement of organizational stability following technological or structural change. For instance, management training programs often generate clarification of new role expectations for both individual role performers and other related system members, while also facilitating the emergence of new informal groupings through which the expectations may be fulfilled. By providing an opportunity to bring difficult problems "out in the open" where they can be discussed in a nonthreatening manner, training facilitates the formation of new cliques and compatibility groups. Particularly for individuals considered marginal either before or after an organizational change, training may provide the only opportunity to reestablish realistic communication and affiliation networks and may constitute a mechanism for readmission into the mainstream of organizational life. In this sense, managerial training may result in the crystallization of new self-images for those experiencing change.

In a therapeutic sense, training also appears to fulfill the emotional needs of those involved in change. A pleasant feeling of well-being tends to be generated by participation in training sessions. Out of this euphoria may come a smoother functioning organization, one in which the sharing of anxiety produces emotionally satisfying results.

Similarly, as a result of providing the trainee with an opportunity to share his problems with others, training ceremonials usually foster discovery by the trainee that he is not the only individual experiencing uncertainty about the "right thing to do." In this manner many trainees come to understand that their own feelings of isolation and frustration are not only shared by others but also are caused by common experiences. This therapeutic value is perhaps best illustrated by requests for the formation of a kind of "supervisors anonymous" where former trainees can meet periodically and discuss mutual problems.

Equally as important, training also indicates the organization cares about the problems of its people. By asking persons to attend a training program and involving them in its ceremonials (sending formal memoranda to them, placing telephone calls to their place of work, and presenting graduation certificates), the organization indicates it does know they exist. This feeling of inclusion increases the sense of identification of each trainee with the organization. Attendance at training sessions, formal memos, telephone calls, and certificates are all visible symbols of the trainee's importance. At the same time, such extensive formal recognition helps to convince trainees that they are and will be performing tasks of significance. Thus, training has a therapeutic commitment-producing effect in addition to that of maintaining consensus.

In short, whether or not training accomplishes its stated objectives, it clearly serves as a mechanism both for preventing the tensions surrounding change from disrupting an organization and for socializing neophyte role occupants to new expectations and clique patterns. Training also enables the organization, acting through the personnel administrator, to minister to the emotional needs of system members in somewhat the same manner as a religious organization serves the religious needs of believers through its clergy.

Not only do the traditional activities performed by personnel administrators legitimate many types of organizational changes, they also serve to remove or reduce anxieties concerning certain status quo conditions. As one examines facets of organizational life, it becomes obvious there are many anxieties which arise from "the way things are today." Many of these appear to surround the distribution of rewards and authority in organizations, and at least two activities normally assigned to personnel administrators directly effect the perpetuation of internal system structures serving to allocate rewards and authority.

Questions of the appropriateness of wage and other reward differentials are resolved through appeals to established job evaluation procedures. The utilization of such symbols to legitimate the status quo tends to be effective because wage and salary programs employ apparently rational, scientific techniques involving the determination and manipulation of quantitative rather than qualitative measures. Yet in our interviews, several personnel administrators defined job evaluation as "the systematic application of bias to the ranking of jobs," implying that while job evaluation may have the virtue of consistency, it is far from being scientific. Any practitioner can point, of course, to sources of error in these programs: jobs raised in order to meet competitive labor market conditions or jobs designed for a specific individual and then evaluated to give him sufficient salary potential. The main organizational value of job evaluation lies not in its ability to precisely weigh jobs, but rather in its "scientific sounding" approach to this problem. In turn, this in and of itself, is sufficient to justify (from the perspective of organizational members) existing salary structures, thereby reducing organizational anxieties surrounding the differential distribution of rewards.

For much the same reason, performance appraisal programs serve to buttress the current distribution of authority in organizations. Regardless of the procedures employed, implicit in the implementation of performance appraisal programs is a recognition by both the superior and subordinate of their role relationships. That is, the mere act of appraising performance reminds the superior that he is the superior (or else why evaluate performance?) and the subordinate that he is a subordinate (or else why participate in the evaluation?). In short, the mere act of participation in the process of performance appraisal reinforces and legitimates organizational authority structures.

Symbolic embodiment of organizational values

In part, ceremonials affect perceptions and expectations by providing symbols which remind members of central organizational values. In much the same manner that the Senate of the United States employs a chaplain to symbolize its concern for religion and the righteousness of each member, the personnel administrator symbolizes the corporate organization's concern for fair and equitable treatment of organizational members. Through a process of association similar to that previously discussed in terms of legitimation, the personnel administrator's existence imputes such a concern to each and every organizational member, particularly "members of management."

In reality, then, the personnel administrator provides a visible symbol (to both members of the organization and outsiders) of the ideal towards which the organization strives in dealing with employees: an ideal which, because it is an ideal, need never be attained. The mere provision of this symbol reminds system members of their responsibilities for the human aspects of their organizational roles. It may be that the basic function of the personnel administrator is not to *guarantee* the just treatment of individuals but rather to symbolize the organization's *intention* to strive toward equitable behavior.

The insider-outsider

As previously discussed, the personnel administrator serves to represent general societal values of fairness and justice to the organization and its members. This means that the personnel administrator functions as an insider-outsider: he performs a role inside the organization which advocates the position of those interests outside the organization. This inevitably marks the personnel role as different from other organizational roles concerned primarily with internal matters. Such a peculiar function may generate doubts about the organizational loyalty of personnel role performers. This uncertainty contributes to feelings of organizational marginality and poses one of the most serious dilemmas confronting personnel practitioners. On the one hand, the successful conduct of the role is dependent on the administrator's relationship with other organizational roles. Yet the very nature of this insider-outsider function (i.e., as an advocate of outside organizational values) cuts personnel administrators off from meaningful relationships with the role performers over whom they must exert influence. This marginality and conflict often causes personnel administrators to physically and psychologically withdraw by becoming extensively and actively involved in external organizational activities such as community work, activities of chambers of commerce, and professional groups.

This insider-outsider role has another dimension. As a representative of extraorganizational concerns, by definition the personnel administrator becomes a nonparticipant in organizational struggles between employees and superiors. As a nonparticipant (or at least a relative neutral), he is in a position to receive "secret information" from both sides. A parallel might be drawn between the priest, who is in a position to receive information from parishioners concerning their sins, weaknesses, and transgressions, and the personnel administrator, who is in a position to receive information from organizational members about their machinations and organizational transgressions.

This access to secret knowledge brings, at one and the same time, considerable power and pain. For instance, such knowledge about organizational members can be potentially dangerous to them. The best defense against leakage of this threatening information is to structure the possessor's role so that he has only minimal contact with other persons in the organization who might capitalize on such information[19] as well as attempt to discredit the possessor. Such actions by system members tend to further exacerbate the marginality of personnel administrators.

Nevertheless, because of possession of secret information, personnel administrators are often in a position to accrue considerable potential

19. For a discussion of the importance of controlling the visibility aspects of role behavior see *ibid.* chaps. 3, 5, and 6.

power over certain individuals within their organizations. The possession of secret knowledge enables the administrator to exchange silence on certain issues for benefits such as status, deference, inclusion, etc. Thus, the phenomenon is often seen of public inclusion of the personnel administrator in high councils but a private discounting of the views of this role occupant as other organizational officials balance the need to prevent the personnel administrator from using the knowledge he possesses with their desires to retain control of the enterprise.

Summary

Ceremonials are an important aspect of organizational life. The analysis of ceremonials may be particularly relevant to the attainment of organizational goals which concern the building and maintenance of the organization over time. In respect to personnel administrators, relevant ceremonials serve to facilitate the resolution of problems associated with organizational selection, role transition, organizational and technological change, and the maintenance or legitimation of authority structures—all problems which must be managed if the organization is to survive.

The analysis of ceremonial activities has three interesting implications. First, by providing relatively satisfying, apparently simple solutions to complex and perplexing problems, ceremonials tend to perpetuate themselves. As with the creation of communities, they tend to "outlive their usefulness." Second, ceremonials probably render organizational life, with all of its buzzing impersonality, more tolerable. This may be a major functional value of ceremonials in organizations. Finally, as a result of continual assumptions concerning the effectiveness of ceremonials in resolving organizational problems and the fact that ceremonials often outlast the substantive reasons which gave rise to them, ceremonials may generate unintended and unwarranted organizational resistance to change.

Researchers in general have avoided examining the ceremonial dimensions of organizations and the manner in which organizations utilize ceremonials. This area offers a rich field for further scientific research into understanding, explanation, and prediction of organizational behavior.

Symbols, Patterns, and Settings: An Optimistic Case for Getting Things Done

Thomas J. Peters

The most important decisions are often the least apparent. —Karl Weick

What tools come to mind when you think about changing an organization? If you came up through the ranks in the 1950s and 1960s, the answer is quite likely to be divisionalizing and developing a strategic planning system. Shifting the organizational structure and inventing new processes are still options for change. But increasingly thorny and overlapping international, competitive, and regulatory problems call for increasingly complex responses—and such responses are getting increasingly difficult to devise and problematical in their application.

It is reasonable to propose, however, that an effective set of change tools is actually embedded in senior management's daily message sending and receiving activities, and that these tools can be managed in such a way as to energize and redirect massive, lumbering business and government institutions. The tools will be characterized as symbols (the raw material), patterns (the systematic use of the raw material), and settings (the showcase for the systematic use).

It is not suggested that these tools merely be added to the traditional arsenal of formal change instruments—primarily structure and process. Rather, it will be argued that historically effective prescriptions are losing some of their impact, and their formal replacements—such as the matrix structure—have comparatively little leverage. Moreover, the typical top management is seldom around for much more than five or six years—too little time in which to leave a distinctive and productive stamp on a large, history-bound institution solely by means of the available formal change alternatives. Hence effective change may increasingly depend on systematic use of the informal change mechanisms, derived from coherent daily actions.

Some speculations

My thesis in this article is that there are a variety of practical controlled change tools appropriate to today's complex and ambiguous organization settings. Most have been around a long time and need only to be consciously packaged and managed. Some are rather new. Few have been thought of as major instruments for achieving organizational redirection. Almost all are associated with the informal organization.

Figure 1 arrays some of these change tools along the previously noted dimensions of controllability and speed of change, and figure 2 presents some mundane change tools. By briefly assessing the reasons for the failure or obsolescence of the conventional tools and their successors (shown here as having drifted to the low-control, low-speed category), a very general rationale for the nature of the new change-tool candidates can be developed. Then each new category of tools can be assessed in turn.

There are at least two reasons why the conventional solutions have failed to achieve their full promise or have declined in effectiveness. One is that none of them takes time explicitly into account. In the case of structural solutions, management typically miscalculates in two different ways. On the one hand, it grossly underestimates the growing time lag between changed structure and changed behavior. On the other hand, it overestimates their durability under growing environmental pressures and consequently tends to leave them in place long after they have outlived their effectiveness.

The second reason for the weakness of conventional solutions is over- or underdetermination. Several solutions seem to rest on an overestimation of

Speed of Short-Term Change

		Low	High
Control Over Direction of Change	High	Manipulation of symbols—a Patterns of activity —b Settings for interaction—c 1	Single element structural thrust focusers Total systems of top managers interaction Dominating value 2
	Low	4 Overdetermined approaches: • Complex planning systems • Multiple project teams • Matrix structures Underdetermined approaches: • Bottom-up team building	3 Change for change sake: • Structure • Senior managers

Figure 1. Speculation about current change tools

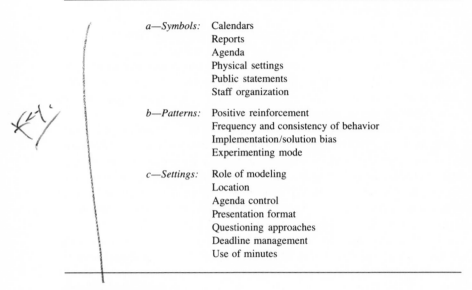

a—Symbols: Calendars
Reports
Agenda
Physical settings
Public statements
Staff organization

b—Patterns: Positive reinforcement
Frequency and consistency of behavior
Implementation/solution bias
Experimenting mode

c—Settings: Role of modeling
Location
Agenda control
Presentation format
Questioning approaches
Deadline management
Use of minutes

Figure 2. Mundane tools

managers' ability to determine the best way to accomplish great purposes—overdetermination. For example, complex planning systems, multiple project teams, and the matrix structure proceed from the implicit
assumption that effective organizing flows from figuring out the correct
wiring diagram—an assumption increasingly at odds with today's organizational tasks. Kopper's chief executive officer, Fletcher Byrom, recently
remarked, "Of all the things that I have observed about corporations, the
most disturbing has been a tendency toward over-organization, producing a
rigidity that is intolerable in an era of rapidly accelerating change."

At the other end of the spectrum—underdetermination—bottom-up
team building has been based on the opposite presumption: Overall organizational purposes can be largely ignored; seeding effective new behavior
patterns at the bottom of the organization or in ranks of middle management will somehow eventuate in desirable organizational performance
levels.

The proposed "new" change tools partially address both issues. First,
they explicitly take time into account, recognizing both that change typically comes slowly as the result of the application of many tools and that
the organizational focus of prime importance today is temporary and will
almost certainly have changed substantially four or five years hence. Second, they are tools of the experimenter: That is, they neither assume an
ability to fix organizational arrangements with much precision—the failing

of overdetermination—nor do they ignore purposiveness—the failing of underdetermination.

Obsession with the mundane

Cell 1 of figure 1 (high-control, low-speed change), the realm of what my colleagues and I have come to call "mundane tools," reflects the notion that the management of change—small or large—is inextricably bound up with the mundane occurrences that fill an executive's calendar.

By definition, managing the daily stream of activities might be said to consist of the manipulation of symbols, the creation of patterns of activity, and the staging of occasions for interaction. The mundane tools are proposed as direct alternatives to structural manipulation and other grand solutions to strategic organization needs. Conscious experimentation with these tools can provide a sound basis for controlled, purposive change.

Manipulation of symbols

Because they have so often been applied by the media to the performances of politicians intent on reshaping or repairing an image, the terms *symbolic behavior* and *symbol manipulation* have lately acquired something of a pejorative connotation: symbol vs. substance. In a much more basic sense, however, symbols are the very stuff of management behavior. Executives, after all, do not synthesize chemicals or operate lift trucks; they deal in symbols. And their overt verbal communications are only part of the story. Consciously or unconsciously, the senior executive is constantly acting out the vision and goals he is trying to realize in an organization that is typically far too vast and complex for him to control directly.

What mundane tools might best aid the executive interested in effecting change through symbol manipulation? To signal watchers, which includes nearly everyone in his organization, there is no truer test of what he really thinks is important than the way he spends his time. As Eli Ginsberg and Ewing W. Reilley have noted: "Those a few echelons from the top are always alert to the chief executive. Although they attach importance to what he says, they will be truly impressed only by what he does."

Is he serious about making a major acquisition? The gossip surrounding his calendar—Has he seen the investment banker?—provides clues for senior and junior management alike.

As reported in *Fortune*, Roy Ash's early activities after assuming the reins at Addressograph-Multigraph suggest mastery of the calendar and other mundane tools:

> Instead of immediately starting to revamp the company, Ash spent his first several months visiting its widely scattered operations and politely asking a lot of searching questions. . . . His predecessors had always summoned subordinates to the headquarters building, which had long

lived up to its official name, the Tower. Rather than announcing his ideas, Ash demonstrated them. He left his office door open, placing his own intercom calls to arrange meetings, and always questioned people in person, not in writing. Then he removed some of the company's copying machines "to stop breeding paperwork." Spotting a well-written complaint from an important customer in Minneapolis, Ash quickly flew off to visit him. As he now explains, "I wanted the word to get around our organization that I'm aware of what's going on." Ash's next dramatic step to reshape company attitudes will be moving its headquarters to Los Angeles . . . he justifies the move primarily on psychological grounds. "We must place ourselves in a setting where—partly through osmosis—we get a different idea of our future." For much the same reason, he wants to change the corporation's name, too.

Calendar behavior includes review of reports and the use of agenda and minutes to shape expectations. What kinds of questions is the executive asking? Does he seem to focus on control of operating costs, quality, market share? How is his memory about what was "assumed" last month? Last quarter? What kinds of feedback is he giving? What sorts of issues get onto his agenda?

Other symbolic actions include the use of physical settings and public statements. By attending operating meetings in the field, the top man can provide vital evidence of his concerns and the directions he wants to pursue. By touching or ignoring a particular theme, a public statement—boilerplate to a skeptical outsider—can lead to a rash of activity. In a talk to investment bankers, a president devoted a paragraph to new departures in an R&D area that had previously been underfunded. Almost overnight, a wealth of new proposals began bubbling up from a previously disenchanted segment of the labs.

Last, his use of his personal staff—its size, their perquisites, how much probing he allows them to do—will indicate, not only the chief executive's style of doing business, but the direction of his substantive concerns as well.

The executive's ability to manage the use of symbols is at the heart of the case for optimism. Literally at his fingertips, he has powerful tools—his day-timer and phone—for testing the possibilities of change and, over time, substantially shifting the focus of the organization.

Patterns of activity

Success or failure in exploiting these simple tools is seen in the pattern of their use. Richard E. Neustadt in *Presidential Power* maintained:

> The professional reputation of a President in Washington is made or altered by the man himself. No one can guard it for him; no one saves

him from himself. . . . His general reputation will be shaped by signs of pattern in the things he says and does. These are the words and actions he has chosen, day by day.

In short, the mundane tools that involve the creation and manipulation of symbols over time have impact to the extent that they reshape beliefs and expectations. Frequent, consistent, positive reinforcement is an unparalleled shaper of expectations—and, therefore, inducer of change.

Patterns of positive reinforcement can be applied in at least two ways: (1) using praise and designing positive reinforcement schemes for individuals or groups, and (2) allowing the bad to be displaced by the good, instead of trying to legislate it out of existence.

The White House, for example, has historically made meticulous use of the tools of praise. Selecting the attendees for major events and controlling the use of various classes of presidential letters of praise is a key activity controlled by very senior staff and the president himself.

Along the same lines, a research vice-president, responsible for about 2,000 scientists, has his executive assistant provide him with a sample of about 50 reports produced each month. He sends personal notes to the authors, often junior, of the best half-dozen or so.

Without touching on the complex ramifications of reinforcement theory, these instances merely support the point that senior managers are signal transmitters, and signals take on meaning as they are reiterated. Moreover, there is ample evidence that giving prominence to positive efforts and exposing them to the light of day induces constructive change far more effectively than trying to discourage undesired activities through negative reinforcement. As an associate of mine succinctly observed, "It's a hell of a lot easier to add a new solution than attack an old problem." An example illustrates the point in a broader context:

The information system unit of a multibillion-dollar conglomerate had a disastrously bad reputation. Rather than "clean house" or develop better procedures, the vice-president/systems installed, with some fanfare, "Six Programs of Excellence." Six reasonably sizable projects—out of an agenda of over 100—were singled out for intensive management attention. The effort was designed to build, from the inside out, a reputation for excellence that would gradually increase user confidence and group motivation alike.

Frequency and consistency are two other primary attributes of effective pattern shaping. A pattern of frequent and consistent small successes is such a powerful shaper of expectations that its creation may be worth the deferral of ambitious short-term goals:

In one large company, the top team wished to establish a climate in which new product development would be viewed more favorably by all divisional managers. Rather than seeking an optimal product slate the first year—with the attendant likelihood of a high failure rate—the top team instead consistently supported small new product thrusts that gradually "made believers out of the operators."

Since consistency becomes a driving force in inducing major change over time, the executive committed to change ought to be constantly on the lookout for opportunities to reinforce activities, even trivial activities, that are congruent with his eventual purpose. He scours his in-basket for solutions—bits of completed action—to be singled out as exemplars of some larger theme. Support of completed actions typically generates further actions consistent with the rewarded behavior. The executive who keeps on testing tools to produce this result will find that by varying his patterns of reinforcement he can substantially influence people's behavior over time, often several levels down in the organization. (Figure 3 offers advice to pattern shapers based on my research.)

Settings for interaction

The third class of mundane tools is settings. Senior management's development of a symbolic pattern of activities occurs somewhere. These are some of the setting-variables that can directly reinforce or attenuate the impact of the symbolic message:

Presence or absence of top managers

Psychologists now agree on the high impact of modeling behavior—the most significant finding of the last decade, according to many. The senior executive's presence and his minor actions can bring to life and rather precisely shape an institutional point of view—about investment, competitive response, the importance of tight controls. The careers of top executives abundantly reflect their intuitive awareness of this point.

Location of groups and meetings

Moving a meeting or a staff unit or a new activity is often a dramatic signal that something new is afoot. At one company, the previously isolated top team began holding meetings in the field, thus signaling a sincere intent to make decentralization work after three previous failures.

Agenda control

Since agenda directly symbolize priorities, agenda management can be a potent tool. A division's top team changed its basic approach to management to suddenly devoting more than half its meeting time to issues of project implementation, previously a relatively minor item on its agenda. To cope with the new questions they were getting from the top, managers throughout the organization were soon following suit.

The world is a stream of problems that can be activated, bound in new ways, or bypassed.

His associates are pattern watchers and are acutely aware of his and their impact, over time, on each other.

Above all, timing is important.

An early step in analyzing a situation is careful assessment of the levers he does or does not control.

Most change occurs incrementally, and major change typically emerges over a long period of time.

Much of the change induced in subordinates results from consciously acting as a model himself.

Frequent rewards—directed at small, completed actions—effectively shape behavior over time.

Good questioning, focusing on the short term, helps him and his subordinates learn about system responses to small nudges one way or another.

Creating change in organizations is facilitated by unusual juxtaposition of traditional elements with small problem-making subunits that seed changes.

Long-term goals are of secondary importance since control of change follows from learning about multiple, small, real-time adjustments.

Consistency in delivering small, positive outcomes is an efficient and effective way to manipulate others' perceptions when attempting to induce change.

Patience, persistence, self-control, and attention to the mundane are often keys to achieving small, consistent outcomes.

Surprise should usually be avoided in an attempt to present stable expectations to peers, subordinates, and bosses.

It is possible approximately to calculate the opportunity value of others' and one's own time, thus substantially increasing the ability to pick change opportunities.

Adding new solutions is often better than tackling old problems; that is, as much or more change and learning can ensue from the effective implementation of new solutions as from time-consuming efforts to overcome typically deep-seated resistance to old problems.

Figure 3. Guiding assertions for the pattern shaper

Attendance

Who attends which meetings, and who presents material, can signal new approaches to management and new substantive directions. When one company president decided to force his vice-presidents, instead of junior staff, to present reviews and proposals, the atmosphere of his meetings perceptibly changed. All at once, heated battles between analytic guns-for-hire over numerical nuances were replaced by sober discussion of the issues.

Presentation/decision memorandum formats

Format control can shift managers' focus to new issues and fundamentally reshape the process of organizational learning. One management team vastly improved its approach to problem solving by meticulously starting every decision presentation with a historical review of "the five key assumptions." At a second major corporation, the chief executive brought to life his major theme—focus on the competition—by requiring all decision documents to include much greater depth of competitive analysis.

Questioning approaches

Among the clearest indicators of the direction or redirection of interest are the sorts of questions the top team consistently asks. Accounts of the working methods of Roy Ash, Harold Geneen, and others stress their unique questioning style and its pervasive effect on the issues the organization worries about. For instance, *Forbes* describes how A. W. Clausen of the Bank of America shifted concern from revenue to profit: "Ask an officer, 'How's business,' and you'd immediately hear how many loans he's made. I tried to leave my stamp by making everyone aware of profit."

Approaches to follow-up

Effective use of minutes, ticklers, and history can become the core of top management's real control system. Genuine accountability was introduced into a lax management organization by introducing a "blue blazer" system that made follow-up a way of life. In tracking issues, whenever operating executives' proposals had been modified by staff, the impact of the changes was explicitly noted. This put the staff and its contribution on stage. Accountability was further substantially sharpened by revamping a previous forecast-tracking procedure to highlight assumptions and outcomes.

Professor Serge Muscovici has asserted that:

> Social status, leadership, majority pressure . . . are not decisive factors in social influence. A minority can modify the opinions and norms of a majority, irrespective of their relative power or social status, as long as, all other things being equal, the organization of its actions and the expression of its opinions and objectives obey the conditions . . . of consistency, autonomy, investment, and fairness.

Fairness takes on added meaning in the context of mundane management tools, intended as they are to shape expectations, over time, through minor shifts of emphasis. To be effective, the management of expectations must be unfailingly honest, realistic, and consistent. Violation of this property, especially if perceived as intentional, automatically destroys the effectiveness of patterned symbolic manipulation.

Richard Neustadt captures the essence of the use of mundane tools:

> [Franklin D. Roosevelt] had a strong feeling for a cardinal fact in gov-
> ernment: That Presidents don't act on policies, program, or personnel
> in the abstract; they act in the concrete as they meet deadlines set by
> due dates, act on documents awaiting signatures, vacant posts awaiting
> appointees, officials seeking interviews, newsmen seeking answers,
> audiences waiting for a speech.

Note that the tools he mentions are all at hand. Though rarely disruptive or
threatening, they have the potential to revolutionize an organization's ways
of thinking and doing over time—particularly if, instead of being used intuitively and implicitly, they are consciously packaged and managed.

Major change via temporary focus

Big bureaucracies are run largely on inertia. Salesmen make their calls,
products roll off the line, and checks get processed without any intervention by senior management. The task of today's slate of top managers,
then, might well be viewed as time-bound: "How do we make a distinctive, productive difference over the next four years?" Or, "How do we
leave our mark?"

It has been suggested above that certain prescriptions—undertaking
structural shake-ups or introducing new formal processes—are less effective than they once were in altering corporate perspectives. Constructing
temporary systems to redirect the organization's attention and energies may
be a better way to coax along institutional change. The high-impact devices
proposed for this purpose are a natural extension of the mundane tools just
discussed, in that in and of themselves they act as strong signals (or accumulations of symbols) of attention to new corporate directions.

Major—but limited—shifts in emphasis have been accomplished by
public and private bureaucracies through three kinds of temporary focusing
mechanisms: single-element focusers, systems of interaction, and dominating values. Each of these focusing mechanisms is discussed below.

Single-element focusers

To begin with, single-element focusers have been used time and again as
a strategic signaling and implementing device. Consider how General
Motors, a massive bureaucracy by any definition, recently adapted more
swiftly than any other major automobile maker to the need to downsize its
entire product line:

> The project center [says *Fortune*] was probably GM's single most im-
> portant managerial tool in carrying out that bold decision. . . . It has
> eliminated a great deal of redundant effort, and has speeded numerous

new technologies into production. Its success . . . rests on the same delicate balance between the powers of persuasion and coercion that underlines GM's basic system of coordinated decentralization.

Some other business examples of single-element focusers similarly wrested the attention of major organizations—temporarily—to something new:

Harris Corporation created an interdivisional technology manager to oversee transfer of technology—Harris's "main strategic thrust"—between previously isolated groups.

Product family managers—three to five senior men with small staffs— were introduced as a means of wrenching the attention of two huge functional bureaucracies toward the marketplace; the creation of these high-visibility positions was thought to be a clearer, more efficient signal of strategic redirection than a major structural shift. Similarly, the establishment of just one job, executive vice-president for marketing, at White Consolidated is credited with sprucing up the long-stagnant sales of White's newly acquired Westinghouse appliance group.

ITT's product group managers are a free-wheeling band of central staff problem solvers and questioners who have brought a common market-based orientation to a highly diversified conglomerate.

An oil company's central technology staff (a roving group of top-ranking geologists and engineers) has markedly upgraded exploration and production quality.

In surveying these and other instances of success, some common threads can be identified (see figure 4). Most important of these is singleness of focus. That is, the single-element focuser should not be confused with multiple-team project management. Its effectiveness rests on achieving a limited, temporary focus on one, or at most two, major new items. Note, also, that the structural manifestations tend to be about half staff, half line. On one hand, the focusing element often has the look of a traditional staff unit, but its manager, as the unmistakable agent of the top team's highest priority, visibly intrudes on operating managers' territory.

Kenneth Arrow, the Nobel laureate economist, describes an analogous approach to galvanizing massive government institutions into acting on new agenda: "Franklin D. Roosevelt . . . saw the need of assigning new tasks to new bureaus even though according to some logic [such a task] belonged in the sphere of an existing department." Congressional Budget Office Deputy Director Robert Levine summarizes the thesis this way:

Since it seems impossible . . . to change overall public bureaucratic systems substantially either by changing their direction at the top by devices like program budgeting, or by changing their culture à la orga-

Success Characteristic	Related Failure Mode
Focus: Limited number of "devices," no more than two and preferably one.	Use—usually simultaneously—of many devices (e.g., teams, meetings) dilutes attention and can become just a bureaucratic encumbrance.
Focus within focus: The limited device must, moreover, have a limited agenda and not take on everything at once.	Limited devices charged with turning the world around in 12 months are likely to fail (i.e., a failure of expectation).
Incumbent: Manned with a very senior contender(s) for the top.	Selection of good men, but not those recognized as members of "the top ten" or surefire top ten contenders.
Start-up: Either a pilot element (e.g., one product family manager of an eventual set of five) or a "pilot decision," (e.g., a visible output—perhaps a decision—by the new event/process) will affect acceptance.	Groups/processes invented, but no clear sign of early progress or shift of emphasis.
Need: A clear-cut, agreed-upon business need for the element exists.	The new element's agenda is not clear and/or is not viewed as urgent.
CEO role: CEO is reinforcer of project *and* lets it make its mark.	CEO nonsupporter or a supporter but preempts the new role by continuing to play the game by the old rules.
Conscience: Systems—formal or informal—to "watch" the top team and ensure that actions are being taken consistent with the purpose of the shift.	Element "implemented," but top team regularly takes decisions inconsistent with purpose.
Implementation duration: Even though single device, implementation should be expected to take a couple of years at least.	Since it is only a simple new element, put it in place and let it go.

Figure 4. Attributes of single-element focusing devices

nization development, it may be useful to look for a third class of solutions . . . specifically, trying to treat bureaucratic units as if they were competing business units. . . . Even if it worked very well, this would be less well than program budgeting or organization development if they worked well. But the contention here is that in the real world this alternative concept is substantially more likely to work.

System of interaction

Attention-directing organization elements are only the first of the three high-impact focusing mechanisms to be considered here. The second is the construction of a coherent system of senior management interaction, again with the purpose of shifting management attention either to some new direction or to some new method of reaching overall consensus. Under some circumstances, this second mechanism might even be preferred to the first. On the one hand, a system of forums has perhaps less symbolic impact than a single high-visibility element. On the other hand, however, such a system does directly manipulate the agenda of senior managers.

Systems of forums designed to turn top management's eyes to new horizons range from one company's five "management forums"—a formal system of interaction designed to force regular discussion of strategic issues—to a president's regular informal breakfast meetings where senior executives, free of their staffs and the attendant bureaucratic insulation, engage in untrammeled discussion of key issues.

One particularly striking class of forums is special operating or strategic review sessions. Texas Instruments, ITT, and Emerson Electric, among others, focus top-management direction setting in regular sessions where— as everyone in the organization knows—"things get done" or "the buck stops." Another notable example is cited by *Fortune:*

> One of the enduring questions of management, a subject of constant concern and endless analysis, is how a large corporation can best monitor and direct operations spread over many industries and throughout many parts of the world. A number of companies have sought the answer in ponderous and elaborate management mechanisms. . . . But there is at least one large company whose top management continues to rely on plain, old-fashioned, face-to-face contact. Richard B. Loynd, the president and chief operating officer of Eltra Corp . . . visits each of Eltra's thirteen divisions as many as eight times a year, and puts managers through formal grillings that last several hours at a time. The people at Eltra call this the "hands-on" management technique. Loynd says: "I think I spend more time with our operating people than the president of any other major company."

Invariably, like the single-element focusers, these systems are temporary in nature. Since most of them tend to become rigid and lose their unique value in the course of time, they need to be modified at intervals. One executive reports:

> The monthly breakfast meeting finally got the chairman and his operating presidents away from staff. For two years these sessions, preliminary to the regular monthly review, became the real decision-making/enervating forum. But then the staffs caught on. One by one, *they* began coming to breakfast.

Dominating value

The discussion of change mechanisms has had a consistent undercurrent. The three classes of mundane tools have been presented as apparently trivial signaling devices for redirecting organizational attention and energy over time toward a theme, while the first two major change tools have been characterized as just larger-scale or agglomerated devices for the same purpose.

One final tool, which may be labeled the *dominating* value, addresses the role and utilization of the theme itself. It is, on the one hand, more delicate than the other tools, in that its use demands consummate political commitment-building skills and a shrewd sense of timing. In another sense it is more robust than the others, in that, if handled effectively, it can generate substantial, sustained energy in large institutions. For the senior manager, therefore, thinking about and acting on the value management process is, although imprecise, extremely practical.

Business researchers have coined various terms for an effective, predominant institutional belief. Richard Normann calls it a business idea or growth idea. He devotes an entire book, *Management and Statesmanship*, to documenting a case for the power of an effective, simply articulated business idea and describing the unique role and leverage of top management in indirectly guiding the process of belief establishment and change. He argues that "the interpretation of ongoing and historical events and the associated adjustment and regulation of the dominating idea is probably the most crucial of the processes occurring in the company."

Some other recent scholarly work, well grounded in the leading edge of social science findings, provides a corroborating point of view. Andrew Pettigrew's anthropological study of the creation of organization culture is representative:

> One way of approaching the study of the entrepreneur's relationship with his organization is to consider the entrepreneur as a symbol creator, an ideologue, a formulator of organizational vocabularies, and a maker of ritual and myth. Stylistic components of a vision, which may be crucial, might include the presence of a dramatically significant series of events, rooting the vision back into history, and thus indicating the vision was more than a fad. Visions with simple, yet ambiguous content expressed in symbolic language are not only likely to be potent consciousness raisers, but also flexible enough to sustain the ravages of time and therefore the certitude of events. Visions contain new and old terminology perhaps organized into metaphors with which it is hoped to create new meanings. Words can move people from a state of familiarity to a state of awareness. Some people have the capacity to make words walk. I suspect this is one of the unexplored characteristics of successful entrepreneurs.

Louis Pondy, in "Leadership is a Language Game," quite similarly equates leadership effectiveness with the capacity to achieve what he calls "language renewal."

Roy Ash puts the same notion in more concrete terms:

At a sufficiently high level of abstraction, he says, "all businesses are the same." Ash's plans for testing that theory are summed up in the notes that he continually pencils on yellow legal pads. One of the most revealing of these notes says: "Develop a much greater attachment of everybody to the bottom line—more agony and ecstasy." As he sees it, the really important change in a company is a process of psychological transformation.

If one combs the literature for the lessons extracted by business leaders, the crucial role of a central belief emerges. The biographies of Cordiner at GE, Vail at AT&T, Greenewalt at Du Pont, and Watson at IBM all stress the quest to give operational force and meaning to a dominant, though imprecise, idea. Such accounts may be dismissed as self-serving, but it would seem a bit more cynical than even these times call for to write off the extraordinary consistency of so many closing statements.

Among active business leaders, the pattern of evidence is repeated. Richard Pascale, for example, has described the management style of several particularly effective chief executive officers. He notes the recurrence of a simple, overarching theme captured in a few words: for example, Harold Geneen's ceaseless "search for the unshakable facts," reflected in all kinds of organizational arrangements from structural contrivances—his controllers reporting to the chief executive and his intrusive product group managers—through interaction mechanisms—the famed ITT monthly review sessions. Further examples dot the business press:

A. W. Clausen at Bank of America: "Stay around Tom Clausen for about 15 minutes and he'll talk about laying pipe," says *Forbes*. "That's his shorthand for anticipating events and readying a response. Subordinates lay pipe to Clausen when they tell him about potential problems; he lays the pipe the other way when he sketches his expectations. The expression isn't especially catchy, the process isn't particularly glamorous. But it does help to explain why Bank of America isn't facing huge loan losses—and this big, slow-moving tortoise seems perfectly able to keep up with the flashier, more dynamic hares."

John DeButts at AT&T incessantly uses the term "the system is the solution." The concept, professed by DeButts in every setting from management meetings to television commercials, is aimed at starting the process of shifting the massive million-person Bell System's focus to the marketplace.

Tom Jones at Northrup, Fortune notes, has been particularly successful at gaining more than a fair share of defense contracts—largely, he believes, by bringing to life the theme "Everybody at Northrup is in marketing."

Walter Spencer at Sherwin Williams, according to *Forbes,* spent his five years as CEO working to introduce a "marketing orientation" into a previously manufacturing-dominated institution. Says Spencer: "When you take a 100-year old company and change the culture of the organization, and try to do that in Cleveland's traditional business setting—well, it takes time; you just have to keep hammering away at everybody. . . . The changeover to marketing is probably irreversible now. It's not complete, but we've brought along a lot of young managers with that philosophy, and once you've taken a company this far, you can't go back."

When the scholarly research and the anecdotal evidence are drawn together, some characteristic attributes of an effective dominating value can be discussed:

It is both loose and tight. That is, it connotes a clear directional emphasis—focus on the competition, stand for quality, become low-cost producer—but ample latitude for supporting initiatives.

It must, almost always, emerge rather than be imposed. Though it may be crystallized in a succinct phrase, it usually represents the end product of time-consuming consensus-building processes that may have gone on for a year or more.

Just as it cannot be improved by fiat, it cannot be changed at will. Typically, a major shift in the dominant belief can be brought about only when an important change is perceived to be at hand. The process of gaining commitment requires so much emotional commitment and institutional energy that it can be repeated only infrequently.

It has a reasonably predictable life cycle. Beginning with a great deal of latitude, it becomes progressively less flexible over time—though never approaching the rigidity of a quantified goal.

It may be a definition or characterization of the past, meant primarily to mark the end of a period and provide the energy to start a search for new modes of organizational behavior. For example, one might choose to label the past five years as "the era of tight control" in order to suggest that something now coming to an end should be replaced with something new, as yet unspecified.

It imposes choices. Despite the general nature of most effective beliefs, they do require management to face up to the limits of the organization's capacities. Of course, any huge enterprise does a bit of everything, but, for example, a choice to stress controls, if effectively implemented, is likely also a choice not to push harder for new products.

It can be anything from a general management principle to a reasonably specific major business decision. At the management-principles end, it can become a commitment to something like "fact-based analysis." At the business-decision end, it can be a commitment to a revised position for a key product line. In the middle are hybrids such as "enhanced focus on competition."

It suggests movement (e.g., toward becoming the industry quality leader or dominating a particular market niche), thus implying some

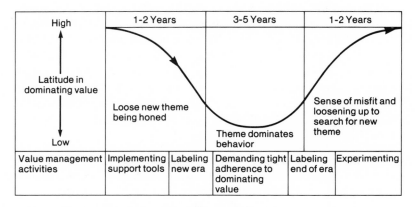

	1-2 Years		3-5 Years	1-2 Years	
High ↑ Latitude in dominating value ↓ Low	Loose new theme being honed		Theme dominates behavior	Sense of misfit and loosening up to search for new theme	
Value management activities	Implementing support tools	Labeling new era	Demanding tight adherence to dominating value	Labeling end of era	Experimenting

Figure 5. Five- to nine-year cycle of strategic transition

sort of tension or imbalance. Few leaders have been noted for achieving balance. Most have been known for going from somewhere to somewhere else.

Figure 5 gives a graphic portrayal of the essentials of the process I have been discussing. It depicts a five- to nine-year cycle of strategic transition marked by the tightening, executing, loosening, and redirecting search for an operational dominating value.

Change for change's sake

At least one significant tool remains to be considered: namely, change for its own sake.

This is the device assigned, in figure 1, to cell 3 (low-control, high-speed change). Sometimes things are such a muddle that significant change for its own sake is a good bet to produce, on balance, a more desirable outcome than any directionally managed program.

In *The Economist,* Norman McRae recently observed:

> . . . the most successful companies have been those restless enough to be unsure what their management styles should be. Successful big American corporations today will often centralize their policy making, and get a significant initial gain in effectiveness; but then, as time passes, will find that this does not work because the central planners do not know what is really going on out in the field. So these corporations will then decentralize, and get a significant initial gain in effectiveness. This constant reorganization is in fact very sensible, and is a main reason why I judge that big American corporations are still the most efficient day-to-day business operators in the world.

A somewhat less radical dose of the same medicine is the rather arbitrary reshuffling of top team member responsibilities, even when it results in a seemingly less rational match of skills to tasks. A fresh juxtaposition of perspectives, per se, is often of value.

At least one word of warning about high-early impact, low-control pre-scriptions is in order. The secret of their success is novelty. Routine reorga-nizing or all-too-regular shake-ups of top team assignments all too readily evoke the sense of déjà vu. "Nobody on the top team has been in the same job for more than 15 months," remarks an executive of a high-technology company. "Of course, all they do is trade bureaucratic barbs. That's all they've got. No one sees the results of his own initiatives."

Although it certainly merits much more discussion, the analysis of this last class of tools must necessarily be cut short at this point.

In conclusion: Limits and optimism

The purpose of this essay has been twofold: first, to provide a simple classi-fication of change tools and some speculative hypotheses in support of the case for pessimism about the old favorites among them; second, to suggest that for the alert senior manager, today's organizational garbage cans are still full of powerful change tools—tools that he uses intuitively, and there-fore not systematically, but which nevertheless are numerous and poten-tially powerful enough to justify a measure of optimism.

A limited measure, to be sure. Even with a mastery of all the change tools reviewed here, today's senior manager is unlikely to be able to de-velop real consensus, commitment, and change in more than a single direc-tion. Richard Neustadt's metaphor captures the essence of his role:

> Presidential power is the power to persuade. Underneath our images
> of Presidents-in-boots, astride decisions, are the half-observed realities
> of Presidents-in-sneakers, stirrups in hand, trying to induce particular
> department heads . . . to climb aboard.

As he tries to coax his senior colleagues aboard, the senior executive has at his command a variety of settings—settings in which he can experi-ment, implement, and build patterns to provide a general conception of what's possible. He can, with luck and to a limited extent, grasp control of the signaling system to point a general direction and mark out limited areas of expected new institutional excellence. By adroitly managing agenda, he can nudge the day-to-day decision-making system, thus simultaneously im-parting new preferences and testing new initiatives.

And some day, in retrospect, he may be able to see himself as an experi-menter who attempted to build consensus on a practical (and flexible) vi-sion of what was possible over a five-year horizon, and through incessant attention to the implementation of small, adaptive steps, eventually made that vision a reality.

If so, he should be well content.

Selected bibliography

Richard Pascale in "Three Chief Executives: The Effect of Style on Implementation" (Research Paper 357, Stanford Graduate School of Business) developed, with the subjects' cooperation, detailed case studies of Harold Geneen, Roy Ash, and Ed Carlson. He meticulously describes the links between their everyday behavior patterns, supporting organizational systems, and effectiveness.

John Kotter and Paul Lawrence in *Mayors in Action* (Wiley, 1974) discuss in a series of case studies the relationship, for example, between mayoral agenda setting and implementation success.

Four studies of bureaucratic politics offer particularly detailed analyses of the mundane attributes of influence accumulation and exercise: Graham Allison's *Essence of Decision* (Little, Brown, 1971); Edward Banfield's *Political Influence* (Free Press, 1961); Robert Caro's *The Power Broker* (Knopf, 1974); and Richard Neustadt's *Presidential Power* (Wiley, 1960).

Henry Mintzberg's unique observational study of senior executives, *The Nature of Managerial Work* (Harper & Row, 1973), vividly portrays the fragmented nature of real senior-management activity. If one finds his analysis credible, then presumably the kinds of change levers discussed in this article are of particular importance.

H. Edward Wrapp's "Good Managers Don't Make Policy Decisions" (*Harvard Business Review,* September–October 1967) and James Quinn's "Strategic Goals: Process and Politics" (*Sloan Management Review,* Fall 1977) provide good examples of effective muddling-about processes that typically attend development of what is called a "dominating value" in this paper.

The notion of organizations as temporary systems discussed in the paper is treated at length by E. J. Miller and A. K. Rice in *Systems of Organization* (Tavistock, 1967).

Last, James March and Johan Olsen's *Ambiguity and Choice* (Universitelforlaget: Norway, 1976) proposes and supports a novel, complex model of organizational choice. The decision-making environment they describe clearly calls for radically different management prescriptions. The tools offered in this paper seem, to me, to be reasonably consistent with their view of the world.

Fitting New Employees into the Company Culture
Richard Pascale

What corporate strategy was in the 1970s, corporate culture is becoming in the 1980s. Companies worry about whether theirs is right for them, consultants hawk advice on the subject, executives wonder if there's anything in it that can help them manage better. A strong culture—a set of shared values, norms, and beliefs that get everybody heading in the same direction—is common to all the companies held up as paragons in the best-seller *In Search of Excellence*.

There is, however, one aspect of culture that nobody seems to want to talk about. This is the process by which newly hired employees are made part of a company's culture. It may be called learning the ropes, being taught "the way we do things here at XYZ Corp.," or simply training. Almost no one calls it by its precise social-science name—socialization.

To American ears, attuned by Constitution and conviction to the full expression of individuality, socialization tends to sound alien and vaguely sinister. Some equate it with the propagation of socialism—which it isn't—but even when it is correctly understood as the development of social conformity, the prospect makes most of us cringe. How many companies caught up in the corporate culture fad will be quite as enthusiastic when they finally grasp that "creating a strong culture" is a nice way of saying that employees have to be more comprehensively socialized?

The tradition at most American corporations is to err in the other direction, to be culturally permissive, to let employees do their own thing to a remarkable degree. We are guided by a philosophy, initially articulated by John Locke, Thomas Hobbes, and Adam Smith, that says that individuals free to choose make the most efficient decisions. The independence of the parts makes for a greater sum. Trendy campaigns to build a strong corporate culture run into trouble when employees are asked to give up some of their individuality for the common good.

The crux of the dilemma is this: We are opposed to the manipulation of individuals for organizational purposes. At the same time we increasingly realize that a degree of social uniformity enables organizations to work better. One need not look to Japan to see the benefits of it. Many of the great American companies that thrive from one generation to the next— IBM, Procter & Gamble, Morgan Guaranty Trust—are organizations that have perfected their processes of socialization. Virtually none talk explicitly about socialization; they may not even be conscious of precisely what they are doing. Moreover, when one examines any particular aspect of their policy toward people—how they recruit or train or compensate— little stands out as unusual. But when the pieces are assembled, what emerges is an awesome internal consistency that powerfully shapes behavior.

It's time to take socialization out of the closet. If some degree of it is necessary for organizations to be effective, then the challenge for managers is to reconcile this necessity with traditional American independence.

Probably the best guide available on how to socialize people properly is what the IBMs and the P&Gs actually do. Looking at the winners company by company, one finds that, with slight variations, they all put new employees through what might be called the seven steps of socialization:

Step one. The company subjects candidates for employment to a selection process so rigorous that it often seems designed to discourage individuals rather than encourage them to take the job. By grilling the applicant, telling him or her the bad side as well as the good, and making sure not to oversell, strong-culture companies prod the job applicant to take himself out of contention if he, who presumably knows more about himself than any recruiter, thinks the organization won't fit his style and values.

Consider the way Procter & Gamble hires people for entry level positions in brand management. The first person who interviews the applicant is drawn not from the human resources department, but from an elite cadre of line managers who have been trained with lectures, videotapes, films, practice interviews, and role playing. These interviewers use what they've learned to probe each applicant for such qualities as the ability to "turn out high volumes of excellent work," to "identify and understand problems," and to "reach thoroughly substantiated and well-reasoned conclusions that lead to action." Initially, each candidate undergoes at least two interviews and takes a test of his general knowledge. If he passes, he's flown to P&G headquarters in Cincinnati, where he goes through a day of one-on-one interviews and a group interview over lunch.

The New York investment banking house of Morgan Stanley encourages people it is thinking of hiring to discuss the demands of the job with their spouses, girlfriends, or boyfriends—new recruits sometimes work 100 hours a week. The firm's managing directors and their wives take promising candidates and their spouses or companions out to dinner to bring home to them what they will face. The point is to get a person who will not be happy within Morgan's culture because of the way his family feels to eliminate himself from consideration for a job there.

This kind of rigorous screening might seem an invitation to hire only people who fit the mold of present employees. In fact, it often *is* harder for companies with strong cultures to accept individuals different from the prevailing type.

Step two. The company subjects the newly hired individual to experiences calculated to induce humility and to make him question his prior behavior, beliefs, and values. By lessening the recruit's comfort with himself, the company hopes to promote openness toward its own norms and values.

This may sound like brainwashing or boot camp, but it usually just takes the form of pouring on more work than the newcomer can possibly do. IBM and Morgan Guaranty socialize with training programs in which, to quote one participant, "You work every night until 2 A.M. on your own material, and then help others." Procter & Gamble achieves the same result with what might be called upending experiences—requiring a recent college graduate to color in a map of sales territories, for example. The message is clear: while you may be accomplished in many respects, you are in kindergarten as far as what you know about this organization.

Humility isn't the only feeling brought on by long hours of intense work that carry the individual close to his or her limit. When everybody's vulnerability runs high, one also tends to become close to one's colleagues. Companies sometimes intensify this cohesiveness by not letting trainees out of the pressure cooker for very long—everyone has so much work to do that he doesn't have time to see people outside the company or reestablish a more normal social distance from his co-workers.

Morgan Stanley, for instance, expects newly hired associates to work 12- to 14- hour days and most weekends. Their lunches are not the Lucullan repasts that MBAs fantasize about, but are typically confined to 30 minutes in the unprepossessing cafeteria. One can observe similar patterns—long hours, exhausting travel schedules, and almost total immersion in casework—at law firms and consulting outfits. Do recruits chafe under such discipline? Not that much, apparently. Socialization is a bit like exercise—it's probably easier to reconcile yourself to it while you're young.

Step three. Companies send the newly humble recruits into the trenches, pushing them to master one of the disciplines at the core of the company's business. The newcomer's promotions are tied to how he does in that discipline.

In the course of the individual's first few months with the company, his universe of experience has increasingly narrowed down to the organization's culture. The company, having got him to open his mind to its way of doing business, now cements that orientation by putting him in the field and giving him lots of carefully monitored experience. It rewards his progress with promotions at predictable intervals.

While IBM hires some MBAs and a few older professionals with prior work experience, almost all of them start at the same level as recruits from college and go through the same training programs. It takes about 15 years, for example, to become a financial controller. At Morgan Stanley and consulting firms like McKinsey, new associates must similarly work their way up through the ranks. There is almost never a quick way to jump a few rungs on the ladder.

The gains from this approach are cumulative. For starters, when all trainees understand there is just one step-by-step career path, it reduces politicking. Since they are being evaluated on how they do over the long haul, they are less tempted to cut corners or go for short-term victories. By the time they reach senior positions they understand the business not as a financial abstraction, but as a reality of people they know and skills they've learned. They can communicate with people in the lowest ranks in the shorthand of shared experience.

Step four. At every stage of the new manager's career, the company measures the operating results he has achieved and rewards him accordingly. It does this with systems that are comprehensive and consistent. These systems focus particularly on those aspects of the business that make for competitive success and for the perpetuation of the corporation's values.

Procter & Gamble, for instance, measures managers on three factors it deems critical to a brand's success: building volume, building profit, and conducting planned change—altering a product to make it more effective or more satisfying to the customer in some other way. Information from the outside world—market-share figures, say—is used in the measuring along with financial data. Performance appraisals focus on these criteria as well as on general managerial skill.

IBM uses similar interlocking systems to track adherence to one of its major values, respect for the dignity of the individual. The company monitors this with surveys of employee morale; "Speak Up," a confidential suggestion box; a widely proclaimed policy of having the boss's door open to any subordinates who want to talk; so-called skip-level interviews, in which a subordinate can skip over a couple of organizational levels to discuss a grievance with senior management; and informal social contacts between senior managers and lower level employees. Management moves quickly when any of these systems turns up a problem.

The IBM culture includes a mechanism for disciplining someone who has violated one of the corporate norms—handling his subordinates too harshly, say, or being overzealous against the competition. The malefactor will be assigned to what is called the penalty box—typically, a fairly meaningless job at the same level, sometimes in a less desirable location. A branch manager in Chicago might be moved to a nebulous staff position at headquarters. To the outsider, penalty box assignments look like just another job rotation, but insiders know that the benched manager is out of the game temporarily.

The penalty box provides a place to hold a manager while the mistakes he's made and the hard feelings they've engendered are gradually forgotten. The mechanism lends substance to the belief, widespread among IBM employees, that the company won't fire anybody capriciously. The penalty box's existence says, in effect, that in the career of strong, effective managers there are times when one steps on toes. The penalty box lets someone who has stepped too hard contemplate his error and return to play another day.

Step five. All along the way, the company promotes adherence to its transcendent values, those overarching purposes that rise way above the day-to-day imperative to make a buck. At the AT&T of yore, for example, the transcendent value was guaranteeing phone service to customers through any emergency. Identification with such a value enables the employee to accept the personal sacrifices the company asks of him.

Placing oneself at the service of an organization entails real costs. There are long hours of work, weekends apart from one's family, bosses one has to endure, criticism that seems unfair, job assignments that are inconvenient or undesirable. The countervailing force making for commitment to the company in these circumstances is the organization's set of transcendent values that connect its purpose to human values of a higher order than just those of the marketplace—values such as serving mankind, providing a first-class product for society, or helping people learn and grow.

Someone going to work for Delta Air Lines will be told again and again about the "Delta family feeling." Everything that's said makes the point that Delta's values sometimes require sacrifices—management takes pay cuts during lean times, senior flight attendants and pilots voluntarily work fewer hours per week so the company won't have to lay off more-junior employees. Candidates who accept employment with Delta tend to buy into this quid pro quo, agreeing in effect that keeping the Delta family healthy justifies the sacrifices that the family exacts.

Step six. The company constantly harps on watershed events in the organization's history that reaffirm the importance of the firm's culture. Folklore reinforces a code of conduct—how we do things around here.

All companies have their stories, but at corporations that socialize well the morals of these stories all tend to point in the same direction. In the old Bell System, story after story extolled Bell employees who made heroic sacrifices to keep the phones working. The Bell folklore was so powerful that when natural disaster struck, all elements of a one-million-member organization were able to pull together, cut corners, violate normal procedures, even do things that would not look good when measured by usual job performance criteria—all in the interest of restoring phone service. Folklore, when well understood, can legitimize special channels for moving an organization in a hurry.

Step seven. The company supplies promising individuals with role models. These models are consistent—each exemplary manager displays the same traits.

Nothing communicates more powerfully to younger professionals within an organization than the example of peers or superiors who are recognized as winners and who also share common qualities. The protégé watches the role model make presentations, handle conflict, and write memos, then tries to duplicate the traits that seem to work most effectively.

Strong-culture firms regard role models as constituting the most powerful long-term training program available. Because other elements of the culture are consistent, the people who emerge as role models are consistent. P&G's brand managers, for example, exhibit extraordinary consistency in several traits—they're almost all analytical, energetic, and adept at motivating others. Unfortunately most firms leave the emergence of role models to chance. Some on the fast track seem to be whizzes at analysis, others are skilled at leading people, others seem astute at politics: the result for those below is confusion as to what it *really* takes to succeed. For example, the companies that formerly made up the Bell System have a strong need to become more market oriented and aggressive. Yet the Bell culture continues to discriminate against potential fast-trackers who, judged by the values of the older monopoly culture, are too aggressive.

Many companies can point to certain organizational practices that look like one or two of the seven steps, but rarely are all seven managed in a well-coordinated effort. It is *consistency* across all seven steps of the socialization process that results in a strongly cohesive culture that endures.

When one understands the seven steps, one can better appreciate the case for socialization. All organizations require a degree of order and consistency. They can achieve this through explicit procedures and formal controls or through implicit social controls. American companies, on the whole, tend to rely more on formal controls. The result is that management often appears rigid, bureaucratic, and given to oversteering. A United Technologies executive laments, "I came from the Bell system. Compared with AT&T, this is a weak culture and there is little socialization. But of course there is still need for controls. So they put handcuffs on you, shackle you to every nickel, track every item of inventory, monitor every movement in production and head count. They control you by the balance sheet."

At most American companies, an inordinate amount of energy gets used up in fighting "the system." But when an organization can come up with a strong, consistent set of implicit understandings, it has effectively established for itself a body of common law to supplement its formal rules. This enables it to use formal systems as they are supposed to be used—as tools rather than straitjackets. An IBM manager, conversant with the concept of socialization, puts it this way: "Socialization acts as a fine-tuning device; it helps us make sense out of the procedures and quantitative measures. Any number of times I've been faced with a situation where the right thing for the measurement system was X and the right thing for IBM was Y. I've always been counseled to tilt toward what was right for IBM in the long term and what was right for our people. They pay us a lot to do that. Formal controls, without coherent values and culture, are too crude a compass to steer by."

Organizations that socialize effectively use their cultures to manage ambiguity, ever present in such tricky matters as business politics and personal relationships. This tends to free up time and energy. More goes toward getting the job done and focusing on external considerations like the competition and the customer. "At IBM you spend 50% of your time managing the internal context," states a former IBMer, now at ITT. "At most companies it's more like 75%." A marketing manager who worked at Atari before it got new management recalls: "You can't imagine how much time and energy around here went into politics. You had to determine who was on first base this month in order to figure out how to obtain what you needed to get the job done. There were no rules. There were no clear values. Two of the men at the top stood for diametrically opposite things. Your bosses were constantly changing. All this meant that you never had time to develop a routine way for getting things done at the interface between your job and the next guy's. Without rules for working with one another, a lot of people got hurt, got burned out, and were never taught the 'Atari way' of doing things because there wasn't an Atari way."

The absence of cultural guidelines makes organizational life capricious. This is so because success as a manager requires managing not only the substance of the business but also, increasingly, managing one's role and relationships. When social roles are unclear, no one is speaking the same language; communication and trust break down. A person's power to get things done in a company seldom depends on his title and formal authority alone. In great measure it rests on his track record, reputation, knowledge, and network of relationships. In effect, the power to implement change and execute business strategies depends heavily on what might be called one's social currency—as in money—something a person accumulates over time. Strong-culture firms empower employees, helping them build this currency by supplying continuity and clarity.

Continuity and clarity also help reduce the anxiety people feel about their careers. Mixed signals about rewards, promotions, career paths, criteria for being on the "fast track" or a candidate for termination inevitably generate a lot of gossip, game playing, and unproductive expenditure of energy. Only the naive think that these matters can be entirely resolved by provisions in a policy manual. The reality is that many criteria of success for middle- and senior-level positions can't be articulated in writing. The rules tend to be communicated and enforced via relatively subtle cues. When the socialization process is weak, the cues tend to be poorly or inconsistently communicated.

Look carefully at career patterns in most companies. Ambitious professionals strive to learn the ropes, but there are as many "ropes" as there are individuals who have made their way to the top. So the aspirant picks an approach, and if it happens to coincide with how his superiors do things, he's on the fast track. Commonly, though, the approach that works with one superior is offensive to another. "As a younger manager, I was always taught to touch bases and solicit input before moving ahead," a manager at a Santa Clara, California, electronics firm says, "and it always worked. But at a higher level, with a different boss, my base-touching was equated with being political. The organization doesn't forewarn you when it changes signals. A lot of good people leave owing to misunderstandings of this kind." The human cost of the failure to socialize tends to go largely unrecognized.

What about the cost of conformity? A senior vice president of IBM asserts: "Conformity among IBM employees has often been described as stultifying in terms of dress, behavior, and lifestyle. There is, in fact, strong pressure to adhere to certain norms of superficial behavior, and much more intensely to the three tenets of the company philosophy—respect for the dignity of the individual, first-rate customer service, and excellence. These are the benchmarks. Between them there is wide latitude for divergence in opinions and behavior."

A P&G executive echoes this thought: "There is a great deal of consistency around here in how certain things are done, and these are rather critical to our sustained success. Beyond that, there are very few hard and fast rules. People on the outside might portray our culture as imposing lockstep uniformity. It doesn't feel rigid when you're inside. It feels like it accommodates you. And best of all, you know the game you're in—you know whether you're playing soccer or football; you can find out very clearly what it takes to succeed and you can bank your career on that."

It is useful to distinguish here between norms that are central to the business's success and social conventions that signal commitment and belonging. The former are essential in that they ensure consistency in executing the company's strategy. The latter are the organizational equivalent of shaking hands. They are social conventions that make it easier for people to be comfortable with one another. One need not observe all of them, but one wants to reassure the organization that one is on the team. An important aspect of this second set of social values is that, like a handshake, they are usually not experienced as oppressive. Partly this is because adherence doesn't require much thought or deliberation, just as most people don't worry much about their individuality being compromised by the custom of shaking hands.

The aim of socialization is to establish a base of shared attitudes, habits, and values that foster cooperation, integrity, and communication. But without the natural rough-and-tumble friction between competing co-workers, some might argue, there will be little innovation. The record does not bear this out. Consider 3M or Bell Labs. Both are highly innovative institutions—and both remain so by fostering social rules that reward innovation. Socialization does not necessarily discourage competition between employees. Employees compete hard at IBM, P&G, major consulting firms, law firms, and outstanding financial institutions like Morgan Guaranty and Morgan Stanley.

There is, of course, the danger of strong-culture firms becoming incestuous and myopic—what came to be known in the early days of the Japanese auto invasion as the General Motors syndrome. Most opponents of socialization rally around this argument. But what one learns from observing the likes of IBM and P&G is that their cultures keep them constantly facing outward. Most companies like this tend to guard against the danger of complacency by having as one element of their culture an *obsession* with some facet of their performance in the marketplace. For example, McDonald's has an obsessive concern for quality control, IBM for customer service, 3M for innovation. These obsessions make for a lot of fire drills. But they also serve as the organizational equivalent of calisthenics, keeping people fit for the day when the emergency is real. When, on the other hand, the central cultural concern points inward rather than outward—as seems to be the case, say, with Delta Air Lines' focus on "family feeling"—the strong-culture company may be riding for a fall.

Revolutions begin with an assault on awareness. It is time to be more candid and clear-minded about socialization. Between our espoused individualism and the reality of most companies lies a zone where organizational and individual interests overlap. If we can manage our ambivalence about socialization, we can make our organizations more effective. Equally important, we can reduce the human costs that arise today as individuals stumble along in careers with companies that fail to articulate ends and means coherently and understandably for all employees.

11   Strategy, Structure, and Adaptation

The reader has noticed that we've been moving, section by section, from the smaller to the larger, from the single person to the group to the whole organization. This section and the next continue on that track. They look at managing in the large context. This one focuses particularly on overall strategies for trying to change the organization so that it can keep up with, and even lead, a changing world.

The three pieces in this section are all practical pieces, all oriented toward helping the manager to select and implement a broad, somewhat long-term strategy. John Kotter and Leonard Schlesinger consider how managers actually do select strategies, and what makes for effective choices.

The second paper, by James Brian Quinn, argues for a particular approach to strategy. He shows the advantages of an incremental approach rather than a master plan approach; this is an idea that should remind the reader of an earlier part of this book, section 2, which was about alternative ways of thinking and problem solving.

And the third piece, by Eric Flamholtz, offers help on an absolutely critical issue for those small companies blessed by their own success. The issue is, of course, finding an appropriate strategy for growth. Many entrepreneurial start-up organizations have found that early successes have sown the seeds of later failures. The entrepreneurial way of managing the start-up almost always runs into trouble as the organization grows. The entrepreneurial style almost always gives way to more analytical "professional" styles. But must it? Must those two alternatives clash, destructively, often to the point of destroying what has been so beautifully and laboriously built?

The strategy question never goes away. It's there when we try to figure out whether to start something, and if so, what and how. It's there when we succeed and have to figure out how to keep our now-adolescent child healthy and growing; and it's there in middle age and old age as we try to figure out how to deal with those new hotshot young competitors and how to pass the baton to a new generation.

Choosing Strategies
for Change

John P. Kotter and
Leonard A. Schlesinger

It must be considered that there is nothing more difficult to carry out, nor more doubtful of success, nor more dangerous to handle, than to initiate a new order of things.[1]

In 1973, The Conference Board asked 13 eminent authorities to speculate what significant management issues and problems would develop over the next 20 years. One of the strongest themes that runs through their subsequent reports is a concern for the ability of organizations to respond to environmental change. As one person wrote: "It follows that an acceleration in the rate of change will result in an increasing need for reorganization. Reorganization is usually feared, because it means disturbance of the status quo, a threat to the people's vested interests in their jobs, and an upset to established ways of doing things. For these reasons, needed reorganization is often deferred, with a resulting loss in effectiveness and an increase in costs."[2]

Subsequent events have confirmed the importance of this concern about organizational change. Today, more and more managers must deal with new government regulations, new products, growth, increased competition, technological developments, and a changing work force. In response, most companies or divisions of major corporations find that they must undertake moderate organizational changes at least once a year and major changes every four or five.[3]

Few organizational change efforts tend to be complete failures, but few tend to be entirely successful either. Most efforts encounter problems; they often take longer than expected and desired, they sometimes kill morale, and they often cost a great deal in terms of managerial time or emotional upheaval. More than a few organizations have not even tried to initiate needed changes because the managers involved were afraid that they were simply incapable of successfully implementing them.

Reprinted with permission from *Harvard Business Review,* March-April 1979, 106–13. © 1979 by the President and Fellows of Harvard College. All rights reserved.

1. Niccolò Machiavelli, *The Prince.*

2. Marvin Bower and C. Lee Walton, Jr., "Gearing a business to the future," in *Challenge to Leadership* (New York: The Conference Board, 1973), p. 126.

3. For recent evidence on the frequency of changes, see Stephen A. Allen, "Organizational choice and general influence networks for diversified companies," *Academy of Management Journal,* September 1978, p. 341.

In this article, we first describe various causes for resistance to change and then outline a systematic way to select a strategy and set of specific approaches for implementing an organizational change effort. The methods described are based on our analyses of dozens of successful and unsuccessful organizational changes.

Diagnosing resistance

Organizational change efforts often run into some form of human resistance. Although experienced managers are generally all too aware of this fact, surprisingly few take time before an organizational change to assess systematically who might resist the change initiative and for what reasons. Instead, using past experiences as guidelines, managers all too often apply a simple set of beliefs—such as "engineers will probably resist the change because they are independent and suspicious of top management." This limited approach can create serious problems. Because of the many different ways in which individuals and groups can react to change, correct assessments are often not intuitively obvious and require careful thought.

Of course, all people who are affected by change experience some emotional turmoil. Even changes that appear to be "positive" or "rational" involve loss and uncertainty.[4] Nevertheless, for a number of different reasons, individuals or groups can react very differently to change—from passively resisting it, to aggressively trying to undermine it, to sincerely embracing it.

To predict what form their resistance might take, managers need to be aware of the four most common reasons people resist change. These include: a desire not to lose something of value, a misunderstanding of the change and its implications, a belief that the change does not make sense for the organization, and a low tolerance for change.

Parochial self-interest

One major reason people resist organizational change is that they think they will lose something of value as a result. In these cases, because people focus on their own best interests and not on those of the total organization, resistance often results in "politics" or "political behavior."[5] Consider these two examples:

> After a number of years of rapid growth, the president of an organization decided that its size demanded the creation of a new staff function—New Product Planning and Development—to be headed by a vice

---

4. For example, see Robert A. Luke, Jr., "A structural approach to organizational change," *Journal of Applied Behavioral Science,* September–October 1973, p. 611.

5. For a discussion of power and politics in corporations, see Abraham Zaleznik and Manfred F. R. Kets de Vries, *Power and the Corporate Mind* (Boston: Houghton Mifflin, 1975), chap. 6; and Robert H. Miles, *Macro Organizational Behavior* (Pacific Palisades, Calif.: Goodyear, 1978), chap. 4.

president. Operationally, this change eliminated most of the decision-making power that the vice presidents of marketing, engineering, and production had over new products. Inasmuch as new products were very important in this organization, the change also reduced the vice presidents' status which, together with power, was very important to them.

During the two months after the president announced his idea for a new product vice president, the existing vice presidents each came up with six or seven reasons the new arrangement might not work. Their objections grew louder and louder until the president shelved the idea.

A manufacturing company had traditionally employed a large group of personnel people as counselors and "father confessors" to its production employees. This group of counselors tended to exhibit high morale because of the professional satisfaction they received from the "helping relationships" they had with employees. When a new performance appraisal system was installed, every six months the counselors were required to provide each employee's supervisor with a written evaluation of the employee's "emotional maturity," "promotional potential," and so forth.

As some of the personnel people immediately recognized, the change would alter their relationships from a peer and helper to more of a boss and evaluator with most of the employees. Predictably, the personnel counselors resisted the change. While publicly arguing that the new system was not as good for the company as the old one, they privately put as much pressure as possible on the personnel vice president until he significantly altered the new system.

Political behavior sometimes emerges before and during organizational change efforts when what is in the best interests of one individual or group is not in the best interests of the total organization or of other individuals and groups.

While political behavior sometimes takes the form of two or more armed camps publicly fighting things out, it usually is much more subtle. In many cases, it occurs completely under the surface of public dialogue. Although scheming and ruthless individuals sometimes initiate power struggles, more often than not those who do are people who view their potential loss from change as an unfair violation of their implicit, or psychological, contract with the organization.[6]

Misunderstanding and lack of trust

People also resist change when they do not understand its implications and perceive that it might cost them much more than they will gain. Such situa-

---

6. See Edgar H. Schein, *Organizational Psychology* (Englewood Cliffs, N.J.: Prentice-Hall, 1965), p. 44.

tions often occur when trust is lacking between the person initiating the change and the employees.[7] Here is an example:

> When the president of a small midwestern company announced to his managers that the company would implement a flexible working schedule for all employees, it never occurred to him that he might run into resistance. He had been introduced to the concept at a management seminar and decided to use it to make working conditions at his company more attractive, particularly to clerical and plant personnel.
>
> Shortly after the announcement, numerous rumors began to circulate among plant employees—none of whom really knew what flexible working hours meant and many of whom were distrustful of the manufacturing vice president. One rumor, for instance, suggested that flexible hours meant that most people would have to work whenever their supervisors asked them to—including evenings and weekends. The employee association, a local union, held a quick meeting and then presented the management with a nonnegotiable demand that the flexible hours concept be dropped. The president, caught completely by surprise, complied.

Few organizations can be characterized as having a high level of trust between employees and managers; consequently, it is easy for misunderstandings to develop when change is introduced. Unless managers surface misunderstandings and clarify them rapidly, they can lead to resistance. And that resistance can easily catch change initiators by surprise, especially if they assume that people only resist change when it is not in their best interest.

Different assessments

Another common reason people resist organizational change is that they assess the situation differently from their managers or those initiating the change and see more costs than benefits resulting from the change, not only for themselves but for their company as well. For example:

> The president of one moderate-size bank was shocked by his staff's analysis of the bank's real estate investment trust (REIT) loans. This complicated analysis suggested that the bank could easily lose up to $10 million and that the possible losses were increasing each month by 20 percent. Within a week, the president drew up a plan to reorganize the part of the bank that managed REITs. Because of his concern for the bank's stock price, however, he chose not to release the staff report to anyone except the new REIT section manager.
>
> The reorganization immediately ran into massive resistance from the people involved. The group sentiment, as articulated by one per-

7. See Chris Argyris, *Intervention Theory and Method* (Reading, Mass.: Addison-Wesley, 1970), p. 70.

son, was: "Has he gone mad? Why in God's name is he tearing apart this section of the bank? His actions have already cost us three very good people [who quit], and have crippled a new program we were implementing [which the president was unaware of] to reduce our loan losses."

Managers who initiate change often assume both that they have all the relevant information required to conduct an adequate organization analysis and that those who will be affected by the change have the same facts, when neither assumption is correct. In either case, the difference in information that groups work with often leads to differences in analyses, which in turn can lead to resistance. Moreover, if the analysis made by those not initiating the change is more accurate than that derived by the initiators, resistance is obviously "good" for the organization. But this likelihood is not obvious to some managers who assume that resistance is always bad and therefore always fight it.[8]

Low tolerance for change

People also resist change because they fear they will not be able to develop the new skills and behavior that will be required of them. All human beings are limited in their ability to change, with some people much more limited than others.[9] Organizational change can inadvertently require people to change too much, too quickly.

Peter F. Drucker has argued that the major obstacle to organizational growth is managers' inability to change their attitudes and behavior as rapidly as their organizations require.[10] Even when managers intellectually understand the need for changes in the way they operate, they sometimes are emotionally unable to make the transition.

It is because of people's limited tolerance for change that individuals will sometimes resist a change even when they realize it is a good one. For example, a person who receives a significantly more important job as a result of an organizational change will probably be very happy. But it is just as possible for such a person also to feel uneasy and to resist giving up certain aspects of the current situation. A new and very different job will require new and different behavior, new and different relationships, as well as the loss of some satisfactory current activities and relationships. If the changes are significant and the individual's tolerance for change is low, he might begin actively to resist the change for reasons even he does not consciously understand.

8. See Paul R. Lawrence, "How to deal with resistance to change," *Harvard Business Review,* May–June 1954, p. 49; reprinted as *Harvard Business Review* Classic, January–February 1969, p. 4.

9. For a discussion of resistance that is personality based, see Goodwin Watson, "Resistance to change," in *The Planning of Change,* eds. Warren G. Bennis, Kenneth F. Benne, and Robert Chin (New York: Holt, Rinehart, and Winston, 1969), p. 489.

10. Peter F. Drucker, *The Practice of Management* (New York: Harper and Row, 1954).

People also sometimes resist organizational change to save face; to go along with the change would be, they think, an admission that some of their previous decisions or beliefs were wrong. Or they might resist because of peer group pressure or because of a supervisor's attitude. Indeed, there are probably an endless number of reasons why people resist change.[11]

Assessing which of the many possibilities might apply to those who will be affected by a change is important because it can help a manager select an appropriate way to overcome resistance. Without an accurate diagnosis of possibilities of resistance, a manager can easily get bogged down during the change process with very costly problems.

Dealing with resistance

Many managers underestimate not only the variety of ways people can react to organizational change, but also the ways they can positively influence specific individuals and groups during a change. And, again because of past experiences, managers sometimes do not have an accurate understanding of the advantages and disadvantages of the methods with which they *are* familiar.

Education and communication

One of the most common ways to overcome resistance to change is to educate people about it beforehand. Communication of ideas helps people see the need for and the logic of a change. The education process can involve one-on-one discussions, presentations to groups, or memos and reports. For example, as a part of an effort to make changes in a division's structure and in measurement and reward systems, a division manager put together a one-hour audiovisual presentation that explained the changes and the reasons for them. Over a four-month period, he made this presentation no less than a dozen times to groups of 20 or 30 corporate and division managers.

An education and communication program can be ideal when resistance is based on inadequate or inaccurate information and analysis, especially if the initiators need the resistors' help in implementing the change. But some managers overlook the fact that a program of this sort requires a good relationship between initiators and resistors or that the latter may not believe what they hear. It also requires time and effort, particularly if a lot of people are involved.

Participation and involvement

If the initiators involve the potential resistors in some aspect of the design and implementation of the change, they can often forestall resistance. With

11. For a general discussion of resistance and reasons for it, see chap. 3 in Gerald Zaltman and Robert Duncan, *Strategies for Planned Change* (New York: John Wiley, 1977).

a participative change effort, the initiators listen to the people the change involves and use their advice. To illustrate:

The head of a small financial services company once created a task force to help design and implement changes in his company's reward system. The task force was composed of eight second- and third-level managers from different parts of the company. The president's specific charter to them was that they recommend changes in the company's benefit package. They were given six months and asked to file a brief progress report with the president once a month. After they had made their recommendations, which the president largely accepted, they were asked to help the company's personnel director implement them.

We have found that many managers have quite strong feelings about participation—sometimes positive and sometimes negative. That is, some managers feel that there should always be participation during change efforts, while others feel this is virtually always a mistake. Both attitudes can create problems for a manager, because neither is very realistic.

When change initiators believe they do not have all the information they need to design and implement a change, or when they need the whole-hearted commitment of others to do so, involving others makes very good sense. Considerable research has demonstrated that, in general, participation leads to commitment, not merely compliance.[12] In some instances, commitment is needed for the change to be a success. Nevertheless, the participation process does have its drawbacks. Not only can it lead to a poor solution if the process is not carefully managed, but also it can be enormously time-consuming. When the change must be made immediately, it can take simply too long to involve others.

Facilitation and support

Another way that managers can deal with potential resistance to change is by being supportive. This process might include providing training in new skills, or giving employees time off after a demanding period, or simply listening and providing emotional support. For example:

Management in one rapidly growing electronics company devised a way to help people adjust to frequent organizational changes. First, management staffed its human resource department with four counselors who spent most of their time talking to people who were feeling "burnt out" or who were having difficulty adjusting to new jobs. Second, on a selective basis, management offered people four-week minisabbaticals that involved some reflective or educational activity away from work. And, finally, it spent a great deal of money on in-house education and training programs.

12. See, for example, Alfred J. Marrow, David F. Bowers, and Stanley E. Seashore, *Management by Participation* (New York: Harper and Row, 1967).

Facilitation and support are most helpful when fear and anxiety lie at the heart of resistance. Seasoned, tough managers often overlook or ignore this kind of resistance, as well as the efficacy of facilitative ways of dealing with it. The basic drawback of this approach is that it can be time-consuming and expensive and still fail.[13] If time, money, and patience just are not available, then using supportive methods is not very practical.

Negotiation and agreement

Another way to deal with resistance is to offer incentives to active or potential resistors. For instance, management could give a union a higher wage rate in return for a work rule change; it could increase an individual's pension benefits in return for an early retirement. Here is an example of negotiated agreements:

> In a large manufacturing company, the divisions were very interdependent. One division manager wanted to make some major changes in his organization. Yet, because of the interdependence, he recognized that he would be forcing some inconvenience and change on other divisions as well. To prevent top managers in other divisions from undermining his efforts, the division manager negotiated a written agreement with each. The agreement specified the outcomes the other division managers would receive and when, as well as the kinds of cooperation that he would receive from them in return during the change process. Later, whenever the division managers complained about his changes or the change process itself, he could point to the negotiated agreements.

Negotiation is particularly appropriate when it is clear that someone is going to lose out as a result of a change and yet his or her power to resist is significant. Negotiated agreements can be a relatively easy way to avoid major resistance, though, like some other processes, they may become expensive. And once a manager makes it clear that he will negotiate to avoid major resistance, he opens himself up to the possibility of blackmail.[14]

Manipulation and co-optation

In some situations, managers also resort to covert attempts to influence others. Manipulation, in this context, normally involves the very selective use of information and the conscious structuring of events.

One common form of manipulation is co-optation. Co-opting an individual usually involves giving him or her a desirable role in the design or implementation of the change. Co-opting a group involves giving one of its

---

13. Zaltman and Duncan, *Strategies for Planned Change,* chap. 4.
14. For an excellent discussion of negotiation, see Gerald I. Nierenberg, *The Art of Negotiating* (Birmingham, Ala.: Cornerstone, 1968).

leaders, or someone it respects, a key role in the design or implementation of a change. This is not a form of participation, however, because the initiators do not want the advice of the co-opted, merely his or her endorsement. For example:

One division manager in a large multibusiness corporation invited the corporate human relations vice president, a close friend of the president, to help him and his key staff diagnose some problems the division was having. Because of his busy schedule, the corporate vice president was not able to do much of the actual information gathering or analysis himself, thus limiting his own influence on the diagnoses. But his presence at key meetings helped commit him to the diagnoses as well as the solutions the group designed. The commitment was subsequently very important because the president, at least initially, did not like some of the proposed changes. Nevertheless, after discussion with his human relations vice president, he did not try to block them.

Under certain circumstances co-optation can be a relatively inexpensive and easy way to gain an individual's or a group's support (cheaper, for example, than negotiation and quicker than participation). Nevertheless, it has its drawbacks. If people feel they are being tricked into not resisting, are not being treated equally, or are being lied to, they may respond very negatively. More than one manager has found that, by his effort to give some subordinate a sense of participation through co-optation, he created more resistance than if he had done nothing. In addition, co-optation can create a different kind of problem if those co-opted use their ability to influence the design and implementation of changes in ways that are not in the best interests of the organization.

Other forms of manipulation have drawbacks also, sometimes to an even greater degree. Most people are likely to greet what they perceive as covert treatment and/or lies with a negative response. Furthermore, if a manager develops a reputation as a manipulator, it can undermine his ability to use needed approaches such as education/communication and participation/involvement. At the extreme, it can even ruin his career.

Nevertheless, people do manipulate others successfully—particularly when all other tactics are not feasible or have failed.[15] Having no other alternative and not enough time to educate, involve, or support people, and without the power or other resources to negotiate, coerce, and co-opt them, managers have resorted to manipulating information channels in order to scare people into thinking there is a crisis coming which they can avoid only by changing.

15. See John P. Kotter, "Power, dependence, and effective management," *Harvard Business Review,* July–August 1977, p. 125.

Explicit and implicit coercion

Finally, managers often deal with resistance coercively. Here they essentially force people to accept a change by explicitly or implicitly threatening them (with the loss of jobs, promotion possibilities, and so forth) or by actually firing or transferring them. As with manipulation, using coercion is a risky process because inevitably people strongly resent forced change. But in situations where speed is essential and where the changes will not be popular, regardless of how they are introduced, coercion may be the manager's only option.

Successful organizational change efforts are always characterized by the skillful application of a number of these approaches, often in very different combinations. However, successful efforts share two characteristics: managers employ the approaches with a sensitivity to their strengths and limitations (see exhibit 1) and appraise the situation realistically.

The most common mistake managers make is to use only one approach or a limited set of them *regardless of the situation*. A surprisingly large number of managers have this problem. This would include the hard-boiled boss who often coerces people, the people-oriented manager who constantly tries to involve and support his people, the cynical boss who always manipulates and co-opts others, the intellectual manager who relies heavily on education and communication, and the lawyerlike manager who usually tries to negotiate.[16]

A second common mistake that managers make is to approach change in a disjointed and incremental way that is not a part of a clearly considered strategy.

Choice of strategy

In approaching an organizational change situation, managers explicitly or implicitly make strategic choices regarding the speed of the effort, the amount of preplanning, the involvement of others, and the relative emphasis they will give to different approaches. Successful change efforts seem to be those where these choices both are internally consistent and fit some key situational variables.

The strategic options available to managers can be usefully thought of as existing on a continuum (see exhibit 2).[17] At one end of the continuum, the change strategy calls for a very rapid implementation, a clear plan of action, and little involvement of others. This type of strategy mows over

16. Ibid., p. 135.
17. See Larry E. Greiner, "Patterns of organization change," *Harvard Business Review*, May–June 1967, p. 119; and Larry E. Greiner and Louis B. Barnes, "Organization change and development," in *Organizational Change and Development*, eds. Gene W. Dalton and Paul R. Lawrence (Homewood, Ill.: Richard D. Irwin, 1970), p. 3. © 1970 by Richard D. Irwin, Inc.

Approach	Commonly used in situations	Advantages	Drawbacks
Education + communication	Where there is a lack of information or inaccurate information and analysis	Once persuaded, people will often help with the implementation of the change	Can be very time-consuming if lots of people are involved
Participation + involvement	Where the initiators do not have all the information they need to design the change, and where others have considerable power to resist	People who participate will be committed to implementing change, and any relevant information they have will be integrated into the change plan	Can be very time-consuming if participators design an inappropriate change
Facilitation + support	Where people are resisting because of adjustment problems	No other approach works as well with adjustment problems	Can be time-consuming, expensive, and still fail
Negotiation + agreement	Where someone or some group will clearly lose out in a change, and where that group has considerable power to resist	Sometimes it is a relatively easy way to avoid major resistance	Can be too expensive in many cases if it alerts others to negotiate for compliance
Manipulation + co-optation	Where other tactics will not work or are too expensive	It can be a relatively quick and inexpensive solution to resistance problems	Can lead to future problems if people feel manipulated
Explicit + implicit coercion	Where speed is essential and the change initiators possess considerable power	It is speedy and can overcome any kind of resistance	Can be risky if it leaves people mad at the initiators

Exhibit 1. Methods for dealing with resistance to change

←————————————————————————————————————→

Fast:	Slower:
Clearly planned.	Not clearly planned at the beginning.
Little involvement of others.	Lots of involvement of others.
Attempt to overcome any resistance.	Attempt to minimize any resistance.

Key situational variables:

The amount and type of resistance that is anticipated.

The position of the initiators vis-à-vis the resistors (in terms of power, trust, and so forth).

The locus of relevant data for designing the change, and of needed energy for implementing it.

The stakes involved (e.g., the presence or lack of presence of a crisis, the consequences of resistance and lack of change).

Exhibit 2. Strategic continuum

any resistance and, at the extreme, would result in a fait accompli. At the other end of the continuum, the strategy would call for a much slower change process, a less clear plan, and involvement on the part of many people other than the change initiators. This type of strategy is designed to reduce resistance to a minimum.[18]

The further to the left one operates on the continuum in exhibit 2, the more one tends to be coercive and the less one tends to use the other approaches—especially participation; the converse also holds.

Organizational change efforts that are based on inconsistent strategies tend to run into predictable problems. For example, efforts that are not clearly planned in advance and yet are implemented quickly tend to become bogged down owing to unanticipated problems. Efforts that involve a large number of people but are implemented quickly usually become either stalled or less participative.

Situational factors

Exactly where a change effort should be strategically positioned on the continuum in exhibit 2 depends on four factors:

1. The amount and kind of resistance that is anticipated. All other factors being equal, the greater the anticipated resistance, the more difficult it

18. For a good discussion of an approach that attempts to minimize resistance, see Renato Tagiuri, "Notes on the Management of Change: Implication of Postulating a Need for Competence," in John P. Kotter, Vijay Sathe, and Leonard A. Schlesinger, *Organization* (Homewood, Ill.: Richard D. Irwin, Inc., 1979).

will be simply to overwhelm it, and the more a manager will need to move toward the right on the continuum to find ways to reduce some of it.[19]

2. *The position of the initiator vis-à-vis the resistors, especially with regard to power.* The less power the initiator has with respect to others, the more the initiating manager *must* move to the left on the continuum.[20] Conversely, the stronger the initiator's position, the more he or she can move to the right.

3. *The person who has the relevant data for designing the change and the energy for implementing it.* The more the initiators anticipate that they will need information and commitment from others to help design and implement the change, the more they must move to the right.[21] Gaining useful information and commitment requires time and the involvement of others.

4. *The stakes involved.* The greater the short-run potential for risks to organizational performance and survival if the present situation is not changed, the more one must move to the left.

Organizational change efforts that ignore these factors inevitably run into problems. A common mistake some managers make, for example, is to move too quickly and involve too few people despite the fact that they do not have all the information they really need to design the change correctly.

Insofar as these factors still leave a manager with some choice of where to operate on the continuum, it is probably best to select a point as far to the right as possible for both economic and social reasons. Forcing change on people can have just too many negative side effects over both the short and the long term. Change efforts using the strategies on the right of the continuum can often help develop an organization and its people in useful ways.[22]

In some cases, however, knowing the four factors may not give a manager a comfortable and obvious choice. Consider a situation where a manager has a weak position vis-à-vis the people whom he thinks need a change and yet is faced with serious consequences if the change is not implemented immediately. Such a manager is clearly in a bind. If he somehow is not able to increase his power in the situation, he will be forced to choose some compromise strategy and to live through difficult times.

Implications for managers

A manager can improve his chance of success in an organizational change effort by:

19. Jay W. Lorsch, "Managing Change," in *Organizational Behavior and Administration,* eds. Paul R. Lawrence, Louis B. Barnes, and Jay W. Lorsch (Homewood, Ill.: Richard D. Irwin, 1976), p. 676.

20. Ibid.

21. Ibid.

22. Michael Beer, *Organization Change and Development: A Systems View* (Pacific Palisades, Calif.: Goodyear, 1979).

1. Conducting an organizational analysis that identifies the current situation, problems, and the forces that are possible causes of those problems. The analysis should specify the actual importance of the problems, the speed with which the problems must be addressed if additional problems are to be avoided, and the kinds of changes that are generally needed.

2. Conducting an analysis of factors relevant to producing the needed changes. This analysis should focus on questions of who might resist the change, why, and how much; who has information that is needed to design the change, and whose cooperation is essential in implementing it; and what is the position of the initiator vis-à-vis other relevant parties in terms of power, trust, normal modes of interaction, and so forth.

3. Selecting a change strategy, based on the previous analysis, that specifies the speed of change, the amount of preplanning, and the degree of involvement of others; that selects specific tactics for use with various individuals and groups; and that is internally consistent.

4. Monitoring the implementation process. No matter how good a job one does of initially selecting a change strategy and tactics, something unexpected will eventually occur during implementation. Only by carefully monitoring the process can one identify the unexpected in a timely fashion and react to it intelligently.

Interpersonal skills, of course, are the key to using this analysis. But even the most outstanding interpersonal skills will not make up for a poor choice of strategy and tactics. And in a business world that continues to become more and more dynamic, the consequences of poor implementation choices will become increasingly severe.

Managing Strategies Incrementally

James Brian Quinn

Introduction

In a recently completed study of large companies undergoing strategic change (1), I found that managers purposely guided important actions *incrementally* toward strategies embodying many of the structural principles of elegant formal strategies. In these concerns the approach was neither "anti-planning" nor an abrogation of the hard intellectual thought processes required for formal strategic analyses. In fact, formal planning was usually an essential building block in the step by step processes executives used to develop overall strategies. But for good reasons, they relied on much more evolutionary practices than this model usually implies (16, 10, 42). Their approach might at first seem to be disjointed or muddling (20), but on closer analysis the rationale behind their incremental approach to strategy formulation was so powerful that it perhaps provides a normative model for most strategic decisions. Why and how do effective executives manage in this mode?

From broad to specific

Strategy deals with the unknowable (2). In the beginning, it is literally impossible to predict all the important events and forces which might possibly shape the future of the enterprise—much less the total effect of their interactions. The best that executives can do is to forecast the forces *most likely* to impinge on the company's future and the probable nature and range of their potential impacts (18). From these they can define broadly and flexibly what they would like to do, i.e., their *vision* of success (32). Then successful strategists try to build a *resource base* and a *posture* that is so strong and flexible that the enterprise can survive and prosper toward its vision despite all but the most devastating events. They consciously seek a market/technological/product scope within which their concerns can be "preeminent" despite their resource limits (17). Then, when possible, they

Reprinted with permission from OMEGA 10, no. 6:613–27. © 1982 by Pergamon Press, Ltd.

place some "side bets": (a) to decrease the risk of catastrophic failure or (b) to offer the company added future options (6).

Instead of seeking ultimate specificity in their overall strategies, executives in my study accepted much ambiguity (50). They initially worked out in their own minds—and shared with selected colleagues—only a few integrating concepts, principles, or philosophies that would help rationalize and guide the company's overall movements. They proceeded step by step from the early generalities toward later specifics (30), clarifying the strategy incrementally as events permitted or dictated. In early stages they consciously avoided over-precise statements which might impair the flexibility or imagination needed to exploit new information or opportunities (37). They constantly reassessed the future, found new congruencies as events unfurled, and blended the organization's skills and resources into new balances of concentration and risk dispersion as external forces and internal potentials intersected to suggest better, but never perfect, alignments. The process was dynamic with neither a real beginning nor end.

In the hands of skillful executives incrementalism is not merely reactive as some have suggested (3). Incrementalism can be a purposeful, powerful management technique for integrating the analytical, behavioral, political and timing aspects of strategy formulation.

Why incrementalism?

There are five basic reasons for using careful incrementalism in strategy formulation. It helps executives:

1. improve the quality of information available for strategic decisions;
2. deal with the different lead times and sequencing problems involved in major decisions;
3. stimulate flexibility, creativity, and opportunism in pursuing desired goals;
4. overcome political and emotional barriers to change;
5. create the personal and organizational commitment needed to implement strategies effectively.

Specific examples will demonstrate how incrementalism contributes in various common and difficult strategic situations.

Precipitating events

No matter how carefully executives plan, external events—over which they have essentially no control—can precipitate urgent, piecemeal, interim decisions with critical long-term strategic consequences (16). Early decisions made under stress can create new thrusts, precedents or opportunities that are difficult to reverse later. Recognizing this, top executives often deal with precipitating events in an incremental fashion. Early commitments are kept formative, tentative and subject to later review. In some cases, neither the company nor external players can understand the full implications of alternative actions. All want to test assumptions and have a chance to learn from and adapt to the others' responses (31), for example:

> When I was in the office of Esso France's president our discussions were interrupted several times by announcements that the country was being shut down by political turmoil and that various activist groups had taken over one or another of Esso's facilities. Instead of ending our conversation to take some action, the president quietly said, "Right now we must merely find out what is going on. Then we must wait until the situation clarifies enough to know what to do." It took several days to clarify the demands of the activists, to undertand the forces at play, and to participate effectively in coalitions. Haste could have set in motion forces which would have permanently damaged the French company's strategic position.

Further information has a value. So effective executives consciously try to keep their options open until they better understand how later events may affect their enterprise, their various constituencies, and their power bases. Logic dictates that critical decisions should be made as late as possible consistent with the information available (26); this usually means incrementally. But crisis decisions do not provide the sole—or central—rationale for incrementalism in strategy formulation. Other aspects of strategy do.

Technology development

Although one can, and should, lay out the broad goals and a planned framework for R&D activities, the precise directions that R&D may project the company can only be understood step by step as scientists uncover new phenomena, amplify discoveries, reduce concepts to practice, build prototypes, and interact with potential users. Throughout this process a wise management will maintain its options and proceed incrementally from broad visions toward final specific positioning strategies (38). The latter pattern is often significantly affected by where break-throughs occur, their timing, and relative economic potentials, none of which can be accurately predicted when the program begins. For example:

> Pilkington's entire worldwide strategy would have been markedly changed if its float glass program had not had a bit of luck at a crucial moment. When a pouring spout on its experimental glass facility broke, the accident led to solution of the final bottleneck in the revolutionary new process which then dominated the industry for 20 years. On the other hand, if Pilkington's fiberglass programs had been relatively more successful earlier, the company's whole strategy might well have shifted in other directions (40).
>
> Similarly today, Genentech must see which of its genetically engineered products and processes can be reduced to practice first and which

will perform safely and effectively in life systems, before it defines much of its eventual strategy. Even now it appears that Genentech's early positioning may be in animal disease prevention, not in the glamorous human health areas it first envisioned.

Recognizing the need for flexibility in technical strategies in the U.S. Defense Department companies like IBM and Xerox have developed "phased program planning" systems. They make concrete decisions only on the current phase of a project. They continue to introduce data from further technical findings and user interactions (48) into program decisions as long as possible until truly fixed commitments must be made for plants, components or major facilities. This added information often positions the new technology differently and more effectively than earlier formal analysis suggested—with important consequences for strategy.

Acquisition/diversification programs

Acquisition/diversification strategies also require an incremental approach for maximum effectiveness. Formal analyses can lay out broad goals for such programs, define the criteria candidate companies must meet, set priorities for the search, build needed resource and organizational flexibilities, and anticipate potential problems in integrating new units into the enterprise (22). But so much depends on the availability, sequencing, conditions of purchase and specific management characteristics of the individual companies acquired that successful acquisition programs must proceed flexibly and opportunistically, interactively reshaping initial visions and strategies as concrete potentials emerge (47). This is especially important for large single acquisitions where each new unit markedly changes the company's overall strategic capabilities. For example:

> Continental Group would have a very different strategic posture today if it had purchased Peabody Coal instead of Richmond Insurance. Yet both would have made viable "fourth legs" for Continental's business at the time of their consideration. And the acquisition of one might have preempted the other (40).
>
> Similarly, Seagram's unsuccessful billion dollar attempts to acquire St. Joe Minerals and CONOCO will probably lead to a completely different future strategic posture than it once anticipated. Yet such divergent results are common hazards of acquisition strategies.

Even in acquiring smaller companies, the final impact of a diversification program will be determined by whether and when specific candidates become available (24)—always a somewhat random process. Some of the most successful acquisitions come "over the transom," as Steak and Ale did for Pillsbury (40), to a flexibly prepared company. One can rarely completely foresee how such acquisitions will fit and blend into a new strategy until at least the key pieces are known and in place. For example:

General Mills very carefully laid out the criteria for its early 1970s acquisitions in the classic manner. Its intentions were: (1) to expand in food-related fields, (2) to develop new growth centers based on its skills at marketing to the homemaker. The consensus was that the majority of the resources should go to food-related areas. Almost the exact opposite occurred. Because of external factors beyond its control, the company had a good selection of candidates in non-foods areas and few in foods. By 1973 General Mills had diversified into a wide array of new areas from toys to creative crafts to fine clothing, with high impact on its total posture (40).

In addition to handling such sequencing and timing considerations, incremental processes also assist in achieving the crucial psychological and power shifts which so significantly affect a program's overall directions and consequences. Properly used, they step by step help to create the broad conceptual consensus, risk-taking attitudes and adaptive dynamics critical to success. Most important among these processes are:

1. generating the initial psychological commitment to diversify outside of familiar fields;
2. building a sufficient "comfort factor" about risk-taking for key managers to actually commit resources to new areas;
3. systematically realigning the enterprise's resources and organization structure so it can move opportunistically;
4. empowering an "activist" whose career depends upon the success of the diversification program;
5. shortening lines of communication from the activist to the highest decision authorities;
6. overcoming political resistance to redirecting funds;
7. actively changing the company's past ethos as new attitudes, potentials and power centers emerge (31).

Each of these processes can affect the timing and direction of the strategy as much as any formal analysis. Each has its own timing imperatives. And each interacts with other decision processes and the random appearance of acquisition candidates to redirect initially planned actions, time scales and results in unexpected ways. Complexities are so great that few diversification programs end up as initially envisioned. Experienced managers recognize this and manage their acquisition programs incrementally, reshaping their broad early visions flexibly, step by step, as new opportunities, acquired competences and executive personalities merge to create new potential patterns for success. Until these patterns are clear, acquisition goals are kept general and are rarely explicitly announced. For example:

As George Wiessman, chief architect of Philip Morris' successful acquisition program, said: "We don't announce growth goals in new areas because we don't want to get trapped into doing something stupid. We might be tempted to acquire a company when we shouldn't. Or we might hang on to an operation we really should sell off. Public statements can sometimes generate powerful expectations—internally and externally—that can pressure you to do the wrong thing."

Major reorganizations

Macro organizational changes tend to be associated with most major corporate strategy shifts (9). Like most other important strategic decisions, these moves are also typically handled incrementally *and* outside the formal planning process. Why?

Their effects on personal or power relationships preclude discussion in the open forums and reports of formal planning. Top executives have to think through the new roles, capabilities and probable individual reactions of the many principals affected. They may have to wait for the promotion or retirement of a valued colleague before making a particular desired change. Then they frequently have to bring in, train, or test new people for substantial periods before they can staff key posts with confidence. As individuals' potentials, performance, personal drives, and relationships to other team members develop, top managers may substantially modify major elements in their original organization concept as well as the overall corporate strategy. For example:

> At General Mills, Charles Bell brought in a new team of outside professional managers under General Rawlings. This team redefined the company's problems and opportunities in ways the prior management could not have foreseen. Over a period of time they divested many divisions which had been the core of the old business. These divestitures released funds for acquisitions in new areas, thus automatically increasing the visibility and power of the new controllership-financial group brought in by Rawlings. But with fewer large divisions competing for funds, the Consumer Foods Group also rapidly grew in importance. This ultimately led to the choice of the Consumer Foods Head, James MacFarland, for the corporation's next CEO—and set the direction of General Mills' future strategy (40).

Successful reorganizations, other than those made in crises, tend to proceed opportunistically, step by step, selectively moving people and unit structures toward a broadly conceived organizational goal which is constantly modified and rarely articulated in detail until the most important psychological and structural pieces finally fit together. An overall concept of "decentralization", "SBUs" or "global product units" may prevail throughout. But if adequate allowance is made for testing, flexibility and feedback, the final formulation may bear little likeness to initial conceptions. And the outcome is usually an improvement.

Government–external relations strategies

Government–external relations strategies also require incremental formulation. Such strategies typically deal with very large scale forces, mostly beyond the company's direct control. Data tend to be very soft, often can only be subjectively sensed, and may be costly or impossible to quantify. The way outside individuals or groups will respond to a particular stimulus is difficult to predict. Yet these forces can be very powerful relative to the company. And their potential attack modes can be so diverse that it is physically impossible to lay out probabilistic decision diagrams that have much meaning. Bizarre actions of outsiders can determine final outcomes. Results are unpredictable and error costs extreme. Hence, the most rational seeming and best intended strategies can be converted into disasters unless they are interactively developed and tested. For example:

> In the 1960s General Motors found that technical discussions of cost vs. benefit tradeoffs were useless against demagogic slogans like "smog kills" or "GM is the worst polluter in the world." Despite assisting in the basic studies that defined automotive exhausts as a major causative factor in smog, GM publicly resisted some early attempts to impose effluent standards as "beyond the state of the art." Then later, after successfully completing the costly and risky ($100 million) development of the catalytic converter, GM had its earlier concerns thrown in its face as "foot dragging" or "lying" about technical potentials. As one executive said, "You were damned if you did and damned if you didn't." Only after prolonged interactions with regulators, legislators and public interest groups did GM truly understand the needs and pressure potentials of its opponents. Area by area it experimented with better ways to communicate with various interests. Only then could it identify effective patterns to mold into its overall corporate strategy (31).

Other strategies

Other strategies, like those for divestitures, capital access, international relations, human resources development etc., are so sensitive that they too are usually determined in subsystems outside the forums of formal planning. The timing imperatives of each subsystem or strategic area tend to drive its decisions out of synchronization with the others. Consequently just as managers move forward incrementally with each strategic area, they also must proceed incrementally toward a total strategy (25). They constantly try, both intuitively and analytically, to integrate their actions into a cohesive pattern as they go along. But rarely do all the pieces fit neatly and totally in detail at any specific instant, especially at the moment annual plans are due.

Formal planning increments too

In most cases formal planning itself should be a part of the incremental process. Most sophisticated managements purposely design their plans to be "living" or "evergreen." They are best thought of as frameworks to guide and provide consistency for future decisions made incrementally. To act otherwise is to deny that further information has a value. Properly developed, such systems are very useful—indeed essential—as components of the strategic process: they teach managers about the future and extend the time horizon of detailed plans; they serve as important vehicles for involving lower level managers and forcing negotiations on goals and program balances throughout the organization; in the planning guidelines issued from the top and in the commitment patterns they eventually set forth, they systematize and confirm incrementally made strategic decisions. Annual planning provides a critical interface between strategic and tactical commitments. It is the *sine qua non* of all decentralization and sensible management control (44).

But in my sample, annual planning was rarely the source point for major new strategies—and certainly not for overall corporate strategies. These evolved from the kinds of incremental processes described above.

Formulation and implementation blur

In large organizations overall strategies rarely burst forth full blown from even the best strategic studies (28). Even MacArthur's brilliant "island hopping" strategy was slowly synthesized from a series of studies, political interactions, tests and early failures (23). Executives tend to adopt only a piece of a given study's total recommendations and leave other key elements to be defined as new information becomes available, politics permit or specific opportunities or thrusts crystallize. Overall strategies *emerge* organically as executives link together and create order out of a series of partially overlapping processes and interacting decisions that may span years (12). Such incrementalism is a conscious adaptation to the psychological and informational problems of getting an ever changing group of people with diverse talents and interests to work together effectively in a continually dynamic environment.

The lines between strategy formulation and implementation constantly blur. Some parts of a major strategy will be in early awareness building stages, other parts in analytical stages, others in experimental phases, others in unpredictable flux or crisis situations, and still others in introduction or implementation modes which require later modification. Partial implementation of large scale strategies must be underway even as other formulation efforts go forward. Thoughtful executives treat each step in the formulation process as an integral part of implementation. They see that key people are informed, involved and committed in developing their particular phases of the strategy. They build existing momenta into the strategy, wherever possible. And they constantly try to see that essential interim decisions—like facilities, technology, or personal selections—help implant or flexibly support intuitively perceived strategic thrusts that may not yet be worked out in detail. Because of such dynamics it may be misleading to think that in large organizations one can realistically first formulate a detailed overall strategy, announce it, and then proceed to implant it. Much more subtle, interrelated, continuous evolutionary processes tend to dominate strategy development in these circumstances.

Managing incrementalism

How can one proactively manage strategy formulation in this mode? One executive provided perhaps the most articulate short statement of the overall approach:

> Typically you start with a general concern, vaguely felt. Next, you roll an issue around in your mind until you think you have a conclusion that makes sense for the company. Then you go out and sort of post the idea without being too wedded to its details. You then start hearing the arguments pro and con, and some very good refinements of the idea usually emerge. Then you pull the idea in and put some resources together to study it so it can be put forward as more of a formal presentation. You wait for "stimuli occurrences" or "crises," and launch pieces of the idea to help in these situations. But they lead toward your ultimate aim. You know where you want to get. You'd like to get there in six months. But it may take three years, or you may not get there at all. And when you do get there, you don't know whether it was originally your own idea—or somebody else had reached the same conclusion before you and just got you on board for it. You never know (40).

Because of differences in organizational form, management style, and the content of individual decisions, no single paradigm holds for all strategic decisions (37). But my study suggests that executives tend to utilize somewhat similar incremental processes as they manage complex strategy shifts. A few glimpses follow:

Leading the formal information system

Rarely do the earliest signals for strategic change come from the company's formal horizon scanning, planning or reporting systems. Instead, initial sensing of needs for major strategic changes is often described as "something you feel uneasy about," "inconsistencies" or "anomalies" (31) between the enterprise's current posture and some general perception of its future environment (29). Effective managers establish multiple credible internal and external sources to obtain objective information about their enterprise and its surrounding environments (50). They use these networks to short-circuit all the careful screens their organizations build up "to tell the top only what it wants to hear" (4). They actively search beyond their organization's formal information systems, deeming the latter to be too historical, tradition oriented or extrapolative to pinpoint needed basic changes in time (8). For example:

> To avoid their own natural biases, executives who are aggressively seeking new potential opportunities or threats make sure their networks include people who look at the world quite differently from the dominating culture of the enterprise. Some companies have structured "devil's advocates" into their planning processes for this purpose. Others have undertaken "aggressor company" exercises to simulate how intelligent aggressors could best attack their patents, markets, or desired future positions. Still others—like Xerox—have commissioned groups of known independent thinkers to make special studies, with the extensive help of outside consultants and authorities, to ensure top managers view changing environments analytically and creatively.

Building organizational awareness

This may be essential when key players do not have enough information or psychological stimulation to voluntarily change their past action patterns or to investigate options creatively. At early stages, successful change managers seem to consciously generate and consider a broad array of alternatives (50). While tapping the "collective wit" of the organization, they try to build awareness and concern about new issues. They assemble objective data to argue against preconceived ideas or blindly followed past practices. Yet they want to avoid prematurely threatening power centers that might kill important changes before potential supporters really know what is at stake and can bring broader interests to bear. At this stage, management processes are rarely directive. Instead they are likely to involve studying, challenging, questioning, listening, talking to creative people outside ordinary decision channels, generating options, but purposely avoiding irreversible commitments (15). For example:

> In the early 1970s there was a glut in world oil supplies. Nevertheless, GM's Chief Economist began to project an increased US dependency on foreign oil and higher future prices. These concerns led the Board in 1972 to create an *ad hoc* energy task force of key executives under David Collier. The group's report in May 1973 "created a good deal of discussion around the company" in the months before the oil embargo hit. "We were trying to get other people to think about the issue," said Richard Gerstenberg, then chairman of GM. These discussions provided an important backdrop for the crucial downsizing decisions made during the embargo period (40).

Executives may want their colleagues to be more knowledgeable about such major issues and help think through ramifications clearly before taking specific actions (25). They want to avoid being the prime supporter of a losing idea or having the organization attack or slavishly adopt "the boss's solution" and having to change it as more evidence becomes available. Even though top executives may not have in mind specific solutions to an emerging problem they can proactively guide early steps in intuitively desired directions by defining the issues staffs investigate, selecting the people who make the investigations, and controlling the reporting process. They may not terminate this "diagnostic phase" (29) until they have identified potential proponents and opponents of various positions and are sure that enough people will "get on board" to make a solution work.

Building credibility/changing symbols

Symbols may help managers signal to the organization that certain types of changes are coming, even when specific solutions are not yet in hand. Knowing they cannot communicate directly with the thousands who must carry out a strategy, many executives purposely undertake a few highly visible symbolic actions which wordlessly convey complex messages they could never communicate as well, or as credibly, in verbal terms. Through word of mouth the informal grapevine can amplify signals of a pending change in ways no formal communication could (41). For example:

> In GM's downsizing decision, engineers said one of top management's early decisions affected the credibility of the whole weight-reduction program: "Initially, we proposed a program using a lot of aluminum and substitute materials to meet the new mass targets. But this would have meant a very high cost, and would have strained the suppliers' aluminum capacity. However, when we presented this program to management, they said, 'Okay, if necessary, we'll do it.' They didn't back down. We began to understand then that they were dead serious. Feeling that the company would spend the money was critical to the success of the entire mass reduction effort" (40).

Organizations often need such symbolic moves, or decisions they regard as symbolic, to verify the intention of a new strategy or to build credibility behind one in its initial stages. Without such actions people may interpret even forceful verbiage as mere rhetoric and delay their commitment to new thrusts.

Legitimizing new viewpoints

This will often involve planned delays, since top managers may purposely create discussion forums or allow slack time for their organizations to talk through threatening issues, work out the implications of new solutions, or gain an improved information base that permits new options to be evaluated objectively in comparison with more familiar alternatives. Because of familiarity, solutions which arise out of executives' prior experience are perceived as having lower risks (or potential costs) than newer alternatives that are more attractive when viewed objectively. In many cases, strategic concepts which are at first strongly resisted can gain acceptance and positive commitment simply by the passage of time and open discussion of new information—when executives do not exacerbate hostility by pushing them too fast from the top (11). Many top executives, planners and change agents consciously arrange for such "gestation periods" and find that the concept itself is frequently made more effective by the resulting feedback and acceptance. For example:

> When William Spoor took over as CEO at Pillsbury, one of the biggest issues he faced was whether to stay in or get out of the Pillsbury Farms' chicken business. Management was deeply split on the question. Spoor asked all key protagonists for position papers and purposely commissioned two papers on each side for the Board. He invited consultants' views and visited Ralston Purina, which had undergone a similar divestiture. He got an estimate from Lehman Brothers as to the division's value. All this went to the Board which debated the issue for months. A key event occurred when Lehman found a potential European buyer at a good price. Finally, when the vote was taken only one person—Pillsbury Farms' original champion—voted for retention (40).

Tactical shifts and partial solutions

These are typical steps in developing a new overall strategic posture and early problem resolutions are likely to be partial, tentative or experimental (24). Beginning moves are often handled as mere tactical adjustments in the enterprise's existing posture and as such they encounter little opposition. Executives can often obtain agreement to a series of small programs when a broad objective change would encounter too much opposition. Such programs allow the guiding executive to maintain the enterprise's ongoing strengths while shifting momentum—at the margin—toward new needs (12). At this stage, top executives themselves may not yet comprehend the full nature or extent of the strategic shifts they are beginning (7). They can still experiment with partial new approaches without risking the viability of the total enterprise, while their broad early steps can legitimately lead to a variety of different success scenarios (29). For example:

> Following the Collier report, when the oil embargo hit in fall 1973, General Motors responded at first by merely increasing production of its existing small cars. Then as the crisis deepened, it added another partial solution, the subcompact "T car"—the Chevette—and accelerated the Seville's development cycle. As economy appeared more saleable, executives set an initial target of removing 400 pounds from

big-car bodies in 1977. Then as fuel economy pressures persisted and engineering feasibilities offered greater confidence, this target was tightened further to 800-1000 pounds (3 miles per gallon). No step by itself shifted the company's total strategic posture until the full downsizing of all lines was agreed upon. But each partial solution built confidence and commitment toward a new direction.

As events unfurl, the solutions to several initially unrelated problems tend to flow together into a new synthesis. When possible, strategic logic (risk minimization) dictate starting broad initiatives that can be flexibly guided in any of several possible desirable directions (50).

Broadening political support

Broadening political support for emerging new thrusts is frequently an essential and consciously proactive step in major strategy changes. Committees, task forces or retreats tend to be favored mechanisms. By selecting such groups' chairmen, membership, timing and agenda the guiding executive can largely influence and predict a desired outcome, yet nudge other executives toward a consensus (24). The careful executive, of course, still maintains complete control over these "advisory" processes through his various influence and veto potentials. In addition to facilitating smooth implementation, many managers report that interactive consensus building also improves the quality of the strategic decisions themselves and helps achieve positive and innovative assistance when things otherwise would go wrong. For example:

> Shortly after he became CEO of General Mills, James MacFarland took his 35 top people on a three day retreat to discuss "how to move a good company to greatness." He wanted the views of others in defining greatness and their active participation in achieving it. Working in groups of six to eight, the management team defined what the characteristics of a great company were from various points of view, what General Mill's shortcomings were, and what main thrusts were needed to overcome these. Over time, these broad visions, goals and programs were converted into charters for various divisions and groups. They became the initial guidelines for the company's very successful and flexible development over the next decade (40).

Overcoming opposition

Overcoming opposition is almost always necessary at some stage. Careful executives realize that they must deal with the support the preceding strategy had. They try not to unnecessarily alienate managers from the earlier era, whose talents they may need in future ventures, through a frontal assault on old approaches. Instead, they persuade individuals toward new concepts whenever possible, co-opt or neutralize serious opposition if necessary (43), or move through zones of indifference (5) where early changes will not be disastrously opposed. Under the best circumstances, they find "no lose" situations that activate all important players positively towards new common goals. For example:

> After the goodness to greatness conference described above, General Mills had two major strategic thrusts: (1) to expand internally and through acquisitions in food related areas and (2) to acquire new growth centers based on General Mills' marketing skills. Neither of the two critical power centers—the more traditional product groups nor the strong finance acquisition group—was foreclosed from participation and active involvement in the new strategy. In fact, both were stimulated to support it for their own future benefit.

Successful executives tend to honor legitimate differences in views concerning even major directions and note that initial opponents often thoughtfully shape new strategies in more effective directions. Some may become active supporters as new information emerges to change their views. But consensus is not always possible. Strong minded executives sometimes disagree to the point where they must be moved to positions of less influence or stimulated to leave. And timing can dictate very firm top level direction at key junctures.

Consciously structured flexibility

Flexibility is essential in dealing with the many "unknowables" in the total environment. One cannot possibly predict the precise form or timing of all important threats and opportunities the firm may encounter. Logic dictates therefore that managers purposely design flexibility into their organizations and have resources ready to deploy incrementally as events demand. This requires:

1. proactive horizon scanning to identify the general range, scale, and impact of the opportunities and threats the firm is most likely to encounter;
2. creating sufficient resource buffers, or slacks, to respond as events actually do unfurl;
3. developing and positioning "champions" who will be motivated to take advantage of specific opportunities as they occur;
4. shortening decision lines between such persons and the top for rapid system response.

These—rather than pre-capsuled (and shelved) programs to respond to stimuli which never occur quite as expected—are the keys to real contingency planning.

The concept of resource buffers perhaps requires some amplification to suggest their strategic nature. For example:

Exxon set up its Exploration Group to purposely undertake the higher risks and longer-term investments necessary to search for oil in new areas, and thus to reduce the potential impact on Exxon if there were sudden unpredictable changes in the availability of Middle East oil.

Instead of hoarding cash, Pillsbury and General Mills sold off unprofitable businesses and cleaned up their financial statements to improve their access to external capital sources for acquisitions. Such access in essence provided the protection of a cash buffer without its investment.

IBM's large R&D facility and its project team approach to development assured that it had a pool of people it could quickly shift among various projects to exploit interesting new technologies opportunistically as they developed.

With such flexible patterns designed into the strategy the enterprise is proactively ready to move on those thrusts that by their very nature may have to evolve incrementally.

Trial balloons and systematic waiting

These are often the next steps for prepared strategists. As Roosevelt awaited a critical event like Pearl Harbor, the strategists may have to wait patiently for the proper option or precipitating event to appear. For example:

The availability of desired acquisitions or real estate may depend upon a death, divorce, fiscal crisis, management change or erratic economic break. Technological advances may await new knowledge, inventions or lucky accidents. Or planned market entries may not be wise until new legislation, trade agreements or competitive shake outs occur. Very often the optimum strategy depends on the timing and sequence of such random events. For example the timing and nature of SDS Inc.'s availability was a proximate cause of both the date and results of this first Xerox entry into computers.

Executives may also consciously launch trial concepts like Mr. McColough's "Architecture of Information" or Mr. Spoor's "Super Box" in order to attract options and concrete proposals. Usually these trial balloons are phrased in very broad contextual terms. Without making a commitment to any specific solution, the executive activates the organization's creative abilities (46). This approach keeps the manager's own options open until substantive alternatives can be evaluated against each other and against concrete current realities. And it prevents practical line managers from rejecting desirable strategic shifts because they are forced to compare "paper options" against what they see as well-defined, urgent needs.

Creating pockets of commitment

This may be necessary for entirely new strategic thrusts. The executive may encourage exploratory projects to test options, create necessary skills or technologies or build commitment for several possible options deep within the organization. Initial projects may be kept small, partial, or *ad hoc,* not forming a comprehensive program of seeming to be integrated into a cohesive strategy. At this stage guiding executives may merely provide broad goals, a proper climate and flexible resource support, without being identified with specific projects (46). In this way they can avoid escalating attention to any one solution too soon or losing personal credibility if it fails. But they can stimulate those options which lead in desired directions, set higher hurdles for those that do not or quietly have them killed some levels below to maintain their own flexibility. Executives can then keep their own options open, control premature momentum, openly back only winners and select the right moment to blend several successful thrusts into a broader program or concept (49). They can delay their own final decisions on a total thrust until the last moment, thus obtaining the best possible match-up between the company's capabilities, psychological commitments, and changing market needs. For example:

> For years IBM has made the technical "shoot out" a portion of its style in managing development programs. They allow various teams to work independently on alternative approaches to a desired solution. Then they have the teams demonstrate their approach in a prototype competition. Top management maintains the right of ultimate choice. But the winning team is already committed to its approach and ready to champion it in the organization. Such parallel development improves each team's motivation to invent and progress, enhances the quality of information used to critique each approach, creates genuine options, and allows final choices to be made as near the marketplace as possible. By increasing the effectiveness of decisions, the efficiency of development improves despite the apparent cost of parallel development.
>
> Similar techniques have been used by Bell Laboratories. Pilkington, United Technology, and other successful technical groups.

Crystallizing focus

Crystallizing focus at critical points in the process is, of course, vital. Sometimes executives will state a few key goals at an early stage to generate action or cohesion in a difficult or crisis situation. But for reasons noted, guiding executives often purposely keep early goal statements vague and commitments broad and tentative (37). Then as they develop information or consensus on desirable thrusts, they may use their prestige or power to push or crystallize a particular formulation. Despite adhering to the rhetoric of specific goal setting, most executives in my study were careful not to state many new strategic objectives in concrete terms until they had carefully built consensus among key players (21). To do otherwise might inadvertently centralize their organizations, preempt interesting options, provide a common focus for otherwise fragmented opposition, or cause the organization to undertake undesirable actions just to carry out a stated commitment. Because the net direction of an organization's goals ultimately reflects a negotiated balance among the imperatives felt by the dominant executive coalition (33) and the most important power centers and stakeholders in the enterprise (14), the last thing an executive wants is to weaken his or her position by creating an unintended counter coalition. When to crystallize viewpoints and when to maintain open options is one of the true arts of strategic management. For example:

> The principal stockholder in a $200 million drilling company wanted the company to grow relatively rapidly by selective acquisitions. But when its Board representative presented a detailed plan outlining proposed areas for growth and diversification, the proposal was stymied. Other Board members—based on limited experience—took a rigid stance on one specific aspect of the plan, acquisition of "service companies" supporting the line. No progress was made until the principal stockholder went back and sold the Board on an idea they all could accept, growth through acquisition. As Board members became comfortable with this broad concept it became possible later to reintroduce the idea of "service companies" and allay the Board's fears with a specific example.

Formalizing commitment

This is the final step in formulation. As partial consensus emerges, the guiding executive may crystallize events by stating a few broad goals in more specific terms for internal consumption. Finally when sufficient general acceptance exists and the timing is right, the decision may appear in more public pronouncements. For example, as General Mills divested several of its major "old line" divisions its annual reports began to state these as moves "to concentrate on the company's strengths" and "to intensify General Mills' efforts in the convenience foods field," statements which it would have been unwise or impolitic to make until many of the actual divestitures had taken place and a new management coalition and consensus had emerged.

As each major new thrust comes into focus strategic managers insure that some individual(s) feel responsible for its execution. Plans are locked into programs or budgets, and control and reward systems are aligned to reflect intended strategic emphases (10). Since so much has been written on this subject, I will avoid details here.

Continuing dynamics and mutating consensus

Unless continuing dynamics and mutating consensus quickly follow initial implementation, old crusades become the new conventional wisdom and the organization fails to prepare itself for new concerns and concepts. In trying to build commitment, executives often surround themselves with people who strongly identify with the new strategy. These supporters can rapidly become systematic screens against new views. Even as the organization arrives at its new consensus, guiding executives must move to insure that this too does not become inflexible. Effective strategic managers therefore immediately introduce new focus and stimuli at the top to begin mutating the very strategic thrusts they have just solidified—a most difficult but essential psychological task. Thus strategy formulation in successful large organizations becomes a continuous evolving, political, consensus building process with neither a finite beginning nor end.

Not a linear process

While generation of a strategy generally flows along the sequence presented, stages are by no means orderly or discrete. Few executives manage the process through all phases linearly. Any single decision may well involve numerous loops back to earlier stages as unexpected issues are encountered. Or decision times may become extremely compressed and require short circuiting leaps forward when crises suddenly appear and options narrow precipitously. The strategy's ultimate development involves a series of nested partial decisions (in each strategic area) interacting with similar decisions in all other areas and with a constantly changing resource base. Pfiffner (35) has aptly described the process as "like fermentation in biochemistry, rather than an industrial assembly line." The validity of a strategy lies not in its pristine clarity or rigorously maintained structure, but in its capacity to capture the initiative, to deal with unknowable events, to redeploy and concentrate resources as new opportunities and thrusts emerge and thus to use resources most effectively toward selected goals.

Each major segment of a strategy is likely to be in a different phase of its development—from initial awareness toward ultimate commitment—at any given moment. The real integration of all these components into a total enterprise strategy takes place primarily in the minds of individual top executives. Some portions of the strategy may be seen the same way by all, but each executive may legitimately perceive the overall balance of goals and thrusts slightly differently (29). Some differences may be openly expressed as issues to be resolved when new information becomes available; others may remain unstated, hidden agendas to emerge at later dates; still others may be masked by accepting a broad statement of intention that accommodates many divergent views within its seeming consensus—while a more specific statement might be divisive. Events often move almost imperceptibly from awareness, to concern, to experiments, to options, to partial acceptance, to momenta, to consensus, to formal reinforcement. The process is so continuous that it may be hard to discern the particular point in time when specific clear-cut decisions are made.

Integrating the strategy

Nevertheless, the total pattern of actions, though incremental, does not remain piecemeal in well-managed organizations. Effective executives constantly reassess the total organization, its capacities and needs as related to surrounding environments. They seek new cohesive patterns which integrate interim decisions made in subordinate strategies. To coordinate these decisions cross-sectionally, wise managers use a variety of formal and informal techniques.

They see that the teams developing subordinate strategies have overlapping members. They require periodic briefings and reviews for higher echelon groups to bring a total corporate view to bear and to learn from those with more detailed knowledge. They use formal planning techniques to interrelate and evaluate resources required, benefits sought and risks undertaken. Some use highly developed scenario techniques or complex forecasting models to better understand basic relationships among specific subsystems, the total enterprise, and its critical environments. Others create specialized staffs, "devil's advocates," or "contention teams" to make sure that all important aspects receive thorough evaluation. These techniques help in specific situations. But two other concepts lie at the core of most strategic integration.

Concentrating on a few key thrusts

Strategic managers constantly seek to distil out a few (six to ten) "central themes" that draw the firm's diverse existing activities and new probes into common cause (45). Once identified, these help maintain focus and consistency in the strategy. They make it easier to discuss and monitor intended directions. In ideal circumstances, these themes can be converted into a matrix of strategic "thrusts" or "missions" cutting across divisional plans and dominating other criteria used to rank divisional commitments (39). Each division's plans have to show *enough* effort to accomplish its share of each thrust, even though this means overriding short-term present-value or rate-of-return rankings on projects within the division (34). Texas Instruments and General Electric Company have provided some well publicized formal models for doing this. Unfortunately, few companies seem able to implement such complex planning systems without generating voluminous paperwork, large planning bureaucracies and undesirable rigidities in the plans themselves.

As noted, careful professionalism in planning can pay high dividends. Nevertheless, few effective planners rely primarily on annual planning processes to create overall strategies. In larger companies they often delegate those procedures to subordinates while they focus on other models of intervention. In parallel with the concepts developed above, they carefully orchestrate ad hoc efforts designed to:

1. *teach* top managers about the future;
2. *sense* developing strategic needs early;
3. *build executive awareness* about options;
4. *broaden support* and comfort levels for action;
5. *crystallize* and communicate partial consensus as it emerges;
6. *stimulate* a few key executives' personal commitment toward new options;
7. *build attitudes,* communication channels and resource buffers that make the organization more *flexible* toward change.

These interventions take on many different forms. One can only suggest—not catalogue—interesting approaches here.

Teaching (the chief planner of a large chemical company):

"For the price of one professional and his secretary, I can design for myself and a few key executives a biweekly series of seminars led by the very best people in the world. There's just no comparison between the potential impact of the two investments. And keeping my staff to minimum levels avoids political exposure."

Commitment (the vice president of strategic planning of a large information products company):

"I move when I know a top executive is about to make a speech or internal presentation where a reference about the future would be useful. I brief him or his speech-writers on potentially exciting developments or ideas I think may be ready for public exposure. Sometimes this is just a device to increase the executive's awareness of needs the company must respond to. Once an executive has spoken publicly about an issue, he is much more likely to feel he understands it and is committed to doing something about it. If I can get him to implicitly endorse a goal or a specific option in public, he will feel even more committed."

Such "whispering in the ears of the gods" helps create awareness and set the hook of initial commitment in key people. As a coalescing idea picks up momentum, planners often seek out its main sources of support and opposition and develop further processes to "assess" it or increase its psychological and potential viability.

Momentum (a very effective chief planner of a large consumer products company):

"I may first have to build up a more adequate data base on the subject. Then I arrange for some articulate proponents or neutral parties to prepare background papers on the topic with no recommended actions presented. As these endeavors accumulate weight and/or support, I may set up an informational meeting or two to inquire where we should go from here and what the prime concerns of opponents are. My office can often coordinate the accumulation of necessary data for the next stage of discussions. Finally, if necessary, I can arrange for a line executive to establish a carefully selected committee to look into the issue and come forward with recommendations. Of, if I can get a particular manager to sponsor the idea, it can be put forward as a trial balloon in his next formal plan."

Such legitimate interventions can help a new option over the hurdles of ignorance and suspicion it always encounters. As the idea gains momentum, planners can further stimulate its acceptance by having their staffs prepare special studies on it and by including inquiries about it in the instructions issued for drawing up long-range plans. Finally, as consensus emerges, they see that the concept appears in the assumptions, goals, and formal strategy statements of various groups. But this is the terminus of the strategy process. Not the essence of it.

Coalition management

At the heart of all controlled strategy development lies coalition management. Top managers operate at a confluence of pressures from: stockholders, environmentalists, government bodies, customers, suppliers, distributors, producing units, marketing groups, technologists, unions, special issue activists, individual employees, ambitious executives and so on, where knowledgeable people of good will can easily disagree on a proper balance of actions. In response to changing pressures and coalitions among these groups, the top management team continuously forms and re-forms its own coalitions aligned around specific decisions. These represent various members' different values and interests concerning the particular issue at hand and are sources of constant negotiations and implied bargains among the leadership group (43).

Most major strategic moves tend to assist some interests—and executives' careers—at the expense of others. Consequently, each set of interests can serve as a check on the others and thus help maintain the breadth and balance of the overall strategy. Some managements try to insure that all important policies have representation or access at the top. And the guiding executive group may continuously adjust the number, power or proximity of these access points to maintain a desired balance and focus (51). People selection and coalition management are the ultimate controls top executives have in guiding and coordinating their companies' strategies. These must be managed with sophistication and care to achieve desired degrees of stimulation, objectivity, cohesion and dynamism. The following quotations, the first by a CEO, the second by Robert Hatfield when Chairman of Continental Group, make the point well:

> "If good people share the same values, they will instinctively act together. We must know how people will respond intuitively when they are thousands of miles away. . . . We work hard and consciously to understand each other and where we are going. If we know these things and communicate openly, our actions will be sensible and cohesive. Yet we'll have the flexibility to deal with changing environments. These—and the choice of top-flight people—are our real controls for coordinating strategy development."

> "How do you manage the strategic process? It all comes down to people: selecting people. First, you look for people with certain general characteristics. They have to be bright, energetic, flexible, with high integrity or they won't be adaptive and last in the long run. Among these, you look for the best people with the kinds of experience and interests likely to lead the company in directions you want it to go. But you have to be careful with this. You don't want just 'yes' men on the directions you believe in. You want people who can help you think out new approaches too. Finally, you purposely team people with somewhat different interests, skills, and management styles. You let them push and tug a bit to make sure different approaches get considered. And you do a lot of chatting and informal questioning to make sure you stay informed and can intervene if you have to."

Conclusions

In recent years, there has been an increasing chorus of discontent concerning corporate strategic planning. Many managers are concerned that despite elaborate strategic planning systems, costly staffs for this purpose, and major commitments of their own time, their most elaborate strategies get implemented poorly, if at all. These executives and their companies have generally fallen into the classic trap of thinking about strategy formulation and implementation as separate sequential processes. They have relied on the awesome rationality of their formally derived strategies and the inherent power of their positions to cause their organizations to respond. When this does not occur, they become bewildered, if not frustrated and angry.

Instead, successful managers who operate logically and proactively in an incremental mode build the seeds of understanding, identity and commitment into the very processes which create their strategies. Careful incrementalism allows them to improve the quality of information used in decisions and deal with the practical policies of change—while they step by step build the organization's momentum toward the new strategy and the psychological motivation to carry it through. In large enterprises strategy formulation and implementation are largely overlapping, simultaneous and continuous functions. In their formulation processes, successful strategic managers generally create the awareness, concern, options, initial movement, personal identity and organizational commitment that cause the strategy to be already flowing toward effective and flexible implementation before it is ever—if ever—announced in detail.

Notes and references

1. *The Study* (pub. 1980, see [39]). From diverse industries a sample of some ten multibillion dollar companies was selected. Each had recently undergone major strategic changes. Important participants were asked how the overall strategy and each of its important components had come about. With each company's help I tried to document all statements as carefully as possible from both primary and secondary sources. These materials were integrated and published in a series of detailed case studies which make up the data base I refer to here. Participating companies were: General Mills, Inc. and Pillsbury Company (consumable products); Exxon Corporation and Continental Group (basic processes); Xerox Corporation and Pilkington Brothers, Ltd. (advanced technology); and General Motors Corporation, Chrysler Corporation, and Volvo AB (consumer durables).

2. Ansoff, H. I. (1965) *Corporate Strategy: An Analytic Approach to Business Policy for Growth and Expansion.* New York: McGraw-Hill.

3. Ansoff, H. I. (1972) The concept of strategic management. *Journal of Business Policy* 2(4):2–7.

4. Argyris, C. (1977) Double loop learning in organizations. *Harvard Business Review* 55(5):115–25.

5. Barnard, C. I. (1938) *The Functions of the Executive* (Cambridge, Mass.: Harvard University Press) provides perhaps the first reference to the concept of the "zone of indifference."

6. Bower, J. L. (1970) Planning within the firm, *American Economic Review* 60(2):186–94, notes that executives place such diversifying side bets to reduce their personal risk as well as corporate risk.

7. Carter, E. E. (1970) A behavioral theory approach to firm investment and acquisition decisions (Ph.D. diss, Carnegie-Mellon University) notes that initial goal consensus by the dominant coalition is by no means common.

8. Carter, E. E. (1971) The behavioral theory of the firm and top-level corporate decisions, *Administrative Science Quarterly* 16(4):413–28, describes active search processes by executives to define new problems, not just to respond to recognized problems.

9. Chandler, A. D. (1962) *Strategy and Structure: Chapters in the History of the Industrial Enterprise.* Cambridge, Mass.: MIT Press.

10. Cohen, K. J., and R. M. Cyert (1973) Strategy: Formulation, implementation, and monitoring. *Journal of Business* 46(3):349–67.

11. Cyert, R. M., W. R. Dill, and J. G. March (1958) The role of expectations in business decision making. *Administrative Science Quarterly* 3(3):307–40.

12. Cyert, R. M., and J. G. March (1965) *A Behavioral Theory of the Firm*. Englewood Cliffs, N.J.: Prentice-Hall.

13. Daniel, D. R. (1966) Reorganizing for results. *Harvard Business Review* 44(6):96–104.

14. Georgiou, P. (1973) The goal paradigm and notes towards a counter paradigm, *Administrative Science Quarterly* 18(3):291–310, suggests a wider negotiation involving lower level task groups as well.

15. Gilmore, F. F. (1973) Overcoming the perils of advocacy in corporate planning. *California Management Review* 15(3):127–37.

16. Guth, W. D. (1971) Formulating organizational objectives and strategy: A systematic approach, *Journal of Business Policy* 2(1):24–31, provides an excellent example of this approach.

17. Henderson, B. (1981) *The Concept of Strategy* (Boston, Mass.: Boston Consulting Group) describes this process in Social Darwinist terms that, as in the biological analogue, successful companies are those which assume the specific differentiating characteristics necessary to outperform all others in their selected niches.

18. Klein, H. (1981) Environmental analysis and forecasting. *Journal of Business Strategy* 1(3).

19. Lindblom, C. E. (1968) *The Policy-Making Process* (Englewood Cliffs, N.J.: Prentice-Hall) notes that the incremental manager is a shrewd, resourceful problem solver, wrestling bravely with a universe he is wise enough to know is too big for him.

20. Lindblom, C. E. (1959) The science of "muddling through," *Public Administrative Review* 19(2):79–88, is the classic statement of this approach.

21. Locke, E. A. (1968) Toward a theory of task motivation and incentives, *Organizational Behavior and Human Performance* 3(2):157–89, suggests that assigned goals have effect only to the extent that they are accepted and internalized by the subordinate.

22. Mace, M. L., and G. G. Montgomery (1962) Management Problems of Corporate Acquisitions (Boston, Mass.: Harvard University) laid out the classic pattern for this approach.

23. Manchester, W. (1978) *American Caesar: Douglas MacArthur, 1880–1964*. Boston, Mass.: Little Brown.

24. March, J. G., and J. P. Olsen (1976) (with contributions by S. Christensen, M. D. Cohen, H. Enderud, K. Kreiner, P. Romelaer, K. Rommetveit, P. Stava, and S. S. Weiner) *Ambiguity and Choice in Organizations* (Bergen, Norway: Universitetsforlaget) suggest that these suggestions become garbage cans of ideas unless properly guided.

25. March, J. G. and H. A. Simon (1958) Cognitive limits on rationality, in *Organizations* (New York: John Wiley); note that as members of the top management coalition sponsor an idea a process of "uncertainty absorption" takes place. People begin to judge the competency of the sponsor rather than the evidence presented, and that individual's credibility and power suffer if the result is wrong.

26. Marschak, J. (1954) Toward an economic theory of organizations and information. In *Decision Processes,* edited by R. M. Thrall, C. H. Coombs, and R. L. Davis. New York: John Wiley.

27. Mintzberg, H. (1973) *The Nature of Managerial Work.* New York: Harper & Row.

28. Mintzberg, H. (1973) Strategy-making in three modes, *California Management Review* 16(2):44–53, cites different modes of strategy formation as well. Elements of all three modes were seen in the largest companies of my sample, but all were linked by incrementalism.

29. Mintzberg, H., P. Raisinghani, and A. Theoret (1976) The structure of "unstructured" decision processes. *Administrative Science Quarterly* 21(2):246–75.

30. Newall, A., and H. A. Simon (1972) *Human Problem Solving* (Englewood Cliffs, N.J.: Prentice-Hall) note that when faced with complex contextual decisions, executives tend to break them down into sub-decisions to which more routinized or understood decision procedures can be applied.

31. Normann, R. (1977) *Management for Growth,* translated by N. Adler. New York: John Wiley.

32. Pascale, R., and A. Athos (1981) *The Art of Japanese Management* (Cambridge, Mass.: Harvard University Press) suggest that perhaps the most distinguishing characteristic of most successfully managed U.S. companies is the clear presence of a "superordinate goal" that becomes a portion of the value system influencing all major decisions on a day-to-day basis.

33. Perrow, C. (1961) The analysis of goals in complex organizations, *American Sociological Review* 26(1):854–66, stresses a dominant coalition which negotiates key goals relationships within itself and uses its combined power to enforce these as organizational goals.

34. Pfeffer, J., G. R. Salancik, and H. Leblebici (1976) The effect of uncertainty on the use of social influence in organizational decision making. *Administrative Science Quarterly* 21(2):227–45.

35. Pfiffner, J. M. (1960) Administrative rationality. *Public Administration Review* 20(3):227–45.

36. Quinn, J. B. (1961) Long range planning of industrial research. *Harvard Business Review* 39(4).

37. Quinn, J. B. (1977) Strategic goals: Process and politics, *Sloan Management Review* 19(1), develops this argument in depth.

38. Quinn, J. B. (1979) Technological innovation, entrepreneurship, and strategy, *Sloan Management Review* 20(3), amplifies this concept.

39. Quinn, J. B. (1980) *Strategies for Change: Logical Incrementalism.* (Homewood, Ill.: Dow Jones Irwin) develops the argument in depth.

40. Quotation from a copyrighted case by James Brian Quinn (1977–81), Dartmouth College, Hanover, N.H. Available upon request.

41. Rhenman, E. (1973) *Organization Theory for Long-Range Planning.* New York: John Wiley.

42. Rothschild, W. E. (1976) *Putting it all Together: A Guide to Strategic Thinking.* New York: AMACOM.

43. Sayles, L. R. (1964) *Managerial Behavior: Administration in Complex Organizations* (New York: McGraw-Hill) provides an excellent overview of the processes involved.

44. Schaffer, W. B. (1973) What have we learned about corporate planning? *Management Review* 62(8):19–26, lists other benefits, but these were repeatedly confirmed by top managers.

45. Smalter, D. J., and R. L. Ruggles (1966) Six business lessons from the pentagon, *Harvard Business Review* 44(2):64–75, develop this form of missions planning in detail.

46. Soelberg, P. O. (1967) Unprogrammed decision making, *Industrial Management Review* 8(2):19–29, develops a similar concept he calls a "trap search."

47. Vancil, R. F., and P. Lorange (1975) Strategic planning in diversified companies, *Harvard Business Review* 53(1):81–90, also note that formal strategic planning is inappropriate for acquisition planning beyond setting broad goals and guidelines.

48. von Hipple, E. (1977) The dominant role of the user in semiconductor and electronic process innovation. *IEEE Transactions* EM24(2).

49. Witte, E. (1972) Field research on complex decision-making processes—the phase theorem, *International Studies of Management and Organization* 2(2):156–82, notes up to 51 specific decisions in observed strategic processes which had to be blended over a several-year time frame.

50. Wrapp, H. E. (1967) Good managers don't make policy decisions. *Harvard Business Review* 45(5):91–99.

51. Zaleznik, A. (1970) Power and politics in organizational life, *Harvard Business Review* 48(3), develops this thesis. He notes that confusing compliance with commitment is one of the most common and difficult problems of strategic implementation. Often organizational commitment may override personal interest if the former is carefully developed.

Managing the Stages of
Organizational Growth
Eric G. Flamholtz

One of the critical challenges facing the CEO of a rapidly growing entrepreneurial company is to cope simultaneously with the endless day-to-day
problems of a developing organization while keeping an eye on its future
direction. Most CEOs of such companies are going through the process of
building a company for the first time, and this is, in many ways, akin to
navigating unchartered waters in a leaky rowboat with an inexperienced
crew while surrounded by a school of sharks. The sea is unfamiliar, the
boat is clumsy, the skills needed are not readily apparent or not fully developed, and there is a constant reminder of the high costs of an error in
judgment.

Just as the skipper of the boat might wish for a guide to facilitate naviga-
tion, training, and ship repair, the CEO of the entrepreneurial company
may frequently wish for a guide to building the firm. It would also be
useful for the skipper to learn that others before him or her have made the
voyage successfully, and perhaps even to hear about some of the lessons
they learned in the process.

Purpose

This article is addressed to the CEO who is faced with the special challenge
of building an entrepreneurial company. It presents a framework for understanding and managing the stages of organizational growth from the inception of a new venture to development as a mature firm. It provides a way of
understanding the critical management issues facing a developing organization at each stage and a guide to when those stages will occur in the organizational life-cycle. It also offers some insight into what must be done to
successfully build the organization, not only at each particular stage but
over the cycle as a whole.

Overview of the framework

Four major ideas are included in this framework:

1. There are six key tasks or prerequisites that all organizations must perform satisfactorily in order to develop a successful entity.
2. The six key tasks are always being performed to some extent in any organization at any given time, but they do not always receive (or need to receive) the same degree of emphasis at a particular point in time.
3. The achievement of the six key organizational tasks can be viewed as a developmental process, with each task requiring development at a different stage of organizational growth.
4. The failure to satisfactorily perform one or more of these developmental tasks will lead to a variety of organizational problems or "growing pains."

We shall begin by describing the key tasks of developing a successful organization and then discuss their role at each stage of organizational growth.

The critical tasks of organizational success

Based on an analysis of the experience of actual organizations (both successful and unsuccessful) as well as research on organization effectiveness, six key dimensions emerge as essential for building a successful organization:

1. Identification and definition of a viable *market niche* to serve;
2. Development of *products and/or services* appropriate to the firm's chosen market niche;
3. Acquisition and/or development of the *resources* required to operate the firm;
4. Development of the *operational systems* necessary for the firm to function on a day-to-day basis;
5. Development of the *management systems* required for the overall functioning of the organization on a long-term basis; and
6. Development of the *organizational culture* that management feels is necessary to guide the firm.

The nature of each of the critical tasks of developing a successful organization is described below.

Identification of a market niche

The most fundamental prerequisite to developing a successful organization involves the identification and definition of a firm's market and, if feasible, a "market niche." A market involves the present and potential buyers of the goods and/or services which a firm intends to produce and sell.

A "market niche" is a place within a market where a firm can potentially develop a comparative (competitive) advantage in providing goods and/or services to satisfy customer needs.

The first challenge to organizational survival or success is to identify a market need for a good or service to which the firm will seek to respond. This can be either a need that has not yet been recognized by other firms or a need currently satisfied by existing firms. However, the chances for organizational success are enhanced to the extent that the firm has identified a need that is not being adequately fulfilled, or where there is little competition.

This challenge is faced by all new ventures; indeed, it is the challenge for a new venture to overcome. It has, however, also been the critical test of many growing concerns and has even brought many once proud and great firms to near ruin or total demise. On the contrary, many firms have achieved great success merely because they were one of the first in a new market. For example, Apple Computers grew from a small entrepreneurship in a garage to a $500 million publicly held firm in a few years because its founders identified the market for a "personal" computer. Similarly, Dreyer's, a manufacturer of ice cream (which is a relatively undifferentiated product) grew within five years from sales of $14.4 million in 1978 to $55.8 million in 1982 because the company saw and cultivated a market niche between the "super premium ice creams" such as Haägen-Dazs and the generic (commodity) ice cream of most supermarkets.

Although some firms have been successful because they identified and clearly defined a market niche, others have foundered either because they failed to define a niche or because they mistakenly abandoned their historical niche. For example, a medium-sized national firm that manufactured and sold specialty clothing wished to "upgrade" its image and products and become a boutique with a high-fashion orientation. However, it failed to recognize that its historical market was the "medium" market, and its efforts were unsuccessful.

Many firms are able to survive merely because they have been able to identify a market need for certain goods or services; however, those firms that achieve great success frequently do so because they have identified not only a market need but also a potential niche that they have then proceeded to capture.

In brief, the foundation for an organization's ultimate success is the firm's market niche. The ability to identify a market niche is the most basic prerequisite for organizational success. Thus, the first phase of developing a successful organization must emphasize the definition of the firm's markets and potential niches.

This process will, of course, involve the use of strategic market planning to identify potential customers, their needs, etc. It will also involve laying out the strategy of how the firm plans to compete with others for its share of the intended market.

Development of products and/or services

A second task facing the organization involves "productization." This is the process of analyzing the needs of present and potential customers in order to design the products and/or services that will satisfy their needs.

Although many firms are able to correctly perceive a market need, they are not necessarily able to develop a product that is capable of satisfying that need adequately. For example, the firms of Silicon Valley were able to identify the need for a "64K chip"; however, the market for that product ultimately came to be dominated by Japanese companies and Motorola because of the ability of the latter to mass-produce the chip with a higher degree of reliability. Thus, being the first is not necessarily sufficient.

The productization process involves not only the design of a "product" (defined here to include services as well), but also the ability to produce it. For a service firm, the ability to "produce" a product involves the firm's "service delivery system," which is the mechanism through which services are provided to customers.

Productization is not simply the problem of relatively new or small companies; it faces large, well-established firms as well. Indeed, it can even face whole industries. For example, the U.S. automobile industry was unsuccessful during the 1970s in productizing their products to meet the changing needs of their market, including the need for reliable, fuel-efficient, economical automobiles. Hence, they permitted the emergence of a powerful competitor in the Japanese into a market that they once dominated.

The development of successful products depends to a great extent on effective strategic market planning. This involves understanding who your potential customers are, what their needs are, how they buy, and what they perceive to be value in a product.

The success of the productization task depends, to a very great extent, on the success of defining the firm's market niche. The greater the degree to which there has been a good understanding of the market's needs, the more likely that the productization process will be effective in satisfying those needs. Thus, the productization task is the second level in building a successful organization.

Acquisition and development of resources

The third major task facing organizations concerns the need to acquire and develop additional resources required to facilitate its present and anticipated future growth. A firm may have identified a market and products, but not have sufficient resources to compete effectively. For example, small competitors in the soft-drink industry face the need to be low-cost producers. This requires high-speed bottling lines, but at a cost of $1 million a line the smaller firms simply cannot afford them.

A firm's success in identifying a market niche and productization will create increased demand for its products and/or services. This, in turn, will stretch the firm's resources very thin. The organization will suddenly find that it requires additional physical resources (space, equipment, etc.), financial resources, and human resources. The need for people resources, especially management, will become particularly acute. At this stage of development, there is irony in the fact that the firm's own success has created a new set of problems.

Development of operational systems

To function effectively a firm must not only produce a product or service but also administer the basic day-to-day operations reasonably well. This involves the functions of accounting, billings, collections, advertising, personnel recruiting and training, sales, production, delivery and related systems. Thus, the fourth task in building a successful organization concerns the development of the systems needed to facilitate the day-to-day operations of the firm—the "operational systems."

Typically, firms that are confronted by the tasks of developing their market niche and products tend to neglect the development of the operational systems required to run their organizations on a day-to-day basis, except to the extent necessary to keep functioning. As a firm grows in size, there is an ever-increasing amount of strain put on such basic operating systems as accounting, billing and collections, accounts payable, the production or service delivery system, the marketing and advertising systems, the recruitment and training systems, and related systems.

In brief, as a firm grows in size it tends to quickly outgrow the administrative systems available to operate it. For example, in one electrical components distribution firm with more than $200 million in annual revenue, salespeople were continually infuriated when they found that deliveries could not be made of products they had sold because the firm's inventory records were hopelessly incorrect. Similarly, a medium-sized residential real estate firm with annual revenue of about $10 million found that it required almost one year of effort and embarrassment to correct its accounting records after the firm's "bookkeeper" retired. A $100 million consumer products manufacturer encountered problems with materials that had to be returned to vendors because there was simply insufficient warehouse space to house the purchases (a fact that no one noticed until the deliveries were at the door). A $15 million industrial abrasives distributor found itself facing constant problems in keeping track of customer orders and in knowing what was in inventory. The firm's inventory control system, which was fine when annual sales were $3–5 million, had simply become overloaded at the higher sales volume, causing one manager to remark that "nothing is ever stored around here where any intelligent person could reasonably expect to find it."

Table 1. Symptoms of organizational growing pains

---

1. People feel "There are not enough hours in the day."
2. People are spending too much time putting out fires.
3. Many people are not aware of what each other is doing.
4. There is a lack of understanding about where the firm is headed.
5. There is not a sufficient number of good managers.
6. Everybody feels "I have to do it myself, if I want to get it done correctly."
7. Most people feel "Our meetings are a waste of time."
8. When plans are made, there is very little follow-up and things just don't get done.
9. Some people have begun to feel insecure about their place in the firm.
10. The firm has continued to grow in sales but not in profits.

When firms have grown rapidly and neglected the operational systems needed to run their business (for the understandable reason that they have been too busy making money to devote the effort to developing such systems), they tend to experience a variety of "organizational growing pains," as shown in table 1.

Development of management systems

The fifth task required to build a successful organization is to develop the management systems required to facilitate the long-run growth and development of the firm. The management systems required include systems for planning, organization, management development and control.

The planning system refers to the process of planning for the overall development of the organization as well as for scheduling and budgeting operations. It involves the processes of strategic planning, operational planning, and contingency planning. A firm may do planning but lack a planning system. The "organization structure" of the firm involves how people are organized, who reports to whom and how activities are coordinated. All firms have some organization structure (formal or informal), but not necessarily the correct structure for their needs. The management development system refers to the process of planned development of the people needed to run an organization as it grows. The "control system" refers to the set of processes (budgeting, goal setting) and mechanisms (performance appraisal) used to influence the behavior of people so that they are motivated to achieve organizational objectives. In brief, to function effectively all organizations must have a satisfactory set of management systems.

Until the firm reaches a certain size (which tends to differ for each firm), it can typically operate without formal management systems. The planning that tends to be done is in the head of the entrepreneur, and is frequently done on an ad hoc basis. The organizational structure, if it exists, tends to be informal with ill-defined responsibilities, which may well overlap several people. Management development tends to be "on-the-job training," which basically means that "you're on your own." When control systems are used in such organizations, they tend to use the accounting system as a basis of organizational control rather than a broader concept of management control.

The basic symptom of organizational growing pains at this level of development is the decreasing ability of the original entrepreneur or senior executive to control all that is happening.

Developing the corporate culture

Just as all people have personalities, all organizations have a culture—a set of shared values, beliefs and norms that govern how people are expected to operate the business on a day-to-day basis. Although all firms have cultures (which can be identified by trained observers), the culture may be implicit rather than explicit.

Values refer to what the organization believes is important with respect to product quality, customer service, treatment of people, etc. Beliefs are the ideas that people in the corporation hold about themselves as individuals and about the firm as an entity. Norms refer to the unwritten rules that guide day-to-day interactions and behavior, including language, dress and the use of humor.

This sixth challenge in building a successful organization is to institutionalize the corporate culture.

The pyramid of organizational development

Taken together, these six key tasks of building a successful organization comprise a "pyramid of organizational development"; that is, they comprise a series of sequential steps or tasks that must be performed in an integrated fashion in order to develop a successful organizational entity (see fig. 1).

The six key tasks forming the pyramid must all be performed successfully in order for the overall organization to function successfully. The pyramid should not be viewed as suggesting that the six key tasks are developed totally independently at different times; rather, all of the six are essential to the functioning of a firm at any given time, but each will achieve a different degree of development at different stages in an organization's growth process, as described below.

Stages of organizational growth

Four different stages of growth for a firm to develop to organizational maturity can be identified: (1) the new venture stage; (2) the expansion stage; (3) the professionalizing stage; and (4) the consolidation stage.

At each of these stages, one or more of the critical tasks of organizational development receives attention until the organization has finally achieved maturity and success. The stages of growth and the related critical

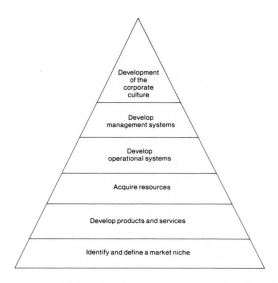

Figure 1. The pyramid of organizational development

development areas as well as the approximate size (measured in millions of dollars of sales revenues) at which an organization will pass through each stage is shown in table 2 and described below. It should be noted that this framework applies to a division of a large company as well as to an independent organization. Thus it applies, for example, to a $175 million division of a $3.5 billion firm.

Stage 1: The new venture

Stage 1 of organizational growth involves the inception of a new venture. In Stage 1, the critical issues for management are (1) to identify the markets and/or niche(s) which will be served and (2) to develop the products (services) appropriate to those selected market segments.

Table 2. Stages of organizational growth from a new venture to maturity

Stage	Stage description	Critical developmental areas	Approximate organizational size ($ millions of sales)
1.	New venture	Markets and "products"	Less than $5
2.	Expansion	Resources and operational systems	$5 to $25
3.	Professionaliza-tion	Management systems	$25 to $100
4.	Consolidation	Corporate culture	$100 to $500

Stage 1 typically occurs for organizations from the time they have virtually no sales until they reach approximately $5 million. During Stage 1, the firm will have to perform all of the critical tasks of organizational success; however, the relative emphasis will be on the first two tasks: defining markets and developing products. This is represented schematically in the pyramid shown in figure 2.

In brief, the major concern during Stage 1 is survival. Do we have a viable market and product?

Stage 2: Expansion

If an organization successfully completes the key developmental tasks of Stage 1, it will reach Stage 2. This stage involves the rapid growth or expansion of the firm in terms of sales revenue, number of employees, etc. For most firms, the rapid growth that characterizes Stage 2 begins at about the $5 million sales level, though it can occur at lower or higher levels.

Stage 2 presents a new set of developmental problems or challenges. Organizational resources are, as noted above, stretched to the limit, as increasing sales require a seemingly endless increase in people, financing, equipment, space, etc. Similarly, the firm's day-to-day operational systems for recruiting, production or service delivery, purchasing, accounting, collections, and payables are virtually overwhelmed by the sheer amount of product or service being "pushed out the door."

The major problems that occur during Stage 2 are the problems of

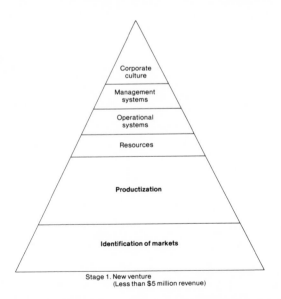

Figure 2. Degree of emphasis in pyramid of organizational development for a Stage 1 firm

growth rather than those of survival. It is during this stage that "horror stories" begin to accumulate:

Salespeople who sell product they know is in inventory only to learn that someone else has grabbed it for their customers.

The same vendor's invoices are paid two and three times, while another vendor screams at having not been paid in six months.

A precipitous drop in product quality for unknown reasons.

Sharply increased turnover just when the company needs more personnel.

Missing letters, files, and reports that cause confusion, loss of time, and embarrassment.

Senior executives who find themselves scheduled to be in two cities in two states for important meetings on the same day at the same time, or who arrive in a distant city and learn they are a day early.

The most typical symptoms of organizational growing pains have been shown previously in table 1.

The nature of the relative emphasis on each key developmental area during Stage 2 in the organizational development pyramid is shown schematically in figure 3.

Stage 3: Professionalization

Somewhere during the period of explosive growth that forms Stage 2, senior management realizes (or ought to realize) that there is a need for a

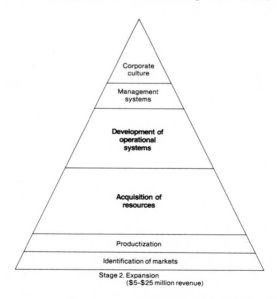

Figure 3. Degree of emphasis in pyramid of organizational development for a Stage 2 firm

qualitative change in the nature of the firm. The firm cannot merely add people, money, equipment, and space and cope with its growth; rather, the firm must undergo a transition or metamorphosis and become a somewhat different type of organization.

Until this point, the firm has been entrepreneurial. It has operated with a considerable degree of informality. Indeed, it may have lacked well-defined goals, responsibilities, plans, controls, etc., and still prospered. However, once a critical size has been achieved, what is required is to increasingly formalize many of these same things and processes that have been informally done. The need for this transition typically occurs by the time an organization has reached approximately $25 million in sales. For some firms it may occur sooner, whereas for others it may be somewhat later.

The sheer size of the organization now requires more formal plans, regularly scheduled meetings, defined organizational roles and responsibilities, a performance appraisal system, and management control systems. This requires a planned program of organizational development—that is, a program to develop the key systems required to manage the new entity that the firm has now become. This is the fifth key developmental area described above.

In addition, a change is also required in the skills and capabilities of the people who manage the firm. Until this point, it was possible to be more of a doer or hands-on manager than a professional manager. What is increasingly required are people who are adept at administering the firm: planning, organization, motivation, leadership, and control. Thus, individual managers are also faced with personal transitions. They must increasingly think and act as managers, not merely in title but in behavior and psychology.

The nature of the relative emphasis on each key developmental area in the organizational pyramid during Stage 3 is shown schematically in figure 4.

Stage 4: Consolidation

Stage 4 presents a different type of problem in building a successful organization. Once the organization has made the transition to a professionally managed firm with workable systems for planning, organization, management development, and control, the firm must turn its attention to an intangible but nevertheless real and significant asset: the corporate culture.

During the growth that occurred to get a firm to Stage 4 (which typically seems to occur at about $100 million in sales), the firm has brought in new "waves" of people. The first wave occurred when the firm was relatively small and informal during Stage 1. During this period, the firm's culture (values, beliefs, and norms) were transmitted by direct day-to-day contact between the founder(s) and personnel. The diffusion or transmission of

Figure 4. Degree of emphasis in pyramid of organizational development for a Stage 3 firm

culture was a byproduct of what the firm did. Virtually "everybody knew everybody else" and what the firm wanted to achieve and how.

During Stage 2, the rapid expansion of the firm brought in a new wave of people. These people were "socialized" to a considerable degree by the first wave; that is, the first wave transmitted the culture to the next generation. However, at some level of organizational size, especially with the development of disbursed geographical operations, the informal socialization process becomes more attenuated and less effective. The sheer number of new people simply overwhelms the informal socialization system.

By the time a firm reaches $100 million in revenues, a third wave of people has joined the organization and the informal socialization system is simply no longer adequate to do what it once did so well. At this stage, the firm must develop a more formal method of consciously transmitting the corporate culture throughout the organization.

The nature of the relative emphasis on each key developmental area during Stage 4 is represented in figure 5.

Organizational characteristics during different growth stages

The previous sections have examined the six essential areas of organizational development, the four stages of organizational growth, and the degree of emphasis required in each development area during each stage of growth. Table 3 summarizes the characteristics of organizations for each of the key developmental areas during each stage of growth.

Figure 5. Degree of emphasis in pyramid of organizational development for a Stage 4 firm

Table 3. Organizational characteristics during each stage of growth

Key organizational development areas	Stages of organizational growth			
	1	2	3	4
Overall management focus during stage	Make & sell	Expand resources & products	Build the management infrastructure	Spread the culture
Corporate culture	Informal but understood	Attenuating	Tenuous	Explicitly defined
Management systems	Informal	Informal	Formalizing	Formal
Operational systems	Basic	Developing	Well-developed	Well-developed
Resources	Thin	Stretched thin	Increasing surplus	Strong
Products	Develop core products	New products	Established products	Established products
Markets	Define markets & niche	Market	Well-defined market	Well-defined market

Implications of the framework

The previous sections have presented a framework for understanding what is necessary to build a successful organization. What are the implications of this framework for corporate managers and leaders?

There are four major implications:

1. There are six basic tasks that must be performed by all organizations if they wish to be successful. Although not all of the tasks or building blocks are equally important, they are all essential prerequisites to organizational success. Thus, the six tasks should be viewed as "key organizational development areas."
2. The six key developmental areas are hierarchical in nature; that is, some are more fundamental prerequisites than others. This means that some must be developed to a greater extent earlier than others to facilitate organizational growth.
3. An organization achieves the key tasks as part of an ongoing developmental process. In the process of developing a successful organization, the organization will encounter the need to build its capability in each of the key developmental areas at different stages of organizational growth.
4. The failure to adequately perform one or more key developmental tasks will inevitably lead to "organizational growing pains."

Action steps for the CEO

Given the framework presented above, what should the CEOs or senior management of a rapidly growing entrepreneurial organization do? They must apply the framework to their own organization and identify its current stage of development, as well as the extent to which the organization has strengths or weaknesses in each of the six key development areas.

The first step in the process for doing this analysis may be termed an "organizational development evaluation or audit." Its primary purpose is to determine what the current degree of organizational development is and what needs to be done to improve it. Such an organizational evaluation can either be done internally or with the assistance of an experienced independent consultant.

Once the organizational evaluation has been completed, the CEO together with advisers must develop a master plan or blueprint for building the organization's capabilities to enable it to function successfully at its current or next stage of development. This plan ought to include specific goals and action plans for their implementation. Typically, the first step in this process involves strategic planning and involves people at various organizational levels.

The third step in the process involves actually implementing the desired organizational changes. This will involve the development of new organizational systems (planning, organization, control). It will also involve development of management's capabilities through corporate educational programs. Finally, it may involve planning changes in the corporate culture.

It must be noted that the steps and process outlined above are quite complex in practice. For a Stage 1 firm, the process will typically require one to two years to make the necessary transitions; in a Stage 4 firm, three years or more may well be required. During this process, some people may leave the firm, either voluntarily or not.

Based on experience with firms going through these changes, we can conclude that where the process is suitably designed and well-executed, the firm will emerge stronger and more successful. If the required changes are not made or if they are poorly conceived and executed, a firm may well find itself with stunted growth, lower profitability, and, perhaps, eventually in a corporate graveyard.

12

Organizations and Their Environments

Onward, upward, and outward! Organizations don't live in a vacuum. There's a big world out there. It's more active, more crowded, more volatile, more international than ever. And it won't slow down. Managing an organization today isn't what it was 50 years ago. The roads were empty then. What your company was manufacturing in January it would also be manufacturing in December and the next December, too! Maybe, if it was a daring company, it might go so far as to add a new color to its line.

But now almost all organizations live right square in the middle of urban jungles. Traffic's very heavy—even at midnight. Abrasive, difficult competitors are everywhere. Government regulators are looking over everybody's shoulders. Uncertainty is pervasive; and when uncertainty is high anxiety usually follows.

How can organizations grow and prosper in such dynamic environments? Or at least how can they survive?

This last section of our book raises those managerial issues—issues of the manager's role in coping with and even shaping the organization's environment. It isn't easy, but it can be done.

One thing it takes to manage the environment is time. Modern CEOs have to devote very large chunks of their time and energy to what's *outside* their organizations—to dealing with government, community, competitors, suppliers, and, most of all, customers. The amount of time the typical CEO devotes to those outside issues has much more than doubled in just the decade from the mid-seventies to the mid-eighties. It's a crowded world out there, and steering the organizations through it has become a major part of the managing process.

All three of the articles in this last section are about organizations and their environments, as well as about the manager's role in trying to manage those organization-environment relationships. Harold Leavitt et al. provide a set of categories, of alternative methods that organizations use to try to cope with those intrusive and obtrusive environments. The methods range from pulling into their shells like turtles, to "proactively" trying to make the environment adapt to the organization. There are costs and there are benefits to every alternative, but in today's world those ratios are quite different than in years past.

David Boje and Terance Wolfe carry the proactive idea a step further. They show how managers can actually develop that organization-environment relationship in ways that provide benefits to both.

Our closing paper, Jeffrey Pfeffer's article on the institutional functions of the manager, provides an appropriate closing for our book. It remaps the managing job to include the outside, institution-building, societal role of the manager. But it reminds us that the managing job also includes all that inside stuff, too. Managing, after all, is about action; but it's also about planning and organizing, and it's about imagining and creating. Doing any of those things effectively requires a lot of savvy about two constantly changing and critical factors: people, and that big world that surrounds our little piece of managerial turf.

Strategies for Survival: How Organizations Cope with Their Worlds
Harold J. Leavitt, William R. Dill, and Henry B. Eyring

The relationship between an organization and the world is much like the relationship between an individual and the world. We can learn a great deal about an individual without knowing anything at all about his world. We can understand his nervous system, his digestive system, his respiratory system, and the ways in which they articulate. But if we want to extend our understanding, we must find out how he copes with his environment. We must understand not only the structure of his nervous system but how it responds to external stimuli, not only the nature of his respiratory system but how it is affected by the atmosphere in which he breathes. We must understand the environmental limits of survival.

We must also understand how the individual copes with *changes* in his environment. Somehow organisms do manage to adjust to change, and sometimes they even manage to change the world so that it adjusts to them. When the world turns cold, they learn to build igloos, to insulate themselves from unpleasant environments to which they cannot or will not adapt. They even learn to create environments that they positively prefer. They condition and purify the air—usually after they have polluted it.

This complex relationship between the organism and its environment has a counterpart in the exchange between the organization and its environment. Sometimes the adaptation is inadequate; when the organization meets an environment it cannot cope with, it dies. What are the points at which an organization comes into contact with its environment? The list is long, but finite. Consider, for example, a small retail store. It lives at a location, an address. This address, this shop is in a neighborhood in a town in a nation. It is made of brick and mortar. That means it has been in contact with neighbors and plumbers and carpenters. The shop presumably sells something it has bought from someone else. So there is always the interface with the community of suppliers at one end and customers at the other.

Those are some obvious points of environmental contact, the proximate

From Harold V. Leavitt, William R. Dill, and Henry B. Eyring, *The Organizational World*. © 1977 by Harcourt Brace Jovanovich, Inc. Reprinted by permission of the publisher.

ones. But there are others. How about municipal services? The policeman
on the beat and the fire department? Insurance companies? The PTA that
claims the retail shop is selling dirty books to teen-agers? The black community that claims it sells racist books? There are employees, too, who are
citizens of the community. They want shorter hours and higher pay.

In a multitude of ways even the small shop finds itself in a complex exchange with its environment, not just passively but in critically active
ways. Its survival and growth depend on its ability to maintain and build
those relationships in ways that provide the shop with what it needs. If it is
a white-owned shop in a black ghetto, or a psychedelic shop in a straight,
middle-class town, it may not survive. In certain areas, if it is a shop that
refuses to pay off the cops, it may not survive even if it obeys all the laws.
So if it *has* survived, it has perforce been shaped, perhaps brainwashed, by
the forces that its particular environment exerts upon it.

But the shop can also shape its environment—to some extent. The
books it sells—including the dirty ones—may influence the community.
The style and design of its storefront may influence the architecture of
neighboring stores. Its entrepreneurial activities may bring in all sorts of
people from other areas.

Sense organs and survival

First, a generalization: the less sensitive an organization is to its environment, the less likely it is to survive. The dress shop that doesn't understand
the style preferences or budgets of local women is not likely to flourish.
The shop owner cannot assume that the dresses that sell in Istanbul will sell
just as well in Fort Wayne.

That generalization seems obvious enough. But the converse does not.
It does *not* follow that the greater an organization's capacity to sense its
environment, the *more* likely it is to survive. For an organization with
good sensors can survive only if it *also* possesses the capacity to modify its
behavior in response to the information it receives. Indeed, if it has no
mechanism for adapting to that information, its fine sensors may become
downright destructive. Suppose, for example, that I am very sensitive to
pain but I am paralyzed. If a pin is stuck into me I cannot move away.
I would be better off if I weren't sensitive to pain at all.

Consider some recent developments in the Catholic church. Ritual texts
have been translated from Latin into the language of the local community
as a means of bringing church and community closer together. Priests have
been encouraged to show more awareness of the problems of their communities. The church, as it were, is trying to improve its capacity to sense
what is going on at the interface between its parishes and its parishioners.

But let us suppose—only for the sake of supposition—that no other
changes take place within the structure of the church. Suppose that the new
information now entering the system through the parish priest has nowhere

to go, that the people "upstairs" either don't listen to it or don't know what to do with it. Is the church better off than it was before? In one way it is. The local priest can deal with some problems he failed to sense before. But organizationally, the church may be in trouble. For now it is faced with priests sensitive to urgent problems but frustrated by their inability to prompt responsive action at higher levels.

Internal communication, muscle, and survival

To be effective, then, a sensing mechanism must be tied into an internal mechanism for communicating and processing what is sensed, and a set of "muscles" for responding to what it processes. Without those mechanisms, a good sensing system may make the organization *less* capable of survival than an organization that is sealed off in its own shell, unaware of what is going on around it. The slow, insensitive, hard-shelled turtle can cope with its environment by closing itself off. A sensitive, but still slow, soft-shelled turtle would be vulnerable indeed.

This is another way of saying that an organization needs to be internally coherent to deal with its environment. The system needs to be a full system, with all its parts sensibly related to one another. Good sensors need to be connected to a brain and accompanying muscles. Several different systems may be coherent in their own ways and may work reasonably well, but some work better than others in particular environments.

Some alternative designs for survival

Let's consider four internally coherent ways in which organizations can sense and respond to environments.

Imperviousness: The withdrawal model

Some organizations deal with the world by shutting it out—by rolling up into a spiny ball and hoping their unattractive exterior will discourage enemies. Many religious and utopian groups, and some communes, have tried to drop out of the world. To a lesser degree withdrawal has also been the route of some government agencies, and in a less extreme way the route of some American railroads.

They try actively to eliminate any sense of the world around them. Some companies, for example, discourage their people from joining professional groups by suggesting that such activities are disloyal and that the time thus wasted might better be spent within the company. Such organizations are more concerned with sheer survival than with growth or adaptation. Their primary reaction to a changing environment is to find better ways of *not* responding to it—harder shells, tighter restrictions.

Why should any organization want to insulate itself from the world? For much the same reason that ancient cities walled themselves in—to protect what they valued from predators *who valued different things*. For the same reason that many youth communes are hidden in the woods—to permit their members to do their thing without persecution or attack. And for the same reason that the early Mormons settled in Salt Lake City.

Organizations build shells when they want to protect, in their existing forms, their values, their possessions, their beliefs, their people. But there is another reason, too. An organization that is impervious to its environment is not easily shaken from its routines; it is not "distracted" from its objectives, because it does not pay attention to things that might be distracting. It does not push panic buttons, because it does not hear the cries of fire. So an impervious exterior also helps provide for single-minded concentration.

Today, universities are active places, more active than they used to be. Professors are out consulting and carrying on field research. Students, no longer the hub of the university's universe, complain simultaneously of the "irrelevance" of their courses and of the university's multiple connections with other power groups in the environment. Are they asking for a return to isolation? If so, would "relevance" to the current world still be possible?

Or consider the diplomatic services of most nations. Diplomats act as organizational sense organs as well as muscles. One of their functions is to send home relevant intelligence about their host country. To do that, they must really get to know the host country. Yet almost all the world's diplomatic services carefully rotate their people every few years. One reason is the fear that their diplomats will become too sensitive, too understanding, and therefore too sympathetic with the host's problems, and hence may become more representational of the host than reportorial about it. Don't such rotation schemes contribute, in a mild way, to imperviousness from certain types of information?

In many companies salesmen serve as important sense organs. They work outside the organization, spending their time with customers. But they are sometimes reluctant to report back unpleasant information about the company's products or behavior because they know that home-office executives prefer not to hear such news.

And consider the old model of the mental hospital. It was a model of isolation. Get the patients out into the woods, into a walled asylum. Let few visitors in and few patients out. Minimize contact between patient and the world. And how about the model of the convent?

Selective imperviousness

So far we have considered the organization that closes off *all* environmental inputs. In the long run, especially in a changing environment, such complete imperviousness is disastrous for most organizations in the modern world.

Suppose we are the managers of an organization that foresees the danger of such isolation and wants to avoid it. But we are understandably concerned lest our people be seduced into immorality or disloyalty by exposure to the temptations of the world. And we also want to act upon our environment, to sell our product or to proselytize our religion or to enrich the coffers of our native country. How can we act intelligently upon an environment that we dare not let our people sense too well? We cannot. So we compromise. We sense, but we keep what we sense from penetrating too deeply into our organization. We hold the world at arm's length, in a gingerly fashion, and perhaps distastefully; but at least we look at it, and then act upon it.

Consider English colonialism. The English trained their men in England, in English schools and English universities. They trained them long and well so that their colonial officers would be true Englishmen. Then they sent them off to India with English manners and English dinner jackets to govern the heathen. Those officers carried England with them. They drank tea and dressed for dinner as though they were in London—and to that degree they remained impervious to their environment. They were little concerned about the inappropriateness of English evening dress to the Indian climate.

But they did not *ignore* their environment. They even learned a bit of the local language. They identified local leaders. They trained local people. They set up an intelligence network to learn about local affairs. And, being English, they were polite. They learned local protocol and respected it. Yet never for a moment did they consider going native. Never did they identify with their environment, blend into it, participate in it. No snake charmers for them. They sensed the world they were in, but because they were strongly socialized into their home culture, they remained outside it.

Japanese businessmen working abroad are masters of selective imperviousness. They learn the local ways quickly, designing and marketing their products to fit local practices, but they remain culturally and organizationally Japanese.

For an organization to ensure that its people will sense well and yet not be shaken by what they sense requires a very high level of socialization of its members—high loyalty, high commitment. And the organization must police the whole process, for even strong company men may backslide. One major British company used to check up on its field managers periodically to make sure they were maintaining their British identity. "We know there's a problem," one executive said, "when a manager in Borneo stops dressing for dinner. Then it's time to bring him back to London."

Adaptiveness: The organizational chameleon

As the world changes, it becomes more difficult for organizations to sense their environment and still remain independent of it. The British could remain British in India as long as India remained a colony. It is much more difficult for them to remain British and also effective in an economically expanding, independent India, where Indian, American, Japanese, and Russian competitors abound; where the environment is active, turbulent, and differentiated rather than passive and submissive.

One alternative for the organization confronting such an active environment is the opposite of imperviousness. It is to *adapt* to the local environment, to develop good sense organs and to use the information that comes in to make the organization as much a part of the local scene as possible. The adaptive organization, in effect, goes native. It becomes part of the environment. In Rome it is Roman. In Thailand it is Thai. It joins the local clubs, hires local people, and behaves in the approved local way.

There is something seductively attractive about this alternative. It seems to be respectful of local culture, polite, nonintrusive.

But there are many dangers for the organization in such behavior. Your people in Thailand may become so understanding of the Thais' needs and problems that they show more concern for Thai welfare than for your own. Or your people may be rejected by the host for trying to be what they are not. And adaptive behavior is mostly responsive rather than active, forever modifying itself to fit the world. In a volatile, rapidly changing world, an adaptive organization may find itself trying to change its behavior from day to day, blown about by political and social winds.

An ethical danger also arises for the organization that tries too hard to adapt. Should it be adaptive to *any* environment regardless of the conditions that exist there? Should it offer bribes where bribes are commonplace? Should it be racist where the society is racist? Should it treat employees as slaves because that is the societal model? The British colonialists carried not only their tea but their British standards of morality, justice, decency, fair play. Old-fashioned as those standards may now seem, they were high standards around which the organization could stand proud and honorable, whatever the local behavior.

So beware the siren of extreme organizational adaptiveness—your organization may become a chameleon.

Action-adaptation

The impervious organization shuts itself off, neither permitting change within itself nor creating change in its environment. The selectively impervious organization rejects any stimuli that may induce change in itself but tries actively to modify the environment. The adaptive organization accepts its environment and changes itself to meet it.

But there is still another alternative. An organization may be *both* adaptive *and* active. It may change itself to live with its environment and at the same time alter its environment.

For many organizations, altering the environment is part of their normal work. Public health organizations would be of little use if they did not erase malaria and reduce infantile mortality and thereby significantly alter their environment. Agricultural agencies would be of little use if they did not change the behavior of farmers and the nature of farming.

The prime purpose, after all, of many organizations is to change their worlds. There is a story about two shoe salesmen who were sent to open up a remote African market. The first salesman cabled home: "No one here wears shoes. Sales situation hopeless. Cancel all shipments." The second salesman cabled: "No one here yet wears shoes. Ship all you can."

But a dilemma arises. How can an organization be *of* its environment and still change it? Clearly the first place to look for an answer is in the environment itself. In some environments, like Los Angeles, change is a normal attribute of the environment. A Tibetan organization can move into Los Angeles to sell mothers on the idea of feeding their infants curdled yak's milk, and few will think it very strange. The Tibetan salesmen could easily, if they were sensitive, make themselves quite at home in that turbulent, competitive, shifting environment. The complexity and rapidity of change make almost anything possible. But let the same salesmen try to peddle their yak milk in stable, traditional Charleston, South Carolina, and things will be different.

But can we also adapt to a passive, relatively unchanging environment, and simultaneously change it? That seems almost a logical contradiction.

One possibility, however, may be to try a *sequential* process. First, adapt to the environment, then change it from within. The problem here, of course, is that once the organization has adapted, it may no longer be interested in creating the change it had originally wanted.

One of the great problems for many organizations in the next few years will be to devise some appropriate blend of action with adaptation—a blend that allows the organization to maintain its own identity, to effect change in its environment, and yet to "belong" to that environment. The issues involved in working out such a path are not just issues of efficiency. They are also ethical, ecological, and human issues.

Organizational tuning

An adult organization, again like an adult person, is not infinitely flexible. It is limited in what it can do, limited by its tasks, its personality, and its history. It may wish to be adaptive and yet be unable to adapt without undertaking major internal redesign. It needs to be "tuned."

Some organizations are appropriately tuned to their environment; some are overtuned; some undertuned. A delicately tuned automobile may be great for the racetrack but not for day-to-day city driving. A highly sensitive organization, alert to every change around it, may do very well in a subtle environment where small news items create large public response and casual remarks portend large changes, where minor shifts in consumer tastes can kill an unresponsive product line. But put such a highly sensitive organization into a stolid, stable, non-competitive environment and it may be paralyzed by its own sensitivity, overresponding to noise that is fundamentally irrelevant to the organization's activities. Organizations with a strong marketing orientation sometimes get into trouble in foreign environments for that very reason. Marketing people generally are highly sensitive to consumer signals. University faculties sometimes overrespond to local signals, too, even when the cost of responding fully to *all* those signals may be much too great for the university to bear. But organizations dominated by production people or technological people are apt to err in the opposite direction.

Overcentralized and undercentralized organizations

Consider, also, the relationship between the degree of centralization in an organization and its ability to cope with its environment. In some settings a high degree of centralization, as in a field army, is a major source of the organization's power. The centralization of control may permit a small force to overcome a larger, loosely organized enemy force with poor internal communication and no central decision points.

But that same centralized organizational design may be a source of weakness in other settings. For one thing, a lucky shot at the brain of a highly centralized organization can kill it. The Norman abbeys in England suffered such a fate. They were excellently, tightly organized communities. But they had single, identifiable heads—the abbots. When Henry VIII decided to get rid of the abbeys, he did so very easily by getting rid of the abbots. And the rest of the organization fell apart.

Conversely, some historical reports indicate that General de Gaulle advocated a *federal* rather than a central form of government for postwar Germany, because—it is said—he believed that decentralized federalism would *prevent* Germany from rapidly regaining its strength. France, after all, had a strong centralist tradition. In fact, Germany came back very fast, probably in large part because of its multiple, relatively loose federal form. It is much harder to chop off the many heads of a federalized government than to chop off the one head of a highly centralized one.

Centralized organizations, as we suggested in the chapter on organizations abroad, have other weaknesses in certain environments. Communication lines are long, for one thing. If issues must go all the way to the top for decision, reaction may be too slow in a rapidly changing environment.

On the other hand, units of highly decentralized organizations may be too adaptive, too ready to take on local color and local loyalty. Such organizations may collapse for lack of controlling bonds from the top.

The strategies of imperviousness, adaptation, and action

Viewed historically, which of these strategies has worked best, under what conditions?

Imperviousness has tended to work when the goals of the organization either do not require much interaction with the environment, or when the environment is very stable. The scholarly monk can do his work quite well if he is left alone. But as interdependence and change increase, imperviousness becomes less useful. The plumbing-fixture manufacturers of France can go on making obsolete toilets as long as the French maintain their existing attitudes toward toilets. But when tourists start fussing, and Hilton hotels start appearing, and Frenchmen come back from abroad, the pressure for change builds up.

But, since impervious organizations are, by definition, insensitive, we should not expect them to change steadily in response to steadily mounting pressures. It is only when the temperature reaches the boiling point that the turtle may decide to stick its head and feet out of its shell and move. And then it may be too late.

When does selective imperviousness work? First, when the organization succeeds in indoctrinating its members deeply into its organizational beliefs and standards. Selective imperviousness requires a kind of absolute faith, an ardor, a commitment to carry one's message out to the world, to get others to do things our way. And that seems to be getting harder to do each year.

Selective imperviousness also works well in relatively undifferentiated, placid, noncompetitive environments. British colonialists and the early Jesuits had a sort of monopoly over the environments in which they worked. But now there are the Russians and the Cubans and the Chinese, and, oddly enough, the locals, all in the same place.

To take the distant, formal, standoffish role implied by such selective imperviousness becomes very risky in turbulent settings. Not only was that true for the early British; the same is true for the contemporary American company that insists on operating in the American way in Latin America, or in the urban way in a rural setting. It must offer an extraordinary product or service if it expects to remain unsullied in the intricate networks of a briskly moving but foreign environment.

Adaptation, as we have seen, is a fine strategy—for survival. Taking on the local coloring, going native, will usually help an organization to stay locally alive; but it is not likely to produce innovation or to influence the environment. Indeed, it may generate serious *internal* problems for the organization's members. For most of us are not perfectly adaptive. We cannot become one with our environments even if we want to. Our history, our education, our values don't permit it.

Some form of an active-adaptive strategy appears almost a necessity for contemporary organizations, both because of the nature of the modern organization and the nature of the modern environment. G.E. cannot be French, but it must be quasi-French if it is to build and sell computers in France. Certainly France cannot be suborned into the G.E. way; but on the other hand, G.E. had better not be fully suborned into the French way.

Redesigning oneself

So what is left? Interaction rather than isolation. Patience rather than pre-cipitousness. Modification rather than conversion. A world, that is to say, of talk and compromise; of incremental changes on the outside accompanied by incremental adaptive changes on the inside; of both sensitivity and identity.

That is a difficult task, but organizations can work at it. To succeed, they need a good sensing apparatus with which to learn about their environment, good action apparatus with which to respond to and influence their environment, and, most of all, good internal communication and decision apparatus with which to do two things: (1) to convert what they sense into appropriate action, and (2) to modify and redesign themselves.

One important difference between man and organization is that man is born with sense organs, brain, and muscles. Organizations must make their own. They can choose to be blind or to see with many eyes, to build lots of action muscle or little, and to devise an effective internal communication and decision mechanism or a faulty one.

Yet most organizations do not treat these problems as a conscious part of their self-design. Their sense organs, especially, tend to develop helter-skelter as an ancillary product of trying to buy or sell or lobby. The internal mechanisms for processing what they sense are often highly dependent on personalities and prejudices. Organizations hire salesmen to sell, not to lis-ten. And often what the salesman hears, he cannot successfully transmit back into the organization. Sales meetings typically include little listening. The communication is one way, from company to salesman. Similarly, or-ganizations hire scientists to do R&D, not to keep up with their profession. But the scientist who listens to his profession often produces highly useful work for the organization.

Only in recent years has the issue of organizational sensing begun to be examined consciously. Unfortunately, "organizational intelligence" is the phrase often used to describe this process; but that phrase, adapted from the diplomatic and military worlds, connotes spying on an enemy. That is not the central problem. The central problem is knowing one's world.

Summary

Organizations use several different strategies for coping with their environ-ments. All those strategies involve sensing the environment, processing what is sensed, and acting.

Some organizations use a strategy of "imperviousness," sensing little and acting little. This strategy is useful for organizations that want to iso-late themselves from change, but it is increasingly difficult to implement in a volatile world.

Other organizations are "selectively impervious." They try to sense the environment and act in response to it, but they also make sure they do not enter into it. Such organizations presocialize their people and require strong commitment and loyalty.

Still other organizations try to sense their environment and to become one with it. That "adaptive" strategy has some limited use for survival, but it does little to foster growth or innovation.

The strategy of "action-adaptation" involves changing both oneself and one's environment interactively. But it is easier to adapt to and to change active, volatile environments than passive ones.

In any strategy, however, one central problem is the tuning of the organization's behavior to the particular state of its particular environment. Appropriate tuning means organizational responsiveness that is neither too strong nor too weak for the organization's environment.

The degree of centralization in an organization affects its tuning. Organizations too centralized for their environment become rigid and slow to respond. Overly decentralized organizations may become too locally adaptive, too hard to control.

Organizations have a distinct advantage over individuals in coping with this problem: they can redesign their own sense organs, brains, and muscles into a system consistent with the strategies they choose.

Notes and references

A good background for this chapter may be found in works on "open-systems theory," such as E. Trist and F. E. Emery, "The Causal Texture of Organizational Environments," *Human Relations* 18 (1965), pp. 21–32, in which the authors categorize environments into the types we have used in our discussion. This article is also reprinted in F. E. Emery, ed., *Systems Thinking* (London: Penguin Books, 1969).

On the ways in which organizations try to cope, we have borrowed liberally from J. D. Thompson, *Organizations in Action* (New York: McGraw-Hill, 1967).

On the problems of trying to understand foreign environments, we suggest W. J. Lederer and E. Burdick, *The Ugly American* (New York: Norton, 1958).

Tom Wolfe's fascinating piece on the naiveté of white officialdom in understanding black culture is also useful: *Radical Chic and Mau-Mauing the Flak Catchers* (New York: Bantam Books, 1970).

On organizational intelligence, see H. L. Wilensky, *Organizational Intelligence* (New York: Basic Books, 1967).

Transorganizational Development: Contributions to Theory and Practice
David M. Boje and
Terance J. Wolfe

Recent experience indicates that government no longer has the resources or the commitment to provide substantive solutions to complex social problems. The current turmoil in the automobile industry provides a concrete illustration. Plant closures have resulted from the introduction of new technology combined with cutbacks in demand and increasing foreign competition. Surrounding communities have been confronted with higher rates of unemployment and community decline. Local economies have been strained due to the growth of unemployed, low-skilled workers. The demand for products and services has decreased, and threatened the livelihood of local merchants. Social service agencies have been pressured to provide welfare relief, job retraining, and career and psychological counseling. Entire communities, then, have been affected by these actions.

Organizations and communities affected by these problems are interested in the generation and implementation of alternative strategies. Complex problems require new organizational forms for their resolution. The formation of interorganizational "networks" among public, private and grassroot organizations is one strategy that has emerged to meet this need. Networks are recurring patterns of communication and resource exchange (Boje and Whetten 1981). They offer a method for pooling and sharing information among interested parties, as well as achieving the economies of scale necessary for concerted progress.

To date, research on interorganizational relations has been directed toward the morphological description of preexisting networks of organizations (Aldrich 1979; Knoke & Rogers 1977; van de Ven et al. 1977; Galaskiewicz 1979; Boje & Whetten 1981). Stable structures in predictable environments dealing with certain and narrowly defined issues have been examined (Motamedi 1978). These settings have made the research task manageable. However, they have failed to provide the necessary guidance for working with the complex problems of creating and changing networks in the turbulent environments of today's society.

The important task has begun to shift from network structure to an understanding of the process of "networking." Concerned individuals, groups, and organizations have found it difficult to form networks capable of responding to collective interests. This has led to a demand for a new breed of organizational development (OD) change agent. These specialists would take as their target of change the relationships among self-interested components of the environment that have a stake in a problem's resolution. The term *transorganizational development* (TD) has been applied to this area of consultation (Cummings 1984).

Conventional organization development change strategies may be inappropriately applied to the formation of networks. This is likely to occur inasmuch as we lack sufficient theory to guide our actions. Interorganizational networks present the consultant with a novel set of challenges. These may necessitate the creation of more "activist oriented" strategies that take into account the unique context of problem situations.

The purpose of this paper is to delineate a set of TD change strategies that can aid the networking process. We begin with a brief review of transorganizational development. Then, drawing on the literature of symbolic interactionism, a description of the concept of negotiating contexts and its importance to understanding TD theory is presented. Finally, a set of strategies are presented which can aid the consultant in the development of dynamic interorganizational networks. They include methods for mobilizing new networks, changing existing networks, and reframing the collective definitions that bind networks together. The strategies are presented in terms of the increasing degree of activism required by the consultant for producing transorganizational change.

Transorganizational development theory

The origins of transorganizational development theory can be traced to the early work of Culbert, Elden, McWhinney, Schmidt, and Tannenbaum (1972). They were reporting on the efforts of the Graduate School of Management at UCLA to refocus the field of OD.

> OD must move beyond (but certainly not leave) the single organization as its primary focus of attention. We call this shift in focus from intra-organizational change to interorganizational change and social change the emergence of a transorganizational perspective. . . . In this broader, less structured context, central issues like policy making, directionality, power relations and conflict management become important, and we intend to explore them in practice. Hence our label, transorganizational practice. [p. 2]

In a separate effort, Thayer (1973) defines transorganizational as

> . . . the innumerable occasions when individuals from different organizations and suborganizations work together to solve an existing problem. . . . The effective functions are performed partly inside each separate organization and partly outside, for the cooperative venture is

itself a new organization. The emphasis on the "trans" helps us see that things occur both through and beyond individual permanent organizations, and that we can no longer visualize each such organization as a closed system. [p. 12]

Given this definition, there are many frequently occurring situations that can properly be regarded as "transorganizational." Interagency cooperation in the public sector, competitive and collaborative arrangements in the private sector, public interest groups, and social change movements (Motamedi 1978), as well as "transnational" and "transgovernmental" relations (Keohane and Nye 1974), are all examples of transorganizational phenomena. Twelve years after the UCLA challenge, research and practice in TD continue to be limited by conventional organization development technology (Kaplan 1980).

Transorganizational development practice, as defined here, refers to those strategies and actions designed to create or modify networks. The consultant's role in TD practice is to aid participants in the decision-making and action-taking processes necessary to either gain entry into, or improve their standing in, the network. This requires a theory that treats the network as an open and dynamic system with a common purpose, as well as operating within a context that has constantly changing boundaries.

Negotiating contexts

Network participants are interested parties who have a stake in particular outcomes and depend on the network for the accomplishment of their goals. Mason (1969, 1978) refers to these individuals, groups, and organizations as stakeholders. Their interactions occur within a larger problem-oriented environment.

There are three interdependent attributes that characterize the environment or context within which network interactions take place. First, interactions are governed by a negotiation process in which network participants "collectively define" their organizing (i.e., problem) issues. Second, "domains" are created as stakeholders identify their special interests in these issues. Finally, "exchanges" link participants together in interdependent relations. Stakeholder networks operate within negotiating contexts (Kling and Gerson 1977, 1978) that are collectively defined through their interactions and reflect their special interests. These contexts are dynamic and changing, and they vary as new problems become salient and old issues recede.

Collective definition. Crucial to the process of network formation is the development of collective definitions. Lang and Lang (1961, p. 43) describe collective definitions as "the process by which cognitive assessments are brought in line with one another so that some common and plausible assessments emerge." Blumer (1971, p. 298) notes that social issues are rooted in "processes of collective definition." Networking depends on the continual negotiation of collective definitions as participants develop mutual understanding of their common issues.

From experience, each participant defines a unique view of the environment. As stakeholders independently experience a common shock or crisis, they describe their context in a similar language. Shared experiences and a common language contribute to their sense of a joint fate (e.g., Reaganomics, right-to-lifers, Watts riots). Recent changes in the California automobile industry provide an illustration of the emergence of a collective definition.

California automobile manufacturers have been systematically curtailing their level of operations since 1980 when Ford closed its Pico Rivera plant. This was rapidly followed by Mack Truck's Hayward plant, GM's Fremont and Southgate plants (March 1982), and Ford's last West Coast plant, in San Jose (Mann 1984). By 1982, GM's Van Nuys plant, which produces Camaros and Firebirds, was the last remaining auto assembly plant in California. In October of that year, the second shift—roughly 2,500 workers—was laid off and the plant was threatened with closure. On May 13, 1983, in the face of a recall of the second shift, the UAW Local held a rally to protest future job security. The "Campaign to Keep GM Van Nuys Open" has become a rallying point for local, state, and national labor leaders, politicians, welfare and public interest groups, and community action agencies. The "campaign" continues today and drew national attention during the 1984 GM–UAW contract negotiations.

Local private industry councils (PICs) have been created to address issues of unemployment and retraining. Their development reflects the changing context of networking as stakeholder actions alter the definition of the situation. Collective definitions are shaped by delicate processes internal to the network itself, such as rumor mills, as well as by more stable and recurring network interactions.

Domains. Each stakeholder is simultaneously "hanging on to" and "letting go of" a range of issues. These issues define the stakeholder's domain and refer to investments in particular outcomes (e.g., product, service, technology, function, location, logic, skill, language, client). Negotiating contexts do not include all of the domain issues of every stakeholder; therefore, their inclusion and combination is of strategic importance.

If a stakeholder's domain includes issues relevant to an emerging problem, such as plant closures, then that stakeholder will have a vested interest in the negotiating contexts that influence network formation. Stakeholders may adjust their domain boundaries, broadening or constricting them, as they attempt to move toward or away from issues that differentially affect their access to resources.

The "Campaign to Keep GM Van Nuys Open" played an important role in the GM–UAW contract negotiations. It significantly influenced the UAW emphasis on job security and company-provided retraining funds. Yet, the Van Nuys Local refrained from endorsing the national contract because they did not feel it adequately addressed their security needs. In this case, the "campaign" was unsuccessful in broadening its domain boundary to include the national union.

Exchange. The third attribute of negotiating contexts is exchange. It deals with the interdependent nature of stakeholders in a network. Interdependence develops through stakeholder exchanges around problems that go beyond the scope and capacity of their separate efforts. Stakeholders recognize this interdependence when they realize that their actions can affect, and be affected by, others—even those with whom they are not directly exchanging products, services, and information. This sense of correlated fate, which emerges and grows through environmental interaction, serves to bind stakeholders together.

When the Southgate GM auto assembly plant closed, the union aligned itself with Los Angeles County to obtain a variety of social service programs for unemployed auto workers that the union could not provide on its own. Meanwhile, GM worked with the private industry council administered through Los Angeles city government. In both cases, patterns of exchange were created by the situation which had not previously existed.

In sum, negotiating contexts are subject to the influences of the larger environment. As boundaries change through interaction, different aspects of the environment become important. Contexts are open systems; they incorporate salient aspects of the environment, process them through individual and organizational activity, and distribute transformed output back into the larger environment. Figure 1 lists a number of environmental forces that affect negotiating contexts and contribute to their definition.

Economic or market conditions affect the supply of capital and the distribution of products and services within negotiating contexts—for example, the impact of Japanese imports on the U.S. auto market. Social and cultural conditions of organizations and communities determine the behavioral world of their participants as when card-carrying auto workers are not readily accepted in the white-collar environment of aerospace firms. Political and ideological persuasions create factions that influence and define stakeholder alignments such as between county- and city-sponsored social services. Technical and scientific developments make relationships among actors easier or more difficult to facilitate, such as the influence of robotics on the skill requirements of autoworkers. The natural or physical setting affects the costs of information and resource transfer; it is less costly to communicate between local organizations, more costly between the national union and GM headquarters and the president's task force on hi-tech solutions to displaced workers. The complex pattern of interrelationships

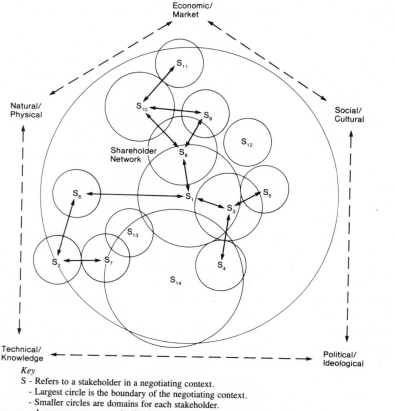

Economic/
Market

Natural/
Physical

Social/
Cultural

Shareholder
Network

Technical/
Knowledge

Political/
Ideological

Key

S - Refers to a stakeholder in a negotiating context.
- Largest circle is the boundary of the negotiating context.
- Smaller circles are domains for each stakeholder.
◄ - - ► - A resource or communication link between two stakeholders.
◄——► - Interdependence between environmental forces of change. Lines interlinking all forces have been
omitted for clarity.

Figure 1. Negotiating context

among these various environmental forces contribute to the turbulence of
negotiating contexts (Emery and Trist 1965). Yet, this very turbulence
dramatizes their interdependence.

Figure 1 summarizes what has been stated thus far. Networks (see
arrows) occur within negotiating contexts. Through networking, stakeholders collectively recognize and define a range of contextual issues. Each
stakeholder carves out domains within the negotiating contexts (represented by the smaller circles in figure 1), which are composed of a range of
self-interested issues. These issues define stakeholders' investments in particular outcomes such as technologies, products, and benefits. The overlapping circles draw attention to the overlap in issues. Finally, negotiating
contexts themselves are open systems; they import inputs from the larger
environment, undertake conversion processes, and redistribute outputs.
Since many environmental forces influence negotiating contexts, consult-

ing to an entire transorganizational network is significantly different from consulting to a single organization.

Implications for practice. As can be seen from the foregoing, transorganizational development concerns itself with the relationships between a variety of stakeholders as they attempt to pursue their self-interests. Stakeholders create collective problem definitions as they engage in exchanges regarding domain issues within negotiating contexts. Each has its own unique set of issues but overlaps and linkages are of concern to the consultant. The consultant seeks to aid the development of effective networks by mapping the fit between stakeholder domains and facilitating the emergence of collective problem definitions within negotiating contexts. To do so requires a shift in three fundamental OD value premises.

First, OD is oriented to top-down change. Planned change starts with the inclusion of top management to gain their support in efforts designed to trickle down (Argyris 1970). In TD, there is no "top"; however, there is a core of stakeholders, which, by virtue of strategic location at the crossroads of communication and resource channels, occupies a central position in emerging or stable networks (Boje and Whetten 1981)—for example, the constituency of a PIC.

In contrast to conventional OD strategies, effective TD may necessitate an "activist grassroots" approach by aiding less powerful organizations, communities, or national interest groups (e.g., S_{12}, S_{13}, and S_{14} in figure 1). These can connect up with and redirect the coordinating core, thereby enhancing the overall health of the network and broadening the negotiating contexts. Healthy negotiating contexts balance stakeholder networking in ways that optimize exchanges, identify domains, and form collective definitions.

In figure 1, the core stakeholders (S_1, S_3, S_6, S_8) of the network can be seen as providing a limited coordination function to the three sets of otherwise "loosely coupled" (Weick 1976) stakeholder networks (S_1: S_3-S_6-S_8, S_3: S_4-S_5, S_6: S_2-S_7, S_8: S_9-S_{10}-S_{11}). Change from the top under these conditions can mean increasing the core's grip on the less dominant periphery (e.g., S_4, S_5, S_7, and S_{11}) in ways that may be dysfunctional to other stakeholders—for example, force, coercion, or other forms of pressure tactics designed to induce participation.

Second, OD contains unquestioned assumptions about the superiority of humanistic social science. TD change strategies can involve mobilizing opposing coalitions, extending an existing network to include stakeholders outside the current problem boundaries, introducing competing organizational forms, or creating alternative definitions of the issues. Humanistic OD is at odds with networking needs that dictate breaking up a hierarchy of prestige, altering a pattern of resource allocation, introducing domain dissensus, and dissolving self-serving empires that are often prevalent in the public and private sectors.

Finally, conventional OD strategies of trust building, consensus seeking, and collaboration are likely to be impotent in many TD efforts. Organizations that have attained dominance in the face of competition for scarce resources are not predisposed to collaborative solutions. Once a network evolves an entrenched pecking order, it adapts more readily to the survival needs of that order than to the constraints of the negotiating contexts. Contextual needs, such as the redistribution of resources, may go unmet. In sum, TD (1) requires a holistic "network to negotiating contexts" framework, (2) is activist oriented, and (3) involves the exercise of power to bring about significant change.

Transorganizational development practice

Given this theoretical framework, the practice of transorganizational development will be situationally influenced by the needs of affected individuals, groups, and organizations as they attempt to create effective, problem-oriented strategies for goal achievement. There are three broad strategies in TD: mobilizing new networks, changing existing networks, and reframing collective definitions. They vary in their degree of activism. The technology for mobilizing new networks is most akin to traditional OD interventions and the least activist in its orientation. Altering the strategic balance or composition of existing networks, and breaking down and reconstructing collective definitions require more radical approaches. These approaches demonstrate the need for a transorganizational development practice that takes the consultant beyond the technology and intervention style of traditional OD (Brown 1980; Cummings 1984). Each of these will be reviewed in turn.

Mobilizing new networks

Organizations and individuals do not exist in isolation. They are involved in a variety of input and output exchanges. Turbulent environments preclude organizations and individuals from recognizing shared interests, and this limits their involvement with each other. The intervention task is to induce networking. This requires that the separate domain concerns of individuals and organizations be broadened to develop an appreciation for collective action within interdependent contexts.

Developing collective definitions. Networks form for a variety of reasons. First, they form when there is a recognized self-interest among concerned parties. Stakeholders will act to obtain greater access over available resources or to reduce uncertainty in their shared environment. For example, Cesar Chavez and the United Farm Workers, as well as other local unions and community organizations, attended the "Campaign to Keep GM Van Nuys Open" rally. Second, networks form in response to external sanctions (Laumann, Galaskiewicz, and Marsden 1978), such as the threat of plant closure. Third, network participation can be legislatively mandated. In sum, networking requires recognition of common inducement issues.

Successful transorganizational networking is dependent upon the formation and development of collective definitions. The realization that one's own concerns and interests are shared by others (e.g., layoff, unemployment) leads to voluntary participation of stakeholders in the network. The definitional process serves to focus network participants on shared problems and experiences, and it contributes to the emergence of a common direction.

Collective definitions can be created as stakeholders are brought together to explore common interests. They may examine issues that require widespread support, consume large amounts of resources, necessitate action taking, introduce turbulence, and reveal correlated fate.

When correlated fate can be demonstrated, individuals, groups, and organizations from other negotiating contexts are drawn in based on vested interests and create new contexts of interdependent relationships. The TD consultant must actively manage this process of growth, and create the conditions that facilitate the sharing of definitions. Failure to do so may result in stakeholders going in disparate ways, undermining their own efficiency, and contributing to a breakdown in the network's goal accomplishment. For example, city agencies committed to helping the unemployed may work at odds with each other unless their common interests, resources, and objectives can be identified and agreed upon.

Identifying domains. Domains can be identified by explicitly mapping both the inducements and contributions of potential stakeholders. Inducements are the goals, rewards, and satisfactions that stakeholders seek to obtain through their network participation. Contributions are those services and resources they provide in the belief that, as a result, their objectives will be satisfied (March and Simon 1958).

Network mapping has been proposed as a technique for making stakeholders more aware of each other (Mason 1978; Mason, Mitroff, and Emshoff 1978). Using this method, participants who have a stake in the network's outcomes are identified, respective inducements and contributions are shared and examined, and assumptions about the impact of future stakeholder behavior are systematically explored. In this way, stakeholder interests are defined and established, and a context is created for future bargaining and exchange.

Facilitating exchanges. To be effective, a network must create a method for estimating individual contributions, identifying and expressing solution preferences, and discovering the penalties, traps, and responsibilities of participation. A process of exchange enables stakeholders to recognize their functional relationships to one another and to reveal their individual contributions to collective goal achievement. If stakeholders do not perceive their common direction the network will lack the basis for becoming a distinct entity. Members will not be able to agree upon their joint task, and concerted action taking will not be possible.

Stakeholder exchanges depend on the consultant's skill in setting up a process for expressing alternative definitions of the negotiating contexts and examining similarities and differences. This will enable network participants to converge on collective issues. Open system planning (Jayaram 1976), strategic assumption surfacing (Mason, Mitroff, and Emshoff 1978), and shared learning (Goodman and Huff 1978) are group conference procedures that can aid the exchange process. The change agent can play a catalytic role by aiding the development of a temporary organization characterized by a collective focus and a shared identity.

Network leadership. Developing collective definitions, identifying domains, and facilitating exchanges are in and of themselves insufficient to mobilize a new network. At some point a core nucleus must crystallize to articulate, symbolize, direct, and channel loosely organized stakeholders (Lang and Lang 1961). This core nucleus becomes the basis for network leadership.

As participants' fields of vision expand beyond their own self-interests through network exchanges a blurring of stakeholder domains is likely to ensue. This will lead to network members taking behavioral cues from a core of stakeholders. This core becomes a symbol in whose name specific functions get articulated and performed—for example, the mayor's task force on plant closures. Trist (1979) refers to this group as the referent point by which other stakeholders orient themselves in their mutual interactions.

Figure 2 illustrates the relationship between the TD consultant, network leadership, and the extended network. This core group is integral to the network's problem-defining, problem-solving, and action-taking strategies. It is through their efforts that the network gets shaped, communication occurs, and outcomes are created. They target strategies that mobilize other stakeholders into action and draw them into the issue.

In sum, tactics for creating a network include developing collective definitions, identifying domains, facilitating exchanges, and channeling network leadership. Mobilizing a new network is vastly different from modifying an existing one or redefining stakeholder perspectives in an entenched network. These require conflict interventions that make structural realignments and alternative collective definitions possible. For clarity of presentation, we will treat structure and definition as separate topics.

Changing existing networks

Networks operate within dynamic negotiating contexts. This creates ambiguity, which has several consequences. First, it inhibits the development of

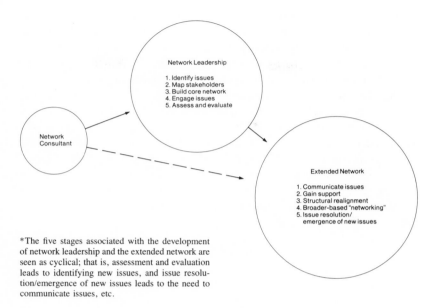

Network Leadership

1. Identify issues
2. Map stakeholders
3. Build core network
4. Engage issues
5. Assess and evaluate

Network
Consultant

Extended Network

1. Communicate issues
2. Gain support
3. Structural realignment
4. Broader-based "networking"
5. Issue resolution/
   emergence of new issues

*The five stages associated with the development
of network leadership and the extended network are
seen as cyclical; that is, assessment and evaluation
leads to identifying new issues, and issue resolu-
tion/emergence of new issues leads to the need to
communicate issues, etc.

Figure 2. A networking approach to problem solving

stakeholder consensus regarding problem definition, identification of resources, participants' stakes, and strategies for action. Second, it produces
apathy and a reluctance to change. Third, there is a tendency for networks
to retrench when issue salience decreases. Finally, network structure is resistant to change. Each of these has implications for transorganizational
practice. The methods for dealing with them require an increasingly activist theory of intervention.

Existing networks can be changed in several ways. The degree of association between network participants can be varied through information
and resource exchanges. Control can be exerted over the type, quantity,
and quality of inputs that enter the network from the external environment.
Communication channels can be modified producing conditions of slack or
overload. Finally, competing organizational or structural forms can be introduced to instigate the network to action. Each of these strategies are detailed below.

Strategic coupling. Coupling binds stakeholders together. It occurs through
the exchanges that stakeholders have about their domain issues. The degree
of coupling within a network has an important impact on its effectiveness.
Loose coupling in a network leads to more adaptability (Simon 1962;
Weick 1976; Aldrich 1977; Pfeffer and Salancik 1978). Alternatively, tight
coupling leads to more rigidity and less responsiveness to change (Oshry

1976; Alderfer 1980; Brown 1980). The amount of coupling necessary will vary depending on the turbulence or uncertainty of the external environment, as well as on stakeholder preferences.

Stakeholders have varying preferences for the degree of coupling that exists within a network. These preferences are likely to be influenced by the stakeholders' strategic assessments of the impact of the change on their access to the network's resources and power bases.

Assuming power is relational (Wolfe 1959; Emerson 1962; Cartwright and Zander 1968; Cook 1977), the power structure of a network can be modified by changing its "strategic couplings." The darkened circle in figure 3 represents a dominant network position. Arrows have been drawn to indicate which couplings, if removed, would significantly alter the power relations. The dotted lines represent the couplings that, if created, would also change the balance of power.

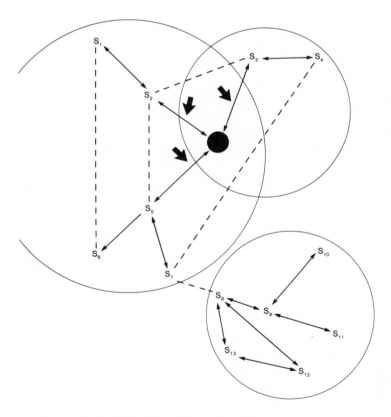

Figure 3. Modifications in an existing network

For example, if S_2 "couples" with S_3 and S_5, then dependence on the dominant position to mediate their exchanges will be lessened. In this way, broader-based network support can be created and additional opportunities for carrying out exchanges, discovering domains, and developing collective definitions will present themselves. Coupling of this nature can initially be used to extend the network by incorporating new members and identifying new resources.

In sum, tightly coupled networks are more vulnerable to external disturbances than loosely coupled. The impact of a conflict episode in one part can be felt in all parts of a tightly coupled network. Loose coupling, on the other hand, mitigates rapid communication, and network participants may be unaware of circumstances and events affecting other members.

Extending or contracting inputs. Varying the inputs to negotiating contexts can be used to change existing networks. Increasing the amount and variety of environmental inputs will strain the network's information processing capabilities and lead to structural changes (Lawrence and Lorsch 1967). As information-processing needs increase, the organization necessary for handling these requirements becomes more complex (Galbraith 1973, 1977; Pondy and Mitroff 1978).

Structural change can also be stimulated by curtailing the resource flow to a network. Weick (1977) points out that many attempts have been made to change bureaucracies by pouring in large doses of resources. When the existing power structure is firmly entrenched, this strategy frequently serves only to strengthen their control. When resources that maintain structural variety are contracted, efforts to create new alignments and redefine goals are quickly undertaken (Culbert and McDonough 1980). This is evidenced by the more conservative economic goals being accepted under "Reaganomics," in particular the attempt to dismantle the large public bureaucracies.

In cases where extending or contracting inputs are not sufficient to readjust the boundaries of the negotiating contexts and alter the power structure, disruptive nonviolent tactics may be called for. Such tactics may include overloading communication channels, violating the normative structure, and transmitting ambiguous messages.

Disrupting current operations. Information overload, deviations from accepted channels, and transmission of ambiguous messages are all ways of inducing conflict (Robbins 1974) and thereby restructuring a network. Structure can be modified by overloading the central positions of a network with information-processing demands. As demands increase, it will be necessary for the dominant core to coordinate its actions and to buffer the expectations placed on it. With increasing demands the costs of coordination begin to outweigh the power advantages of centralization. This can lead the network to a strategy of decentralization and the decoupling of subsystems such as the leadership core.

Network restructuring can also occur as a result of violating system norms. Engaging in behaviors that are not normally regarded as acceptable may call attention to dysfunctional aspects of the system (Haley 1969; Smith 1975). An unequal distribution of network resources, an imbalance in the concentration of power, and injustices perpetrated against one sub-group (e.g., blacks, women) to the benefit of others illustrate system be-haviors that perpetuate the status quo. Given the turbulent environment of most networks, such system maintenance behaviors may, in fact, be de-structive. Grassroots lobbying is one way of producing change outside of accepted channels.

Finally, communicating ambiguous messages to various stakeholders can also be effective for heightening the level of conflict and bringing about network change. This strategy is most useful when the network is tightly coupled or, though loosely coupled, actively attempting to strengthen its connections. A tightly coupled network is characterized by heavy informa-tion exchange. When stakeholders communicate their varying perceptions about ambiguous messages, doubt and uncertainty will be introduced. This will raise the level of tension and conflict. Communicating ambiguous messages to a loosely coupled network attempting to strengthen its connec-tions will increase recognition of the need for exchanging information and creating a coherent structure.

Introducing competing forms. The final strategy for changing existing net-works is the introduction of competing structural forms. Organizational structures are created to satisfy particular purposes. However, needs and purposes vary over time, environments become more volatile, and the level of differentiation and integration must change (Lawrence and Lorsch 1967). Frequently those who have the organizational leverage to influence deci-sions and respond to external changes are too enmeshed in the situation to read the signs—a situation much akin to Henry Ford's willingness to "give them any color car they want as long as it's black." Under these conditions, introducing a competing structural form can lead to the redesign of an existing structure.

The impact of health maintenance organizations (HMOs) on traditional health-care delivery illustrates this method (Saward and Fleming 1980). Prior to the emergence of HMOs, physicians practicing in private-care hos-pitals aided their own self-interests by *adding* costs due to the increased participation of third-party funders such as the federal government (Medi-care, Medicaid). However, within the HMO the physicians' self-interests are aided by *controlling* costs, since bonus or salary increases are dependent on meeting operating budgets. The strength of this competition has prompted major reforms in the traditional structure. In a similar way, the emergence of UPS and Federal Express has produced significant changes in the U.S. Postal Service. Competing organizational forms, then, can lead to the modification or change of existing networks.

To summarize, several strategies have been presented for changing existing networks. They vary in variety and their degree of activism. Strategic coupling can be used to modify the existing balance of power and to develop broader-based network support. Varying the inputs to negotiating contexts can lead to greater network differentiation or new alignments and goal redefinition. Current operations can be disrupted through a variety of nonviolent tactics, including information overload, norm violations, and strategic transmittal of ambiguous messages. Finally, existing networks can be induced to change by the emergence of competing structural forms. In the next section the focus will be on how collective definitions can be reframed to provide new strength and direction to an existing network.

Reframing collective definitions

Negotiating contexts and domains are created and maintained by definitional processes, which can themselves become targets of change. Here, "definitional" refers to shared logics of rationality and legitimacy of action (Lang and Lang 1961) that are often conveyed between stakeholders. Stories of past events provide a logic for understanding present decisions (Boje, Fedor, and Rowland 1981). In this light it can be seen how legislative attempts to alter resource-exchange patterns usually fail: they don't take into consideration the unifying and driving power of collective definitions.

Network hierarchies are maintained by beliefs in precedence, by shared definitions of appropriate and inappropriate collective behavior, and by mutual respect for territorial domains. Each of these constitutes a logic frame that helps to define expected behavior. Breaking stakeholders' deepset frames by adopting new languages, introducing alternative historical rationalizations, and constructing new organizing myths are the most activist of the TD change strategies. They address fundamental changes in the shared system of meaning. They challenge and attempt to reconstruct the network's culture.

Creating a new language. A new language and vocabulary can be introduced that provide alternative meanings to stakeholder relationships and change the way negotiating contexts get framed. People use language to communicate experience. Through interactions they create a common language and a shared system of meaning. Stakeholders who have networked together based on common interest develop a vocabulary that symbolizes their relationships. This vocabulary and the existing relationships may become dysfunctional over time as conditions and participants change. The TD consultant can influence the network by intervening into the language system.

To modify the language used to map out stakeholder relations it is necessary to identify and define existing terms in use. Terms enter a given network language because of their descriptive power; they often define the nature of the relationship, provide clues to the power and influence structure, and are emotionally laden. Consider the following examples drawn from a social service agency. They are terms used by one agency to describe other public and private agencies in the manpower training sector: crown prince, kingdom, empire builder, domain.

These terms are descriptive of a feudal system. The logic frame employed is from the perspective of a low power position. The occupants see themselves as having no rights or claims, but understand that their role is to serve a kingdom in which others are the beneficiaries.

In this case, the change strategy requires substituting a new symbolic language, one that has the ability to redirect the attention of stakeholders. The following conversions illustrate this point: crown prince = catalyst; kingdom = shared fate; empire builder = peacemaker; domain = jurisdiction.

In the social service illustration, counselors, clients, and administrators could be brought together to create new labels for themselves, their domains, and their negotiating contexts. The metaphors of feudalism (power over, submission, status quo) imply different system functions, roles, and energy than the metaphors of democracy (power to, equality, growth and change). Consultants capable of helping clients construct new orienting metaphors can open them up to alternative networking possibilities.

Intervening into a network's language system is likely to produce resistance. Change strategies that attempt to modify the language system will be more effective if they provide new interpretations to old terms, rather than abandoning or destroying existing frameworks (Vickers 1965).

Rewriting history. One method for changing stakeholders is to modify their interpretations of the past. The actions of a social system at one point in time are shaped by its own and others' actions at previous points in time. The historical rendering of an event or series of events molds the perceptions and interpretations that participants and observers ascribe to them. Historians are familiar with how countries rewrite their histories to rationalize, and thereby legitimize, their current patterns of behavior (Ravitch 1977). For example, Indians can be framed as barbarians obstructing settlement, partners in reclaiming the West, disenfranchised, or as victims of white imperialism.

History is told in stories, and it is through stories that the TD consultant learns about the client structure and intervenes into the client system. The consultant is told stories that highlight victories over current enemies, identify values that are sacred and unchangeable, and promote the soundness of the network's actions. Stories are told that are designed to influence the intervention strategy, circumscribe the change target, and expose the criteria for assessing intervention success or failure.

At the transorganizational development level, the consultant is interested in reconstructing stories about (*a*) how the network started, (*b*) what critical dramas occurred during its evolution, (*c*) who the key leaders and organizations were and how their values shaped the outcome, and (*d*) why the dramas had the impact they did. The consultant can help to accent those dramas that provide important lessons for current circumstances, that preserve contemporary values, and that support alternative futures capable of meeting community needs.

Myth making. Networks can be revitalized through the creation of new images of organizational possibilities for social action. Social systems use myths to communicate information about their structure, values, customs, and norms. A mythological structure is created in which the fundamental beliefs, goals, and aspirations of the participants are embodied in a set of people and events that are both real and to some extent imaginary. They are based on *real* people and events, but are embellished with the passage of time.

An actual person or event that had a significant impact in the shaping of the organization or network acquires a "superhuman" quality. Within this mythical figure or event the promise of the future still seems possible. The "American dream," "from rags to riches," "only in America," and "working your way to the top" are all mythical qualities of the American value system. They are used to motivate stakeholders, mobilize individual and collective action, and invigorate the pursuit of shared goals.

Social revolutionaries have used myth making as a strategy for changing social and organizational structures in dramatic ways. Setting goals that transcend current realities and indicate directions for future change has the potential for unleashing individual energy and commitment. New myths enable the network to gain control or influence over issues and align itself with alternative stakeholders. This is the tactic of many advocacy groups— for example, the Coalition for Economic Survival in Los Angeles.

To be effective, this strategy requires images that inspire individuals to ignore outdated bureaucratic rules, to discount dysfunctional traditions, to challenge historical assumptions, and to shed the onus of legislative futility. In this way, the change agent truly is a revolutionary. The interventionist engages in a strategy of bringing about change from within by working with existing stakeholders.

In this section a set of methods have been described that represent the most activist of the TD change strategies. Intervening into the meaning system of an existing social structure requires a radical departure from existing change technology. Several methods were described. They include creating a new language and thereby reshaping participants' interpretive schemas, rewriting history to modify their sense of reality, and engaging in revolutionary myth making to invigorate the process of change by providing new directions and renewed commitment.

In reviewing the macro-level change interventions proposed here, there are several assumptions worth considering. First, just as intraorganizational systems undergo constant change, so also do stakeholder networks, where the frequency of linkages between members is less and the strength of their associations is weaker. Second, despite the characteristic looseness of networks, there are critical linkages, which, when modified, create ripple effects throughout the system. Third, there is a constant tension between equality and greater status differentiation. Finally, and most important, change efforts that take the network in its entirety as the target of change will produce more influential and longer-lasting community effects than those efforts directed toward single organization interventions.

Implications

The transorganizational development strategies outlined here are summarized in table 1. They have been arranged based on the increasing level of activism required on the part of the change agent.

This paper has addressed two important issues for the field of transorganizational development. First, strategies for stakeholder networking will need to be more "activist" oriented in order to cope with the loosely

Table 1. Transorganizational development strategies

	Low TD Activism
1. *Mobilizing new networks* 　　Developing collective definitions 　　Identifying domains 　　Facilitating exchanges 　　Network leadership	
2. *Changing existing networks* 　　Strategic coupling 　　Extending or contracting inputs 　　Disrupting current operations 　　Introducing competing forms	
3. *Reframing collective definitions* 　　Creating a new language 　　Rewriting history 　　Myth making	
	High TD Activism

coupled and political nature of social issues. Second, TD practice will have to incorporate system-wide strategies to bring about permanent change.

These results provide us with five useful clues about networking. First, alternative networks are not easily mobilized. Second, if change efforts are not internalized by participants, a targeted network will regress to its former equilibrium position in terms of subsystem alignments and power differentials. Third, TD consultants will be required to take sides, to mobilize new coalitions, and to take less value-neutral roles if they hope to be effective in overcoming existing structures. Fourth, the network will have to be more responsive to the negotiating contexts within which it is embedded than to the domain interests of its stakeholders. Finally, to minimize resistance, interventions into a network's meaning system will have to focus on changing the meaning of existing labels rather than substituting new or alternative frameworks.

To be successful, transorganizational development demands more activist-oriented, system-wide change efforts—even revolutionary efforts—especially when cooperative strategies are neither feasible nor powerful enough to make a difference.

Bibliography

Alderfer, Clayton P. Consulting to Underbounded Systems. In C. P. Alderfer and C. L. Cooper (eds.), *Advances in Experiential Social Processes,* vol. 2, 267–95. New York: Wiley, 1980.

Aldrich, Howard. Visionaries and Villains: The Politics of Designing Interorganizational Relations. In E. Burack and A. Negandhi (eds.), *Organization Design: Theoretical Perspectives and Empirical Findings,* 23–40. Kent, Ohio: Kent State University Press, 1977.

Aldrich, Howard. *Organizations and Environments.* Englewood Cliffs, N.J.: Prentice-Hall, 1979.

Argyris, Chris. *Intervention Theory and Method: A Behavioral Science View.* Reading, Mass.: Addison-Wesley, 1970.

Blumer, Herbert. Social Problems as Collective Behavior. *Social Problems,* Winter 1971.

Boje, David M. and David A. Whetten. Effects of Organizational Strategies and Contextual Constraints on Centrality and Attributions of Influence in Interorganizational Networks. *Administrative Science Quarterly* 26 (1981), 378–95.

Boje, David M., Don Fedor, and Kendrith Rowland. Myth-Making: A Qualitative Step in OD Interventions. *Journal of Applied Behavioral Science* 18 (1982), 17–28.

Brown, L. Dave. Planned Change in Underorganized Systems. In T. G. Cummings (ed.), *Systems Theory for Organization Development,* 181–203. New York: Wiley, 1980.

Cartwright, Dorwin, and Alvin Zander (eds.). *Group Dynamics: Research and Theory,* 3d ed. New York: Harper and Row, 1968.

Cook, Karen S. Exchange and Power in Networks of Interorganizational Relations. *Sociological Quarterly* 18 (Winter 1977), 62–82.

Culbert, Samuel A., James M. Elden, Will McWhinney, Warren Schmidt, and Robert Tannenbaum. Trans-Organizational Praxis: A Search Beyond Organizational Development. *International Associations* 24, no. 10 (1972).

Culbert, Samuel A., and John J. McDonough. *The Invisible War: Pursuing Self-Interests at Work.* New York: Wiley, 1980.

Cummings, Thomas G. Transorganizational Development. In B. M. Staw and L. L. Cummings (eds.), *Research in Organizational Behavior,* vol. 6, 367–422. Greenwich, Conn.: JAI Press, 1984.

Emerson, Richard M. Power-Dependence Relations. *American Sociological Review* 27, no. 1 (1962), 31–40.

Emery, Fred, and Eric Trist. The Causal Texture of Organizational Environments. *Human Relations* 18 (1965), 21–32.

Galaskiewicz, Joseph. *Exchange Networks and Community Politics.* Beverly Hills, Calif.: Sage, 1979.

Galbraith, Jay. *Designing Complex Organizations.* Reading, Mass.: Addison-Wesley, 1973.

Galbraith, Jay. *Organization Design.* Reading, Mass.: Addison-Wesley, 1977.

Goodman, Richard A., and Anne Sigismund Huff. Enriching Policy Premises for an Ambiguous World. In J. W. Sutherland (ed.), *Management Handbook for Public Administrators,* 334–61. New York: Van Nostrand, 1978.

Haley, Jay. *The Power Tactics of Jesus Christ.* New York: Grossman, 1969.

Jayaram, G. K. Open System Planning. In W. G. Bennis, K. D. Benne, R. Chin, and K. Corey (eds.), *The Planning of Change,* 3d ed., 175–83. New York: Holt, Rinehart & Winston, 1976.

Kaplan, Robert E. Intervention in a Loosely Organized System: An Encounter with Non-being. Technical Report No. 15. Greensboro, N.C.: Center for Creative Leadership, 1980.

Keohane, Robert O., and Joseph S. Nye. Transgovernmental Relations and International Organizations. *World Politics* 27, no. 1 (1974), 39–62.

Kling, Rob, and Elihu M. Gerson. The Social Dynamics of Technical Innovation in the Computing World. *Symbolic Interaction* 1, no. 1 (1977), 132–46.

Kling, Rob, and Elihu M. Gerson. Patterns of Segmentation and Intersection in the Computing World. *Symbolic Interaction* 1, no. 2 (1978), 24–43.

Knoke, David, and David L. Rogers. A Block Modeling Analysis of Interorganizational Networks. Unpublished paper, Indiana University, 1977.

Lang, Kurt, and Gladys E. Lang. *Collective Dynamics.* New York: Thomas Crowell, Co., 1961.

Laumann, Edward O., Joseph Galaskiewicz, and Peter V. Marsden. Community Structure as Interorganizational Linkages. *Annual Review of Sociology* 4 (1978), 455–84.

Lawrence, Paul R., and Jay W. Lorsch. *Organizations and Environments.* Boston: Division of Research, Graduate School of Business Administration, Harvard University, 1967.

Mann, Eric. Workers and Community Take on G.M. *The Nation* 238, no. 5 (1984), 145, 161–63.

March, James G., and Herbert Simon. *Organizations.* New York: Wiley, 1958.

Mason, Richard O. A Dialectical Approach to Strategic Planning. *Management Science* 15 (1969), B403–B414.

Mason, Richard O. Management by Multiple Advocacy. Unpublished working paper, UCLA, Study Center in Public Services Management and Policy, 1978.

Mason, Richard O., Ian Mitroff, and James Emshoff. Strategic Assumption Making: Arriving at Policy through Dialectics. Unpublished mimeograph, UCLA, 1978.

Motamedi, Kurt. The Evolution from Interorganizational Design to Transorganizational Development. Paper presented at the Academy of Management Meetings, San Francisco, 1978.

Oshry, Barry. *Notes on the Power and Systems Perspective.* Boston: Power and Systems, Inc., 1976.

Pfeffer, Jeffrey, and Gerald R. Salancik. *The External Control of Organizations: A Resource Dependence Perspective.* New York: Harper and Row, 1978.

Pondy, Louis R., and Ian Mitroff. Beyond Open Systems. Paper presented at the Academy of Management Meetings, 1976 (revised).

Ravitch, Diane. *The Revisionist Revised.* New York: Basic Books, 1977.

Robbins, Stephen P. *Managing Organizational Conflict: A Nontraditional Approach.* Englewood Cliffs, N.J.: Prentice-Hall, 1974.

Saward, Ernest W., and Scott Fleming. Health Maintenance Organizations. *Scientific American* 243 (1980), 47–53.

Simon, Herbert. The Architecture of Complexity. *Proceedings of the American Philosophical Society* 106 (December 1962), 467–82.

Smith, Ken K. The Values and Dangers of Power Conflict. *Contemporary Australian Management* 3 (1975), 19–23.

Thayer, Frederick G. *An End to Hierarchy! An End to Competition!* New York: Franklin Watts, 1973.

Trist, Eric. Referent Organizations and the Development of Interorganizational Domains. Distinguished lecture to the Academy of Management Meetings, Atlanta, 1979.

Van de Ven, Andrew H., Gordon Walker, and Jennie Liston. Coordination Patterns within an Interorganizational Network. *Human Relations* 32, no. 1 (1979), 19–36.

Vickers, Geoffrey. *The Art of Judgement: A Study of Policy Making.* New York: Basic Books, 1965.

Weick, Karl E. Educational Organizations as Loosely Coupled Systems. *Administrative Science Quarterly* 21, no. 1 (1976), 1–18.

Weick, Karl E. Organization Design: Organizations as Self Designing Systems. *Organizational Dynamics* 6, no. 2 (1977), 31–46.

Wolfe, Donald. Power and Authority in the Family. In D. Cartwright (ed.), *Studies in Social Power,* 99–117. Ann Arbor: University of Michigan, Institute for Social Research, 1959.

Beyond Management and the Worker: The Institutional Function of Management
Jeffrey Pfeffer

Theory, research, and education in the field of organizational behavior and management have been dominated by a concern for the management of people *within* organizations. The question of how to make workers more productive has stood as the foundation for management theory and practice since the time of Frederick Taylor. Such an emphasis neglects the institutional function of management. While managing people within organizations is critical, managing the organization's relationships with other organizations such as competitors, creditors, suppliers, and governmental agencies is frequently as critical to the firm's success.

Parsons (1) noted that there were three levels in organizations: (a) the technical level, where the technology of the organization was used to produce some product or service; (b) the administrative level, which coordinated and supervised the technical level; and (c) the institutional level, which was concerned with the organization's legitimacy and with organization-environment relations. Organization and management theory has primarily concentrated on administrative-level problems, frequently at very low hierarchical levels in organizations.

Practicing managers and some researchers do recognize the importance of the institutional context in which the firm operates. There is increasing use of institutional advertising, and executives from the oil industry, among others, have been active in projecting their organizations' views in a variety of contexts. Mintzberg (2) has identified the liaison role as one of ten roles managers fill. Other authors explicitly have noted the importance of relating the organization to other organizations (3, 4).

Saying that the institutional function is important is different from developing a theory of the organization's relationships with other organizations, a theory which can potentially guide the manager's strategic actions in performing the function of institutional management. Such a theory is needed, and data are accumulating to construct such a theory.

The purposes of this article are (*a*) to present evidence of the importance of the institutional function of management, and (*b*) to review data consistent with a model of institutional management. This model argues that managers behave as if they were seeking to manage and reduce uncertainty and interdependence arising from the firm's relationships with other organizations. Several strategic responses to interorganizational exchange, including their advantages and disadvantages, are considered.

Institutional problems of organizations

Organizations are open social systems, engaged in constant and important transactions with other organizations in their environments. Business firms transact with customer and supplier organizations, and with sources of credit; they interact on the federal and local level with regulatory and legal authorities which are concerned with pollution, taxes, antitrust, equal employment, and myriad other issues. Because firms do interact with these other organizations, two consequences follow. First, organizations face uncertainty. If an organization were a closed system so that it could completely control and predict all the variables that affected its operation, the organization could make technically rational, maximizing decisions and anticipate the consequences of its actions. As an open system, transacting with important external organizations, the firm does not have control over many of the important factors that affect its operations. Because organizations are open, they are affected by events outside their boundaries.

Second, organizations are interdependent with other organizations with which they exchange resources, information, or personnel, and thus open to influence by them. The extent of this influence is likely to be a function of the importance of the resource obtained, and inversely related to the ease with which the resource can be procured from alternative sources (5, 6). Interdependence is problematic and troublesome. Managers do not like to be dependent on factors outside their control. Interdependence is especially troublesome if there are few alternative sources, so the external organization is particularly important to the firm.

Interdependence and uncertainty interact in their effects on organizations. One of the principal functions of the institutional level of the firm is the management of this interdependence and uncertainty.

The importance of institutional management

Katz and Kahn (7) noted that organizations may pursue two complementary paths to effectiveness. The first is to be as efficient as possible, and thereby obtain a competitive advantage with respect to other firms. Under this strategy, the firm succeeds because it operates so efficiently that it achieves a competitive advantage in the market. The second strategy, termed "political," involves the establishment of favorable exchange relationships based on considerations that do not relate strictly to price, quality, service, or efficiency. Winning an order because of the firm's product and cost characteristics would be an example of the strategy of efficiency; winning the order because of interlocks in the directorates of the organizations involved, or because of family connections between executives in the two organizations, would illustrate political strategies.

The uses and consequences of political strategies for achieving organizational success have infrequently been empirically examined. Hirsch (8) has recently compared the ethical drug and record industries, noting great similarities between them. Both sell their products through gatekeepers or intermediaries—in the case of pharmaceuticals, through doctors who must write the prescriptions, and in the case of records, through disc jockeys who determine air time and, consequently, exposure. Both sell products with relatively short life cycles, and both industries place great emphasis on new products and product innovation. Both depend on the legal environment of patents, copyrights, and trademarks for market protection.

Hirsch noted that the rate of return for the average pharmaceutical firm during the period 1956–1966 was more than double the rate of return for the average firm in the record industry. Finding no evidence that would enable him to attribute the striking differences in profitability to factors associated with internal structural arrangements, Hirsch concluded that at least one factor affecting the relative profitability of the two industries is the ability to manage their institutional environments, and more specifically, the control over distribution, patent and copyright protection, and the prediction of adoption by the independent gatekeepers.

In a review of the history of both industries, Hirsch indicated that in pharmaceuticals, control over entry was achieved by (a) amending the patent laws to permit the patenting of naturally occurring substances, antibiotics, and (b) instituting a long and expensive licensing procedure required before drugs could be manufactured and marketed, administered by the Food and Drug Administration (FDA). In contrast, record firms have much less protection under the copyright laws; as a consequence, entry is less controlled, leading to more competition and lower profits. While there are other differences between the industries, including size and expenditures on research and development, Hirsch argued that at least some of the success of drug firms derives from their ability to control entry and their ability to control information channels relating to their product through the use of detail personnel and advertising in the American Medical Association journals. Retail price maintenance, tariff protection, and licensing to restrict entry are other examples of practices that are part of the organization's institutional environment and may profoundly affect its success.

Managing uncertainty and interdependence

The organization, requiring transactions with other organizations and uncertain about their future performance, has available a variety of strategies that can be used to manage uncertainty and interdependence. Firms face two problems in their institutional relationships: (*a*) managing the uncertainty caused by the unpredictable actions of competitors; and (*b*) managing the uncertainty resulting from noncompetitive interdependence with suppliers, creditors, government agencies, and customers. In both instances, the same set of strategic responses is available: merger, to completely absorb the interdependence and resulting uncertainty; joint ventures; interlocking directorates, to partially absorb the interdependence; the movement and selective recruiting of executives and other personnel, to develop interorganizational linkages; regulation, to provide government enforced stability; and other political activity to reduce competition, protect markets and sources of supply, and otherwise manage the organization's environment.

Because organizations are open systems, each strategy is limited in its effect. While merger or some other interorganizational linkage may manage one source of organizational dependence, it probably at the same time makes the organizations dependent on yet other organizations. For example, while regulation may eliminate effective price competition and restrict entry into the industry (9–11), the regulated organizations then face the uncertainties involved in dealing with the regulatory agency. Moreover, in reducing uncertainty for itself, the organization must bargain away some of its own discretion (6). One can view institutional management as an exchange process—the organization assures itself of needed resources, but at the same time, must promise certain predictable behaviors in return. Keeping these qualifications in mind, evidence on use of the various strategies of institutional management is reviewed.

Merger

There are three reasons an organization may seek to merge—first, to reduce competition by absorbing an important competitor organization; second, to manage interdependence with either sources of input or purchasers of output by absorbing them; and third, to diversify operations and thereby lessen dependence on the present organizations with which it exchanges (12). While merger among competing organizations is presumably proscribed by the antitrust laws, enforcement resources are limited, and major consolidations do take place.

In analyzing patterns of interorganizational behavior, one can either ask executives in the organizations involved the reasons for the action, or alternatively, one can develop a hypothetical model of behavior which is then tested with the available data. Talking with organizational executives may not provide the real reasons behind interorganizational activity since (*a*) different persons may see and interpret the same action in different ways, (*b*) persons may infer after the fact the motives for the action or decision, and (*c*) persons may not be motivated to tell the complete truth about the reasons for the behavior. Much of the existing literature on interorganizational linkage activity, therefore, uses the method of empirically testing the deductions from a hypothetical model of interorganizational behavior.

The classic expressed rationale for merger has been to increase the profits or the value of the shares of the firm. In a series of studies beginning as early as 1921, researchers have been unable to demonstrate that merger active firms are more profitable or have higher stock prices following the merger activity. This literature has been summarized by Reid (13), who asserts that mergers are made for growth, and that growth is sought because of the relationship between firm size and managerial salaries.

Growth, however, does not provide information concerning the desired characteristics of the acquired firm. Under a growth objective, any merger is equivalent to any other of the same size. Pfeffer (12) has argued that mergers are undertaken to manage organizational interdependence. Examining the proportion of merger activity occuring within the same 2-digit SIC industry category, he found that the highest proportion of within-industry mergers occurred in industries of intermediate concentration. The theoretical argument was that in industries with many competitors, the absorption of a single one did little to reduce competitive uncertainty. At the other extreme, with only a few competitors, merger would more likely be scrutinized by the antitrust authorities and coordination could instead be achieved through more informal arrangements, such as price leadership.

The same study investigated the second reason to merge: to absorb the uncertainty among organizations vertically related to each other, as in a buyer-seller relationship. He found that it was possible to explain 40 percent of the variation in the distribution of merger activity over industries on the basis of resource interdependence, measured by estimates of the transactions flows between sectors of the economy. On an individual industry basis, in two-thirds of the cases a measure of transactions interdependence accounted for 65 percent or more of the variation in the pattern of merger activity. The study indicated that it was possible to account for the industry of the likely merger partner firm by considering the extent to which firms in the two industries exchanged resources.

While absorption of suppliers or customers will reduce the firm's uncertainty by bringing critical contingencies within the boundaries of the organization, this strategy has some distinct costs. One danger is that the process of vertical integration creates a larger organization which is increasingly tied to a single industry.

The third reason for merger is diversification. Occasionally, the organization is confronted by interdependence it cannot absorb, either because of resource or legal limitations. Through diversifying its activities, the organization does not reduce the uncertainty, but makes the particular contingency less critical for its success and well-being. Diversification provides the organization with a way of avoiding, rather than absorbing, problematic interdependence.

Merger represents the most complete solution to situations of organizational interdependence, as it involves the total absorption of either a competitor or a vertically related organization, or the acquisition of an organization operating in another area. Because it does involve total absorption, merger requires more resources and is a more visible and substantial form of interorganizational linkage.

Joint ventures

Closely related to merger is the joint venture: the creation of a jointly owned, but independent organization by two or more separate parent firms. Merger involves the total pooling of assets by two or more organizations. In a joint venture, some assets of each of several parent organizations are used, and thus only a partial pooling of resources is involved (14). For a variety of reasons, joint ventures have been prosecuted less frequently and less successfully than mergers, making joint ventures particularly appropriate as a way of coping with competitive interdependence.

The joint subsidiary can have several effects on competitive interdependence and uncertainty. First, it can reduce the extent of new competition. Instead of both firms entering a market, they can combine some of their assets and create a joint subsidiary to enter the market. Second, since joint subsidiaries are typically staffed, particularly at the higher executive levels, with personnel drawn from the parent firms, the joint subsidiary becomes another location for the management of competing firms to meet. Most importantly, the joint subsidiary must set price and output levels, make new product development and marketing decisions and decisions about its advertising policies. Consequently, the parent organizations are brought into association in a setting in which exactly those aspects of the competitive relationship must be jointly determined.

In a study of joint ventures among manufacturing and oil and gas companies during the period 1960–71, Pfeffer and Nowak (15, 16) found that 56 percent involved parent firms operating in the same two-digit industry. Further, in 36 percent of the 166 joint ventures studied, the joint subsidiary operated in the same industry as *both* parent organizations. As in the case of mergers, the proportion of joint venture activities undertaken with other firms in the same industry was related to the concentration of the firm's industry being intermediate. The relationship between concentration and the proportion of joint ventures undertaken within the same industry accounted for some 25 percent of the variation in the pattern of joint venture activities.

In addition to considering the use of joint ventures in coping with competitive interdependence, the Pfeffer and Nowak study of joint ventures examined the extent to which the creation of joint subsidiaries was related to patterns of transaction interdependence across industries. While the correlations between the proportion of transactions and the proportion of joint ventures undertaken between industry pairs were lower than in the case of mergers, statistically significant relationships between this form of interorganizational linkage activity and patterns of resource exchange were observed. The difference between mergers and joint ventures appears to be that mergers are used relatively more to cope with buyer-seller interdependence, and joint ventures are more highly related to considerations of coping with competitive uncertainty.

Co-optation and interlocking directorates

Co-optation is a venerable strategy for managing interdependence between organizations. Co-optation involves the partial absorption of another organization through the placing of a representative of that organization on the board of the focal organization. Corporations frequently place bankers on their boards; hospitals and universities offer trustee positions to prominent business leaders; and community action agencies develop advisory boards populated with active and strong community political figures.

As a strategy for coping with interdependence, co-optation involves some particular problems and considerations. For example, a representative of the external organization is brought into the focal organization, while still retaining his or her original organizational membership. Co-optation is based on creating a conflict of interest within the co-opted person. To what extent should one pursue the goals and interests of one's organization of principal affiliation, and to what extent should one favor the interests of the co-opting organization? From the point of view of the co-opting organization, the individual should favor its interests, but not to the point where he or she loses credibility in the parent organization, because at that point, the individual ceases to be useful in ensuring that organization's support. Thus, co-optation requires striking a balance between the pressures to identify with either the parent or co-opting institution.

Furthermore, since co-optation involves less than total absorption of the other organization, there is the risk that the co-opted representative will not have enough influence or control in the principal organization to ensure the desired decisions. Of course, it is possible to co-opt more than a single representative. This is frequently done when relationships with the co-opted organization are particularly uncertain and critical. Co-optation may be the most feasible strategy when total absorption is impossible due to financial or legal constraints.

Interlocks in the boards of directors of competing organizations provide a possible strategy for coping with competitive interdependence and the resulting uncertainty. The underlying argument is that in order to manage interorganizational relationships, information must be exchanged, usually through a joint subsidiary or interlocking directorate. While interlocks among competitors are ostensibly illegal, until very recently there was practically no prosecution of this practice. In a 1965 study, a subcommittee of the House Judiciary Committee found more than 300 cases in which direct competitors had interlocking boards of directors (17). In a study of the extent of interlocking among competing organizations in a sample of 109 manufacturing organizations, Pfeffer and Nowak (3) found that the proportion of directors on the board from direct competitors was higher for firms operating in industries in which concentration was intermediate. This result is consistent with the result found for joint ventures and mergers as well. In all three instances, linkages among competing organizations occurred more frequently when concentration was in an intermediate range.

Analyses of co-optation through the use of boards of directors have not been confined to business firms. Price (18) argued that the principal function of the boards of the Oregon Fish and Game Commissions was to link the organizations to their environments. Zald (19) found that the composition of YMCA boards in Chicago matched the demography of their operating areas, and affected the organizations' effectiveness, particularly in raising money. Pfeffer (20) examined the size, composition, and function of hospital boards of directors, finding that variables of organizational context, such as ownership, source of funds, and location, were important explanatory factors. He also found a relationship between co-optation and organizational effectiveness. In 1972, he (21) found that regulated firms, firms with a higher proportion of debt in their capital structures, and larger firms tended to have more outside directors. Allen (22) also found that size of the board and the use of co-optation was predicted by the size of a firm, but did not replicate Pfeffer's earlier finding of a relationship between the organization's capital structure and the proportion of directors from financial institutions. In a study of utility boards, Pfeffer (23) noted that the composition of the board tended to correlate with the demographics of the area in which the utility was regulated.

The evidence is consistent with the strategy of organizations using their boards of directors to co-opt external organizations and manage problematic interdependence. The role of the board of directors is seen not as the provision of management expertise or control, but more generally as a means of managing problematic aspects of an organization's institutional environment.

Executive recruitment

Information also is transferred among organizations through the movement of personnel. The difference between movement of executives between organizations and co-optation is that in the latter case, the person linking the two organizations retains membership in both organizations. In the case of personnel movement, dual organizational membership is not maintained. When people change jobs, they take with themselves information about the operations, policies, and values of their previous employers, as well as contacts in the organization. In a study of the movement of faculty among schools of business, Baty et al. (24) found that similar orientations and curricula developed among schools exchanging personnel. The movement of personnel is one method by which new techniques of management and new marketing and product ideas are diffused through a set of organizations.

Occasionally, the movement of executives between organizations has been viewed as intensifying, rather than reducing, competition. Companies have been distressed by the raiding of trade secrets and managerial expertise by other organizations. While this perspective must be recognized, the exchange of personnel among organizations is a revered method of conflict *reduction* between organizations (25). Personnel movement inevitably involves sharing information among a set of organizations.

If executive movement is a form of interfirm linkage designed to manage competitive relationships, the proportion of executives recruited from within the same industry should be highest at intermediate levels of industrial concentration. Examining the three top executive positions in twenty different manufacturing industries, the evidence on executive backgrounds was found to be consistent with this argument (26). The proportion of high-level executives with previous jobs in the same industry but in a different company was found to be negatively related to the number of firms in the industry. The larger the number of firms, the less likely that a single link among competitors will substantially reduce uncertainty, but the larger the available supply of external executive talent. The data indicated no support for a supply argument, but supported the premise that interorganizational linkages are used to manage interdependence and uncertainty.

The use of executive movement to manage noncompetitive interorganizational relationships is quite prevalent. The often-cited movement of personnel between the Defense Department and major defense contractors is only one example, because there is extensive movement of personnel between many government departments and industries interested in the agencies' decisions. The explanation is frequently proposed that organizations are acquiring these personnel because of their expertise. The expertise explanation is frequently difficult to separate from the alternative that personnel are being exchanged to enhance interorganizational relationships. Regardless of the motivation, exchanging personnel inevitably involves the transfer of information and access to the other organization. It is conceptually possible to control for the effect of expertise—in other words, taking expertise into account, is there evidence that recruiting patterns reflect the influence of factors related to institutional management?

Regulation

Occasionally, institutional relationships are managed through recourse to political intervention. The reduction of competition and its associated uncertainty may be accomplished through regulation. Regulation, however, is a risky strategy for organizations to pursue. While regulation most frequently benefits the regulated industry (9, 10), the industry and firms have no assurance that regulatory authority will not be used against their interests. Regulation is very hard to repeal. Successful use of regulation requires that the firm and industry face little or no powerful political opposition, and that the political future can be accurately forecast.

The benefits of regulation to those being regulated have been extensively reviewed (11, 27). Regulation frequently has been sought by the regulated industry. Currently, trucking firms are among the biggest supporters of continued regulation of trucking. Since the Civil Aeronautics Board was created in 1938, no new trunk carriers have been started. Jordan (28) found that air rates on intrastate (hence not regulated by the CAB) airlines within California are frequently 25 percent or more lower than fares on comparable routes of regulated carriers. Estimates of the effects of regulation on prices in electric utilities, airlines, trucking, and natural gas have indicated that regulation either increases price or has no effect.

The theory behind these outcomes is still unclear. One approach suggests that regulation is created for the public benefit, but after the initial legislative attention, the regulatory process is captured by the firms subject to regulation. Another approach proposes that regulation, like other goods, is acquired subject to supply and demand considerations (11). Political scientists, focusing on the operation of interest groups, argue that regulatory agencies are "captured" by organized and well-financed interests. Government intervention in the market can solve many of the interdependence problems faced by firms. Regulation is most often accomplished by restriction of entry and the fixing of prices, which tend to reduce market uncertainties. Markets may be actually allocated to firms, and with the reduction of risk, regulation may make access to capital easier. Regulation may alter the organization's relationships with suppliers and customers. One theory of why the railroads were interested in the creation of the Interstate Commerce Commission (ICC) in 1887 was that large users were continually demanding and winning discriminatory rate reductions, disturbing the price stability of railroad price fixing cartels. By forbidding price discrimination and enforcing this regulation, the ICC strengthened the railroads' position with respect to large customers (29).

Political activity

Regulation is only one specific form of organizational activity in governmental processes. Business attempts to affect competition through the operation of the tariff laws date back to the 1700's (30). Epstein (31) provided one of the more complete summaries of the history of corporate involvement in politics and the inevitability of such action. The government has the power of coercion, possessed legally by no other social institution. Furthermore, legislation and regulation affect most of our economic institutions and markets, either indirectly through taxation, or more directly through purchasing, market protection, or market creation. For example, taxes on margarine only recently came to an end. Federal taxes, imposed in 1886 as a protectionist measure for dairy interests, were removed in 1950, but a law outlawing the sale of oleo in its colored form lasted until 1967 in Wisconsin.

As with regulation, political activities carry both benefits and risks. The risk arises because once government intervention in an issue on behalf of a firm or industry is sought, then political intervention becomes legitimated, regardless of whose interests are helped or hurt. The firm that seeks favorable tax legislation runs the risk of creating a setting in which it is equally legitimate to be exposed to very unfavorable legislation. After an issue is opened to government intervention, neither side will find it easy to claim that further government action is illegitimate.

In learning to cope with a particular institutional environment, the team may be unprepared for new uncertainties caused by the change of fundamental institutional relationships, including the opening of price competition, new entry and the lack of protection from overseas competition.

Conclusion

The institutional function of management involves managing the organization's relationships with other organizations. Table 1 presents strategies of institutional management with their principal advantages and disadvantages. From observation of organizational activities, the most common response to interdependence with external organizations seems to be the attempt to develop some form of interorganizational linkage to ensure the continuation of favorable relationships with important organizations in the environment.

All such interfirm linkages have costs, with the most fundamental being the loss of the organization's autonomy. In return for the certainty that one's competitors will not engage in predatory price cutting, one must provide assurances about one's own behavior. For example, cooptation involves the possibility of acquiring the support of an external organization, but at the same time the firm gives up some degree of privacy over its internal information and some control over its operations and decisions.

Variables affecting responses to the organization's environment can be specified. Actions taken to manage interdependencies are related to the extent of the interdependence and its importance to the organization. The response to competitive interdependence is related to measures of industry

Table 1. Advantages and disadvantages of strategies of institutional management

Strategy	Advantages	Disadvantages
Merger	Completely absorbs interdependence	Requires resources sufficient to acquire another organization May be proscribed by antitrust laws, or infeasible for other reasons (e.g., a governmental unit cannot be absorbed by a firm)
Joint ventures	Can be used for sharing risks and costs associated with large, or technologically advanced activities Can be used to partially pool resources and coordinate activities	Is available only for certain types of organizations, though less restricted than merger (COMSAT, for instance, brings together government and business)
Co-optation	Relatively inexpensive	May not provide enough coordination or linkage between organizations to ensure performance Co-opted person may lose credibility in original organization
Personnel movement	Relatively inexpensive Almost universally possible	Person loses identification with original organization, lessening influence there Linkage is based on knowledge and familiarity, and on a few persons at most, not on basic structural relationships
Regulation	Enables organization to benefit from the coercive power of the government	Regulation may be used to harm the organization's interests
Political activity	Enables organization to use government to modify and enhance environment	Government intervention, once legitimated, may be used against the organization as well as for its benefit

structure, and particularly to the necessity and feasibility of developing informal, interorganizational structures. Two important issues remain. First, is effective institutional management associated with favorable outcomes to the organization? Second, given the importance of institutional management, why are some organizations more successful than others at this task?

The effect of institutional management on firm performance is difficult to measure, and seldom has been examined. To examine the effect of successful institutional management, an outcome measure is needed. Profit is only one possibility, because there is evidence that the reduction of uncertainty may be sought regardless of its effect on profit (32). Whatever criterion is chosen is affected by many factors. To attribute a result to institutional management, other causes must be controlled. Nevertheless, institutional management receives a great deal of management attention in some firms and a firm's interorganizational relationships may be important to its success and survival.

Of even more fundamental interest is the question of why some firms are able to develop more effective strategic responses to their institutional environments. It is possible that effective institutional management requires fundamentally different structures of top management, or the development of excess managerial capacity, or the development of particular types of information systems. It is easier to find successful institutional management than to identify critical variables enabling it to develop in the first place. For example, some universities have better relationships with their state legislatures than do others. It is possible to retrospectively infer explanations as to why this is so. What remains to be done is to explain those factors that could be designed into an organization initially to ensure effective institutional management in the future.

Considering its probable importance to the firm, the institutional function of management has received much less concern than it warrants. It is time that this aspect of management receives the systematic attention long reserved for motivational productivity problems associated with relationships between management and workers.

References

1. Parsons, Talcott. *Structure and Process in Modern Societies* (Glencoe, Illinois: Free Press, 1960).

2. Mintzberg, Henry. *The Nature of Managerial Work* (New York: Harper and Row, 1973).

3. Pfeffer, Jeffrey, and Phillip Nowak. "Organizational Context and Interorganizational Linkages Among Corporations." Unpublished manuscript (Berkeley: University of California).

4. Whyte, William F. *Street Corner Society* (Chicago: University of Chicago Press, 1955).

5. Jacobs, David. "Dependency and Vulnerability: An Exchange Approach to the Control of Organizations," *Administrative Science Quarterly* 19 (1974), 45–49.

6. Thompson, James D. *Organizations in Action* (New York: McGraw Hill, 1967).

7. Katz, Daniel, and Robert L. Kahn. *The Social Psychology of Organizations* (New York: John Wiley, 1966).

8. Hirsch, Paul M. "Organizational Effectiveness and the Institutional Environment," *Administrative Science Quarterly* 20 (1975), 327–44.

9. Jordan, William A. "Producer, Protection, Prior Market Structure and the Effects of Government Regulation," *Journal of Law and Economics* 15 (1972), 151–76.

10. Pfeffer, Jeffrey. "Administrative Regulation and Licensing: Social Problem or Solution? *Social Problems* 21 (1974), 468–79.

11. Posner, Richard A. "Theories of Economic Regulation," *Bell Journal of Economics and Management Science* 5 (1974), 335–58.

12. Pfeffer, Jeffrey. "Merger as a Response to Organizational Interdependence," *Administrative Science Quarterly* 17 (1972), 382–94.

13. Reid, Samuel R. *Mergers, Managers, and the Economy* (New York: McGraw-Hill, 1968).

14. Bernstein, Lewis. "Joint Ventures in the Light of Recent Antitrust Developments," *The Antitrust Bulletin* 10 (1965), 25–29.

15. Pfeffer, Jeffrey, and Phillip Nowak. "Joint Ventures and Interorganizational Interdependence," *Administrative Science Quarterly,* in press.

16. Pfeffer, Jeffrey and Phillip Nowak. "Patterns of Joint Venture Activity: Implications for Antitrust Policy," *The Antitrust Bulletin,* in press.

17. House of Representatives, Staff Report to the Antitrust Subcommittee of the Committee on the Judiciary. *Interlocks in Corporate Management* (Washington, D.C.: U.S. Government Printing Office, 1965).

18. Price, James L. "The Impact of Governing Boards on Organizational Effectiveness and Morale," *Administrative Science Quarterly* 8 (1963), 361–78.

19. Zald, Mayer N. "Urban Differentiation, Characteristics of Boards of Directors and Organizational Effectiveness," *American Journal of Sociology* 73 (1967), 261–72.

20. Pfeffer, Jeffrey. "Size, Composition and Function of Hospital Boards of Directors: A Study of Organization-Environment Linkage," *Administrative Science Quarterly* 18 (1973), 349–64.

21. Pfeffer, Jeffrey. "Size and Composition of Corporate Boards of Directors: The Organization and its Environment," *Administrative Science Quarterly* 17 (1972), 218–28.

22. Allen, Michael Patrick. "The Structure of Interorganizational Elite Co-optation: Interlocking Corporate Directorates," *American Sociological Review* 39 (1971), 393–406.

23. Pfeffer, Jeffrey. "Co-optation and the Composition of Electric Utility Boards of Directors," *Pacific Sociological Review* 17 (1974), 333–63.

24. Baty, Gordon B., William M. Evan, and Terry W. Rothermel. "Personnel Flows as Interorganizational Relations," *Administrative Science Quarterly* 16 (1971), 430–43.

25. Stern, Louis W., Brian Sterthal, and C. Samuel Craig. "Managing

Conflict in Distribution Channels: A Laboratory Study," *Journal of Marketing Research* 10 (1973), 169–79.

26. Pfeffer, Jeffrey, and Huseyin Leblebici. "Executive Recruitment and the Development of Interfirm Organizations," *Administrative Science Quarterly* 18 (1973), 449–61.

27. Stigler, George J. "The Theory of Economic Regulation," *Bell Journal of Economics and Management Science* 2 (1971), 3–21.

28. Jordan, William A. *Airline Regulation in America: Effects and Imperfections* (Baltimore: Johns Hopkins University Press, 1970).

29. MacAvoy, Paul W. *The Economic Effects of Regulation* (Cambridge, Mass.: MIT Press, 1965).

30. Bauer, Raymond A., Ithiel de Sola Pool, and Lewis Anthony Dexter. *American Business and Public Policy* (New York: Atherton Press, 1968).

31. Epstein, Edwin M. *The Corporation in American Politics* (Englewood Cliffs, New Jersey: Prentice-Hall, 1969).

32. Caves, Richard E. "Uncertainty, Market Structure, and Performance: Galbraith as Conventional Wisdom," in J. W. Markham and G. F. Papanek (eds.), *Industrial Organization and Economic Development* (Boston: Houghton Mifflin, 1970), pp. 283–302.